Studies in Anglo-Saxon History VII

SLAVERY IN EARLY MEDIAEVAL ENGLAND

Slaves were part of the fabric of English society throughout the Anglo-Saxon era and on into the twelfth century but, as the base of the social pyramid, English slaves have left no known written records. However, there are extensive references to them throughout the documents and writings of the period. This important study, in an area which has hitherto attracted little scholarly attention, seeks to assemble the evidence, drawn from a variety of sources in Old English and Latin, to convey a picture of slaves and slavery in England, viewed against the background of English society as a whole. From this detailed examination a composite picture emerges, showing who the slaves were and how they came to be enslaved; their rights and obligations; how they were freed and the nature of this freedom; how the institution changed; and how it related to the appearance of serfdom, which came to characterise post-Conquest English rural society. The study concludes with an extensive appendix on the vernacular terminology of slavery, revealing that the concepts of enslavement were embedded in the religious imagery of the period.

DAVID PELTERET is a Senior Research Fellow at King's College London.

STUDIES IN ANGLO-SAXON HISTORY

General Editor: John Hines

ISSN 0950–3412

Already published

SLAVERY IN EARLY MEDIAEVAL ENGLAND

FROM THE REIGN OF ALFRED UNTIL THE TWELFTH CENTURY

DAVID A. E. PELTERET

THE BOYDELL PRESS

First published 1995
The Boydell Press, Woodbridge
Reprinted in paperback 2001

Transferred to digital printing

ISBN 978–0–85115–399–5 hardback
ISBN 978–0–85115–829–7 paperback

The Boydell Press is an imprint of Boydell & Brewer Ltd
PO Box 9, Woodbridge, Suffolk IP12 3DF, UK
and of Boydell & Brewer Inc.
668 Mount Hope Ave, Rochester, NY 14620-2731, USA
website: www.boydellandbrewer.com

A CIP catalogue record for this book is available
from the British Library

Library of Congress Catalog Card Number 94–33021

This publication is printed on acid-free paper

CONTENTS

LIST OF TABLES

TO HELEN

ACKNOWLEDGMENTS

Any study of the past is in some measure an exercise in autobiography, however 'objectively' it is presented. The debts I owe in writing this work reach far back into my past and I should like here to acknowledge at least some of them. Maurice Pope, Theo Haarhoff and John Atkinson played a large role in bringing alive for me the languages, literature and history of the Classical World at the University of Cape Town; Leslie Casson neatly deflected me into the study of early English by giving me a junior teaching job there. The stimulating, fraught and tragic land of South Africa of the '50s and '60s inculcated in me an acute awareness of the disparities in power that can exist within a society, thereby prompting me to ask questions about the most disadvantaged members of early English society, questions that have rarely exercised Anglo-Saxon historians. My old school, Rondebosch Boys' High, awarded me its Overseas Scholarship, which provided me with the means to study in England and to observe the lineal descendant of Anglo-Saxon society at first hand. Paul Hyams encouraged me one rainy night at a party on the outskirts of London to pursue these questions, and the generosity of the Centre for Medieval Studies at the University of Toronto provided me with the financial means to do so. Michael Sheehan was an exacting critic but tactful, generous with his time (at the cost of his own scholarship), and possessed of the humility that sought never to impose his personal perspectives on his student.

This work was put aside for many years. Had not Chris Chippindale generously arranged to have the original study optically scanned, I doubt whether I would have had the fortitude to start the exacting task of making the extensive revisions that the passage of time rendered necessary. The staff of the Dictionary of Old English under Toni Healey have been ever tolerant of and helpful towards someone who has dropped in and out of their office in an unpredictable way. Nancy Spears and Ian and David McDougall have been of especial assistance. Successive Principals of New College in the University of Toronto – and in the case of this book, Ted Chamberlin and Fred Case – have always encouraged me to pursue my academic endeavours in concert with my administrative responsibilities, and my colleagues at the College have provided the friendship and support that has enabled me to do so. None of them will resent my singling out Clara De Abreu in particular, whose kindnesses to me over the past fourteen years have been legion: without her assistance in a multitude of ways this study would not have reached completion.

It is always a pleasure to acknowledge the help received from librarians: amongst the many libraries that have been used for this study, I have especially drawn on the knowledge of the staff of the Students' Room at the British Library, London; the Bodleian Library, Oxford; the Pontifical Institute of Mediaeval Studies, Toronto; and the John P. Robarts Library and the Thomas Fisher Rare Book Room at the University of Toronto. Graham Bradshaw has acquired books

Acknowledgements

for the University of Toronto's library at my request that were not in its collections; and Robin Healey and Anne Jocz have been most helpful in locating volumes for me.

I have been enriched by information and advice from a number of scholars: Roy Hart in Peterborough, David Roffe in Sheffield, David Howlett and Bruce Mitchell in Oxford, Simon Keynes in Cambridge, Richard Lee and the Revd D. M. Stanley in Toronto, Allen Frantzen[1] in Chicago, and Milton Gatch in New York have all contributed specific items of information, though none should be held responsible for the uses to which I have put their scholarship. My thanks, too, to Christopher Dyer, who as the originally anonymous reader of an earlier draft of this book offered some useful suggestions. John Parry cast his expert editorial eye over the Introduction and spared me from making several gaffes. Richard Sharpe and Patrick Wormald in Oxford have provided me with moral support in various ways. Ursula Schaeffer, then in Freiburg-im-Breisgau, offered me practical help in the form of hospitality and the use of her car, which enabled me to travel from Germany to Switzerland to examine Bern, Burgerbibliothek, MS. 671.

Paul Hyams has kindly permitted me to quote from his Oxford Ph.D. dissertation and David Roffe likewise has allowed me to quote from a letter he had sent me. Cambridge University Press has generously sanctioned my using material first published in the journal *Anglo-Saxon England*.

Helen Rowett has shown me great kindness and affection: to her this book is dedicated.

---

[1] I regret that the volume he co-edited with Douglas Moffat, *The Work of Work: Servitude, Slavery, and Labor in Medieval England* (Glasgow 1994), came to hand too late to be used by me. Readers of this book should especially see Frantzen's introductory essay and the papers by Karras on gender issues, Girsch on the Old English terminology for slaves, Ruffing on Ælfric's *Colloquy*, Samson on the end of mediaeval slavery, and Brady on Irish servitude (where some archaeological evidence for ploughs is presented).

MANUMISSIONS AND STATUS DOCUMENTS: CONCORDANCE TO THE PRINCIPAL EDITIONS

There are a large number of Anglo-Saxon documents in Latin and Old English recording the freeing of persons, which have generally, if loosely, been called 'manumissions'. There are also two lists of serfs and an associated document, which will be termed 'status documents' in this book. No comprehensive edition of all these records exists. They will be referred to below as *Manumissions* and *Status Documents* and have been assigned the numbers I propose to give them in a future edition. Concordances are given here to Ker, *Catalogue* and to the following editions:

B   *Cartularium Saxonicum*, ed. Birch

C   Craster, 'Some Anglo-Saxon records of the See of Durham'

D   Dickins, 'The beheaded manumission in Exeter Book', in *The Early Cultures of North-West Europe*, edd. Fox & Dickins, pp. 363–67 + one plate

E   *Hand-Book to the Land-Charters and Other Saxonic Documents*, ed. Earle

F   Förster, 'Die Freilassungsurkunden des Bodmin-Evangeliars', in *A Grammatical Miscellany offered to Otto Jespersen*, edd. Bøgholm *et al.*, pp. 77–99

FT   Förster, *Der Flussname Themse und seine Sippe*, pp. 788–95

H   *Select English Historical Documents*, ed. & transl. Harmer

Hi   Hickes, *Dissertatio Epistolaris ad Bartholomaeum Showere*, in *ibid.*, *De Antiquae Litteraturae Septentrionalis Utilitate*

K   *Codex Diplomaticus Ævi Saxonici*, ed. Kemble

M   Meritt, 'Old English entries in a manuscript at Bern'

P   Pelteret, 'Two Old English lists of serfs'

T   *Diplomatarium Anglicum Ævi Saxonici*, ed. Thorpe

W   Wanley, *Librorum Veterum Septentrionalium . . . Catalogus Historico-Criticus*

The text will be identified by the page number in the edition followed either by the number assigned it by the editor in parentheses or, if unnumbered, by the number of the document on a particular page without parentheses (no. 1 on any given page being the first document to *start* on that page). The dates are those suggested by the editors, corrected on occasion by Ker in his *Catalogue*. These should be regarded as provisional: further examination of the manuscripts and of the names occurring in these records may permit a closer delimitation of when they were entered in the various manuscripts.

I. MANUMISSIONS

No.	Manuscript	Date	Ker	Principal Editions
1.1	BL Royal 1 B vii	924 x 925 x	246	T622, BII.315(639), H32(19)
2.1	Bern, Burger-bibliothek 971	925 x 950	6c	M346(3), FT794(2a)
2.2	Bern, Burger-bibliothek 971	925 x 950	6c	M346(4), FT795(2b)
3.1	BL Add. 9381	ca 1075	26	KIV.308.2, T623.2, F83(1)
3.2	BL Add. 9381	950 x 1000	126	KIV.308.3, T623.3. F83(2)
3.3	BL Add. 9381	959 x 993	126	KIV.308.4, T623.4, F83(3)
3.4	BL Add. 9381	x 1025	126	KIV.309.1, T623.5, F83(4)
3.5	BL Add. 9381	959 x 993	126	KIV.309.2, T623.6, F83(5)
3.6	BL Add. 9381	959 x 993	126	KIV.309.3, T624.1, F84(7)
3.7	BL Add. 9381	x 1000	126	KIV.309.4, T624.2, F84(8)
3.8	BL Add. 9381	x 1000	126	KIV.309.5, T624.3, F85(9)
3.9	BL Add. 9381	x 1000	126	KIV.309.6, T624.4, E272(9), F85(10)
3.10	BL Add. 9381	939 x 946	126	KIV.309.7, T624.5, F85(11)
3.11	BL Add. 9381	939 x 946	126	KIV.310.1, T624.6, F85(12)
3.12	BL Add. 9381	939 x 946	126	KIV.310.1, T624.6, F85(13)
3.13	BL Add. 9381	939 x 946	126	KIV.310.2, T624.7, F86(14)
3.14	BL Add. 9381	946 x 993	126	KIV.310.3, T624.8, F86(15)
3.15	BL Add. 9381	959 x 993	126	KIV.310.4, T625.1, F86(16)
3.16	BL Add. 9381	959 x 971	126	KIV.310.5, T625.2, F86(17)
3.17	BL Add. 9381	978 x 1016	126	KIV.310.6, T625.3, F87(18)
3.18	BL Add. 9381	1000 x 1025	126	KIV.311.1, T625.4, F87(19)
3.19	BL Add. 9381	978 x 1016	126	KIV.311.2, T625.5, F88(20)
3.20	BL Add. 9381	1000 x 1025	126	KIV.311,3, T625.6. F88(21)
3.21	BL Add. 9381	978 x 1016	126	KIV.311.4, T625.7. F88(22)
3.22	BL Add. 9381	ca 1000	126	KIV.312.1, F89(23)
3.23	BL Add. 9381	959 x 993	126	KIV.312.2, T626.1, F89(24)
3.24	BL Add. 9381	959 x 975	126	KIV.312.3, T626.2, F90(25)
3.25	BL Add. 9381	946 x 953	126	KIV.312.4, T626.3, E272(23), F90(26)
3.26	BL Add. 9381	946 x 993	126	KIV.312.5, T626.4, E272(24), F90(27)
3.27	BL Add. 9381	x 1000	126	KIV.312.6, T626.5, F91(28)
3.28	BL Add. 9381	955 x 959 x	126	KIV.313.1. T626.6, E272(26), F91(29)
3.29	BL Add. 9381	ca 1075	126	KIV.313.2, T627.1, E273(27), F91(30)
3.30	BL Add. 9381	ca 1075	126	KIV.313.3, T627.2, E273(28), F92(31)
3.31	BL Add. 9381	959 x 975 x	126	KIV.313.4, T628.1, F92(32)
3.32	BL Add. 9381	959 x 975 x	126	KIV.313.4, T628.1, F92(32)
3.33	BL Add. 9381	ca 1075	126	KIV.314.1, T628.2, E274(30), F93(33)
3.34	BL Add. 9381	959 x 975 x	126	KIV.314.2, T629.1. F93(34)
3.35	BL Add. 9381	978 x 1025	126	KIV.314.3, T629.2, F94(35)
3.36	BL Add. 9381	946 x 953	126	KIV.314.4, T629.3, F94(36)
3.37	BL Add. 9381	1075 x 1100	126	KIV.315.1, T629.4, E274(34), F94(37)
3.38	BL Add. 9381	x 1000	126	KIV.315.2. T629.5. F95(38)
3.39	BL Add. 9381	959 x 975 x	126	KIV.315.3, T629.6, E274(36), F95(39)
3.40	BL Add. 9381	959 x 975 x	126	KIV.315.3, T629.6, E274(36), F95(40)
3.41	BL Add. 9381	978 x 1016	126	KIV.315.4, T630.1, F96(41)
3.42	BL Add. 9381	959 x 975 x	126	KIV.315.5, T630.2, F96(42)

No.	Manuscript	Date	Ker	Principal Editions
3.43	BL Add. 9381	939 x 993	126	KIV.315.6, T630.3, F96(43)
3.44	BL Add. 9381	959 x 993	126	KIV.316.1, T630.4, F96(44)
3.45	BL Add. 9381	950 x 1000	126	KIV.316.2, T630.5, F97(45)
3.46	BL Add. 9381	959 x 975	126	KIV.316.3, T630.6, F97(46)
3.47	BL Add. 9381	959 x 975	126	KIV.316.3–4, T630.6–7, F98(47)
3.48	BL Add. 9381	959 x 975	126	KIV.316.4, T630.7. F98(48)
3.49	BL Add. 9381	959 x 975	126	KIV.316.5, T631.1, F98(49)
3.50	BL Add. 9381	959 x 975	126	KIV.316.6, T631.2, F99(50)
3.51	BL Add. 9381	978 x 1016	126	KIV.317.5, T631.3, F99(51)
4.1	Cotton Tib. B V	955 x 959	194c	T623.1
4.2	Cotton Tib. B V	1000 x 1025	194a	KVI.211.3, T644.2
5.1	Bodley 579	1046 x 1100	315e	Hi12.1, T638.1, E253(5)
5.2	Bodley 579	x 1097	315c	Hi12.2, T638.2, E253(4)
5.3	Bodley 579	x 1097	315c	Hi13.2, T639.1, E253(1)
5.4	Bodley 579	1042 x 1066	315e	Hi13.1, T638.3, E254(3)
5.5	Bodley 579	x 1097	315c	Hi13.3, T639.2, E254(2)
5.6	Bodley 579	1030 x 1050	315e	E254.3, BIII.536(1245)
5.7	Bodley 579	1030 x 1050	315e	E254.4, BIII.536(1246)
5.8	Bodley 579	1030 x 1050	315e	E255.1, BIII.536(1247)
5.9	Bodley 579	1030 x 1050	315e	E255.2, BIII.537(1248)
5.10	Bodley 579	1030 x 1050	315e	E255.2, BIII.537(1248)
5.11	Bodley 579	1030 x 1050	315e	E255.2, BIII.537(1249)
5.12	Bodley 579	1030 x 1050	315e	E255.2, BIII.537(1250)
5.13	Bodley 579	1030 x 1050	315e	E255.2, BIII.538(1251)
5.14	Bodley 579	1030 x 1050	315e	E255.3, BIII.538(1252)
5.15	Bodley 579	1030 x 1050	315e	E256.1, BIII.538(1253)
5.16	Bodley 579	x 1097	315d	Hi13.4, T639.3, E256.3
6.1	Cotton Domit. vii	ca 1050	147a	T621, E275.1. BIII.358(1254)
6.2	Cotton Domit. vii	ca 1050	147a	T621, E275.i, BIII.359(1254)
7.1	[Cotton Otho B.ix]	1030x1040	176c	Bodleian James 18, p. 43, C190.1
7.2	[Cotton Otho B.ix]	1030 x1040	176d	Bodleian James 18, p. 42, C190.2
7.3	[Cotton Otho B.ix]	1030 x1040	176e	W238, col. 1 (V)
7.4	[Cotton Otho B.ix]	1030 x1040	176f	Bodleian James 18, p. 43, C191.1
8.1	CCCC 140	1075 x 1087	35.2	Hi22.1, T642.1, E269(6)
8.2	CCCC 140	1075 x 1087	35.2	Hi22.2, T642.2, E269(7)
8.3	CCCC 140	1075 x 1087	35.2	Hi22.3, T642.3. E269(11)
8.4	CCCC 140	1088 x 1122	35.2	Hi22.4. T643.4, E269(13)
8.5	CCCC 140	1088 x 1122	35.2	Hi22.5, T642.4, E270(14)
8.6	CCCC 140	1075 x 1087	35.2	Hi22.6, T642.5. E270(8)
8.7	CCCC 140	1088 x 1122	35.2	T644.1, E270(15)
8.8	CCCC 140	1065 x 1066	35.2	Hi23.1, T643.1, E271(12)
8.9	CCCC 140	1061 x 1065	35.2	Hi23.2, T643.2, E271(9)
8.10	CCCC 140	1061 x 1065	35.2	Hi23.3, T643.3, E271(10)
8.11	CCCC 111	1075 x 1087	35.8	Hi9.2, T640.1, E268(1)
8.12	CCCC 111	1075 x 1087	35.8	Hi10.2, T641.1, E268(2)
8.13	CCCC 111	1075 x 1087	35.8	Hi10.3. T641.2, E268(3)
8.14	CCCC 111	1075 x 1057	35.8	Bi10.1, T641.3, E268(4)
8.15	CCCC 111	1075 x 1087	35.8	Hi10.4, T641.4, E269(5)
9.1	Exeter 3501	1143	20.9	Hi14.1
9.2	Exeter 3501	ca 1133	20.13	Hi15.7, T645.2, E257.1

No.	Manuscript	Date	Ker	Principal Editions
9.3	Exeter 3501	*ca* 1133	20.13	Hi16.1, T646.1, E257.2
9.4	Exeter 3501	*ca* 1133	20.13	T648.2, E258.1
9.5	Exeter 3501	1137 x 1142	20.13	Hi15.5, T645.1, E258.2
9.6	Exeter 3501	x 1129	20.13	Hi15.2, T632.1, E258.3
9.7	Exeter 3501	1125 x 1130	20.13	Hi15.1, T631.4, E259.1
9.8	Exeter 3501	x 1133	20.13	Hi18.1, T633.2. E259.2
9.9	Exeter 3501	*ca* 1133	20.13	Hi15.6, T648.1, E259.3
9.10	Exeter 3501	*ca* 1133	20.13	Hi14.2, T634.3
9.11	Exeter 3501	1090 x 1130	20.13	T622 (partial), D366
9.12	Exeter 3501	3 x 13 June 1133	20.13	Hi16.2, T646.2, E260.2
9.13	Exeter 3501	1072 x 1103	20.13	T635.1. E261.1
9.14	Exeter 3501	1072 x 1103	20.13	Hi15.4, T633.1. E261.2
9.15	Exeter 3501	1072 x 1103	20.13	T635.2, E262.1
9.16	Exeter 3501	1072 x 1103	20.13	T648.3, E262.2
9.17	Exeter 3501	1072 x 1103	20.13	T637.1, E262.3
9.18	Exeter 3501	1072 x 1103	20.13	Hi15.3, T632.2. E262.4
9.19	Exeter 3501	1072 x 1103	20.13	T634.2, E263.1
9.20	Exeter 3501	x 1093	20.13	T637.2, E263.2
9.21	Exeter 3501	1072 x 1103	20.13	T635.3, E263.3
9.22	Exeter 3501	1072 x 1103	20.13	T636.1, E264.1
9.23	Exeter 3501	1072 x 1103	20.13	T636.2, E264.2
9.24	Exeter 3501	1072 x 1103	20.5	T634.3

II. STATUS DOCUMENTS

No.	Manuscript	Date	Ker	Principal Editions
1.1	Cotton Tib. B.v	*ca* 1000	22	Hi28n, T649–51, KVI.211.4, E276–7, P472–3
2.1	*Textus Roffensis*	1058 x 1075	373B	P493.1
2.2	*Textus Roffensis*	1058 x 1075	373B	KIV.305.2(865), T644.3, P493.2

INTRODUCTION

The existence of slavery as an integral part of early English society for over half a millennium comes as a considerable surprise to most people. The fervour with which 'Rule, Britannia' is sung annually on the last night of the Promenade Concerts in London shows that the proud assertion made in this paean to nationalism that 'Britons never will be slaves' accords with a self-image of the singers which has also been projected onto the English past.[1] Many historians of Anglo-Saxon England have shared in the creation of this image. Studies of Anglo-Saxon kingship and aristocracy abound but rarely will the word 'slave' appear in the index of an Anglo-Saxon history textbook.[2] It is not the purpose of this study to examine why slaves have excited so little interest amongst Anglo-Saxonists. Instead this book will explore what can be learnt about those people called 'slaves' who helped perpetuate English society and who participated in the shaping of the English countryside from the reign of King Alfred of Wessex up to the twelfth century.

THE PROBLEM OF DEFINITION

What is a 'slave'? D. B. Davis in his excellent study of slavery in Western culture has discerned three distinguishing factors which, when operating outside the sphere of the family, define a person as a slave: 'his person is the property of another man, his will is subject to his owner's authority, and his labor or services are obtained through coercion.'[3]

This definition may be considered satisfactory at a general level of discussion, but when one comes to compare slavery as it existed in various societies, or within a single society at different periods in its history, the definition proves to be inadequate and, indeed, inaccurate. For instance, the criterion of being the property of another person needs to be qualified in the case of slaves in China during the Han and T'ang dynasties. Technically they were owned by the emperor, but it was the emperor in his role as representative of the state rather than

---

[1] Probably most of the singers are unaware that the song comes from Thomas Arne's opera *Alfred: A Masque* and that they are thus celebrating indirectly one of the greatest of the Anglo-Saxon kings. See Cummings, *Dr Arne and 'Rule, Britannia'*, and Scott, 'Arne's "Alfred" '; for an edition of the music (though not in the version sung at the Proms) and the libretto see *Alfred*, ed. Scott. The words are usually ascribed to the author of *The Seasons*, James Thomson: see *The Complete Poetical Works*, ed. Robertson, p. 422.

[2] For royalty see Rosenthal, 'A historiographical survey'. Amongst studies on the aristocracy see especially Dumville, 'The ætheling'; Hart, 'Athelstan "Half-King" and his family', reprinted in a revised form in *idem*, *The Danelaw*, Chapter XXI; and Williams, '*Princeps Merciorum gentis*'.

[3] Davis, *The Problem of Slavery in Western Culture*, p. 31.

in his personal capacity, because the slavery of this period appears to have had a penal character to it.[4] Another exception can be found in Roman law, where under certain circumstances a slave might have no master at all and was instead considered to be a *res nullius* (that is, something that is not owned).[5]

Two further examples from Rome and China help illustrate the wide differences that have existed between slave systems. In Roman law slaves were usually someone's property (apart from the exception just mentioned) and so they were deemed to be a 'thing', as has been the case in many other legal systems.[6] The Chinese, on the other hand, did not draw the seemingly logical conclusion that if slaves were property they were 'things' rather than human beings.[7] The investigations of M. I. Finley into some Classical Greek societies showed that even amongst peoples speaking a common language there could be wide variation between one society and another. A slave in the Crete of the Gortynian code, for instance, had a different set of rights and obligations from one living in Athens. Furthermore, Finley found that there could be a continuum of statuses between slaves and freemen, with people living 'between slavery and freedom' who cannot adequately be described by means of a general definition.[8]

In consequence, Finley put forward a typology whereby different status groups within a society at a given point in history could be delineated. He suggested that seven features should be examined:

(1) power over a man's labour and movements; (2) power to punish; (3) claims to property, or power over things – a complex of elements requiring further differentiation both in its range (from *peculium* to full ownership) and in its application to different categories of things (e.g. cattle or land or agricultural produce or money); (4) privileges and liabilities in legal action, such as immunity from arbitrary seizure or the capacity to sue or be sued; (5) privileges in the area of the family: marriage, succession, and so on; (6) privileges of social mobility, such as manumission or enfranchisement (and their inverse); and (7) privileges and duties in the sacral, political, and military spheres.[9]

These are all socio-legal in nature, and an eighth aspect, which is socio-psychological, should also be included: that of esteem. For instance, slaves in the Roman imperial bureaucracy would probably have been considered – both by themselves and by other members of the society – to have a higher status than a *colonus* living on a *latifundium*.

---

4 See Pulleyblank, 'The origins and nature of chattel slavery in China'. Patterson has pointed out in *Slavery and Social Death* that '[a]s a legal fact, there never existed a slaveholding society, ancient or modern, that did not recognize the slave as a person in law' (p. 22).

5 Buckland, *The Roman Law of Slavery*, p. 2.

6 It should be noted, however, that in keeping with Patterson's comments above (n. 4) slaves are also referred to as persons in Roman law. For a discussion of this see Buckland, *The Roman Law of Slavery*, pp. 3–5.

7 Pulleyblank, 'The origins and nature of chattel slavery in China', 213. The opposition 'thing/person' is, of course, a modern Western cultural construct; it was evidently not felt to be a binary opposite in Chinese society.

8 'The servile statuses of ancient Greece'; 'Between slavery and freedom'. See also the collection of papers, *Slavery in Classical Antiquity*, ed. Finley.

9 'The servile statuses of ancient Greece', 188. The typology is also given, in slightly more detail, in 'Between slavery and freedom', 247–8.

Finley's typology offers a means whereby a slave can be defined with more precision, something which is particularly valuable for comparative purposes. The typology does not, however, point to which group should be labelled as 'slaves' in the first place. Here historians have to exercise their own judgment as to which status group should be so defined.[10] It will always be used of a group of persons who are in some way regarded as property, though not all such persons will be called slaves. Usually it will also apply to that group in society having the least rights. Only with many more detailed studies of servile groups in a variety of societies and at different periods in world history will it be possible perhaps to agree on a general definition of a 'slave'. Such a definition will likely embrace more than the three characteristics listed in Davis's definition, with a select combination of some of these being deemed sufficient to categorise a person as a slave.

SLAVERY IN ENGLAND: THE PROBLEMS

As Finley's work has shown, the decision as to which group in a society can be called 'slaves' must be dependent on the terminology of status employed by that society. The Anglo-Saxons had a very large vocabulary of status terms. Fortunately, in that society one group stands out unambiguously as being viewed as chattels and as having both the fewest rights and the heaviest obligations. The general term for a male member of this group was *þeow*, and, significantly, the Anglo-Saxon translators equated him with the Roman *seruus*, the Latin word most widely used to denote a slave.[11]

The Modern English word 'slave' which is employed to describe this group should not be used interchangeably with the word 'serf'. Though the two terms have been used in the past by some writers as virtual synonyms, a clear distinction can be made between them.[12] Whereas slaves were usually in some way regarded as the property of another person or institution, serfs were not personally owned but instead owed obligations to a person or institution in virtue of their occupancy of land. Both groups were to be found in late Anglo-Saxon England.[13] Unfortunately English uses a single epithet 'servile' for the adjectival form of both 'slave' and 'serf'. In this study, therefore, the usage of the substan-

---

[10] Kopytoff and Miers were so concerned about the semantic load that has been placed on the word 'slavery' that they enclosed it in inverted commas in their general discussion of the phenomenon in Africa. See 'African "slavery" as an institution of marginality', in *Slavery in Africa*, edd. Miers & Kopytoff (note especially their addendum 'A plea on terminology' on pp. 76–8).

[11] For other terms used of slaves see below, chapter I and appendix I.

[12] See Simpson & Weiner, *The Oxford English Dictionary*, XV.7, col. 1, s.v. *serf*. A semantic history of the word 'serf' remains to be written. Bak has discussed some of the conceptual difficulties arising out of the imprecise use of the words 'serf' and 'serfdom' in his paper, 'Serfs and serfdom: words and things'; he observes: 'Briefly, there is a medieval usage, referring to distinct, particular forms of dependence and another, modern one, based on generalized, critical scholarship' (p. 9).

[13] Pelteret, 'The *coliberti* of Domesday Book', 47–9, and Pelteret, 'Two Old English lists of serfs', 474–5.

tive 'slave' will be extended to include an adjectival function as well (for which there is ample semantic precedent in English), while the adjective 'servile' will be retained to refer to serfs or as a generalised term for both groups.

These terminological problems are easily dealt with. There are several other questions about the institution of slavery in England, however, that require considerable investigation. First and foremost, there is the problem of determining its defining characteristics – those features that mark it out from the slavery of Republican Rome, say, or from that of the American Deep South. Other questions are prompted by the nature of Anglo-Saxon society. Here was a people strongly influenced by a religion that held as a central tenet the equality of all in the sight of God. From a modern perspective the coexistence of slavery and the Christian Church would seem to be incompatible. Yet this was not so in Anglo-Saxon England. The attitude of the Church towards the institution of slavery therefore needs to be evaluated. Yet other questions centre on the issue of legal status. What were the causes of enslavement and from what sources were slaves drawn? Conversely, under what circumstances could a slave acquire a new legal status?

The most enigmatic questions posed by Anglo-Saxon slavery, however, do not concern the existence of the institution, but rather how, why, and when it came to disappear. Still widely in evidence at the end of the Anglo-Saxon era as Domesday Book shows,[14] slaves had completely disappeared from the sources less than a century later. From the perspective of an age which has witnessed a struggle extending over two centuries up to the present day to eliminate slavery totally from the world, the rapid disappearance of slavery from England, virtually unremarked upon by writers of that age, is very puzzling.

These are the major issues upon which this study will focus.

SOME EARLIER STUDIES

As early as 1685 the existence of slaves in early English society had been noted by Robert Brady in his book, *A Complete History of England*.[15] When over a century later Samuel Heywood was prompted to compose *A Dissertation upon the Distinctions in Society, and Ranks of the People, under the Anglo-Saxon Governments* (published in London in 1818), he devoted a full chapter to them.[16] Three more decades were to pass before the appearance of the first social history of early England to be based on a sound knowledge of a wide range of Anglo-Saxon sources: John Mitchell Kemble's *The Saxons in England*, published in

---

[14] See below, chapter VII.
[15] See, for example, his explanation of the word 'serui' on p. 206, n. (f): 'Servi Servants, or rather Slaves (for *Servus* in Classick Authors never signifies otherwise) were of two sorts, better or worse, or Predial and Personal. . . . The Personal Servants or Slaves had nothing of their own, but what they gained was their Lords who fed and kept them. These and their Children were slaves. . . .' He also discusses them in his 'General Preface', pp. lx–lxi, and on pp. 82–3.
[16] Chapter VI, pp. 355–424.

1849. His survey included a chapter on slaves which is still the longest and most wide-ranging treatment of this Anglo-Saxon class yet written.[17]

Kemble's interpretation of slavery was shaped by his overall conception of the beginnings of English society. In what has become known as the 'Germanist' view of early Anglo-Saxon England, he argued that the society was fundamentally Germanic, there being little continuity from the preceding Romano-British people and culture.[18] The basic group in Anglo-Saxon society he felt to be the 'free' *ceorlas*, who formed communities based originally on kinship. There were rights of common in certain lands, but in addition each freeman held an equal amount of land, a hide of 33½ acres. Kemble considered that Anglo-Saxon society moved in the direction of a reduction in freedom owing to an increase in the power of lordship and the decline of the free peasant cultivator.

In his discussion of slavery Kemble began by analysing the causes of slavery in order to distinguish groupings within the slave-class as a whole. In his view the principal cause of slavery was war, although voluntary servitude, arising out of the poverty caused by over-population, and penal servitude were contributory sources. The original slaves were Britons, hence the Old English *wealh* and *wyln* as terms for a slave.

Those who were not completely free he divided into two groups: (1) 'those who have been partially dispossessed by conquest, but retain their personal freedom in some degree' (the *lætas* of Kent should be counted amongst this number, he felt), and (2) 'the mere chattels of a lord who can dispose of them at his pleasure'.[19] The latter class Kemble in turn divided into slaves *casu* (that is, those who became slaves 'by the fortune of war, by marriage, by settlement, by voluntary surrender, by crime, by superior legal power, and by illegal power or injustice')[20] and slaves *natura* (that is, by birth).

Kemble then turned to the manumission of slaves. He regarded christianity as the primary cause of emancipation: '[I]t was the especial honour and glory of Christianity, that while it broke the spiritual bonds of sin, it ever actively laboured to relieve the heavy burthen of social servitude.'[21] His interpretation of the freedom granted was influenced by his view that Anglo-Saxon society made landed possession and the exercise of political and public rights inseparable. This meant that complete manumission would, in Kemble's terms, have had to involve the whole community, since otherwise those freed could neither have received land (unless their lords gave it to them) nor could they have been granted political rights. Since the Anglo-Saxon wills afford no evidence of such public involvement, he concluded that on being granted freedom a person would have remained on the lord's estate but would not have been subject to servile disabilities. The rights granted by manumission, therefore, were limited and

---

[17] The edition cited is the 1876 one revised by Birch. The pagination of the two editions, however, is the same and the changes made in the chapter on slaves seem to be minimal. The section on slaves (termed 'serfs' by Kemble) is in volume I, chapter VIII, pp. 185–227.

[18] For the history of some of the ideas lying behind this thesis see Stephenson, 'The problem of the common man in early medieval Europe'.

[19] Kemble, *The Saxons in England*, I.193.

[20] *Ibid.*, I.194.

[21] *Ibid.*, I.211.

subject to agreement between the lord and slave prior to the conferral of freedom. The types of manumission ceremony were divided by him into two classes, ecclesiastical and civil. Ecclesiastical manumission (by which he meant an act of freeing that took place in a church) was the commonest. Civil manumission included manumission at the crossroads and possibly the conferral of freedom by charter.[22]

Kemble's division of slaves into *serui casu* and *serui natura* is rather artificial. Furthermore, he was forced to use Continental evidence to suggest other sources of slaves (such as those who allegedly lost free status through marriage to a slave), since he could not find evidence of these in English records. Nevertheless he rightly perceived that there were some differences between slaves that came about because of how they acquired their status. His work in general has the distinction of highlighting most of the problems that any study of slavery would have to examine, and he justly recognised that this subject could not be treated in isolation from a consideration of the overall structure of early English society.

Frederic Seebohm in *The English Village Community*, first published in 1876, was likewise interested in the structure of Anglo-Saxon society as a whole, though in his methodology and in the conclusions he drew from the evidence, he was poles apart from Kemble.[23] He attempted to move backwards in time from the known to the unknown. His primary interest was in the manor, and he sought to understand how it functioned in practical terms by using both contemporary and ancient evidence.

Seebohm suggested that the manor had already appeared in Roman times and that perhaps the Roman fields had been arranged in a three-field system. When the Anglo-Saxons invaded the country the land probably became *terra regis*, but he considered it unlikely that the system of land management changed. 'It is most probable that whenever German conquerors descended upon an already peopled country where agriculture was carried on as it was in Britain, their comparatively small numbers, and still further their own dislike to (*sic*) agricultural pursuits and liking for lordship, and familiarity with servile tenants in the old country, would induce them to place the conquered people in the position of serfs, as the Germans of Tacitus seem to have done, making them do the agriculture by customary methods.'[24] He regarded it as improbable that the original inhabitants were all exterminated, but even if they were, it did not follow that they were replaced by free village communities. The *hams* and *tuns* of the early settlements he considered were 'generally speaking, and for the most part from the first, practically *manors* with communities in *serfdom* upon them'.[25] The general movement of English history Seebohm felt was for most of the people an upward one. 'Certainly during the 1,200 years over which the direct English evidence extends the tendency has been towards more and more of freedom.'[26]

---

[22] Kemble was – rightly – doubtful whether there were any manumissions by charter on the Frankish model. He cites on p. 223 *Manumission*, §8.1 as a possible example, but this should be interpreted differently. See below, p. 159.

[23] Quotations are taken from the fourth edition of 1890.

[24] Seebohm, *The English Village Community*, pp. 418–19.

[25] *Ibid.*, p. 423.

[26] *Ibid.*, p. 438.

Seebohm's arguments in favour of social continuity from Roman times have not in general found favour, though most scholars would now concede that the break was not always an absolute one.[27] His differences with Kemble over the Germanist position created a somewhat artificial debate based on rather too simplistic a notion of 'freedom'. His main contribution was to insist that the historical evidence must be interpreted in the light of the realities of rural life and agriculture.

Just such a sensitivity to the subtleties of rural life is exhibited in Frederic William Maitland's outstanding *Domesday Book and Beyond*,[28] published in 1897. This is one of a number of works that have been prompted to discuss slavery because of its widespread presence in Domesday Book. Maitland had no doubt that the *serui* of Domesday Book should be described as 'slaves' rather than 'serfs'. Nevertheless, he warned against thinking of the slave as a thing – although he doubted whether 'a grossly barbarous age' could understand the juridical notion of a person.[29] His awareness of this imprecision led him to conclude that degrees of servitude were possible. From this viewpoint 'the *theów* or *servus* is like to appear as the unfreest of persons rather than as no person but a thing.'[30] In this observation he anticipated Finley's arguments in favour of a 'continuum of statuses'.

Maitland felt that by the eleventh century the law was acting in such a fashion as to blur the distinction between slave and free. With the growth of lordship, lords were becoming responsible for producing their free dependants in court, just as they had had to do with their slaves. The development of private courts also led to both bond and free appearing before them. Furthermore, the slave had long been able to acquire a *peculium*, a practice supported by the Church. Thus, by the eleventh century a slave, while not possessing proprietary rights, could nevertheless occupy land and possess goods that could not be tampered with, provided certain customary services were performed for the lord.

In spite of this Maitland concluded that there was in the eleventh century a definite legal barrier between slaves and others: '[W]e may say that every man who was not a *theów* was in some definite legal sense a free man.'[31] He did not, however, attempt to define this 'legal sense'. We may hazard the guess that there were two reasons for his failure to do so. In the first place, he was attempting to apply concepts drawn from a sophisticated legal system to the relatively simple Anglo-Saxon one and then he was also seeking to define a social class solely in legal terms. He was, however, sensible of this latter weakness: '[W]e ought to

---

[27] Finberg argued in 'Roman and Saxon Withington' in his book, *Lucerna*, pp. 21–65, that there was a degree of continuity on the Gloucestershire manorial estate of Withington. For more certain evidence of continuity see Chadwick, 'The British or Celtic part in the population of England', in *Angles and Britons*. Since the publication of these studies, it has been realised that the term 'continuity' itself is imprecise and requires further definition. The distinctions between continuity of a settlement site, continuity of population, and continuity of occupation of a place are explored by Janssen in 'Some major aspects of Frankish and medieval settlement in the Rhineland', in *Medieval Settlement*, ed. Sawyer, especially p. 41.

[28] Slaves are discussed on pp. 23–36 in a section confusingly entitled 'The serfs'.

[29] Maitland, *Domesday Book and Beyond*, p. 27.

[30] *Ibid.*, p. 28.

[31] *Ibid.*, p. 30.

observe that the economic stratification of society may cut the legal stratification.'[32] He pointed out how in the south-west of Britain, where slaves abounded, there were instances in Domesday Book where slaves had arable land and oxen. On the other hand, there were probably freemen who worked full-time for a lord.

As for the decline of slavery, Maitland regarded the Church as having had an influence on the improvement of the slave's lot. Yet paradoxically it harmed the position of the poorer freeman, since by teaching that the slave was a person rather than a thing the Church helped to blur the social divisions further, something which, he pointed out, was already evident under Cnut.

Though he did not take his train of thought far enough, Maitland offers us an important insight in his perception that a social class cannot be defined simply in legal or in economic terms, but that a combination of these factors must be involved.

Maitland's contemporary, Paul Vinogradoff, reveals a debt to both Seebohm and Maitland in his writings. Like Seebohm, he was interested in the manor. His assessment of the part slavery played in Anglo-Saxon society as a whole he set forth in his 1905 study, *The Growth of the Manor*.[33] Like Maitland, Vinogradoff favoured Kemble's views about the existence of a free peasantry. Insofar as these peasants were warriors, they were able to acquire slaves through warfare, and the more successful of them would also have had the resources to purchase them. Those who were less successful would soon have had to engage in agriculture themselves, since the freeman essentially had to be both a farmer and a soldier. With both slave and free engaged in farming a blurring of the distinction between them took place. Vinogradoff argued that slavery is unsuited to an undeveloped agricultural economy because it demands the management of human resources. It is much easier to give a slave a plot of land and let him render services in kind as repayment. Vinogradoff's general position, therefore, does not differ much from Maitland's.

He considered that the variation in density between the number of slaves living in the east and those to be found in the west of England supported his overall interpretation, arguing that the reason for the difference in numbers lay in 'the development of larger complexes of property in the West, which afforded a more convenient field for the use of slave labour than the scattered and generally small households of the Danes.'[34]

On manorial estates, therefore, manpower was originally derived from slaves retained to work the land needed by the lord himself. To these were added in the course of time free 'boorborn' men. Because these men performed the same tasks as slaves, their condition approached that of servitude. Their numbers were swollen by many others: the kinless, the criminal, those broken by war and misfortune, and landless younger brothers and their descendants. These last could be paid by being given land to cultivate for themselves, a practice which he suggested then spread from free labourers to slaves. Thus, manorialism, in Vinogradoff's view, led to a merging of statuses. As slavery disappeared in the

---

[32] *Ibid.*, p. 33.
[33] First published in 1905. The more accessible second edition of 1911 is used here. Slaves are discussed on pp. 332–6.
[34] Vinogradoff, *The Growth of the Manor*, p. 203.

Norman period, 'bondage became more general, and infected classes and persons which [*sic*] had originally been free from it.'[35]

In his *English Society in the Eleventh Century* published in 1908 Vinogradoff returned to a brief consideration of slaves, this time more closely based on the evidence of Domesday Book.[36] While Anglo-Saxon charters had implied that slavery was an essential part of the society, Domesday Book suggests that slavery was in an advanced state of decay. Vinogradoff explained this change by positing that a reclassification of the servile classes took place in the eleventh century. In that century descendants of slaves were to be found among two groups: serfs, who were domestic and home-farm servants, and *geburas*, who are to be identified with some of the *bordarii* and *uillani* of Domesday Book. These formed a transitional group between the personally-enslaved and the serfs of the glebe. This social change was aided by a 'mighty current of emancipation' in the eleventh century.[37] The freedmen passed into the class of the *bordarii*. Without discussion, he concluded that the disappearance of slavery was due to religious influences and economic conditions. This appears to represent something of a shift from the position taken in *The Growth of the Manor*, where he had asserted that economic and social reasons lay behind the growth in manumission, rather than religion and philanthropy.[38]

Both Maitland and Vinogradoff have advanced our understanding of slavery by pointing to the economic foundations of late Anglo-Saxon society and by drawing attention to changes that took place in the position of the lower ranks of the 'free' peasantry. They thus show that social change was very complex in the eleventh century, and that Kemble's argument that religious reasons lay behind the disappearance of slavery is at best inadequate.

A fresh insight into the disappearance of slavery was provided in 1954 by M. M. Postan in his study of the English estate labourer in the twelfth and thirteenth centuries.[39] He accepted the probability that slaves were more abundant before 1066. By that date they were agricultural labourers working permanently on the manor. Many of these were ploughmen, as earlier work by Round had shown.[40] This is evidenced by the correlation of two slaves to one plough to be seen in many of the Domesday Book entries. Some of these entries, however, record a lower proportion of slaves to ploughs. Postan pointed out that this deficiency is frequently made good by *bouarii*: 'It suggests that the connexion between the slave and the *bovarius* was not only functional, i.e. not only a matter of jobs, but also historical, i.e. a matter of dates; that the slave and the *bovarius* represented two consecutive phases in the evolution in manorial labour.'[41] He accepted that there was some difference in status between the *bouarius*, who was a serf, and the slave. But while they differed in status, they performed the same economic function, and so in the course of time the slave became transformed into a

[35] *Ibid.*, p. 333.
[36] *Ibid.*, pp. 463–70.
[37] *Ibid.*, p. 468.
[38] *English Society*, p. 470; cf. *The Growth of the Manor*, p. 333.
[39] Postan, *The Famulus*.
[40] See below, p. 194 and n. 35.
[41] Postan, *The Famulus*, p. 8.

bouarius. He did not, of course, suggest that all slaves became *bouarii* – there were other jobs to be done on the manors of the twelfth century and no doubt this applied equally in the previous century. It is not unlikely that persons chosen to perform these other tasks were also drawn from the ranks of the slaves. The absorption of slaves into the dependent landholders Postan regarded as having started by 1086, but he felt this had not progressed far enough to have eliminated slaves who were employed in the lord's *curia* or household.

The advantage to be gained from assigning slaves land to develop rather than have them live in the *curia* was seen by Postan as the main reason behind the change in the status of slaves, rather than the influence of the Church's teaching or the act of granting freedom. He pointed out that the Normans inherited large areas of undeveloped land. When these lands were situated in a lord's demesne his best course of action lay in creating smallholdings, which enabled the land to be developed while maintaining the supply of servants needed on the demesne.

Another study on English rural life should be discussed here, although slaves receive only incidental attention in it. T. H. Aston in his paper published in 1958 entitled 'The origins of the manor in England' set out to rebut the then prevailing Germanist view on the late development of the manor.[42] He argued that there was insufficient time for the rise of landlordship and the appearance of manorialism to have taken place between the alleged flourishing of the free peasant society – supposedly found up until the ninth-century laws – and the twelfth century, by which time demesne and labour services were in a decline. Aston suggested instead that Anglo-Saxon society was organised on the basis of lordship from the beginning, and that already by the seventh century most lords had some tenants. He regarded the absence of freedmen as a class outside of Kent and the Danelaw to be very important in shaping this society. 'The legal depression of the ordinary manorial tenantry . . . has one of its origins in this easy and widespread absorption of freedmen, in which those of free birth were so obviously liable to suffer.'[43]

Aston portrayed manorialism in England as a complex process going back 'to that organisation of settlement and agriculture which, so our place-names seem to tell us, was already old when Ine described it in his laws'.[44] As an example of the complexity that could arise, he pointed to the contrary effects that good lordship could bring: the lord might help fragment the manor by giving grants of land to freedmen, yet by his dominance also promote unity by having persons commend themselves to him.

In a supplement to his original paper, published a quarter of a century later, he turned his attention especially to population and settlement trends. He accepted the orthodox view that population, and hence settlement, expanded over the centuries of the Anglo-Saxon era.[45] The various forms which this settlement took lay behind the 'growth of the manor' – but the expansion also led to a growth in economic freedom for the peasantry through assarting and reclamation, especially in the Scandinavianised part of England.

[42] Reprinted in *Social Relations and Ideas*, edd. Aston *et al.*, pp. 1–25.

[43] Aston, 'The origins', p. 70 (= *Social Relations and Ideas*, p. 12).

[44] Aston, 'The origins', p. 83 (= *Social Relations and Ideas*, p. 25).

[45] 'A postscript', in *Social Relations and Ideas*, edd. Aston *et al.*, pp. 26–43.

Aston's paper and its supplement serve a useful purpose in reasserting what was basically the view of Seebohm, namely, that the manor must be seen as having its roots in Anglo-Saxon society well before the eleventh century and that the process cannot be separated from the institution of slavery. Population trends and consequent settlement patterns need also to be factored into any assessment of social change.

His work was, however, one of synthesis covering a wide geographic area. What is needed now are studies based on a geographically delimited areas. This has been done in an especially illuminating fashion by John Blair in his *Early Medieval Surrey: Landholding, Church and Settlement Before 1300*, published in 1991. His suggestions about the development of the manor are particularly helpful. He has accepted Aston's views about the antiquity of the unitary manor, while also arguing that multi-vill or 'federative' manors too were early: both types were to be found co-existing over a period of some centuries. In his view the expanding thegnly class of late Anglo-Saxon England put pressure on all these land units. 'Whatever was happening elsewhere, the landlords of late Saxon Surrey had no disposition to amalgamate their manors into compact blocks. By the Conquest we have already reached the stage at which land was usually exploited in self-contained units of normal manor size, run from their own centres; correspondingly, the "federative" structure was in decline.'[46] He has acknowledged that the biggest estates belonging to bishops and monasteries appear to have remained more stable, but even they showed signs of subinfeudation from the 1070s onwards, thus continuing a trend that had begun in the Anglo-Saxon period. The driving force here was economic growth – and the multi-vill estates had much under-developed land. The consequence is that 'later Saxon and Norman Surrey was increasingly dominated by "normal" manors comparable to, or smaller than, the average parish.'[47] What gives his interpretation some general application is that this outcome is also evident in the West Midlands, where, as he has noted, 'nearly half the charter units are coterminous with parishes'.[48] The antiquity and stability of manors offer us an explanation as to how manorial custom could arise; and the change in the size of manors in the tenth to twelfth centuries together with the dynamic of economic growth that lay behind this change will provide us with a key to transformations in status within rural society. As we shall see, Continental historians have also identified agricultural growth as a crucial element in the disappearance of slavery.

Henry Loyn's *The Free Anglo-Saxon* is a brief inaugural lecture that was delivered in 1975 on the occasion of his appointment to the Chair in Medieval History at Cardiff. It merits attention as one of only a handful of papers by British scholars devoted specifically to the topic of slavery. More importantly, his address elegantly and with sound judgment has touched on a number of themes that will be explored further in this book. He has defined a freeman as one 'who possessed full standing in law'; '[t]he practical tests (as opposed to legal concern with status) relating to what was or was not free seem increasingly to depend on obligations, particularly obligation to pay and an obligation in

---

[46] *Early Medieval Surrey*, p. 31.
[47] *Loc. cit.*
[48] *Ibid.*, pp. 31–2.

11

matters of justice.'[49] The concept of freedom itself was complex and subject to gradations. Slavery eventually 'withered away'.[50] The slave trade ceased for a variety of reasons: the Vikings became settled; the Church was reformed and gained power; and the Normans imposed discipline and order. With respect to the disappearance of the slavery that had been recorded in Domesday Book, '[a]s the idea of felony grew stronger the significance of status, free or unfree, diminished.'[51] The growing power of money in the economy between 950 and 1150 weakened the distinctions between free and unfree. 'Status diminishes in importance by the side of ability to pay', and in the case of English society this led to the depression in status of those formerly free but also to the rejection of 'the savager attributes of Anglo-Saxon slavery.'[52]

Apart from these studies comparatively little of value has been written on specific aspects of Anglo-Saxon slavery.[53] But mention should be made of the chapters on Domesday Book published in the *Victoria County Histories*, particularly those written by Horace Round,[54] and of two papers on slavery in Domesday Book by H. B. Clarke and John Moore, which will be discussed in chapter VII.[55] The slave trade as it affected Wales and Ireland has also been thoroughly investigated.[56]

From the study of slavery in England we must now turn to wider issues: first, to consider a few works that have examined slavery as an economic phenomenon; then, to a recent study on slavery as a world phenomenon; and finally, to some current investigations into slavery in mediaeval Western Europe.

For an economic perspective on slavery it is natural to turn to Karl Marx. In point of fact, Marx did not have a great deal to say on the subject as he was more interested in what he saw as the later stages of economic development, the transitions from feudalism to capitalism and then to communism. His views on the early middle ages received their fullest expression in his *Formen die der kapitalistischen Produktion vorhergehen*, written in 1857–8. This work has as yet had comparatively little impact because it was published only in 1953, and another eleven years were to pass before it appeared in an English translation.[57]

---

49 *The Free Anglo-Saxon*, pp. 5 and 10.
50 *Ibid.*, p. 11.
51 *Ibid.*, p. 12.
52 *Ibid.*, pp. 13 and 14.
53 I. Jastrow's *Zur strafrechtlichen Stellung der Sklaven bei Deutschen und Angelsachsen* has been superseded *Die Gesetze*, ed. Liebermann. Wright's 'On slavery, as it existed in England during the Saxon era', and Warren's 'Slavery and serfdom in England', do not repay the effort of reading.
54 Round contributed chapters on Domesday to the Bedfordshire, Berkshire, Essex, Hampshire, Herefordshire, Hertfordshire, Northamptonshire, Somerset, Surrey, Sussex, Warwickshire, and Worcestershire volumes.
55 Clarke, 'Domesday slavery (adjusted for slaves)'; Moore, 'Domesday slavery'.
56 'Wales and the mediaeval slave trade'; Holm, 'The slave trade of Dublin'.
57 Translated as *Pre-Capitalist Economic Formations* by J. Cohen and edited with an excellent introduction, to which I am much indebted, by E. J. Hobsbawm (London, 1964). I have used the American edition published in New York in 1965, from which all citations have been taken. Marx did not prepare this work for publication and the text is frequently obscure and ambiguous.

In this study Marx formulated rather more closely his theory of the periodisation of history first enunciated in his *German Ideology* of 1845–6. The earliest form of society he considered to be based on communal property. This centred on the kinship group, though there could be modifications in the division of labour through the rise of chiefs and the use of slaves. Changes in the communal form of property led to corresponding changes in the social division of labour. Various stages could then follow. Anglo-Saxon society seems best to fit what he termed the Germanic stage. This was based on a class system, having a certain measure of private property, and thus containing, in Marx's terms, contradictions that would ultimately lead to its demise. This stage was based on slavery, but unfortunately Marx did not discuss the internal contradictions of Germanic slavery, largely because, as Hobsbawm has pointed out: '[H]e is not concerned with the internal dynamics of pre-capitalist systems except in so far as they explain the preconditions of capitalism.'[58] To gain some insight into Marx's mode of thinking, therefore, it is necessary to look at his views on Ancient society, particularly that of Rome, which was also based on slavery.

The Roman citizen was fundamentally a landowner. With the threat posed by other communities wanting to take over Roman territory and the need for more land for an expanding population, war became a primary occupation. 'Evolution of slavery, concentration of landed property, exchange, a monetary economy, conquest. etc.'[59] are in some measure compatible with such a tribal society and allow limited evolution 'but once the limits are transcended, decay and disintegration ensue.'[60] There are two reasons for this. The existence of private property implies the possibility of losing it, and with it the basis of one's citizenship. In a time of rapid economic development this is more likely. Slavery is the second contradiction in the system. With the need to restrict citizenship to the conquerors, enslavement of the conquered results. 'Thus the preservation of the ancient community implies the destruction of the conditions upon which it rests, and turns into its opposite'[61] because, as Hobsbawm has explained: 'The "commonwealth", first represented by all citizens, is represented by the aristocratic patricians, who remain the only ones to be full landowners against the lesser men and the slaves and by the citizens against the non-citizens and slaves.'[62]

Marx's contribution lies not in his presentation of a model explaining the details of mediaeval social change but rather in his providing a means whereby the material may be interpreted. This is based on the stresses caused within a society through the contradictions inherent in private property, of which the ownership of persons as a means of production forms an integral part. His theory of the periodisation of history is provocative, but more detailed analytic studies like the present one will have to be done before it can be seen whether such a theory is truly viable and can be formulated with precision.

A couple of decades ago a vigorous debate took place among economic historians over the reasons for the decline of slavery.[63] On the whole their

[58] *Ibid.*, p. 43.   [59] *Ibid.*, p. 83.
[60] *Loc. cit.*   [61] *Ibid.*, p. 93.
[62] *Ibid.*, p. 40.
[63] The debate appeared principally in the *Journal of Economic History*. See especially Domar, 'The causes of slavery or serfdom: a hypothesis', where the importance of the land-labour

writings are not very helpful for this study, either because their works contain methodological weaknesses or because they have suggested approaches that are precluded by the nature of the extant English evidence. Most of their publications are also characterised by a concentration on economic perspectives to the exclusion of other viewpoints. One study that is sympathetic to the interests of the social historian, however, is John Hicks's *A Theory of Economic History*, which is concerned with determining why Europe moved over to a free labour system from one that had used slaves.[64] As we shall see, the conclusions that he came to are basically those arrived at by Marc Bloch, except that they are presented in more strictly economic terms.

Hicks suggested that the choice of using slave labour as opposed to free labour comes down to the relative costs of the two methods per unit of time, assuming that they are of equal efficiency. 'If slave labour is plentiful, it will drive out free labour; but if free labour is relatively plentiful, it will drive out slavery. They are competing sources; when both are used the availability of one affects the value (wage or capital value) of the other.'[65] The only qualification that he felt needed to be added is that there is a general tendency not to enslave one's own people. He therefore suggested that during the economic expansion of the early middle ages slaves were expensive and so were undercut by free labour. Isolated from sources of slaves, Western Europe adopted the free labour system and this had become well established by the time an alternative source of supply, Africa, was opened up. Though this theory is a very generalised one and certainly simplistic, Hicks's work offers confirmation of a contention made earlier by Bloch that a continuous supply of people was necessary for the perpetuation of slavery.

The perspective of Marx and Hicks was essentially a synoptic one. A similar approach to the phenomenon of slavery itself was attempted by H. J. Nieboer in 1900 in his study, *Slavery as an Industrial System: Ethnological Researches*. This was a brave attempt for its time[66] but it has now been superseded by Orlando Patterson's *Slavery and Social Death: A Comparative Study*, published in 1982, which has been able to draw on a further eight decades of research into slavery round the world. Patterson has concentrated a great deal on the symbolic aspects of slavery because in his view language and symbol reveal patterns of thought. He has suggested that the powerlessness of slaves 'always originated (or was conceived of as having originated) as a substitute for death. . . .'[67] Furthermore, the slave was 'natally alienated': 'Alienated from all "rights" or claims of birth, he ceased to belong in his own right to any legitimate social order. All

ratio is discussed, but the words 'slave' and 'serf' are used interchangeably. For criticisms see North & Thomas, 'The rise and fall of the manorial system: a theoretical model', who are in turn taken to task for their model by Jones, 'The rise and fall of the manorial system: a critical comment'. Patterson also presents some criticisms of Domar's arguments in 'The structural origins of slavery', in *Comparative Perspectives on Slavery in New World Plantation Societies*, edd. Rubin & Tuden.

[64] Oxford, 1969. For slavery, see especially pp. 123–34.
[65] Hicks, *A Theory of Economic History*, p. 132.
[66] For some criticisms of Nieboer's views, see Patterson, 'The structural origins of slavery'.
[67] Patterson, *Slavery and Social Death*, p. 5.

slaves experienced, at the very least, a secular excommunication.'[68] A consequence of powerlessness was that the slave had no honour (a concept that I have expressed above as 'esteem'). This concept of honour has led Patterson to a definition of slavery that is based on the perspective of personal relations: '*slavery is the permanent, violent domination of natally alienated and generally dishonored persons.*'[69] He has paid particular attention to manumission because he has not regarded slavery as a static condition. 'Enslavement, slavery, and manumission are not merely related events; they are one and the same process in different phases.'[70] The rate of manumission was dependent on several factors. Women tend to be freed more than men, largely because of sexual relations that form between them and their masters or other free males.[71] Rates are particularly influenced by economic or military shocks to a society (except in the case of small lineage-based ones).[72] On the other hand, in his view monotheistic religions, such as christianity, have had, with only isolated exceptions, no influence on the rate of manumission. 'Christianity had no effect on the rate of manumission in medieval Europe. Indeed, church-owned slaves were often the last to receive their freedom. . . .'[73] One of his major conclusions is a challenging one for this study: 'The inherent instability of the slave relation has been one of the major findings of this work.'[74] This poses the question as to why slavery survived for seven centuries in England. He has noted that '[u]p to a certain point it was possible for slavery to flourish without marked social or cultural consequences; this was the case, for example, in tenth- and early eleventh-century England and Han China.'[75] Naturally, in examining slavery as a world-wide phenomenon, he could not be expected to follow through on the questions begged by statements such as the last one. These and other views he has expressed in this stimulating work will need to be explored in the pages that follow.

Slavery can be said to have been a normal feature of early mediaeval European societies.[76] Many of its characteristics (such as the forms of manumission) were shaped by the slavery of the late Roman world. Most historians, however, have tended to treat English slavery in isolation from that obtaining on the Continent. An exception to this was Marc Bloch, who included English slavery in his synoptic analysis of aspects of early mediaeval European slavery in his paper, 'How and Why Ancient Slavery Came to an End'.[77]

Noting that war has always been a rich source of slaves, Bloch pointed out that

---

[68] *Loc. cit.*
[69] *Ibid.*, p. 13 (Patterson's italics).
[70] *Ibid.*, p. 296.
[71] *Ibid.*, p. 263.
[72] *Ibid.*, p. 285.
[73] *Ibid.*, p. 275, citing Verlinden, *L'Esclavage dans l'Europe médiévale*, I.84.
[74] Patterson, *Slavery and Social Death*, p. 336.
[75] *Ibid.*, p. 341.
[76] For a very brief introduction to early medieval slavery see Phillips, *Slavery from Roman Times to the Early Transatlantic Trade*, pp. 43–65. Other studies include Heers, *Esclaves et domestiques au moyen âge dans le monde méditerranéen* and Milani, *La schiavitù nel pensiero politico. Dai Greci al basso medio evo*. More detailed regional studies are mentioned in n. 118 below.
[77] The French version is to be found in his *Mélanges historiques*, I.261–85. The English translation is in *Slavery and Serfdom in the Middle Ages*, transl. Beer, from which all citations are taken. For further comments on slavery and serfdom see also his *Feudal Society*, transl. Manyon, 2 vols.

the conflicts during the late Roman empire fostered an increase in slaves through captivity in war, acquisition through trade, and voluntary enslavement because of poverty. At the same time there was a growth in the practice of giving slaves land and then utilising some of their time and the products of their labour, rather than exploiting them like domestic animals. This came about because of a major agrarian change. There were fewer large estates, and slaves became less suitable than tenants for working these estates. Bloch argued that this was because slaves, being a perishable asset, gave a poor return and also because they were poor breeders. Once the supply began to drop, their value went up, and there was an ecomomic change in the direction of tenancy. Furthermore, Germanic society did not offer the economic conditions suitable for large-scale enterprise that imperial Roman society had.

In the Carolingian period the custom of the manor extended its protection during the second half of the ninth century to the slave-tenant, replacing a master's arbitrary power by rules drawn from local tradition. Slavery thus came to differ from the ancient type. In addition, from that century on the number of slaves decreased rapidly, except in England, where the change is only apparent in the eleventh-century Domesday Book. Bloch concluded this was because English society evolved more slowly: 'Serfdom, which there as elsewhere had to absorb so many former slaves, was scarcely established before the Norman conquest, no more than was the regime of the fief and vassalage – and the coincidence is significant.'[78]

Bloch then turned to the role of religion in this social change. Christian thinkers saw servitude as stemming from the Fall. Though all were equal before God, 'attempting to reform the established social order from top to bottom in the hope of bringing about the triumph of a happiness that was in itself impossible could only be a vain undertaking.'[79] The Church, in fact, served to strengthen slavery by not permitting slaves to enter the priesthood. On the other hand, it did recognise the religious validity of slave marriages and encouraged manumission as an act of piety. Both these factors aided in the transformation of slavery.

The motives for manumission were likely, however, to be mixed: 'as well as being a good act about whose nature slave owners were far from indifferent, the freeing of slaves constituted an operation from which economic conditions of the moment had removed all danger, revealing nothing but its advantages.'[80] Thus, although people could be manumitted without obligations to their former masters, more usually their lords retained some power over them. Masters could then be compensated through taxation and levies for the services they had formerly received from their slaves. Nevertheless, the overall consequence of manumission was that slavery became 'like a reservoir that constantly emptied itself at the top, at an accelerating pace'.[81]

Bloch then examined the rise of serfdom. He noted that the concept of freedom itself underwent a change, 'to the extent that a whole crowd of men who would have passed as free came to see their condition thenceforth considered as unfree.'[82] Though the serfs' burdens were heavy, they possessed different legal

---

[78] Bloch, 'How and why', p. 26.
[79] *Ibid.*, p. 12.
[80] *Ibid.*, p. 15.
[81] *Ibid.*, pp. 18–19.
[82] *Ibid.*, p. 20.

characteristics from slaves and also differed in the economic sphere in that their lords did not own their labour power; most importantly, their duties were limited by custom.

A new word, *esclave*, arose to describe the old class of slaves, proving that serfdom was indeed something different. The word was an ethnic name for the Slavic people, pointing to the old practice of enslaving foreigners. But in this christianity had a decisive influence. '[I]n limiting the area where masters and slave traders could legally supply themselves to the space beyond the boundaries of the Catholic world, if it did not entirely dry up the recruitment for slavery, it at least reduced the source to a very thin trickle.'[83] The Celts in Britain, who fell outside the *ciuitas christiana*, were thus legitimate prey, which provides another major reason for the long duration of slavery in England.

Bloch made a valuable contribution in ascribing the increase in manumission to a coincidence of religious feeling with economic self-interest. He has also raised an interesting problem in pointing to the lateness in the decline of slavery in England. His view that this was due to the late appearance of manorialism there needs, however, some modification in the light of Aston's and Blair's work.

Historians since Bloch's time have placed less stress on the servile nature of mediaeval society, accepting that there was a wide range of statuses in the countryside of Europe. Georges Duby in particular has argued in his book *Rural Economy and Country Life*, first published in French in 1962, that throughout western Europe there was in the period around the year 1000 'a reapportionment of authority' whereby 'the mass of labouring peasants, whether proprietors or tenants, were subject to the private domination of a few leaders.'[84] This change he finds most striking in France. In the north of that country the reduction in the authority of the king in the first half of the tenth century was followed in the south some fifty years later by a weakening in the power of the count. The 'peace of God' movement balanced this change. The transformation in the power structure led to an enhancement of the influence of local castellans, who appropriated at the local level the power or *ban* formerly exercised by the king. The claims of castellans to the right to control law and order led to assertions by them, not just to levy fines and exact punishment for crimes, but also to tax the peasantry (though not the castellans' relatives, friends, and vassals) for providing them with protection. By the second half of the eleventh century the distinction between a man of servile condition (a *seruus*) and a freeman (a *francus*) had disappeared: 'All that mattered for the lord of the *ban* and for his officials was the fact that they were workers, which brought all peasants residing in the territory of the castle within the power of the *sire* and his authority to raise taxes.'[85] This process was nowhere uniform or complete: many persons escaped the castellans' power and became dependants of noble families and religious establishments who defended 'their men' against the claims of castellans. The effects of this domestic lordship was also a merging of statuses: 'There ceased to be any distinction between slaves and free men amongst the "men of

---

[83] *Ibid.*, p. 25.
[84] Duby, *Rural Economy and Country Life*, p. 187. The French title of the book is *L'Économie rurale et la vie des campagnes dans l'Occident médiéval*.
[85] *Ibid.*, p. 188.

17

the house".'[86] Duby has acknowledged that the pattern was rather different in England. 'Inside the "manor", authority over men and over land, domestic lordship and land lordship, coincided. On the other hand the autonomous *seigneurie banale*, the independent territorial lordship, did not, properly speaking, exist at all. William the Conqueror held all the castles.'[87] Duby's discussion of the *seigneurie banale* has been important in later discussions of rural serfdom, though in *Rural Economy and Country Life* he was not interested in slavery *per se* and so did not address the English evidence on this issue. For our purposes, his insight that lords ceased to have an interest in the niceties of rural socio-legal distinctions amongst the peasantry will be useful – though, as we shall see, the evidence suggests that in the case of England it was the traumatic blow to the body politic delivered by the Norman Conquest that provided the new lords with the power to ignore distinctions between slave and free amongst the peasantry.

Mediaeval slavery has been a matter of continuing interest to Continental scholars and a number of recent studies deserve mention here because of their relevance to this book. Pierre Dockès's *Medieval Slavery and Liberation*, originally published in French as *La Libération médiévale* in 1979, has taken its inspiration from Marx. His work, which is heavily dependent on secondary sources, portrays slavery as 'ending' in continental western Europe several times during late antiquity and the early middle ages. He thinks that 'between the fifth and the seventh centuries the social structure was based chiefly on free peasants and tenants, relatively little exploited (as compared with previous periods)' but that 'the tendency, particularly during the eighth and the first part of the ninth century, was toward a revival of the great estate, gang slavery, subjugation of the poor free peasants, and increase in the burden on the poor tenants'.[88] This in turn was followed by a time of crisis in the late ninth century which led to the establishment of a new, feudal mode of production. This period of crisis was fueled in part by strong resistance from the peasant masses against their overlords. 'Thus it is possible that between the final demise of slavery in the West (accompanied by crises of the manorial economy and governmental authority) and the forging of a new coalition by the masters based on a new type of seigniory, there intervened a period of unrest – not only a time of insecurity, when vagabond bands of robbers, both native and foreign, roamed the countryside, but also a time of collective freedom, of revenge by the free peasantry, and of reduced exploitation.'[89] Once the mode of production changed, the availability of slaves through conquest and trade could not lead to a revival of slavery: '[O]ur view is that revival of the slave trade within or near the borders of a country in which the slave system has disappeared does not bring that system back to life, and furthermore, a slackening of the slave trade in a society in which the slave system is flourishing does not destroy that system.'[90]

In general, Dockès's arguments are not very convincing. As we shall see later, there is some evidence in the laws and also in the writings of Wulfstan that slaves in Anglo-Saxon England took advantage of the upheavals caused by the successive waves of invasions from Scandinavia in the late ninth century and at the

---

[86] *Ibid.*, p. 190.
[87] *Ibid.*, p. 194.
[88] *Medieval Slavery and Liberation*, p. 101.
[89] *Ibid.*, pp. 104–105.
[90] *Ibid.*, p. 141.

end of the tenth century to escape and some apparently even joined in actions against their erstwhile masters. Slave revolts *per se* do not, however, seem to have had much significance in the demise of mediaeval slavery. The best that can be said for this viewpoint is that it emphasises that slavery is a gross form of human exploitation and that those subject to it will frequently seek to evade it, though flight and poor labour-productivity are more likely than collective revolt. As for the slave trade, we shall see that both its presence and its demise in England must be viewed as contributory factors to the presence and demise of slavery itself. On the other hand, Dockès's emphasis on the concept of crisis when the reasons for the disappearance of slavery are being considered, an idea that is also central to Patterson's thinking, will prove to be useful.

Just as Dockès has followed in the footsteps of Marx, so Pierre Bonnassie is a disciple of Marc Bloch. His most important paper on slavery, 'The survival and extinction of the slave system in the early medieval West (fourth to eleventh centuries)', first published in French in 1985, is in fact dedicated to the memory of Marc Bloch.[91] He has swum against the current of contemporary historiographic opinion by arguing that in two respects the Church *did* have a part to play in the demise of mediaeval slavery: 'The consensus necessary to the maintenance of the slave system was . . . undermined at two levels: the free poor ceased to see slaves as the cattle they were designated as by the rich and forbidden to frequent by the law; the slaves found in the sacraments which they received the justification for their aspiration to the human condition and, in consequence, to liberty.'[92] As for the procurement of slaves, he has noted that '[i]n the early Middle Ages, slave labour was frequently being procured from a neighbouring province (through the wars of razzia of the Merovingian period), even from the same locality (through the system of enslavement for debt, the sale of children and judicial condemnations).'[93] A slave who was familiar with the local language and customs was thus '*less and less de-socialised*' (his italics)[94] and his continued status as a slave depended on a consensus between slave and free which by then hardly existed. These two factors modified social behaviour. Economic factors, however, also need to be taken into account. The dissemination of the labour-saving device of the water-mill, especially in the ninth to eleventh centuries, the development of the frontal yoke for oxen, and the invention of the horse harness, which came into general use in the two centuries after *ca* 850 leading to a quintupling of productive equine labour, all assisted in increased productivity causing 'a redeployment of labour, which itself generated a liberation of rural slaves'.[95] The great estate was ill-suited, in his view, to this kind of economic development; instead the dynamism of small peasant holdings was what fostered the change. In response the great estates 'were decentralised, broken up and dispersed. They, too, established offshoots.'[96] Enfranchisement of former slaves followed, not, as Bloch considered, in a time of recession, but rather in the context of economic growth.

In Bonnassie's view the disappearance of slavery took place over the whole of

---

[91] In his *From Slavery to Feudalism in South-Western Europe*, transl. Birrell, pp. 1–59.
[92] *Ibid.*, p. 32. [93] *Ibid.*, pp. 36–7.
[94] *Ibid.*, p. 37. [95] *Ibid.*, p. 41.
[96] *Ibid.*, p. 45.

the early middle ages. The institution reached its maximum diffusion in the sixth century and the beginning of the seventh. In the Mediterranean and to a lesser degree in Gaul changes occurred in the century after that: slaves no longer were willing to be accepted as animals and when labour was scarce because of plagues, they rebelled. Charlemagne attempted to revive slavery but the institution was to undergo yet another crisis, its final one in southern Europe, at the end of the tenth and the beginning of the eleventh: 'At this point, everything combined to promote the extinction of slavery, all the factors tending to its disappearance operated simultaneously':[97] adherence to christian beliefs became general among the peasantry; technical progress became diffused; agrarian expansion promoted mobility of labour; and state structures broke down and with them the repression that the State could exercise. At this point in southern Europe briefly 'society was free (juridically) from any form of servitude.'[98] This was intolerable to the 'ruling class', who then imposed new burdens on the free peasantry, leading to the serfdom of the feudal period. He has conceded that in northern Europe, where he has felt slavery was 'later in being widely established',[99] the change is less apparent and some continuity between slavery and serfdom can be detected. 'It should not be permitted,' he has observed, 'to obscure the essential truth, that is of a discontinuity – the death of a very old social order (the slave system) and the forms of subjection associated with it, the birth of a new society (feudal society) and new types of dependence.'[100]

Bonnassie's outstanding essay provides a new synthesis on mediaeval slavery in the early middle ages in southern Europe. I seriously question his assumption that late Roman slavery automatically led to the slavery of the middle ages except in the juridical sphere, since slavery in the Empire seems to have been more an urban and domestic phenomenon than an agrarian one.[101] Thus, when he writes, 'The slave regime was reconstituted more solidly than ever by the barbarian monarchies',[102] I would place the emphasis on the word 'reconstituted' and question the content of the abstract phrase 'slave regime'. He has also put little stock in the importance of a continuing supply of slaves for maintaining a slave system. Nevertheless, his observations on the chronology of slavery's demise is useful.

There seems to be a general consensus that the early mediaeval centuries saw an expansion of agriculture – indeed, a conference held in 1988 at the Abbey of Flaran was devoted to this topic: its proceedings are a useful introduction to the thinking of a number of social historians from England and the Continent on mediaeval slavery.[103] One of the contributors was Adriaan Verhulst, whose area of interest lies further north than Bonnassie's, in the region of the Rhine. In his paper, 'Comparative study of the classic manorial system to the east and the west

---

[97] *Ibid.*, p. 55.   [98] *Ibid.*, p. 57.
[99] *Ibid.*, p. 58.   [100] *Ibid.*, pp. 58–9.
[101] See, for example, Macmullen, 'Late Roman slavery', though one should bear in mind the qualificatory remarks of Samson, 'Slavery, the Roman legacy', in *Fifth-Century Gaul*, edd. Drinkwater & Elton.
[102] Bonnassie, 'The survival and extinction of the slave system', p. 52.
[103] *La Croissance agricole du haut moyen âge.*

of the Rhine in the Carolingian era',[104] he has argued that east of the Rhine those subject to week-work (the free and semi-free) and those required to engage in daily labour (the slaves) were in two quite different juridical categories. In contrast, west of the Rhine the distinction seems already to have been in the process of disappearing in the ninth century. Where in the former area there was an increase in duties imposed on slaves, west of the Rhine the increase in agricultural service fell on the free and semi-free; it was imposed by proprietors and only weakly resisted by the peasantry, possibly because of pressures caused by increasing population. 'In the light of the evidence for a majority of slaves and unfree to the east of the Rhine, we are led to believe, therefore, that in the central and western parts of the Frankish kingdom the seigneurial offensive was made on the free and semi-free because of the lack of the unfree.'[105] But the small number of slaves in the west then requires an explanation. Probably a combination of factors caused this: the cohabitation of the free and unfree, enfranchisements, the practice of giving slaves their own plots – in short, the greater economic development of the west over the east. He has agreed with Bonnassie against Bloch that the giving of plots to slaves was not a consequence of the sources of supply drying up nor of the increased cost of employing them on the demesne. Instead, it was the result of their increased recruitment, which he has seen as the consequence of a natural demographic increase, while the overlords' response in turn was a cause of population increase. Verhulst has supported Bonnassie's case that small peasant exploitation of resources provided an impulse for economic expansion, but in his view this cannot be detached from 'the great manorial development and more especially of its "reserve" [that is, its undeveloped lands kept for hunting].'[106]

Two other explorations of the social structure of early medieval western Europe should be mentioned, partly to illustrate that the renewed enthusiasm for the investigation of peasant social structures has not led to a consensus. Guy Bois's *The Transformation of the Year One Thousand. The Village of Lournand from Antiquity to Feudalism*, translated by Jean Birrell in 1992 from the 1989 French original, *La Mutation de l'an mil. Lournand, village mâconnais de l'antiquité au féodalisme*, is a study of a single French village with a focus on the tenth century. Bois has drawn attention to the survival of slavery into that century but has also stressed how important a relatively few independent land-holders were in preserving slavery on their small estates, while on great estates the distinction between slaves and free peasants became increasingly unclear. The former aristocratic class, with its dependence on slaves, was doomed to be displaced by a new feudal class which seized the power formally exercised by

---

[104] 'Étude comparative du régime domanial classique à l'est et à l'ouest du Rhin à l'époque carolingienne', in *ibid.*, pp. 87–101.

[105] 'Devant l'évidence d'une majorité d'esclaves et de non-libres à l'est du Rhin, nous sommes amenés à croire, par conséquent, que dans les régions centrales et occidentales du royaume franc l'offensive seigneuriale a porté sur les libres et demi-libres à cause du manque de non-libres': *ibid.*, p. 100.

[106] 'la grande exploitation seigneuriale et plus particulièrement de sa "réserve" ': *ibid.*, p. 101. Verhulst's review article, 'The decline of slavery and the economic expansion of the early middle ages', should also be consulted for other recent studies and for his comments on some of the papers delivered at the 1988 Flaran conference.

the state and extended their dominion over all peasants, freeman and slave alike. Feudalism itself fostered a fresh relationship between towns and the countryside, encouraging a new mercantilism based on the market. Like other recent social historians, he has stressed the importance of economic growth, the consequences of which include social destabilisation. All this he has argued led to a transformation from the antique order to feudalism that was abrupt and revolutionary, taking place in the Mâconnais in the course of a mere quarter of a century or less. Some of his claims will seem rather obvious, except perhaps to some dogmatic Marxists and *Annalistes* writing within the French historiographic tradition: '[T]here is no justification for claiming that it [the global process of change about which he is writing] was dominated by the primacy of any specific "instance" (economic, social, political or ideological). A crude materialism, determined at all costs to give priority to the economic factor, is here as naive and dangerous as the speculative idealism for which only mentalities count.'[107] The most dramatic of his assertions is that Lournand can be taken as indicative of a social change that swept western Europe. Even Georges Duby, whose earlier claims for the centrality of the year 1000 in the shift to feudalism Bois has accepted, is cool in his preface to Bois's monograph;[108] Verhulst (whose insights Bois has praised)[109] has written a hostile review article of his book[110] and an English historian has recently been no less dismissive.[111]

From the point of view of this present study, Paul Freedman's *The Origins of Peasant Servitude in Medieval Catalonia*, published in 1991, is most valuable for illustrating how wide the differences were between various regions of Western Europe during the period from the ninth to the twelfth centuries and for stressing how effective laws can be in subjecting peasants to their lords. In Catalonia during the ninth and tenth centuries areas won back from Islamic domination were settled by free men who worked small parcels of land. Bonassie had argued that these should be seen as 'peasant allods' but Freedman has suggested that they rapidly became tenures subject to annual payments to lords, though they were not initially subject to labour services.[112] Only with the collapse of the authority of the counts of Barcelona following the death of Count Ramon Borrell in 1017 were local lords able to usurp public authority, enabling them to bring about changes in the forms of tenure of the local peasantry and so reducing their rights, which thereby led to their enserfment. The focus of his book is on the rise and fall of this serfdom in north-eastern Spain between the eleventh and fifteenth centuries. Both from the point of view of its chronology and its concentration on serfdom his study would seem to be peripheral to this work. But because legal texts form a major source of information about slaves in the late Anglo-Saxon period, it is important to assess how useful laws really are in shaping a society and in providing a portrayal of its social realities, for it could

[107] Bois, *The Transformation of the Year One Thousand*, p. 166.
[108] 'And criticised this book will be, perhaps in part demolished, but therein lies its value.' Preface by Georges Duby in Bois, *The Transformation of the Year One Thousand*, p. x.
[109] *Ibid.*, p. 7.
[110] Verhulst, 'The decline of slavery'.
[111] Dunbabin, [review of Bois, *La Mutation de l'an mil*].
[112] Freedman, *The Origins of Peasant Servitude*, p. 64.

easily be argued that medieval legal codes are artificial constructs and thus provide treacherous material for recreating the past. In discussing the bondsmen known in Catalonia in the thirteenth century and later as *Remences*, Freedman powerfully argues: 'Although not all tenants in Old Catalonia were *Remences*, the elaboration of laws arbitrarily defining them as such tended to debase the social condition of many previously free peasants. It is my contention that far from being vestigial or artificial, servile institutions constituted a mechanism by which lords ruled and gained the profits of their tenants' labor.'[113] Though, of course, it does not logically follow that the importance of Catalan legal documents validate our using English legal materials for the same purposes, his arguments do show that legal materials should not be lightly dismissed.

Finally, brief mention must be made of Ruth Mazo Karras's thorough survey of Nordic evidence in her fine book, *Slavery and Society in Medieval Scandinavia*, published in 1988. Because of the nature of her source material, she has concentrated on the period from the twelfth to the fourteenth centuries, which falls outside the focus of this study, but her initial chapter is devoted to slavery in the early mediaeval period in general and, in particular, the concepts of 'freedom' and 'unfreedom'. In this last respect her work has more in common with German than Anglo-Saxon scholarship.[114] She has rightly seen that in defining a slave one has to bear in mind the social, economic, and legal spheres of human activity, and her discussion, which does not lend itself easily to summary, illustrates the difficulty of providing a universal definition for this category of persons. She has put forward four characteristics that might define a mediaeval European slave: such a person is one who lacks 'all or most of the rights accorded to others [of the same age and sex] in the particular society'; is 'an outsider who does not belong in a kin group or the community'; is one who 'labors under the direct control of the owner or the owner's representative'; and is one who is seen by contemporaries as a member of 'a distinct status group, the lowest in society'.[115] After a review of the evidence on slavery in Roman Italy, Carolingian France, and Anglo-Saxon England, she has concluded, like Bonnassie and Verhulst, that 'the end of slavery as a means of forcing labor came not because of a decline in the supply of slaves but rather because of a switch to a new means of agricultural organization.'[116] Next she has treated of the difference between freedom and unfreedom, in her view an important distinction in general terms in the middle ages. 'A spectrum of personal statuses is a more appropriate description of actual social relations than a slave-free dichotomy, but that dichotomy nonetheless existed in the minds of medieval writers'; one who was deemed to fall into the category of 'unfree' was endowed with 'a real social stigma'.[117] (Indeed, we shall see a couple of examples of this sense of social stigma in our texts.) This summary does not do justice to the complexity of the

---

[113] *Ibid.*, pp. 3–4.
[114] See, for example, Schott, 'Freiheit, Freie', in *Lexicon des Mittelalters*, volume IV, columns 896–901, and the extensive bibliography there cited.
[115] Karras, *Slavery and Society in Medieval Scandinavia*, p. 11.
[116] *Ibid.*, p. 36.
[117] *Ibid.*, p. 38.

issues Karras has examined in her monograph, which finds mention here because this book will be wrestling with the same issues of definition.

We may conclude this highly selective review of the subject by observing that as far as the historical analysis of slavery in England is concerned the general trend has been to show that the problems are much more complex than had originally been thought. Slaves, it has been emphasised, functioned in the social, legal, and economic spheres of society. Their position cannot be understood unless the position of other social classes is also examined. The disappearance of slavery must be linked with transformations that were taking place in other aspects of Anglo-Saxon society. Perhaps the major transformation lay in the development of the manor as an economic unit, a process which is now perceived as having started earlier than the eleventh century. This implies that the decline in slavery, too, was not a rapid social change, and that the reasons for its disappearance were likely to be as complex as developments that took place in the society as a whole. Religious, social, economic, and legal grounds have been put forward as the reasons for its disappearance. But since slavery in England has not received the detailed attention that the similar phenomenon in Byzantium, France, the Iberian peninsula, Iceland, Italy, and Scandinavia has had from scholars,[118] one may still fairly repeat the observation of H. G. Richardson and G. O. Sayles: 'The reasons for the disappearance of slavery and the cessation of the slave trade in the twelfth century are obscure.'[119]

THE CHANGING NATURE OF SOCIETY IN THE ANGLO-SAXON ERA

The work of Kemble, Seebohm, and Finley has shown that one must have a sense of the overall shape and development of Anglo-Saxon society in order to place the slaves, who formed but one constituent element of that society, in perspective.

By the time England moves into the light of history in the seventh century, there already existed certain large socio-political groupings such as the people of Kent and of Wessex. The evidence of place-names consisting of a man's name followed by *-ingas*, such as Reading and Hastings ('the people of Rad' and 'the people of Hæsta'),[120] and the names and hidages preserved in the eighth-century

---

[118] For Byzantium and Italy see Verlinden, *L'Esclavage dans l'Europe médiévale*, II; for France and the Iberian Peninsula, Verlinden, *L'Esclavage dans l'Europe médiévale*, I; for Iceland, Árni Pálsson, 'Um lok þrældóms á Íslandi', Foote, 'Þrælahald á Íslandi', and Wilde-Stockmeyer, *Sklaverei auf Island*. See also Karras's study, 'Concubinage and slavery in the Viking age', in which she attempts to get behind the Scandinavian laws and literary sources back to the Viking period; unfortunately English Danelaw sources do not seem to have anything useful to say about this topic. Williams, *Thraldom in Ancient Iceland*, is of little value.

[119] *The Governance of Mediaeval England*, p. 121, n. 5.

[120] The view that *-ingas* names go back to the earliest period of the Anglo-Saxon settlement, as expressed by Smith in 'Place-names and the Anglo-Saxon settlement', 75–7, has long been discarded by place-name experts. The names are still held to be early but are now considered to represent a secondary colonisation from sites represented by the earliest burials: see Gelling, *Signposts to the Past*, pp. 106–10.

Tribal Hidage[121] suggest that there were many bands of people linked – if we can draw historical conclusions from the highly literary Cynewulf and Cyneheard episode in the *Anglo-Saxon Chronicle*[122] – by ties of kinship and sworn allegiance. How to describe these groupings is problematic. For instance, German-speaking historians have tried to grapple with the difficulty of defining the so-called *gentes* in the Continental Latin sources.[123] Historical terminology is inadequate in such instances, and it is more useful to employ anthropological insights to describe these groups of varying size, social structure, and survivability.

We might best visualise Anglo-Saxon England of the sixth to ninth centuries as being a congeries of chiefdoms and tribes.[124] The term 'tribe' has been a source of dissatisfaction, particularly amongst students of African societies,[125] but it remains a useful concept in an anthropological context. The distinction between tribes and chiefdoms also has value, provided the definitions of these

---

[121] For an introduction to the Tribal Hidage with attempts to identify the geographic location of the various peoples mentioned in it see Hart, 'The Tribal Hidage'; Davies & Vierck, 'The contexts of Tribal Hidage'; and Hill, *An Atlas of Anglo-Saxon England*, pp. 76–7, figs. 136–8.

[122] For the literary nature of the Cynewulf and Cyneheard episode see especially Waterhouse, 'The theme and structure of 755 *Anglo-Saxon Chronicle*'. Ferro has attempted to retrieve some historical details from the rhetorical structure of this piece in 'The king in the doorway', in *Kings and Kingship*, ed. Rosenthal, pp. 17–30.

[123] Wolfram, *History of the Goths*, transl. Dunlap, pp. 5–18. Wolfram has warned against using the word *gens*, which appears in the sources: 'Whoever uses the word *gens* must be aware of the many variations it embraces' (p. 12) – but while he was aware of the terminological problem, he cannot be said to have found a solution to it. His pupil, Walter Pohl, has also grappled with this difficulty in *Die Awaren*, especially pp. 15–17 and 215–21.

[124] In this distinction I am following the terminology employed by Service in his *Primitive Social Organization*, although this should not be interpreted as implying my acceptance in full of his evolutionary approach. I have found his analysis more comprehensive and his terminology more satisfactory than Fried's 'On the evolution of social stratification and the state', in *Culture in History*, ed. Diamond. Although Service's ideas have been subject to criticism, the concept of 'chiefdom' remains a useful one, as a seminar held in 1988 to explore the concept showed: see *Chiefdoms: Power, Economy, and Ideology*, ed. Earle. In the following discussion it has not always been possible to avoid using the words 'tribe' and 'tribal' in a more general sense, but 'chiefdom' is always used in the technical sense employed by Service.

[125] Southall initiated some of the criticism of the word 'tribe' by pointing to its imprecision in his paper 'The illusion of tribe', and Roland Oliver has some illuminating observations on how the tribal concept was shaped by colonialism: see *The African Experience*, p. 185 and cf. pp. 147–8 (where he also notes that kingship 'could function admirably in a community of five or ten thousand people' with a court 'consisting of wives, children, young men-at-arms and clan elders acting as councillors and courtiers' numbering between one and two hundred people: he could well be describing early Anglo-Saxon kingdoms!) Ekeh in 'Social Anthropology and two contrasting uses of tribalism in Africa' has noted (pp. 687–8) that 'outside Africa tribalism continues to be used in its anthropological sense, whereas inside Africa tribalism is widely used in its other meaning. . . . As used by Africans, tribalism in post-colonial Africa refers to the abhorrence for the abuse of common opportunities and public goods (that is, those owned in common by various ethnic groups) through manifestation of undue preferences for persons of one's own ethnic grouping.' In this study, 'tribe' and 'tribal' will not be used in the pejorative sense employed by Africans and Africanists.

terms are not pressed too closely.[126] Chiefdoms possess a much tighter structure than tribes and have greater coercive power over the ordering of society.

Chiefs in Anglo-Saxon England were called *cyningas*.[127] Because of the continuity of this office over the past fifteen hundred years it is natural to use the modern cognate 'kings' to describe them, but it must be remembered that in the early centuries of the Anglo-Saxon era they were not heads of states as their modern successors are. Some of the early chiefs who possessed extraordinary power and skill may have been regarded as paramount chiefs over several chiefdoms, though the belief that such a chieftaincy conferred on its holder the title of *Bretwealda* appears to be an increasingly dubious proposition.[128] Clearly the members of the various chiefdoms recognised some ethnic affinity with one another, but it was to take till after the Conquest for the barriers between chiefdoms to be broken down completely.[129] The ties of a tribe or chiefdom to a particular place remained strong at the end of the ninth century.[130] The tribal sense of belonging probably weakened in the succeeding two centuries, but it should not be underrated, even in the time of Edward the Confessor, whose financial strength still derived from the old West-Saxon counties.[131]

During the early centuries of the Anglo-Saxon era the size of the country

---

[126] Tainter in *The Collapse of Complex Societies*, pp. 29–31, has some cogent criticisms of the typological approach towards the classification of societies, though he also has conceded (p. 29): 'In some respects, evolutionary typologies of human societies are useful in that they facilitate initial communication and comparison.'

[127] Early Anglo-Saxon kingship has been discussed by Wallace-Hadrill, *Early Germanic Kingship in England and on the Continent*; Chaney, *The Cult of Kingship in Anglo-Saxon England*; *The Origins of Anglo-Saxon Kingdoms*, ed. Bassett; Kirby, *The Earliest English Kings*; and Yorke, *Kings and Kingdoms in Early Anglo-Saxon England*. None can be said to have adopted an anthropological perspective.

[128] On Bretwealdas see John, *Orbis Britanniae*, pp. 6ff., and Wallace-Hadrill, *Early Germanic Kingship*, pp. 109ff., and references there cited. Bede, *Historia Ecclesiastica*, II.5 (*Bede's Ecclesiastical History*, edd. & transl. Colgrave & Mynors, pp. 148 and 150) mentions seven such kings; the A Version of the *Anglo-Saxon Chronicle* s.a. 827 adds an eighth (see *Two of the Saxon Chronicles Parallel*, s.a. 827 [ed. Plummer, p. 60.25–6]). More recently the term has been called into question and we may wonder whether Bede was not trying to impose the same kind of typology on the recent past as we today seek to apply to that period: see Wormald, 'Bede, the *Bretwaldas* and the origins of the *Gens Anglorum*', in *Ideal and Reality in Frankish and Anglo-Saxon Society*, ed. Wormald with Bullough & Collins.

[129] Bede's *Historia Ecclesiastica Gentis Anglorum* by its very title indicates this underlying feeling of unity, in addition to affording numerous examples within the text itself of intercourse between the various chiefdoms. Wormald discusses this issue of unity in 'Bede, the *Bretwaldas* and the origins of the *Gens Anglorum*', in *Ideal and Reality*, ed. Wormald with Bullough & Collins.

[130] Note that Alfred's primary source of landed wealth lay in Somerset, which Maddicott describes as '[t]he Alfredian heartland' (Balzaretti *et al.*, 'Debate: Trade, industry and the wealth of King Alfred', 184, and cf. Madicott, 'Trade, industry and the wealth of King Alfred', 46.) The maps in Hill, *An Atlas of Anglo-Saxon England*, pp. 84–91, show that apart from the expansionist Æthelstan, the itineraries of Alfred and his successors up to the reign of Edgar remained primarily in Wessex and Kent (which had been won from the Mercians).

[131] As late as Edward the Confessor's reign, the most organised system of food renders for the royal court was based in Wiltshire, Somerset, and Dorset, the centre of the old kingdom of Wessex, although it must be noted that such renders were by then also drawn from widely scattered parts of the country: see Stafford, 'The "farm of one night" ', especially p. 492.

relative to the numbers of the invaders may have encouraged fissiparous tenden-
cies, with some chiefdoms breaking down into various tribal groups, just as
happened when the Maoris settled New Zealand. But the weaker social structure
of these tribes meant that they could easily succumb through war to the greater
cohesive power of neighbouring chiefdoms. The advantages of the latter form of
social organisation are such, in fact, that some tribes will voluntarily join a
chiefdom.[132]

It would be a mistake to interpret early Anglo-Saxon history up to the reign of
Alfred in straightforward evolutionary terms, with the population of England
evolving from tribes into chiefdoms and ultimately into a state. Different parts of
the country at different times can be seen to have moved between these various
social forms.[133] Take Mercia in the time of Offa, for instance. In the latter part of
Offa's reign a process of absorption of weaker social units into the larger entity
of Mercia seems to have taken place. The Hwicce are one such group that came
under Mercian domination, and the *subreguli* mentioned in the sources of the
time of Offa perhaps can be seen as leaders of other tribes or minor chiefdoms
that had come under Mercia's sway.[134] For a time it appears also to have absorbed
the kingdom of Lindsey and Kent. By the end of Offa's reign in 796 Mercia
clearly had risen to the level of a chiefdom and possessed many elements of a
state:[135] it had the coercive power to ensure the construction of Offa's Dyke;[136] an
archbishopric had been established at Lichfield, providing both the religious and
administrative expertise necessary for the running of a state;[137] and Offa may
even have inaugurated a burghal system to protect this nascent state, which in

132 On the Maoris Service has observed: 'For example, the Polynesians who settled New Zealand found a wide-open environment to expand into, so that frontier-like pioneering was
possible and a leader of low hereditary position could nevertheless by charismatic force gain
a following and raise his status by achievement in carving out a new domain' (*Primitive
Social Organization*, p. 152).
133 Tainter has examined in *The Collapse of Complex Societies* the phenomenon of social
collapse, which is particularly applicable to Anglo-Saxon society right up to the tenth
century. One of the limitations of the evolutionary schema is that it implies a movement
towards greater social complexity. Tainter has observed (*ibid.*, p. 38): 'Collapse offers an
interesting perspective for the typological approach. It is a process of major, rapid change
from one structurally stable level to another. This is the type of change that evolutionary
typologies imply, but in the reverse direction.'
134 On the Mercians see Stenton's classic essay, 'The supremacy of the Mercian kings'. On the
Hwicce see Smith, 'The *Hwicce*', in *Medieval and Linguistic Studies in Honor of Francis
Peabody Magoun*, edd. Bessinger & Creed. Hooke has examined the landholdings of the
region in *The Anglo-Saxon Landscape* and Sims-Williams has provided a very sophisticated
analysis of its history in *Religion and Literature in Western England 600–800*, especially
chapter II.
135 Anglo-Saxonists have not been much interested in analysing the process of state formation:
this has rather been the province of anthropologists and archaeologists. Historians could
benefit much from some of the comparative material and formulations to be found in *The
Early State*, edd. Claessen & Skalník, and *The Study of the State*, edd. Claessen & Skalník –
though they would also find much to disagree with. (I owe these two references to Professor
Richard Lee.) Only D. P. Kirby among Anglo-Saxonists has shown any awareness of this
work (see his *The Earliest English Kings*, p. 24, n. 11).
136 On Offa's Dyke see Noble, *Offa's Dyke Reviewed*, ed. Gelling. For a map and a brief
discussion see Hill, *An Atlas of Anglo-Saxon England*, p. 75, fig. 135.
137 Godfrey, 'The archbishopric of Lichfield'.

turn might have fostered a growth in trade.[138] The presence of an *emporium* in Mercian London able to trade with other markets such as those at Ipswich, *Hamwic* (modern Southampton), and Quentovic in France,[139] aided by an incipient coinage in the form of *sceattas*,[140] meant that, economically-speaking, Mercia was ready for 'take off'. And yet it all came to nought. Offa was unable to found a dynasty; within a few years of his death Lichfield lost its archiepiscopal status; and the Scandinavian incursions of the ninth century disrupted the trading networks.

The process had to start all over again nearly a century later under the leadership of Alfred of Wessex. Alfred's situation, so carefully delineated by the intellectual circle round him,[141] suggests that at first he was little more than a tribal leader. By the end of his reign, however, his kingdom appears to have risen to the status of a chiefdom.[142] His successors were to expand the power of Wessex widely through England, so that by the reign of Edgar, three-quarters of a century later, we can again see the elements of a state. A strong system of *burh*s fostered trade and the presence of port-reeves ensured the king's control over this trade through the imposition of tolls.[143] External trade (possibly in wool)[144] had led to the importation of silver,[145] the minting of which was so

---

[138] This has been suggested by Haslam in 'Market and fortress in England in the reign of Offa', though it is a conjecture based on rather flimsy evidence. The words, 'might have fostered a growth in trade', have been chosen with care: for the hazards of imputing economic motives to the early medieval kings see Balzaretti in Balzaretti *et al.*, 'Debate: Trade, industry and the wealth of King Alfred', 142–50.

[139] On *emporia* see Hodges, *Dark Age Economics*, especially chapter III, and *The Anglo-Saxon Achievement*, chapter IV. Several papers in the 1986 conference volume, *The Rebirth of Towns in the West AD 700–1050*, edd. Hodges & Hobley, discuss specific towns, though it must be remembered that new evidence and interpretations are constantly being brought forward in this field: see Vince, 'The economic basis of Anglo-Saxon London' (pp. 83–92); Wade, 'Ipswich' (pp. 93–100); and Brisbane, 'Hamwic (Saxon Southampton)' (pp. 101–8). Vince has provided a more general introduction to the early medieval archaeology of London in *Saxon London*. David Hill believes that he has found the site of Quentovic; if correct, our knowledge about cross-Channel trade in the Middle Saxon period should increase tremendously.

[140] Blunt, 'The coinage of Offa', in *Anglo-Saxon Coins*, ed. Dolley, p. 39.

[141] Davis, 'Alfred the Great: propaganda and truth'.

[142] His control over Kent and apparent hegemony over Mercia reveal the typical absorption of weaker social structures into a more powerful chiefdom.

[143] On the *burh* see Hill, 'The Burghal Hidage'; Radford, 'The later pre-Conquest boroughs and their defences'; and Hill, *An Atlas of Anglo-Saxon England*, pp. 85–6, figs. 149–53. Sawyer briefly discusses tolls in 'Kings and merchants', in *Early Medieval Kingship*, edd. Sawyer & Wood, pp. 143–4; see also *Anglo-Saxon Writs*, ed. & transl. Harmer, pp. 76–8.

[144] This suggestion, made by Sawyer in 'The wealth of England in the eleventh century', pp. 161–3, seems very plausible, though the written sources say little. Archaeological evidence, however, is now speaking out: at Lincoln, for instance, a marked increase in sheep bones compared to those of cattle is noticeable after the mid-tenth century and there is other evidence from this period that sheep were being kept for wool. For further information and references to the archaeological literature see Richards, *The English Heritage Book of Viking Age England*, pp. 71 and 73.

[145] Silver was discovered in the Harz mountains in northern Germany in the 960s, which Sawyer has claimed in 'The wealth of England', pp. 160–1, was the source of the vast numbers of silver coins that were minted in England in the late tenth and the early eleventh centuries.

firmly under the control of the king that he could initiate the process of regularly reissuing coins.[146] The re-establishment of monasteries provided education, thereby fostering the administrative expertise necessary for the managing of the increasingly complex relationships that existed within the society. Record keeping, whether in the form of tax-receipts, land-charters or even manumission-documents, could now be undertaken. By the time of the Norman conquest, the sophisticated administrative apparatus necessary to support a state was in place.[147]

But let us go back a bit and examine in more detail the pre-state formations, namely, the tribe and the chiefdom. The warp and woof of these entities lay in the dynamics of social relations and in the social classes that developed. First, social relations. In a tribal society order is maintained mainly through the feud. This device can, of course, be highly destructive of the social fabric. Chiefdoms reduce feuding through the imposition of authority. The authority derives not from coercive power (which characterises the state) but from hierarchy. This marks a major distinction between tribes and chiefdoms; as Service has observed: '[B]ands and tribes are egalitarian, chiefdoms are profoundly inegalitarian.'[148]

In the light of this we should not be surprised that the first legislative acts of the Anglo-Saxon kings illustrate their support for the ritualisation of feud by laying down a scale of monetary compensation for injuries caused. Nor should we be surprised (*pace* Richardson and Sayles)[149] that in the earliest code, promulgated by Æthelberht of Kent, we find that representatives of the Church were protected by the highest wergeld, for by accepting the spiritual power vested in the clergy, Æthelberht was legitimising and reinforcing his own authority.

The statuses that develop out of the inegalitarian nature of chiefdoms can take various forms. Among the Anglo-Saxons there seem to have been three major divisions, the nobility, the *ceorlas*, and the slaves. This tripartite structure may have had Indo-European roots.[150] As far as the nobility is concerned, the early and widespread references to lordship in Anglo-Saxon sources preclude the belief that the Germanic invaders of England formed egalitarian societies. A

---

[146] Michael Dolley'a arguments in favour of a regular six-year *renouatio monetae* from late in the reign of Edgar onwards suggest the kind of neatness about an historical process that should make any historian suspicious. Ian Stewart has suggested that the process was much more imprecise and subject to particular circumstances, a case that is altogether more convincing: see his 'Coinage and recoinage after Edgar's reform', in *Studies in Late Anglo-Saxon Coinage*, ed. Jonsson.

[147] For a thought-provoking introduction see Campbell's rather vaguely titled paper, 'Some agents and agencies of the late Anglo-Saxon state', in *Domesday Studies*, ed. Holt. Keynes has provided a thorough and illuminating examination of the charter evidence in *The Diplomas of King Æthelred 'The Unready'*.

[148] Service, *Primitive Social Organization*, p. 140.

[149] Richardson & Sayles, *Law and Legislation*, pp. 1–4.

[150] Cf. Pearson's statement in 'Some aspects of social mobility in early historic Indo-European societies', 155: '[T]here is general agreement that early historic Indo-European societies were commonly characterized by an hierarchical system of functional classes which included a warrior nobility, a class of freemen farmers and artisans, and a class of slave laborers.' On the medieval notion of social tripartition see Hill, '*Rígsþula*: some medieval christian analogues', 86 and n. 15.

nobility should rather be seen as having been an integral part of every chiefdom and was probably present in incipient form in many tribes. This nobility most likely was endogamous within its class: it preserved itself by marrying, if necessary, others of the same class from outside the chiefdom.[151] In all probability it reserved for itself the right to fight, although in the conditions of the earliest settlement the nobility may on occasion have been forced to draw on other members of society in order for the social group as a whole to survive.[152] Death in war and physical, mental, or temperamental incapacity must have reduced the fortunes of many noble families. There is no evidence, however, that the early English tribes possessed a caste structure on the Indian model, and it seems likely that entrée into the nobility was permitted to the exceptionally able (and those who simply were lucky), although probably in the more important chiefdoms this occurred only over several generations. The sixhundredmen of the early laws may possibly represent such a group in transition towards nobility.[153]

A nobility of this kind need not have been particularly large in any one chiefdom, since the number needed for fighting is unlikely to have been very great. Vast warrior bands should be removed from one's mind; common sense and the evidence go against this. Anglo-Saxon society was based primarily on subsistence agriculture, although certain more successful chiefdoms must have had substantial surpluses to have produced or acquired wealth of the kind

[151] This is particularly evident, of course, in royal marriages. Bertha, the wife of Æthelberht of Kent, came from Merovingian Gaul; Æthelthryth, daughter of Anna of East Anglia, was married first to an ealdorman of the South Gyrwas and then to Egfrith, who was later to become King of Northumbria. (For references to the latter see Bede, *Historia Ecclesiastica Gentis Anglorum*, ed. Plummer, II.234ff. and Index, s.v. *Aedilthryd*.)

[152] The problem of whether fighting was done by all freemen or only by a warrior class is one of the most controversial in Anglo-Saxon studies. Stenton was probably the leading proponent of the view that all freemen owed military service; see his *Anglo-Saxon England*, pp. 290–1. The contrary view that warfare was the prerogative of the nobility was taken by Eric John, especially in 'English feudalism and the structure of Anglo-Saxon society' (*Orbis Britanniae*, pp. 128–53). Richardson and Sayles in their essay 'The Old English military system', in *The Governance of Mediaeval England*, pp. 42–61, came close to John's views in regarding the *miles* of Bede's day as 'a young man, unmarried and of noble birth, in the service of the king or the royal family' who in time 'might gain advancement, acquire an estate, and become a *comes*, a *gesith*' (pp. 57–8). They did compromise, however, by saying (p. 51): 'We are prepared to accept as a historical fact a universal obligation upon freemen, by custom or from necessity, to bear arms for the purpose of local defence.' Abels has thought that the *ceorlas* mentioned as being liable to a fine of thirty shillings as *fierdwite* in Ine, §51 were like the Continental *Königsfreien*, whose duties included attendance in the king's host. He has argued that 'fyrd service in seventh-century Wessex was an obligation of king's men. . . . As with the ceorls, only those nobles who were bound to the king by the tie of lordship were obliged to serve him with arms.' (*Lordship and Military Obligation in Anglo-Saxon England*, p. 22.) I still incline to John's view that the duty of the *ceorl* was to supply provisions for the king's army: cf. n. 160 below. It is possible that later on, with the growth of towns and the weakening of the tribal structure, freemen became involved in defence duties. But the slighting reference to Dunnere as an *unorne ceorl* ('simple ceorl') in the *Battle of Maldon*, line 255 (*Anglo-Saxon Minor Poems*, ed. Dobbie, p. 14) shows that as late as the end of the tenth century participation by a non-noble was unusual and noteworthy.

[153] For an alternative explanation of the sixhundredmen see Seebohm, *Tribal Custom in Anglo-Saxon Law*, pp. 396–401.

represented by the Sutton Hoo treasure.[154] But on the whole there would simply not have been enough food available to permit large bodies of men to be away from the land. This assertion is supported by Ine, §13.1, which states that an army (*here*) was any body containing more than thirty-five men.[155]

Those warriors who participated successfully in war were rewarded by the king with a grant of superiority over a portion of tribal territory.[156] Such a grant might have included some land that would then be worked by those owned by the warriors (in other words, by slaves), but it would also have embraced territory that was farmed by non-noble members of the chiefdom, who were obliged to support the warrior and his family as a *quid pro quo* for his martial services. This superiority evidently was held by precarious tenure and so could be lost: the memory of this practice is preserved, for instance, in the Old English poem *Deor*, whose narrator, supplanted in his lord's favour by another poet, laments the loss of the lands that had been granted him.[157]

The vast majority of the members of the chiefdom were agriculturalists, termed *ceorlas* by the Anglo-Saxons. In order to support the nobility as well as their own families, the *ceorlas* were granted the right to exploit land that was held in superiority by the king or his nobles, to whom they in return made a render known as *feorm*.[158] As John has pointed out, this right did not confer ownership; all land was ultimately vested in the chiefdom as represented by the king.[159] But

---

[154] Merovingian coins and Byzantine objects such as the spoons and bowls in the Sutton Hoo treasure are evidence of trading in luxury goods that by their very nature imply surpluses over and above a subsistence level of existence. For the Sutton Hoo treasure see Bruce-Mitford, *The Sutton Hoo Ship-Burial*, and for brief introductions, Evans, *The Sutton Hoo Ship Burial* and Green, *Sutton Hoo*. One might add that the acceptance of christianity by a king would also require surpluses in order to support the ecclesiastical hierarchy. Chaney's chapter, 'The economics of ruler-cult in Anglo-Saxon law', in his book, *The Cult of Kingship in Anglo-Saxon England*, unfortunately does not examine the economic production of the early chiefdoms from this point of view.

[155] This point is emphasised and illustrated by Richardson and Sayles, 'The Old English military system', in *The Governance of Mediaeval England*. Cf. their comment (p. 53): 'Large mediaeval armies never existed except in the imagination of historians, contemporary or modern. The limitations imposed by supplies of arms and food, by discipline and, above all, by distance were inescapable and insuperable.' See also Sawyer, 'The density of the Danish settlement in England', 5.

[156] For the concept of 'superiority' and the arguments centring on it see John, *Orbis Britanniae*, pp. 99ff.

[157] *Deor* (*The Exeter Book*, edd. Krapp & Dobbie, pp. 178–9).

[158] A king would make a progress through his territory during the course of the year, supported *en route* by food renders from his lands. The progress can still be seen in an attenuated form in Queen Elizabeth II's annual migration between Balmoral, Sandringham, and Buckingham Palace. For the practice among Germanic kings see Peyer, 'Das Reisekönigtum des Mittelalters'. This activity is a world-wide one among pre-state societies, as Kobishchanow has pointed out in 'The phenomenon of *gafol* and its transformation', in *Early State Dynamics*, edd. Claessen & Van der Velde, p. 108. (Linguistic difficulties and intellectual isolation led him to borrow from Old English the inaccurate term *gafol* instead of *feorm* to describe the phenomenon.) Both Stafford in 'The "farm of one night" ' and Charles-Edwards, 'Early medieval kingships in the British Isles', in *The Origins of Anglo-Saxon Kingdoms*, ed. Bassett, have examined the practice in Anglo-Saxon society.

[159] Although I do not support him in all the details, in general I accept John's position as set out in 'Folkland reconsidered', in *Orbis Britanniae*, pp. 64–127.

in practice the right to work the land granted to a *ceorl* through his membership of the chiefdom would have made it unlikely that a family could be dispossessed of this land, unless the status of its members fell through misdemeanour or misfortune. To this extent the land farmed by *ceorlas* was *de facto* heritable. *Ceorlas* should not be regarded as serfs or members of a rudimentary feudal society. Their duty to support the king and the nobility was inherent in *their membership of the chiefdom*, not in their possession of a particular portion of land.[160] Membership of the chiefdom gave the *ceorl* the privilege of being recognised by its law. He was accorded a legal status, which in turn granted him a wergeld. As a member of the chiefdom he was deemed to be 'free'.[161] In practical terms what this meant was that he could appeal to the protection of the customary law of the chiefdom in order to gain redress if wronged.

In the case of the third group in the chiefdom, the slaves, we cannot tell whether any were drawn from within a tribe or chiefdom in the earlier stages of the settlement of England. The later laws record the presence of *witeþeowas*, men enslaved as a punishment.[162] They had no recourse to the protection of the law and were regarded as chattels rather than persons. As such they were 'unfree', that is, they were not recognised as members of the chiefdom. There seems to be a natural tendency in human societies against the enslavement of one's own people, so we may assume that *witeþeowas* formed neither a large nor a stable element in any chiefdom.[163]

So far the different elements in the social structure of tribes and chiefdoms have been discussed in isolation from one another. What changes in the social classes did contacts between the various classes bring?

The early Anglo-Saxons must have come to Britain chiefly as infiltrators and conquerors.[164] The result was the disintegration of Romanised British

---

[160] It is apparent from the story of Imma in Bede, *Historia Ecclesiastica*, IV.22(20) (*Bede's Ecclesiastical History*, edd. & transl. Colgrave & Mynors, pp. 400–5) (text and translation) that the function of the *ceorl* in a battle such as the one in which he was captured was to give the logistic support necessary to enable the thegn to fight. *Ceorl*, like *cyning*, survives in Modern English but its current form 'churl' has suffered a debasement in meaning and so is not used in this book with one exception, where is is necessary for literary reasons (see p. 94, n. 66, below).

[161] Here Stenton with his old Germanist views on the 'free' peasantry seems at his most dated. Abels has a full discussion of the issue in chapter I of his *Lordship and Military Obligation*.

[162] *Witeþeowas* are not mentioned in Æthelberht's code but he failed to state what sanctions would be imposed if, for instance, a freeman was unable to pay his wergeld on being convicted of adultery. Penal slavery could have been the sanction in such a case. On the other hand, Wihtred, §26 lays down that a king may sell a man across the sea if he is caught with stolen property on him, which might imply that penal slavery *sensu stricto* was not know in Kent (*Die Gesetze*, ed. Liebermann, I.14). But the nearly contemporary laws of Ine prove that it was a familiar punishment among the West Saxons: Riggs, *Criminal Asylum in Anglo-Saxon Law*, p. 14 and n. 35, has pointed out that his laws, in fact, imply three types of penal bondage.

[163] The classic example is the 'jubilee year', observed by the Old Testament Hebrews every seventh year, when slaves of Hebrew ethnic origin were released: see Cohn, 'Slavery', in *Encyclopaedia Judaica*, ed. Roth, volume XIV, col. 1656.

[164] The volume of work on this subject grows annually. For a recent review of the evidence that is sympathetic to the point of view both of the historian and of the archaeologist see Higham, *Rome, Britain and the Anglo-Saxons*.

society[165] and the gradual conquest of the rest of the indigenous Celtic peoples in that part of Britain which came to be known as England. The effect of the latter conquest was the enslavement of a certain number of the indigenous inhabitants.[166] These slaves had much the same status as the *witeþeowas*, with the significant difference that they had never been members of the chiefdom or tribe, and so were less likely than the *witeþeowas* to be admitted into its membership (in other words, become 'free'). Regrettably, we are able to perceive only the most shadowy outlines of these early slaves. There appear to be a number of instances in pagan England of the ritual killing of persons on the death of a powerful figure: these unfortunates may have been slaves.[167] Possibly as our knowledge of cemetery archaeology grows, we may also discern those who were in the lowest social stratum, though the disappearance of artefacts from burials once christianity had been adopted makes this a faint hope.[168]

Conquest did not inevitably involve enslavement. In an agrarian society mass enslavement must always have been difficult: it may have been possible if there was a general social collapse attendant on conquest but more usually in analogous societies subject peoples have been traded to others, thereby removing the captives from their original place of settlement.[169] Often the indigenous society must have been left more or less intact but with tributary dues imposed on it.[170] If this society was sufficiently large, the tribal law might even have been forced to recognise the rights of the conquered people, merely indicating their subject position by according them a lower legal status than the members of the

---

[165] Agreement on the nature and extent of this disintegration has not been reached by scholars. Cf. the comments on p. 7 and n. 27 above.

[166] Cf. the comments of Gildas in his *De Excidio et Conquestu Britanniae*, §25, quoted below, p. 100 and n. 93.

[167] This is still a controversial interpretation. For possible examples see Dickinson, *Cuddesdon and Dorchester-on-Thames, Oxfordshire*, pp. 23–4 (a group of burials discovered in the nineteenth century and inadequately described at the time), and Carver, 'The Anglo-Saxon cemetery at Sutton Hoo: an interim report', in *The Age of Sutton Hoo*, ed. Carver (recently excavated burials at Sutton Hoo about which the excavator has declared [p. 355]: 'I feel obliged to suggest that the eastern group of graves is destined to be interpreted as a ritual area, contemporary with the mounds and involving human sacrifice around a tree.') Cf. Davidson, 'Human sacrifice in the late pagan period in north western Europe', in *ibid.*, pp. 331–40.

[168] Recent work has begun to refine our interpretations of cemetery evidence. Some studies that focus on British evidence include a volume of conference proceedings, *Anglo-Saxon Cemeteries 1979*, ed. Rahtz *et al.*; Boddington, 'Raunds, Northamptonshire: analysis of a country churchyard'; Boddington, 'Models of burial, settlement and worship: the final phase reviewed', in *Anglo-Saxon Cemeteries: A Reappraisal*, ed. Southworth; and Härke, ' "Warrior graves"? The background of the Anglo-Saxon weapon burial rite'.

[169] Oliver, *The African Experience*, chapter X, 'Masters and slaves', especially p. 116; Patterson, *Slavery and Social Death*, p. 170.

[170] This I think was the form taken by the *imperium* referred to by Bede (*Historia Ecclesiastica*, I.25 and II.5, and the notes to Plummer's edition, II.43 and 85). It is absurd to believe that, for instance, when Oswig 'also subjected the greater part of the Pictish race to the dominion of the English', he reduced them to slavery (*Historia Ecclesiastica*, III.24, and Plummer's notes, II.186–7; translation in *Bede's Ecclesiastical History*, edd. & transl. Colgrave & Mynors, p. 295) – an Anglo-Saxon chiefdom would not have possessed the numbers and resources to emulate what the Romans had done on occasion.

conquering group. This seems to have been the case with the *Wealas* of Ine's code.[171]

Since the Anglo-Saxons possessed a warrior aristocracy, war was in consequence not something that merely took place between them and the indigenous peoples: inter-tribal warfare amongst the invading peoples themselves was an ever-recurring phenomenon.[172] The fight in 679 between the Mercians and the Northumbrians in which the thegn Imma was captured is only one of many examples.[173] In this instance Imma escaped the death that should have been his fate because he was initially thought to be a *ceorl* rather than a warrior: instead he was sold to a slaver. Internecine warfare of this kind must have been a constant source of slaves in all parts of the country during the earlier centuries.[174]

As has already been indicated, movement in or out of the slave class could take place, just as with the nobility. War, crime, or misfortune added to the number of the unfree. Conversely, it was also possible for slaves to become freemen over the course of several generations. For instance, those called *lætas* in the earliest Kentish code probably represent former slaves undergoing this status change.[175]

Into this somewhat fluid but status-oriented society at the end of the sixth century came not merely a new religion (almost always a source of social change) but also the expertise necessary to institutionalise it.[176] The agent of change was the land-charter and the law it represented. Whether one sees Augustine or Theodore as the introducer of the charter into England does not matter here: what is important is that a device was incorporated into Anglo-Saxon law in the seventh century that enabled superiority over land to be transferred *permanently* into the hands of an institution. This was a radical change and one of lasting importance in shaping the society.[177] For with it came the means to accumulate land free from the risks of confiscation that had marked earlier

---

[171] Ine, §§23.3, 24.2, 32, 33, 54.2, and 74 (*Die Gesetze*, ed. Liebermann, I.100, 102, 114, and 120).

[172] The prevalence of warfare is the central point of R. M. T. Hill's paper, 'Holy kings – the bane of seventh-century society'. Eric John has also emphasised this point: 'Anglo-Saxon society was so violent that a central fact of its politics, its way of life, even, was fighting and making war' (*Orbis Britanniae*, p. 132), though one should note that John is really referring to the waging of war by one class within that society. The functional view suggested above of the aristocracy as a warrior class makes this continual warfare easily understandable (see n. 152 above). The warrior and martial ethos of Old English literature, especially the poetry, continues to fascinate scholars, as we can see in Hermann's study, *Allegories of War*. Strangely enough, little consideration has been given to warfare from a comparativist perspective since Chadwick's *The Heroic Age* was published in 1912. For inspiration scholars might do well to look at *The Anthropology of War*, ed. Haas.

[173] Cited in n. 160 above.

[174] For other examples see Pelteret, 'Slave raiding and slave trading in early England', and chapter II below.

[175] Seebohm, *Tribal Custom in Anglo-Saxon Law*, p. 484; cf. Pearson, 'Some aspects of social mobility', 159. See further below, appendix I, s.v. *læt*.

[176] For an insightful survey see Mayr-Harting, *The Coming of Christianity to Anglo-Saxon England*.

[177] On the introduction of the charter into England see the review article by Brooks, 'Anglo-Saxon charters: the work of the last twenty years', especially pp. 216–17, and references there cited.

grants, which had been dependant on satisfactory service being rendered by its holders. No wonder, then, that the nobility were interested in this, as Bede records.[178] From the land, after all, came economic power, and through that the means of gaining political power. Evidently by the early eighth century individual members of the nobility were succeeding in acquiring powers over land that were becoming vested permanently in their families.[179]

This portrayal of the early Anglo-Saxon chiefdoms contains most of the seeds of change that were to grow over the succeeding centuries of the Anglo-Saxon era. The two most important were the underlying feeling of some sort of common ethnic identity, which was masked so long as inter-tribal warfare prevailed, and the right to alienate permanently from the chiefdom the superiority over land, thereby allowing it to pass into the hands of one class. With the former lay the possibility of uniting the country under a leader drawn from a single chiefdom. Offa approached it in the eighth century, but it was the successes of Alfred against the Vikings in the late ninth century and the concomitant weakening of the other Anglo-Saxon chiefdoms by these invaders that laid the foundations for unification under a national leader, which was finally attained only by the Normans.

The second tendency presented the possibility of developing a manorial economy, with the workers on these estates finding their lives increasingly under the sway of local lords rather than being governed by the customs observed by the chiefdom as a whole. Such an economy demanded growth in innovative custom since the customary law of the tribe was inadequate in this sphere. This growth took place at two levels. In Alfred's laws one finds the first legislation promulgated by an Anglo-Saxon king to be drawn consciously from various tribal codes. With the growing power of the West Saxons Alfred's code probably came to apply to more peoples than just the inhabitants of Wessex. As a collection of laws governing a chiefdom, it was too broad, however, to cover the local circumstances that arose from the new economic conditions imposed by manorialism. Control over day-to-day relationships passed into the hands of those who had the power over landed estates, or their deputies. Estates differed in size and organisation. Thus systems of manorial law had to evolve which were designed to deal with purely local circumstances where the tribal bond was of little or no importance.

The process of development of the manor itself is still being worked out by Anglo-Saxon historians.[180] The subject is bedevilled by a lack of historical and demographic information. Advances are most likely to be made in the fields of landscape studies and archaeology but as yet there is no consensus on the nature of Anglo-Saxon settlement, especially in the Middle Saxon period (that is, the

---

[178] *Councils*, edd. Haddan & Stubbs, III.314–25 (text); *English Historical Documents c. 550–1042*, §170 (transl. Whitelock, pp. 799–810) (translation).

[179] On this see John, *Land Tenure in Early England, passim*, and 'Folkland reconsidered', in *Orbis Britanniae*, pp. 64–127.

[180] Cf. Aston's 'The origins of the manor in England *with* A postscript' and Blair's *Early Medieval Surrey*.

seventh to ninth centuries).[181] Here one can but attempt an outline, which a decade hence may be seen to need revision in the light of new insights and information.

Roman Britain appears to have been densely populated. The size and comparative rarity of cemeteries in the early Anglo-Saxon period surely bespeaks a major population decline (though this belief has been questioned).[182] Estates in the early Anglo-Saxon centuries are thus likely in the main to have been extensive and probably often drew on a variety of land-types in order to be self-sufficient.[183] The growing use of the land-charter for the acquisition of property by the nobility permitted closer utilisation of agrarian resources, and wills facilitated, perhaps inadvertently, the division of formerly huge and diverse estates into units that could be more closely managed.[184] This process was disrupted by frequent inter-tribal warfare and the Viking incursions.

Only with the transformation of the various chiefdoms into a nascent state in the late tenth century was the kind of stability available to enable the manor, with its demesne and peasant fields, to develop. The volume of land-charters and wills from the latter part of the tenth century onwards should thus be seen as an expression of the development of the manor rather than just a chance survival of documents whose forerunners had been destroyed by the Viking upheavals.

[181] Some of the evidence has been reviewed by Hamerow in 'Settlement mobility and the "Middle Saxon Shift" '.

[182] After mentioning that regional studies are producing increasing evidence of a high density of settlement in late Roman Britain, Peter Salway has observed in *Roman Britain*, pp. 544–5: 'If other regional and local studies confirm these calculations, we should no longer be comparing Roman Britain with 1086 (recent work on Domesday Book suggests 1.75 to 2.25 million) but with England in the middle of the fourteenth century shortly before the Black Death, when a figure towards the upper end of the range 4.5 to 6 million is currently thought likely.' Salway's suggestion of a densely settled late Roman Britain has gained widespread support. Peter Sawyer, ever ready to challenge orthodoxies, has questioned the view that Anglo-Saxon settlement 'developed by a more or less continuous process of growth, from small beginnings made by early colonists after the collapse of Roman authority until the early fourteenth century'; instead, he has argued that 'the rural resources of England were almost as fully exploited in the seventh century as they were in the eleventh' ('Introduction: Early medieval English settlement', in *Medieval Settlement*, ed. Sawyer, pp. 1 and 2). Sawyer did not directly address the issue of population growth or decline but his use of the phrase 'fully exploited' implies that the population remained static. I, like most Anglo-Saxonists, find this interpretation difficult to accept.

[183] Whether the multiple-estate model that has been propounded over the past thirty years by Glanville Jones in a variety of papers (for example, 'Multiple estates and early settlement', in *Medieval Settlement*, ed. Sawyer) will eventually come to be accepted remains to be seen. Gregson, 'The multiple estate model: an adequate framework for analysis of early territorial organisation?', in *The Borders*, ed. Clack & Ivy, is one discordant voice. The debate was joined in two papers in the *Journal of Historical Geography*: Gregson, 'The multiple estate model: some critical questions' and Jones, 'Multiple estates perceived'. That large early estates frequently controlled a variety of land types seems indubitable, whether they were the dens in the Weald attached to Kentish estates used for the grazing of pigs (see Witney, *The Jutish Forest*, pp. 56–77) or the upland areas and river valleys that have shaped some of the modern parishes in the chalklands of southern England (see Taylor, *Village and Farmstead*, p. 150 and his map of Charminster, Dorset, on p. 149), or simply a variety of topography in a more compact estate as in Plaish in Shropshire (see Robinson, 'Mapping the Anglo-Saxon landscape').

[184] *Anglo-Saxon Wills*, ed. & transl. Whitelock, *passim*.

Archaeological evidence in support of this picture is now starting to accumulate. Agricultural expansion into formerly marginal lands, nucleation of villages, the surprising appearance of a fortified manor at Goltho in Lincolnshire, all point to the tenth century as a crucial period of change in land usage.[185] The growth of towns with their attendant trade rendered unnecessary the old multiple estate, with its diversity of land-types (woodland, upland pasture, meadow, and field);[186] the will and the land-charter were available as tools to permit its break-up. The tenth century possibly even saw the initiation of the three-field system in the Midlands of England:[187] the social inequalities and the administrative tools were certainly then available to bring about such a change. The development of the various forms of the manor that were to become characteristic of the post-Conquest period encouraged the growth of local custom governing the day-to-day activities, duties, and relationships of those working on these estates. In a few lucky instances, such as the *Rectitudines Singularum Personarum* and the Tidenham custumal, we are able to come in direct contact with this local custom.[188]

Inevitably these changing economic and social conditions had an impact on personal status and the laws defining status. One of the tasks of this book is to assess how Anglo-Saxon slaves were affected by these changes.

---

[185] For a survey of some of the recent archaeological findings, see Hodges, *The Anglo-Saxon Achievement*, pp. 166–77. On Goltho, see Beresford *et al.*, *Goltho*; Hodges has claimed that the phase 3 fortified manor there should be ascribed to the early to mid-tenth century (*Anglo-Saxon Achievement*, p. 170).

[186] *Anglo-Saxon Towns in Southern England*, ed. Haslam; *The Rebirth of Towns in the West*, edd. Hodges & Hobley.

[187] Caution is called for here, since the evidence is still limited and open to reinterpretation. I have come down on the side of Glenn Foard, who has pointed to 'evidence of a comprehensive replanning of the settlement, agricultural and administrative landscape over a large part of England in the late Saxon period', the part of England in question being the area 'which was characterized in the medieval period by open fields and nucleated villages' (review of *Anglo-Saxon Settlements*, ed. Hooke, 253). Support for pre-Conquest changes in estate management also comes from another quarter: Stafford's study of Edward the Confessor's food renders. She has observed with respect to the royal estates in 'The "farm of one night" ', 498: 'But there is evidence to suggest that in some cases Domesday reveals not simply an ancient system surviving intact, but also the results of the dynamic management of the demesne managers of more recent history.' On the other hand, we should note that Beresford and Hurst now consider that the evidence for replanning at Wharram Percy, first thought to date from the tenth century, should, in fact, be dated to the twelfth century: see their *English Heritage Book of Wharram Percy Deserted Medieval Village*, p. 96. This and other evidence has inclined Biddick in 'People and things: power in early English development', to place the nucleation of settlement later, 'possibly as late as the twelfth century' (p. 7), though she has wisely not taken a final position on this as the evidence is still being assessed.

[188] On the *Rectitudines Singularum Personarum* and the Tidenham custumal, see chapter VI below.

THE SCOPE OF THIS STUDY

Nora Chadwick has observed that in the exploration of early mediaeval history 'selection plays hardly any part because our sources are so few that every scrap of material is precious. For synthesis we have to substitute the detective instinct, and seek to determine the importance of the significantly little.'[189] Nowhere is this more true than in the study of slavery in England. In a society where writing was the preserve almost entirely of the Church and tended therefore to serve its interests, slaves, who were excluded by canon law from ecclesiastical positions and by tribal law from participation in the government of the society, receive only incidental mention in most documents of the period.

The nature of the source material itself places further restrictions on the kinds of information about slaves that are available to us. To determine the various types of slave and freedman status in Anglo-Saxon society one must examine the vernacular terminology; to comprehend the attitudes of the free towards slaves one has to examine literary documents such as homilies and saints' lives; to learn about the rights and obligations of a slave one has to turn to the laws; to understand the slave-owners' attitudes towards manumission one must read the wills; to discover the process of manumission itself one has to analyse the manumission-documents; to put the slave in an economic perspective within late Anglo-Saxon society one must take into consideration the land-charters and custumals; finally, to ascertain the patterns of ownership and distribution of slaves, as well as the reduction in their numbers in certain areas, one has to delve into Domesday Book. Thus each type of source tends to reveal a different facet of slavery, in large measure because of its literary genre.[190]

The limited amount of information on slavery and the shaping of that information by the nature of the sources have dictated the unusual approach adopted in this book. Instead of employing the thematic approach of the historian, the structure of this work is determined by the nature of the sources, a methodology more usually employed in literary studies. We shall start by looking at the Old English terminology employed to denote slaves, slavery, freedmen, and freedom. The study then will turn to an analysis of what the different genres of source material reveal about slavery in England. This concentration on the varying types of evidence will enable us to discern patterns that would otherwise be lost if a more conventional thematic approach were adopted, such as the increase in manumissions in the wills and the changing nature of the freedom granted in the manumission-documents.

In two instances, however, it seems worthwhile to break out of a framework

---

[189] Chadwick *et al.*, *Studies in the Early British Church*, p. 20.

[190] 'Literature' is here being used in a much wider sense than simply *'belles lettres'*. In this I share the outlook of the late Angus Cameron, who argued from the point of view of a literary critic that our perspective on Old English literature should embrace *all* prose writings, as well as poetry: 'My mild reproach to the earlier literary historians is that they have given a great deal of time to a small number of texts and have merely catalogued or ignored the rest' ('The boundaries of Old English literature', in *The Anglo-Saxons: Synthesis and Achievement*, edd. Woods & Pelteret, p. 34).

shaped by genre. Ælfric and Wulfstan stand apart from other authors of the late Anglo-Saxon period because of the volume and range of their literary production. Ælfric is particularly noteworthy for his homiletic writings, Wulfstan for his secular legislation and ecclesiastical regulations. Both produced works in other genres. To fragment their respective *oeuvres* would be to mask, if not distort, the views on slavery of two of the leading writers of the age. Ælfric's works, therefore, will be treated as a whole in the chapter on literary materials and Wulfstan's in the chapter on legislation.

Even with the adoption of this approach certain themes will be seen to be present throughout the book. These centre on the questions about the existence of slavery in Anglo-Saxon England that were raised in the second section of this chapter. The Conclusion will draw these themes together. First, a profile of the Anglo-Saxon slave will be presented, employing the model suggested by Finley. Then the disappearance of slavery in England will be discussed. This will be followed by an examination of the attitude of the Church towards slaves and slavery. Finally, the relationship of slavery in England to the institution as it existed in early mediaeval societies elsewhere in western Europe will be assessed.

The nature of the evidence has also dictated the chronological limits of this book. Any attempt to deal fully with slavery in England prior to the late ninth century would demand that a number of wider problems be tackled first. For much of the earlier period the written material presents severe difficulties. For the seventh century one is primarily dependent on the early laws; but their function and relationship to contemporary European codes still need to be evaluated – a book in itself. The laws place a monetary value on injuries and on different classes of people. Philip Grierson has called into question earlier interpretations of the coinage mentioned in these laws, which means that views of scholars like H. M. Chadwick on the structure of primitive Anglo-Saxon tribes may need to be revised.[191] For the late seventh and the eighth century land-charters become available, but the interpretation of this evidence is also subject to controversy,[192] and one is sorely hampered by outmoded editions.[193] Written sources for the first few centuries of the Anglo-Saxon era can be supplemented by place-name and archaeological data. Much of this, however, is still ambiguous: frequently one is now at the stage of being able to ask more intelligent questions rather than finding it possible to answer them.[194]

For these reasons, the reign of King Alfred of Wessex (872–899) has been

---

[191] Grierson, 'La Fonction sociale de la monnaie en Angleterre aux VIIe–VIIIe siècles', in *Moneta e scambi nell'alto medioevo*, pp. 341–62; 'La discussione', *ibid.*, pp. 363–85; Chadwick, *Studies on Anglo-Saxon Institutions*, especially pp. 156–60.

[192] See the reviews of John's *Land Tenure* by Grosjean and Whitelock; cf. also the comments of Bullough, 'Anglo-Saxon institutions and early English society', 652–3, and Brookes, 'Anglo-Saxon charters'.

[193] The British Academy and the Royal Historical Society are now jointly sponsoring the editing of all the extant Anglo-Saxon land-charters.

[194] See Higham, *Rome, Britain and the Anglo-Saxons*, especially p. 209. Some of the complexity involved in place-name interpretation is shown in Dodgson's discussion of *-ham/-hamm* names, 'Place-names from *hām*, distinguished from *hamm* names', and Gelling's two books, *Place-Names in the Landscape* and *Signposts to the Past*.

taken as the starting point for this study. From his reign onwards literary and legal sources increase considerably. Earlier evidence, however, will occasionally be utilised when it can elucidate problems that appear subsequent to 872. The terminal point of the book is dictated by when the evidence for slavery in England peters out – sometime in the second quarter of the twelfth century. By ignoring the political date of 1066 we can exploit the riches of Domesday Book, an extremely valuable source of evidence about English slavery, and we can also rise to the challenge posed by one of the most important questions about English slavery, the reasons for its disappearance from the country.

Our quest, it is sad to say, will not enable us to get to know many individual slaves. Often the evidence will frustrate us because it will fail to answer our questions. Yet by devoting some of our time to recovering the lives of these unknown people from the early centuries of English history, we implicitly declare the value of our present existence.

I

ÞEOW AND *ÞEOWEN, ÞRÆLL* AND *ÞIR*: THE LINGUISTIC EVIDENCE ON SLAVERY

The Anglo-Saxons possessed an extensive terminology of servitude and free-dom. There are several reasons for this large vocabulary. Since slavery was an integral part of Anglo-Saxon society, a sizeable lexicon was needed to express the diverse relationships fostered by this institution. Slavery was also part and parcel of the mixed Scandinavian and Anglo-Saxon society of the Danelaw. As the two peoples integrated some Scandinavian words for slaves were adopted into Old English. The Anglo-Saxon language was also influenced by ideas drawn from a quite different sphere. Biblical writers and the early christian Church Fathers, influenced by the omnipresent institution of slavery, had employed the terminology of servitude and freedom to express the nature of Humanity's relationship to God and the devil. The translation of these theological texts into Old English led to an expansion of the Old English vocabulary and an enlarge-ment of the senses of existing words. Then, too, the Latin vocabulary of land law employed the vocabulary of servitude to a certain extent, thereby extending the semantic range of English vocabulary yet further.

In this chapter these influences will be examined in turn. The semantics of individual words will not be our primary concern: the emphasis rather will be on what the vocabulary reveals about the institution of slavery within Anglo-Saxon society.

THE INDIGENOUS OLD ENGLISH TERMINOLOGY OF SERVITUDE AND FREEDOM

For the sake of convenience the Old English terminology relating to slavery is best divided into two groups: words used to describe slavery itself and vocabu-lary employed to denote the transformation of status from slave to freeman.

The main Old English word used to describe a slave was *þeow*. Remarkably stable in meaning, it seems always to have referred to someone who was in a legal state of servitude. It carried no implications as to how that state was acquired, nor does the word ever seem to have gained pejorative overtones. Perhaps because it was so tied to a defined legal institution, it eventually dropped out of use in Middle English to be replaced by the two words, *thrall* (which seems to have possessed a pejorative connotation even in Old English)[1]

---

[1] See below, appendix I, s.v. *þræl*.

41

and *slave*, which came into English via French in the thirteenth century after the native institution had disappeared. As long as 'slave' remained a definable legal category *þeow* survived; when the law finally caught up with social and economic reality by dropping the category, the word itself was doomed. Its last appearance in writing in any of its forms (apart from its resurrection as an archaism in the nineteenth century) was in 1400, and significantly the fourteenth-century citations in the *Oxford English Dictionary* always record it in phrases like *þeuwe and þral* and *thewe & freo*, where clearly it is a fossilised relic.

Þeow as the general word for someone in a legal state of slavery was particularly rich in derivatives. There was a feminine equivalent, *þeowen*, 'a female slave', and also several diminutive forms, *þeowling*, 'a slave', *þeowincel*, 'a little or young slave', and through the abstract noun *þeowet*, *þeowetling*, 'a young slave'. To express the abstract state of slavery the words *þeowet*, *þeowdom*, and *þeowdomhad* were used. *Þeow* seems to have retained its legal connotation in most of its compounds; only in the case of *þeowdom* ('a state of legal servitude' and hence 'service') and *þeow(i)an* ('to serve as a slave' and hence 'to serve') does the root seem to have lost this legal sense.

In terms of early Anglo-Saxon law a slave possessed no legal personality but was a chattel. This is brought out by the word *æht*, 'something owned by a person', 'property', which then gained the specialised sense 'some*one* owned by a person', 'a slave'. As a piece of property a slave could be bought and sold. The verb used to denote the purchase of a slave is *bicgan (æt)*. *Bebicgan* is the only verb recorded as denoting the selling of persons, but the presence of the noun *mannsilen*, 'the sale of a person', probably indicates that *sellan* was used as well. The compound *ceapcniht* is used of 'a young person who is for sale'. From the point of view of an owner, a slave could be described as a *freohsceatt*, 'a person who could be freely disposed of'. A slave who was legally owned was called a *rihtþeow*.

Probably all slave-owning societies find it difficult to regard a slave simply as an object. The ambivalent attitude of Anglo-Saxon society over whether to view a slave as a chattel or a fellow human-being is reflected in the vocabulary. A number of words used of males or females in general gained the specialised meaning of 'slave'. The word *mann*, originally 'a human-being of either sex' and then 'a male human-being', acquired a further sense 'a male human-being belonging to someone else', 'a slave'. The feminine cognate, *mennen*, is found only in the sense 'a female slave'. Two other nouns referring to women in general, *wifmann*, 'a woman', and *mægden-mann*, 'a young woman', were also used of female slaves in certain contexts. Three such general words for women gained this specialised meaning as against only one for men perhaps because of the closer personal contact women slaves had with their masters in their positions as domestic servants or concubines.

That a person could be a slave for a variety of reasons is reflected in the vocabulary. For some it was a condition that one was born into: the compounds *þeowboren* and *þeowbyrd*, 'born a slave', supply proof of this. Criminal conviction was another reason. The prefix *wite-* was used in these cases, appearing in the substantive *witeþeow*, 'one who has become a slave as a punishment', 'a penal slave', and the adjectival equivalent *witefæst*, 'enslaved as a punishment'. *Nid-*, which denoted force, was also employed: it appears in the words *nidþeow* and *nidþeowetling*, 'a person who is compulsorily enslaved' (the diminutive suffix here presumably being pejorative).

In the early Anglo-Saxon period people were enslaved mainly through subjugation in war.[2] It is surprising, therefore, that this source of slaves received hardly any recognition in Old English. The gloss *hæftincel*, 'a young male slave', suggests that the simplex *hæft*, 'a captive', also possessed an unattested sense 'slave'. Presumably this latter sense of *hæft* did not survive because once captives had been integrated into the economic structure of the tribe it seemed inappropriate to describe their servile descendants by such a term.

An indirect indication of conquest as a source of slaves is provided by the words *wealh*, *wiln*, and the diminutive form of the latter, *wilnincel*.[3] *Wealh* seems to have had as its original meaning 'a foreigner'. It was early used to indicate 'a foreigner of British origin', 'a Celt'. In English sources (mainly south-western) it also acquired the sense 'a Celtic slave' or simply 'a slave', presumably because many of the conquered Celts in the south-west of Britain were enslaved by the Anglo-Saxons. In this it shows the same semantic development as the word *slave* itself, which is cognate with *Slav*.[4] *Wiln* is derived from *wealh*, with the addition of the feminine suffix *-en*. Since *wiln* displays *i*-mutation, a phonological change that can be dated to *ca* A.D. 700,[5] the suffix must have been added before then. It is never found in the sense 'Celtic woman' and may have had a wider dialectal distribution than *wealh*, though it still appears to have been a southern word. In the light of this evidence it seem probable that it was derived from *wealh* in its original sense of 'a foreigner'. Both *hæftincel* and *wealh* indicate the importance of people taken from outside the tribe as a source of slaves, and in the case of the latter word, specifically those of Celtic origin.

There are four other examples in Old English of masculine nouns with feminine cognates that denote slaves: *man/mennen*, *scealc/scielcen*, *þegn/þignen*, and *þeow/þeowen*. The first three feminine nouns have undergone *i*-mutation[6] and so are very early borrowings. This seems to indicate that there was no tendency to enslave members of only one sex.

A number of Old English words point to the use of young people as slaves. The words *þegn* (cognate with τέκνον, 'child', 'son'),[7] *cniht*, 'a youth', and *wencel*, 'a child', are all attested as designating a slave in certain instances. Young slaves were denoted by the addition of the diminutive suffixes *-incel*[8] and

---

[2] On the evidence for this see below, pp. 70–4.

[3] Faull, 'The semantic development of Old English *wealh*', is an important study. For further discussion of this word see s.v. *wealh* in appendix I below, where further references to studies of the use of *wealh* in place-names are given. Cf. also below, appendix I, s.vv. *wiln* and *wilnincel*.

[4] Verlinden, 'L'Origine de *sclavus* = esclave'.

[5] Campbell, *Old English Grammar*, pp. 71–85.

[6] *Þeowen* might also have been borrowed early but in West Saxon the effect of *i*-mutation would have been hidden by a later sound change (Campbell, *Old English Grammar*, p. 81, §202); **þiowen* might have been expected in non-West-Saxon texts, but the form *þeowen* here could have appeared through analogy with *þeow* or under the influence of the standard West-Saxon literary dialect.

[7] The word is discussed by Green, *The Carolingian Lord*, pp. 98–106.

[8] Peters has propounded the view that *-incel* is a suffix without dialectal significance in Old

-*ling* to the base word, though we must also allow for the possible use of the diminutive in a derogatory sense devoid of any implications of age, as we have already seen in *nydþeowetling*.[9] Words employing diminutive suffixes are *hæft-incel, inbyrdling, þeowetling, þeowincel,* and *wilnincel.* The word *fostorling,* 'a child adopted as a household slave', presumably reveals the fate of some children who were orphaned.

Several words indicate the occupational function of the slave. Thus *þegn,* frequently attested in the sense 'servant', is also found in the sense 'slave' in the mid-tenth-century dialect of the Northumbrian scribe Aldred. Even in Aldred's dialect, however, this sense seems to have been on the decline in the face of an alternative specialised sense which became common in late Old English, 'a freeman who serves a noble or a king'. *Weorcþeow,* 'a slave who works', is found only in poetry, but is probably of ancient origin because a cognate is found in Old Norse. An occupational term with a complex semantic history is the word *esne.* Its earliest attested sense is 'a hired labourer', already a specialised meaning. It then acquired the sense 'a slave', presumably via an unattested sense 'one who labours'. This newer meaning does not seem to have been limited to any particular region as has been alleged;[10] it is attested in this sense from Kent, Wessex, and the North. The word was also used as a personal name and had a further sense of 'a man'. Possibly because of the ambiguity between this last sense and the sense 'slave' it passed out of use in the Middle English period. *Birele,* 'a female (?cup-)bearer', derived from *beran,* 'to bear', appears in the Laws of Æthelberht, §§14 and 16. The occupation seems to have been limited originally to slaves (possibly captives in war), although in later usage the masculine form was used to denote the honorific position of butler in an aristocratic household.

A second group of words arose out of the manumission process involving the change in status from slave to freeman. The manumittor was called a *freolsgefa* or *freotgifa* (both words are *hapax legomena*). The act itself was described by the verb *(ge)freogan,* and the action was called a *freotgift* or *freot,* the latter word also being used to describe the document recording the act.

The person freed was known in the earliest Kentish laws as a *læt,* which appears to have been a legal status differing in some degree from that of an ordinary freeman. The term disappears thereafter, however, and survives only in the word *freolæta,* 'a freedman', itself an old Germanic compound as other Germanic dialects attest.[11] An apparent synonym for the latter word is *freotmann.* Apart from the *lætas,* freedmen had no separately defined legal status in Anglo-Saxon law. Because of the rarity of the words for 'manumittor' and

---

English but that in any case it probably ceased to be productive well before the end of the Old English period: see 'Two suffixes reconsidered', especially pp. 116–17.

9 It is possible that the suffix -*ling,* having lost its diminutive force in some words, in turn sometimes lost its derogatory connotation over time: in the word *þeowling* the suffix seems to be quite neutral in connotation.

10 Gutmacher, 'Der Wortschatz des althochdeutschen Tatian', 68, s.v. *asni.*

11 Old High German *frîlaz, frîlâz;* Middle Dutch *vrilaet.* See Carr, *Nominal Compounds in Germanic,* p. 117.

'freedman', it seems reasonable to assume that indeed there was no difference in status between freedmen and freemen outside of Kent and, later on, the Danelaw.

Most of the words that have been discussed deal with the slave as a person with a status defined by law. Since the Anglo-Saxons lived in an agrarian society, it was natural for them also to define persons in terms of land. This becomes particularly apparent late in the period, when the pattern of land-holding changed from precarious tenure to manorialism, with a consequent shift in socio-legal relationships. The change is illuminated by the use of two prefixes that were particularly productive of words, *in-*, 'associated with the (demesne) household', and *æhte-*, 'associated with the manorial demesne'. Neither of these prefixes in themselves implied any kind of legal status. Thus *inhired*, 'a household', defined persons sociologically rather than legally. Where these compounds do refer to slaves, the unfree status is denoted either by the root word (for example, *inþinen*) or by the socio-economic role of the person referred to. Often this role has to be deduced from the literary context in which the word is found. An example is *æhteswan*, 'a swineherd connected with the demesne'. The word as used in the *Rectitudines Singularum Personarum*, §7 does not in itself indicate legal status, but a later clause shows that all who performed this role were slaves.[12]

Obviously when legal status was linked to socio-economic role, changes in one sphere could lead to changes in the other. This is best illustrated by the word *æhteman*, 'a man associated with the demesne'. As used in the *Rectitudines* it is possible that it refers to persons who were slaves, but elsewhere it seems to be the general term for a labourer on the manorial demesne whose ties were with the land rather than directly with a master – in other words, one who was a serf.[13]

Those in a manorial sphere who were not slaves but who were legally bound to engage in labour services were *weorcwyrðe*. If they were permitted to depart from an estate they were called *færwyrðe*. Another term used to describe them was *færfrige*. Here the prefix *fær-* denotes the freedom 'to go' from the land; this must be contrasted with the earlier term *folcfrige* applied to slaves who were freed, where the freedom was granted in respect of the tribe rather than the land. In the documents recording the granting of freedom from contractual obligations to an estate the verbs that came to be used were *alisan*, *lisan*, and *onlisan* (*ut*), 'to release', rather than *freogan*, 'to free'. When such a release was purchased rather than granted voluntarily by the overlord the verb used was (*ge*)*bicgan* (*ut*).

In the tenth and eleventh centuries, which was a time of rapid change in England when ties to an estate became more significant than those to a specific people, terminology appropriate to the old legal status of slave coexisted with that denoting the newer status of serf.

---

12 See below, appendix I, s.v. *æhteman*.
13 Pelteret, 'Two Old English lists of serfs', 497–500.

THE SCANDINAVIAN INFLUENCE

As the name 'Danelaw' implies, much of tenth-century England was influenced by Norse legal practices. Scandinavian law recognised slavery but employed a somewhat different legal terminology from that used by the Anglo-Saxons. Texts in Old English from the Danelaw are rare, so the impact of Scandinavian vocabulary on Old English appears to be less than it actually may have been. A number English words of Old Norse origin and one loan-translation show, however, that some aspects of the Scandinavian law of slavery operated in England.

The Old Norse word for a slave was *þræl*. This appears from the tenth century onwards in Old English texts of northern provenance and in the works of Wulfstan, who had northern connexions. In these works it either replaces or is used as an alternative to *þeow*. Unlike the latter word it has not been lost to the English language, possibly because it acquired through metaphorical use connotations that *þeow* did not possess. *Þræl* differed from *þeow* in. not having a feminine cognate. The feminine equivalent was *þir*, which appears as a gloss to John 18:17 in the Northumbrian Rushworth and Lindisfarne Gospels. Female slaves are mentioned much less frequently than male slaves in the sources, so the rarity of *þir* is not necessarily an indication of the frequency of its usage in England.

Freedmen in some of the early Norse laws were divided into two classes, each having a defined set of rights and obligations. Those in the higher class possessing a larger degree of personal freedom were called *leysingar*. This word appears only once in the sources, in association with another word, *healffreo*, which probably represents the second category of freedmen, the *frjálsgjafar*.[14] The words bear testimony to the existence in the Danelaw of Scandinavian legal practices governing the manumitted which do not appear to have been part of indigenous Anglo-Saxon law.[15]

THE VOCABULARY OF SERVITUDE AND FREEDOM IN ENGLISH
TRANSLATIONS OF LATIN RELIGIOUS TEXTS

The translation of religious writings from Latin into Old English was a prominent aspect of Anglo-Saxon scholarship from at least the time of King Alfred on. Pre-eminent, of course, was the Bible, but Lives of Saints and even Bede's *Historia Ecclesiastica* were englished. As will be discussed in chapter II the imagery of slavery and freedom was integral to christian thought, so that the vernacular words expressing these concepts are relatively common in such translations. Much of this terminology must have been newly coined, but some of the words possibly also represent contemporary social and legal terms that have chanced not to survive in the extant secular sources.

---

[14] See below, appendix I, s.vv. *healf-freoh, lising*.
[15] For a more detailed discussion see Pelteret, 'Slavery in the Danelaw', in *Social Approaches to Viking Studies*, ed. Samson, pp. 185–6.

The christian concept of Christ as Redeemer and His crucifixion as a redemption of Humanity was particularly productive of new words in Old English. Among the words for 'redeemer' are *alisend, eftlisend, freolsend, gefreogend, lisend,* and *onlisend;* for 'redemption' *alisendness, alising, alisness, eftlising, onlisness,* and *tolising;* and the verbal equivalent, 'to redeem', is represented by *gefreolsian, lisan,* and *onlisan.* It is possible that some of these words were also used for 'manumittor of slaves', 'manumission', and 'to manumit', but it is more likely that most were created to meet the exigencies of Old English poetic style, which demanded numerous synonyms.

Occasionally the requirements of the Latin encouraged the translator to coin compounds, which again was an Old English poetic practice. This appears to be the case with the words *efenþeow(a), efenþegn, efne-esne,* 'fellow slave', and *efenþeowen,* 'fellow slave-woman', where the prefix *efen- (efne-)* seems to have been used to represent the Latin *con-* in the words *conseruus* and *conserua.* These vernacular words appear to have gained wider currency in homiletic writing as a result of having been used in scriptural translations.

The words *þeowhad* and *geþeowtian* are preserved only in translations of Latin texts, where they are used in the context of religious imagery. They are likely, however, to represent indigenous legal terminology. The Old English *Bede* uses in passages that are paraphrases of the original the word *þeowhad,* which means 'the condition of being a slave'. The Old English *Honorius,* extant in a twelfth-century manuscript, is the only source to preserve *geþeowtian,* 'to enslave'.

Over forty words expressing aspects of slavery and freedom are employed in translations of religious writings. These had the effect, therefore, of extending and entrenching this type of vocabulary in Old English. The social consequence of this extensive vocabulary and its association with religious literature was that it was virtually impossible for an Anglo-Saxon to see slavery as being other than inherent in the human condition.[16]

THE VOCABULARY OF SERVITUDE AND FREEDOM IN THE LAND-CHARTERS

Old English documents such as the land-charters frequently utilise the terminology of servitude and freedom to describe legal transactions involving immovable property, chiefly land, a practice that has not been generally commented upon. There are at least twenty-three words that are employed in this sphere. Some of these are compounds likely to have been used only in the context of land law, such as *freolsboc,* 'a land-charter granting superiority over land with freedom from the jurisdiction of others', and *sundorfreodom,* 'a special right'. Others are merely extensions of an existing sense used to cover this new legal context, as in *freodom,* which acquired several senses in the realm of land law, and *þeowet,* 'service due from a property to an overlord'.

---

[16] See further below, pp. 68–70.

A few of the words, however, are now preserved only in their new legal context but may originally have been used of persons. *Nidþeowian*, extant only in a single legal text with the sense 'to force a property to render dues to one', almost certainly had an earlier sense 'to compulsorily enslave a person' (cf. the substantive *nidþeow*). *Freols*, which came to denote a land-charter, may possibly have developed this meaning via an earlier unattested sense of 'a manumission-document'. The words *freolsdom* and *frigness*, both meaning 'immunity', 'freedom of land from dues', perhaps also denoted 'the state enjoyed by a freeman', though there is no hint of this in extant texts.

THE SOCIAL SIGNIFICANCE OF THE OLD ENGLISH TERMINOLOGY OF SERVITUDE AND FREEDOM

Vocabulary is often a pointer to the importance of an object or institution to the speakers of a language. The range of terminology concerned with slavery in Old English is proof of how central this institution was in Anglo-Saxon society. Even when some of the words have been explained away as synonyms in a language that favoured a superfluity of such words, the fact remains that an extensive vocabulary developed covering most aspects of the institution. There were words to denote the origins of slaves through birth (*þeowboren*, *þeow-byrde*), crime (*witeþeow*), necessity (*nidþeowetling*), or capture in war (*hæft*); their age (*þeowincel*, etc.); their lack of legal personality (*æht*); and their occupational function (*weorcþeow*, *esne*). Slavery itself was described through a range of abstract nouns (*þeowdom*, *þeowhad*, etc.). Words employing connotations that arose from dialect geography (*þræl* vs. *þeow*) or which were expressive of attitudes of mind (the diminutive suffix in *þeowetling*) are also to be found.

Another set of words described the change in status from slave to freeman. This included words to denote in abstract terms the new status acquired (*freodom*, *freols*), to imply a distinction from the former status held (*freotmann*, *freolæta*), and to relate this status to the society as a whole (*folcfrige*). In the case of persons subject to Scandinavian law, those who were freed gained a status that differed from ordinary freemen (*healffreo*, *lising*). The early disappearance of the word *læt*, the comparative rarity of the words *freolæta* and *freotmann*, and the extreme rarity of words for 'manumittor' suggest, however, that this legal differentiation did not obtain in areas defined by late Anglo-Saxon law.

The influence of christian writings on the size of the servile lexicon is manifest and, as has been discussed, the vocabulary of slavery and freedom was also adapted for use in land law, thereby revealing how far the concepts of servitude and freedom had passed into the thought patterns of the Anglo-Saxons.

The vocabulary shows that the institution of slavery was not a static one. The rise of a terminology in which persons were described through their relationship to a landed estate (*in-*, *æhte-*) rather than by legal status (*þeow-*) indicates a transformation in the economic structure of late Anglo-Saxon society involving a greater emphasis on obligations to the land than on allegiance to a people, which concomitantly involved a transformation of slavery into serfdom.

What the texts of the period have to say about the various aspects of slavery alluded to in the vocabulary – the acceptance of the institution by moralists of the period, the laws governing slavery, the process of status change from slave to freeman, and the transformation of slavery into serfdom – will be the subject of the subsequent chapters of this book.

II

'THE WORK IS HARD, BECAUSE I AM NOT FREE':
SLAVES AND SLAVERY IN THE LITERARY SOURCES

In a sense all written sources could be considered to be 'literary' in that they can be assigned to various genres whose characteristics are definable. Conceived more narrowly, however, 'Literature' can be defined as that body of writing with some emotive or philosophical content such as poetry, homily, history, or biography; material of a specifically legal or administrative nature may be excluded. Evidence drawn from literature more strictly delimited in this way will form the basis of the present chapter. These writings afford insights usually denied us by non-literary sources, such as some of the emotive aspects of socio-legal relationships, insights which are here so important for assessing the role of slaves in Anglo-Saxon society.

In the examination that follows the emphasis will be placed on vernacular literature, but the relevant Latin sources will also be discussed.[1] We shall start by exploring the portrayal of slaves as they appear in various categories of literature. Chronology has dictated the order in which these categories are considered. First we shall survey Old English poetry.[2] Most early English vernacular poetry is preserved in manuscripts of the late tenth century but much of the subject matter is derived from pre-Alfredian times.[3] The next major group of texts that survive are the translations of the Alfredian revival. These texts belong to various literary genres but for our purposes it is useful to examine them as a group because they reveal how Anglo-Saxons of a particular age interpreted in their own words literature composed in another era in Latin. This category is followed by the chronologically more diffuse genre of Saints' Lives, composed in the tenth century or later. Finally, homilies by Ælfric and anonymous writers dating mostly from the first half of the eleventh century conclude this section.

---

[1] All vernacular sources listed in Sections A and B of Cameron's 'A List', in *A Plan*, edd. Frank & Cameron, have been read for this chapter, with the exception of documents that have not been edited, and penitential texts, laws, charters, and records, which are discussed in later chapters of this book. As for the Latin sources, in addition to those cited below, the Lives relevant to the period that are listed in *A Bibliography of English History to 1485*, ed. Graves, have been consulted.

[2] Quotations and line references will be drawn from the volumes of the series The Anglo-Saxon Poetic Records, edd. Krapp & Dobbie, I–VI (New York & London 1931–53).

[3] For example, *Deor*, lines 38–41 (*The Exeter Book*, edd. Krapp & Dobbie, p. 179), records the early practice of holding land by precarious tenure in return for service to the king. Some of the poems may, of course, have been composed as late as the tenth century.

The second part of the chapter will concentrate on certain themes scattered through the literary sources. Here genre itself plays a lesser role in shaping the ideas expressed.

THE PORTRAYAL OF SLAVERY IN VARIOUS GENRES OF ANGLO-SAXON LITERATURE

OLD ENGLISH POETRY

The humbler aspects of Anglo-Saxon life are confined in Old English poetry almost exclusively to the *Riddles*.[4] These poems, which may go back to the eighth century[5] and which follow a tradition that is different from the rest of the vernacular poetry, often have as their answers such commonplace objects as a plough, rake, or key. It is entirely appropriate, therefore, that the lower ranks of Anglo-Saxon society, the *ceorlas* and the slaves, should be used as a source of imagery in these works.

About eight riddles appear to contain references to persons of servile status.[6] *Riddle*, §12 is particularly informative. It declares:

> Gif me feorh losað,   fæste binde
> swearte Wealas,   hwilum sellan men.
> . . .
>
> . . .   Hwilum feorran broht
> wonfeax Wale   wegeð ond þyð,
> dol druncmennen,   deorcum nihtum,
> wæteð in wætre,   wyrmeð hwilum
> fægre to fyre;   me on fæðme sticaþ
> hygegalan hond,   hwyrfeð geneahhe,
> swifeð me geond sweartne.

> If life is taken from me, I bind fast the dark Welsh, and sometimes better men. . . . Sometimes a dark-haired Welsh-woman, brought from afar, a foolish drunken servant-girl, on dark nights lifts and presses me, wets me in water, sometimes warms me well at the fire; sticks into my bosom her wanton hand, turns me around often, sweeps across my blackness.[7]

---

[4] *The Exeter Book*, edd. Krapp & Dobbie, pp. 180–210, 224–5, and 229–43; also edited in *The Exeter Book, Part II*, ed. & transl. Mackie, and *The Old English Riddles*, ed. Williamson.

[5] On the problems of dating the *Riddles* see *ibid.*, pp. 5–12.

[6] *Riddle*, §§22, 43, and 54 mention the *esne*. In §43 *esne* and *hlaford*, denoting the body and soul respectively, are described as siblings, so *esne* here perhaps means 'a free servant'. But the analogy does not seem to be worked out very carefully. *Riddle*, §§52, 71, and possibly 88 contain the words *wealh* (m) and *wale* (f). In the first two the words seem to mean 'Celt'; the riddles would have an ironic impact if they meant 'slave' as well, but there is no evidence within the poems for assigning this sense to them. A *þeow* may be referred to in *Riddle*, §64 (see *The Exeter Book*, edd. Krapp & Dobbie, pp. 367–8). For *ceorlas* see *Riddle*, §§25 and 27; Gleissner discusses the *ceorles dohtor* mentioned in the former riddle in *Die 'zweideutigen' altenglischen Rätsel*, pp. 201–4.

[7] *The Exeter Book*, edd. Krapp & Dobbie, p. 186; translation in *The Exeter Book*, ed. & transl. Mackie, II.101–3. For another edition, see *The Old English Riddles*, ed. Williamson, p. 74,

To interpret this, one must take into account the verbal ambiguities in the passage. Ambiguity is an important feature of Old English poetry, as has been stressed by Fred Robinson, who has pointed to a number of examples in the *Riddles*.[8] Here it is to be found in the epithets *swearte* and *wonfeax*, and the substantives *wealas* and *wale*. The epithets primarily denote physical appearance: *wonfeax* ('dark-haired') seems to be synonymous with *swearte* ('swarthy'). Both words, however, have strong pejorative connotations. *Wonfeax* in itself implies a comparison with blond hair, a stereotypical characteristic of the Germanic peoples. Elsewhere in the *Riddles hwitloccedu* ('blond-haired') is specifically used as a sign of high status.[9] *Wonfeax*, therefore, suggests a correspondingly low status. That this is not an unreasonable deduction is indicated by the other phrases used of the *wonfeax wale*. She is a *dol druncmennen* (which, if the text is correct, is the only place in Old English literature where a drunken woman is referred to), and she possesses a *hygegalan hond*. *Swearte* is directly contrasted with the epithet *sellan*, 'better', which appears in the next half line in the riddle. The implied comparison between black-haired Celts and blond-haired Anglo-Saxons suggests that those referred to as *sellan* were Anglo-Saxons. Such men would hardly be mentioned in these terms if they were criminals, so they can only be men bound after capture in war, a common motif in Old English literature. This supports the semantic evidence already discussed that war was a major source of slaves; such slaves evidently were especially of Celtic stock, though they were also sometimes (*hwilum*) of Anglo-Saxon origin.

Swearte has pejorative connotations, as is evident from its use elsewhere in Old English poetry, where it describes hell (*landa sweartost*),[10] devils ('engla and deofla . . . hwitra and sweartra'),[11] the raven, symbol of death in war (*hræfen . . . sweart*),[12] and, in a metaphorical sense, sin (*sweartra synna*).[13] In this passage its contrast with *sellan*, which can also mean 'morally/spiritually better', heightens its association with sin and the devil. This is particularly interesting for the history of ideas as it provides an early example of the association through imagery of physical appearance with moral qualities.

The riddle also reveals the close link in ideas between 'Celt' and 'slave'. While the epithet *wonfeax* and the phrase *feorran brohte* suggest that the primary

---

no. 10. Whitman provides an alternative prose translation in *Old English Riddles*, pp. 170–1; for a freer verse translation see *A Feast of Creatures*, transl. Williamson, p. 70. Most scholars believe the solution to be 'leather' or 'ox-hide'; Williamson, *The Old English Riddles*, argues (pp. 166–7) that it is 'ox'. For a possible alternative meaning of the word *swifeð* see Gleissner, *Die 'zweideutigen' altenglischen Rätsel*, p. 342. There seems to be little reason for emending *druncmennen* as suggested by Grein and Holthausen: see *The Exeter Book*, edd. Krapp & Dobbie, p. 328, and *The Old English Riddles*, ed. Williamson, p. 167.

[8] Robinson, 'Lexicography and literary criticism'.

[9] *Riddle*, §80.4; cf. *Riddle*, §42.3, *hwitloc*. The association of hair-colour with social status is also to be found in the Icelandic *Rígsþula*, which lends credence to Hill's suggestion that the latter poem has an insular origin (though he appears to lean towards a Celtic rather than Anglo-Saxon understanding of the word 'insular'): see his '*Rígsþula*: some medieval Christian analogues', 87–8.

[10] *Genesis B*, line 487 (*The Junius Manuscript*, ed. Krapp, p. 18).

[11] *Christ C*, lines 895–8 (*The Exeter Book*, edd. Krapp & Dobbie, p. 28).

[12] *Finnsburh*, lines 34–5 (*Beowulf and Judith*, ed. Dobbie, p. 4).

[13] *Juliana*, line 313 (*The Exeter Book*, edd. Krapp & Dobbie, p. 122).

meaning of *wale* is 'Celtish woman', the phrase *dol druncmennen* acts as a poetic amplification that suggests the meaning of *wale* is instead 'slave woman'.[14] The riddle illustrates, therefore, the importance of the Celts as sources of slaves.

Given the mundane solution of the riddle, undoubtedly one of the pleasures in reading the poem derives from the sexual ambiguity that runs through it. Sexual innuendo was not a characteristic of Old English epic poetry and it is a reasonable inference that a generally disdainful attitude towards Celts and slaves permitted its use here, where the poetic form of the riddle evidently licensed subject matter that would have been impermissible in the aristocratic world of heroic poetry.

Outside the *Riddles* Old English poetry has virtually nothing to say about slavery. Some earlier critics would have contested this statement by asserting that in *Beowulf* the man who stole the cup from the dragon hoard was a slave, and that the names Wealhþeow and Ongynþeow indicate that these persons were of servile origin. Davis, Gordon, and Damico have brought forward evidence that casts doubt on these views, although more recently it has been claimed that Wealhtheow's name does indeed suggest that she had been a slave.[15] It would have been surprising if slavery were alluded to in *Beowulf*, since Old English poetry in general portrays only an aristocracy of warriors. To have introduced a slave, or even an ordinary freeman, would have been inappropriate in such an heroic world where all men were *eorlas*, a word which itself denotes aristocratic status. Thus for Beowulf to have died as a result of the action of a slave would have reduced his stature. Only in the very late *Seasons of Fasting*, thought to have been composed by someone in the Wulfstanian circle, does one find a passing reference to a slave: 'Who can make a thrall's peace with his lord, if he has previously angered him greatly, and does not make it good, but daily renews by his actions the injury of the old offence?'[16] The world of Anglo-Saxon poetry is that of the thegnly class; the rest of the society tended to be ignored. This

---

[14] The phrase *wonfah wale* also appears in *Riddle*, §52 (*Riddle*, §50, in *The Old English Riddles*, ed. Williamson). Damico suggests in *Beowulf's Wealhtheow*, p. 59, that the activity the *Wale* engages in in the latter riddle 'suggests a coalescence of the ethnic and status senses of the term'.

[15] Davis, in *Beowulf*, facs. ed. Zupitza, p. 103, n. 16, stated that he considered the damaged word in *Beowulf*, line 2223 to be þegn, not þeow, as some editors have read. Andersson has rejected both readings and instead proposed þeof in 'The thief in *Beowulf*', especially pp. 495–6. For Gordon's explanations of names ending in -þeow see 'Wealhþeow and related names'. His views have been taken considerably further by Damico in *Beowulf's Wealhtheow*, pp. 58–68. Recently T. D. Hill has argued that the name indeed means 'foreign slave'. He has claimed that 'by marrying someone of low status or no status whatever, a king can affirm implicitly or explicitly the absolute gulf between himself and even the mightiest of his subjects' and has provided some Continental examples of this practice: see his ' "Wealhtheow" as a foreign slave', 108. The problem of Wealhtheow's name thus cannot be said to have been resolved.

[16]   Hwa mæg þyngian   þreale hwilcum
    wiþ his arwesan,   gyf he him ærur hæfð
    bitere onbolgen,   and þæs bote ne deð,
    ac þa æbyligþe   ealdere wrohte,
    dæghwamlice   dædum niwað?

Seasons of Fasting, lines 195–9 (*The Anglo-Saxon Minor Poems*, ed. Dobbie, p. 103). Translation from Sisam, *Studies*, p. 51. Even in this work the ethos is fundamentally aristocratic, as

applied as much to the *ceorlas* as to the slaves; even the late *Battle of Maldon*, composed some time after 991, only grudgingly acknowledges that *ceorlas* were being used in the *fyrd*.[17]

A prominent feature of the literary revival under King Alfred was the stimulus given to the translation of Latin texts into the vernacular. Their late ninth-century date gives a unity to a group of works which are, in fact, drawn from a number of literary genres.

Translations have the greatest significance for the historian of ideas when the translator departs from the original text. One such departure that appears in the Alfredian *Orosius* is of signal importance to this study. Orosius writes:

At that time, too, the Volsinians, the most flourishing of the Etruscan peoples, almost perished as a result of their wantonness. After making licence a habit, they indiscriminately freed their slaves, invited them to banquets, and honoured them with marriage. The liberated slaves (*libertini*), admitted to a share of power, criminally plotted to usurp complete rule of the state, and relieved of the yoke of slavery, were consumed with the desire for revolution. Once free, they cursed those masters whom they as slaves had devotedly loved, because they remembered that these men had once been their masters. The liberated slaves then conspired to commit a crime and claimed the captured city for their class alone. So great were their numbers that they accomplished their rash purpose without real resistance. They criminally appropriated the property and wives of their masters, and forced the latter to go into distant exile. These wretched and destitute exiles betook themselves to Rome. Here they displayed their misery and tearfully pleaded their cause. They were avenged and restored to their former position through the stern rule of the Romans.[18]

Russom has pointed out in 'A Germanic concept of nobility', 1–15, especially p. 13. For the ascription of the poem to Wulfstan's circle, see Sisam, *Studies*, p. 50. It should be noted that *þræl* was much used by Wulfstan to denote a slave (see below, pp. 94–5 and 99, and appendix I, s.v. *þræl*).

[17] Though praising his bravery, the poet in *The Battle of Maldon*, line 256 (*The Anglo-Saxon Minor Poems*, ed. Dobbie, p. 14) describes Dunnere as an *unorne ceorl* ('simple *ceorl*'). For a discussion of the word *unorne* see *The Battle of Maldon*, ed. Gordon, p. 57. Locherbie-Cameron has suggested that the name, derived from OE *dun*, 'dingy', 'dun-coloured', is a 'dismissive reference to his family's status': see her chapter 'The men named in the poem', in *The Battle of Maldon AD 991*, ed. Scragg, pp. 239–40, and see also *ibid.*, pp. 243–4.

[18] 'Tunc etiam Uulsinienses, Etruscorum florentissimi, luxurie paene perierunt. nam cum, licentia in consuetudinem prorogata, seruos suos passim liberos facerent, conuiuiis allegarent, coniugiis honestarent: libertini in partem potestatis recepti plenitudinem per scelus usurpare meditati sunt et liberati seruitutis iugo, ambitu dominationis arserunt et quos dominos subditi aequanimiter dilexerunt, eos iam liberi, quod dominos fuisse meminerant, exsecrati sunt. itaque conspirantes in facinus libertini – quorum tanta manus fuit, ut sine controuersia auso potirentur – correptam urbem suo tantum generi uindicant, patrimonia coniugiaque dominorum sibi per scelus usurpant, extorres dominos procul abigunt, qui miseri, exules egentesque Romam deferuntur: ubi ostentata miseria querelaque defleta, per Romanorum seueritatem et uindicati sunt et restituti.' *Pauli Orosii Historiarum adversus Paganos Libri VII*, IV.5.3–5 (ed. Zangemeister, p. 215) (text); *Seven Books of History against the Pagans*, transl. Raymond, p. 160 (translation).

The translator, who gave a free rendering of the original, did not interpret *libertinus* as a freedman, as Orosius intended, but instead used it to denote 'a son of a freed slave', a post-Classical sense attested in Isidore of Seville's *Etymologies* and some Anglo-Saxon glossaries:[19]

In those days the Ulcinienses and that people, the Etruscans, almost completely destroyed themselves because of their own foolishness because they freed some of their slaves and also were too gentle and forgiving to them all. Then it was displeasing to their *ceorlas* that the slaves were freed and they would not be. Then they plotted against the lords, and the slaves with them, until they were more powerful than them, and they afterwards drove them out completely from the land and married those who had earlier been their mistresses. Then afterwards the lords sought the Romans and they helped them so that they regained their own again.[20]

Now, although the translator has strayed far from the meaning of Orosius's text, his translation presumably made sense to him.[21] One may thus legitimately draw conclusions about the nature of his society from what he has written here. He considers that the Etruscans were granting their slaves a more desirable freedom than that which the *ceorlas* possessed. At first sight this seems most puzzling, as *ceorlas* appear to be freemen in Alfred's laws.[22] Clearly, therefore, in his translation he could not have had in mind the freedom conferred by tribal law. But as has been mentioned, under manorial custom a man could be granted another type of freedom. He could become *færfrige*, that is, be released from the custom of the manor and permitted to leave the estate.[23] Presumably this was the kind of freedom that the translator considered the *ceorlas* did not possess. We may reasonably assume that he made this change in his translation because it approximated to the world that he knew. If this deduction is correct, it is the first indication that personal status as defined by the law of the tribe was being superseded by a status that was dependent on a person's relationship to the land. This required a change in the concept of freedom. Thus, from being a set of

[19] Janet Bately has made this suggestion in her edition, *The Old English Orosius*, p. 274, commentary to p. 87.19–20.

[20] 'On ðæm dagum Ulcinienses 7 Thrusci ða folc forneah ealle forwurdon for hiora agnum dysige, for þæm þe hie sume heora þeowas gefreodon 7 eac him eallum wurdon to milde 7 to forgiefene. Þa ofþuhte heora ceorlum þæt mon þa þeowas freode 7 hi nolde. Þa wiðsawon hie þæm hlafordum 7 þa þeowas mid him, oþ hie wyldran wæron þonne hie 7 hie siþþan mid ealle of þæm earde adrifon [7 him to wifum dydon þa þe ær wæran heora hlæfdian]. Þa siþþan gesohton þa hlafordas Romane, 7 hi him gefylstan þæt hie eft to hiora agnum becoman.' Text in *The Old English Orosius*, ed. Bately, p. 87.16–24. See also Finberg (to whom credit must be given for being the first to point out the importance of this text) in *The Agrarian History of England*, I.ii: *A.D. 43–1042*, ed. Finberg, p. 451.

[21] Bately, 'King Alfred and the Latin MSS of Orosius' History', has shown that Alfred's translation is not as inaccurate as had been believed, since it seems to have been based on manuscripts containing variant readings. The translator also made additions from various sources: see *The Old English Orosius*, ed. Bately, pp. lv–lxxii, and further references cited there. Bately does not suggest, however, that this passage is based on such variant readings or additions.

[22] Alfred, §43 (*Die Gesetze*, ed. Liebermann, I.78); cf. Alfred, §10 (*Die Gesetze*, ed. Liebermann, I.56).

[23] See above, p. 45 and below, appendix I, s.v. *færfrige*.

rights and obligations defined by the law of the tribe freedom was evidently beginning to denote the possession of the right to be released from a manorial estate and its custom.

A similar portrayal of a society based not on tribal allegiance but on socio-economic function appears in another translation made under Alfred's aegis, that of Boethius's *Consolatio Philosophiae*. In an addition to the Latin text the translator writes: '[T]hus a king's raw material and instruments of rule are a well-peopled land, and he must have men of prayer, men of war, and men of work.'[24] It was a view that was to gain popularity a century later.[25]

Both translations, therefore, present a perspective on society different from that evident in the laws, where there is a clear distinction between slave and free. Instead, through the presentation of society in socio-economic terms the distinction becomes unimportant and leads to an alternative conception of freedom that is not based on tribal allegiance.

Where Latin texts that incidentally mention slaves are accurately turned into Old English, it is much more difficult to assess the historical impact of the references to slaves. A translation extant in several manuscripts, though, provides *prima facie* evidence that its contents were well known and thus, potentially at least, could shape attitudes within the society. Among such translations of wide popularity and circulation pre-eminence must be given to Bede's *Historia Ecclesiastica* and Gregory the Great's *Cura Pastoralis*.

The Old English version of Bede's *Historia Ecclesiastica* survives in seven manuscripts, a large number for a vernacular text.[26] Notable incidents concerning slaves in this work include Pope Gregory's alleged meeting with Anglian slave boys, the capture and sale into slavery of the thegn Imma, and Bishop Wilfrid's freeing of 250 slaves at Selsey.[27] The first two stories were later used by Ælfric, though there is no evidence that this translation was his source.[28] As will be mentioned in the next section, the example of Wilfrid, together with similar incidents recorded in other Saints' Lives, may have been a factor in influencing the growth of manumission in the tenth century.[29] In the case of the *Cura*

---

[24] '[Þ] bið þonne cyninges [*andweorc 7*] *his* tol mid to ricsianne, *Þ he* hæbbe his lond fullmonnad; he sceal habban gebedmen *7 fyrdmen* 7 weorcmen.' *King Alfred's Old English Version of Boethius de Consolatione Philosophiae*, §17 (ed. Sedgefield, p. 40.15–18) (text); *King Alfred's Version of the Consolations of Boethius*, §17 (transl. Sedgefield, p. 41) (translation). On the addition see Payne, *King Alfred and Boethius*, pp. 64–5. The history of the concept is examined by Duby, *The Three Orders*, transl. Goldhammer, especially pp. 99–109, where a strongly French slant is evident in the interpretation.

[25] Ælfric expresses it in three of his works: 'On the Old and New Testament' ('Letter to Sigeweard'), lines 1207–20, in the *The Old English Version of the Heptateuch*, ed. Crawford, pp. 71–2; in his 'Passio Sanctorum Machabeorum', lines 812ff., in *Ælfric's Lives of Saints*, ed. & transl. Skeat, II.120–2; and in his Latin letter to Wulfstan, in *Die Hirtenbriefe Ælfrics*, §2a.14 (ed. Fehr, p. 225.20–1). Wulfstan adopted it in his *Institutes of Polity*: see *Die 'Institutes of Polity, Civil and Ecclesiastical'*, §§24–9 and 31–6 (ed. Jost, pp. 55–6), and it also appears in *Wulfstan*, §50 (ed. Napier, p. 267.9–17).

[26] Cameron 'A List', in *A Plan*, edd. Frank & Cameron, pp. 120–1, §B.9.6.

[27] *The Old English Version of Bede's Ecclesiastical History*, II.1, IV.13, and IV.23 (ed. & transl. Miller, I.1.96–9, I.2.306–7, and I.2.326–31) (text and translation).

[28] See below, pp. 62–3.

[29] See below, p. 60 and table IV, pp. 129–30.

Pastoralis, the six extant manuscripts of the vernacular translation also suggest that this work was widely read in England.[30] Gregory does not say much about slavery but in chapter XXIX he asserts: 'It is also to be made known to the masters that they are presumptuous towards God for his own gift, if they do not understand that those who are subject to them.by the dispensation of God are equals and associates in their nature. The slave is to be told to know that he is not independent of his master. It is to be made known to the master that he is to understand that he is the fellow-slave of his slave.'[31] This acceptance of the institution of slavery, which at the same time asserts the equality before God of everyone, slave and free, can be seen recurring in the thought of Ælfric and Wulfstan.[32]

SAINTS' LIVES

Among the Saints' Lives composed in the late tenth and the eleventh centuries, those of St Swithhun and St Wulfstan of Worcester provide direct evidence about social conditions in England. In addition, slaves are mentioned in a number of the translations made from Latin sources in Ælfric's Third Series of *Catholic Homilies*.

The *Life of St Swithhun* is found in several versions. The saint's biography was first written in 981 in prose by Lantfred, who was probably a monk from Fleury.[33] This was later epitomised.[34] At some time between 992 and 994 Wulfstan the Cantor composed a verse account based on Lantfred's *Life*,[35] and

---

30 On the manuscripts of *Cura Pastoralis* see Cameron, 'A List', in *A Plan*, edd. Frank & Cameron, p. 119, §B.9.1.

31 'Ðæm hlafordum is eac to cyðanne ðætte hie wið Gode ofermodgiað for his agenre gife, gif hie ne ongietað ðæt þa bioð hiera gelican & hiera efngemæccean on hiera gecynde, ða þe him underðiedde bioð ðurh Godes gesceafte. Ðæm ðeowan is to cyðonne ðæt he wiete ðæt he nis freoh wið his hlaford. Ðæm hlaforde is to cyðonne ðæt he ongite ðæt he is efnðeow his ðeowe.' *King Alfred's West-Saxon Version of Gregory's Pastoral Care*, §29 (ed. & transl. Sweet, p. 200.10–20) (text in the Cotton manuscripts' version); *ibid.*, p. 201 (translation; emended).

32 See below, pp. 64 and 89–90.

33 The evidence for Lantfred's origin is briefly set out in *Wulfstan of Winchester*, edd. & transl. Lapidge & Winterbottom, p. xciv, n. 192.

34 The relationship between the two versions is not clear. The epitome is edited under the title *Historia Translationis et Miraculorum Auctore, ut videtur, Lantfredo a, Monacho Wintoniensi in Anglia*, in *Acta Sanctorum Iulii . . . Tomus I*, edd. Ianning *et al.*, pp. 292–3, and the *Miracula*, in *ibid.*, pp. 294–9. This latter version is based on the incomplete Roma, Biblioteca Apostolica Vaticana, MS. Regina Suecia 566 (*olim* 769), and needs to be supplemented by Sauvage's edition, based on Rouen, Bibliothèque municipale, MS. U.107 (1385), 'Sancti Swithuni Wintoniensis episcopi translatio et miracula auctore Lantfredo'.

35 Wulfstan's metrical version is described in *Wulfstan of Winchester*, edd. & transl. Lapidge & Winterbottom, p. xcv as 'a hexametrical contrafactum of Lantfred's text'. The precise relationship between this account and Lantfred's remains, however, to be worked out. Wulfstan adds to Lantfred's account of Flodoald's slave (*Historia Translationis et Miraculorum*, II.33–7, in *Acta Sanctorum Iulii . . . Tomus I*, ed. Ianning *et al.*, p. 298) the significant additional facts that the reeve's name was Eadric and that he had charge of the royal vill of Calne (*ibid.*, II.36–7). It would appear from this that Wulfstan based his version on Lantfred's but that he added information gained from other (probably local) sources. We may expect to have a better understanding of the relationship between the versions once Michael Lapidge's study,

between 992 and 1002 Ælfric composed another Life containing 17 out of the 35 episodes that appear in Lantfred's biography.[36] The analysis that follows is based mainly on Lantfred's earlier prose version.

As with so many Saint's Lives the selection of incidents recorded in the bio graphy of Swithhun was influenced by the miracles described in the New Testa- ment. Thus the loosing of fetters, described in Acts 16 and reappearing in numerous hagiographical works, occurs no less than three times in the *Life of St Swithhun*. A small slave girl (*ancillula*), manacled hand and foot for some slight misdeed and due to be beaten for it, found on praying to the saint that her leg-irons fell off during the night, enabling her to run off to Swithhun's tomb in Winchester, where her master found her the next day and freed her.[37] Similarly, another slave who had been placed in foot fetters for his failure to carry out some task had them miraculously loosed when he prayed at the tomb of the saint.[38] And a northern slave-woman, who had been stolen and subsequently sold in Winchester, was placed in chains by her new mistress when the latter noticed her talking to her erstwhile master, who had appeared in the city.[39] The slave somehow made her way to the church where Swithhun's body lay and miraculously appeared next to the altar above which Swithhun was entombed, in spite of a priest who was guarding it. Unfortunately the story tails off inconse- quentially, but it is clear that her current owner, who is described as 'a very bad mistress' (*pessima domina*), was fearful that the slave would prefer to go back to her old master. These anecdotes imply that the fettering of slaves was used primarily for custody and as a punishment. Unlike the slaves in some societies, they evidently did not work in chain gangs.

These three incidents have a particular resonance because we have the means to recapture these scenes through our imaginations. The site of Swithhun's tomb is known from the excavations of Martin Biddle and his team: the spot is marked by a stone slab outside the present cathedral at Winchester. Perhaps more spectac- ularly we actually know what the shackles may have looked like, for among the wealth of metalwork found at Winchester were fetters attached to locks, dating

---

The Cult of St Swithun, appears in print (forthcoming in Winchester Studies 4, *The Anglo-Saxon Minsters of Winchester*, Part II). Lapidge and Winterbottom provide a very useful introduction to the literary form of the *translatio* on pp. cvi–cvii of their edition of Wulfstan's *Life of St Æthelwold*. Wulfstan's *Narratio metrica de Sancto Swithuno* has been edited by Campbell in *Frithegodi Monachi Breuiloquium*. For the legal aspects of this latter account, which are less germane here than the social information, see Whitelock, 'Wulfstan Cantor and Anglo-Saxon law', 87 and 92. Whitelock appears not to have been aware that Wulfstan's work was based on Lantfred's prose account as she nowhere mentioned the latter in her paper.

[36] *Ælfric's Lives of the Saints*, §21 (ed. & transl. Skeat, pp. 440–73). On the date of composition see Clemoes, 'The chronology of Ælfric's works', in *The Anglo-Saxons*, ed. Clemoes, pp. 212–47, especially p. 244.

[37] *Miracula*, I.5, in *Acta Sanctorum Iulii . . . Tomus I*, edd. Ianning *et al.*, p. 294.

[38] This incident is preserved in the Rouen manuscript and in Wulfstan the Cantor's version. For the text see 'Sancti Swithuni Wintoniensis episcopi translatio et miracula auctore Lantfredo', §51(1) (ed. Sauvage, p. 406), and *Narratio metrica*, II.1147–66, in *Frithegodi Monachi Breuiloquium*, ed. Campbell, p. 177.

[39] *Miracula*, II.23–8, in *Acta Sanctorum Iulii . . . Tomus I*, edd. Ianning *et al.*, p. 297.

from perhaps the eleventh century.[40] Only recently have human shackles been recognised for what they are – formerly they were thought to be horse fetters – and the evidence for these objects in Western Europe has not been fully assembled.[41] This is one field in which archaeologists can make a contribution towards our knowledge of slavery, though care will be needed in the interpretation of the material because the evidence for prisons and imprisonment in Anglo-Saxon England (where shackles may well have been employed) has also yet to be assessed.

St Swithhun played the central role in another incident involving a slave belonging to a wealthy trader called Flodoald.[42] This account suggests that the master had a genuine affection for his slave. The slave had been arrested and condemned to the ordeal of hot iron by a reeve over the objections of his master,[43] who not merely offered to give the reeve his slave instead, but also offered him a pound of silver, which itself could be the price of a slave.[44] The reeve rejected these offers, but through the intervention of the saint he was unable to see the slave's burns when, after the statutory period of time, the bandages were removed.

These stories in the *Life of St Swithhun* establish the saint as one who protected slaves both against injustice and cruelty. *The Life of St Wulfstan*, written sometime after his death in 1096 in Old English but now extant only in a Latin translation by William of Malmesbury, shows the saint going even further than this: Wulfstan actively went out and opposed the Bristol slave trade.[45]

These two Lives as a whole show that the genre was essentially a literature of the nobility, just as Old English poetry was. Unlike the interest in martial prowess characteristic of the hero of epic poetry, however, the saintly hero was instead actively concerned with the position of slaves within society. This concern is also to be seen in Ælfric's collection of Lives drawn from the *Uitae Patrum*.[46] In this collection the saints, who like the Germanic hero were often

---

[40] Goodall, 'Locks and keys', in *Object and Economy in Medieval Winchester*, ed. Biddle, pp. 1011–12, §§3671–5; see also plate LXIII and figure 314.

[41] Joachim Henning has provided an invaluable catalogue and typological analysis of the shackles that have been found in Eastern Europe and Germany in 'Gefangenenfesseln im slawischen Siedlungsraum', though in my view he is too inclined to interpret them as evidence of slavery rather than considering their possible use for the detention and punishment of criminals. Similar shackles have been found at Lagore crannog in Ireland: Scott in 'Iron "slave-collars" from Lagor crannog' has suggested that they might be for hunting dogs but Mytum in *The Origins of Early Christian Ireland* (p. 144) thinks that they could have been for high status hostages.

[42] *Miracula*, II.33–7, in *Acta Sanctorum Iulii . . . Tomus I*, edd. Ianning *et al.*, p. 298.

[43] Paul Hyams has discussed the incident from a legal point of view in 'Trial by ordeal', in *On the Laws and Customs of England*, edd. Arnold *et al.*, pp. 93–5. For another subtle analysis of the ordeal see Brown, 'Society and the supernatural'. Robert Bartlett has provided a wide ranging examination of the topic in *Trial by Fire and Water*.

[44] *Miracula*, II.34, in *Acta Sanctorum Iulii . . . Tomus I*, edd. Ianning *et al.*, p. 298. Cf. below, pp. 86–7 and 107.

[45] *The Vita Wulfstani*, II.20 (ed. Darlington, pp. 43–4). Mason has discussed this version in *St Wulfstan of Worcester*, pp. 289–94.

[46] See Rosenthal, *The 'Vitae Patrum' in Old and Middle English Literature*; Ott, *Ueber die Quellen der Heiligenleben in Ælfrics Lives of Saints*; and Loomis, 'Further sources of Ælfric's

nobly-born (*æðel-boren*), influenced a number of men to manumit their slaves. Thus Florus offered his gold and silver to God 'and freed his slaves before the altar' on being converted by St Maur.[47] Chromatius and his son were first baptised by St Sebastian the Martyr, who then also baptised their household (*inn-hyrede*) and estate-workers (*æhtamannum*) numbering over a thousand people. Chromatius thereupon forgave all his debts, freed his slaves and distributed property (*feoh*) to them.[48] One Gallicanus freed no less than five thousand people and gave them goods.[49]

These actions are strikingly like those of Bishop Wilfrid in the seventh century. On receiving the peninsula of Selsey as a gift, he freed and baptised 250 men and women living there.[50] Wilfrid's possible motivation for engaging in this act and its precise meaning in legal terms are best deferred to the discussion of manumission in chapter V below. Here consideration must be given to the influence that the vernacular version of this story may have had on later Anglo-Saxon England, something about which one must concede it is impossible to attain any certainty. It is fair to say that Wilfrid is portrayed by Bede as a significant figure in the early history of the English Church and his status as a saint invested his actions with an aura of sanctity. Furthermore, his freeing of slaves illustrated a fulfilment of Christ's injunction to 'sell all you have and give to the poor'. At the very least, then, one may suggest that the vernacular version of the story existed together with the *Lives* of Saint Swithhun and St Wulfstan as another source which served to foster an attitude of mind among slave owners in the late tenth and the eleventh century favouring the manumission of large proportions of the slaves living on their estates.[51]

HOMILIES

Ælfric, abbot of Eynsham, composed the largest extant body of homilies written in Old English[52] and in consequence he is one of the few writers of the Anglo-Saxon period whose ideas on slavery we can piece together into a coherent whole. To do this properly we will also need to look also at a non-homiletic work

---

Saints' Lives'. Considerable advances are currently being made in identifying Ælfric's sources: for recent work the reader is advised to consult the *Fontes Anglo-Saxonici* database at the University of Manchester, which is being edited by Donald Scragg & Michael Lapidge.

47 'and his menn gefreode ætforan ðam weofode', *Ælfric' Lives of Saints*, §6.239 (ed. & transl. Skeat, p. 162).

48 *Ibid.*, §5.307–14 (p. 136).

49 *Ibid.*, §7.381 (p. 192).

50 *The Old English Version of Bede's Ecclesiastical History*, IV.13 (ed. Miller, I.2.304–7) (Old English text and translation) = *Bede's Ecclesiastical History*, IV.13 (edd. & transl. Colgrave & Mynors, pp. 374–7) (Latin text and translation).

51 For the possible ecclesiastical influence of Bede's Latin version of this story see chapter IV below.

52 Translations of both series of Ælfric's *Catholic Homilies* and texts of the First Series are taken from *The Sermones Catholici*, ed. & transl. Thorpe. The translations have been silently emended to replace 'servant' with 'slave' and to eliminate archaisms and obvious errors. Texts of the Second Series are drawn from *Ælfric's Catholic Homilies*, ed. Godden, cross-referenced to Thorpe for the sake of convenience.

of his, the *Colloquy*.[53] After we have surveyed his ideas, we will turn to examining references to slaves in the anonymous homilies.[54]

A. *The Homilies of Ælfric*

In Ælfric's homilies slavery, which is portrayed mainly in metaphorical terms, has the purpose of illustrating Humanity's relation to the Devil and to God. As creatures tainted by evil, Humankind is several times described by Ælfric as being a slave of sin. Using Christ's words, 'Verily, verily I say unto you, Each of those who work sin shall then be the slave of sin',[55] he depicts every vice a person engages in as a devil set over him, like a master over a slave. In another passage an avaricious person is compared to a slave, who unlike a lord could not own property: 'Verily he is not lord of those possessions, when he cannot distribute them, but he is the slave of those possessions, when he wholly serves them.'[56]

When sin is personified as the Devil, the lord-slave dichotomy is particularly valuable to him as an image. For example, the total control exercised by a master over a slave, a control reducible only by manumission, appears in Ælfric's typological interpretation of the exile of the Hebrew people in Egypt: 'As the Almighty God then delivered his people from the king Pharaoh, and led them to the country which he had promised to Abraham and his offspring, so also he delivers daily his chosen from the old devil, and releases them from his thraldom and from this world of toil, and leads them to the eternal country for which we were created.'[57] Christ's death as a release from this control is employed in another similar passage on the exile: 'The Israelitish people were delivered from sudden death, and from Pharaoh's thraldom through the offering of the lamb, which was a betokening of Christ's passion, through which we are redeemed from eternal death and the power of the cruel devil. . . .'[58]

Another aspect of slavery underlying the image of servitude to the Devil

---

53 *Ælfric's Colloquy*, ed. Garmonsway.

54 Though Archbishop Wulfstan also wrote homilies, most of his views on slaves were embodied in secular legislation and collections of ecclesiastical regulations. So as not to fragment his thinking on slaves, treatment of his homilies will be deferred to chapter III, where the whole corpus of his writings will be considered.

55 'Soð, soð ic eow secge, ælc ðæra ðe synne wyrcð he bið þonne ðære synne ðeow.' *Ælfric's Catholic Homilies*, §13.76–7 (ed. Godden, p. 129) = *The Sermones Catholici*, II.15 (ed. & transl. Thorpe, p. 228.8–9).

56 'Witodlice ne bið he þæra æhta hlaford, þonne he hi dælan ne mæg, ac he bið þæra æhta ðeowa, þonne he him eallunga þeowað. . . .' *The Sermones Catholici*, I.4 (ed. & transl. Thorpe, p. 66.5–7).

57 'Swa swa se ælmihtiga God ða his folc ahredde wið þone cyning pharao, and hi lædde to ðam earde þe he Abrahame and his ofspringe behet, swa eac he arett dæghwomlice his gecorenan wið þone ealdan deofol, and hi alyst fram hie ðeowte and from ðyssere geswincfullan worulde, and gelæt hi to ðam ecan eðele ðe we to gesceapene wæron.' *Ælfric's Catholic Homilies*, §12.180–6 (ed. Godden, p. 115) = *The Sermones Catholici*, II.13 (ed. & transl. Thorpe, p. 200.10–16).

58 'Dæt Israhela folc wearð ahredd fram þam færlican deaðe, and fram Pharaones ðeowte þurh þæs lambes offrunge, ðe hæfde getacnunge Cristes ðrowunge, ðurh ða we sind alysede fram ðam ecum deaðe and þæs reðan deofles anwealde. . . .' *Ælfric's Catholic Homilies*, §15.43–7 (ed. Godden, p. 151) = *The Sermones Catholici*, II.15 (ed. & transl. Thorpe, p. 264.34ff.)

derived from its being a state that could be entered into through capture in war. For example, Ælfric describes the Babylonian exile in these terms: 'The king of the heavenly Jerusalem is Christ; of the infamous Babylon the devil is king, who wars on the sinful, and leads them captives to the hellish city, in devilish thraldom.'[59]

The image of enslavement to sin and the Devil depicts slavery as an involuntary state advantageous to the owner (in this case, the Devil). Enslavement to God, on the other hand, is a state that is beneficial to the slave (who here represents Humanity). This then makes slavery a commendable state. A confusion of these two aspects is evident in one passage where he describes those who obey God's orders as friends because they act voluntarily and with a knowledge of God's purposes, unlike the slave. He then unconsciously slips back into describing those obedient to God's will as 'God's slaves' in the midst of this discussion:

The apostles and all those who obey God's commandments, are called his friends. He said, 'I call you not slaves, because the slave knows not what his lord does.' The lord takes not his slave as a counsellor, but takes his faithful friends, and to them opens his will. So also God manifests his secrets to those who inwardly love him; and the slave, that is, he who is slave to sins, is cut off from God's counsel. Awe is twofold, and service is twofold. One awe is without love, the other is with love, and it is holy and pure. So also one service is compulsory without love, the other is voluntary with love, which befits God's slaves. The Lord took from us the name of slave, and called us His friends, if we perform His will.[60]

Apart from using the slave in figurative terms, Ælfric also employed as examples two of Bede's stories which had slaves as central characters. The first tells of Gregory's encounter with Anglian slaves in Rome, related in order to explain why he came to send missionaries to convert the Anglo-Saxons.[61] Of the slaves Ælfric declares that 'they were men white of body and of comely countenance, with noble heads of hair',[62] which prompts Gregory to observe: 'Alas that

---

[59] 'Ðære heofonlican Hierusalem cyning is Crist; þære scandlican Babilonian cyning is deofol, se geheregað þa synfullan, and gehæfte to þære hellican byrig gelæt to deoflicum ðeowte.' *Ælfric's Catholic Homilies*, §4.243–6 (ed. Godden, p. 37) = *The Sermones Catholici*, II.4 (ed. & transl. Thorpe, p. 66.32–4).

[60] 'Þa apostoli and ealle ða þe Godes bebodum gehyrsumiað beoð his frynd gecigede. He cwæð, "Ne hate ic eow ðeowan, for ðan þe se ðeowa nat hwæt his hlaford deð." Ne nymð se hlaford his ðeowan him to rædboran, ac nimð his holdan frynd, and him geopenað his willan. Swa eac God geswutelað his digelnyssa ðam ðe hine inweardlice lufiað; and se ðeowa, þæt is, se ðe synnum þeowað, bið ascyred fram Godes ræde. Ege is twyfeald, and ðeowdom is twyfeald. An ege is butan lufe, oðer is mid lufe, and se is halig and clæne. Swa eac oðer ðeowt neadunge buton lufe, oðer is sylfwilles mid lufe, se gedafenað Godes ðeowum. Drihten genam of us þæs ðeowan naman, and het us His frynd, gif we His willan gewyrcað.' *Ælfric's Catholic Homilies*, §35.38–49 (ed. Godden, p. 300) = *The Sermones Catholici*, II.40 (ed. & transl. Thorpe, p. 522.29ff.)

[61] *Ælfric's Catholic Homilies*, §9.53ff. (ed. Godden, p. 74) = *The Sermones Catholici*, II.9 (ed. & transl. Thorpe, p. 120.14ff.); *Bede's Ecclesiastical History*, II.1 (edd. & transl. Colgrave & Mynors, pp. 132–5).

[62] 'þa wæron hwites lichaman and fægeres andwlitan menn, and æðellice gefexode.' *Ælfric's Catholic Homilies*, §9.57–8 (ed. Godden, p. 74) = *The Sermones Catholici*, II.9 (ed. & transl. Thorpe, p. 120.18–19).

men of such fair appearance should be subject to the swart devil.'[63] Ælfric has here embellished his source by introducing the 'swart devil', thereby suggesting a link between physical appearance and moral qualities, a notion that was perhaps implicit in the Bedan account but is not openly alluded to. As we have seen earlier, this same association of ideas occurs in *Riddle*, §12.

His second *exemplum* is the story of Imma, a young Northumbrian thegn wounded and captured in battle, and subsequently sold into slavery.[64] The story is told in order to illustrate the efficacy of the Mass. Ælfric preserves the outline of the story, but fails to mention Imma's subterfuge of pretending to be a *ceorl* in order to save his life – presumably because it was no longer the practice to slaughter warrior captives and also possibly because *ceorlas* may have been regularly fighting in the *fyrd* by his time. With renewed Viking attacks in the late tenth century enslavement through capture in war must have increased the impact of the illustration.

Ælfric did not ignore, however, the position of slaves in the world around him. Like other mediaeval thinkers he accepted slavery and cited with approval Paul's injunction to slaves to obey their masters and for their masters to be gentle with their slaves.[65] He went on, however, to draw a distinction between temporal lordship and servitude on the one hand, and the equality of all in the sight of God on the other: 'The master and the slave call alike to the Heavenly Father in their Pater noster. They are both men born in the world, and they will have from God whatsoever they shall have merited. Every servitude will be ended in this present life, save of those only who minister to sins, they will have everlasting servitude, and others will be free, although they in life long before had served.'[66]

This theological observation that all people are equal in the sight of God led him to conclude that all share a common humanity: '. . . as Christ said in His Gospel, "He who does the will of my Father who is in heaven, he is my brother, and my mother, and my sister." Now therefore all Christian men, whether high or low, noble or ignoble, and the lord, and the slave, are all brothers, and have all one Father in heaven. . . . As boldly may the slave call God his Father as the king. We are all alike before God. . . .'[67] He illustrated this by pointing to Christ's

---

[63] 'Wa la wa þæt swa fægeres hiwes menn sindon ðam sweartan deofle underðeodde.' *Ælfric's Catholic Homilies*, §9.65–6 (ed. Godden, p. 74) = *The Sermones Catholici*, II.9 (ed. & transl. Thorpe, p. 120.26–7).

[64] *Ælfric's Catholic Homilies*, §21.143 (ed. Godden, p. 204) = *The Sermones Catholici*, II.24 (ed. & transl. Thorpe, p. 357.22ff.); *Bede's Ecclesiatical History*, IV.22(20) (edd. & transl. Colgrave & Mynors, pp. 400–5).

[65] *Ælfric's Catholic Homilies*, §19.215–21 (ed. Godden, pp. 186–7) = *The Sermones Catholici*, II.22 (ed. & transl. Thorpe, p. 326.21–7).

[66] 'Se hlaford and se ðeowa gelice clypiað to ðam Heofonlican Fæder on heora Paternostre. Begen hi sind men on middanearde accenede, and hi habbað æt Gode swa hu swa hi geearniað. Ælc ðeowt bið geendod on ðisum andweardan life, buton ðæra anra þe synnum ðeowiað, hi habbað ecne ðeowt, and ða oðre beoð frige, ðeah ðe hi on life lange ær ðeowdon.' *Ælfric's Catholic Homilies*, §19.221–7 (ed. Godden, p. 187) = *The Sermones Catholici*, II.22 (ed. & transl. Thorpe, p. 326.27–33).

[67] '. . . swa swa Crist cwæð on his godspelle, "Se ðe wyrcð mines Fæder willan seðe is on heofonum, he bið min broðer, and min moder, and min sweoster." Forði nu ealle cristene men, ægðer ge ríce ge heane, ge æðelborene ge unæðelborene, and se hlaford, and se ðeowa, ealle hí sind gebroðra, and ealle hí habbað ænne Fæder on heofonum. . . . Eallswa bealdlice mot se

behaviour related in John 4:46–53, where Jesus healed the 'under-king's son' by pronouncing the words of healing without submitting to the official's request that He return to his home to do this, in contrast to the personal visit Jesus made in order to cure the servant of the more lowly centurion, as told in Luke 7:3–10.[68]

Though Ælfric was drawing on New Testament precedent in emphasising the common humanity of all people, slave and free, he was going counter to the traditional Anglo-Saxon legal view of a slave. But he was not alone in this. As will be seen later, there were forces moving in this direction from Alfred's time on, if not before.[69] Ælfric's contribution lay in expressing the idea with such clarity. His friend Wulfstan was to accept this viewpoint (even to the extent of using some of Ælfric's very phraseology)[70] and through Wulfstan the idea gained wider currency by being incorporated into royal laws and ecclesiastical regulations.

Thus, while Ælfric's homilies display a humane attitude towards slaves, they also show very clearly how a moralist of that age was completely at home with the institution of slavery through inheriting a set of images and stories that depended for their impact on an acceptance of slavery as a natural part of the social order.

Ælfric's sensitivity to the position of slaves is particularly evident in his little textbook called the *Colloquy*, which was designed to enlarge a school pupil's vocabulary. Understanding of this work has been greatly advanced by Garmonsway and Anderson.[71] We now know that it is an example of a literary genre that goes back to a fourth-century collection of exercises and vocabulary lists known as the *Hermeneumata Pseudo-Dositheana*.[72] The *Colloquy* itself Anderson thinks arose in a monastic context: '[I]t is possible for us to see the unifying theme of the *Colloquy* as an expression of the Benedictine monastic ideal, derived from the Rule, of an orderly and well-regulated life within the confines of an economically self-sufficient community devoted to the service of God – a community separate from the world but at the same time a microcosmic image of it, in which each monastic craftsman contributes in his own way to the general welfare.'[73]

Among the figures who have a role in the *Colloquy* is the ploughman. Anderson rightly sees him as representing the *laboratores*, in mediaeval thinking held to be one of the three estates that constituted society.[74] Ælfric does not make him the only representative of this group. Instead he draws upon another tradition by

---

ðeowa clypigan God him to Fæder ealswa se cyning. Ealle we sind gelice ætforan Gode. . . .'
The Sermones Catholici, I.19 (ed. & transl. Thorpe, p. 260.16–25) (text); *ibid.*, p. 261 (translation; slightly emended).

[68] *The Sermones Catholici*, I.8 (ed. & transl. Thorpe, p. 128.25–7). The under-king's son is called *þone ætheling* by Ælfric.

[69] See below, pp. 83–5.

[70] See below, pp. 89–90 and n. 38.

[71] Garmonsway, 'The development of the Colloquy', in *The Anglo-Saxons*, ed. Clemoes; Anderson, 'Social idealism in Ælfric's *Colloquy*'.

[72] Garmonsway, 'The development of the Colloquy', in *The Anglo-Saxons*, ed. Clemoes, pp. 252–4.

[73] Anderson, 'Social idealism in Ælfric's *Colloquy*', p. 159.

[74] *Ibid.*, p. 157. See above, p. 56 and n. 24.

having the carpenter and smith also vie for this position. Like the debate that precedes this on the value of the baker and the cook, it can be seen as part of 'a more general tradition of school debate over the relative merits of various crafts and callings'.[75] Where the ploughman differs from the carpenter and smith is that he possesses a different legal status because he was not a free person. The verbal portrayal of the ploughman is worth quoting *in extenso*:

'What have you to say, ploughman? How do you undertake your work?'
'Oh, my lord, I work excessively. I go out at day-break, goading the oxen to the field, and I join them to the plough; there is not a winter so harsh that I dare lurk at home for fear of my master. But after yoking the oxen and securing the ploughshare and coulter to the plough, throughout the whole day I must plough a full acre or more.'
'Have you a companion?'
'I have a boy spurring on the oxen with a whip, who even now is hoarse with the cold and the shouting.'
'Do you do anything else during the day?'
'I certainly do more. I must fill the stalls of the oxen with hay and supply them with water and carry their dung outside. Oh! Oh! The work is hard. Yes, the work is hard, because I am not free.'[76]

Though things like the ploughshare and coulter have been included in order to introduce Latin agricultural vocabulary, the passage conveys an accurate verbal depiction of a ploughing scene. The mournful lament is what distinguishes the ploughman from other figures in the *Colloquy* and indeed from other servile figures in Anglo-Saxon sources: Ælfric has succeeded in portraying his plough-man as a living human being by going beyond a description of his occupation to permitting his ploughman to reveal his personal feelings through his own words. The ploughman's expression of his unhappiness caused by his lack of freedom is far more powerful than any external description of his personal misfortune could have been. It is the only example in Anglo-Saxon literature of the life of the slave *as told from the viewpoint of the slave*. This is not because the Anglo-Saxons were unable to perceive a literary creation from within – the lament of Satan in *Genesis B* is proof of that. Rather it is indicative of the social gulf that existed between those who produced the literature and those who were slaves. Ælfric marks himself out as being exceptional by being able to bridge that gulf in this passage.

---

[75] *Ibid.*, p. 156.
[76] 'Quid dicis tu, arator? Quomodo exerces opus tuum?'
  'O, mi domine, nimium laboro. Exeo diluculo minando boues ad campum, et iungo eos ad aratrum; non est tam aspira hiems ut audeam latere domi pro timore domini mei, sed iunctis bobus, et confirmato uomere et cultro aratro, omni die debeo arare integrum agrum aut plus.'
  'Habes aliquem socium?'
  'Habeo quendam puerum minantem boues cum stimulo, qui etiam modo raucus est pre frigore et clamatione.'
  'Quid amplius facis in die?'
  'Certe adhuc plus facio. Debeo implere presepia boum feno, et adaquare eos, et fimum eorum portare foras. O! O! magnus labor. Etiam, magnus labor est, quia non sum liber.' *Ælfric's Colloquy*, lines 22–35 (ed. Garmonsway, pp. 20–1). On the ploughman and the plough see further below, pp. 199–202.

We should not, however, allow sentiment to cause us to ignore precisely what the text says: 'Yes, the work is hard, *because* (*quia*) I am not free.' The key word is 'because' and its significance becomes apparent if we apply the corollary of the sentence: 'No, the work is not hard, because I am free.' Consciously or unconsciously Ælfric has perceived another truth, namely, that the state of slavery does not provide an incentive for productive labour. It would be foolish, of course, to suggest that the demanding nature of the ploughman's work would change with any transformation in his legal status: the implication of this passage is that his *perception* of the onerous nature of his work would change. If a privileged person like Ælfric understood this, so might landlords, who thus might have been persuaded to manumit slaves because it could potentially be in their own economic self-interest.

B. *Anonymous Homilies*

The anonymous homilies, like those composed by Ælfric, also utilise the imagery of servitude. This imagery will be examined more fully in the next section of this chapter. Here instead we might note how the anonymous homilies reveal another dimension of the Church's impact on slavery not apparent in Ælfric's writings. Under the influence of the penitential discipline so actively promoted by Ælfric's contemporary, Wulfstan, several of the homilies strongly support the practice of fasting. In so doing they emphasise that slaves were not exempt from these ecclesiastical regulations. Thus in the sermon *Be mistlican gelimpan* the homilist declares that slaves are to be freed from work and granted church privileges in order that they might fast the more willingly and do what work they wish for themselves.[77] This is an obvious reference to the four holidays granted slaves in Alfred, §43, which will be examined in the next chapter.[78] If they failed to fast properly they were to be beaten (*þolian þære hyde*), in contrast to freemen, who could pay a fine varying from thirty pence in the case of a *bonda* to thirty shillings in that of a thegn. But the differentiation in punishment between slave and freeman is less important than the fact that both were subject to common ecclesiastical duties. The acquisition of common obligations was to be as important for the disappearance of slavery from England as the possession of common rights was.

The same wording concerning the free days is used in a homily that enjoined a special fast in order to win Divine favour in meeting the difficulties that had arisen out of the arrival of 'a great army', an obvious reference to one of the Viking incursions in the reign of Æthelred.[79] The appearance of these regulations in more than one source suggests that they had some general application. The obligation of everyone to observe ecclesiastical regulations is also emphasised in the sermon *Ad populum dominicii diebus*, where Christ is made to declare that all who did not keep the Sabbath were to be excommunicated from God and have no fellowship with Christ and His angels for ever.[80]

A Lenten homily, recorded in a mid-eleventh-century script, implicitly recog-

---

[77] *Wulfstan*, §35.19ff. (ed. Napier, p. 171); variant version in *ibid*. §36.23–27 (p. 173).
[78] See below, p. 85 and n. 21.
[79] *Wulfstan*, §39.24ff. (ed. Napier, pp. 180–1).
[80] *Ibid*., §57 (p. 296.30ff.)

nises that the slave's lot was nevertheless still harsher than a freeman's.[81] It permits slaves, children below the age of twelve, and poor people to fast only till noon on three days rather than to 3.00 p.m. In addition they could eat what they could get except for meat (usually dairy products, fish, and eggs were proscribed)[82] and partake of a small evening meal, presumably on each day of the fast. Regulations on this matter must have varied, however; the directions for the use of a confessor that emanated from Wulfstan's circle decreed that *all* should fast till 3.00 p.m.[83]

From one point of view these regulations may be said to have perpetuated the *status quo* by retaining corporal punishment for slaves who breached the regulations and by associating them with the young and the poor. Yet in their insistence that slaves were subject to these obligations they showed that in this sphere there was no distinction between free and unfree. They asserted the equality of all before God, a concept that received strong support from both Ælfric and Wulfstan. Furthermore, in releasing slaves from the full severity of the rules on fasting one cleric at least gave practical expression to this perception by his humane consideration of the economic position of slaves, whose physical labours must have been heavy and food frequently inadequate.

This survey of the literature shows that it was not in the nature of these texts for the slave to play anything other than a peripheral role. Nevertheless both the Saint's Life and the Homily disclose forces within the society which were pushing towards the eventual elimination of the slave status. The Saint's Life featured a hero whose actions included helping slaves and promoting their manumission. The homilies meanwhile encouraged the blurring of the distinctions between slave and free by emphasising the equality of all in the sight of God and by insisting that slaves as well as freemen be subject to ecclesiastical regulations on fasting. These forces were in operation from at least the time of Alfred, when it came to be realised that slavery involved more than just a legal status conferred by membership of the tribe.

SOME THEMES IN THE LITERARY SOURCES

Scattered through the literary sources are many incidental references to slaves and slavery unrelated to the nature of the genre, which, when assembled, supply some very useful information. One theme, the concept of enslavement to God and to the Devil, has already been touched on. This will be examined further here, together with two other themes, the sources of slaves and the nature of the slave trade.

---

[81] Ker, 'Three Old English texts', in *The Anglo-Saxons*, ed. Clemoes, pp. 267, 270–2, and 278–9.

[82] *Das altenglische Bussbuch*, ed. Spindler, p. 170.14–15 and p. 203, 'Glossar', s.v. *hwīt*.

[83] Ker, 'Three Old English texts', in *The Anglo-Saxons*, ed. Clemoes, p. 276.10–12. *Wulfstan*, §29.16–19 (ed. Napier, p. 136), decrees that all over the age of twelve should fast till 3.00 p.m. at Lent, during the four Ember periods and the martyrs' mass-nights (*mæsse-æfenas*). On Wulfstan's possible influence on the matter of fasting, see below, pp. 92–3.

THE HISTORICAL IMPLICATIONS OF THE METAPHOR OF SLAVERY IN ANGLO-SAXON RELIGIOUS THINKING

As slavery was such an integral part of ancient society it is not surprising that slaves appear fairly frequently in both the Old and New Testaments. And as people tend to visualise the abstract world of the spirit in terms of the concrete world round them, it is also not surprising that the relationship between Humanity and God – and Humanity and the Devil – was apprehended in servile terms. Thus Mary sings in her hymn of praise:

> My soul doth magnify the Lord,
> And my spirit hath rejoiced in God my Saviour,
> For he has regarded the low estate of his handmaiden:
> For, behold, from henceforth all generations shall call me blessed.[84]

Many others, patriarch, king, and disciple of Jesus alike, are described as slaves of God.[85]

Under the influence of the Authorised Version the biblical word 'slave' has been replaced in modern christian religious discourse by 'servant', the social class nearest to that of a slave in societies that no longer possess slaves.[86] Yet the antecedent Hebrew, Greek, Latin, and Old English versions of the Bible were unambiguous in their use of the legal status word 'slave'.[87] Biblical scholars are only now starting to realise how important it is to know something about slavery in the ancient world in order to understand the nature of the theological concepts expressed in the Bible.[88] This is no less true of the Anglo-Saxon age, when the nature of slavery in that society shaped the reader's understanding of the biblical text. On the other hand, the imagery reflected back on the society by taking slavery and the idea of redemption from slavery for granted, thereby giving the Anglo-Saxon reader no grounds for questioning the institution.[89]

---

[84] Luke 1:46–8. Note the contrast between 'lord' ($\kappa\acute{v}\varrho\iota o\varsigma$) and 'slave' ($\delta o\tilde{v}\lambda o\varsigma$). The background to this vocabulary is briefly discussed and further references given in Nock, *Early Gentile Christianity and its Hellenistic Background*, pp. 32–5. The implications of this specific passage from Luke has been explored by Vogt in 'Ecce Ancilla Domini', in his *Ancient Slavery and the Ideal of Man*, transl. Wiedemann, pp. 146–69. Note especially his comment on p. 147 that 'the phrase "handmaid of the Lord" obscures the radical significance contained in the terms $\delta o\acute{v}\lambda\eta$ and *ancilla* in the world of Greek and Roman antiquity and in the Israel of this period'.

[85] I Chronicles 6:49 (Moses); I Kings 3:6 (David); James 1:1 (James).

[86] Chaucer is already occasionally using the word in scriptural passages; see, for example, *The Parson's Tale*, line 629, in *The Riverside Chaucer*, ed. Benson, p. 308.

[87] Hebrew *'ebed*, Greek $\delta o\tilde{v}\lambda o\varsigma$, Latin *seruus*, Old English *þeow* are the most common words used in these contexts. Goodspeed, *Problems of New Testament Translation*, p. 140, has pointed out that 'slave' appears only in Revelation 18:13 in the Authorised Version of the New Testament, whereas the Greek text records $\delta o\tilde{v}\lambda o\varsigma$ 121 times.

[88] Bartchy, *MAΛΛΟN XPHΣAI*; Goodspeed, *Problems of New Testament Translation*, pp. 139–41; Vogt, 'Ecce Ancillae Domini'. I owe the first two references to the Revd D. M. Stanley of Regis College, Toronto.

[89] Anstey in his review of Davis, *The Problem of Slavery in the Age of Revolution*, has suggested that the imagery continued to have an impact on Western ideas on slavery in that the Evangelicals expounded the doctrine of salvation in terms of the 'bedrock concept' of redemption. If he is correct, the Evangelicals must have emphasised slavery to the Devil as an

Some aspects of the imagery of servitude and its relation to other image clusters are worth exploring further in order to understand its impact on the Anglo-Saxons' perception of slavery. Ælfric's homilies have shown that slavery as an image of Humanity's spiritual state was used in two different ways. In one respect it represented a state of obedience beneficial to the slave as a type of Humanity; in another it represented a state of domination by the overlord, that is, the Devil. Ælfric does not seem to have perceived the distinctions in the use of this imagery. There is some evidence, however, that Wulfstan was at least sub-consciously aware of it. He uses the word *þræl* several times when referring to a slave of the Devil but never uses it of a slave of God, thereby giving *þræl* a pejorative connotation.[90]

Another aspect of the institution of slavery that appears in biblical imagery is the portrayal of Christ as a manumittor or redeemer. In Old English Christ was called *(A)lisend* and the act of redemption was expressed by the verb *(a)lisan*, the latter being a word that is also employed in the manumission-documents.[91] The image of Christ as redeemer was also used in two other related image clusters, so that it is frequently difficult to say which is being referred to. The first is the image of imprisonment. Often those imprisoned are portrayed as being bound in fetters, particularly, as has been mentioned, in Saints' Lives.[92] This encouraged the metaphorical development of the concept, so that Christ's death came to be portrayed as an act of redemption of Humankind from the Devil's imprisonment or from his fetters.[93] The second image cluster portrayed the life of Humanity in terms of war. Paul's likening of the christian virtues to items forming part of a soldier's martial equipment had established the image of the *miles christianus*, a notion that was particularly attractive to the Anglo-Saxons with their warrior ethos.[94] A christian in Old English literature is often called *Godes þegn*, God's servant, a description most often used in the poetry but also not infrequently employed in prose writings as well.[95] The Old Testament accounts of war, such as the fighting that led to the Babylonian captivity, permitted this image to be developed further. The state of sin came to be described figuratively as captivity to the Devil, with Christ acting through His death as a redeemer of Humanity from such captivity.[96] With capture in war often leading to a life of slavery and with Christ being viewed in a martial context as a redeemer, it was easy for this image cluster to become associated with that of servitude.[97]

unnatural state rather than slavery to God as a natural one. This would explain why they came to question the institution.

[90] See below, appendix I, s.v. *þræl*.
[91] See further below, table V, pp. 153–4, and appendix I, s.vv. *alisend, alisan*.
[92] Above, pp. 58–9.
[93] For imprisonment in hell see, for example, *The Sermones Catholici*, I.19 (ed. & transl. Thorpe, p. 266.34–5).
[94] Ephesians 6:11ff.
[95] For example, *The Sermones Catholici*, I.27 (ed. & transl. Thorpe, p. 386.17).
[96] The idea is quite common in Ælfric's writings. See, for example, *The Sermones Catholici*, I.36 (ed. & transl. Thorpe, p. 546.33–5).
[97] Some of the imagery examined in this paragraph, notably bondage and the release from that state, has been fruitfully explored from a rather different perspective in Rendall, 'Bondage and freeing from bondage'.

Slavery as an established feature of the ancient and early mediaeval world formalised the existence of differences in power between one person and another, just as religion formalised the differences in power between Humanity and the surrounding world. It was a natural development, therefore, to use the former as a metaphor to illustrate the latter. Christianity inherited this metaphor and expanded its use so that slavery came to be visualised as inherent in Humanity's relationship to God, thereby in turn legitimising the secular institution of slavery. Because slavery was central to the religious imagery, we can readily comprehend how moralists came to accept it as a 'natural' institution whose legitimacy was not questioned.

THE SOURCES OF SLAVES

War has always been a major source of human labour in slave-owning societies. The Anglo-Saxons were no exception to this generalisation, and there is ample evidence to show that at least until the eighth century wars of conquest and inter-tribal strife were a fertile source of slaves.[98] In fact, the Anglo-Saxons probably continued to take slaves in war right into the tenth century. The *Anglo-Saxon Chronicle*, for instance, records that in 909 King Edward led a combined West-Saxon and Mercian force against the Danes in the North, where, in addition to killing many Danes, it 'ravaged very severely the territory of the northern army, both men and all kinds of cattle'.[99] The use of the word *wealh* in the sense of 'slave' in the late southern sources suggests that many Celts must also have been enslaved when Æthelstan finally conquered the south-west of England.[100]

Nevertheless, from the ninth to the eleventh centuries it was mainly the Norsemen who enslaved many in England by capturing them in war. We still imperfectly understand the sources of this Scandinavian restlessness: technological developments in naval architecture certainly played a part, though whether as a cause or an effect is still a matter of debate.[101] Whatever the reasons, the consequence was that the Norse became widely recorded as slavers in Europe. Perhaps as early as 761 they seized captives in a raid on Makhor in Mauretania, and people were taken in raids on Spain in 844 and 859 x 861. Although some were ransomed, not all were so fortunate: a number of Moors captured during the second attack on Spain ended up in Ireland.[102]

It is ironic that these early references to the Vikings as slavers should depict inhabitants of Islamic realms as their victims, for we are now beginning to

---

[98] See Levison, *England and the Continent in the Eighth Century*, pp. 5 and 8–9, and Lohaus, *Die Merowinger und England*, pp. 39–42.

[99] 'heo gehergade swiðe micel on þæm norð here, ægðer ge on mannum ge on gehwelces cynnes yrfe. . . .' *Two of the Saxon Chronicles Parallel*, ed. Plummer, I.94.28ff. (910 A) (text); *English Historical Documents c.500–1042*, §1 (transl. Whitelock, p. 210, s.a. 909).

[100] See below, appendix I, s.v. *wealh*.

[101] Peter Sawyer has postulated that the growth of trade stimulated the developments: see his *Kings and Vikings*, pp. 75–7.

[102] The early date for the attack on Africa was argued by Melvinger in *Les Premières Incursions des Vikings en Occident*, pp. 129–64. Texts and discussion on the later attacks is to be found in Dozy, *Recherches sur l'histoire et la littérature de l'Espagne*, II.250–86, and Stefánsson, 'The Vikings in Spain', 37 and 41. For Moors in Ireland see *Annals of Ireland: Three Fragments*, ed. & transl. O'Donovan, pp. 158–63.

realise that it was the explosive expansion of Islam in the eighth and ninth centuries that stimulated the slave trade and created a demand that the Scandinavians proved very willing to meet. We are still groping our way towards a understanding of the macro-economic forces that the spread of Islamic civilisation unleashed and a detailed discussion would take us too far from the topic in hand.[103] A brief excursus will, however, provide a context for local events in England. The reckless growth in the ninth century of Baghdad and Samarra, 120 kilometres upstream, demanded extensive labour resources, and the caliphs possessed in abundance the silver to purchase humans that would enable them to carry out their building programmes.[104] By the end of the tenth century their extravagance had exhausted their treasury, but elsewhere there were other Islamic rulers who had chosen another conspicuous form of displaying their wealth that also required a plentiful supply of human beings, namely, the acquisition of women as personal possessions and of the eunuchs required to staff their dwellings. At one point the caliph of Cordoba had a harem of over 6000 and his counterpart in Cairo had twice that number.[105] The Scandinavians proved ready to meet this demand by drawing on peoples from right across Europe. Ireland, for instance, was a good source of slaves according to the sagas.[106] One captive who ended up in Iceland rather than in the world of Islam was Melkorka, the Irish princess who plays such an important role in *Laxdœla Saga*.[107] And slaves of Slavic origin were used by Scandinavians as a major trading item with Islamic merchants in eastern Europe.[108]

Once the Norse settled in Ireland they used it as a base from which to make slave raids on the west coast of Britain.[109] For example, when Ólafr the White and Ivarr the Boneless returned to Dublin in 871, 'a great multitude of men, English, Britons, and Picts, were brought by them to Ireland, in captivity'.[110] Thereafter no part of the British coastline was really safe from attacks by marauding Vikings. There are specific reports of the capture of men in the first

---

[103] Alexander Murray has provided an elegant synthesis in a book that has not received the attention it deserves, *Reason and Society in the Middle Ages*, pp. 35–57.

[104] See the stimulating introduction to Abbasid Baghdad and Samarra by Hodges and Whitehouse in *Mohammed, Charlemagne & the Origins of Europe*. Their synthesis needs revision and refinement but their attempt to include evidence that extends beyond national, and indeed continental, boundaries is admirable.

[105] For the Cordoba and Cairo harems see Lombard, *The Golden Age of Islam*, p. 195. Additional figures revealing the Islamic realms' capacity for importing slaves can be found in Murray, *Reason and Society in the Middle Ages*, p. 50.

[106] For a discussion of the evidence see Smyth, *Scandinavian Kings in the British Isles*, chapter XI (pp. 154–68), which should be read in association with Holm's qualifying comments in 'The slave trade of Dublin', 324–5.

[107] *Laxdœla Saga*, §13 (ed. Einar Ólafur Sveinsson, pp. 27–8).

[108] Bolin, 'Mohammed, Charlemagne and Ruric', 30 and references there cited; Sawyer, *The Age of the Vikings*, pp. 193–4.

[109] See Charles, *Old Norse Relations with Wales*, pp. 34–7, and Bromberg, 'Wales and the mediaeval slave trade', 265. On Dublin as a slave-trading centre over the course of several hundred years see Holm, 'The slave trade of Dublin'.

[110] 'et præda maxima hominum Anglorum 7 Britonum 7 Pictorum deducta est secum ad Hiberniam in captiuitate.' *Annals of Ulster*, s.a. 871 (edd. Mac Airt & Mac Niocaill, I.326) (text); *ibid.*, I.327 (translation).

halves of both the tenth and eleventh centuries,[111] but on the basis of the evidence in the *Sermo ad Anglos* it is apparent that people were also enslaved during the the repeated incursions recorded in the *Anglo-Saxon Chronicle* during Æthelred's troubled reign.[112] Some of the captives were undoubtedly taken abroad and sold,[113] while others were probably transported off to the Danelaw.[114]

These Viking raids did not cease with the Norman Conquest according to the biography of Gruffudd ap Cynan, which relates how Hugh, earl of Chester, cunningly got the better of a band of Danes who were demanding slaves: 'Then, moreover, the perjured traitors of Danes who betrayed Gruffyd were expecting the promises which Hugh had promised them, and captives of men, women, youth and maidens; and he paid them like a faithful man to the unfaithful, confirming the divine ordinance, for he had succeeded in collecting all the toothless, deformed, lame, one-eyed, troublesome, feeble hags and offered them in return for their treachery. When they saw this they loosened their fleet, and made for the deep toward Ireland.'[115] The approbation shown by the biographer towards Hugh's conduct is in itself revelatory of contemporary attitudes.

The political upheavals of the eleventh century probably also led to enslavement for some. After the unfortunate Ætheling Alfred had been taken captive in 1036, a number of his companions were sold by Earl Godwine.[116] On landing in the West Country from Ireland in 1052 Earl Harold 'seized for himself what came his way in cattle, men, and property'. Subsequently he and his father were reconciled with the king, but it would be overly sanguine to assume that all those captured regained their freedom.[117] A band of Northumbrians, travelling south to Northampton in 1065 to gain King Edward's recognition of Morcar as their earl instead of Tostig, behaved in a like fashion; reportedly they 'captured many hundreds of people and took them north with them, so that that shire and other neighbouring shires were the worse for it for many years'.[118]

Another disruptive factor in mid-eleventh-century England was the increase

---

[111] *Two of the Saxon Chronicles Parallel*, ed. Plummer, I.101.12–13 (921 A), I.111.14 (943 D), I.141.26ff. (1011 E), and I.166.14ff. (1046 E).

[112] See below, pp. 95–101.

[113] *Two of the Saxon Chronicles Parallel*, ed. Plummer, I.192.8–10 (1064 E).

[114] The widespread evidence of place-names derived from Old Norse *leysingi* implies that slaves were to be found throughout the area, even though Domesday Book does not record their presence in the North-east. See below, appendix I, s.v. *lising*.

[115] 'Eno hagen, ydd oeddynt y bratwyr anudonol o'r Daenysseit a vredychessynt Ruffudd yn aros yr eddiweideon a addawsei Hu uddunt, a cheith o wyr a gwragedd, o weisseon a morynnyon. Ag ynteu a'e talws uddunt hwy megis ffyddlawn y anffyddlawn, yn y kadarnhaei dwywawl lunyeth; kanys neu ry ddaroedd iddaw ar ehang kynullaw holl wrachiot mantach, krwm, kloff, unllygeityawg, gormessawl, diallu, ag eu kynnig uddunt ym pwyth eu bradwryaeth. A phan welsant wynteu hynny, gillwng eu llynghes a wnaethant a chyrchu y dyfynfor parth ag Ywerddon.' *Historia Gruffud Vab Kenan*, ed. Evans, p. 27 (text); *The History of Gruffydd ap Cynan*, ed. & transl. Jones, p. 149 (translation).

[116] *Two of the Saxon Chronicles Parallel*, ed. Plummer, I.158.26 (1036 C).

[117] 'nam him on orfe. 7 on mannum. 7 on æhtum. swa him gewearð.' *Two of the Saxon Chronicles Parallel*, ed. Plummer, I.178.6ff (1052 E) (text); *English Historical Documents 1042–1189*, §1 (transl. Douglas & Greenaway, pp. 125–6) (translation).

[118] 'fela hund manna hi namon. 7 læddon norð mid heom. swa þet seo scyre 7 þa oðra scyre þe þær neh sindon wurdon fela wintra þe wyrsan.' *Two of the Saxon Chronicles Parallel*, ed. Plummer, I.192.8–10 (1064 E) (text); *English Historical Documents, 1042–1189*, §1 (transl.

in predatory raids by the various Celtic-speaking peoples on the periphery of the country. For example, some of the inhabitants of Hereford were carried off in a raid made in 1055 by King Gruffudd ap Llywelyn, who had joined the outlawed Earl Ælfgar with a force from Ireland.[119] Such incursions from Wales must have continued, for we are told that 'many hundreds of men' were liberated by King William when he led an army into the country in 1081.[120] King Malcolm III of Scotland led a series of raids into England, in 1058, 1061, 1070, and 1079. Those unfortunate enough to be captured in the first three raids may well have been enslaved; those taken in 1079 certainly suffered that fate.[121] In 1138 captives seized in a battle between the English and the Picts and Scots at Clitheroe were destined to become slaves.[122] According to the *Annals of Loch Cé* in the same year Scotsmen had also made a raid into 'the north of Saxan' (presumably Westmorland), taking numerous people captive.[123]

The dominance of martial themes and martial imagery in Old English literature may well explain why warfare is recorded as the major source of slaves, even though the disruption that came in its train must also have led large numbers to seek voluntary enslavement in order to get sufficient food to stay alive.[124] The laws make it apparent that crime must also have led to the loss of freedom for a good few people.[125] Yet the only other source of slaves mentioned in the literary texts is the passing reference in the *Life of St Swithhun* discussed earlier to the effect that a slave-woman in Winchester had been stolen in the north of England.[126] As a negotiable asset the slave could of course be stolen like any other item of property. This naturally did not increase the overall stock of slaves, but the number of references to this crime suggest that it was an import-

---

Douglas & Greenaway, p. 142) (translation). On the revolt against Tostig and its background see Kapelle, *The Norman Conquest of the North*, pp. 97–9.

[119] *Two of the Saxon Chronicles Parallel*, ed. Plummer, I.184.28ff. (1055 C). Holm, 'The slave trade of Dublin', discusses (pp. 341–3) the importance of Wales to the Viking slavers in Dublin.

[120] *Two of the Saxon Chronicles Parallel*, ed. Plummer, I.214.12–13 (1081 E).

[121] For the general political background to Malcolm's activities see Kapelle, *The Norman Conquest of the North*, pp. 90–3, 122–4, and 148–53. For Malcolm's attack of 1079 see *Two of the Saxon Chronicles Parallel*, ed. Plummer, I.214.2 (1079 E). Simeon of Durham, who wrongly dates the incursion as 1070, makes it clear that the captives were enslaved: *Historia Regum*, §156, in *Symeonis Monachi Opera Omnia*, ed. Arnold, I.192, translated in *Scottish Annals from English Chroniclers*, transl. Anderson, p. 92. Malcolm led two further invasions into England, in 1091 and 1093, meeting his death on the latter occasion (*Historia Regum*, §174, in *Symeonis Monachi Opera Omnia*, ed. Arnold, I.221–2). There is no record of his taking slaves during his final two attacks.

[122] John of Hexham mentions the battle: see *Symeonis Monachi Opera Omnia*, ed. Arnold, II.291; Richard of Hexham reports that the Picts 'either made them their slaves (*ancillas*) or sold them to other barbarians for cows': *De Gestis Regis Stephani*, fo 41v, in *The Chronicle of Robert of Torigni*, ed. Howlett, p. 157 (text); *Scottish Annals from English Chroniclers*, transl. Anderson, p. 187 (translation).

[123] *The Annals of Loch Cé*, s.a. 1138 (ed. & transl. Hennessy, p. 139). Holm, 'The slave trade of Dublin', has pointed out (p. 341, n. 65) that I erred in ascribing this raid to the Irish in 'Slave trading and slave raiding', 113.

[124] See below, pp. 162–3.

[125] See below, pp. 93, 163, and 247–8.

[126] See above, p. 73.

ant factor in the internal economy of the country. Theft of slaves was proscribed as early as the mid-seventh century in Hlothhere and Eadric, §5, and Ine, §53 laid down the procedure for dealing with an allegation of such a crime. Alfred, §9.2 excluded the theft of a person (*man-ðeof*) from the general category of crimes for which there was a standard penalty. As Swithhun's *Life* shows it remained a problem well into the tenth century. VI Æthelstan, §6.3 established a fine for such a theft, and a stolen female slave was the central issue in a dispute at Yaxley some years later.[127] Wulfstan's strictures against the selling into slavery of freemen might well point to the kidnapping of freemen for sale as a problem in the early eleventh century, a not improbable occurrence in that period of disruption.[128]

THE SLAVE TRADE

There are only scattered references to slave trading – as opposed to slave raiding – in the sources. In consequence one has to depend to some degree on inference in describing its operation, as Bromberg did in his survey of the Welsh slave trade.[129]

Evidence from an unexpected source suggests that by the reign of Alfred we should regard the Anglo-Saxons as major participants in the slave-trade. The *Honorantiae Ciuitatis Papiae*, a text extant in a manuscript of the fifteenth century and later, records a treaty entered into between a *rex Anglorum et Saxonum* and a Lombard king (*rex Langobardorum*) in Pavia.[130] According to the document, Anglo-Saxons entering Lombardy through the mountain passes had been required to empty their bags, which had led to a number of affrays. The treaty exempted Anglo-Saxons from the payment of tolls (the word used is *adecimari*, which literally denotes the payment of tithes) in return for three-yearly payments from the Anglo-Saxon king of such desirable goods as refined silver, long- and short-haired greyhounds, shields, spears, and swords. Though the clause containing this agreement does not specify that these Anglo-Saxons had been tithed nor nor does it indicate what goods they had been bringing with them, the preceding clause in the text declares that all traders entering Lombardy by specific routes had to pay a tithe on horses, male and female slaves, wool, linen, and canvas cloth, tin, and swords.[131] All these were products for which England became famous, and mention of tin is perhaps the clearest indication that the two clauses should be associated with each other. While there is no certain evidence as yet for tin-mining in England between the seventh and the twelfth centuries,[132] Anglo-Saxon pewter ornaments made from a tin/lead alloy

---

[127] See below, p. 166.
[128] See below, pp. 96 and 99.
[129] Bromberg, 'Wales and the mediaeval slave trade'.
[130] *Die 'Honorantie Civitatis Papie'*, edd. Brühl & Violante (text); *Medieval Trade*, 20 (transl. Lopez & Raymond, pp. 56–60) (translation). My thanks to Dr Robin Healey for locating the edition by Brühl & Violante for me.
[131] *Ibid.*, §§1–2 (pp. 17 and 19).
[132] Pounds, 'Mining', in *Dictionary of the Middle Ages*, ed. Strayer, VIII.398, col. 1, and 401, col. 1.

were certainly being made in the tenth century[133] and, given the virtual monopoly of Cornwall and Devon over the supply of tin to Europe in the high middle ages, we may assume that mining had already been resumed there by the end of the ninth century.

The text itself has been much tampered with and it gives no direct evidence as to who the kings in question were. The most recent editors of the text draw on diplomatic evidence to suggest that the agreement could have been drawn up around the year 900, not necessarily by an Anglo-Saxon king himself but by a deputy, such as an archbishop who was travelling *en route* to Rome to receive his *pallium*.[134] This is an attractive suggestion for a number of reasons. The wording of the treaty contains a number of terms characteristic of the Latin used in England,[135] the kind of vocabulary that a cleric might be expected to have known. A good candidate would be Plegmund, archbishop of Canterbury from 890 to 923 and a major figure in Alfred's educational reforms. During Alfred's reign he was in written communication with both Pope Formosus (891–896) and Archbishop Fulk of Rheims; and in 898 he met with Alfred and others to discuss the *instauratio* of London (presumably the establishment of a borough plan). In 908 he took the alms of King Edward the Elder and of the people to Rome, returning thence with relics.[136] He was thus an important administrator. We do not know whether he obtained a *pallium* during Alfred's reign, but, given Alfred's claimed associations with Rome, he was probably encouraged to do so. Following the death of Louis II in 875, central royal power broke down in Italy; sole rulership was not reasserted until Berengar of Friuli did so (and then very weakly) in 902.[137] The final decade of the ninth century was an appropriate time for a local ruler to claim kingship over the old Lombard capital of Pavia. Plegmund's return to Italy in 908 had perhaps in part the purpose of renewing the agreement, now Berengar was – theoretically, at least – in sole command of northern Italy.

Another argument that would strongly favour a date sometime in Alfred's reign for the conclusion of the treaty is that we know that he reached another such agreement with Pope Marinus (882–4) exempting from taxes the quarter in Rome known as the *schola Saxonum*, which was used by Anglo-Saxon merchants.[138] The very existence of this agreement with the pope might have been the cause of the violence in Pavia, when merchants who knew they were exempt from taxes in Rome suddenly found themselves having to pay tribute on entering Italy.

133 Wilson, *Anglo-Saxon Ornamental Metalwork 700–1100*, §§37, 39, 51–4, 134, and 142 (pp. 146–8, 154–7, 201, and 204).
134 *Die 'Honorantie Civitatis Papie'*, edd. Brühl & Violante, pp. 37 (commentary on line 42) and 83, n. 125.
135 *Ibid.*, p. 37 (commentary on lines 40 and 47–8).
136 On Plegmund see Brooks, *The Early History of the Church of Canterbury*, pp. 152–4 and 210–14.
137 For an excellent survey of Italy at this time see Wickham, *Early Medieval Italy*, especially pp. 168–77. He briefly discusses the *Honorantiae* on pp. 89–90.
138 *Asser's Life of King Alfred*, §71 (ed. Stevenson, p. 53) (text); *Alfred the Great*, §71 (transl. Keynes & Lapidge, p. 88). On the *schola Saxonum* see *ibid.*, p. 244, n. 82, and Hoogewerf, 'Friezen, Franken en Saksen te Rome'.

By the late ninth century, Venice, which had also concluded an agreement with Pavia according to the *Honorantiae*,[139] was well-established as a slave-trading port.[140] We might thus envisage a trade-route in slaves between Anglo-Saxon England and the west coast of Italy, whence slaves from English sources could be despatched to Byzantium and to Arab lands in the Near East.

The frequent enactment of legislation against the sale of christians abroad supports the evidence of the *Honorantiae* that Englishmen regularly transported slaves across the sea to sell.[141] Many Anglo-Saxons must also have sold persons stolen or captured in war within the country. Had those at Winchester who sold the stolen northern slave-woman mentioned in the *Life of St Swithhun* or the merchants prevailed upon by St Wulfstan to give up the Bristol slave trade been foreigners, it is likely to have been commented upon. We cannot say, however, whether many of these English traders actually went out and captured the slaves themselves, as many of the Scandinavians certainly did.

Aside from the Anglo-Saxons, the main traders in slaves from the British Isles from the time of Alfred on are likely to have been the Scandinavians. As Peter Sawyer has rightly insisted, not all of them were pirates.[142] The division between the two roles was, of course, not a hard and fast one; raiders in one area could become traders of their booty somewhere else. Unfortunately, the sources preserve no definite evidence for their trading activities (as opposed to their predatory raids) during the first period of the Scandinavian invasions. As for the early eleventh century, William of Malmesbury asserts that in England Cnut's sister used to purchase companies of slaves, especially young women, whom she then exported to Denmark. Even if incorrect in detail, the memory of a slave trade with Denmark after the second period of Viking incursions must be an accurate one.[143]

Information about the centres of slave trading in England is equally exiguous. In a verse satire of 1015 x 1024 the poet Warner of Rouen tells of the sale at *Corbric* (presumably Corbridge in Northumberland) of an Irishman and his wife after they had been captured by some Danes.[144] At the other end of the country Domesday Book in an unusual reference mentions the toll due on the sale of slaves in Lewes, Sussex.[145] The reference in Swithhun's *Life* to the sale of a woman in Winchester just mentioned above and a few possible records of sales from Bath and Bodmin[146] suggest that slaves could be sold at any *port*, as a market town is called in the sources. Several towns were probable centres for the export of slaves abroad, though Bristol is the only one recorded in later sources.

---

[139] *Die 'Honorantie Civitatis Papie'*, §§3–4 (edd. Brühl & Violante, p. 19).

[140] Verlinden, *L'Esclavage*, I.115ff and 130–1.

[141] See below, pp. 91–2.

[142] Sawyer, *The Age of the Vikings*, especially chapter VIII (pp. 177–201).

[143] *Willelmi Malmesbiriensis Monachi De Gestis Regum Anglorum*, II.200 (ed. Stubbs, p. 245). The story seems a little improbable in the light of Wulfstan's success in persuading Cnut to re-enact legislation against the selling of persons out of the country.

[144] Musset, 'Le satiriste Garnier de Rouen et son milieu'; Pelteret, 'Slave trading and slave raiding', 108.

[145] Domesday Book, volume I, fo 26ra.

[146] *Manumission*, §§8.10, 8.11 (Bath); §3.29 (Bodmin).

London is mentioned by Bede,[147] and as a major trading port it almost certainly remained a slave-trading centre long after his time. Though situated inland, York, which remained with some vicissitudes a Danish city from the mid-ninth century until 954, is likely to have been a centre for the export of slaves to Scandinavia.[148] Bromberg suggested that there are also grounds for supposing Chester to have been another exporting town (with Ireland this time as at least an intermediate destination), an interpretation with which Metcalf and Northover have concurred.[149]

The impression one gets from the sources is that from the mid-tenth century on the slave trade was geared mainly to the export of persons abroad, although the internal trade did not cease. Until that time, inter-tribal fighting and the final subjugation of the South-west afforded the opportunity to increase the overall number of slaves within the country. Thereafter the unification of England meant that the main source of slaves lay on the periphery – in other words, Wales and the northern border. The Domesday Book figures imply that any Welsh captured on the borders of Worcestershire and Herefordshire did not remain in the area, and so were presumably exported abroad. Only Gloucestershire among the Welsh border shires had a high proportion of slaves.[150] The existence of the major slave market in Bristol may have been the cause of the large numbers in this area.

The trade continued under the Normans. As has been mentioned, there was a market at Lewes in the 1080s. Only the vigorous opposition of various churchmen was to bring about the termination of the trade. The Bristol slave market proved particularly hard to eradicate. The *Uita Wulfstani*, II.20, mentions that it had been a 'very ancient custom' to buy persons from all over England and transport them to Bristol for eventual sale in Ireland. 'You could see and sigh over rows of wretches bound together with ropes, young people of both sexes whose beautiful appearance and youthful innocence might move barbarians to pity, daily exposed to prostitution, daily offered for sale.'[151] It took the strenuous opposition of Wulfstan of Worcester to bring this activity to a halt there.[152] According to William of Malmesbury, Lanfranc also brought pressure to bear on the somewhat reluctant Conqueror to outlaw the Anglo-Irish slave trade.

---

[147] *Bede's Ecclesiastical History*, IV.22(20) (edd. & transl. Colgrave & Mynors, pp. 400–5).

[148] On the York of this period from an historian's viewpoint see Smyth, *Scandinavian York and Dublin*; for an archaeologist's perspective see Hall, *The Viking Dig*.

[149] Bromberg, 'Wales and the mediaeval slave trade', 265–6; Metcalf and Northover, 'Debasement of the coinage in Southern England', 166. (It should be noted, however, that Madicott has expressed reservations about the interpretations of Metcalf and Northover in 'Trade, industry and the wealth of King Alfred', 13.)

[150] See below, table VII. The situation was a little different in Herefordshire. Here there was a higher percentage of slaves on the border than in the fertile centre of the shire. This has been explained by Nelson in *The Normans in South Wales*, pp. 64–5, as due to the relocation of slaves from royal estates, notably round Radnor, in order to assist in the development of frontier estates.

[151] 'Uideres et gemeres concathenatos funibus miserorum ordines, et utriusque sexus adulescentes; qui liberali forma, etate integra, barbaris miserationi essent, cotidie prostitui, cotidie uenditari.' *The Vita Wulfstani*, §20 (ed. Darlington, p. 43) (text); 'Life of Bishop Wulfstan of Worcester', in *Three Lives of the Last Englishmen*, transl. Swanton, p. 126 (translation).

[152] Mason, *St Wulfstan of Worcester*, pp. 184–6.

Presumably because of the tolls that it gave him, the trade was profitable to the king, and William of Malmesbury declares that he would have been unlikely to have prohibited it 'had not Lanfranc commended it, and Wulfstan, powerful from his sanctity of character, commanded it by episcopal authority'.[153] The prohibition against the trading in slaves enacted in clause 12 of the *Willelmi articuli* may reflect William's legislative response to this ecclesiastical lobbying.

Finally, in 1102 the Council of Westminster completely outlawed the trade in England. Its twenty-eighth canon enjoined, 'That no one is henceforth to presume to carry on that shameful trading whereby heretofore men used in England to be sold like brute beasts'.[154] The reference to 'brute beasts' is less dramatic in its impact, however, when we realise that it is a phrase that is also to be found in Continental sources, both in a letter of Conrad II composed between 1027 and 1029 and in the *Chronica Boemorum*.[155] Furthermore, the decisions of this council may not have received the prominence that Archbishop Anselm had hoped for.[156] Certainly the ruling did not mean that the risk of being enslaved was immediately removed. Apart from the incursions from Celtic lands that have been referred to above, the memory of Bristol as a source of slaves lingered on. Hermann the Monk reports that he was cautioned on a visit to Bristol early in the twelfth century about the way in which Irish traders would suddenly raise anchor and sail away with any unwary visitors, whom they would take abroad and sell to pagans.[157]

Only when there ceased to be a market for slaves in Ireland could such activities come to an end in England. It was as late as 1170 that the Synod of Armagh ordered that any Englishman enslaved in Ireland was to receive his freedom. According to Gerald of Wales, the synod regarded Ireland's subservience to England as a punishment for the enslavement of people by her own merchants, freebooters, and pirates, although it was noted that the English themselves had been as much at fault because they used to sell their children and relatives into slavery when they suffered penury and hunger.[158] Capture and

---

[153] 'nisi quod Lanfrancus laudauerit Wulstanus præceperit, auctoritate episcopali pro conscientia sanctitatis abunde exuberans.' *Willelmi Malmesbiriensis Monachi De Gestis Regum Anglorum*, III.269 (ed. Stubbs, p. 329) (text); *William of Malmesbury's Chronicle of the Kings of England*, transl. Giles, p. 303 (translation).

[154] 'Nequis illud nefarium negotium quo hactenus homines in Anglia solebant uelut bruta animalia uenundari deinceps ullatenus facere praesumat.' *Eadmeri Historia Novorum in Anglia*, ed. Rule, p. 143 (text); *Eadmer's History of Recent Events in England*, transl. Bosanquet, p. 152 (translation). The paragraph division is that given in *Councils and Synods*, edd. Whitelock *et al.*, I.2.687, which should be consulted for the textual evidence on the council.

[155] *Conradi II. Diplomata*, §130 (ed. Bresslau, p. 176) and *Cosmae Pragensis Chronica Boemorum*, ed. Bretholz, p. 92.30. The latter work was completed in 1125 and so it is unclear whether the phrase was a borrowing or, more likely, as Whitelock *et al.* suggested, it was 'something of a commonplace of the period' (*Councils and Synods*, ed. Whitelock *et al.*, I.2.678, n. 4).

[156] The canons had a limited circulation, though Whitelock *et al.* suggested that at least the sexual provisions governing the clergy were enforced for a time (*ibid.*, p. 670).

[157] *Hermanni Monachi De Miraculis S. Mariæ Laudunensis*, II.21 (ed. Migne, cols 985–6).

[158] *Expugnatio Hibernica*, I.18, in *Giraldi Cambrensis Topographia Hibernica, et Expugnatio Hibernica*, ed. Dimock, p. 258; *Expugnatio Hibernica: The Conquest of Ireland by Giraldus*

consequent enslavement abroad remained a hazard of English life, therefore, well after the Westminster Council of 1102.

The evidence reviewed in this chapter reveals how slavery and the recruitment of slaves was an integral part of Anglo-Saxon society. The institution of slavery was never questioned by contemporary moralists, who themselves frequently used the images of the slave and slavery in their writings. There was, however, opposition to the slave trade, although this was probably in large measure because it involved the sale of christians into heathendom.

Cambrensis, §18.5–17 (edd. & transl. Scott & Martin, p. 70); Holm, 'The slave trade of Dublin', 340.

III

'FREE ANNUALLY ONE PENAL SLAVE': LAWS AND PENITENTIALS

Late Anglo-Saxon society was governed by laws that developed from a variety sources. Early written laws had come into being in a tribal context. Collections of these laws, now rather inaccurately called codes, were issued under the names of various kings such as Æthelberht and Ine.[1] As the power of the West Saxons grew at the expense of other tribal groups these laws took on an increasingly national character, especially through their incorporation into Alfred of Wessex's law code. Another kind of law emanated from the Church, which sought by various means to regulate the conduct of society. In addition to securing the incorporation of moral regulations into tribal codes, the Church issued canons, which were promulgated at ecclesiastical councils and were binding on its members. (Sometimes, in fact, it is questionable whether one can draw a clear distinction between tribal and ecclesiastical laws.)[2] Individuals also compiled collections of penances for moral offences. Like the laws and ecclesiastical canons, these penitentials sought to impose a code of conduct on society. In contrast to the laws they probably operated largely through moral suasion, though one must allow for the possibility that they were enforced by the clergy in areas where they held jurisdictional powers, such as on episcopal lands.[3] Finally, the manorial estate also encouraged the growth of a body of custom which sought to regularise the relationships of those living there. By its very nature, however, this kind of law tended to be of local application.

This chapter will concentrate on the laws and rules of moral conduct of tribal and ecclesiastical origin that have a bearing on the institution of slavery. Manorial custom will be examined in chapter VI, where other evidence on landed estates is dealt with. The present chapter is divided into four sections, with the

---

[1] Translations of the Anglo-Saxon laws are taken from *The Laws of the Earliest English Kings*, ed. & transl. Attenborough, and *The Laws of the Kings of England from Edmund to Henry I*, ed. & transl. Robertson. Page references to these works will not be given in this chapter except where there is a possibility of ambiguity.

[2] Wormald has shown the close relationship between church councils and royal legislation in his paper 'In search of King Offa's "Law Code" ', in *People and Places*, edd. Wood & Lund, pp. 25–45.

[3] Frantzen has presented a thorough survey of the Anglo-Saxon penitentials in *The Literature of Penance in Anglo-Saxon England*. He has provided a new introduction in the French translation entitled *La Littérature de la pénitence dans l'Angleterre anglo-saxonne*, transl. Lejeune. (All references in this study will be to the American edition.) See also his paper, 'The tradition of penitentials in Anglo-Saxon England'.

first examining laws promulgated in the name a king from the reign of Alfred up to the time of the early codes issued by Æthelred the Unready. The second sections shifts the focus somewhat. The later codes of Æthelred and several promulgated by Cnut have been shown to have been influenced by the thought and literary style of Archbishop Wulfstan of York, who published regulations of a more ecclesiastical nature and also composed a body of homiletic literature. Because of Wulfstan's stature within Anglo-Saxon society and the wide range of his writings, this section will not limit itself to royal laws which he helped to draft but will discuss all works ascribed to him that contain material relevant to this study. From this wider perspective one can learn not merely about the position of slaves in Wulfstan's time but also take advantage of the rare chance of seeing how a leading member of Anglo-Saxon society viewed slaves and slavery. In the laws promulgated when Wulfstan was archbishop the impact of penitential discipline is very apparent. The third section accordingly will examine how slaves are portrayed in penitentials known to have been in circulation in England during the eleventh century. In the final section we shall explore a number of legal compilations composed in the twelfth century following the long hiatus in the extant legislation after the reign of Cnut. These collections, which contain a certain amount of material on slaves and associated classes, claim to represent the law of an earlier period.

LAW CODES FROM ALFRED TO ÆTHELRED

Early Anglo-Saxon legal codes treated slaves chiefly as chattels: legal regulations dealt with the compensation to lords for wrongs done to their slaves and assigned responsibility for wrongs done by them. Alfred's laws, which date from 892 x 893 or perhaps a little earlier,[4] mark a change in this conception of slaves in that they acknowledged that such persons possessed certain minimal rights.

The Laws of Alfred describe him as *Westseaxna cyning*. The description is important because it implies that his was not a national code but one that had application only to West-Saxon territory. Alfred acknowledged his debt to laws promulgated by Offa of Mercia and Æthelberht of Kent, but he was selective in his borrowing.[5] He disclaimed, but did not exclude, innovation in his legislation.[6]

The code starts with a lengthy Introduction, which draws largely from

---

[4] Liebermann (*Die Gesetze*, III.34) favoured 892 x 893 but Attenborough (*The Laws of the Earliest English Kings*, p. 35) suggested that it might be earlier as Alfred is termed *Angul-Saxonum rex* or *Anglorum Saxonum rex* in Latin documents issued during the latter part of his reign.

[5] Alfred Preface, §49.9 (*Die Gesetze*, ed. Liebermann, I.46).

[6] In the same clause he declared, '. . . many of those which I did not like I rejected with the advice of my councillors, and ordered them to be differently observed. For I dared not presume to set in writing at all many of my own, because it was unknown to me what would please those who should come after us.' ('. . . manege þara þe me ne licodon ic awearp mid minra witena geðeahte, 7 on oðre wisan bebead to healdanne. Forðam ic ne dorste geðristlæcan þara minra awuht fela on gewrit settan, forðam me wæs uncuð, hwæt þæs ðam lician wolde ðe æfter us wæren.') (Translation in *English Historical Documents c.550–1042*, §33 [transl. Whitelock, pp. 408–9].)

chapters 20, 21, 22, and part of 23 of the book of Exodus. This introduction has not received the attention it deserves.[7] It should be seen as integral to Alfred's purposes in issuing these laws. The introduction establishes him in the tradition of Moses, who delivered to his people the Ten Commandments, just as the central portion casts him as a Solomonic figure dispensing wise judgments and the edition of Ine's law with which the text concludes associates him with Nehemiah, whose restoration of the derelict city of Jerusalem led to Ezra's reading the law of Moses before the people.[8] Alfred's translation is especially interesting for its omissions from, and changes to, the biblical text.

Exodus 20 contains the Ten Commandments. Alfred omitted the second commandment and parts of the fourth and tenth ones but otherwise faithfully recorded them. In the best extant manuscripts part of Exodus 20:10, which expands on the fourth commandment, does not appear in his Introduction, §3. Where the Bible says of the sabbath: 'But the seventh day is the sabbath of the lord thy God: in it thou shalt not do any work, thou, nor thy son, nor thy daughter, thy manservant, nor thy maidservant', Alfred merely says: 'Remember to hallow the rest day; work on six days and on the seventh rest', before proceeding to translate Exodus 20:11.[9] In his text there is no explicit injunction that slaves should observe the sabbath, something that is readily understandable in an agrarian society, where animals such as cows need daily attention. We should perhaps not make too much of this, though, as Ine, §§3 and 3.1 barred slaves from working on a Sunday and in our present state of knowledge we cannot be certain of either Alfred's source or the reliability of our texts[10] – but it was to be over a century before there was another explicit prohibition against slaves' working on a Sunday.[11]

Several verses of Exodus 21 contain legal provisions governing the treatment

---

[7] This introduction has been very little discussed by scholars, perhaps because Attenborough omitted it from his translation of Alfred's Code and Dorothy Whitelock included only a few clauses in hers. Turk discussed it in his edition, *The Legal Code of Ælfred the Great*, pp. 30–55, but this work is little known, having been superseded by Liebermann's monumental edition. Frantzen, who has drawn attention to Turk's book in his *King Alfred*, pp. 14–16, has rightly emphasised the importance of this scriptural preface.

[8] I owe the idea of the associations with Solomon and Nehemiah to Dr David Howlett.

[9] 'Gemyne þæt ðu gehalgige þone ræstedæg; wurceað eow VI dagas 7 on þam siofoðan restað eow.' *Die Gesetze*, ed. Liebermann, I.26.

[10] Fournier in 'Le *Liber ex lege Moysi*', 230, pointed to an association between Alfred's text and a canonical collection of apparently Irish origin that contains very similar portions of Exodus, and Frantzen (to whose book I owe the reference) has observed in *King Alfred*, p. 15, that we do not know what version of the Bible Alfred knew. An edition of this text, which is extant in at least four manuscripts, is a *desideratum*. As for the text of Alfred's laws, the purportedly lost version reproduced by William Lambard in his *Archaionomia* in 1568 translates the missing lines from the biblical text: see *Die Gesetze*, ed. Liebermann, I.26, note †, for the text and *ibid.*, I.xxxiii–iv, on Lambard's edition, which Liebermann accepted as genuine. There has been a strong suspicion that Lambard fabricated this text and so extreme caution should be employed in using his edition: for a review of twentieth-century opinions see Robinson, *The Tomb of Beowulf*, pp. 279–80. Eckhardt's 1958 edition of Alfred's Laws, while having the virtue of including his introduction, unfortunately does not advance our understanding of the text: see *Leges Anglo-Saxonum 601–925*, ed. (with a German translation) Eckhardt, pp. 58–173.

[11] See p. 93 below.

of slaves. Exodus 21:2–6 had laid down that a Hebrew slave had to be freed after six years unless he refused to accept his freedom for any reason. This provision appears in translation in Alfred's Introduction, §11, but with changes to the biblical text: 'Hebrew slave' becomes 'christian slave' and the verse 'And if the slave shall plainly say, I love my master, my wife and my children; I will not go out free' is transformed in Old English into 'If the slave then says: "I do not wish to go from my lord nor from my wife nor from my child *nor from my property*." . . .'[12]

The first change implies by its adoption of the qualifying adjective 'christian' that christian and pagan slaves were viewed differently. This hints at the acceptance of the idea that the community of christians took precedence over legal distinctions of rank. It was a view that was to be developed further by Wulfstan. The second change, the addition of a slave's *ierfe* to the reasons why he should not want freedom, acknowledges that a slave might have his own possessions. It implies that slaves were settled and enjoyed normal familial relationships.

The decision to include these provisions on the freeing of slaves may well have been influenced by a canon of the Synod of Chelsea, which met in 816.[13] It declared that on the death of a bishop every Englishman who had been subjected to slavery in his lifetime was to be freed. In addition, when the offices were being said for the deceased bishop in each parish, every priest and abbot had to free three men and give three shillings to each of them.

Whitelock pointed out that Alfred changed Exodus 21:7f. in §12 of his Introduction because the rights of the head of a household were more extensive among the Hebrews than among the Anglo-Saxons, though she did not pursue the matter further.[14] Alfred declares that if a man sells his daughter into slavery, she should not be entirely like slave women (*ðeowu*) and other 'servile women' (*oðru mennenu*),[15] though it is not clear what the distinction between these two categories of person was. The purchaser does not have the authority 'to sell her to a foreign people' ('ut on elðeodig folc to bebycgganne') – but if he does not care for her, he must 'let her go free to a foreign people' ('læte hie freo on elðeodig folc').[16] This has so heavily abbreviated Exodus 21:7–11 that it has completely changed the meaning of the biblical text. The repetition of *on elðeodig folc* is puzzling, since Ine, §11 had prohibited the sale of anyone across the sea and the release of a free-born slave woman to a foreign people has no sanction in Exodus 21:8. We should seriously consider whether the phrase has not accidentally been repeated, though this must have happened at an early stage in the transmission of the text since the Parker Manuscript, which dates from the mid-tenth century, already contains the phrase.[17] *Læte hie freo* would, however, be closer to the *demittet eam* of the Vulgate text.

---

[12] 'Gif se þeowa þonne cweðe: "Nelle ic from minum hlaforde ne from minum wife ne from minum bearne ne from minum ierfe." . . .'

[13] The text of the whole synod appears in *Councils*, edd. Haddan & Stubbs, III.579–84. The legislation referred to appears in chapter X.

[14] 'The prose of Alfred's reign', in *Continuations and Beginnings*, ed. Stanley, p. 95.

[15] 'ne sie hio ealles swa ðeowu swa oðru mennenu.' *Die Gesetze*, ed. Liebermann, I.30.

[16] *Loc. cit.*

[17] Cambridge, Corpus Christi College, MS. 173. On the date of the hand that copied the laws of Alfred-Ine see Ker, *Catalogue*, p. 59.

Whatever our conclusions are about this textual puzzle, Alfred's inclusion of provisions governing the sale of a free-born female offspring into slavery and her treatment thereafter suggests that voluntary enslavement was well-known in his day.

Clauses 17 and 20 of the Introduction, which are translations of Exodus 21:20–21 and 26, attempt to afford the slave some protection. The first clause declares that a lord is guilty if a male or female slave dies at his hands within the day (implying that legal action would be taken against him). The second clause states that a slave who lost an eye because of the action of his or her lord should be freed. One cannot say to what extent these provisions were enforced, but their inclusion in Alfred's legislation does reveal an acceptance that slaves of either sex were entitled to protection against physical abuse.

The main body of the code indicates that changes had taken place in West-Saxon society since the time of Alfred's predecessor, Ine. The latter's legislation, promulgated between 688 and 694, had recognised that the British were an important ethnic group in Wessex, even though many of them appear to have been slaves. No consideration is given to them in Alfred's laws and one must assume that in some measure they had been integrated into Anglo-Saxon society during the intervening two centuries, even though the process still had some way to go as the South-west had not yet been completely subjugated.

Ine's laws had recognised four main status divisions within West-Saxon society: those with a wergeld of 1200 shillings, those whose wergeld was six hundred shillings, *cierliscan men* (whose wergeld is not stated but which appears to have been two hundred shillings), and slaves.[18] By Alfred's time West-Saxon society had become rather more complex with three categories of people, rather than two, below the sixhundredmen. First there were the *ceorlas* themselves. They occupied landed property, though this was not fortified (§40), and they could be slave-owners (§§18.1, 25). Below the *ceorlas* was the category of *esnewyrhtan* or 'hired labourers'.[19] They were definitely not slaves, yet they did not have the right to the same leisure time that ordinary freemen possessed. Instead they were lumped together with slaves when it came to the days that they had to work (§43). They were probably still regarded as members of the tribe but lacked the land which earlier had been a visible symbol of this membership. Slaves remained the lowest on the social scale and were clearly distinguished from freemen in the code. This is apparent from the differing punishments meted out to slave and freeman for wrongdoing: the slave was usually physically chastised whereas the freeman could generally escape this by means of a monetary compensation. Thus, for the rape of a slave by a slave the penalty was castration; anyone else who raped a slave had only to pay a fine (§§25 and 25.1).

Yet Alfred's code provides the first evidence in the laws of the recognition of slaves as more than mere chattels. Particularly informative about changing perceptions is that a woman was required to pay compensation for an act of fornication in the form of cattle and not slaves (§18.1). This implies that slaves

---

[18] Alfred, §§10, 18.1–3, 25, and 25.1; cf. Ine, §§3 and 70 (*Die Gesetze*, ed. Liebermann, I.56, 58, 62, 64; cf. I.90 and 118).

[19] Alfred, §43 (*Die Gesetze*, ed. Liebermann, I.78). On the word see appendix I, s.v. *esne*.

were regarded by some members of society as property just like cattle,[20] but the very promulgation of this provision suggests that this view of them was becoming unacceptable.

A practical expression of this changed perception of the slave appears in clause 43. This declares that on the Wednesday of each of the four Ember weeks slaves could sell anything that they had been given 'in God's name' or which they had acquired in their spare time.[21] The gifts 'in God's name' are explained by a passage in Byrhtferth's *Manual* where he comments that 'on that day they shall rejoice who . . . on the twelve Ember days have made offerings and distributed alms, so as to please and glorify God'.[22] Probably such a distribution of alms was made to the poor in general, but it is important to note that slaves were deemed to be eligible for these alms. In effect, the provision permitted them to own property, something that the laws had not recognised up to this time.

This legislation of Alfred contained the elements of two changes which were to have future significance. It provided the first extant acknowledgment in law that the slave was more than a chattel. This was a developing perception that was to become particularly apparent in the work of Wulfstan. At the same time Alfred's legislation recognised a class of *esnewyrhtan*, whose legal position somewhat blurred the formerly clear legal distinctions between slaves and *ceorlas*.

In the century after Alfred three other items of royal and ecclesiastical legislation directly or indirectly point to an amelioration of the slave's position. According to Ine, §47 a slave could not be summoned to be vouched to warranty for the sale of property claimed to be stolen. But II Æthelstan, §24, promulgated in 929 x 939, states that if goods bought by someone were claimed to be stolen they had to be returned to the seller, whether he was a slave or a freeman. The clause is elliptical but the implication is that the onus would then have been on the seller to prove good title. The law thus acknowledged that the slave could be a principal in a legally recognised act and was answerable at law for it.

Æthelstan's *Ordinance on Charities*, §1 instructed all his reeves to free annually a penally-enslaved man. The *Ordinance* as a whole shows strong ecclesiastical influence, which suggests that the Church continued to maintain the

---

[20] This view of the slave is seen in Alfred and Guthrum, §4, where, presumably to prevent fraud, it was decreed that a purchaser had to know his warrantor when he bought men, horses, or oxen (*Die Gesetze*, ed. Liebermann, I.128).

[21] The Ember days were fasts held on a Wednesday, Friday, and Saturday at four periods in the year. The Old English poem, *The Seasons for Fasting* (in *Anglo-Saxon Minor Poems*, ed. Dobbie, pp. 98–104), seems to indicate that the traditional English dating for the Ember days followed Roman liturgical practice in having the initial fast in the first week of Lent, unlike Frankish and Breton practice, which simply held it in the first week of March, irrespective of the relationship with Lent. The other Ember days were in June in the week after Whitsunday, in September in the week before the autumnal equinox, and in December in the last full week before Christmas. This description is a simplified picture of a liturgical practice that evolved over several centuries. For further details see Willis, *Essays in Early Roman Liturgy*, pp. 51–97, especially pp. 66–7 and 70–4; for a very brief discussion see Hilton, 'The Old English *Seasons for Fasting*', 155.

[22] '... þy dæge blissiað þa þe . . . þa twelf ymbrendagas Gode to þance 7 to wyrðmynte geoffredon 7 ælmessan dældon.' *Byrhtferth's Manual*, ed. & transl. Crawford, p. 240.28–31 (text); *ibid*., p. 241 (translation).

view that it was a charitable act to free a person. This is confirmed by a third post-Alfredian legislative act, a synodal decision that was probably promulgated 990 x 1001.[23] The canon laid down that every bishop should free a man on the death of a fellow bishop; it was optional for abbots and abbesses, on the other hand, to free someone if they wished to. The document highlights what was to be a continuing tension between the inherited body of moral teaching that the Church proclaimed and the desire to preserve the Church itself as a human institution. That *all* bishops now had to free a slave (and not necessarily a penal slave) on the death of a fellow-bishop went further than the Synod of Chelsea's canon, but the exemption of monasteries from this requirement shows the Church seeking to preserve its institutional strength in a period of monastic revival. Yet the canon essentially re-affirmed the *principle* that it was virtuous to manumit, an affirmation that was probably more important than the monastic exemption because the restoration of the Church's authority in the later tenth century inevitably increased the impact of its views on society.

Most of the laws of the tenth century, however, continued to present the slave in economic rather than in human terms. This approach towards the slave as an economic asset appears most tellingly in a tenth-century agreement between the Anglo-Saxons and those of Celtic ethnic origin known now as *Dunsæte*.[24] This set the replacement value of a man (that is, a slave) at one pound. Clause 7 of the agreement lays down his comparative value *vis à vis* other chattels, as the following table shows:

TABLE I: VALUE OF CHATTELS ACCORDING TO *DUNSÆTE*, §7

Chattel	Value
Horse	30 shillings
Mare	20 shillings
Untamed Ass	12 shillings
Ox	30 pence
Cow	24 pence
Pig	8 pence
Man	1 pound[a]
Sheep	1 shilling[b]
Goat	2 pence

[a] 20 shillings in *Quadripartitus*.
[b] The value is that given in *Quadripartitus*.

A man was thus equivalent to a team of oxen but was assessed at only two-thirds the value of a horse.

---

[23] *Councils and Synods*, §53, cc. 5 and 9 (edd. Whitelock *et al.*, I.404–6). On the date see Brotanek, *Texte und Untersuchungen*, pp. 128–9; Whitelock *et al.* preferred to date it as 'early 11th Century'. Darlington discussed the ecclesiastical councils of this period in 'Ecclesiastical reform in the late Old English period'.

[24] Text in *Die Gesetze*, ed. Liebermann, I.374–9.

Æthelstan acknowledged in the draconian measures he took against theft that the slave was an economic asset. IV Æthelstan, §6 insisted on the death penalty for theft in all instances, whether the thief was free or unfree. Eighty slaves of the same sex as the offender had either to stone to death a male thief who was a slave, or, in the case of a female slave, burn her, after which they each had to pay threepence in compensation. The compensation thus amounted to a pound, which both the agreement with the Celts mentioned above and a later agreement made by Æthelred with the Danes in 991 (II Æthelred, §5.1) set as the compensation payable for a slave.[25] By making slaves financially responsible for the death of fellow-slaves convicted of theft (which, incidentally, assumed that slaves would possess some financial assets), Æthelstan neatly obviated the problem of masters shielding their slaves on the grounds that they would be losing property.

As a chattel with an economic value the slave was a tempting object of theft. This crime of *manðeofe* or theft of a person was proscribed in Alfred, §9.2. Æthelstan attempted to stop the crime by setting a fine of half a pound or more for such a theft, depending on the appearance of the slave (VI Æthelstan, §6.3), but as we saw in the last chapter the crime continued after his reign.[26]

In addition to being viewed as chattels, slaves continued to be subject to physical punishment as a consequence of their legal status. Before he introduced his more severe legislation against theft, Æthelstan had stipulated that a slave who had been found guilty (presumably of theft) was to be beaten unless the lord paid double the amount involved (II Æthelstan, §19). Much later in the century I Æthelred, §2 declared that a slave found guilty at the ordeal was to be branded, whereas a freeman was to be fined.

Some slaves sought to escape from these legal disabilities. In the agreements of both Alfred and Æthelred with the Danes the two sides promised not to harbour runaway slaves, but the problem lingered on into the eleventh century.[27] Others took to stealing, so that Edmund had to order the hanging of the leader of any group of slaves guilty of theft, and the lashing and mutilation of the others (III Edmund, §4).

By the end of the tenth century, the legal position of slaves can be said to have been better than it was when Alfred came to the throne, in spite of the harsh legislation that had been enacted since his time. It was acknowledged that slaves could possess property and there was some recognition of other legal rights. Furthermore, ecclesiastical law continued to encourage manumission.

Though the slave's position might have improved, one will hardly get an adequate understanding of the society or of the eventual disappearance of slavery if one ignores the fact that the position of the lower ranks of the free was slowly deteriorating. The presence of free hired labourers or *esnewyrhtan* with reduced rights shows that legal and economic distinctions had already appeared in the ranks of the *ceorlas* by Alfred's time. Another indication of this is the equation with *lisingas* of *ceorlas ðe on gafollande sit*, that is, those who

---

[25] Cf. also *Leis Willelmi*, §7. See *Die Gesetze*, ed. Liebermann, II.692.7e).

[26] For example, see Wulfstan Cantor, *Narratio Metrica de Sancto Swithuno*, §II.78–204, in *Frithegodi Monachi Breuiloquium*, ed. Campbell, pp. 143–7. Cf. above, p. 58.

[27] See below, pp. 98–9.

occupied rented land. This was the terminology employed in an agreement made between Alfred and the Danes in the 880s.[28] As has been mentioned in chapter I, *lisingas* were the higher category of Norse freedmen.[29] They were considered to possess freedom, enjoyed marriage rights, and had the right to dispose of property, but they were subject to certain obligations towards their manumittor and the manumittor's family.

The rent-paying *ceorlas* were still ordinary members of the tribe as both the term *ceorl* and their wergeld of two hundred shillings indicate. Yet unlike ordinary *ceorlas*, who worked what was *de facto* their own land, these men had obligations in the form of *gafol* to the person who controlled the land they worked on.[30] Thus while both the rent-paying *ceorlas* and the *lisingas* were held to possess freedom and enjoyed similar rights, they were also subject to obligations that an ordinary freeman did not have: in the case of the *ceorl* these were owed to his overlord whereas the *lising* owed them to his manumittor. The *esnewyrhtan* and rent-paying *ceorlas* were therefore in some measure dependent on those who controlled the land, that is, the lords. The growth of lordship in the tenth century, fostered by the accumulation of land in manorial estates and encouraged by the kings who sought to use lordship as a means of social control, was the primary cause of the reduction in the rights of freemen.

The first real signs of the limitations imposed by lordship on a person's freedom appear in 924 x 925 when II Edward, §7 insisted that a man had to be released from the service of his overlord before he could be accepted into the service of another. Æthelstan's second code placed him even further under the power of a lord. II Æthelstan, §2 declared that the relatives of lordless men from whom justice could not he obtained had to bring them home[31] and find them a lord. II Æthelstan, §22.2 prohibited a lord from dismissing anyone before he had satisfied all legal demands. If the lord's estates were too extensive for him to act personally as a surety for his men, he was obliged to place them in charge of a reeve. The purpose of Æthelstan's legislation was obviously to use lords as a means of combating lawlessness in the society, but its effect was to enable these lords to reduce the freedom of those who were under their control. They evidently took advantage of the power granted them to prevent freemen from seeking other lords. III Æthelstan, §4.1 aimed at rectifying this by declaring: 'And a lord shall not prohibit a free man from seeking for himself a [new] lord, if he has conducted himself rightly',[32] but it is apparent from the evidence of Wulfstan's *Sermo ad Anglos* that this provision was ineffective.

The consequence of these social and legal changes was that in the manorial sphere economic role rather than membership of the tribe became the determi-

---

[28] Alfred and Guthrum, §2. On the date see Stenton, *Anglo-Saxon England*, p. 260, n. 3. Cf. appendix I, s.v. *lising*.

[29] See above, p. 46 and below, appendix I, s.v. *lising*.

[30] This interpretation follows Stenton, *Anglo-Saxon England*, p. 261, n. 1 and Whitelock in *English Historical Documents c.550–1042*, p. 416, n. 11. As Stenton suggested, the rent-paying *ceorlas* were presumably the *geburas* of the vernacular sources.

[31] Following Whitelock's interpretation of *gehamette* in *English Historical Documents c.550–1042*, p. 418, n. 1.

[32] 'et etiam ne dominus libero homini hlafordsoknam interdicat, si eum recte custodierat' (*Die Gesetze*, ed. Liebermann, I.170). See below, p. 97.

nant of status. This transformation in the position of the *ceorl*, particularly evident in the *Rectitudines Singularum Personarum*, will be examined in more detail in chapter VI. Here it will suffice to observe that through the appearance of a class of person intermediate in position between slaves and freemen and through the growth of local lordship at the expense of the tribal bond the way had been made easier for the eventual demise of slavery.

THE SOCIAL VIEWS OF WULFSTAN AND LEGISLATION CONCERNING SLAVERY PUBLISHED UNDER HIS INFLUENCE

One of the signal advances in Anglo-Saxon studies during recent decades has been the recognition of Archbishop Wulfstan of York[33] as the most important influence on both secular and ecclesiastical law during the early eleventh century.[34] The works in which he had a hand included royal legislation, ecclesiastical regulations, penitential literature, and homilies.[35] The range of this material enables us to go beyond merely using it to deduce the social and legal position of slaves in this period: we also have the rare opportunity of analysing the thinking of a prominent Anglo-Saxon man-of-affairs. We shall take advantage of this opportunity by moving beyond the purely legal material to include all the relevant works in the Wulfstanian canon. After examining his overall view of society and the role of slavery within it, we shall turn to royal legislation issued under his influence. Here certain general themes that concern slaves will dealt with first, followed by a treatment of specific items of information to be found in royal laws. Ecclesiastical regulations will next be examined. Finally, his *Sermo ad Anglos* will be set in its literary-historical context in order to evaluate the significance of its frequent references to slaves.

Wulfstan viewed society as a whole in strongly hierarchical terms. His acceptance of a class structure in society is evident from his use of such compounds as *weofod-þegn*, *mæsseþegn* and *cyric-þegn* (terms apparently coined by him)[36] in order to emphasise the high social standing of the clergy. Here secular terminology was applied to ecclesiastical positions. Changes within the hierarchy he regarded as a special act of God.[37]

At the same time he accepted an egalitarian conception of Humanity as a consequence of Christ's sacrifice for all. He followed Ælfric in this, using almost identical language to express the idea: 'The slave may just as confidently call

---

[33] Bishop of London, 996–1002; bishop of Worcester, 1002–1016x1023; archbishop of York, 1002–1023.

[34] For a biography see Whitelock, 'Archbishop Wulfstan, homilist and statesman'.

[35] D. Bethurum suggested that the *Rectitudines* may be from his circle. As this custumal cannot be proved to be by him consideration of it will be deferred to chapter VI, where other manorial documents are discussed. See Bethurum, 'Episcopal magnificence in the eleventh century', in *Studies in Old English Literature in Honor of Arthur G. Brodeur*, ed. Greenfield, pp. 162–70.

[36] They appear only in writings that have been ascribed to him, other than a single example of *weofoddegn* in one of the anonymous homilies. Cf. Bethurum, 'Six anonymous Old English codes', 461–2.

[37] See below, p. 94 and n. 66.

89

and name as his father his Lord in his *Pater Noster* as the lord may, and the bondwoman just as well as the lady. At an equal price Christ bought the emperor and the powerful king and the poor man, that is, with his own blood. Through that we may perceive and know that we are all brothers and also sisters, when we all call to a single Heavenly Father as often as we chant our *Pater Noster*.'[38] To explain Humanity's relationship to God he drew on the analogy drawn from secular society of the slave's relationship to his master. All christians were slaves of God. The analogy applied particularly to the clergy, who are often described as *Godes þeowas* in his writings.

This egalitarian view of Humankind did not lead him to question the institution of slavery. Yet the equality of all before God and the Grace shown by Him to His 'slaves' led Wulfstan to be concerned about the welfare of those at the bottom of the social hierarchy in general, and slaves in particular. This nexus of ideas is best illustrated by a passage from his ecclesiastical tract, *Episcopus*:

13. It is the responsibility of each lord to protect his compulsorily enslaved men as best he may, because they and those who are free are equally dear to God, and he bought us all for an equal price.

14. All of us are God's own compulsorily enslaved men; and He judges us as we here judge those over whom we have judgment on earth.[39]

Wulfstan interpreted this equality of all to mean that in the secular realm everyone should receive equal protection under the law. VII Æthelred, §6.1 declares: 'And all men, whether poor or rich, shall be entitled to the benefit of the law.'[40] As the passage from *Episcopus* implied, no one should be arbitrarily treated but should be judged according to the law. This did not mean, however, the judgments should be identical for all. The earlier laws varied the punishment according to a person's social rank, and the penitentials, which played such a big part in Wulfstan's thinking, had indicated that everybody's personal circumstances should be taken into account. II Cnut, §68.1*b* therefore advises that in passing judgment 'we must make due allowance and carefully distinguish between age and youth, wealth and poverty, freemen and slaves, the sound and the sick'.[41] In effect, then, the slave was still not regarded as responsible for his

---

[38] 'Ealswa bealdlice se þeowa clypað and namað on his pater noster his drihten him to fæder swa se hlaford, and seo wylen eallswa wel swa seo hlæfdige. Mid gelicum wurðe crist bohte þone kasere and þone rican kyning and þone earming, þæt wæs mid his agenum blode. Be þam we magon ongitan and oncnawan, þæt we synd ealle gebroðra and eac geswustra, þonne we ealle to anum heofenlicum fæder swa oft clypiað, swa we ure pater noster singað.' Printed by Jost, 'Einige Wulfstantexte und ihre Quellen', 272. He pointed out (*loc. cit.*) that Wulfstan took the idea from Ælfric's works. See especially *The Sermones Catholici*, I.19 (ed. & transl. Thorpe, p. 260.23–4), cited above, p. 63, n. 67. Wulfstan also borrowed a phrase from *Ælfric's Catholic Homilies*, §19.221–2 (ed. Godden, p. 187), cited on p. 63, n. 66 above.

[39] '13. Hit bið ælces hlafordes agen þearf, þæt he hie nydþeowum byrge, swa he betst mæge, for ðam þe hy syn Gode efen leofe 7 þa ðe syndon freolse, 7 us ealle he gebohte mid gelican weorðe. 14. Ealle we syndon Godes agene nydþeowan; 7 swa he gedemð us, swa we her demað þam þe we on eorðan dom ofer agan.'

[40] 'Et sit omnis homo dignus iure publico, pauper et diues.'

[41] 'we sceolon medmian 7 gesceadlice todælan ylde 7 geogoþe, welan 7 wædle, freot 7 þeowet, hæle 7 unhæle.'

actions to the same degree that an adult freeman was. In Wulfstan's view, the slave was not, however, a chattel but a fellow human being on the lowest rung of the social ladder. The embodiment of these views in legislation helped give currency to this more humane perception of the slave.

Apart from these trends in thought which are to be seen across the full spectrum of Wulfstan's writings, certain themes are particularly prominent in the secular legislation drafted by him. One such is a preoccupation with the sale of persons out the country. The earliest codes thought to have been influenced by him simply proscribed in virtually identical clauses (V Æthelred, §2 and VI Æthelred, §9) the sale of those innocent of crime out of the country, particularly to the heathen.[42] Subsequent legislation was more explicit. VII Æthelred, §5 made the prohibition against the sale of men abroad general and did not limit it to those innocent of crime.[43] II Cnut, §3 also prohibited the 'all too prevalent practice'[44] of selling men out of the country 'and especially of conveying them into heathen lands',[45] which implies that the trade was between England and both christian and pagan territories.

VII Æthelred, §5 declared that anyone guilty of this offence was to be excommunicated 'unless he repents and makes amends as his bishop shall direct'.[46] This suggests that the legislation was to be enforced in conjunction with the sanctions imposed by penitential discipline.[47] That Wulfstan decided to use legislation to proscribe what seems to have become a serious problem in the early eleventh century may have been influenced by the strong opposition in penitential sources to the sale of christians abroad.[48] As early as 732 Pope Gregory III had condemned the sale of men to the pagans and had said that a penance equivalent to that for homicide should be imposed.[49] A couple of Continental penitentials specifically castigated the practice.[50] Wulfstan almost certainly knew of their opposition to this because a passage in an Old English hand-book for the use of a confessor, which its editor has felt Wulfstan might have had compiled,[51] sternly declares: 'If anyone sells a Christian into heathendom, let him not be worthy of any rest among Christian people unless he buy them whom he sold abroad back again; and if he is not able to do that, may he pay the full value for the sake of God and release another with a second payment

---

[42] On the background to the codes of Æthelred and Cnut, and Wulfstan's role in them, see Sisam, *Studies*, pp. 278–87; Whitelock, 'Wulfstan's authorship of Cnut's laws'; and *A Wulfstan Manuscript*, facs. ed. Loyn, pp. 48–9.

[43] On the ascription of this code to Wulfstan see Whitelock, 'Archbishop Wulfstan, homilist and statesman', 41.

[44] 'alle to swiðe'. On the ascription and dating of this code see Whitelock, 'Wulfstan and the laws of Cnut'.

[45] 'ne on hæðendome huru ne gebringe'.

[46] 'nisi peniteat et emendet, sicut episcopus suus edocebit.'

[47] On the general relationship between penitential discipline and Anglo-Saxon law see Oakley, *English Penitential Discipline and Anglo-Saxon Law*.

[48] See further below, p. 97.

[49] *Die Briefe des heiligen Bonifatius und Lullus*, §28 (ed. Tangl, p. 51.18–23).

[50] Pseudo-Roman Penitential, §[11].19, Pseudo-Cummian, §4.9 (cf. Pseudo-Roman, §7.5), in *Die Bussordnungen der abendländischen Kirche*, ed. Wasserschleben, pp. 374–5, 476, and 369 respectively.

[51] Fowler, 'A late Old English handbook', 6–12, especially p. 12.

and then free that person; and in addition to that may he do penance for fully three years as a confessor may direct; and if he does not have the money with which to release a man, may he do a more severe penance: that is, a full seven years, and may he ever repent.'[52]

Another general concern of Wulfstan's was to impose ecclesiastical customs by means of royal legislation. Three areas that are of particular relevance to this study were support for the poor through the imposition of tithes,[53] the obligation of all to observe fasts and church festivals, and the regulation of sexual relationships.

VII Æthelred, §1.3 imposed a tithe on every thegn and VII Æthelred, §4 enjoined that the produce of every tenth acre should be given to the Church. The first clause also legislated on Peter's Pence. Every *hyremannus* (presumably a hired labourer) was obliged to give Peter's Pence unless he did not have the money, in which case the lord had to pay it.[54] *Rectitudines Singularum Personarum*, §3.4 indicates that this payment was a characteristic duty of a freeman, so the anticipated incapacity of hired workmen to pay this due suggests that economic forces here too were blurring what had formerly been a clear legal distinction between freeman and slave. This is also to be seen in VIII Æthelred, §6, which states that the king and his council had agreed that one third of all tithes should go 'to God's poor and to poverty-stricken slaves'.[55]

As for fasts, the influence of penitential literature on Wulfstan is particularly evident. This first appears in the so-called Treaty of Edward and Guthrum, perhaps the earliest piece of legislation that Wulfstan had a hand in.[56] In clause 8 of this code the penalty for breaking a legally imposed fast was a fine in the case of freemen and a lashing in the case of slaves. Legislation on fasting was extended in VII Æthelred, §2. This decreed that all had to observe a three-day fast on the Monday, Tuesday, and Wednesday preceding Michaelmas. The legislation is linked with the poverty laws in that the food which would have been consumed during that period was to be given to the poor. Slaves were to be exempt from work on the three days 'so that they can fast the better and may make what they want for themselves'.[57] Wihtred, §15 had set a penalty for a slave who did not observe a fast but until the time of Wulfstan there is no further mention of a slave's obligation to do this. (Alfred, §43 had permitted slaves to

---

[52] 'Gyf hwa Cristene man on hæðendom sille, se ne bið wurðe ænigere reste mid Cristenum folce buton he hy bicge eft ham ongean þæt he ut sealde; and gif he þæt don ne mæge, gedæle þæt wurð eal Godes þances and oðerne alyse mid oðrum wurðe, and þæne þonne gefreoge; and þartoeacan betan þreo gear fullice swa swa scrift tæce; and gif he feoh næbbe þæt he man mid alesan mæge, bete þe deoppor: þæt is vii gear fulle, and bereowsige æfre.' *Ibid.*, p. 26.289–96.

[53] For an excellent introduction to early mediaeval poverty legislation see Ullmann, 'Public welfare and social legislation'. Mollat has provided a more general discussion of mediaeval poverty in *The Poor in the Middle Ages*, transl. A. Goldhammer.

[54] The Old English version of this clause, VIIa Æthelred, §5, reads *hiredmanna*, 'member of a household': *Die Gesetze*, ed. Liebermann, I.262.

[55] 'Godes þearfum 7 earman þeowetlingan'.

[56] See Whitelock, 'Wulfstan and the so-called Laws of Edward and Guthrum', especially pp. 18–19.

[57] 'quo melius ieiunare possit, et operetur sibimet quod vult' (VII Æthelred, §2.3, in *Die Gesetze*, ed. Liebermann, I.260).

keep alms given on Ember days but did not state that they should fast.) It seems quite probable that Wulfstan reimposed a custom that had tended to lapse. As the anonymous homilies have shown, others then promoted this as well.[58] In VII Æthelred, §2 slaves were still quite different in status from freemen: whereas a *liber pauper* (*bunda* in the Old English version) had to pay thirty pence for failure to observe a fast, a *seruus* (*þræl* in the Old English) was to be lashed, the typical punishment for a slave. But its real significance lay in its insistence that a slave was subject to the same religious obligations as a freeman. This was, of course, completely consistent with Wulfstan's view that all persons were equal before God.

Another domain in which Wulfstan attempted to ensure the observance of church customs was that of religious festivals. Prohibition against work on a Sunday was a long-established ecclesiastical policy.[59] As far back as the *Lex Baiwariorum* the penalty had been a fine for a freeman and a lashing for a slave.[60] Edward and Guthrum, §7 laid down the same penalty for a slave, although he could compound for his offence by paying a fine or *hydgyld* (another indication that slaves already could possess resources by the end of the tenth century). In the case of a freeman who worked, he 'shall be reduced to slavery, or pay a fine or *lahslit*'.[61] Later Wulfstan was to make this legislation even stiffer: whereas according to Edward and Guthrum a master who forced a slave to work on a church festival had merely to pay a fine or *lahslit*, in II Cnut, §45.3 the master was in addition to lose the slave, who thereby gained his freedom. As in the agreement between Edward and Guthrum, a slave who worked voluntarily could compound for his offence by paying a fine instead of receiving a lashing (II Cnut, §45.2).

Wulfstan also sought to regulate sexual relationships. Edward and Guthrum, §4, in prohibiting incestuous unions, declares that when this occurs the male will become the king's possession and the woman the bishop's 'unless they make compensation before God and the world as the bishop shall prescribe, in accordance with the gravity of the offence'.[62] The concessive clause presumably indicates that penal slavery was only to be the penalty if the persons concerned were unable to pay the fine and fulfil the requirements of the penance imposed (given Wulfstan's interest in penitential discipline this must be the meaning of 'make compensation before God'). Adultery was another activity that he sought to control. II Cnut, §54 declares that a lord will lose a female slave if he commits adultery with her. (Presumably she would then gain her freedom, though this is not stated.) The prohibition in the next sub-clause against a man's having a wife and a concubine suggests that this is one reason why this legislation had to be introduced.

---

[58] See above, p. 66.
[59] The history of this is fully examined in McReavy, 'The Sunday repose from labour'.
[60] *Lex Baiwariorum*, VII.4, in *Leges Baiwariorum*, ed. Schwind, pp. 349–50. The freeman lost the right-hand ox from his plough-team.
[61] 'þolie his freotes oððe gylde wite, lahslite'. On the *lahslit*, which was a fine imposed in the Danelaw, see *Die Gesetze*, ed. Liebermann, II.624–5, s.v. *Rechtsbruchbusse*.
[62] 'butan hit man gebete for Gode 7 for worulde, be þam þe seo dæde sy, swa bisceop getæce'.

Several of Wulfstan's legal tracts contain further information about slaves and slavery.[63] *Grið*, §16 outlines additional grounds for enslavement. If a homicide (Liebermann's interpretation of *forworht man*)[64] reached sanctuary he could save his life by paying his wergeld, by going to gaol, or by entering into life-long servitude (*ece þeowet*). In Wulfstan's tract on oaths, his failure to mention slaves in *Að*, §1 implies that unlike *ceorlas* and twelvehundredmen, their oaths were not legally recognised in Mercia (although, as has been pointed out above, II Æthelstan, §24 had permitted a slave to be named as a guarantor to a sale). Finally, it must be noted that although Domesday Book does not record any slaves in the North, *Norðleoda Laga*, §8 certainly suggests by its reference to free Britons that slaves were to be found there.[65]

Wulfstan's collections of ecclesiastical regulations contain very little on slavery, but there are two illuminating passages. The text of the *Institutes of Polity* in Cambridge, Corpus Christi College, MS. 201 includes an addition which certainly came from his pen:

135. And la, oft hit getimað,   þæt þeowetlingc geearnað
freotes æt ceorle,   and ceorl wyrð þurh eorlgife
þegenlage wyrðe   and þegn wurð þurh cynincges gife
eorldomes wyrðe.

. . .

137. Þonne hwilum þ<u>rh
    Godes gife,   swa ic ær sæde,
þræl wyrð to þegne   and ceorl wyrð to earle,
sangere to sacerde   and bocere to biscpe.[66]

This is a masterpiece of rhetorical balance, but beneath its surface lies a kernel of historical information. It suggests that *ceorlas* still owned slaves in Wulfstan's day. The rhetorical form of the first sentence makes this clear. Each third of the sentence contains a pair of legal status terms (the use of the words *freote* and *þegenlage* shows that Wulfstan was thinking along legal lines). On the other hand, Wulfstan's assertions that *ceorlas* and slaves could often improve their social status should not be taken too seriously, though undoubtedly this happened occasionally, especially during the rapid social changes of the late tenth

[63] On the attribution of *Grið*, *Að*, and *Norðleoda Laga* to Wulfstan see Bethurum, 'Six anonymous Old English codes', 449–63.

[64] *Die Gesetze*, ed. Liebermann, I.471, s.v. 'Todesschuldiger'.

[65] 'And gif he [*sc.* Wilisman] ænig land næbbe 7 þeah freoh sy, forgilde hine man mid LXX scill'.' ('And if he [*sc.* a Briton] does not have any land and yet is free, may the compensation payable for him be seventy shillings.')

[66] '135. And lo! often it happens that a slave acquires freedom from a *ceorl*, and a *ceorl* attains through the gift of an *eorl* the legal rank of thegn, and the thegn attains through the gift of a king the legal rank of an *eorl*.
137. Then at times by the grace of God, as I said before, a thrall becomes a thegn and a churl becomes an earl, a cantor a cleric, and a bookman a bishop.' Text in *Die 'Institutes of Polity, Civil and Ecclesiastical'*, ed. Jost, pp. 256–7. The higher of the two terms forms the lower half of the pair in the succeeding comparison. The *ceorl* in the first comparison must be the same as in the second. Were the word to change in meaning from 'man' to '*ceorl*', it would destroy the point of the sentence.

century.[67] Clause 137, which also appears in *Grið*, §21.2, shows by its wording that the advances he talks of should be interpreted from a literary rather than from a literal point of view. It might be said that a thrall became a thegn because of alliteration and a churl an earl because of assonance.

Wulfstan's treatise on the duties of a bishop, *Episcopus*, gives some insight into the rights lost by men who became *nidþeowas* or slaves by compulsion – presumably men who entered slavery through poverty or starvation (§§10, 11, 13, 14).[68] He orders the clergy to ensure that no christian cause another serious harm, 'neither a lord his men, nor in consequence his compulsorily enslaved man' (§10).[69] The special attention such slaves receive in this text implies that they were subject to abuse: in clause 13 he appeals to theological precepts in an attempt to afford them some protection.[70] Another disability these men suffered is indicated in clause 11, which declares: 'those compulsorily enslaved should work for their lords in the whole district over which he has control'.[71] By entering this state, therefore, the *nidþeow* lost any right he had to remain in a single place.

A more general survey of English society appears in his *Sermo ad Anglos*.[72] This was composed *ca* 1014 with a stylish vividness that places it in many anthologies containing early English prose. The immediacy and urgency of the writing warn one that this is primarily a literary document, composed not as a historical account of Wulfstan's society but as a means of winning his listeners (and readers) to a particular point of view. Literary criteria must therefore be kept in the forefront of one's mind when drawing historical conclusions from the *Sermo*.

In its eschatological interest the *Sermo* fits into a pattern of thinking found elsewhere in Wulfstan's homilies,[73] as well as forming part of a continuing christian tradition of such literature, which in Britain can be traced back to Gildas. But it differs from Wulfstan's other homilies in its frequent references to current events. Various sources have been suggested as influencing the content of the *Sermo*, such as the *De Tribulatione*, possibly by Alcuin, which appears in Cambridge, Corpus Christi College, MS. 190, fo 142, one of the 'Wulfstan' group of manuscripts.[74] The *Sermo* was also influenced by Gildas's *De Excidio Britanniae*.[75] These sources supply some of the details used in the homily, but this does not explain why Wulfstan based its overall structure on contemporary

---

[67] On improvements in social position see F. M. Stenton, 'The thriving of the Anglo-Saxon ceorl', in *Preparatory to Anglo-Saxon England*, ed. D. M. Stenton, pp. 383–93. Runciman in his much more detailed analysis has pointed out that social mobility could be downward as well: 'Accelerating social mobility', especially pp. 13–14 and 24–5.

[68] For the ascription of this text to Wulfstan see Jost, *Wulfstanstudien*, pp. 75ff.

[69] 'ne se hlaford his mannum, ne forðan his nydþeowan'.

[70] Cf. n. 38 above.

[71] 'ða nydþeowan hlaferdum wyrcan ofer ealle þa scire, þe he on scrife'.

[72] All references to the *Sermo Lupi ad Anglos* are to Bethurum's edition in *The Homilies of Wulfstan*, §20, pp. 255–75. Translations are from *English Historical Documents c.550–1042*, §240 (transl. Whitelock, I.928–34).

[73] See the 'Eschatological homilies', in *The Homilies of Wulfstan*, ed. Bethurum, pp. 113–41.

[74] On the sources see *Sermo Lupi ad Anglos*, ed. Whitelock, pp. 35–7.

[75] See below, p. 100.

events. There is, however, a possible source for this. On fos 35v–37r of a Copenhagen manuscript containing several of Wulfstan's works, København, Kongelike Biblioteket, MS. G.K.S. 1595 (4°), there is a *Sermo ad Milites* written by Abbo of St-Germain-des-Prés, an author used elsewhere by Wulfstan.[76] The sermon laments the devastation caused in France by the Normans, which is seen as a Divine punishment for the sins of its inhabitants. In lines 80–6 the social upheavals in England are cited as another example of God's anger. In many ways Abbo's sermon differs greatly from Wulfstan's homiletic style in that it draws on scriptural events for its *exempla*. But it is very similar to the *Sermo* in its opening sentence, and also in its use of the description of social upheaval as a means of getting across its homiletic point: 'Brothers, every day you see how this realm is going to ruin. Our men, serfs (*uillani*) and slaves and bondwomen and all of those who used to keep our farms and plough our lands, whence we should have had both our food and our clothing and with which we used to buy our horses and armour, now are dead or captives.'[77] Admittedly it is not a direct source for Wulfstan's *Sermo* in verbal terms, but in linking religious precepts to current events it may well have influenced his thinking.[78]

The first passage in the *Sermo* to mention slavery declares:

And poor men are sorely deceived and cruelly defrauded and sold far and wide out of this country into the power of foreigners, although quite innocent (*swyþe unforworhte*), and children in the cradle are enslaved for petty theft by cruel injustice widely throughout this people. And the rights of freemen are withdrawn and the rights of slaves are restricted and charitable obligations are curtailed. *Free men are not allowed to keep their independence, nor go where they wish, nor deal with their own property as they wish; and slaves are not allowed to keep what they have gained by toil in their own free time, or what good men have granted them in God's favour, and given them in charity for the love of God. But every charitable obligation which ought by rights to be paid eagerly in God's favour every man decreases or withholds, for injustice is too widely common to men and lawlessness dear to them.* And, in short, God's laws are hated and his precepts despised. And therefore we all through God's anger are frequently disgraced, let him perceive it who can. . . .[79]

[76] I am grateful to Professor Milton McC. Gatch for originally drawing my attention to Abbo's *Sermo*. This sermon was the ultimate source of a paragraph on King Zedechiah in *the Homilies of Wulfstan*, §6.115–21 (ed. Bethurum, pp. 149–50). Bethurum in 'Archbishop Wulfstan's commonplace book', p. 921 and n. 23 (cf. *The Homilies of Wulfstan*, ed. Bethurum, pp. 297–8) suggested that Wulfstan's immediate source was a paragraph in Cambridge, Corpus Christi College, MS. 190, but she was apparently not aware that ultimately this was drawn from Abbo's *Sermo*. Wulfstan almost certainly knew Abbo's *Sermo* directly, as the Copenhagen manuscript contains annotations in his hand: see Ker, 'The handwriting of Archbishop Wulfstan', in *England before the Conquest*, edd. Clemoes & Hughes, pp. 319–21. The sermon is now readily accessible in an edited version with a translation and commentary in Cross & Brown, 'Literary impetus for Wulfstan's *Sermo Lupi*'.

[77] 'Fratres, omni die uidetis cum uadit istud regnum in perditionem. Nostri homines uillani et serui et ancille et toti qui nostras uillas tenebant et nostras terras arabant unde nos et uictum et uestimenta habere deberemus, et unde nos caballos et arma comparabamus, iam sunt mortui aut captiuati.' *Ibid.*, 281 (text); *ibid.*, 285 (translation).

[78] This is explored in *ibid.*, 271–80.

[79] '7 earme men syndan sare beswicene 7 hreowlice besyrwde 7 ut of þysan earde wide gesealde, swyþe unforworhte, fremdum to gewealde, 7 cradolcild geþeowede þurh wælh-

Wulfstan thus begins by opposing the sale of men abroad. As Whitelock pointed out, *unforworhte* in this passage has a concessive sense, and Wulfstan did not mean to imply that criminals could be sold abroad.[80] What he was trying to indicate elliptically was the heinousness of the offence; if it was wrong to sell a guilty man abroad, how much more so was it to sell an innocent one?

The passage fairly clearly indicates that the economic disruptions of the period were forcing freemen into slavery. Poverty and debt must not be under-rated as causes of enslavement, even though, as mentioned above, war tends to be emphasised in the sources.

With regard to the enslavement of children, II Cnut, §21 had implicitly limited responsibility for theft to those over twelve years of age, and II Cnut, §76.2 had sought to prevent the enslavement of children whose parent(s) had commited theft – though it is difficult to see how this could have been effectively prevented. Read in the light of this legislation, the passage in the *Sermo* points to a real problem, though not an unexpected one in a period of social disruption.

The following sentence in the *Sermo* deals with the rights of freemen and slaves. As it stands it is not very specific, but the addition in Cambridge, Corpus Christi College, MS. 201 (possibly by Wulfstan or a contemporary of his)[81] expands this. The rights that freemen were losing were freedom of movement and the power of disposing of their own property. As was pointed out above, III Æthelstan, §4.1 had sought to protect the freedom of movement of such men, which were being restricted by the growth of large estates.[82] The *Sermo* indicates that this legislation had been ineffective. It is also valuable in illustrating that, as so often with economic changes in society, the effects of these transformations were perceived but the forces behind them were not understood and so could not be successfully counteracted. As for the rights of slaves, on the other hand, Wulfstan appears to have had in mind Alfred, §43 and VII Æthelred, §2.3, which as we have seen had extended to slaves' rights of acquiring property during

---

reowe unlaga for lytelre þyfþe wide gynd þas þeode, 7 freoriht fornumene 7 þrælriht ge-nyrwde 7 ælmesriht gewanode. *Frige men ne motan wealdan heora sylfra, ne faran þar hi willað, ne ateon heora agen swa swa hi willað. Ne þrælas ne moton habban þæt hi agon on agenan hwilan mid earfedan gewunnen, ne þæt þæt heom on Godes est gode men geuðon, 7 to ælmesgife for Godes lufan sealdon. Ac æghwilc ælmesriht þe man on Godes est scolde mid rihte georne gelæstan ælc man gelitlað oððe forhealdeð, forðam unriht is to wide mannum gemæne 7 unlaga leofe,* 7, hrædest is to cweþenne, Godes laga laðe 7 lara forsawene. And þæs we habbað ealle þurh Godes yrre bysmor gelome, gecnawe se ðe cunne.' *The Homilies of Wulfstan*, §20 (E I).43–50 (ed. Bethurum, pp. 268–9). All citations will be from her edition of Oxford, Bodleian Library, MS. Hatton 113 (*S.C.* 5210) and London, British Library, Cotton Nero A.i (pp. 267–75) except in the present quotation, where the section between asterisks is taken from the version in Cambridge, Corpus Christi College, MS. 201 (*ibid.*, p. 270.85–91), an addition which Whitelock (*Sermo Lupi*, p. 5) felt may have been composed by Wulfstan. Bethurum in *The Homilies of Wulfstan*, p. 23, did not think it was written by him, but 'if not Wulfstan's, was probably contemporary with him'. Professor James Cross is preparing a facsimile edition of MS. 201 for the Early English Manuscripts in Facsimile series.

[80] *Sermo Lupi*, ed. Whitelock, p. 52; cf. *The Homilies of Wulfstan*, ed. Bethurum, p. 359, note to line 45.

[81] See the previous note.

[82] Above, p. 88.

certain Ember days and fasts.[83] It is not surprising that in a society where there were great differences in power this legislation should have been ineffective in protecting the rights of slaves, who were the lowest in the social hierarchy.

Those who were likely to be in the weakest position of all were female slaves.

And it is shameful to speak of what has happened too widely, and it is terrible to know what too many do often, who commit that miserable deed that they contribute together and buy a woman between them as a joint purchase, and practise foul sin with that one woman, one after another, just like dogs, who do not care about filth; and then sell for a price out of the land into the power of strangers God's creature and his own purchase that he dearly bought.[84]

As a generalisation this is no doubt exaggerated but could well be true of certain cities such as Bristol or York, where country people might be transported to the slave markets there with the purpose of selling them to foreign merchants.[85] The use of female slaves for sexual purposes by their owners has such a long history that it would be surprising if it did not occur in Anglo-Saxon England under certain conditions. But it is unlikely to have been a general condition of ordinary agrarian slavery, where the risk of inciting a slave's kin to revenge would have discouraged it. In a town, however, where kinless souls were being sold for their market value, there would not have been the same inhibitions, and the presence of foreign merchants who might be induced eventually to purchase them would have encouraged this. The sale of close kin such as sons, mothers, or brothers, a practice that Wulfstan also attacks, may well have occurred, though for quite different reasons: poverty and starvation rather than greed were likely to be the economic motivations for this.[86]

There are two passages in the *Sermo* that compare thralls and thegns. The first states:

And lo! how can greater shame befall men through God's anger than often does us for our own deserts? Though any slave runs away from his master and, deserting Christianity, becomes a viking, and after that it comes about that a conflict takes place between thegn and slave, if the slave slays the thegn, no wergeld is paid to any of his kindred; but if the thegn slays the slave whom he owned before, he shall pay the price of a thegn.[87]

---

[83] Above, pp. 85 and 92–3.

[84] 'And scandlic is to specenne þæt geworden is to wide 7 egeslic is to witanne þæt oft doð to manege þe dreogað þa yrmþe, þæt sceotað togædere 7 ane cwenan gemænum ceape bicgad gemæne, 7 wið þa ane fylþe adreogað, an after anum 7 ælc æfter oðrum, hundum gelicost þe for fylþe ne scrifað, 7 syððan wið weorðe syllað of lande feondum to gewealde Godes gesceafte 7 his agenne ceap þe he deore gebohte.' *The Homilies of Wulfstan*, §20.85–91 (ed. Bethurum, p. 270).

[85] On the slave trade in general see above, pp. 74–9.

[86] *The Homilies of Wulfstan*, §20.92–4 (ed. Bethurum, pp. 270–1). For an example of voluntary enslavement in the north of the country see *Manumission*, §6.1, discussed below on pp. 162–3.

[87] 'And la, hu mæg mare scamu þurh Godes yrre mannum gelimpan þonne us deð gelome for agenum gewyrhtum? ðeah þræla hwylc hlaforde ætleape 7 of cristendome to wicinge weorþe, 7 hit æfter þam eft geweorþe þæt wæpengewrixl weorðe gemæne þegene 7 þræle, gif þræl þæne þegen fullice afylle, licge ægylde ealre his mægðe; 7 gif se þegen þæne þræl þe he ær ahte fullice afylle, gylde þegengylde.' *The Homilies of Wulfstan*, §20.100–6 (ed. Bethurum, p. 271).

This literary use of the words *þræl* and *þegn* has already been seen in the *Institutes*.[88] Here Wulfstan has dramatised the reversal of fortune by presenting as a generalised situation a specific encounter between two people of different social ranks who were known to each other. This said, the historical situation that motivated the passage still needs explaining.

The reference becomes clear in the light of the Treaty of Alfred and Guthrum, which was drawn up in the late ninth century. Both the Anglo-Saxons and the Danes agreed not to harbour dissidents joining them from the other side. At the same time the wergeld of a Danish warrior was declared equivalent to that of an Anglo-Saxon noble.[89] An escaped slave who joined a Viking band that chose not to observe the restrictions of the Treaty would quite naturally have been accorded a wergeld equivalent to his confrères. A system of wergeld, however, could function effectively only when there was approximate equality of power between kindreds (thereby making feuds unprofitable) or, better still, where there was coercive power, such as that exercised by a king, which could enforce the paying of wergeld. Where these conditions were not met, it would have been natural for wergeld to be paid by the weaker to the stronger and not vice versa. This is, of course, precisely what Wulfstan was complaining about here.

The second passage to compare thegns and thralls states:

And often a slave binds very fast the thegn who previously was his master and makes him into a slave through God's anger. Alas for the misery, and alas for the public shame which the English now have, all through God's anger. Often two seamen, or maybe three, drive the droves of Christian men from sea to sea, out through this people, huddled together, as a public shame to us all, if we could seriously and rightly feel any shame. But all the insult which we often suffer we repay with honouring those who insult us; we pay them continually and they humiliate us daily; they ravage and they burn, plunder and rob and carry on board; and lo, what else is there in all these events except God's anger clear and visible over this people?[90]

That masters were enslaved by their erstwhile slaves may on occasion have happened, though we should allow for the possibility that Wulfstan was influenced by another literary source here.[91] What is more significant is his

---

[88] Above, pp. 94–5.

[89] Alfred and Guthrum, §§2 and 5 (*Die Gesetze*, ed. Liebermann, I.126 and 128). For this interpretation of the wergeld see Stenton, *Anglo-Saxon England*, p. 261 and n. 1.

[90] 'And oft þræl þæne þegen þe ær wæs his hlaford cnyt swyþe fæste 7 wyrcð him to þræle þurh Godes yrre. Wala þære yrmðe 7 wala þære woroldscame þe nu habbað Engle eal þurh Godes yrre! Oft twegen sæmen oððe þry hwilum drifað þa drafe cristenra manna fram sæ to sæ ut þurh þas þeode gewelede togædere, us eallum to woroldscame, gif we on eornost ænige cuþon ariht understandan. Ac ealne þæne bysmor þe we oft þoliað we gyldað mid weorðscipe þam þe us scendað. We him gyldað singallice, 7 hy us hynað dæghwamlice. Hy hergiað 7 hy bærnað, rypaþ 7 reafiað 7 to scipe lædað; 7 la, hwæt is ænig oðer on eallum þam gelimpum butan Godes yrre ofer þas þeode, swutol 7 gesæne?' *The Homilies of Wulfstan*, §20.117–28 (ed. Bethurum, pp. 271–2).

[91] Abbo of Saint-Germain-des-Prés in his work, *Bella Parisiacae Urbis*, I.184–5, describes in poetic terms the siege of Paris by the Vikings in A.D. 885–6 as follows:
      Efficitur seruus liber, liber quoque seruus
      Uernaque fit dominus, contra dominus quoque uerna.
      ('The slave is made free, the free man a slave/ And the home-born slave becomes master,

suggestion that there were Viking slave-raiding parties at this time. This is the third reference in the *Sermo* to the transport of slaves across the sea.[92] As has already been shown, Wulfstan repeatedly proscribed this practice in the laws. Though his initial feelings against this longstanding practice may have been aroused by penitential teaching on the matter, it must indicate that the trade in human beings had burgeoned with the coming of the Danes.

Nevertheless, it should be noted that this last passage is a factual embellishment of a literary description which appears to have been derived from Gildas's *De Excidio Britanniae*. The latter's description of the uprising of the Anglo-Saxons against the Britons, who had invited these warriors to the island, declares:

In just punishment for the crimes that had gone before, a fire heaped up and nurtured by the hand of the impious easterners spread from sea to sea. It devastated town and country round about, and, once it was alight, it did not die down until it had burned almost the whole surface of the island and was licking the western ocean with its fierce red tongue. . . . So a number of the wretched survivors were caught in the mountains and butchered wholesale. Others, their spirit broken by hunger, went to surrender to the enemy; they were fated to be slaves for ever. . . .'[93]

In the *Sermo* the same themes appear: the sweeping from sea to sea, the devastation and burning, and the enslavement of the inhabitants, all arising out of God's anger towards them.[94]

The *Sermo* thus describes in exaggerated literary terms the social disruptions caused by the renewed Viking incursions in the late tenth and early eleventh centuries. It gives a clear indication that this resulted in an increase in enslavement, not only through capture but also through other economic misfortunes

while on the other hand the master becomes the slave.') Text in *Poetae Latini Aevi Carolini*, IV.1, ed. von Winterfeld, p. 85. Here is exactly the rhetorical paralleling that so appealed to Wulfstan. Although the complete text of the poem now survives only in a single manuscript from Saint-Germain-des-Prés, we know that a copy of the poem formed one of a group of manuscripts bequeathed by Æthelwold to Peterborough Abbey (see Lendinara, 'The Third Book of the *Bella Parisiacae Urbis* by Abbo of Saint-Germain-des-Prés', 73, n. 3, and *eadem*, 'The Abbo Glossary in London, British Library, Cotton Domitian i', 139). Wulfstan seems to have had Fenland connexions and was remembered at Peterborough Abbey for his benefactions (see *The Homilies of Wulfstan*, ed. Bethurum, pp. 35 and 65). Given his interest in Abbo's sermons, he may well have sought out this manuscript.

[92] See also *The Homilies of Wulfstan*, §20.43–5 and 83–4 (ed. Bethurum, pp. 268 and 270).

[93] 'Confouebatur namque ultionis iustae praecedentium scelerum causa de mari usque ad mare ignis orientali sacrilegorum manu exaggeratus, et finitimas quasque ciuitates agrosque populans non quieuit accensus donec cunctam paene exurens insulae superficiem rubra occidentalem trucique oceanum lingua delamberet. . . . Itaque nonnulli miserarum reliquiarum in montibus deprehensi aceruatim iugulabantur: alii fame confecti accedentes manus hostibus dabant in aeuum seruituri. . . .' Gildas, *The Ruin of Britain and Other Works*, §§24–5, ed. & transl. Winterbottom, pp. 97–8 (text); *ibid.*, p. 27 (translation).

[94] Bede used the same passage in his *Historia Ecclesiastica*: see *Bede's Ecclesiastical History*, I.15 (edd. & transl. Colgrave & Mynors, p. 52). This may have been known to Wulfstan. But lines 176–87 (*The Homilies of Wulfstan*, ed. Bethurum, p. 274) seem to have been drawn from a letter of Alcuin, who mentioned Gildas by name and this reference may have led Wulfstan on to his source. On his borrowing from Alcuin see Whitelock, 'Two notes on Ælfric and Wulfstan', 125–6.

such as impoverishment. The social upheaval also led to an infringement upon the rights that had earlier been granted to slaves. What is particularly revealing, however, is that Wulfstan took it for granted that slaves *did* possess rights; he in no wise regarded them as privileges dependent on the charity of the free. This indicates a very different perception of the slave from that to be seen in the earliest Anglo-Saxon laws.

In sum, we see in Wulfstan's writings an acceptance that the slave, as a person who possessed certain rights, was entitled to humane and just treatment. Wulfstan cannot be said to be an original thinker and so did not move ahead of his contemporaries by questioning the institution of slavery itself. Expressing himself vividly and with literary flair, he used his power in both Church and State to seek the acceptance of his views. His own writings show that there were many in society who were not yet prepared to do this. His pleas that slaves be treated well imply that there were those who felt they could arbitrarily abuse them. His attacks on the trading in slaves and their sale abroad may even indicate that this situation was worsening.

Nevertheless, whenever the laws and ecclesiastical regulations that Wulfstan shaped were fully observed, the position of slaves must have improved materially. The regulations on tithes afforded them a greater opportunity to receive alms. They were also permitted more of a chance to acquire property for themselves through their own labour. The servile punishment of a lashing remained, but they could compound for this with a fine. Female slaves were afforded some degree of protection against sexual abuse. Even the renewed insistence that slaves had to observe the obligation to fast indirectly improved their position in that it served to emphasise the common humanity that they shared with the free in the eyes of God.

PENITENTIALS

Alfred's laws had presumed the existence of penitentials but there is little evidence of the widespread presence of penitentials in ninth-century England.[95] By the early eleventh century the situation had changed. The Wulfstanian legislation also presumed that it would be backed by the sanction of penitential discipline; there is manuscript evidence to show that this was not just a pious hope. It is, therefore, appropriate to examine some of the penitentials known in England in the tenth and eleventh centuries here in order to see what they have to say about slavery. Before we can do this, some background discussion is needed, for the interpretation of this material is far from straightforward.

Several Latin penitentials claimed to have been compiled in England in the seventh and eighth centuries, and Irish examples must also have been known.[96]

---

[95] Frantzen, *The Literature of Penance*, pp. 125–7.

[96] There are three allegedly seventh- and eighth-century Anglo-Saxon penitentials that purport to have been written or compiled by Theodore, Bede, and Egbert respectively. In 'The penitentials attributed to Bede', Frantzen has provided evidence to question whether Bede ever compiled the penitential ascribed to him. He has explored the textual complexities of the penances ascribed to Bede and Egbert further in *The Literature of Penance*, pp. 69–77. On Irish influences see *ibid.*, chapters II and III, *passim*.

These influenced later Continental collections but, with the exception of extracts from the early Theodore's Penitential and Egbert's Penitential,[97] they seem not to have circulated in late Anglo-Saxon England. Instead, in the tenth century, the three traditions of penitentials that had developed on the Continent from Insular models became known to the English.[98] Continental manuscripts containing penitential material migrated to England[99] and texts were also copied in various forms in the country itself. This material presents the social historian with several acute problems. First, there is the difficulty of determining precisely *what* texts were known in England: penitentials were frequently abbreviated, rearranged or amalgamated from several sources. Even twentieth-century editions do not make these relationships clear[100] – and for many of the penitentials we are dependent on nineteenth-century editions that do not fully meet the demands of current scholarship. Then there is the difficulty of knowing whether the provisions contained within the penitentials reflected the views of Anglo-Saxons. Finally, there is the even more difficult question of determining how influential these penitentials were on the society as a whole.

Rather than dissecting the complex textual tradition of the late Anglo-Saxon penitentials[101] or assessing the possibly imponderable impact of the Latin penitentials ascribed to Theodore and Egbert that were copied in the late Anglo-Saxon period, we shall instead focus our attention on Old English translations. These are the first penitentials since the Old Irish texts to have been written in the vernacular:[102] their very existence bespeaks a desire for them to be utilised for pastoral purposes. By concentrating on the vernacular versions we can at least be assured that the canons the native translators included struck them as important and so may be taken to mirror, in some measure, concerns of the age and the society. As for the impact of penitential discipline on late Anglo-Saxon England, this is a question that we had best return to after we have reviewed the vernacular evidence.

The translations that we shall consider here are the *Confessionale Pseudo-*

---

97 Extracts from the Latin text of Theodore's Penitential are to be found in London, British Library, MS. Cotton Vespasian D.xv, edited by Finsterwalder in *Die Canones Theodori*, pp. 271–84. Cambridge, Corpus Christi College, MS. 320 also contains a copy. The Old English version is edited by Mone in *Quellen und Forschungen*, pp. 515–27; the complete Latin text is edited by Haddan & Stubbs in *Councils*, III.173–204. For a discussion of Theodore's Penitential see Frantzen, 'The tradition of penitentials', 27–31, and *The Literature of Penance*, pp. 63–9 and 76–80. For its later influence see Frantzen, 'The tradition of penitentials', 44–5 and 53. Egbert's Penitential is to be found in Oxford, Bodleian Library, Bodley MS. 716 (*S.C.* 2630).

98 Frantzen, 'The tradition of penitentials', 36–7, and *The Literature of Penance*, p. 130.

99 For manuscripts that migrated to England see Gneuss, 'A preliminary list of manuscripts', and Rella, 'Continental manuscripts acquired for English centers'.

100 Note Frantzen's strictures on the editions by Raith and Spindler ('The manuscript evidence of the introduction has been misunderstood by the editors': 'The tradition of penitentials', 42) and on Fowler's edition of the 'Handbook for the Use of a Confessor' ('the text needs fresh reconstruction': *ibid.*, 45).

101 See Frantzen, 'The tradition of penitentials'. His published work is an extremely valuable contribution towards our understanding of penitentials in England but his studies reveal how much editorial work remains to be done before further conclusions of wider significance can be made. It is pleasing to know that he is now essaying this major editorial undertaking.

102 I owe this point to Allen Frantzen.

Egberti (which, following Frantzen's suggestion will hereafter be called 'Scrift boc'),[103] the Old English 'Penitential' (largely derived from Halitgar's Penitential),[104] the Old English 'Introduction' (introductory material to the 'Scrift boc' and Old English 'Penitential'),[105] the Canons of Theodore,[106] and the Old English 'Handbook for the Use of a Confessor'.[107] It is noteworthy that with one possible exception none appears in manuscripts that can be dated before the eleventh century, that is, before the time that Wulfstan started influencing Anglo-Saxon legislation.[108] The regulations on slavery in these collections had two main objects: to deal with problems of status and to afford some protection to slaves.

The 'Scrift boc' offered a man remission from one year's fasting if he released slaves. The Old English 'Introduction' added that one's stock of good works was increased by releasing slaves and captives.[109] These texts were here merely recording established Church doctrine – one that the wills show to have been widely followed in the tenth and eleventh centuries.[110]

Two clauses in the 'Scrift boc', both ultimately drawn from Theodore's Penitential, regulated changes in status. The first permitted a father to sell his son into slavery in a time of need, but only up to the age of seven; thereafter he had to to have his son's consent.[111] The second prohibited a spouse from re-marrying for five years after the marriage partner had been taken into captivity: if the missing spouse returned after that time, the one who had remarried had to return to the original partner.[112]

An aspect of status that inevitably posed problems in Anglo-Saxon society stemmed from slave marriages. The Church erected no barriers against the union of a slave and a person of free status. In the case of a marriage between a freeman and a bondwoman entered into with the consent of both partners the

---

[103] Edited in *Das altenglische Bussbuch*, ed. Spindler, pp. 176–94. Additional sections are edited on pp. 170–5. Frantzen has argued in 'The tradition of penitentials', pp. 41–2, that 'Scrift boc' is the term employed by the scribe of Cambridge, Corpus Christi College, MS. 190, and that in consequence this title should now be used in preference to the Latinised title 'Confessional' given to the work by Thorpe.

[104] *Die altenglische Version des Halitgar'schen Bussbuches*, ed. Raith. Again the title is Frantzen's: see his argument in 'The tradition of penitentials', 40–1, as to why the description of the penitential as 'pseudo-Egbertian' is inappropriate.

[105] For the identification and use of the title 'Introduction' see Frantzen, 'The tradition of penitentials', 42–4. It is collated in *Das altenglische Bussbuch*, ed. Spindler, pp. 172–4.

[106] *Quellen und Forschungen*, ed. Mone, pp. 515–27.

[107] Fowler, 'A Late Old English handbook'.

[108] Cambridge, Corpus Christi College, MS. 320, which contains a brief extract from the 'Scrift boc', is assigned a date around the end of the tenth century or beginning of the eleventh in Ker, *Catalogue*, p. 105. For a full list of the manuscripts containing penitentials in Old English see Cameron, 'A list', in *A Plan*, edd. Frank & Cameron, pp. 123–5. For the dating of these I have depended on Ker. The hand of the Latin text of Theodore's Penitential is dated in *Die Canones Theodori*, ed. Finsterwalder, p. 63, as a tenth- or eleventh-century one.

[109] *Das altenglische Bussbuch*, §28 (ed. Spindler, p. 194.490) and *ibid.*, §1 (p. 174.84–5).

[110] See below, chapter V.

[111] *Das altenglische Bussbuch*, §15 (ed. Spindler, p. 183.261–3); cf. *Poenitentiale Theodori*, II.13.1, in *Councils*, edd. Haddan & Stubbs, III.202.

[112] *Das altenglische Bussbuch*, §14 (ed. Spindler, p. 182.237–42); cf. *Poenitentiale Theodori*, §II.12.21–2, in *Councils*, edd. Haddan & Stubbs, III.200.

husband was not permitted to desert her later,[113] thereby protecting the rights of the slave against the claims of the free spouse. The 'Scrift boc' also lays down that when one of the partners to a slave union was freed, the free partner had an obligation to gain freedom for the other.[114] Theodore's Penitential had permitted the person freed to marry a free-born person if the original spouse could not be freed.[115] This, therefore, was a change that was in the interests of the slave, though no doubt it was introduced largely in order to preserve the stability of marriage.

But marriages between slave and free led to difficulties over the status of the children. This does not seem to have been resolved by the Anglo-Saxons. As will be seen later in this chapter, the *Leges Henrici Primi* favoured deriving the status of children from that of the father. The 'Scrift boc' suggests the opposite, however, in its statement that a child of a slave woman remained a slave even if the free father liberated his wife.[116]

Several of the penitential regulations sought to afford slaves some protection against abuse at the hands of their owners. The Old English 'Penitential', §2.3 discouraged hasty punishment of slaves by their masters by prescribing a two-year fast for any master who killed a slave without witnesses.[117] A mistress who beat her bondwoman to death had to fast for seven years if the slave was innocent and three if she was guilty.[118] Neither provision prohibited an owner from killing a slave, but they did attempt to prevent arbitrary killing. The translator interpreted this to mean that a master should take his slave before the hundred court.[119] The 'Scrift boc' attempted to protect slave women against sexual abuse by imposing a year's fast on a master who seduced his bondwoman; if she bore his child, he should free her as well.[120] A vernacular version of the Theodore's Penitential was even stricter. It demanded the release of a woman who had been seduced, in addition to demanding that the seducer should fast for six months.[121] In a provision ultimately derived from the Latin version of Theodore's Penitential the Canons of Theodore declared that provided a slave had obtained property lawfully, no one could deprive him of it without his permission, thus lending ecclesiastical support to the secular legislation permitting a slave to own property.[122]

[113] *Das altenglische Bussbuch*, §13 (ed. Spindler, pp. 181–2.221–3).
[114] *Ibid.*, §13 (p. 181.218–21).
[115] *Poenitentiale Theodori*, II.13.4, in *Councils*, edd. Haddan & Stubbs, III.202. The extract in the Vespasian manuscript (cf. n. 97 above) leaves out the vital main clause, thereby rendering the sentence unintelligible.
[116] *Das altenglische Bussbuch*, §13 (ed. Spindler, p. 182.223–4). Cf. below, pp. 106 and 181.
[117] *Die altenglische Version des Halitgar'schen Bussbuches*, ed. Raith, p. 17.2–4.
[118] *Ibid.*, §2.4 (p. 17.5–9).
[119] *Ibid.*, §2.3 (p. 17.1–2).
[120] *Das altenglische Bussbuch*, §5 (ed. Spindler, p. 177.127–9). The former injunction is a translation of Bede's Penitential, that is, it is derived from the Continential penitential tradition; the latter is from the Irish Finnian's Penitential: see *Councils*, edd. Haddan & Stubbs, III.328, 16, and *The Irish Penitentials*, ed. Bieler, p. 80, 40. My thanks to Allen Frantzen for these references.
[121] *Quellen und Forschungen*, §191 (ed. Mone, p. 525.18–19).
[122] *Ibid.*, §109 (p. 518.17–19); cf. *Poenitentiale Theodori*, II.13.3, in *Councils*, edd. Haddan & Stubbs, III.202.

Apart from prohibiting slaves from working on Sundays,[123] the extant penitentials do not mention that they were subject to any other ecclesiastical obligations. But the ecclesiastical recognition of slave marriages and the obligation imposed in the laws on slaves to obey the regulations on fasting indicate that it is probable that slaves were expected to obey all the other provisions governing personal conduct in the penitentials. The Old English 'Handbook for the Use of a Confessor', which appears to be from Archbishop Wulfstan's circle,[124] contains two provisions, however, that aimed at ameliorating the slave's position. It enjoined a confessor to take into account the personal, financial, and legal position of the penitent. Just as the proud and the humble or the rich and the poor should be shrived differently, so should the confessor discriminate between the free person and the slave in imposing a penance.[125] Furthermore, in making amends for their misdeeds wealthy men were encouraged to free their own slaves and also those belonging to others.[126]

We now must face the difficult question of determining how influential these penitentials were. At one level, we have already answered this: Wulfstan assumed the existence of penitential discipline in the royal legislation that he helped to draft. Insofar as these laws were enforced in the troubled conditions of the first half of the eleventh century, penitentials may be said to have had some direct influence in the shaping of the society. How far they influenced the moral life of the country without invoking the sanction of the laws is more difficult to say. I suspect that once we have a clearer picture of the patterns of distribution of both the Latin and Old English penitentials, we may feel that they had considerable influence in their own right. Even though our leading authority on Anglo-Saxon penitential practice has suggested that it was 'part of the religious life of the few',[127] his own work points to the existence of penitential collections in a number of episcopal churches.[128] Diocesan interest in penance is likely to have filtered down to the local church level through the provision of small penitential handbooks for priestly confessors,[129] though it is in the nature of such texts that few copies will have survived.

If such a judgment is well-founded, one may say that in general the penitentials acted as a moral force within the society by insisting that slaves had both rights and obligations similar to those of the free, thereby weakening (albeit unconsciously) the legal bases for the division between the two.

---

[123] *Quellen und Forschungen*, §91 (ed. Mone, pp. 515–16.28ff.)
[124] Fowler, 'A Late Old English handbook', 6–12.
[125] *Ibid.*, 19, lines 91–6.
[126] *Ibid.*, 29, lines 365–6.
[127] Frantzen, *The Literature of Penance*, p. 201.
[128] See Frantzen, 'The tradition of penitentials', pp. 37, 38, 40, and 49 (Worcester), 37, 38, and 40 (Exeter), and 45–6 (Canterbury).
[129] *Ibid.*, pp. 47–8.

POST-CONQUEST LEGAL COLLECTIONS

None of Cnut's Anglo-Saxon successors has left any legislation in codified form. There are, however, a number of twelfth-century legal collections which purport to preserve Anglo-Saxon and early Norman law. The law-books relevant to this study include the *Leges Henrici Primi*, the *Leges Edwardi Confessoris* and the *Leis Willelmi*. These works are worth examining not merely for their material on slaves (some of which is not to be found in pre-Conquest sources), but also because they provide more details about the fusion of the lower ranks of the free and the unfree.

Most of the information about slaves is contained in the *Leges Henrici Primi*, a compilation that was probably completed between 1116 and 1118.[130] According to this source slaves by birth acquired their status from their fathers (§77), which conflicts with the 'Scrift boc'. We shall encounter other evidence to suggest that legal status descended through the female line,[131] so this may have been an unresolved problem in Anglo-Saxon society – it may perhaps even have varied from area to area.

As for losing the slave status, the compilation continues to recognise manumission as necessary for this change to occur (§78). The regulations here, however, include features from Continental legal practice which seem not to have been followed in England.[132]

In the realm of rights the *Leges* indicate that slaves had gained further protection. A slave's kinsmen were permitted to claim compensation of forty pence in the event of his death. If his killer was a freeman the latter had also to give two gloves and a capon (§70.2 and 4). There seems to be no reason to question the genuineness of this provision on compensation. Its importance lies in the legal recognition that a slave possessed a kindred and was an economic asset to it, though no doubt it was introduced into the laws as a disincentive to harm the lord's property.

The compiler recognised a clear difference in liability for crimes between slaves and freemen. Whereas freemen who engaged as a group in theft were jointly culpable, only one slave out of a group of slaves was to be punished on behalf of all. Nevertheless, they all were jointly liable for compensation (§59.25–25*a*). If a freeman and a slave together committed a theft, the slave was to be beaten and returned to his lord while the freeman had to bear the costs of the fine (§59.24; cf. also §85.4a). For thefts under eightpence, the slave was to be branded and beaten but his lord was the one liable to pay compensation (§59.23).

Two different punishments are laid down in the *Leges* for a slave who killed another slave. In clause 70.2–3 monetary compensation to both the owner and the deceased slave's relatives was due, payable either by the slayer's lord or by the slave himself. If this was not forthcoming the lord had to hand him over to

---

[130] The standard edition is now *Leges Henrici Primi*, ed. & transl. Downer. For the date see *ibid.*, pp. 34–7.
[131] See below, pp. 114–15 and 181.
[132] See below, p. 145, n. 68.

his accusers, pay compensation or send the slave away to look after himself (provided this last was done before the slave was charged). Liebermann linked this clause with Ine, §74.[133] The latter refers, however, to Celtic slaves and makes no mention of any limitation on freeing a slave when charged. The compensation due to relatives is also not mentioned there. It seems more likely that the compiler of the *Leges* is preserving here a genuine but otherwise unknown West-Saxon law.

Clause 70.8 declares, however, that if a freeman kills a freeman or a slave another slave, he himself must die. Downer has suggested that there was an Anglo-Saxon source behind this.[134] If this is indeed so, it runs counter to the principle of monetary compensation for the death of another. It could have been the sort of draconian law that might have been promulgated by Æthelstan but it is difficult, however, to see this as other than a temporary piece of legislation that has fortuitously been preserved here.

The *Leges* thus seem to record some genuine legal traditions about the position of slaves. It is not really possible to determine to what extent these still applied in the twelfth century. The post-Conquest law-books in general are more useful in showing how the free came to share the same rights, obligations, and disabilities as the unfree, particularly through the growth of lordship.

Manbot, the compensatory fine payable to a lord for the death of one of his men, illustrates well the changing status of the so-called freeman. Both *Leges Henrici Primi*, §§70.2 and 70.4 and *Leis Willelmi*, §7 set a slave's *manbot* at twenty shillings, which, as Liebermann pointed out, was the full value of the slave.[135] *Manbot* for a freeman in the *Leis Willelmi*, on the other hand, was only ten shillings in recognition of his free status. But this crucial legal distinction between slave and freeman has disappeared in the *Leges Edwardi Confessoris*, a work probably written in Warwickshire and dating from the period 1130 x 1135.[136] Clause 12.4 states: 'The *manbot* in the Danelaw of a villein and a sokeman is twelve *oras* (that is, one pound), that of freemen three marks (that is, two pounds).'[137] Thus villeins and sokemen had acquired a *manbot* equivalent to that of a slave,[138] and though the law uses Domesday terminology that formerly had designated freemen, they had obviously lost this free status.

There are other indications of the diminution in the rights of those who in Anglo-Saxon times would have been called freemen. According to the *Leges Henrici Primi*, *uillani* (equated with *ceorlas* in §76.6), cottars (*cotseti*) and farthingmen (*ferdingi*) were not permitted to be judges in county and hundred courts (§29.1–1b). Furthermore, if freemen were caught as fugitives, they were to be branded (§59.26), a servile punishment (§59.23). Yet another example of the loss of free status concerns Peter's Pence. Formerly the obligation to pay this

---

[133] *Die Gesetze*, ed. Liebermann, I.588.
[134] *Leges Henrici Primi*, ed. & transl. Downer, pp. 29–30.
[135] *Die Gesetze*, ed. Liebermann, III.287, *Leis Willelmi* 7.2).
[136] *Die Gesetze*, ed. Liebermann, III.340–1, §§4–5.
[137] 'Manbote in Denelaga de uillano et sokeman XII orae, de liberis hominibus III marcas' (*Die Gesetze*, ed. Liebermann, I.638).
[138] *Leis Willelmi*, §2.3ff. shows that in the twelfth century twelve *orae* were reckoned to the pound of twenty shillings.

had been a symbol of free status (see *Rectitudines Singularum Personarum*, §3.4). Wulfstan had been forced to soften this by requiring the lords of very poor men to pay on their behalf (VII Æthelred, §1.3). By the twelfth century this had been extended according to *Leis Willelmi*, §17a to include 'ses bordiers (*bordarios*) e ses bouerz (*bubulcos*) e ses serjanz (*seruientes*)'.[139]

The twelfth-century legal collections thus reveal the culmination of trends evident in the Anglo-Saxon period. Those who had once been called slaves were steadily gaining rights, while those formerly described as freemen were becoming subject to increasingly servile disabilities. There was in consequence a fusion of these two groups into one, bound to an overlord through duties owed on the land the peasantry worked.

[139] *Die Gesetze*, ed. Liebermann, I.504–5.

IV

'AFTER THEIR LIFETIME HALF THE MEN ARE TO BE FREE': THE EVIDENCE OF THE WILLS

Anglo-Saxon wills are evidentiary documents of an act that was originally oral in nature.[1] About sixty are extant in Old English, with twenty-four of these individually and collectively providing information on slavery that is not available in other sources.[2] Numerous other such documents must have disappeared,[3] as is attested by Latin translations of now-lost vernacular wills entered in cartularies and elsewhere.[4] As with the Anglo-Saxon land-charters, many of these translations probably retain only those parts of the original documents that had a bearing on the material interests of the monastic house where the cartulary was written. These interests are unlikely to have extended to the social hierarchy of the estates mentioned and thus the translations frequently must have excluded much that would have absorbed our attention in this study. This is apparent from Æthelgifu's will, where the Latin abstract omits many of the details contained in the vernacular text – details that afford some unique insights into Anglo-Saxon social structure.[5]

The distribution of the extant wills, both in their provenance and in their chronology, is extremely patchy.[6] There is none from Northumbria at all. For the first half of the ninth century the five that survive come from Kent – yet thereafter only four more Kentish wills are known. From the huge territory of Mercia there are but eight wills extant (nine if Æthelgifu's will be included) for the whole Anglo-Saxon period and about fifteen from Wessex. On the other hand, there are over a score from East Anglia, all dating from after Æthelred's reign. Another problem with the wills is that prior to the tenth century they did not usually record bequests other than land.[7] Thus the earlier documents are of little use for the study of peasant social structure,[8] and social changes that

---

[1] Sheehan, *The Will in Medieval England*, p. 20, and Hazeltine, in *Anglo-Saxon Wills*, ed. & transl. Whitelock, p. viii.

[2] These are listed in Sheehan, *The Will in Medieval England*, p. 21, n. 11. To these should be added the will of Æthelgifu discussed below.

[3] *Ibid.*, p. 22 and n. 16.

[4] Listed in *ibid.*, p. 22, n. 15.

[5] *The Will of Æthelgifu*, ed. & transl. Whitelock, pp. 40–1.

[6] For detailed references see Sheehan, *The Will in Medieval England*, p. 23 and nn. 19–25.

[7] *Anglo-Saxon Wills*, ed. & transl. Whitelock, p. 100.

[8] They do contain, of course, useful information on the aristocratic classes through the bequests made and the lists of witnesses recorded.

become apparent in the tenth-century sources may well have had their origin in an earlier period.

In spite of these disadvantages the wills contain extremely valuable evidence about the lower ranks of Anglo-Saxon society, both servile and free. This chapter will concentrate on two wills in particular. The first, the late ninth-century will of King Alfred, is especially informative about the change in status brought about by manumission, and supplies some of the earliest evidence for a concept of freedom that was to be a decisive factor in the decline of slavery in England. The second will, that of an otherwise unknown woman, Æthelgifu, dates from a century later. It highlights the use of the will as a means of manumission, thereby revealing the importance of testamentary acts in the decline of slavery. It also discloses the variety of occupational tasks performed by slaves. The remaining wills will be dealt with more cursorily, with attention being centred on certain information that they have in common, such as the position of *witeþeowas*, the manumission of slaves and the nature of the freedom thereby granted, and the bequest of slaves. When viewed collectively these wills provide decisive evidence for an increase in manumissions in the eleventh century. They also hint at what motivated this increase.

THE WILL OF KING ALFRED

The earliest of the extant wills to contain any provisions about dependent classes is King Alfred's, which dates from the period 873 x 889.[9] Near the end of the document Alfred declares:

And I pray in the name of God and of His saints that none of my kinsmen or legatees oppress any *cyrelif* for whom I have paid. Now the West Saxon council have duly declared to me that I may leave them bond or free, whichever I will. But I desire, for the love of God and for the good of my soul, that they be entitled to their freedom and their choice. And I enjoin in the name of the living God, that no man put pressure upon them either by pecuniary exactions, or by any other means, so as to prevent them from choosing whatsoever man they will.[10]

The most probable meaning of the word *cyrelif* is 'one who entered a state of

---

[9] For the date see *Select English Historical Documents*, ed. & transl. Harmer, p. 92. Another translation of the will is provided by Keynes & Lapidge in *Alfred the Great*, pp. 174–5 and 177–8, with a map of the estates mentioned in the will on p. 176 and useful notes on the text on pp. 313–26. Some of the economic implications of Alfred's will have been explored by Maddicott in 'Trade, industry and the wealth of King Alfred' and the papers it elicited in response: see Balzaretti *et al.*, 'Debate: Trade, industry and the wealth of King Alfred'.

[10] '7 ic bidde on Godes naman 7 on his haligra þæt minra maga nan ne yrfewearda ne geswence nan nænig cyrelif þara þe ic foregeald. 7 me Westseaxena witan to rihte gerehton þæt ic hi mot lætan swa freo swa þeowe, swaðer ic wille. Ac ic for Godes lufan 7 for minre sawle þearfe wylle þæt hy syn heora freolses wyrða 7 hyra cyres. 7 ic on Godes lifiendes naman beode þæt hy nan man ne brocie ne mid feos manunge ne mid nænigum þingum þæt hy ne motan ceosan swylcne mann swylce hy wyllan.' *Select English Historical Documents*, §11 (ed. & transl. Harmer, p. 19.16–24 [text]); *ibid.* (pp. 52–3 [translation, emended]) (= Sawyer, *Anglo-Saxon Charters*, no. 1507).

slavery by choice'.[11] Such men would have lost their legal status of freemen, but as will be seen in chapter VI, this could bring some positive advantages in that the lord was then obliged by custom to provide them with food.[12] In this instance, however, there is a hint that there was another reason for their becoming slaves. Alfred did not merely express fear for their vulnerability after being freed; he specifically enjoined that no one was to impose financial exactions on them. This suggests that they were persons who had got themselves into debt and had subsequently had themselves enslaved by the king, who in turn had then discharged the debts on their behalf. These debts may have arisen not merely out of misfortune or the mismanagement of assets; they could also have resulted from the imposition of fines levied for what today would be considered criminal acts.[13] Enslavement under the king might well have been a gentler fate than the continued indebtedness to, or enslavement under, an interested party.

Alfred evidently felt that it was necessary to get the advice of the West Saxon *witan* before freeing these *cyrelif*, the wording seems to imply that he was not certain whether he could otherwise legitimately do so. It is difficult to see why this should have been the case. Perhaps he had used the folk's resources to buy them and had placed them on folkland occupied by him. In freeing them he then potentially would have been reducing the assets of the estates where they were resident. If these estates were folkland, such an action might well have required the people's approval. In any case, given the evident vulnerability of the persons he was freeing, it was probably wise of him to obtain the approval of the *witan* for his action.

Alfred's use of the phrases 'Ac ic for Godes lufan 7 for minre sawle þearfe' and 'hy . . . motan ceosan swylcne mann swylce hy wyllan' is noteworthy. Both phrases are employed in the later manumission-documents (although the second appears in these texts only twice).[14] This suggests that the manumission ceremony had already acquired some sort of regular legal form among the West Saxons at least fifty years before the earliest extant written record of the act.

Something of the nature of the freedom granted these persons can also be deduced from the will. For Alfred the most important aspect of his grant of freedom was that those freed acquired the right to choose a new overlord. Undoubtedly they would have done this protected by their now-enhanced legal status of freeman under tribal law, although Alfred did not say this. There is the same duality here in the concept of freedom as has been seen in the Orosius passage cited in above chapter II.[15] While the term has reference primarily to rights in a manorial society, it can also imply the possession of rights in a tribal society. In the next two centuries the former aspect was to grow at the expense of the latter.

---

[11] See below, appendix I, s.v. *cyrelif.*

[12] *Rectitudines Singularum Personarum,* §§8–9.1 (*Die Gesetze,* ed. Liebermann, I.449–50). Cf. below, pp. 175–6.

[13] A possible example of this (where, however, the defendant was able to pay for his release) is discussed below, p. 163.

[14] See below, p. 146.

[15] Above, pp. 53–6.

THE WILL OF ÆTHELGIFU

The longest and most informative of the vernacular Anglo-Saxon wills was made by a woman, Æthelgifu, whose identity is uncertain. The detailed vernacular version of her will was found earlier this century in a bundle of documents in an outbuilding at Alderley House in Gloucestershire and was edited and printed as recently as 1968. A few years ago Dr Simon Keynes found another vernacular abstract. The will seems to date from *ca* 990 and mentions estates in Bedfordshire, Hertfordshire, and Northamptonshire.[16] It has long been known through a Latin translation, but a comparison of the two versions shows that the Latin document merely summarised the main provisions of the Old English text and in the process omitted all details of the slave population on the estates. The Old English document, however, presents a number of problems of interpretation, largely because of textual and linguistic difficulties, which regrettably the vernacular abstract does not elucidate. These problems must be addressed first in order to assess the evidence about slavery contained in the will.

On an initial reading it is hard to apprehend the pattern of thought of the testatrix: to modern minds the apparent lack of logic can make the references contained in the document seem baffling. This apparent confusion is compounded by its presumption of knowledge that has since been lost. The text contains a number of syntactic ambiguities, which render interpretation yet more difficult. The punctuation cannot be relied upon to assist in resolving these ambiguities because the extant document is obviously a copy since it displays several instances of scribal corruption.[17]

Our primary task, then, must be to attempt to ascertain the structure of the work. The following broad divisions are discernible: (1) lines 1–2: proem; (2) lines 2–3: the grant of what is presumably Æthelgifu's heriot to the king and his wife; (3) lines 3–44: bequests of lands and associated possessions to various persons and institutions; (4) lines 44–50: bequests of certain moveables, mainly associated with her household; (5) lines 50–59: the dispersal, either by manumission or by bequest, of various persons owned by her; (6) lines 59–66: the background to the litigation concerning her property which justified her right to bequeath the above, together with a request to the king to support the terms of her will and an anathema on those who do not.

When divided in this fashion the document can be seen to possess an underlying logic: in section 3 Æthelgifu makes dispositions involving her estates (basically immoveables, that is, her lands but also goods such as stock and

---

[16] On the date see *The Will of Æthelgifu*, ed. & transl. Whitelock, p. 24. For a map of her bequests to minsters see Blair, 'Introduction: From minster to parish church', in *Minsters and Parish Churches*, ed. Blair, p. 5, fig. 2. Dr Simon Keynes has generously given me a transcript of the abbreviated vernacular version of this will in advance of publication; regrettably this version has not shed any light on some of the interpretive problems that will be discussed in this chapter and in appendix II below. For how the will came to Alderley see Keynes, 'A charter of King Edward the Elder for Islington', 304–5.

[17] Lines 8–9: '7 freoge mon hira cild' (repeated; 'heora' in the abbreviated version); line 10: 'freo<ge>' (erasure); line 12: 'æt langaforda' (repeated); line 33: 'hys stwegyn suna' (faulty word division); line 40: '7 wegen men' (faulty word division).

112

persons associated with them); in section 4 she deals with her household property (basically moveable objects except for the *staðul*, which is probably the homestead itself);[18] and in section 5 she expresses her wishes about her slaves (also moveables, who either are being freed or are being transferred into another's possession – in either case they might well be moving from the estates where they formerly resided). Unfortunately some persons are also freed in the section devoted to the estates (section 3), and there are cross-references between this section and that dealing with the dispersal by manumission and bequest of other slaves (section 5). Furthermore, within sections 3 and 5 the pattern of thought seems to be confused. A close analysis of the text, however, permits one to impose some order on the apparent confusion, but it requires a detailed discussion that may strain many readers' patience. This discussion, therefore, has been placed in appendix II below and here only its conclusions will be utilised. These enable us to tabulate the number of slaves manumitted and bequeathed in the will as follows:

TABLE II: ANALYSIS OF THE SLAVES FREED IN ÆTHELGIFU'S WILL

	1	2	3	4	5	6	7
						Children freed	
					Minimum	(parents	Total
			Couples	Family units	no. of	remain	freed
			without	(parent[s] &	children	slaves)	(cols.
Estates	*Men*	*Women*	*children*	*child[ren])*	*in 4*		*1,2,5,6)*
Oakhurst	4[a]	–	–	1	1	–	5
Gaddesden	3	–	–	1	1	1	5
Langford	10	1	1	1	1	–	12
Clifton	–	–	–	–	–	1	1
Munden	4	3	2	1	1	1	9
Standon	4	4	1	1	1	–	9
Offley	3	5	2	1	3[b]	–	11
Weedon	3	1[c]	–	–	–	–	4
Henlow	1	–	–	–	–	–	1
Unspecified	4	4	–	2	4[d]	1	13
TOTAL	36	18	6	8	12	4	70

[a] It is assumed that Ymma was a man (cf. *The Will of Æthelgifu*, ed. & transl. Whitelock, p. 6, n. 8).

[b] This figure represents the two sons and stepdaughter of Wulfstan of Cockernhoe (line 33).

[c] Sister of Byrhtelm, who was also freed at Weedon (line 36).

[d] This figure represents the eldest and youngest son of Mann the goldsmith and his wife (lines 50–1), and the daughter, Ælfwaru, and child(ren) of Wulfric the huntsman and his wife (line 51). It excludes Mann's *cnapa*, who may not have been related to him.

---

[18] *The Will of Æthelgifu*, ed. & transl. Whitelock, p. 12, n. 14.

TABLE III: ANALYSIS OF THE SLAVES BEQUEATHED IN ÆTHELGIFU'S WILL

	1	2	3	4	5	6	7
			Family units (parent[s] and child[ren])	*Minimum no. of children*	*Couples remain slaves (child[ren] freed)*	*Son remains a slave (parent and rest of family freed)*	*Total bequeathed (cols*
Estates	*Men*	*Women*	*bequeathed*	*in 3*	*freed)*	*family freed)*	*1+2+4+6)*
Oakhurst	1[e]	–	–	–	–	–	1
Gaddesden	9[f,g]	4[f]	–	–	1	–	13
Langford	8[h]	3[h]	2	2	–	–	13
Clifton	1	1	–	–	1	–	2
Stondon	–	1	–	–	–	–	1
Munden	5	2	1	2[i]	1	–	9
Standon	–	–	–	–	–	1[j]	1
Weedon	2	–	–	–	–	–	2
From Munden/ Gaddesden/ Langford	5	–	–	–	–	–	5
Not specified	8	5	–	...	1	–	13
TOTAL	39	16	3	4	4	1	60

[e] Excluded are 'all the others' bequeathed to St Alban's (lines 6–7).
[f] This assumes that the younger swineherd, the two men, Brihtelm's younger son, and Wulfstan and his wife were all located at Gaddesden (lines 40–1).
[g] Following Whitelock's translation of line 41 (cf. *The Will of Æthelgifu*, ed. & transl. Whitelock, p. 10 and n. 16).
[h] This assumes that Edwin the priest, to whom a man was bequeathed, resided at Langford, and that Ælfswyth and the miller's wife with their respective children were located there (lines 16 and 18–19).
[i] Interpreting *heord* in line 21 as 'family'.
[j] This assumes that the 'younger shepherd' given with Eatstan's herd was in fact Eatstan's son (lines 25–6).

These figures provide an opportunity to explore several matters of general interest, including marriage-relationships, the occupations of slaves, and the act of manumission. First, let us examine marriage-relationships. Two references to stepdaughters in the will show that there must have been some sort of legal relationship entered into by slaves that was more than just cohabitation.[19] This relationship, furthermore, could exist between persons of differing legal status, if the interpretation of the evidence given above is correct, thus confirming the evidence from legal and penitential sources already discussed in chapter III. Wulfric the huntsman appears to have been a freeman, since otherwise one would have expected him to have received his freedom when his wife and child(ren) did. If this is so, it would appear that Wulfric's children took their legal status from their mother. This is supported by evidence from Hatfield in

[19] Lines 18, 33.

Hertfordshire[20] and contradicts the late evidence of *Leges Henrici Primi*, §77.1, where the status is derived from the father.[21] These observations on marriage-relationships have important implications for the change from slavery to serf-dom. By A.D. 990 there had been time for a fusion of the various peoples, Scandinavian and Anglo-Saxon, who inhabited the South-east Midland region where Æthelgifu's estates were situated. This fusion, together with the society's unified agricultural base, meant that there no longer existed the kinds of social division that might have helped to preserve a rigid distinction between free and unfree. The acceptance of unions between free and unfree could only have helped to blur yet further the distinctions between the two groups.

Much can be learnt about the occupations of slaves on Anglo-Saxon estates from the will. Most startling is the evidence that Edwin the priest must have been a slave.[22] This was, of course, completely contrary to the canons of the Church, which had long decreed that a slave could not become a priest (though a manu-mitted slave might).[23] It is all the more surprising in the light of the reforming activities of such men as Æthelwold and Dunstan, but possibly the reformers' energies were directed more at the establishment of monastic communities than at the regularisation of practices in what must have been in many cases little more than village churches.[24]

Edwin was not the only slave with religious duties on Æthelgifu's estates. Three young women were granted their freedom in the will, provided they fulfilled the condition to 'sing four psalters every week within thirty days and a psalter every week within twelve months'.[25] They were thus not untutored and perhaps even could read. Whitelock has suggested that Æthelgifu was an un-cloistered nun (a *nunne*) who had formed a small religious community in her household, which would explain how these slave women had acquired their education.[26]

There were several workers with specialised occupations on Æthelgifu's estates. Mann was a goldsmith and Wine a miller.[27] There was also an unnamed fuller.[28] With such a large collection of estates Æthelgifu would have found these workers far more valuable as members of her permanent demesne staff than as

---

[20] See below, p. 181, and Pelteret, 'Two Old English lists of serfs', 489–90.

[21] See further above, pp. 104 and 106.

[22] Line 15.

[23] See *The Will of Æthelgifu*, ed. & transl. Whitelock, p. 32, n. 6.

[24] On village churches see Lennard, *Rural England*, chapter X, 'The village churches' (pp. 288–338), with references there cited. See also Owen, 'Chapelries and rural settlement', in *Medieval Settlement*, ed. Sawyer, pp. 66–71, and *Minsters and Parish Churches*, ed. Blair.

[25] 'singe ælcere wucan iiii sealtereas binnan xxx nihtan 7 on xii mo'n'ðum ælcere wucan sealtere' (lines 51–2).

[26] *The Will of Æthelgifu*, ed. & transl. Whitelock, pp. 33–4.

[27] Lines 50–1 (Mann), 10 (Wine). On mills in England see Lennard, *Rural England*, pp. 278–87; Addyman, 'The Anglo-Saxon house: a new review', 295 and n. 3 together with plate VIIb; Rahtz & Bullough, 'The parts of an Anglo-Saxon mill'; and Holt, *The Mills of Medieval England*, pp. 3–16. The mills from the Anglo-Saxon period that have been excavated are all watermills (though a structure found at Cheddar might be a horsemill: see *ibid.*, pp. 18–19). Windmills first appear in documentary records in England in 1185 (*ibid.*, p. 20).

[28] Line 16.

villeins performing occasional services. This perhaps explains why she did not envisage their release until her estates were to be divided up after her death.

Both Postan and Raftis have emphasised the importance of demesne labourers in the post-Conquest period and have argued that the Anglo-Saxon slave was the forerunner of this economically important group of farm workers.[29] As Raftis has pointed out: 'These labourers were most in demand for permanent services like those of the shepherd, swineherd, oxherd, dairymaids, brewers, malters, etc., since the regular villein had to work his own lands and could only give intermittent services to the lord.'[30] The occupations of a number of slaves on Æthelgifu's estates seems to bear out this contention. Thus the only female slave worker mentioned is a *dæge*, who, significantly, was not freed but was bequeathed to Ælfwold.[31] Though this word is ascribed the meaning of 'a female baker' in a tenth-century glossary,[32] its Middle English usage suggests that its main sense was that of 'dairymaid'.[33] An entry in Domesday Book supports this contention by associating a *uaccarius* or 'cowherd' with a *daia*,[34] a link that makes it improbable that the latter was a baker. The fact that the *uaccarius* and *daia* are mentioned separately from the male and female slaves in this entry underlines their economic importance to the demesne. Æthelgifu probably was unwilling to countenance the dairymaid's release on her death because she realised that she was indispensible to the estate.

Other tasks performed by slaves on Æthelgifu's lands were those of swineherd, shepherd, and ploughman. As in the case of the *dæge* the testatrix betrays a reluctance to free such persons. That there was an economic reason behind this is perhaps most clearly evident in the case of the swineherds.[35] At Oakhurst the swineherd was given with the swine to St Alban's. At Langford the swineherd's son appears to have been given to Ælfnoth, quite possibly because he was expected to take over his father's herd. This was the case at Standon, where

---

[29] Postan, *The Famulus* and Raftis, 'The trends toward serfdom in mediaeval England', 20–1.

[30] *Loc. cit.*

[31] Line 55. These are similar to the sentiments expressed by Agobard of Lyons (769–840) in his tract, *Liber aduersus Legem Gundobaldi*, §3, in *S. Agobardi Lugdunensi Episcopi . . . Opera Omnia*, ed. Migne, col. 114: '. . . omnes fratres effecti, unum Patrem Deum inuocant, seruus et dominus, pauper et diues, indoctus et eruditus, infirmus et fortis, humilis operator et sublimis imperator. Iam nemo alium dedignatur, nemo sub alio se despicit, nemo super alium extollitur.' ('All men are brothers, all invoke one same Father, God: the slave and the master, the poor man and the rich man, the ignorant and the learned, the weak and the strong, the humble worker and the sublime emperor. None of them disdains the other, none judges himself inferior to another, none has been raised above the other.' Translation in Bonnassie, 'From slavery to feudalism in south-western Europe', in *From Slavery to Feudalism in South-Western Europe*, trans. Birrell, p. 54, n. 206, to which study I owe the reference.) Agobard's work is known from only a single manuscript discovered in the seventeenth century and there is no evidence that his writings were disseminated in England. Nevertheless, it might be worth exploring his *oeuvre* to see whether his work had any influence on Wulfstan, especially in the light of the latter's interest in legal matters. On Agobert see Cabaniss, *Agobard of Lyons*.

[32] Wright, *Anglo-Saxon and Old English Vocabularies*, ed. Wülcker, I, col. 277.2.

[33] *The Will of Æthelgifu*, ed. & transl. Whitelock, p. 14, n. 1. On the word see further below, appendix I, s.v. *dæge*.

[34] Under Bushley in Worcestershire: Domesday Book, volume I, fo 180vb. For a full discussion of the word, including this passage from Domesday Book, see below, appendix I, s.v. *dæge*.

[35] Lines 6, 10, 25, 26(2x), 40.

Eatstan and the rest of his family were freed, leaving his son to have charge over the herd. Another swineherd was also freed there but the younger swineherd (presumably Eatstan's son) was given to Leofsige. At Gaddesden the 'younger swineherd' and two other men were given to Ælfgifu. A further herd, which Brihtelm had charge of, was given to Leofwine, together with Brihtelm's younger son and two others.[36]

Sheep feature a number of times in this will, so it is perhaps surprising that there are only two references to shepherds. The first is an instruction that Ælfnoth was to have the younger shepherd and the second, that Æthelweard the priest was to receive the under-shepherd.[37] Since sheep-rearing is not a labour-intensive mode of farming, there may have been fewer shepherds than swine-herds. As with the swineherds, the younger people retained their slave status and were bequeathed with the livestock.

Other English sources, especially Domesday Book, suggest that the most common role for a slave was that of ploughman.[38] Ploughmen as such are not mentioned in this will, but there are two indications that at least some of the slaves who were bequeathed performed this role. Ælfwold was given two plough-teams and four men.[39] Furthermore, Æthelgifu's kinswoman, Leofrun, was given eight oxen and two men.[40] As will be discussed in more detail later, the regular complement of men needed to operate a plough-team was two,[41] and there can be little doubt, therefore, that the men who were bequeathed were, in fact, in charge of the plough-teams.

What is very striking is the range of tasks performed by the slaves on Æthel-gifu's estates. This is important to bear in mind when one considers the processes of social change in late Anglo-Saxon England. When certain economic roles were filled by persons drawn from both the legally free and the legally servile, the distinction between the two legal categories was likely to become irrelevant. Something of this is apparent in the case of those people whose economic duties demanded the help of assistants: Edwin the priest, Wulfric the huntsman, and Mann the goldsmith. These were either former slaves or, in the case of Wulfric, had a wife and children who had been slaves, yet they themselves were given slaves to assist them in their work or had their assistant freed, as in the case of Mann's *cnapa*.[42]

The will specifies that many people were to be manumitted, and it is useful to examine these manumissions to understand more fully the motives for the act and what 'manumission' meant in practice. Æthelgifu states that her manu-missions were to be considered as alms.[43] She herself, therefore, conceived of her motive as being a religious one. But as we have seen, she was not blind to

---

36 Reading *ginran* for manuscript *ginra*: see *The Will of Æthelgifu*, ed. & transl. Whitelock, p. 10, n. 16 and line 41.

37 Lines 10 and 55–6.

38 See below, chapter VII.

39 Line 21.

40 Lines 41–2.

41 Below, pp. 199–200.

42 Edwin: lines 15–19; Wulfric the huntsman: lines 26–7, 50–1, 54; Mann the goldsmith: lines 50–1, 53–4.

43 Line 59.

117

economic factors. Thus, while Whitelock was right in pointing out that there is a tendency in the will to release the children of slaves,[44] this is by no means always the case; as we have seen, a number of younger people who had a role to play on the estate such as the swineherds were not freed.[45] On the other hand, there would be sound economic sense in releasing those who were very old: to free the elderly would give them a well-earned release from daily toil but would also release their owners from having to keep them as their productivity declined; instead their kin would have to provide for them. Dufe 'the Old' might have fallen into this last category.[46]

The meaning of the act of manumission in this will can be determined from the rights and obligations that the document imposed on some of those who were freed. In the case of Edwin the priest one finds that although he was granted his freedom with no apparent direct limitations being placed on him, his mistress did not in fact waive all authority over him.[47] In his case 'freedom' could not have meant to Æthelgifu that Edwin would thereby gain the right to move away and seek whatever lord he wished to serve, since he was given a church. Instead it must have meant that his time was essentially his own, although even this was circumscribed to some extent, for his possession of the church with its half a hide formerly occupied by Wineman (which presumably would have supplied him with some of his food and income) was dependent on his keeping the building in good repair. Moreover, if he wanted Byrhstan's sister as a slave, he had to say three masses a week for a year and intercede for his former mistress and her husband 'for ever'.

Essentially, however, Edwin was given his personal freedom: if he had refused to carry out the duties imposed upon him, he would still have been 'free' and so presumably could have found a lord elsewhere. The same would have applied to Liofing of Henlow, who was freed and in addition was to 'have his land on condition that every year he remembers her and her lord'.[48] Not so the three women, Ælfwaru, Leofrun, and Æthelflæd.[49] Their grant of freedom was different from that of Edwin's in that it was conditional upon their singing the psalter regularly for a year. As Æthelgifu's properties were within the Danelaw, it is

---

[44] *The Will of Æthelgifu*, ed. & transl. Whitelock, p. 35.

[45] In line 25 Eatstan's son is left in charge of the herd for which his father had been responsible. The 'younger swineherd' is given to Ælfgifu in line 40. In line 6 a swineherd is given to St Alban's, but his age is not noted. Finally, the 'younger shepherd' is given to Ælfnoth (line 10) – this may be the under-shepherd (*læssan sceaphirde*) who the will later directs had to go to Æthelweard the priest and be replaced by Godere (lines 55–6). It must be noted, however, that *gingra* can mean 'deputy' with no implications of age: see the tenth-century Bedwyn manumission-document, *Manumission*, §2.1. If, as seems probable, the shepherds in lines 10 and 55–6 were one and the same, the use of *læssa* gives strong support to the meaning 'deputy' in line 10, and possibly also in line 40. On the other hand, *ginra* is definitely used in the sense of 'younger' in line 41. Cf. *The Will of Æthelgifu*, ed. & transl. Whitelock, p. 14, n. 2.

[46] Line 23. In support of this view, one may note that Dufe's son was not freed but was given to George the priest (lines 54–5). Eatstan might have been in the same position (line 25).

[47] Lines 15–19.

[48] 'hæbbe his land on þ gerad þe he <æ>l<c>e gare gemune hy 7 hyre hlaford' (line 53).

[49] Lines 51–2.

possible that she was influenced by Scandinavian legal practice in imposing these conditions on their grant of freedom.[50]

These examples suggest that the people manumitted in this will can be divided into three categories. First, there were those who were simply 'freed' with no limitations placed on their freedom. In economic terms this meant they were given the power to negotiate with whomsoever they wished over the hire of their labour and skills. Second, there were those who were 'freed' but their freedom was implicitly limited by their being offered a source of income that imposed demands upon them. In effect, their choice of overlord was thereby limited – but in consequence they might well have been better off than those in the previous category. Finally, there were those who were 'freed' subject to compliance with certain conditions.

The manumission of Liofing of Henlow already adverted to above provides one further insight into a complex process of social change. Although the will does not specify what his title to the land granted him on emancipation was to be, it is noteworthy that Æthelgifu specified that he was to 'have *his* land'. In other words, the land must have been in his use *before* he was freed. A trend towards giving people land to work on their own responsibility rather than having it administered directly by the overlords themselves must have been widespread in the following century and this is perhaps the clearest instance in the wills of this socio-economic change. In A.D. 990 Liofing's slave status was probably still sufficiently well-defined for him to have gained some legal rights under tribal law on being freed. But once slaves were regularly working land that was to all intents and purposes under their own control, it is easy to see that confusion could arise over why those who fulfilled essentially the same economic functions belonged to the differing legal categories of 'freeman' and 'slave'. The resulting meshing of a new socio-economic order with an existing socio-legal one was in time to lead to a change in the concept of freedom.

What was the overall impact of this will of Æthelgifu's on the phenomenon of slavery? First, one should note that since she distributed her estates among a wide range of beneficiaries, this must have encouraged the release of specialist workers such as the goldsmith, whose presence presumably could have been justified only in the household of an owner of many estates. In the second place, although she did not denude her estates of staff (and, in fact, in the case of the swineherds she seems to have been careful to ensure that people were left to look after the herds), she did free a considerable number of people, including women and children. If Æthelgifu's will is any guide, one may suspect that the cumulative effect of testamentary manumission in the century and a half before the Battle of Hastings (that is, the period when donations other than land came to be recorded in the wills) was immense. As will be shown below, there is evidence to suggest that indeed hers was not an untypical will in this respect.

---

[50] Cf. the comments on *lisingas*, above, p. 46, below, pp. 128–9, and appendix I, s.v. *lising*.

OTHER ANGLO-SAXON WILLS

The two wills that have been examined so far contained references only to slaves who held that status by choice or by birth; they did not mention penally-enslaved men or *witeþeowas*.[51] As has been mentioned, the Synod of Chelsea in 816 had ruled that on the death of a bishop every Englishman who had been reduced to slavery during the bishop's lifetime was to be freed.[52] The relevant canon does not specify that these were *witeþeowas* but it is reasonable to assume that at least they were included in the category of persons to be freed. Do the episcopal wills provide any evidence that this ruling was in fact carried out?

The earliest of the extent episcopal wills is that of Theodred, bishop of London. Whitelock assigned it a date of 942 x 951.[53] The will does not mention *witeþeowas* but it does contain manumissions that might have included them. The bishop bequeathed to St Paul's Church the estates at St Osyth in Essex, Southery in Norfolk, and Tillingham in Essex, but directed that on all of these estates the men were to be freed for his soul's sake. To his nephews he granted properties at Lothingland and Mendham in Suffolk but ordered that half of the men on these lands were to be freed. On the episcopal demesnes at Hoxne in Suffolk and in London he directed that all that was on these estates when he received them was to be left there, with the increase to be shared equally between the Minster[54] and the poor – but on both of these estates the men were to be freed. This applied also to *Wunemannedune* and Sheen in Surrey. The same instructions governed his estate at Dengie in Essex, except that men were not mentioned. At Fulham in Middlesex the estate was to remain as it was 'unless one wishes to free any of my men'.[55] Other estates were left both to private individuals and to churches but there is no mention of personnel.

Perhaps it is important that Theodred drew a distinction between the staff on lands that were ecclesiastical in origin or going to an ecclesiastical foundation and those on lands that were bequeathed to private beneficiaries. On all the ecclesiastical properties with the exception of Fulham whenever slaves are mentioned, all were freed, whereas only some were to be emancipated on the estates bequeathed to his nephews. Fulham, which is mentioned after Hoxne and London and so would appear to have been episcopal demesne, seems thus to have been an exception. It is possible, however, that the slaves at Fulham were the

---

[51] On the legal grounds for the *witeþeow's* status see below, pp. 247–8.

[52] Above, p. 83 and n. 13.

[53] Sawyer, *Anglo-Saxon Charters*, no. 1526, and *Anglo-Saxon Wills*, §1 (ed. & transl. Whitelock, p. 99). I am heavily indebted for the dating of the wills discussed in the remainder of this chapter to Sawyer's catalogue and to Whitelock's edition.

[54] Presumably the minster referred to here is the one at Hoxne. Though there was only a single diocese in East Anglia in the tenth century, it apparently had two centres, one at Hoxne in Suffolk and the other at Elmham in Norfolk. Whitelock considered *minster* in this will to refer to some sort of monastic establishment. See further *Anglo-Saxon Wills*, ed. & transl. Whitelock, p. 101, note to line 25, and p. 102, note to line 31. For its location see Blair, 'Introduction', in *Minsters and Parish Churches*, ed. Blair, p. 4, fig. 1.

[55] 'buten hwe mine manne fre wille'. *Anglo-Saxon Wills*, §1 (ed. & transl. Whitelock, p. 4.22) (text); *ibid.*, p. 5 (translation) (= Sawyer, *Anglo-Saxon Charters*, no. 1526).

bishop's personal property whom he had added to the estate – he referred to them as 'my men' – and that in consequence he did not feel obliged to free them but instead gave them to the Church.

If 'freeing' in this period primarily conferred the right to move off the estate, as it seems to have done later, the economic results, particularly on the episcopal demesne, would have been disastrous if everyone had exercised that right. While it might have been possible to run the estates given to St Paul's if all had left by importing staff from that church's other estates, this could hardly have been done on the episcopal property if it had been denuded of staff. It would appear, then, that what the bishop was doing was changing the men's legal status. This legal change in status might have bestowed the right to seek a new master. In practice, however, it probably meant that most of the populace remained on the estates but worked under more favourable conditions. The most obvious way of doing this would have been by granting them land on the estate and thus setting in motion the process of enserfment.

As one can see, the bishop appears to have felt that on ecclesiastical estates at least, all the labourers should be legally free, even if not necessarily so on estates in private hands. He was thus going further than the canons of the 816 Synod. Instead he was following the precedent of St Wilfrid, who had been memorialised by Bede as having freed the slaves at Selsey on being granted a substantial estate.[56] Given the prestigious position of the Church within Anglo-Saxon society, the influence of an ecclesiastical leader such as Theodred is not to be underrated.

The first extant episcopal will to mention *witeþeowas* is that of Bishop Ælfsige of Winchester, dating from the period 955 x 958. In it he declared: 'I wish that each man penally enslaved who is on the episcopal demesne be freed for my sake and my royal lord's.'[57] The subordinate clause perhaps indicates that there were others living on the bishop's private lands who had been penally enslaved. If so, he was interpreting the Synod's ruling rather narrowly.

Such is not the case with the will of Ælfwold, bishop of Crediton from 988 to 1008 x 1012.[58] He left what must have been a personal estate at Sandford in Devon to the monastery at Crediton, except for the penal slaves. These were presumably to be freed because he later directed that on the episcopal estates (which are not named) all penal slaves were to be freed. In addition he freed on the latter estates all slaves he himself had bought.[59] These slaves were probably not considered to be part of the regular inventory of the episcopal demesne and therefore could be employed as the bishop wished.

The will of Archbishop Ælfric (A.D. 1003 x 1004) does not appear to have been quite so generous with regard to ordinary slaves but he did direct that every

---

[56] See above, pp. 56 and 60.

[57] 'ic wille þæt man gefreoge ælcne witeþeowne mannan þe on þam biscoprice sie for hine and for his cynehlaford.' *Anglo-Saxon Wills*, §4 (ed. & transl. Whitelock p. 16.1–3 [text]); *ibid.*, p. 17 [translation]) (= Sawyer, *Anglo-Saxon Charters*, no. 1491).

[58] *The Crawford Collection of Early Charters and Documents*, §10 (ed. Napier & Stevenson, p. 23) (= Sawyer, *Anglo-Saxon Charters*, no. 1492).

[59] This supplements the evidence for an internal slave trade discussed above pp. 58 and 76–7.

penally enslaved man who was condemned in his time was to be liberated.[60] This provision was fully in line with the canon of 816. The will contains one highly significant provision, which, though it does not concern *witeþeowas*, provides a striking illustration of how status could become confused. From an estate at Dumbleton in Gloucestershire bequeathed by him to the abbey of Abingdon three hides were given to Ælfnoth for his lifetime together with ten oxen and two men, who were presumably ploughmen. To this latter grant Ælfric added a significant rider: 'and they are to be subject to the lordship to which the land belongs'.[61] As Ælfnoth was not permitted to alienate the land, the rider was probably added to prevent him from alienating the men and oxen as well. As such the men's legal position would not have changed; they would still have been slaves. But yet they had undergone a subtle social change vis à vis the society in general and Ælfnoth in particular: when Ælfnoth became their master they would not have belonged to him personally; they would instead have been bound to the *soil*. The legal powers that he would have held over them may still have been those of a master over his slaves *except* that he could not exercise the fundamental right that a slave-owner possessed over his property: that of alienating them. As far as Ælfnoth was concerned the men were no longer slaves but what we today would call serfs. Of course, when the abbey of Abingdon succeeded to the property, the community would technically have had the right to sell or release them but the new principle that Ælfric had introduced would probably have erased the memory of the old one; henceforward they would have been attached to the land, and their rights and obligations would have seemed to stem from their relationship to that land.

Admittedly not all the extant episcopal wills directed that slaves should be freed. The wills of both bishop Ælfric of Elmham (A.D. 1035 or 1037 x 1040)[62] and Bishop Æthelmær of Elmham (A.D. 1047 x 1070)[63] do not mention slaves. Possibly the synod's ruling was not universally observed. It is equally possible, however, that there were no slaves on their estates[64] or, alternatively, that if these bishops had acquired any penal slaves during their lifetime, they made a verbal provision for their release not embodied in the written document.

The Synod's ruling seems to have gained a currency in the course of the tenth century that extended beyond the confines of the ecclesiastical community, since by then one starts to find leading laymen releasing penally enslaved persons. The first lay will to contain such a provision is that of Ælfgifu dating from between

---

[60] *Anglo-Saxon Wills*, §18 (ed. & transl. Whitelock, p. 54.4–5) (= Sawyer, *Anglo-Saxon Charters*, no. 1488).

[61] '7 filgan hi þam lafordscype þe þ land to hyre.' *Anglo-Saxon Wills*, §18 (ed. & transl. Whitelock, p. 52.10) (text); *ibid.*, p. 53 (translation) (= Sawyer, *Anglo-Saxon Charters*, no. 1488). On ploughmen and the size of ploughteams see below, pp. 199–201.

[62] *Anglo-Saxon Wills*, §26 (ed. & transl. Whitelock, p. 70) (= Sawyer, *Anglo-Saxon Charters*, no. 1489).

[63] *Anglo-Saxon Wills*, §35 (ed. & transl. Whitelock, p. 93) (= Sawyer, *Anglo-Saxon Charters*, no. 1499). The date is that given by Hart, *The Early Charters of Eastern England*, p. 94, no. 136.

[64] In Domesday Book numerous estates do not report having any slaves, even in counties where they formed a high percentage of the recorded population. See below, p. 234 and n. 160.

966 and 975.[65] If not the divorced wife of Eadwig, Ælfgifu was certainly of royal descent.[66] She left an estate at Princes Risborough in Buckinghamshire to the Old Minster at Winchester except that 'at each village every penally enslaved man who was subject to her shall be freed'.[67] Another will of the same period (968 x 971) made by Ælfheah, ealdorman of Hampshire, directed that the penal slaves on the estates that he had granted to his friends were to be freed.[68] Finally, the will of Ætheling Æthelstan (A.D. 1014 x 1015) requested that 'every penally enslaved man whom I acquired in the course of jurisdiction be freed.'[69]

It was not only the freeing of penal slaves that began to be practised by the laity. In the eleventh century there is the same trend towards the testamentary manumission of *all* slaves on an estate that one finds in earlier episcopal wills. Wills where all slaves were freed include those of Siflæd (probably late tenth or eleventh century),[70] Wulfsige (A.D. 1022 x 1043),[71] Leofgifu (A.D. 1035 x 1044),[72] Thurketel of Palgrave (eleventh century, probably before 1038),[73] Thurstan's bequest (A.D. 1042 x 1043) and will (A.D. 1043 x 1045),[74] Edwin (the will cannot be dated with precision but Edwin was alive in 1066),[75] and Ketel (A.D. 1052 x 1066).[76]

Two wills did not go as far as these did: both Æthelflæd (A.D. 962 x 991 – probably post-975)[77] and Wulfgyth (A.D. 1046)[78] directed that half the men on

---

[65] *Anglo-Saxon Wills*, §8 (ed. & transl. Whitelock, p. 20) (= Sawyer, *Anglo-Saxon Charters*, no. 1484).

[66] See *Anglo-Saxon Wills*, ed. & transl. Whitelock, pp. 118–19. Cf. *Two of the Saxon Chronicles Parallel*, ed. Plummer, p. 113.24–5 (958 D).

[67] 'man freoge on ælcum tunæ ælne witæþæownæ mann þæ undær hiræ geþeowuð wæs.' *Anglo-Saxon Wills*, §8 (ed. & transl. Whitelock, p. 20.8–9) (text); *ibid.*, p. 21 (translation) (= Sawyer, *Anglo-Saxon Charters*, no. 1484).

[68] *Anglo-Saxon Wills*, §9 (ed. & transl. Whitelock, p. 24.6–8) (= Sawyer, *Anglo-Saxon Charters*, no. 1485).

[69] 'man gefreoge ælcne witefæstne mann þe ic on spræce ahte.' *Anglo-Saxon Wills*, §20 (ed. & transl. Whitelock, p. 56.14–15) (text); *ibid.*, p. 57 (translation) (= Sawyer, *Anglo-Saxon Charters*, no. 1503).

[70] *Anglo-Saxon Wills*, §§37–8 (ed. & transl. Whitelock, pp. 92.18 and 94.4–5) (= Sawyer, *Anglo-Saxon Charters*, no. 1525).

[71] *Anglo-Saxon Wills*, §27 (ed. & transl. Whitelock, p. 74.5) (= Sawyer, *Anglo-Saxon Charters*, no. 1537).

[72] *Anglo-Saxon Wills*, §29 (ed. & transl. Whitelock, p. 76.4–5) (= Sawyer, *Anglo-Saxon Charters*, no. 1521).

[73] *Anglo-Saxon Wills*, §24 (ed. & transl. Whitelock, p. 68.3 and 9) (= Sawyer, *Anglo-Saxon Charters*, no. 1527).

[74] *Anglo-Saxon Wills*, §§30 and 31 (ed. & transl. Whitelock, pp. 78.23 and 80.5, 9, 11, 18, and 21) (= Sawyer, *Anglo-Saxon Charters*, nos 1530 and 1531).

[75] *Anglo-Saxon Wills*, §33 (ed. & transl. Whitelock, p. 86.23–4) (= Sawyer, *Anglo-Saxon Charters*, no. 1516).

[76] *Anglo-Saxon Wills*, §34 (ed. & transl. Whitelock, p. 88.16) (= Sawyer, *Anglo-Saxon Charters*, no. 1519).

[77] *Anglo-Saxon Wills*, §14 (ed. & transl. Whitelock, p. 36.30–1) (= Sawyer, *Anglo-Saxon Charters*, no. 1494).

[78] *Anglo-Saxon Wills*, §32 (ed. & transl. Whitelock, p. 84.16–17) (= Sawyer, *Anglo-Saxon Charters*, no. 1535). Lowe's edition of the will based on the version of Register A at Canterbury Cathedral does not affect the discussion here: see 'A new edition of the will of Wulfgyth'.

their estates were to be freed. Ulf's will (A.D. 1042 x 1066) released thirty men on lands at Aston and Oxhey in Hertforshire, which he bequeathed to St Alban's.[79] The post-Conquest will of Eadnoth recorded in the Ramsey *Chronicon* also released half the men on his estate at *Acleia*, which was granted to Ramsey with a lifetime's usufruct both for the testator and, with respect to one virgate of the estate, also for 'his man', Leofwine.[80] In another post-Conquest will preserved in the *Chronicon* Æthelstan, Mann's son, left land at Chatteris in Cambridgeshire to Ramsey *cum dominio et hominibus* ('with the demesne and the men') but directed that of every thirty men, thirteen chosen by lot were to be manumitted.[81]

Several of these documents call for further comment. Leofgifu's will shows that slaves were involved in domestic as well as purely agricultural duties, and so supplements the information on servile occupations contained in Æthelgifu's will.[82] Both Thurstan's bequest to Christchurch of the land at Wimbish in Essex and Wulfgyth's will directed that the men were to be freed after the death of the immediate family, thus leaving to others any reorganisation of the estates that might have been needed after their manumission.

The will of Ketel contains an exceptionally interesting provision. After freeing the men on an estate at Stisted in Essex he directed: 'And I desire that all the men to whom I grant freedom shall have all things which are in their possession except the land.'[83] In other words, as slaves such men already were in control of property, including land, even if *de iure* they did not own it. The probable nature of this property is described in two other wills made by Thurketel of Palgrave and Siflæd. Thurketel declared of his lands at Palgrave and Whittingham in Suffolk: 'And all my men are to be free, and each is to have his homestead (*toft*) and his cow and his corn for food.'[84] As this stands this is ambiguous. It *could*

[79] *Codex Diplomaticus Aevi Saxonici*, §954 (ed. Kemble, IV.289.20–1) (= Sawyer, *Anglo-Saxon Charters*, no. 1532).

[80] *Chronicon Abbatiæ Rameseiensis*, §107 (ed. Macray, pp. 173–4). *Acleia* may be either Oakley in Bedfordshire or Oakley, a wood near St Ives in Huntingdonshire: see Sawyer, *Anglo-Saxon Charters*, no. 1231. The will is also printed in *Codex Diplomaticus Aevi Saxonici*, §919 (ed. Kemble, IV.257–8) and *Diplomatarium Anglicum Ævi Saxonici*, ed. Thorpe, pp. 585–6.

[81] '. . . per omnes terras suas de xxx hominibus numeratis xiii manumisit, quemadmodum eum sors docuit, ut in quadriuio positi pergerent quocunque uoluissent.' *Chronicon Abbatiæ Rameseiensis*, §33 (ed. Macray, p. 59). Cf. pp. 143–4 and n. 62 below.

[82] 'And ic wille þat alle mine men ben fre on hirde and on tune for me and for þo þe me bigeten.' ('And I desire that all my men shall be free, in the household, and on the estate, for my sake and for those who begot me.') *Anglo-Saxon Wills*, §29 (ed. & transl. Whitelock, p. 78.4–5) (text); *ibid.*, p. 77 (translation) (= Sawyer, *Anglo-Saxon Charters*, no. 1521).

[83] 'And ic wille þat alle þo men þe ic an fre þæt he habben alle þinge þe he vnder hande habben buten þat lond.' *Anglo-Saxon Wills*, §34 (ed. & transl. Whitelock, p. 88.22–3) (text); *ibid.*, p. 89 (translation) (= Sawyer, *Anglo-Saxon Charters*, no. 1519).

[84] 'and alle mine men fre, and ilk habbe his toft and his metecu 7 his metecorn.' *Anglo-Saxon Wills*, §24 (ed. & transl. Whitelock, p. 68.3–4) (text); *ibid.*, p. 69 (translation) (= Sawyer, *Anglo-Saxon Charters*, no. 1527). The toft was the enclosure in which a peasant's homestead was placed, behind which there might be a home field or croft. A good example of this settlement pattern is to be seen in the deserted village of Holworth, though it should be noted that it may date from a couple of centuries after the Norman Conquest: see Rahtz, 'Holworth, Medieval Village Excavation 1958', especially p. 130, fig. 3. An excavated toft at Holworth had interior dimensions of 32 x (at least) 24 metres, an adequate amount of space for fruit and

mean that on being released the men were to be given a toft, cow, etc. In the light of the early eleventh-century *Rectitudines singularum personarum* (possibly of Worcester provenance), it seems more likely that Thurketel was declaring that customary food-rations were to continue after the conferral of freedom. According to *Rectitudines*, §8 an *esne* (a term apparently used for a slave in the document) was entitled to 'twelve pounds of good corn and two carcasses of sheep and one good cow for food'.[85] One may reasonably assume, therefore, that Thurketel's men were also already occupying tofts; what the will did was to confer permanent possession of these tofts on them.

De facto ownership of tofts converted these slaves into what the Middlesex Domesday called *cotarii*. Of the 464 cottars listed in Middlesex, more than half had no land at all, and of the remainder, 49 possessed only the gardens attached to their cottages.[86] One may thus presume that many of the cottars in Domesday Book were also of slave origin.

Siflæd's will of the late tenth or early eleventh century shows the same process at work as in the wills of Ketel and Thurketel. Concerning her property at Marlingford in Norfolk she declared: 'and to my tenants (*landsethlen*) their homesteads as their own possession: and all my men [are to be] free.'[87] While it is not clear what the legal status of these *landsethlen* was – they could have been either slaves or freemen who had settled on the estate as labourers – they had their legal status improved by being granted permanent possession of the cottages, and all were declared legally free.

The wills of Ketel, Thurketel, and Siflæd afford us a precious insight into a significant shift in the structure of the society – nothing less than the creation of a new socio-economic class which today we might call 'serfs'. Formerly slaves, they were now deemed to be 'free', though the rights that this new status conferred were not defined. Clearly one of the rights granted in the three wills, however, was to be able to own immoveable property, but the corollary of this is that the testators obviously did not intend that the freedom given should enable their former slaves to seek a new lord elsewhere. The continued payment of food renders traditionally given to slaves implies that Thurketel wanted his newly freed men still to perform services on his estates. If the holdings of the Middle-

---

vegetables to be grown (see *ibid.*, p. 131, fig. 4). Further discussion of the terms can be found in *Deserted Medieval Villages*, edd. Beresford & Hurst, *passim*, and *Wharram: A Study of Settlement on the Yorkshire Wolds*, I, *Domestic Settlement, 1: Areas 10 and 6*, edd. Andrews & Milne, p. 23. Astill has brought these discussions into line with more recent views in 'Rural settlement: the toft and the croft', in *The Countryside of Medieval England*, edd. Astill & Grant, where he has made a strong case for a regional interpretation of English settlement forms. Pre-Conquest written sources are not of much help here and we shall have to depend on the future findings of archaeologists. On the toft see also below, pp. 175–6.

[85] 'XII pund godes cornes 7 II scipæteras 7 I god metecu.' *Rectitudines Singularum Personarum*, §8 (*Die Gesetze*, ed. Liebermann, I.449) (text); *English Historical Documents 1042–1189*, §172 (trans. Douglas & Greenaway, p. 877) (translation). See below, p. 176.

[86] See below, table XX (p. 226), and Lennard, 'The economic position of the bordars and cottars of Domesday Book'.

[87] 'and ic mine landsethlen here toftes to owen aihte 7 alle mine men fre.' *Anglo-Saxon Wills*, §38 (ed. & transl. Whitelock, p. 94.4–5) (text); *ibid.*, p. 95 (translation) (= Sawyer, *Anglo-Saxon Charters*, no. 1525).

sex cottars are any guide, the properties granted them would have been too small in general for them to have had any other choice but to work on their lord's lands.

The effect of wills such as these was, of course, to make the old tribal definitions of status irrelevant. An example of this process of change is to be seen in Thurketel's will, where he states: 'And [I grant] the moor about my part of which the monks and I contended, for freemen to use, as they did before, both before my death and after.'[88] The use of the word *fremannen* implies that the right to use the common land for the pasture of animals had been limited to men of free status. It is this sort of right that originally must have sharply distinguished a free tribesman from a slave, but with the conferral of free status by Thurketel on all his men the distinction became meaningless.

Thurketel Heyng's eleventh-century will, which probably dates from after 1020, also directed that slaves were to be manumitted. In it Thurketel declared: 'And my men are to be free, those who will work for it (?).'[89] The translation is Whitelock's. The form *ihernan*, which she translated as 'ask for', is a bit of a puzzle. She rejected the view that *ihernan* represents Early West Saxon *giernan*, 'to desire', 'to ask for', on the grounds that this does not give very plausible sense.[90] This depends on how one interprets the nature of the freedom given. If it meant primarily a change in legal status, then indeed the reading would seem implausible. But if the testator regarded it as primarily granting his men the right to move off the estate and choose another lord, then 'those who desire it' (namely, freedom) would seem a quite reasonable translation.

If one nevertheless accepts Whitelock's interpretation, there appear to be two ways in which slaves could have acquired this freedom. Thurketel Heyng may have imposed certain duties on them as a condition of their receiving their freedom (compare the women who were freed on condition that they sang the psalter for Æthelgifu and her husband).[91] Alternatively, they may have been given the opportunity to buy their freedom, perhaps through part-time earnings. Some of the manumission-documents that will be discussed in the next chapter may be the consequence of such a purchase of freedom.[92]

As has been seen from Æthelgifu's testament, wills could bequeath as well as manumit slaves. Further examples of where slaves were bequeathed appear in the will of ?*ca* 950 made by Wynflæd, who may have been a lay-abbess of Shaftesbury.[93] (Like Æthelgifu's will Wynflæd's was a tenth- rather than an eleventh-century document.) Her slaves were to be disposed of as follows:

---

[88] 'and þe mor þe ic 7 þo munekes soken ymbe min del fremannen to note so he er deden, er daye 7 after daye.' *Anglo-Saxon Wills*, §24 (ed. & transl. Whitelock, p. 68.16–18) (text); *ibid.*, p. 69 (translation) (= Sawyer, *Anglo-Saxon Charters*, no. 1527).

[89] 'and mine men fre þo it ihernen wellen.' *Anglo-Saxon Wills*, §25 (ed. & transl. Whitelock, p. 70.13) (text); *ibid.*, p. 71 (translation) (= Sawyer, *Anglo-Saxon Charters*, no. 1528).

[90] *Anglo-Saxon Wills*, ed. & transl. Whitelock, p. 181, note to line 13.

[91] See above, p. 115.

[92] See below, pp. 158–61.

[93] *Anglo-Saxon Wills*, §3 (ed. & transl. Whitelock, pp. 10–15) (= Sawyer, *Anglo-Saxon Charters*, no. 1539). For a map of her bequests to local minsters, see Blair, 'Introduction' in *Minsters and Parish Churches*, ed. Blair, p. 5, fig. 2.

(1) To her daughter, Æthelflæd, she bequeathed the estate at Ebbesborne Wake in Wiltshire with its men and stock (*yrfe*), except such as she might give from it for the good of her soul.

(2) At Charlton Horethorne in Dorset she also granted Æthelflæd the men and the stock 'except the freedmen'.[94]

(3) To Eadgifu she bequeathed a woman-weaver (*ane crencestran*) also called Eadgifu and Æthelgifu, a seamstress (*ane sem<estra>n*).

(4) Eadmær (probably her son) was required to pay her grandson, Eadwold, as much stock and as many men as had been bequeathed him at Avon in Wiltshire; in return Eadwold was to pay him what he wished.

(5) She granted to the community at Shaftesbury the estate at Chinnock in Somerset. She then continued: 'and she owns the stock and the men; this being so, she grants to the community the *geburas* who dwell on the rented land, and the slaves she grants to her son's daughter Eadgifu, and also the stock, except the gift for her soul which must be rendered to Yeovil, [Somerset]'.[95] Of the slaves, however, five were to go to Eadwold; in their place Eadgifu was to receive thirteen others.

(6) Finally, to Æthelflæd, Ealhhelm's daughter, she bequeathed Ælfhere's younger daughter.

A number of slaves were, however, manumitted in the will. These fall into three categories. Two women, Wulfwaru and <...>tthryth, Wynflæd freed unconditionally; each was permitted 'to serve whom she pleases'.[96] In contrast Wulfflæd was to be freed only if she served both Æthelflæd, Wynflæd's daughter, and Eadgifu, her grand-daughter. Here freedom excluded the choice of overlord. 'Freedom' in this context could only mean that Wulfflæd was able to negotiate her terms of service, and perhaps she also gained additional status at law. No apparent limit was placed on the freedom of a third group of twenty-six persons from the estates at Chinnock in Somerset, Charlton Horethorne in Dorset, Faccombe in Hampshire, and Coleshill in Berkshire. Their position differed from that of Wulfwaru, however, in that they were penal slaves belonging to Wynflæd.[97]

The fifth bequest of slaves cited above is perhaps the most illuminating part of the document. Time and again in the wills an estate is granted with its stock and its staff (*mid mete and mid mannum*), but it is never stated whether the persons

---

[94] 'b<ut>an þam freotmannon'. *Anglo-Saxon Wills*, §3 (ed. & transl. Whitelock, p. 10.12–13) (text); *ibid.*, p. 11 (translation) (= Sawyer, *Anglo-Saxon Charters*, no. 1539).

[95] '7 hio ah þæt yrfe 7 þa men þenne an hio þan hywum þara gebura þe on þam gafollande sittað 7 þera þeowra manna hio an hyre syna dehter Eadgyfe 7 þæs yrfes butan þam saulsceatte þe man to Gifle syllan sceal'. *Anglo-Saxon Wills*, §3 (ed. & transl. Whitelock, p. 12.26–9) (text); *ibid.*, p. 13 (translation; emended) (= Sawyer, *Anglo-Saxon Charters*, no. 1539).

[96] 'þam þe hyre leofo<st sy>'. *Anglo-Saxon Wills*, §3 (ed. & transl. Whitelock, p. 10.28) (text); *ibid.*, p. 11 (translation) (= Sawyer, *Anglo-Saxon Charters*, no. 1539).

[97] It should be noted that this implies the existence of private jurisdiction. See further below, p. 177.

are bond or free.[98] Only in this will is there an indication of their status. The text specifically declares that Wynflæd owns (*ah*) the men on the estate at Chinnock and that this category of men is inclusive not only of slaves but also 'þara gebura þe on þam gafollande sittað'. There is no evidence that *geburas* were slaves, although the *Rectitudines* and other sources seem to suggest that they were only on the next rung up in the social hierarchy.[99] What happened was that Wynflæd confused superiority and ownership: she did not *own* the *geburas*; she owned the land and was entitled to the rents that the land brought. Why then did she not grant to her daughter Æthelflæd the freedmen in the second section of her bequest? The answer is probably that the *geburas* still had a different relationship to Wynflæd from that held by the freedmen. The *geburas* were bound to the land; the *freotmenn* were bound to Wynflæd personally. When she granted land where the *geburas* were required to perform certain services, it was easy for her to consider that in some sense she owned these men.[100] In the case of the freedmen the relationship was a more personal one: she could release a slave from all obligations to herself (as in the case of Wulfwaru and <...>tthryth) or release the slave subject to certain conditions (as in the case of Wulfflæd, who had to serve her daughter and grand-daughter). The freedmen at Charlton Horethorne must originally have been slaves granted conditional freedom. We would probably not be far wrong if we believed that the conditions limiting their freedom lasted for Wynflæd's lifetime; after her death they would have been free to look for a new lord and hence she restrained her legatee from exercising power over them.

If this reconstruction is correct, one can understand how a confusion in status between slave and free could arise. A 'free' person such as *gebur*, who farmed a small acreage and in return owed many services to an overlord for it, would appear to be servile because of his intimate connexion with land which was not his and which he could not alienate. He was, in fact, becoming a serf. Nor was a freedman, whose relationship was a personal one with a lord, secure from slipping into the impersonal relationship of being bound to the land. Wynflæd's will sought to protect the freedmen at Charlton from subjection to her daughter, but if they subsequently negotiated to remain on the estate there, it would be easy for the belief to arise that they were permanently attached to the land rather than attached for a limited time to a lord.

Unfortunately there are few other references to freedmen in the wills. Twenty freedmen are mentioned in Wulfwaru's will but the document was probably directing that they be manumitted rather than granting rights over them to the legatee and so is unhelpful in this context.[101] An eleventh-century bequest concerning Wereham in Norfolk leaves 'þo men halffre þeowe 7 lisingar' to St

---

[98] *Anglo-Saxon Wills*, §§7, 10, 13, 15, and 17 (ed. & transl. Whitelock, pp. 18.20–1, 24.18, 32.6, 40.13, 48.12 and 50.4–5) (= Sawyer, *Anglo-Saxon Charters*, nos 1512, 1498, 1487, 1486, and 1536) For charters employing this formula, see below, p. 167, n. 12.

[99] See below, pp. 173–4.

[100] Although Wynflæd may have been confused over the nature of ownership, it is important to note that she still perceived that there were some differences between *geburas* and *þeowan menn*, for she referred to them separately and bequeathed them to different legatees.

[101] *Anglo-Saxon Wills*, §21 (ed. & transl. Whitelock, p. 64.23–4) (= Sawyer, *Anglo-Saxon Charters*, no. 1538). I am here following Whitelock's interpretation in *Anglo-Saxon Wills*, p. 165, note to line 9.

Edmund's Abbey.[102] If indeed *lisingar* are the same as *freotmenn*, one can see here the tendency to include freedmen in the class of serfs. The only other reference to *freotmenn* is ambiguous: Wulfgeat 'grants to God his burial fee, namely, one hide at Tardebigge [in Worcestershire], and one pound of pence, and twenty-six freedmen, for his soul'.[103] I am inclined to take this as a manumission clause (the document thus being a paraphrase of the manumission formula 'Wulfgeat freode X for godes lufe 7 his sawles alisednesse').[104] But if instead one assumes that the men were being given to a specific church, as the soul-scot and hide of land must have been, it suggests that once more freedmen were not being given the choice of an overlord but only the chance to negotiate new terms of service and receive additional legal status.

This investigation into the evidence of the wills permits one to draw a number of conclusions about slaves and the institution of slavery. In the first place, the wills point to a definite increase in the manumission of slaves in East Anglia in the eleventh century. Whereas ecclesiastics and laymen manumitted some penal slaves and others in a number of the tenth-century wills, *all* slaves were freed in virtually every eleventh-century East Anglian will that mentions them, as the following table shows:

TABLE IV: SLAVES FREED IN THE WILLS

K = *Codex Diplomaticus Aevi Saxonici*, ed. Kemble; N = *The Crawford Collection of Early Charters and Documents*, edd. Napier & Stevenson; W = *Anglo-Saxon Wills*, ed. & transl. Whitelock. All are followed by the relevant page and line numbers.

Name of testator	Number in Sawyer, Anglo-Saxon Charters, *and* edition	Date	All wite-þeowas freed	Slaves freed:		
				All	Proportion	Optional
Wynflæd	S 1539, W 12.9–11	?*ca* 950	x			
Bp Theodred	S 1526, W 2.17–18,22; 4.1,17,20,22	942 x 951		x	half	x
Bp Ælfsige	S 1491, W 16.1–3	955 x 958	x			
Ealdorman Ælfheah	S 1485, W 24.6–8	968 x 971	x			
Ælfgifu	S 1484, W 20.7–9	966 x 975	x			
Æthelgifu	S 1497	*ca* 990			approx. half	

---

[102] *Anglo-Saxon Wills*, §36 (ed. & transl. Whitelock, p. 92.11) (= Sawyer, *Anglo-Saxon Charters*, no. 1529). On the syntax of this phrase and the meaning of the term see below, appendix I, s.v. *healf-freoh* adj.

[103] 'geann ærest gode his sawelscættas, þ is I hid æt Tærdebicgan 7 I pund penega. 7 VI 7 twentig freotmonna for his sawle.' *Anglo-Saxon Wills*, §19 (ed. & transl. Whitelock, p. 54.8–9) (text); *ibid.*, p. 55 (translation) (= Sawyer, *Anglo-Saxon Charters*, no. 1534). For a map of his bequests to local minsters see Blair, 'Introduction' in *Minsters and Parish Churches*, ed. Blair, p. 5, fig. 2.

[104] See below, p. 141, n. 49.

Name of testator	Number in Sawyer, Anglo-Saxon Charters, *and* edition	Date	All witeþeowas freed	Slaves freed:		
				All	Proportion	Optional
Æthelflæd	S 1494, W 36.30–2	962 x 991			half	
Siflæd	S 1525, W 92.18;94.4–5	s. x^2 – xi	x			
Abp Ælfric	S 1488, W 54.4–5	1003 x 1004	x			
Bp Ælfwold	S 1492, N 23.3,28–9	1003 x 1012	x		all those bought	
Ætheling Æthelstan	S 1503, W 56.14–15	1015	x			
Thurketel Heyng	S 1528, W 70.13	prob. 1020 x	x			
Thurketel	S 1527, W 68.9	prob. x 1038	x			
Wulfsige	S 1537, W 74.5–6	1022 x 1043	x			
Leofgifu	S 1521, W 78.4–5	1035 x 1044	x			
Thurstan	S 1531, W 80.5,9,18	1043 x 1045	x			
Wulfgyth	S 1535, W 84.16–17	1042 x 1053			half	
Wulf	S 1532, K IV.289.20–1	1042 x 1066			30	
Edwin	S 1516, W 86.23–4	*ca* 1066	x			
Ketel	S 1519, W 88.25	1052 x 1066	x			
Æthelstan Mannson	–	1066 x			13/30	
Eadnoth	K IV.258.23–5	?	half			

The primary intention of the manumissions seems to have been to permit the erstwhile slaves to negotiate new terms of service. They might also have been allowed to move elsewhere, but this right could in practice be circumscribed, either because the slave was granted property that would tie him to the land or because his freedom was dependent on certain conditions being fulfilled. Because these grants of freedom operated only at the end of the testator's life, it is fair to say that the religious motive alleged in many of the wills was indeed the most important one. Economic considerations must, however, have played a part, particularly when large blocks of estates that collectively possessed the resources to support specialist artisans like goldsmiths were being broken up.

Slaves performed a wide range of domestic and agricultural roles on estates, from dairymaids to seamstresses and from priests to ploughmen. This diversity of occupation made it easy to regard the unfree and many of the free as a single group from a legal point of view because of their similar economic positions. Marriage between the free and unfree, for which there is some evidence, must also have helped foster this confusion. As the free were becoming economically tied to the land, it was possible for their lords to see them as in some sense 'owned' with the land. This relationship was different, however, from the earlier servile one: now persons were not tied to someone through his or her personal ownership of them but instead through their occupancy of the land, a change that becomes apparent in the wills from just after the year 1000.

V

'FOR THE SAKE OF HIS SOUL':
MANUMISSION-DOCUMENTS

Many of the wills discussed in the last chapter declared that on the testator's death slaves were to be manumitted. It is appropriate, therefore, to turn now to a group of approximately one hundred and twenty documents in Latin and Old English that in the main have the purpose of recording the bestowal of free status on various people. These documents vary in diplomatic form and, as will be seen, somewhat in purpose. As a class they are referred here to as 'manumission-documents' to distinguish the legal records from the act itself, for which the word 'manumission' is retained. The italicised form, *Manumission*, which is hallowed by usage (though sometimes inaccurate), has been retained when citing specific documents.[1] These texts are a rich source of information on slaves and their acquisition of freedom. The discussion of these records and the legal act that lay behind them can most conveniently be organised into four divisions. The first will examine the history of the practice of manumission in Roman and Germanic law, and will survey the evidence for manumission in Britain prior to Alfred's reign. This is a necessary prolegomenon to the second section, which will aim at elucidating what the manumission-documents record about the practice of freeing persons. A discussion of the nature of the 'freedom' conferred by the act of manumission will then follow. The chapter will conclude with an analysis of the evidence on downward social movement as recorded in the manumission-documents.

THE ROOTS OF THE ANGLO-SAXON CEREMONY OF MANUMISSION

MANUMISSION IN ROMAN LAW

The practice of manumission in England was shaped under the influence of two legal systems, the Roman and the Germanic.[2] Among the Roman forms, the most important in terms of later Anglo-Saxon practice was manumission that

---

[1] The term 'status document', employed by the Toronto *Dictionary of Old English* to describe these miscellaneous records, is in many ways a more appropriate compendious term to use; it has been retained for two lists of serfs and an associated document. All quotations from the *Manumissions* and *Status Documents* are based on my own readings and translations. For a concordance of the principal editions of these documents with the numbering system employed in this book and a list of the approximate dates of the acts see above, pp. xiii–xvi.

[2] For the influence of these two legal systems on mediaeval manumission see Fournier, *Essai sur les Formes*.

took place in a church, *manumissio in sacrosancta ecclesia*.[3] It is not germane to this study to go into the origins of this form, which probably lie in Greek religious custom.[4] What is relevant for us is its adoption into Roman law by Constantine the Great in a series of three regulating edicts.[5] The first edict has been lost, but the second of A.D. 316 and third of A.D. 321 survived to be included in the *Codex Justinianus*.[6]

The second edict laid down that a master might free his slave (1) in a Catholic church[7] (2) in the presence of the people (3) with the priests standing by, and (4) that he should make a documentary record of the proceedings; (5) bishops (to whom the edict was addressed) might, however, free their own slaves in any manner they wished provided their intention was clear. The third law decreed that (1) such a mode of manumission conveyed full Roman citizenship and that (2) slaves could be granted freedom by members of the clergy in a last will or through any form of words; such a grant of freedom would be effective immediately on publication of the will without the need for witnesses or intermediaries.[8] In 392 the Eastern Emperor Arcadius distinguished manumission from other public and private legal acts by not prohibiting it during the fifteen days of Easter, thus emphasising its religious character. Like the two edicts of Constantine, Arcadius's legislation was preserved by Justinian in his great codification compiled in the sixth century.[9]

For reasons that will become apparent shortly, it is worth reviewing the mature form of *manumissio in ecclesia* as it was practised in the early middle ages in Italy, the heart of the old Roman Empire. The legal ceremony seems to have consisted essentially of the following elements.[10] The manumittor presented himself at the church with his slave, accompanied by members of the laity who were to be witnesses there. Entering the building, he stopped before the altar (*ante cornu altaris*) and asked the bishop or senior clergyman of the church to lead his slave round the altar. This the cleric did, making three circuits of it with a candle in his hand, and presenting the slave in the course of this perambulation to a certain number of the clergy and laity. Meanwhile, the manumittor declared that the slave was thenceforth to be considered a free man and was to remain so, having open doors to go where he pleased because he had become a Roman citizen. The ceremony was completed by the drawing up of a document which

---

[3] The most thorough examination of this form in the late Roman and early mediaeval period is by Fabbrini, *La manumissio in ecclesia*; see also Mor, 'La "manumissio in ecclesia" '.

[4] See Mor, 'La "manumissio in ecclesia" ', 80–95.

[5] Sozomen in his *Ecclesiastica Historia* records that there were three laws. The first is presumably to be dated between A.D. 313 and 316. See Cassiodorus-Epiphanius, *Historia Ecclesiastica Tripartita*, I.9.20–1 (ed. Jacob, p. 29).

[6] *Codex Iustinianus*, I.13.1–2, in *Corpus Iuris Civilis*, 9th edn, ed. Krueger, II.67. The third edict is also recorded in *Codex Theodosianus*, IV.7.1, in *Theodosiani Libri XVI*, edd. Mommsen & Krueger, p. 179, conveniently translated in *The Theodosian Code*, transl. Pharr, pp. 87–8. See further, Mor, 'La "manumissio in ecclesia" ', 92–5.

[7] Presumably manumissions performed in a church belonging to Arians or any other group deemed to be heretical were not recognised as legally valid.

[8] This last provision applies *postremo iudicio*, which is somewhat ambiguous: it may be referring only to a death-bed wish. See Buckland, *The Roman Law of Slavery*, p. 451 and n. 1.

[9] *Codex Iustinianus*, III.12.7(8), in *Corpus Iuris Civilis*, ed. Krueger, II.27.

[10] Mor, 'La "manumissio in ecclesia" ', 140–1.

made some reference to Constantine's law; it declared that the slave was protected against any attempt to enslave him and laid down a penalty payable to the church in the event of such an attempt.[11]

The focus on the high altar as the place where a slave was to be freed in this form of manumission came to be extended in the mediaeval period, so that by the eleventh century in France custom had also sanctioned other holy places such as tombs of saints, for example, as being suitable locales for the freeing of slaves. A canon issued by the Council of Limoges in its second session in 1031 suggests that under the influence of Germanic legal practice a place of specifically ecclesiastical significance had ceased to be important in the act of manumission:

Then it always was the custom that whoever wanted to should give his slaves freedom before the altar of the Redeemer or the body of the blessed Martial. . . . Now concerning the freeing of slaves it must be said that it has been permissible to do this either at this place, or before the body of the blessed Martial, or at whatever church the lords should choose, or before the body of a deceased relative, just as we have often seen done in many cities; it was so no doubt in order that the appointed chancellor of that see should record the grant of freedom. For also we see that legal grants of freedom are made before the king at the royal palace or in whatever place the event occurred: indeed the Salic law contains [the provision] that wherever a slave's lord wishes he can release the slave.[12]

Another important Roman legal form was by will, *manumissio per testamentum*. For this type of manumission to be legally valid the legacy had to be expressed in imperative terms imposing a charge upon the testamentary heir. An alternative form that was available to a testator under the Empire was by *fideicommissum*.[13] This could be imposed upon anyone and was expressed in terms of a request. It has been described as 'In essence . . . a trust or confidence reposed upon a person's good faith'.[14] Although it did not have the formalism of the legacy, it was still governed by formal rules. For example, if the testator did not indicate which slave(s) out of a larger number he wanted freed and failed to direct the heir to choose, the gift was void.[15]

---

[11] The freed slave remained under the protection of the church, to which he gave an annual gift of a candle or a *denarius*, but this did not reflect in any way on his liberty. In general, freed slaves would be in need of a legal protector, and such a gift presumably betokened that the slave acknowledged that the Church had taken on this role. Anglo-Saxon law seems to have solved this problem rather differently by permitting the former owner of the slave to retain the ex-slave's *mund* or protection. See further below, p. 138.

[12] 'Denique semper fuit consuetudo, ut quicumque uoluerunt, sursum aut ante altare Redemptoris, aut ante corpus beati Martialis, seruos suos libertati darent. . . . Nunc de seruorum libertate dicendum, quia hanc agere licitum est, uel apud hanc sedem, uel ante corpus beati Martialis, uel ad quamcumque ecclesiam domini elegerint coram testibus, uel ante corpus defuncti proximi, sicut sæpe per plures ciuitates fieri uidemus: ita sane, ut huius sedis nominatiuus cancellarius libertatem scribat. Nam & apud regale palatium, uel in quocumque loco res fuerit, coram rege libertates legitimas fieri cernimus: immo lex Salica continet, ut ubicumque serui dominus uoluerit, potest seruum relaxare.' *Sacrorum Conciliorum Nova et Amplissima Collectio*, ed. Mansi, XIX, cols. 543–4.

[13] See Buckland, *The Roman Law of Slavery*, pp. 442–4, 460ff.

[14] Lee, *The Elements of Roman Law*, 4th edn, p. 242, §360.

[15] Buckland, *The Roman Law of Slavery*, p. 517. On the whole matter of manumission by fideicommissary gift see *ibid.*, chap. XXII, pp. 513–32.

Strictly speaking, a fideicommissary gift of liberty cannot be said to be a testamentary manumission since it had to be completed by a *fiduciarius* and was frequently performed *inter uiuos*.[16] But it is appropriate to consider such gifts under the heading of testamentary manumission since the *fiduciarius* was often directed to free persons in testaments and codicils, and under Justinian legacies and *fideicommissa* were in general merged.[17] Though distinct acts, manumission by *fideicommissa* contained in testaments and those made by legacy had a close relationship. Traces of both forms of testamentary manumission are to be found in Anglo-Saxon practice, though the rule that applied throughout the Empire that slaves could only be freed if they were named (*nominatim*)[18] was not operative.

Manumissions made in a church required a record to be kept, whereas those by *fideicommissum* did not. It was but a small step, of course, to keep a documentary record of fideicommissary manumissions as well (particularly as these acts may well have taken place in a church anyway). Several of the Anglo-Saxon manumission-documents record what appears to be the fulfilment of testamentary wishes.[19]

MANUMISSION IN GERMANIC LAW

Like the Roman *manumissio in ecclesia* Frankish, Bavarian, Burgundian, and Lombard law all knew modes of manumission that had as their basic feature the handing over 'by hand' (*per manum*) of the *manumissus* in the course of the ceremony.[20] Because of this common feature a fusion of the two legal traditions, Germanic and Roman, took place, as Fournier has convincingly demonstrated. An illuminating example of the co-existence of the Germanic and Roman modes occurs in a Lombard formula.[21] This explains that a form known as *manumissio per chartam* (because it involved a written document) had the same legal effect as both the Roman *manumissio in ecclesia* and an indigenous Lombard form described as taking place *in quadriuio* ('at the crossroads').[22]

---

[16] *Ibid.*, p. 513.

[17] *Loc. cit.*

[18] Though the law of 2 B.C. establishing this rule was abolished by Justinian, he retained the rule itself. See Buckland, *The Roman Law of Slavery*, pp. 546–8 and 556–7.

[19] Another late Roman form of manumission was *per chartam*. That this was not an influence on later Anglo-Saxon practice is, I think, sufficiently indicated by such diplomatically informal documents as *Manumission*, §§3.27, 3.32, etc. A capitulary of A.D. 803 specifically laid down that the *manumissor* and *manumissus* had to be present simultaneously during the drawing up of the manumission-document and that the signatures of the agents and witnesses were essential. The Anglo-Saxon manumission-documents all fail in one or more of these respects (notably in regard to the signatures). On *per chartam*, see Fournier, *Essai sur les formes*, pp. 82–7 and references there cited.

[20] See *ibid.*, p. 66.

[21] *Liber Legis Langobardorum Papiniensis*, ed. Boretius, in *Monumenta Germaniae Historica, Legum Tomus IIII*, ed. Pertz, pp. 596–7, no. 8. Cf. Fournier, *Essai sur les formes*, pp. 45ff.

[22] Probably the best known Lombard manumission-document mentioning *manumissio in quadriuio* is that quoted in translation without references by Bloch in 'How and why ancient slavery came to an end', in *Slavery and Serfdom in the Middle Ages*, transl. Beer, p. 17, and by Wallace-Hadrill in *The Barbarian West 400–1000*, 3rd edn, p. 60. It is unfortunate that Bloch must have used Troya's *Codice Diplomatico Longobardo*, §683 (IV.527), instead of

That this last form was well known to the Lombards is attested by clause 224 of the *Edict* promulgated in A.D. 643 by King Rothair. It also illustrates the ramifications of such a status change within the community:

On manumission. He who wishes to free his own man or woman slave shall have that right if it pleases him. He who wishes to make his slave folk-free and a stranger to himself, that is, legally independent (*haamund*), ought to do it thus. The lord shall first hand him over to the hand of another freeman and confirm it by formal action (*per gairthinx*). And the second man shall hand him over to a third in the same manner, and the third shall hand him over to a fourth. And this fourth man shall lead him to a place where four roads meet and give him arrow and whip, and say: 'From these four roads you are free to choose where you wish to go.' If the act is done thus, the former slave will then be legally independent and completely free. Afterwards his patron will not have the right to require any liability of him or of his children. And if he who is made legally independent dies without legal heirs, the king's fisc shall succeed him, not the patron or his heirs.

. . .

III. Likewise he who has been made folkfree and given the choice of four roads, and has not been made legally independent, that is, is not a stranger, shall live with his patron as with a brother or other related free Lombard: that is, if this one who was made folkfree does not leave legitimate sons or daughters when he dies, his patron shall succeed him, as is provided hereafter.[23]

This provision reveals that there was an awareness that manumission potentially involved three parties, the lord, his slave, and the community. A person who was completely free of his lord's legal protection was *(ha)amund*.[24] The first clause lays down how a slave could be granted full freedom both from his lord and by the community by means of customary modes, which are set out in detail.[25] The third clause describes a form of manumission whereby a lord could

---

Schiaparelli's *Codice Diplomatico Longobardo*, pp. 321–7, no. 112 (C text), at p. 325, since otherwise he would probably have been persuaded that the document is a forgery.

[23] '*De manomissionibus*. Si quis seruum suum proprium aut ancillam suam liberos dimittere uoluerit, sit licentia qualiter ei placuerit. Nam qui fulcfree, et a se extraneum, id est haamund, facere uoluerit, sic debit facere. Tradat eum prius in manu alteri homines liberi et per gairthinx ipsum confirmit; et ille secondus tradat in tertium in eodem modo, et tertius tradat in quartum. Et ipse quartus ducat in quadrubium, et thingit in gaida et gisil, et sic dicat: de quattuor uias ubi uolueris ambulare, liberam habeas potestatem. Si sic factum fuerit, tunc erit haamund, et ei manit certa libertas: postea nullam repetitionem patronus aduersus ipsum aut filius eius habeat potestatem requirendi. Et si sine heredes legetimus ipse qui haamund factus est, mortuus fuerit, curtis regia illi succidat, nam non patronus aut heredes patroni.

. . .

(III). Item qui fulcfree fecerit, et quattuor uias ei dederit et haamund a se, id est extraneum non fecerit, talem legem patronus cum ipso uiuat, tamquam si cum fratrem aut cum alio parente suo libero Langobardo: id est si filius aut filias legitimas, qui fulcfree factus est, non demiserit, patronus succidat, sicut supter scriptum est.' *Edictus Rothari*, §224 (ed. Bluhme), in *Monumenta Germaniae Historica, Legum Tomus IIII*, ed. Pertz, pp. 54–5 (text); *The Lombard Laws*, §224 (trans. Drew, p. 96) (translation; emended).

[24] This probably means that he was 'without (*[ha]a-*) protection (*mund*)', that is, not under the protective power of a lord. See further, Van der Rhee, *Die germanischen Wörter*, p. 27; on the forms of the word in the manuscripts see *ibid.*, pp. 26–7.

[25] The second clause dealing with freedom granted in the presence of the king is not relevant here.

retain his powers of protection over a slave while permitting the slave to become *fulcfree*. In both forms a private person would release his slave symbolically *in quadriuio* in order that he might become *fulcfree*.

In addition to taking place *in quadriuio* the Lombard ceremony also involved a solemn declaration *per gairethinx*[26] and the slave had to be handed over *per quartam manum* ('through four hands'). These last two elements could, however, easily be absorbed into the similar rituals observed in the *manumissio in ecclesia*. As the Lombard formula cited above shows, the two ceremonies were held to have the same legal force, and if transported to foreign soil it would be easy for these elements in the Germanic ritual to become contaminated by the ecclesiastical form of freeing, with only the symbolic release at the crossroads remaining distinctive.

Another symbolic act employed in Germanic practice is known as *manumissio per sagittam* ('by arrow').[27] The arrow did not confer freedom in itself but was part of the manumission ceremony. The ceremony is described by Paul the Deacon in his *Historia Langobardorum* as follows: 'Therefore the Lombards, . . . in order that they might increase the number of their warriors, confer liberty upon many whom they deliver from the yoke of bondage, and that the freedom of these may be regarded as established, they confirm it in their accustomed way by an arrow, uttering certain words of their country in confirmation of the fact.'[28] A law of the Ripuarian Franks implies that they too recognised arms as a symbol of a man's freedom: 'But if anyone afterwards alleges to the contrary that someone has sent him away free by an illegal act, that man may have recourse to defend this with his sword.'[29]

The Scandinavians, the second wave of Germanic people to invade England, had distinctive forms of manumission too, which, as has been mentioned earlier, they continued to observe on English soil.[30] Norse law recognised two levels of freedman status. In both forms full legal freedom could only be attained over a period of several generations subsequent to manumission.

Of the various Roman and Germanic ritual elements that were involved in the freeing of a person, the two that appear to have been most important in Anglo-Saxon England were manumission *in ecclesia* and *in quadriuio*.

---

[26] There is some doubt about the exact meaning of this word. Fournier's view (*Essai sur les formes*, p. 61) was that this was a solemn declaration of the intention to free a man, made before witnesses who acted as the guarantors of the act. Van der Rhee in *Die germanischen Wörter*, p. 68, has interpreted the word as originally referring to the assembly (= Old English *þing*) where the person being freed was provided with a spear (= Old English *gar*), which seems more plausible. Van der Rhee has discussed the various forms in which the word appears in the manuscripts in *ibid.*, pp. 67–70.

[27] Fournier, *Essai sur les formes*, pp. 59–60.

[28] 'Igitur Langobardi . . . ut bellatorum possint ampliare numerum, plures a seruili iugo ereptos ad libertatis statum perducunt. Utque rata eorum haberi possit ingenuitas, sanciunt more solito per sagittam, inmurmurantes nihilominus ob rei firmitatem quaedam patria uerba.' *Pauli Historia Langobardorum*, I.13 (edd. Bethmann & Waitz, p. 54) (text); *History of the Langobards by Pauli the Deacon*, trans. Foulke, p. 21 (translation; emended).

[29] 'Sed si quis in postmodum contrarius steterit et dixerit, quod eum quis inlicito ordine ingenuum dimisisset, ipse cum gladio suo hoc studeat defensare.' *Lex Ribuaria*, §60(57).2 (edd. Beyerle & Buchner, p. 108).

[30] Above, pp. 46 and 87–8; below, appendix I, s.v. *lising*.

THE HISTORY OF MANUMISSION IN BRITAIN PRIOR TO ALFRED'S REIGN

The appearance of a group called *lœtas* in the code of Æthelberht of Kent (A.D. 597 x 616) suggests that some of the Anglo-Saxons had an indigenous mode of manumission not unlike that practised by the Norse, in which freedom was conferred by means of a process of inter-generational status change.[31] The *lœtas* are not mentioned again, however, in Anglo-Saxon sources and the mode of manumission that gave rise to this group probably did not survive long after the christianisation of the country.

The earliest recorded manumission in Anglo-Saxon history took place some-time between 681 and 686 at Selsey in Sussex, where, according to Bede, Bishop Wilfrid released 250 people on the eighty-seven hides of land granted him by King Æthelwealh for the purpose of founding a monastery.[32] Though the passage contains some textual problems,[33] its overall thrust is clear: in virtue of the superiority over the land granted to him by the king, Wilfrid conferred free status on a substantial number of persons who had been slaves. Wilfrid may well have been motivated in his actions by practical as much as by religious considerations, and it is highly likely that the freed slaves still owed obligations to his new monastery at Selsey.[34]

The importance of this account is that it was recorded by Bede. Bede was widely read in England and his record of Wilfrid's action was thereby likely to help mould the attitudes towards slavery of the leaders in the society.[35] His account may, for instance, have influenced the bishops at the Synod of Chelsea in 816 to promulgate the canon that ordered all English men on episcopal estates enslaved during the lifetime of a bishop to be freed on the latter's death.[36]

Shortly after Wilfrid's mass freeing of slaves, manumission received formal

---

[31] For detailed evidence on this see below, appendix I, s.v. *lœt.*

[32] Bede, *Historia Ecclesiastica*, IV.13 (*Bede's Ecclesiastical History*, edd. & transl. Colgrave & Mynors, pp. 374 and 376).

[33] John, *Land Tenure in Early England*, pp. 12–15, and 'A note on Bede's use of "facultas" '. John's interpretation has not, in general, met with scholarly approval; Wallace-Hadrill's judgment in *Bede's 'Ecclesiastical History of the English People': A Historical Commentary*, p. 122, may be taken as representative: 'In particular, John's interpretation of Bede's "facultas" . . . must be questioned. I think "means" an adequate translation without reference to any technical sense derived from Roman Law.' See also Whitelock, [review of *Land Tenure*], 1009; and Grosjean, [review of *Land Tenure*].

[34] Although the freeing of slaves was a literary motif in a number of Merovingian Saints' Lives (on which see Pelteret, 'Slave raiding and slave trading', 104–5), Wilfrid here was more probably influenced by Irish practices learned at Lindisfarne than by his travels in Gaul. An estate staffed by slaves (in itself a rare piece of information about early Anglo-Saxon estate organisation) would have required considerable supervision. The freed slaves probably did not leave Selsey but became monastic tenants on the Irish model (known in the Irish secular laws as *manaig* or 'monks'), owing rent in kind and labour services, a relationship that would have demanded less oversight. On the *manach* see Hughes, *The Church in Early Irish Society*, pp. 136–7, and Charles-Edwards, 'The pastoral role of the church in the early Irish laws', in *Pastoral Care Before the Parish*, edd. Blair & Sharpe, p. 67. On Wilfrid see *Saint Wilfrid at Hexham*, ed. Kirby.

[35] On the Latin manuscripts see *Bede's Ecclesiastical History*, edd. Colgrave & Mynors, pp. xxxix–lxi and cf. above, p. 56 and n. 27.

[36] Above, p. 83 and n. 13.

legal sanction. The Kentish king, Wihtred, set out in clause 8 of his code of 695 a form of manumission that clearly is akin to the Roman *manumissio in ecclesia*. The clause states that those given freedom at the altar (*an wiofode freols gefe*) should be granted public rights (*folcfry*), but that their manumittor should retain certain rights in the former slave, viz., possession of his heritage (*erfe*) and wergeld, and guardianship over his family (*munde þare hine*). Apart from a variant form in much later Swedish law, only here and in Lombard law is the term 'folk-free' used.[37] When one remembers that Rothair's *Edict* permitted a master to retain his guardianship over a slave (though it also permitted the former slave to become *haamund*, that is, free from such guardianship), the retention of *mund* by the owner in Wihtred's law implies that there was a link between the two legal systems. This possibility is heightened by the existence of *manumissio in quadriuio*, which was practised by the Anglo-Saxons and Lombards alone among the Germanic peoples.[38]

This evidence suggests either that the two peoples shared a common legal tradition or that the Anglo-Saxons drew on Lombard legal practice. The latter seems more likely in view of the date and place of promulgation of the Anglo-Saxon legislation. No mention of manumission *per se* appears in the earlier Kentish codes of Æthelberht (A.D. 597 x 616) and Hlothhere and Eadric (A.D. 673 x 685). Nor does it occur in the West Saxon laws of Wihtred's contemporary, Ine (A.D. 688 x 694). As ecclesiastical manumission continued throughout the Anglo-Saxon period, it seems most unlikely that Alfred would have excluded from his new edition of these laws any such clauses from other codes had they existed. One may thus reasonably conclude that this is the moment of introduction into Anglo-Saxon law of ecclesiastical manumission. Its introduction was most likely a result of the increasing influence of the Church in the South-east, an outgrowth of the work of Theodore and Hadrian, who had come to Kent from Italy some twenty-five years before. In the light of these known links between Kent and Italy a direct borrowing from Lombard law seems entirely possible.[39]

The effect of this legislation was to give legal sanction to a pious act that had been traditionally advocated by the Church. Indeed the Church might well have fostered this. Manumission certainly continued to be practised in the following

---

[37] In addition to Rothair's *Edict* cited above, p. 135, it appears in the *Leges Liutprandi Regis*, §§9, 23, and 55 (ed. Bluhme, in *Monumenta Germaniae Historica, Legum Tomus IIII*, ed. Pertz, pp. 111, 118, and 129). The Old Swedish form is *folkfraels*. On *fulcfree* see Van der Rhee, *Die germanischen Wörte*, pp. 59–62 and further references cited on p. 60, n. 307; also Brunner, *Deutsche Rechtsgeschichte*, 2nd. edn, I.144, n. 50.

[38] For the relationship between the Lombards and other peoples in Italy see Wickham, *Early Medieval Italy*, pp. 64–79, especially pp. 69–70, for the close relationship between Lombard and Roman law.

[39] Margaret Deanesly discussed the cosmopolitan background of Theodore and Hadrian in *The Pre-Conquest Church in England*, 2nd edn, pp. 104–6. The closest parallel to the Anglo-Saxon practice that I have been able to find in sources other than Lombard ones is a formula in the *Formulae Salicae Merkelianae*, §13(b) (in *Formulae Merowingici et Karolini Aevi*, ed. Zeumer, p. 246): '. . . agat, pergat, portas apertas, ciues Romani, parte qua ambulare uoluerit in quattuor angulis terrae omni tempore uite suae licentiam habeat et faciat de semetipso quicquid uoluerit.' ('. . . may he, as a citizen in the territory of the Romans, have the freedom at all times in his life of doing, going, <having> open doors, wherever he wishes to walk in the four corners of the earth, and let him do with himself what he wills.')

century, as a curious letter of Boniface written to the abbess Eadburga of Thanet in 716 proves. In this letter Boniface related the vision of a monk of Wenlock.[40] His monastic informant had told him that he had seen the tormented soul of a fellow monk to whom he had administered the last rites. The monk's suffering had been brought about by the failure of his brother (*germanus*) to free a slave woman whom the two had held in common but whom the dying man had ordered to be released *pro anima eius* ('for the sake of his soul') in what was obviously a death-bed will. The manumission that the brother should have carried out would simply have been the consequence of this oral will. It is noteworthy that Boniface used the formula *pro anima eius*. This is appropriate to a pious death-bed action but is also a formula that frequently appears in the later manumission-documents. The story illustrates how the forms of the two legal acts of making a will and performing a manumission could come to be associated.[41] Boniface's account also reveals both that the importance of manumission as a religious act was firmly imprinted in the Anglo-Saxon mind by the early eighth century and that there was social pressure within the society to enforce such an act.

Thus, while there is little information on manumission in the seventh and eighth centuries, the evidence shows that there had been one act of manumission in which a substantial number of persons had been freed and which had been recorded in a source that was widely read; that a law had been promulgated which sanctioned such an act; and that there is some indication society believed these legal acts should be enforced.

In the following century King Alfred introduced a law permitting a slave to own property. This opened up the possibility that slaves could purchase their own freedom, although nowhere is this explicitly stated in his code. Interestingly enough, the earliest British record of a manumission exemplifies just this. Dating from A.D. 840, the document is not Anglo-Saxon in origin but Welsh. It appears amongst various legal records entered in the St Chad Gospels,[42] and as it is nearly a century older than the earliest extant Anglo-Saxon manumission-documents, it suggests the possibility that the English practice of recording manumissions in gospel books was borrowed from the Celts.[43]

This Welsh document records a grant of liberty not merely to the slave who

---

[40] *Die Briefe des Heiligen Bonifatius und Lullus*, §10 (ed. Tangl, p. 13.22ff.) Translated in *The Letters of Saint Boniface*, transl. Emerton, p. 30. P. Sims-Williams has made the letter much more intelligible by placing it in its religious and cultural context in his study, *Religion and Literature in Western England 600–800*, pp. 243–72.

[41] In Roman law, however, *manumissio in ecclesia mortis causa* and *manumissio testamento* were quite distinct, as Fabbrini pointed out in *La manumissio in ecclesia*, pp. 141–2 and 146–7.

[42] Edited by Evans in *The Text of the Book of Llan Dâv*, p. xlvi. The text is fairly accurate, but does contain a faulty reading as I have found from an examination of the original in Lichfield, Cathedral Library, St Chad Gospels.

[43] This suggestion is strengthened by Wendy Davies's argument that the form of many of the manumission-documents, such as those in the Bodmin Gospels, follows Celtic diplomatic practice, which was derived from late Roman vulgar law. This interpretation, presented in her paper, 'The Latin charter-tradition', in *Ireland in Early Mediaeval Europe*, edd. Whitelock *et al.*, pp. 258–80, merits further investigation.

purchased his freedom but also to his descendants in perpetuity, so the act apparently involved a legal change in status and not just the right to move from an estate. The purchase price seems high, particularly as it involves only a single person. It implies that in Welsh society in the mid-ninth century a slave could acquire money that was regarded as *de facto* his own. If this existed generally as a right among the Welsh, it would provide a possible source of influence on Alfred's apparently innovative legislation permitting a slave to keep the fruits of his spare-time labours or alms given him on Ember days.[44] One of Alfred's circle (and later his biographer), Asser, was a Welshman, and may even have been a relative of the Bishop Nobis listed as one of the witnesses in the St Chad manumission-document.[45] Asser thus could even have been the person who introduced these ideas into West-Saxon society.[46]

THE CEREMONY OF MANUMISSION IN THE ANGLO-SAXON MANUMISSION-DOCUMENTS

The preceding sketch has shown that the Anglo-Saxons were quick to adopt into their legal system the religious form of manumission sanctioned by Roman law. They did not remain isolated from the changes that this form of manumission underwent on the Continent, nor were they immune to the influence of modes of manumission practised there by other Germanic tribes. In keeping with Roman legal practice they made records of such acts and even extended this to cover acts that were not strictly-speaking manumissions at all. In general, reports of these acts were entered in gospel books, thereby both emphasising the religious character of the act of manumission and ensuring that the record of the ceremony was preserved.[47] The approximately one hundred and twenty surviving examples of this category of document range in date from 924 x 925 to the middle of the twelfth century. Apart from four records from the Durham area and two documents concerning serfs from Kent, they are all of south-western provenance, principally from the environs of Bodmin, Exeter, and Bath. They originally were recorded in nine manuscripts, with fifty manumission-documents appearing in the Bodmin Gospels alone; a further twenty-four are to be found in the Exeter Book and sixteen in the Leofric Missal (both associated with Exeter); fifteen are

---

[44] Alfred, §43 (Liebermann, *Gesetze*, I.78).

[45] *Asser's Life of King Alfred*, ed. Stevenson, new impression, p. lxxi and n. 3.

[46] On Asser see *Asser's 'Life of King Alfred'*, transl. Keynes & Lapidge, pp. 48–58.

[47] Davies has pointed out in 'The Latin charter-tradition' (in *Ireland in Early Mediaeval Europe*, edd. Whitelock *et al.*, p. 275): 'The act of transfer before witnesses had become increasingly more significant than an agreement to transfer property and Constantine had introduced legislation which insisted on the performance of the proper procedure and on the registration of transactions. Witnesses to past transactions might be recalled in cases of dispute. From the fourth century, therefore, both records and witnesses (and the recording of witnesses) acquired a new significance. . . .' The recording of the legal act with the names of the witnesses in a sacred book eliminated the problem felt in other jurisdictions of how to deal with disputes when the witnesses to the act had died (see *ibid.*, pp. 275–6): the sanctity of the book could bestow sanctity on the record and thereby ensure its veracity.

entered in Cambridge, Corpus Christi College, MSS. 140 and 111 from Bath.[48] The following is a characteristic example of one such record, a Bodmin document of A.D. 1075 x 1100:

Here is made known in this book that Alweald freed (*gefreode*) Hwatu for his soul at Padstow for his lifetime and after his lifetime, in the presence of Algar and Godric and Wulloth and Gryfyith and Bleythcuf and Solomon. And may he have the curse of God and St Petroc and all the saints of heaven who violates what has been done. Amen.[49]

After the initial notificatory formula in this text the name of the manumittor is stated, and then that of the person freed. The reason for the release and the place where the freeing took place is followed by a list of witnesses present at the ceremony. The document concludes with an anathema.

Some of the later documents record the purchase of freedom. An example is one of *ca* 1090 in the Leofric Missal:

Here is made known in this book that Æthelgifu 'the Good' released (*alysde*) Hig and Dunna and their progeny from Manegot for 13 mancuses. And Einulf the portreeve and Godric 'Buttock' took the toll in the presence of Manleof and Leofweard 'the Lame' and Leofwine, his brother, and Ælfric, son of Happ, and Sweinn the shieldmaker. And may he have God's curse who may ever reverse this, always into eternity. Amen.[50]

In addition to the replacement of the verb *gefreode*, a slight but important change, this document adds the price of the release and records the payment of toll.

[48] The manumission-documents are now to be found in the following manuscripts: Bern, Burgerbibliothek, MS. 671; Cambridge, Corpus Christi College, MSS. 140 + 111; Exeter, Cathedral Library, MS. 3501 (Exeter Book) + Cambridge, University Library, MS. Ii.2.11 (1744); London, British Library, MS. Royal 1.B.vii, MS. Additional 9381 (Bodmin Gospels), MS. Cotton Domitian vii (Durham *Liber Uitae*), MS. Cotton Tiberius B.v, volume I; and Oxford, Bodleian Library, MS. Bodley 579 (*S.C.* 2675) (Leofric Missal). The records in the burnt London, British Library, MS. Cotton Otho B.ix, are preserved in Oxford, Bodleian Library, MS. James 18 (*S.C.* 3855), pp. 42–3, and in Wanley, *Librorum Veterum Septentrionalium . . . Catalogus*, p. 238. Maidstone, Kent County Archives Office, DRc/R1 (*olim* Rochester, Cathedral Library, A.3.5) (*Textus Roffensis*) contains two status documents; MS. Cotton Tiberius B.v, volume I a third. For cross references to printed editions see 'Manumissions and Status Documents: Concordances with the Principal Editions' above, pp. xiii–xvi. The Bodmin records were discussed by Jenner in 'The manumissions in the Bodmin Gospels', and, with respect to the relative merits of Padstow as opposed to Bodmin for the performance of some of these acts, by Olson in *Early Celtic Monasteries in Cornwall*, pp. 71–2. The Exeter ones were examined by Förster in *The Exeter Book of Old English Poetry*, edd. Chambers *et al.*, pp. 44–54, and by Rose-Troup in 'Exeter manumissions and quittances'. See also Rowe, 'Anglo-Saxon manumissions'.

[49] 'Hær cyð on þyson bec þ Ælwold gefreode Hwatu far hys sawle a Petrocys stow a deg'y'e 7 æfter degye an Ælgerys gewytnisse 7 Godric 7 Wulloð 7 Gryfyið 7 Bleyðcuf 7 Salaman. 7 hebbe he Godes curs 7 Sanctus Petrocus 7 æalle welkynes sanctas, þe þ brece, ðæ ydon ys. Amen.' *Manumission*, §3.37.

[50] 'Her kyð on þisse bec þ Æilgyuu Gode alysde Hig 7 Dunna 7 heora ofspring æt Mangode to XIII mancson. 7 Æignulf portgerefa 7 Godric Gupa namon þ toll, on Manlefes gewittnisse 7 on Leowerdes Healta 7 on Leowines, his broþor, 7 on Ælfrices Map Happes 7 on Sweignis scyldwirhta. 7 hæbbe he Godes curs þe þis æfre undo á on ecnysse. Amen.' *Manumission*, §5.2.

These two documents show that there was wide variation both in the diplomatic form and in the formulas employed in this class of record. By examining the constituent elements of records like these we can deduce a great deal about the act of manumission. In the first four sections that follow we shall look at the mechanics of the ceremony, including the various forms of manumission, the formulas employed during the ceremony, the timing of the act, and the witnesses who were present. Sections 5 to 7 will centre on the motivations for the act. This primarily concerns the manumittors, who are examined first, but, as mentioned, some documents show that the unfree also sought to purchase freedom. From here we shall proceed to an examination of the cost of these releases and the toll that was paid.

1. MODES OF MANUMISSION RECORDED IN THE DOCUMENTS

A. *Manumissio in Ecclesia*

i. At the Altar.   The majority of the Bodmin manumission-documents declare that a person had been freed *super altare Sancti Petroci* 'on the altar of St Petroc' (or, in the Old English equivalent of this, *uppan St Petrocys wefode*).[51] This is not the same phraseology used in Continental manumission-documents. The prepositions *super*, *uppan*, and *æt* leave one in doubt as to whether the ritual of walking round the altar was followed.

The altar is not mentioned in the manumission-documents to be found in other manuscripts. However, since these documents usually list bishops and priests as witnesses and invoke in the anathema clause the name of the patron saint of the church in whose gospel book the record was entered (such as St Peter, St Mary, and St Cuthbert), it is reasonable to assume that many of the manumission ceremonies took place in a church at the altar.[52]

ii. At Other Sacred Places.   A few of the documents reveal that the manumission ceremony did not necessarily always take place at the high altar: it could be held in the presence of a saint's relics in a church,[53] at a relative's tomb,[54] or even in a newly-consecrated church *porticus*.[55]

Manumission over a saint's relics was a contemporary Continental practice, as the canon issued by the Council of Limoges shows. Initially, no doubt, the association with a saint was made because a reliquary containing his or her remains was associated with the high altar. It was a quite reasonable development, then, for the ceremony to be transferred to the saint's tomb or to another place in the church where the relics were kept. A further transfer to an especially sacred part of the church on the occasion of its consecration would be a natural extension of this, particularly in view of the large number of the faithful who would have gathered at the spot.

---

[51] Latin: *Manumission*, §§3.1–4, 3.7–8, 3.10–11, 3.14–21, 3.23–4, 3.26, 3.30–31, 3.34–6, 3.38–40, 3.42–4, 3.51; Old English: *Manumission*, §§3.29, 3.46, 3.47.

[52] A clear example of this is *Manumission*, §9.12.

[53] *Manumission*, §3.28: *on Petroc reliquias* ('on Petroc's relics').

[54] *Manumission*, §9.6: *ouer his fæder lic* ('over his father's body').

[55] *Manumission*, §9.19: St Mary's *portic*.

Yet another logical extension of this practice would be to have the ceremony wherever the relics of a highly-regarded person were to be found. There are two Anglo-Saxon manumission-documents that show that this did in fact happen. The first records how a woman was freed by Æthelflæd for her soul and that of her husband, Ealdorman Æthelweard, on the bell of St Petroc, a famous relic of the saint.[56] The second tells of the release of a woman and her family by Marh for king Eadwig *on his agen reliquias*.[57] In both instances the initial freeing was confirmed at St Petroc's Church (in one case, on St Petroc's relics). In the first manumission the woman's husband freed her in the church; in the second, it was apparently also some other party who was required to free the woman and her family at the church. There are three possible explanations for these double manumissions. One is that the practice of freeing on relics away from a church was a recent innovation without the full force of law. The second is that the release away from a church, although legal, would not have afforded the protection by the Church that manumission within a church would have.[58] The third possibility is that the documents were recording manumissions made by the testators (Æthelflæd and Marh respectively) *mortis causa*, that is, because of their impending death; these legal acts were subsequently confirmed publicly in fulfilment of the terms of the verbal will. This last possibility seems the most attractive.

B. *Manumissio in Quadriuio*

Four brief manumission-documents, one of which is only partly legible, record the freeing of persons at the crossroads. They are all entries in the Leofric Missal dating from between 1031 and 1050, and record manumissions that took place in Devon, at Okehampton and Boasley (both in Lifton Hundred), and at High Bray (in Shirwell Hundred).[59] A fifth document records that a release took place *on tune*, which may refer to a ceremony at a similar location.[60]

As these manumissions are of a south-western provenance one might assume that these are isolated records of a Celtic custom were it not for the Latin paraphrase of an Anglo-Saxon will of *ca* 986 preserved in the Ramsey *Chronicon*.[61] This will records that thirteen out of every thirty men chosen by lot were to be freed from estates at Chatteris and Wold, near Witchford in Cambridgeshire, 'so that placed at the crossroads they should go wherever they wished'.[62]

---

[56] *Manumission*, §3.21. On the bell see Doble, *The Saints of Cornwall*, IV.158.

[57] 'on his own relics' (*Manumission*, §3.28). Several interpretations of the phrase are possible. They could be relics owned by the manumittor, Marh, or the relics belonging to, or obtained by, King Eadwig. But it could also mean 'on his own remains', which would then indicate that the act took place after Eadwig's death in 959.

[58] But *Manumission*, §8.5 is the only example that hints that the Church might have taken on this obligation.

[59] *Manumission*, §§5.6, 5.9, 5.13, 5.15.

[60] *Manumission*, §3.25.

[61] *Chronicon Abbatiae Rameseiensis*, §33 (ed. Macray, p. 59). The document is no. 21 in Hart's *Early Charters of Eastern England*, pp. 29, 45, and 101–2. He has discussed it in detail in *The Danelaw*, pp. 613–23.

[62] 'ut in quadriuio positi pergerent quocunque uoluissent'. This is the only document that mentions the use of the lot (*sors*) in determining who was to be freed. Some of the wills

This proves that manumission at the crossroads was widespread, being found right across the southern half of England.[63]

Reichel suggested that the practice stemmed from the custom of erecting stone crosses at the intersection of roads.[64] These, he claimed, fulfilled the function of parish churches. He thus appears to have interpreted these documents as recording a form of *manumissio in ecclesia* without the *ecclesia*. But his theory seems weak on several grounds. Though crosses, in later times at least, were erected in the marketplace in the centre of a town, he cited no evidence to support his view that they were generally erected at crossroads. In any case, by the time these manumissions took place the main function of a cross had probably become that of a sepulchral monument.[65] By the eleventh century parish churches must have been on the increase; had the religious significance of the stone cross rather than the symbolism of the crossroads been the important factor in the ceremony, it would probably have been transferred to the local church by this time.

Warren's suggestion that this was a Continental borrowing, adopted from the Lombards, the only other Germanic people known to have practised the custom, is more plausible. Though the Lombards continued this custom until the twelfth century, the wide diffusion of the practice in southern England implies that it was unlikely to be a recent importation. Since Theodore and Hadrian may have been the source of the Lombard features evident in the form of manumission prescribed by Wihtred in his late seventh-century code of laws,[66] it seems not unreasonable to see *manumissio in quadriuio* as a Lombard feature that was also introduced through the agency of these men. This hypothesis gains support from the manuscripts of Rothair's edict of 643. Some of these manuscripts contain the word *fulcfree* but there are many more examples of variant forms of *fulfree* lacking the *c*. Van der Rhee has argued that this phonological change had taken place by the year 700.[67] If the Anglo-Saxon practice was borrowed from Lombard sources, the form of the Old English word implies that borrowing occurred

mention the freeing of a proportion of men without naming them (above, table IV), and it is possible that in this document lies the explanation of how they were chosen.

[63] It is a measure of the lack of interest shown by scholars in these documents that this practice has attracted so little attention. Kemble conjectured, on the basis of Continental evidence and the will of Æthelstan Mannesune, which freed slaves at Ramsey Abbey, that the custom existed in England but he overlooked, or was unaware of, the entries in the Leofric Missal (*The Saxons in England*, I.221–2). The latter documents were subsequently printed by Davidson, 'Some Anglo-Saxon boundaries', pp. 417–19. F. E. Warren quoted several of the documents from the Leofric Missal in verification of Kemble's conjecture in his edition, *The Leofric Missal*, p. lix. The Ramsey *Chronicon* document is mentioned in connexion with the Lombard practice but without further discussion by Grimm, *Deutsche Rechtsaltertümer*, 4th edn, edd. Heusler & Hübner, I.459. These appear to be the only references to the Anglo-Saxon practice in the secondary literature, apart from Reichel's observation cited in the following note.

[64] Reichel, 'The Devonshire "Domesday" ', p. 269, n. 32.

[65] Stone, *Sculpture in Britain: The Middle Ages*, 2nd edn, p. 10.

[66] Above, p. 138.

[67] Van der Rhee, *Die germanischen Wörter*, observes (p. 61): 'Wir müssen also annehmen, dass das Wort – während es um 643 noch allgemein gebräuchlich zu sein scheint – um 700 im Langobardischen zu *fulfrea* vereinfacht oder durch *fulfrea* ersetzt wurde.'

before the end of the seventh century since the cognate form in Old English is *folcfreo*. If the practice of freeing at the crossroads was indeed of this antiquity in England, it would explain why in the eleventh century the ceremony could be found as far apart as Okehampton in Devon and the environs of Ramsey Abbey in Huntingdonshire.[68]

2. THE FORMULAS USED IN MANUMISSION CEREMONIES

If there was a set text that was followed at manumission ceremonies, it does not survive. All that is extant is a Latin benediction for such a ceremony written in a tenth-century hand in Oxford, Bodleian Library, MS. Bodley 572 (*S.C.* 2026), fo 40r.[69] It is preceded by an early eleventh-century vernacular rubric 'Þær man freod ma<. . . . .>', and reads: 'per libertatem hominis istius quem liberemur in terris, libertatem suorum dona consequi percipere mereamur peccatorum.'[70] It seems likely, however, that the manumission-documents themselves preserve traces of the formulas used in manumission ceremonies.

Harmer has drawn attention to stylistic devices such as alliteration, rhyme, assonance, and parallelism in formulas used in Old English writs.[71] The employment of balanced phrases utilising these devices, while an ancient feature of the language, is particularly to be seen in the prose of the tenth and eleventh centuries. Traces of this practice are evident in a number of the manumission-

---

[68] Twelfth-century sources mention three further kinds of manumission, but it is unlikely that they were practised by the Anglo-Saxons and no manumission-document records them. The Roman *per portas apertas* ('through open doors') occurs in *Leges Henrici Primi*, §78.1 (ed. Downer, p. 242), a clause probably based on Continental sources. *Manumissio per arma* ('through arms') is referred to the same clause of the *Leges* and in *Willelmi Articuli Londoniis Retractati*, §15.1 (*Die Gesetze*, ed. Liebermann, I.491). The former source mentions it in connexion with the county and hundred, which might suggest that this mode was adapted from Continental sources for English purposes, but even if this was so, there is no evidence that it was a mode employed in the eleventh century. A late twelfth-century manumission which released a man in order that he might go on Richard I's crusade possibly employed this mode, but this is only conjecture and the document recording this appears, with its two companion pieces, to be unique (see Stenton, 'Early manumissions at Staunton, Nottinghamshire'). The third type, known by the German maxim '(Stadt)luft macht frei', conferred freedom on a man if he managed to remain for a year and a day in a town without being claimed back by his master. The earliest extant English regulation on the matter, the *Consuetudines* of the town of Newcastle-upon-Tyne in the reign of Henry I (1100–1135), conferred such a right on *rustici*, but this custumal was compiled in the time of Henry II (1155–1165). (It is printed in *Select Charters*, ed. Stubbs, 9th edn, rev. Davis, pp. 132–4.) Though this custom may have existed in the preceding century in a city such as London, it is only likely to have applied widely with the growth of urbanisation in the twelfth century.

[69] Ker, *Catalogue*, §313 (pp. 376–7).

[70] Rubric in *ibid.*, p. 377; text in *Councils*, edd. Haddan & Stubbs, I.697. The Latin text appears to be corrupt. *Mereatur* is an interlinear insertion. Haddan and Stubbs suggested *dona* represents *donator* (p. 698, n. *d*). A possible translation is: 'Through the freedom of that man whom we free on earth, may the giver deserve to finally attain freedom from his sins.' If correct, these words imply that the actual words of release were pronounced by someone other than the manumittor, presumably the officiating priest.

[71] *Anglo-Saxon Writs*, ed. & transl. Harmer, pp. 85–92. For a collection of such formulas, which does not, however, cite any of the examples given here, see Hoffmann, *Reimformeln im Westgermanischen*.

documents. Extended passages of rhythmical prose are not to be found (probably because of the numerous names) but several examples of two-stress phraseology occur. One example which also displays alliteration is *fryo 7 fœrewyrþe* (*Manumission*, §4.1) and frequently in the Exeter Book one finds *freoh 7 saccles*. An interesting example of the latter phrase used in association with several other two-stress phrases is found in *Manumission*, §9.11:

> Áluric hine clípaõ
> fréoh 7 sáccles
> á tune 7 óf tune
> for Gódes lúue.

A variant form of this phraseology occurs in *Manumission*, §9.9:

> Wíllelm de la Brúgere
> cwǽõ sáccles
> Wúlwærd õane wébba
> ínna tune 7 út of tune
> of élce cráfigge.

Another phrase that appears several times is *to cepe 7 to tolle* (*Manumission*, §§5.5, 9.14, 9.16). One late Bodmin document uses a phrase that also occurs in a number of Old English writs, *a degye 7 æfter degye* (*Manumission*, §3.37). In her discussion of the formulas of this kind that are to be found in other legal documents, Harmer concluded: 'It is reasonable to suppose that in such cases we have a record of the actual words spoken when the agreement in question was made verbally before witnesses.'[72] This conclusion would seem to be equally valid for the manumission formulas cited above.

The frequent mention of freedom, either in its verbal, adjectival, or nominal forms (*freode, freoh, freols*) makes it probable that one of these words was also used in the course of the ceremony. This is implied in *Manumission*, §1.1, where after declaring that King Æthelstan had 'freed' a man the record goes on to state in direct speech that he granted to the child what he had granted to the father. In the same document the use of the first person in the anathema indicates that it was also part of the manumission ceremony and not simply a standard formula entered by the scribe in the gospel book.

Another apparently direct statement is an imperative clause employed in an Exeter Book manumission-document: '7 let him ceosa hlaford, loc hwær hig wolde' (*Manumission*, §9.19). An indirect form of this appears in another document, *Manumission*, §9.22. As has been seen in chapter IV, this phrase can be traced right back to Alfred's will. It is probable, however, that the phrase was a later incorporation into the manumission ceremony when lordship had become more important than the tribal tie.

---

[72] *Anglo-Saxon Writs*, ed. & transl. Harmer, p. 87.

3. WHEN MANUMISSION CEREMONIES WERE HELD

While virtually all the manumission-documents lack a dating clause,[73] a few do record that the ceremony was associated with a church festival. At Bodmin two men were freed on the feast of St Michael, that is, on Michaelmas Day, 29 September (*Manumission*, §3.13), and a woman was freed on the vigil of the Advent (*Manumission*, §3.30). Several of the Leofric Missal manumissions are associated with the solstice: there were two separate manumissions that took place on the evening of Midsummer's Mass (*Manumission*, §§5.6, 5.15); another took place on Midsummer's Mass Day (*Manumission*, §5.14); a fourth was held three weeks before Midsummer (*Manumission*, §5.13); and yet another took place on Midwinter's Mass Day (*Manumission*, §5.12). Two manumission ceremonies were held on days that were not in themselves feast days but had a sacred significance locally: the one took place on the day that Bishop Osbern hallowed St Mary's *portic* (*Manumission*, §9.19) and the other when the remains of Bishops Osbern and Leofric were transferred from the Old Minster at Exeter to the New (*Manumission*, §9.12).[74]

Releasing a person on a feast day or on the occasion of a notable event would have had the advantage that there would be likely to be a congregation of people present and so the event could receive a maximum amount of publicity. But there may also have been another dimension present here. As already mentioned, Arcadius had sanctioned the manumission of persons during the most sacred period of the Church's calendar, the fifteen days of Easter. Manumission possibly thereby became associated with sacred events and the documents mentioned above may reflect this. Even if some of these documents are to be regarded as post-Anglo-Saxon quittances rather than true manumissions, *Manumission*, §3.13 (which dates from the time of Edgar or shortly thereafter) proves that it was not simply a post-Conquest custom.[75]

4. THE WITNESSES

Many of the documents give a list of the witnesses present at the ceremony. Again the influence of the Roman *manumissio in ecclesia* can be seen in that the documents frequently record that leading members of the clergy and laity were in attendance.[76] Thus in *Manumission*, §1.1, where King Æthelstan is the manumittor, a provost of an unknown congregation (*hired*)[77] and a reeve (presumably

---

[73] *Manumission*, §9.1 is dated, but it differs from all other documents in that it closely follows Continental forms. Davies, 'The Latin charter-tradition', in *Ireland in Early Mediaeval Europe*, edd. Whitelock *et al.*, p. 262, has pointed to the absence of a final dating clause as one of the distinctive features of Celtic charters.

[74] On the latter event see Rose-Troup, *The Consecration of the Norman Minster at Exeter*.

[75] See below, 'The rights conferred by manumission'.

[76] Cf. above, p. 132.

[77] Wanley, *Librorum Veterum Septentrionalium . . . Catalogus Historico-Criticus*, p. 181, declared that the gospel book in which this manumission-document once appeared (London, British Library, MS. Royal 1.B.vii) was 'olim, ut videtur, Ecclesiæ Christi Salvatoris in Cantuaria', but unfortunately he did not state on what evidence he based this assertion. Keynes has questioned the acription of the manuscript to Canterbury in 'King Athelstan's Books', in *Learning and Literature in Anglo-Saxon England*, edd. Lapidge & Gneuss, pp.

147

the king's reeve) are witnesses. Several record the presence of a bishop as a witness.[78] Sometimes, however, apart from the manumittor, only the clergy are noted as being present as witnesses.[79] It would appear that the number of witnesses was not important; documents mentioning only one, two, or three clerical witnesses[80] appear side by side with others mentioning all the clergy of a congregation.

The purpose of having the clergy present as witnesses was no doubt in part dictated by the need to ensure the veracity of the act, in addition to lending it religious significance. Rothair's *Edict* shows that the Germanic peoples were well aware that such an act required recognition by the community. The Anglo-Saxons were no exception to this, as is shown by some of the documents in which the members of hundred of the area are recorded as witnesses.[81] Unfortunately, little is known about the early hundred court but presumably freemen were required to attend it.[82] Their presence ensured that the freed person was recognised as now being one of their number. A more important reason, perhaps, was to ensure that those responsible for local law-keeping were aware that someone who had just been freed was moving about the district legally. This is most clearly suggested by *Manumission*, §5.16, where not merely the members of Wonford hundred at Holcombe were present at the ceremony but also those living at Exeter, some four miles away.

5. THE MANUMITTORS

A number of prominent persons act as manumittors in these documents, some of whom can be identified from other sources. The earliest Anglo-Saxon manu-mission-document (*Manumission*, §1.1) records King Æthelstan (924–939) as being the manumittor. The Bodmin documents associate every king from Edmund to Æthelred II with manumissions, with the exception of King Edward the Younger. Edmund (939–946) is a manumittor in three documents (*Manumission*, §§3.10–12). His successor, Eadred (949–955), is not mentioned as a manumittor but two documents (*Manumission*, §§3.25 and 3.36) recorded the release of persons for his soul. King Eadwig (955–959) is a manumittor in one document (*Manumission*, §4.1) and had persons released for his soul in another (*Manumission*, §3.49). Similarly Edgar (959–975) only released once (*Manumission*, §3.24) but is mentioned frequently in other documents (*Manumission*,

---

185–9; he has argued that the manuscript belonged instead to the king and that 'the *hired* mentioned in the manumission is perhaps more likely to be a reference to the royal household itself (or more particularly to its religious component), than to the community of some (unspecified) religious house' (p. 188).

[78] *Manumission*, §§3.16, 3.21, 3.42, 3.44, 3.50 (proof of status), 4.1, ?9.10, 9.12.

[79] *Manumission*, §§3.5–8, 3.10, 3.13–16, 3.19, 3.20, 3.25, 3.26, 3.28, 3.32, 3.34–6, ?3.38, 3.41–4, 3.46, 3.47, 3.49, 5.6, ?5.7, 5.8 (witnesses of document only), 5.10–12, 5.14, 5.15, 7.2, 7.4, 8.1 (buying out), 8.3, 8.6 (buying out), 8.14 (buying out).

[80] One present: *Manumission*, §§5.12, 8.7 (possibly not a priest); two present: *Manumission*, §§3.8, 3.23; three present: *Manumission*, §3.14.

[81] The hundred is mentioned in *Manumission*, §§9.5 (Alphington), 9.17 and 9.18 (Cowick Barton), 9.1 and 9.22 (Exeter), and 9.24 (Topsham).

[82] On the hundred and hundred court see Holdsworth, *A History of English Law*, 7th edn, rev. Goodhart & Hanbury, I.7–12, with references there cited.

§§3.6, 3.31, 3.39, 3.40, 3.42, 3.46, 3.47, and 3.49). Æthelred II (978 x 979–1016) is the manumittor in a single document (*Manumission*, §3.17). Whether the manumissions which mention that they were being performed for the king's soul were carried out on the king's orders, resulted from a royal testamentary manumission, or were at the behest of some other person (perhaps to get the king's support for the act) is not possible to say.

The clergy were also frequent manumittors. Wulfsige, bishop of Cornwall (959 x 963–x 963) released many (*Manumission*, §§3.3, 3.6, 3.15, 3.39, 3.40, 3.46, 3.47, and 3.49), though quite a few of these were for the soul of King Edgar. In *Manumission*, §3.15 the bishop is a co-manumittor with the clergy of St Petroc's, who are also manumittors in *Manumission*, §§3.13 and 3.36 (in the latter case, also for the soul of King Eadred). Several persons were also manumitted for the soul of Æthelgar, bishop of Crediton (934–953) (*Manumission*, §3.25). Beyond Cornwall, some were freed for John de Villula, bishop of Bath (1090–1122), and for the congregation of Bath (*Manumission*, §§8.4, 8.7), who were also remembered in a manumission (*Manumission*, §8.15) made by Abbot Ælsige (*ca* 1075–1087). In a special ceremony marking the transfer of the remains of Bishops Leofric and Osbern from the Old to the New Minster at Exeter, Bishop William Warelwast of Exeter (A.D. 1107 x 1137) freed a man for his own soul and those of the late bishops (*Manumission*, §9.12). Another Exeter ecclesiast, Ælfric the canon, is recorded as releasing a man from someone else (*Manumission*, §9.11). None of the episcopal manumissions is explicit enough, however, for one to be able to assert that the Synod of Chelsea's canon on the freeing of slaves on episcopal demesnes provided the motivation for the releases recorded.

A number of ealdormen and other officials are mentioned in the documents. Ordgar and his descendants appear several times as manumittors (*Manumission*, §§3.8, 3.16, and 5.8). There is a manumission for Ordgar (*Manumission*, §5.11) and several may have been performed by Ordgar II's wife (*Manumission*, §§5.9 and 5.13–15). Ealdorman Æthelweard and his wife, Æthelflæd, are manumittors in a single document (*Manumission*, §3.21). In one instance in the Bodmin Gospels persons were freed for a hundredman, Maccos (*Manumission*, §3.30); he is otherwise unknown except as a receiver of toll in another manumission (*Manumission*, §3.29). Aðelicc (that is, Alice), sister of Richard, sheriff of Devon (*Manumission*, §9.5), is known from other sources.[83]

Among the prominent people from whom releases were purchased were Abbot Ælsige and the congregation of Bath (*Manumission*, §§8.1, 8.2); John, bishop of Bath, and the congregation there (*Manumission*, §8.4); and Bishop Geoffrey of Coutances (*Manumission*, §9.20).[84]

Thus over a third of the documents record that the manumittors were persons of high social standing, including kings, bishops, and ealdormen. As the wealthiest and most powerful members of the society they could, of course, afford to free others and were able to ensure that such releases were recorded in

---

[83] See Rose-Troup, 'Exeter manumissions and quittances', 420 and 428–9.
[84] Ælfsige, abbot of St Peter's, Bath (x1075–1087); John, bishop of Wells (1088–1090) and subsequently of Bath (1090–1122); Geoffrey de Montbray, bishop of Coutances (1048–1093).

documentary form. What is significant, however, is that these people felt it necessary to manumit slaves in the first place. It is another indication of the powerful impulsion within the society from at least the tenth century on to free slaves, an impulsion that could only be reinforced by the example provided by such prominent persons.

6. THE REASONS FOR MANUMISSION

The primary reason stated in the documents for manumission is piety: like a litany phrases such as *pro anima sua* ('for the sake of his soul') run through the series of texts.[85] As Bloch has pointed out, there were undoubtedly other reasons hidden behind the standard formulas, but little can be said about these on the basis of the manumission-documents. The Church had had a long history of encouraging manumission as a pious act, as we have seen; the performance of the ceremony within a church and the recording of the event in a gospel book only served to emphasise this. There is no reason to doubt, therefore, that there was a measure of truth in the assertion that the act was done for the good of a person's soul. But this should be taken literally: it was primarily a self-interested act on the part of the manumittor and did not necessarily arise out of any humane considerations for the slave.[86]

Impending death can act as a powerful incentive to good works, and a number of the manumission-documents seem to illustrate this. For instance, the freeing of several people in a variety of places on Ordgar's behalf 'when he lay sick' (*Manumission*, §5.8) suggests this. Eadgifu, who may have been his wife,[87] also freed one person on his behalf (*Manumission*, §5.11) and was the manumittor in several other acts (*Manumission*, §§5.9, 5.13–15). All these might have been in fulfilment of a death-bed will by Ordgar, though this is not stated. And as has been suggested above, the two documents recording apparent 'double' manumissions (*Manumission*, §§3.28, 3.21) may be confirmations of grants of liberty bestowed by deathbed wills.[88]

In documents where a payment is recorded, release for the purpose of marriage may have been a motive. This might explain the freeing of Edith from an estate by Leofgar the baker (*Manumission*, §9.20), who is elsewhere mentioned as being her husband (*Manumission*, §9.8). Similarly, when Æthelsige removed his daughter and granddaughter from one family for the period of the bishop's lifetime and replaced them with other persons (*Status Document*, §2.2), it is possible that the daughter was to (re-)marry, and that instead of paying for her release he was arranging for others to join the estate. In both instances,

---

[85] Davies has noted that this is a Celtic formula used in Wales, the south-west of England, and Brittany; elsewhere the phrase 'is extremely common in all twelfth-century and later material but surprisingly rare before that' ('The Latin charter-tradition', in *Ireland in Early Mediaeval Europe*, edd. Whitelock *et al.*, p. 270).

[86] The freeing of men chosen by lot or of a proportion of unnamed persons, mentioned in n. 62 above, illustrates this.

[87] On Ordgar and his family see Finberg, 'The house of Ordgar and the foundation of Tavistock Abbey', and 'Childe's tomb', in *Lucerna*, pp. 186–203.

[88] See above, p. 143.

however, there is a strong possibility that these documents concern serfs rather than slaves.[89]

7. ASSOCIATED LEGAL TRANSACTIONS

A. *Transactions at the Church Door*

Two late eleventh-century documents included among the records in the Bodmin Gospels, *Manumission*, §§3.29 and 3.33, involve transactions at the church door. These texts throw an interesting sidelight on late eleventh-century legal practice and underline the true nature of the manumission ceremony. They are the earliest references in England to a well-attested practice of transacting legal business at a church door. It was there, for instance, that the legal aspects of marriage such as the handing over of the dower took place prior to the religious ceremony.[90] *Manumission*, §3.29 records two transactions. First, it tells of the purchase by one Æthelsige of a female slave, Ongynethel, and her son at the church door at Bodmin and the payment of an attendant toll. The two were then taken by Æthelsige to the altar and freed. The second record (*Manumission*, §3.33), though included among records of manumissions, is rather different in nature from them. The document states that one Putrael had made himself liable to compulsory enslavement by Ælfric. He then solicited the support of Boia, Ælfric's brother, who successfully negotiated with Ælfric. The deed records that he paid Ælfric and Boia in cash and kind, thereby ensuring that thenceforward he and his offspring would remain *freols 7 saccles*, a term which we shall return to when we come to consider the rights granted by manumission. The act took place before several priests, a deacon, a provost, and the bishop's steward, in addition to members of the laity. Like the sale of Ongynethel, this transaction was a purely legal one. Putrael was due to suffer a legal change in status, which he was able to avoid by means of a payment. No church ceremony is recorded as following. The purpose of engaging in the transaction outside a church would seem to have been twofold: first, it was a public place, so that the legal act would become well known, and second, it ensured that the act would be recorded in a gospel book, especially since there were priests in attendance.

These acts emphasise that manumission was regarded as a religious as well as a legal act. This is made clear in the case of Ongynethel: although she was bought at the church door, she was released *within* the church. It supports the contention that the features of Roman Law to be found in Anglo-Saxon England were transmitted there through ecclesiastical channels.[91]

---

[89] See further below, 'The rights conferred by manumission'.

[90] The best-known literary reference to this practice is in Chaucer's *Canterbury Tales*, where the Wife of Bath declares: 'Housbondes at chirche dore I have had fyve'. ('The Wife of Bath's Prologue', line 6; cf. 'General Prologue', line 460, in *The Riverside Chaucer*, ed. Benson, pp. 105 and 30.) On the practice, see Margulies, 'The marriages and the wealth of the Wife of Bath', 210–14.

[91] On Roman Law in England see Vinogradoff, 'Das Buchland', in *idem*, *The Collected Papers of Paul Vinogradoff*, I.168–91. See also his *Roman Law in Medieval Europe*, 2nd edn, rev. De Zulueta.

B. Payments Recorded in the Documents

Twenty-eight of the documents record a payment made in connexion with the release of a person. As a legal transaction without religious overtones, such an act would not have taken place in a church but at a place like the church door (*Manumission*, §3.29) or in a dwelling (*Manumission*, §9.15). It is important to recognise that, though these documents are recorded in gospel books and have much the same form as those recording acts of manumission, it cannot be assumed that a religious ceremony followed the legal transaction: none of the texts record any pious motive on the part of the manumittor, and the record concerning Ongynethel and her son (*Manumission*, §3.29) alone among the documents mentions that the freeing took place at the altar. As will be discussed in the section below on the rights conferred by manumission, at least some of these texts, therefore, should be viewed as quittance documents recording the release of serfs from an estate rather than recording a change in status from slave to freeman.

The documents provide the following information on the costs of purchasing person or of releasing someone from an estate:

TABLE V: DETAILS OF PAYMENTS RECORDED IN
THE MANUMISSION-DOCUMENTS

No.	Locality	Date	Manumittor(s)	Those manumitted or released	Nature of the Release	Cost
2.1	Great Bedwyn, Wilts.	925 x 950	Edwin granted Wynsige & Æthelnoth, his men, that they ...	Beorhtgyth (f)	moston a don ut	10 mancuses
2.2	Great Bedwyn, Wilts.	925 x 950	Edwin granted to her <Ecgwynn> that she ...	Ecgwynn (f)	moste a don ut of	10 mancuses of silver
8.9	?Bath	1061 x 1065	Wulfwine	Ælfgyth (f)	bohte æt	half a pound
8.10	?Bath	1061 x 1065	Æthelsige	Wynric	bohte æt	2 oras of gold ('mid anon yre golde')
8.8	?Bath	1065 x 1066	Æthelmær	Sæthryth (f)	bohte æt	3 mancuses
3.29	Bodmin, Cornwall	ca 1075	Æthelsige	Ongynethel (f) and her son, Gythiccael	bohte æt... 7 freode	half a pound and fourpence toll
8.1	Bath	1075 x 1087	Ælfwig	himself	hæfð geboht ut æt	2 pounds ('mid anon punde')
8.11	Bath	1075 x 1087	Leofnoth	himself and his offspring	hæfð geboht ut æt	5 oras & 12 sheep

152

No.	Locality	Date	Manumittor(s)	Those manumitted or released	Nature of the Release	Cost
8.13	?Bath	1075 x 1087	Æthelsige	Hildesige, his son	hæfð geboht ut æt	60 pence
8.14	North-stoke, Devon	1075 x 1087	Godwig	Leofgifu the *dæge* and her offspring	hæfð geboht æt	half a pound
9.20 9.8	?Bishop's Clyst, Devon	x 1093	Leofgar	Edith his wife	alisde ut æt	30 pence
5.2	?Devon	x 1097	Æthelgifu	Hig & Dunna & their offspring	alysde æt	13 mancuses
5.3	Cowick Barton, Devon	x 1097	Godwine	himself & his wife & his offspring	bohte æt	15 shillings
5.5	?Devon	x 1097	Eadgifu	Gladu	bohte æt... to cepe 7 to tolle	half a pound
5.16	Holcombe, Devon	x 1097	Brihtmær	himself & Ælfgifu, his wife, & their children & their offspring	hæfð geboht æt	2 pounds
9.14	?Cullompton, Devon	1072 x 1103	Teolling	Alweard & Eadwine, his brother	gebohte æt... to cepe 7 to tolle	7 mancuses
9.15	?Exeter	1072 x 1103	Leofwine & Ealdgyth, his wife	Ælfhild (f)	gebohton æt	64 pence
9.16	?Topsham, Devon	1072 x 1103	Wulfweard	Leofede	bohte æt... to cepe 7 to tolle	5 shillings
9.17	?Cowick Barton, Devon	1072 x 1103	Regenhere	Ælfgyth (f)	bohte at	5 shilling
9.18	Cowick Barton, Devon	1072 x 1103	Sæwine	himself	bohte at	10 shillings
9.21	?Exeter	1072 x 1103	Huscarl	himself	lisde wið	40 pence
9.22	St James Church in Heavitree, Devon	1072 x 1103	Leofwine	himself & his offspring	bohte æt	half a pound
9.23	?Exeter	1072 x 1103	Edith	herself & her offspring	bohte at	24 pence
9.24	Topsham, Devon	1072 x 1103	Eadmær	Leofhild, his kinswoman	hæfð alised ut of...at	24 pence

No.	Locality	Date	Manumittor(s)	Those manumitted or released	Nature of the Release	Cost
8.4	?Lyncombe, Somerset	1088 x 1122	Sæwine	Sideflæd (f)	hafuþ geboht ut æt	50 shillings & ? pence
8.5	?Bath	1088 x 1122	John	Gunnhildr (f)	hæfð geboht æt	half a pound
9.11	Exeter	1090 x 1133	Ælfric the canon of Exeter	Ragnaldr	alisde at	2 shillings

To interpret these figures it is necessary first to review the nature of Anglo-Saxon currency. At the time of the manumissions the pound was probably calculated as being equivalent to 240 pence or twenty shillings.[92] Eight mancuses and probably fifteen ores made up a pound;[93] if calculated in silver pence (the basic unit of currency), they were worth thirty and sixteen pence respectively. But as *Manumission*, §8.10 reminds one, these units of account could also represent a weight of gold, which may have had a value eleven times that of silver.[94]

The figures recorded in the documents vary widely, from two shillings to over fifty shillings. A quarter of them, however, give the cost of release as half a pound and several more put this at five shillings (that is, a quarter of a pound). The laws enable one to suggest what some of the bases of assessment were. For example, if it be assumed that the unknown number of pence in *Manumission*, §8.4 covered the cost of the toll (the text is defective at that point) the fifty shillings paid may have been the equivalent of a slave's wergeld: Ine, §23.3 states that the normal wergeld for a slave was sixty shillings but sometimes was fifty shillings. VI Æthelstan, §6.3 sets the compensation payable for a slave who had been stolen at half a pound. This appears to have been a fine, presumably levied to recompense the owner for the loss of the slave's services. It would be natural to estimate the cost to an owner of the release of a person as being equivalent to this, which would account for the frequency of this figure in the records. *Leges Henrici Primi*, §78.3 sets the manumission payment at thirty pence. There was only one transaction in which this was the sum paid (*Manumission*, §§9.8/9.20), but in three cases it was two shillings (*Manumission*, §§9.11, 9.23, and 9.24) and in one instance (*Manumission*, §9.21) forty pence.

The figures do seem to indicate that there was a reduction in the cost of release from the tenth to the twelfth centuries. This reflects the changing nature of social relationships over this period. As the *ceorlas* gradually came under the

---

[92] Liebermann argued (*Die Gesetze*, II.640, s.v. *Schilling*) that the shilling of twelve pennies was introduced between 1000 and 1066 in England.

[93] IV Æthelred, §9.2 (*Die Gesetze*, ed. Liebermann, I.236) gives the ratio as fifteen ores to the pound; *Leges Edwardi Confessoris*, §12.4 (*Die Gesetze*, ed. Liebermann, I.638) and *Leis Willelme*, §2.3ff. (*Die Gesetze*, ed. Liebermann, I.494) as twelve to the pound.

[94] On the ratio of gold to silver at various times in Anglo-Saxon history see Chadwick, *Studies on Anglo-Saxon Institutions*, pp. 47–51, 54–60, and 158–9.

control of manorial custom, so the number of persons seeking a release from an estate must have gone up. A *ceorl's* tribal status as a freeman would have made it difficult to assess the cost of such a release at the same amount as that of a slave. This would account for part of the wide disparity in the late eleventh-century figures: some of those released may have been *ceorlas* while others were slaves. At this time their tribal status would still have been remembered, even though this status was becoming increasingly irrelevant in economic terms.

Other factors are also likely to have been at play in this transitional period. Undoubtedly many of the sums paid must have been the result of negotiation and would have been based on economic factors such as the number of persons being released and their value to the estate, both in terms of their skills and the general availability of manpower. Personal factors such as the generosity or piety of the manorial overlords and the degree of friendship or distance that existed between them and the persons seeking their freedom would also have influenced the size of the payment. Manorial custom, which varied from estate to estate, would have been yet another factor in determining the amount paid. The high figure of ten mancuses paid at Great Bedwyn in Wiltshire in the early tenth century for what appears to be the release of a *gebur* and the low one of two shillings paid in the vicinity of Exeter in the late eleventh century are likely, therefore, to have been a consequence both of the date of the release and of local custom.

C. Toll

Toll was a tax on the sale of goods levied usually, but not exclusively, on behalf of the king.[95] Fourteen of the manumission-documents mention the payment of toll. All date from the eleventh century or later. Two of these appear to describe the purchase of slaves, one of whom was then released; eight seem to record the release of persons from estates; and four are ambiguous as to whether the act was the purchase of a slave or a release from an estate.[96]

As we have seen, the manumission-documents appear to change in function over time. From being a record of the change in status from slave to freeman they transmute into being an attestation of the release of a person from an estate. The same sort of shift seems to have taken place in the function of the toll. Originally toll would have been exacted on the sale of persons because they were negotiable assets like any other chattel. When a man bought his release from an estate, he was, in effect, buying himself, as the formula *bohte hine æt* ('bought himself from') shows. It was natural, then, to exact toll for this sort of transaction.

As toll was levied for a sale, there is no reason to believe that it was part of the manumission ceremony when an owner was granting someone liberty without there being any payment involved. Thus, the only Bodmin manumission-document to mention the payment of toll is the one already discussed recording the prior purchase of a woman at the church door for the purpose of manumission at the altar (*Manumission*, §3.29). Unfortunately, it is not possible to

---

[95] On toll see *Anglo-Saxon Writs*, ed. & transl. Harmer, pp. 76–8.

[96] *Manumission*, §§4.2 (purchase); 3.29 (purchase and release); 5.2, 5.3, 5.16, 9.7, 9.17, 9.18, 9.21, 9.22 (release); 5.5, 9.14–16 (ambiguous).

assess how frequently the latter purchase-and-manumission transaction occurred. Most of the rest of the Bodmin documents describe a grant of *manumissio in ecclesia* without recording any payment. One may legitimately assume that these transactions did not involve a monetary payment and so there was no reason for toll to be exacted.

Domesday Book, volume I, fo 26ra, declares that fourpence was the customary toll paid on the sale of a man in the town of Lewes in Sussex. This sum is also mentioned in the Bodmin document of *ca* 1075 already discussed, as is the case with an Exeter document of *ca* 1133, which appears to record a release from an estate (*Manumission*, §9.3). Presumably, therefore, this was a uniform tax payable throughout England for manumissions and quittances.

Toll appears to have been collected by the port reeve. He was the chief officer of a market town or trading centre (*port*). I Edward, §1 had ordered that commercial transactions had to be witnessed by him or other trustworthy witnesses. Eight of the manumission-documents report that toll was collected by this officer or someone acting on his behalf.[97] Four of the remaining documents mention that the toll was collected by the same man, Alfred 'Neck', and as he is recorded as doing this on the king's behalf, it is probable that he was also a port reeve.[98] In *Manumission*, §9.16 the receiver of toll is called simply 'reeve of Topsham' but this is likely to be the same sort of officer. Only in *Manumission*, §4.2 is toll reported to have been collected by someone other than a reeve: in this instance it was collected by a beadle, but the port reeve acted as a witness and it is possible that the beadle was his assistant.

THE RIGHTS CONFERRED BY MANUMISSION

The most difficult problem posed by the manumission-documents must now be faced: the nature of the rights conferred on those manumitted. Because of the regional variations that existed in Anglo-Saxon custom and law, it seems wisest to make the provenance of the documents the basis for this examination, since the records were written down at or near the place where the act was performed. We shall first examine the largest single group of manumission-documents. All of Cornish origin, they are entered in the Bodmin Gospels and are the only ones specifically to mention manumission at the altar. The next to be analysed will be the tenth-century records from Great Bedwyn and the eleventh-century ones from Bath. These deal mainly with the purchase of freedom, and appear to be records of quittances from estates rather than declarations of a change in tribal status. Having in mind the contrasting nature of the acts that these records preserve, we will then turn to the manumission-documents from Exeter, which have the longest chronological span of records from any one area and also display the greatest variation in their diplomatic formulas. Finally, a few other documents from the south-east and north of England will provide evidence that

---

[97] *Manumission*, §§3.29, 5.2, 5.5, 5.16, 9.7, 9.14, 9.21 (on behalf of the port reeve), 9.22.

[98] *Manumission*, §§5.3, 9.15, 9.17, 9.18.

manumission as practised in the south-west was also to be found elsewhere in England.

The fifty manumission-documents in the Bodmin Gospels recorded acts covering a time-span of over a hundred and fifty years. Thirty-three of them date from approximately 946 to 1000. *Manumission*, §§3.4, 3.7–9, 3.17–21, 3.27, 3.35, 3.38, 3.41, and 3.51 are from the end of the tenth or the first quarter of the eleventh century and *Manumission*, §§3.29, 3.30, and 3.33 date from the last quarter of the eleventh century. Though these records were entered in the gospel book over a long period of time, there is a considerable measure of uniformity in the formulas employed. Most of them declare, 'Haec sunt nomina illorum hominum quos liberauit X' ('These are the names of those men whom X freed'), or more simply *X liberauit Y* ('X freed Y'). Many go on to state that this was done *super altare Sancti Petroci* ('on the altar of St Petroc') and also frequently contain a movent clause such as *pro anima sua* ('for his soul'). The Old English equivalent of the Latin formulas is 'þes sint þa menn X freode . . . for hys sawle . . . on Petrocys wefode'. Both the Latin and Old English formulas are to be found throughout the period that these records were kept.

The use of the phrase *super altare Sancti Petroci*, recording as it does a formal act of *manumissio in ecclesia*, suggests that the verb *liberare* used in these documents must have the sense 'to confer the status of a free person on some-one'. One may conclude from these records that the legal status of 'slave' continued to be recognised throughout the eleventh century in the Bodmin area. Two records in the Bodmin Gospels that are rather different from the rest of the manumission-documents verify this. The first is the report of the purchase at the church door and subsequent freeing of Ongynethel and her son (*Manumission*, §3.29) and the second (*Manumission*, §3.33) the settlement in which Putrael managed to prevent his own compulsory enslavement (with the words *þeowian*, 'to enslave', and *nydþeowetling*, 'one who is compulsorily enslaved', being used). Both are late eleventh-century documents and leave no doubt that the legal status of a slave is being referred to.

It must not be thought, however, that freemen in the Bodmin area were immune from the socio-economic forces operating elsewhere in England. As early as 959 x 975 a group of men found it necessary to have entered in the Bodmin Gospels a report of their successful defence against the 'accusation of evil men' (*accussatione malorum*) that they were descendants of *coloni* or serfs of the king (*Manumission*, §3.50). This status was clearly disadvantageous enough for them to want it to be publicly declared that they did not fall into this category.[99] Some light is thrown on what was at stake by two entries made in the early to mid-tenth century in a gospel book now to be found in Bern (*Manumission*, §§2.1 and 2.2). These record the permission granted to two women to leave the *geburland* on which they were living in Great Bedwyn (Wiltshire). The verb used is *gedon ut*, and they give the recipients the right to be *færfrige*. It is quite clear from analogous linguistic forms that *geburland* means 'land occupied by *geburas*'.[100] According to the *Rectitudines*, *geburas* were not slaves but they

---

[99] This document is discussed in more detail below, pp. 182–3.
[100] Toller, *Supplement*, p. 393, col. 2, s.v. *geref-land*; Campbell, *Enlarged Addenda and Corrigenda*, p. 61, col. 1, s.v. *þegnland*.

did owe regular and heavy services for the land they held. In terms of the tribal laws, however, they could only have fallen into the general category of *ceorl* and so were legally free. On the other hand, in terms of the manorial economy they are best described as serfs. The right of being *færfrige*, when read in conjunction with the verb *don ut*, can only mean 'free (that is, with the right) to go'. The Bedwyn documents should thus be read as records of quittances. They do not attest the bestowal of a new status on the persons concerned but merely declare that they have been granted permission to leave an estate and go elsewhere.[101]

These documents verify the conclusions drawn from the passage on the Vulsinienses in the Alfredian *Orosius*.[102] They show that in the first half of the tenth century there were persons who were not slaves but who nevertheless had to get permission to leave an estate. The seeds of confusion between the two types of free status were already present. Those leaving were declared to be 'free', though the epithet was qualified by the prefix *fær-*. What is more, the act was performed in the presence of the clergy (though there is no indication that it took place in a church), and was recorded in a gospel book just like the manumission of slaves would have been. The diplomatic form employed differed from the record of the freeing of a slave only in its mention of the payment made for the release and in the absence of a movent clause.

The similarity in the recording of manumissions and quittances leads to some ambiguity of interpretation when one turns to a Bath gospel book of a century later. Now divided into two manuscripts, Cambridge, Corpus Christi College, MSS. 140 + 111, this gospel book contains fifteen documents, ranging in date from *ca* 1065 to 1090 (and possibly, in three instances, as late as 1122).[103] The three earliest documents, *Manumission*, §§8.8–10, record the purchase of persons from the abbot. All three use the formula *bohte æt* ('bought from'), and all mention a payment made to the abbot. There is no reason to believe that these record the manumission of the persons bought: *Manumission* §8.8, in fact, specifies that the person who was purchased should only be freed after the death of the purchaser and his wife. One may conclude, therefore, that these three documents simply record the buying of slaves, one of whom was to be permitted to change her legal status and become free (*beo . . . freoh*) on the death of her owner.

At least one other Bath document seems to be a record of a purchase. *Manumission*, §8.5 declares that John (de Villula, bishop of Wells and subsequently Bath) had bought a woman and entrusted her (*hi betæht*) to the monastery of St Peter's at Bath. Whether she lost her slave status in the course of this transaction cannot be said.

Two further documents, *Manumission*, §§8.2 and 8.4, employ the *bohte æt* formula, but they add the phrase *to ecum freote* ('to eternal freedom'). They may

---

[101] Pelteret, 'The *coliberti* of Domesday Book', 48.

[102] See above, pp. 55–6.

[103] *Manumission*, §§8.4, 8.5, and 8.7 mention John de Villula, who was bishop of Wells from 1088 to 1090. He then moved his see to Wells, where he remained bishop until 1122. The document may thus be as early as 1088 or as late as 1122, but since the *hired* at Bath were recorded as being present, the acts presumably took place in Bath at much the same time as the other Bath acts, in other words, in the early 1090s.

thus be viewed as recording either a quittance from an estate or the manumission of a slave. In the first document the freedom of a woman and her children is bought by her father, which may incline one to believe that he was seeking to change their status rather than enable them to leave their estate. In the second, which also concerns a woman and children, the purchase price is half a pound, which as has been pointed out above is a sum associated with a slave.[104]

The phrase *to ecum freote* occurs in several other Bath documents. In *Manumission*, §8.3 it appears to refer to free legal status as the verb used is *synd gefreod* and the document contains the movent clause *for Ælsiges abbodes sawle* ('for Abbot Ælfsige's soul'). It does not state that the freeing was done in church but the witnesses to the act were the ecclesiastical congregation (*hired*). Yet the phrase is also used in association with the verbal phrase *bohte ut æt* ('bought out from') in *Manumission*, §§8.1, 8.4, and 8.13. Now it could be argued that these were slaves purchasing their free status for the purpose of leaving the estate. But two other documents, *Manumission*, §§8.11 and 8.10, make this very unlikely as they record a purchase price in the one case of two gold ores and in the other of five ores and twelve sheep. These amounts make it far more likely that they were serfs working their own lands which gave them the resources to pay these sums. Another apparent quittance is *Manumission*, §8.6, which uses the same phrase *hæfþ gedon ut* as the Bedwyn documents of a century earlier.

The Bath records seems to mark a truly transitional phase in the society. They use the same overall diplomatic form and very similar phraseology to record both manumissions and quittances. There was still an awareness on the part of the overlords that there was some difference between slaves and serfs, but it was deemed appropriate to use the same form of documentation to record their respective changes in status and it was also felt to be acceptable to use the word *freot* ('freedom') to describe both the legal status of a free person and the right to leave an estate. But in the course of time as slaves became fewer in number it must obviously have been freedom of movement that became the more important concept.

Exeter provides a very varied group of documents covering the longest time-span of any centre, from 955 x 959 to 1143. The earliest of these, *Manumission*, §4.1, declares that King Eadwig ordered a churchwarden to free a man (*het gefreon*). The grant conferred the right to be *fryo 7 færewyrþe*. *Færewyrþe* does not appear elsewhere, but on the analogy of similar formations it seems to mean 'having the legal right to go (?from an estate)'. As this is a right given *in addition* to that of being 'free' it does not seem satisfactory to interpret this as a quittance like the contemporary Bedwyn documents, where the word *færfrige* appears. The use of the verb *gefreon* and the presence of the bishop and the ecclesiastical congregation at Exeter suggests rather that it records the granting of legal freedom to a slave. If this is correct, it is another confirmation that by the tenth century the act of freeing was viewed as having two components: that of conferring a new legal status (*freoh*) and that of granting permission to move away (*færewyrþe*). Both components could be operative in a grant of freedom but it was not necessary for both to apply.

---

[104] See above, p. 154.

The next group of Exeter manumission-documents dates from 1030 x 1050. The records are to be found in the Leofric Missal (*Manumission*, §§5.6–15). All use the verb *freode* and four of them mention that the freeing was done at the crossroads. Given the historical background to freeing at such a spot, these documents must record an act involving a legal status-change from slave to freeman. The verb *freode* is used in the same sense in *Manumission*, §5.1, a record entered some time after 1046 in the Missal. This mentions that before manumission the woman had been bought and toll had been paid, as in *Manumission*, §3.29. The anathema clause invokes a curse against any who would enslave her (*gebywie*), which implies that she had been a slave.

As is the case with the Bath documents, the Exeter texts also record quittances from estates. The earliest one dates from 1042 x 1066 (though it was entered somewhat later), when a man released himself, his wife and child(ren) out of the estate at Topsham in Devon from Hunewine ('lysde . . . æt Hunewine . . . ut of Toppeshamlande'). The same formula appears in a number of other Exeter Book documents from late in the same century (*Manumission*, §§9.8, 9.11, 9.20, 9.21, and 9.24). Two of the latest documents in the Leofric Missal (*Manumission*, §§5.5 and 5.16) and a number of the Exeter Book documents (*Manumission*, §§9.7, 9.13–18, 9.22, and 9.23) use the verb *bohte æt*, where the purchasers are often buying their own freedom. *Manumission*, §§9.7 and 9.13 mention the estate from which the purchaser was buying himself and *Manumission*, §9.22 adds the highly significant phrase 'to ceosende him hlaford 7 his ofspring swa hwær swa hig woldon' ('to choose for himself a lord and his offspring wherever they wish'). In all these cases the most reasonable explanation is that they record the release of serfs from an estate.

Several of the documents from late in the eleventh century introduce a new phrase, *freoh and sacles* (*Manumission*, §§9.7, 9.11–13, and 9.17), and several more use the phrase *sacles . . . of elcre craurigge* (*Manumission*, §§9.2, 9.5, and 9.9)[105] or just the word *sacles* (*Manumission*, §§9.3 and 9.4). Two documents, *Manumission*, §§3.33 and 9.8, give some indication of the meaning of *sacles of elcre craurigge*. When Putrael made a settlement with Ælfric releasing him from the threat of enslavement, he was declared to be 'æfre freols 7 saccles fram þam dæge wið Ælfrice . . .' ('forever free and *sacles* from that day from Ælfric . . .'). In another legal suit Hubert is stated to have *cræfede . . . mid unrihte* Leofgar's wife, whom Leofgar had *alysde ut at Gosfreige bisceope*, a fact attested in another document, *Manumission*, §9.20, where she is declared to have been 'alysde . . . ut . . . æfre ma freoh 7 saccles'. When read in combination, it appears that *cræfede* must mean 'laid legal claim to' and that *sacles* must mean something like 'free from any legal obligation'.[106]

Such a phrase as *freoh and sacles* would then be particularly appropriate in the case of someone seeking a release from an estate. In most instances where the phrase appears, it looks as if the majority of those seeking their release were serfs. But there is some indication that the phrase could also be used of a slave. In June 1133, when the remains of Bishops Leofric and Osbern were moved to

---

[105] *Craurigge*, following Celtic orthographic practice, has 'gg' for Old English [ŋg].

[106] On *sac* see *Anglo-Saxon Writs*, ed. & transl. Harmer, pp. 74–6.

the New Minster at Exeter at the time of its consecration, Bishop William of Exeter freed (*freode*) Wulfric 'Pig' 'for the love of God and St Mary and all Christ's saints and for the bishops' souls and for the redemption of his (own) soul' (*Manumission*, §9.12).[107] Late though this be, it appears to be a record of the old ceremony of the manumitting a slave.

There are two other late examples of such a manumission. In *Manumission*, §9.19, on the occasion of the hallowing of a *porticus* at Exeter some time in the last quarter of the eleventh century, someone was freed (*freode*) for the good of a person's soul. The document goes on to state: 'And let him choose a lord wherever he wishes to look.'[108] Some time before 1129 Walter 'freed Æthelgifu within St Peter's Minster over his father's body for the redemption of his father's soul and his own' (*Manumission*, §9.6).[109]

The Exeter documents suggest that the act of freeing was coming to be regarded as involving a release of a person from an estate. This was already present as an element in the freeing of slaves in the tenth century but increasingly came to apply to those whose tribal status was that of a freeman but who nevertheless were tied by various obligations to the lands they lived on. The similarity in the rights granted by manumission and by quittance led to a similarity in the form in which they were recorded, so the precise nature of some of the documents is difficult to interpret. Yet slavery definitely appears to have remained a living institution in both Bodmin and Exeter throughout the eleventh century and in Exeter it may even have survived as late as the 1130s.

Chance has dictated that most of the manumission-documents should have a south-western provenance. A few survivals from other areas show that the practice of recording manumissions (especially in gospel books) was widespread in England and that changes similar to those evidenced in the Exeter documents took place elsewhere. The earliest Old English manumission-document dates from 924 x 925 and is recorded in a manuscript that may have belonged to King Æthelstan himself (*Manumission*, §1.1).[110] It declares that very soon after Æthelstan became king he freed (*gefreod*) a man. There is no reason to doubt that this was the manumission of a slave, possibly from the royal household. Since two of the very latest of the Exeter manumission-documents (*Manumission*, §§9.12 and 9.19) show that the act could be associated with notable events, this early tenth-century manumission may have been connected in some way with Æthelstan's accession to the throne. We should note that this document specifies that the son of the person freed should enjoy the same benefits as his father. This shows that a grant of freedom to a slave did not automatically confer free status on living descendants and explains why a number of other manumission-documents mention offspring as well as parents. Six records from Durham (one now lost) from the period 1030 x 1050 testify to the practice of manumission in Northumbria (*Manumission*, §§6.1, 6.2, and 7.1–4). The operative words in

---

[107] 'for Godes luue 7 Sancte Marie 7 ealle Cristes halgene 7 for þara bisceopa saule 7 for his saule to alisednesse.' Cf. n. 74 above.

[108] '7 let him ceasa hlaford, loc hwær hig wolde.'

[109] 'ureode Aþeluue inna Sanctes Petres Minstre ouer his fæder lic, his feder saule to alisednisse 7 his'.

[110] See n. 77 above.

these documents are *geaf freols* ('gave freedom'), *(ge)freod* and *gefreolsad* ('freed'). One must assume that all these record the conferral of a new legal status. Finally, we should not forget the *Textus Roffensis* record already mentioned, *Status Document*, §2.2, in which we are told Æthelsige 'has lent for Bishop Sigeweard's lifetime [1058 x 1075] his daughter and her daughter from Tottel's kin, and has placed other persons in there'.[111] This appears to be a modified form of quittance: the man's descendants were temporarily leaving an estate (*gelæned ut*) and other were coming in to take their place (*gedon in* – contrast the opposite process, *gedon ut*). This exhibits the same practice seen in the Bath and Exeter documents of recording the bestowal of freedom of movement on those who appear to have been serfs.

To sum up then. The act of freeing a slave implied both the conferral of a new legal status and the right to move away (*fryo 7 færewyrþe*). The serf shared with the slave the lack of the latter right. Those who possessed freedom of movement were deemed *færewyrþe* but they could also be called *færfreoh*, which shows the start in the shift in meaning of the words *freogan*, *freoh* and *freols/freot* away from denoting a legal status to indicating the right to leave an estate. The evidence suggests that the right of freedom of movement became more important in the latter part of the eleventh century and that the persons desiring it should be looked upon more as serfs than as slaves, though the slave status probably survived in the South-west into the twelfth century. That the lords chose to use very similar diplomatic forms to record both manumissions and quittances suggests that the differences in tribal status of those they were freeing ceased in the course of time to be very important to them.

DOWNWARD SOCIAL MOVEMENT IN THE MANUMISSION-DOCUMENTS

Four of the manumission-documents supply some information about the diminution in social status of freemen in the late Anglo-Saxon period.[112] The first, an eleventh-century entry in the Durham *Liber Uitae*, *Manumission*, §6.1, records the manumission by a woman of a group of people 'whose heads she took in exchange for food in those evil days.'[113] (Presumably they had symbolised their enslavement to her by putting their heads in her hands: the hand was a symbol of power among the Anglo-Saxons, and, of course, it was used by the Romans when freeing a person as the word 'manumission' implies.)[114] Why 'those days' were 'evil' is not specified, but the disruption to life caused by invasion, feud, and acts of God such as drought or flood must in an agricultural society have posed an ever-present threat to food production. As will be discussed in the following

---

111 'hæfð gelened be Siwordes dægge biscpes his dohter 7 hiore dohter ut of Totteles cynne, 7 hæfð oþra mænn þærinn gedon'. Cf. above, p. 150. For further discussion of the document see below, p. 182 and nn. 81–3.
112 Runciman, 'Accelerating social mobility', is the best general guide to this topic.
113 'þe heo nam heora heafod for hyra mete on þam yflum dagum.'
114 For the Anglo-Saxon symbolism see *Select English Historical Documents*, ed. & transl. Harmer, p. 102, note to line 25. On Roman manumission see Weiss, in *Paulys Realencyclopädie der classischen Altertumswissenschaft*, edd. Wissowa & Kroll, XIV.2, cols 1366–77, s.v. *Manumissio*.

chapter, slaves were entitled by custom to receive comestibles from their owners.[115] To hungry people an assurance of food would have outweighed the disadvantages of a reduced legal status and the conditions of the age argue that voluntary enslavement is likely to have been a fairly common phenomenon, even though this Durham document is the only direct evidence for this practice.

The second document, *Manumission*, §3.33, which records the payment by Putrael of eight oxen (in other words, a plough-team) to Ælfric and sixty pence to Boia in order to prevent his enslavement by Ælfric, has already been mentioned. The grounds for his enslavement are not stated. The payments Putrael made to exculpate himself suggest that this cannot be an instance of debt-slavery. It is more likely that Putrael was guilty of some misdeed that laid him open to enslavement by Ælfric. As has already mentioned, it is evidence that the term 'slave' still denoted legal status in the final quarter of the eleventh century and was not simply a fossilised term that had lingered on from the Anglo-Saxon period.

The path of downward movement, however, did not necessarily lead only to enslavement. There were other obligations incurred and losses of rights beyond those that simply involved a change in legal status. Mention has already been made of the declaration made in the presence of Bishop Wulfsige Comoyre of Cornwall (959 x 993) and other priests by some sons and grandchildren that their fathers had not been serfs of the king (*Manumission*, §3.50).[116] Another record (*Manumission*, §9.8) reports how Hubert of Bishop's Clyst in Devon made an unjust legal claim to the wife of Leofgar the baker after she had been properly freed from the estate there in the time of Geoffrey de Montbray, bishop of Coutances (who died in 1093). Through their assertion of free status in a gospel book these persons may have succeeded in preserving their rights. Others were likely to have been less fortunate. Those who lost their free status would not necessarily have descended into slavery, however, but would have incurred servile obligations, as in the case of Leofgar's wife, who probably would have had to return to the estate at Bishop's Clyst had her defence failed.

None of the last three documents can be considered a record of a manumission and strictly speaking they should not have been dealt with in this chapter. But they were entered among the manumission-documents in gospel books and share a similarity of diplomatic form with these documents. From the perspective of the scribe these records, like the records of manumissions and quittances, were testifying to the waiving of claims over persons whose legal status varied. This lack of concern over precision in defining legal status was likely to have been shared by the Norman overlords, to whom differences in status among their estate workers as defined by Anglo-Saxon legal practice would not have held much significance.

---

[115] See below, pp. 175–6.
[116] On Bishop Wulfsige see Picken, 'Bishop Wulfsige Comoere'. See further below, p. 182.

VI

'WITH THE LAND AND THE MEN':
CHARTERS, SURVEYS, AND CUSTUMALS

The preceding two chapters have largely concerned themselves with the status of slaves on estates and how that status was changed through manumission. Comparatively little was said about the relationships between slaves and others on these estates. In this chapter we shall have the opportunity to explore these relationships as they are portrayed in various kinds of estate document, especially the land-charter. The advent of the land-charter permitted land formerly held by precarious tenure to be accumulated and passed on from one generation to another. This innovation in Anglo-Saxon legal practice facilitated the growth of a body of custom that came into being in order to regulate the rights and duties of those living on these estates. The estates themselves will have varied widely in size and economic structure, being influenced by such diverse factors as topography and the life histories of individuals. The response to this diversity will have resulted in an equally wide range of custom. Yet in spite of the variety of custom that undoubtedly existed, some level of generalisation is possible. One terminological generalisation that will find frequent use in this chapter is the word 'manor', denoting a landed estate that included a home farm. The term is imprecise but, provided we recognise its imprecision, is still useful at a level of general discourse. The growth of the body of custom that developed on manors is especially evident in three groups of documents that deal with the transfer and use of land: the land-charters themselves, recording the granting of superiority over landed property; surveys and custumals, describing the rights and obligations of those living on estates; and a miscellaneous group of documents that include lists and accounts, relating to the detailed administration of particular properties.

LAND-CHARTERS[1]

There are over 1050 documents that purport to represent charters, writs, and other records issued in England between the accession of Alfred and the death of Harold. Most of these deal, in whole or in part, with land transactions. In addition there are 63 records of bounds, and approximately 180 further docu-

[1] All Anglo-Saxon charters listed in Sawyer's *Anglo-Saxon Charters* from the time of King Alfred on have been examined, with the exception of unpublished documents. Because of the volume of the material it has been necessary to rely on the unsatisfactory editions of Kemble

ments are known to have existed but are now either incomplete or have been lost.[2] Because the Anglo-Saxons used Lombard diplomatic models to document their land transactions, they contain less information than might be expected about those resident on the properties.[3] Nevertheless, there are a number of documents that mention the inhabitants of estates. These can also be divided into three groups, which will be examined in turn. First, a few charters mention slaves directly. Then, several more refer to persons whose legal status is uncertain. Finally, a larger group disclose a social change that is of fundamental importance to this study: the subjection to landed proprietors of persons who under the law of the tribe would have been considered to be freemen.

Among the charters that mention slaves are four leases that record a number of slaves who were to be returned with the property on termination of the lease. At some point before late May in 1023 the abbot and monastic community at Evesham leased four and a half hides at Norton in Worcestershire to one Æthelmær.[4] At the termination of the lease one man, six oxen, twenty sheep, and twenty acres of sown corn had to be given to the monastery. Similarly, in a post-Conquest lease granted to Ealdgyth by Walcher, bishop of Durham, sometime between 1071 and 1080, an agreement (*mana*) was reached that on her death or departure from the estate the bishop should receive eight oxen, twelve cows, and four men.[5] Presumably the men in these two leases were part of the

---

and Birch, with the latter being followed wherever possible. In the case of the vernacular documents, *Select English Historical Documents*, ed. & transl. Harmer, *Anglo-Saxon Writs*, ed. & transl. Harmer, and *Anglo-Saxon Charters*, ed. & transl. Robertson, have been preferred. For post-Conquest charters Davis, *Regesta*, I, has been used, supplemented by the Errata and Addenda noted in volume II, edd. Johnson & Cronne. Since Sawyer published his immensely valuable catalogue, a number of additional charters have come to light. The document published by Brooks *et al.*, 'A new charter of King Edgar', does not make mention of slaves. There are nine other unrecorded charters from the reigns of Æthelstan to Æthelred to be found in the 'Ilford Hospital Book' at Hatfield House in Hertfordshire but these have still to be published: see Bascombe, 'Two charters of King Suebred of Essex', in *An Essex Tribute*, ed. Neale, p. 85, where only seven are mentioned; in a personal communication, Dr Simon Keynes has informed me that seven are tenth century and two were issued by Æthelred and are dated 1013. Dr Keynes has recently discovered a number of transcripts of Anglo-Saxon charters in Brussels and London. He has provided an introduction to the Brussels material in 'A lost cartulary of St Albans Abbey'; an edition of the extant extracts from six unrecorded charters from a manuscript in London in 'The lost Cartulary of Abbotsbury', 225–30 and 232; and an edition of a further London charter in 'A charter of King Edward the Elder for Islington'. His forthcoming book, *Anglo-Saxon Charters: Archives and Single Sheets*, will prove to be an invaluable guide to such sources.

2   The figures are based on Sawyer's *Anglo-Saxon Charters*. Excluded are wills and manumission-documents.

3   Brooks's 'Anglo-Saxon charters: the work of the last twenty years' remains useful, though it was written two decades ago.

4   *Anglo-Saxon Charters*, §81 (ed. & transl. Robertson, p. 156) (= Sawyer, *Anglo-Saxon Charters*, no. 1423). The document mentions the existence of waste, which was presumably caused by the Danish ravages in the time of Æthelred. This would account for the paucity of stock. See *Anglo-Saxon Charters*, ed. & transl. Robertson, p. 404.

5   *Anglo-Saxon Charters*, appendix I, §2 (ed. & transl. Robertson, p. 230); for the date, see *ibid.*, p. 480. Given the late date of the document, however, one cannot be confident that the men were slaves. As will be seen, the *gebur* was customarily granted two oxen, in other words, a quarter of a plough team, on entry to an estate (see below, p. 174). In this agreement the

original assets of the estate at the time of the lease, though it is also possible that they were being added to the stock of the estate as part of the reimbursement by the lessee for the use of the land.

Two other leases apparently recorded slaves in order to prevent the lessee from stripping the estates of their assets. Seven slaves are mentioned in an inventory of the stock of an estate at Beddington in Surrey leased to King Edward by the Winchester monastic community in 899 x 908.[6] In the lease of an estate at Luddington in Warwickshire to a certain Fulder by the monks of Worcester in the eleventh century it was specified that he should return the land after three years 'with the full equipment supplied him by the community', which included twelve slaves in addition to two teams of oxen, one hundred sheep, and fifty fothers of corn.[7]

Significantly, in each of these four documents the lessor was either a religious community or a bishop. Once more one sees the conservative aspect of the Church as an institution. By discouraging the alienation of its property, it was also inhibiting the trend towards the increased freeing of slaves evident on secular estates.

Three other charters mention slaves. Each implicitly depicts the slave as a valuable chattel. The first is an interesting account of an imbroglio that resulted from the theft of a woman at Yaxley in Huntingdonshire some time before 968.[8] The alleged owner, Ælfsige, found the slave in the possession of one Wulfstan, who vouched Æthelstan of Sunbury to warranty. Æthelstan acknowledged the sale, but when required to appear to produce his warrantor (*geteama*) failed to turn up. Æthelstan then handed the woman over to the plaintiff, Ælfsige, and paid him two pounds in compensation. (This may have been the value placed on a slave in some areas since it is also recorded as the release price in two manumission-documents.)[9] Though the matter did not end there, it is sufficient to show that slaves were a marketable commodity and gives another rare insight into the theft of slaves for the purposes of trading them within the country.[10] Slaves also appear in two marriage agreements of the second decade of the eleventh century from widely separate parts of the country, Worcestershire and

Lotharingian bishop Walcher was seeking to ensure that the estate was not denuded of staff, a ploughteam, and livestock; the status of the staff may well have been an irrelevance to him. W. E. Kapelle has ascribed to Walcher a heavy responsibility for increasing the peasantry's obligations on his Northumbrian estates: see *The Norman Conquest of the North*, pp. 185–9.

[6] *Cartularium Saxonicum*, §618 (ed. Birch, II.282) (text); *English Historical Documents c.550–1042*, §101 (transl. Whitelock, pp. 543–4) (translation) (= Sawyer, *Anglo-Saxon Charters*, no. 1444). For the date, I have followed Whitelock; Sawyer suggests 900 x 909.

[7] 'mid swa myclum swa se hired him on hand sette'. *Anglo-Saxon Charters*, §79 (ed. & transl. Robertson, p. 154.5–6) (text); *ibid.*, p. 155 (translation) (= Sawyer, *Anglo-Saxon Charters*, no. 1421).

[8] *Anglo-Saxon Charters*, §44 (ed. & transl. Robertson, pp. 90–2) (= Sawyer, *Anglo-Saxon Charters*, no. 1447). Listed by Wormald, 'A handlist of Anglo-Saxon lawsuits', 261, §38, and see also *ibid.*, pp. 248, 252, 256, 271–2, 276, and 280.

[9] See above, pp. 152–3, table V.

[10] The document implies that the same legal procedures were being employed in the alleged case of theft as had been laid down three centuries earlier in Hlothhere and Eadric, §5 (*Die Gesetze*, ed. Liebermann, I.9–10).

Kent.[11] They record the bestowal of thirty and ten men respectively on the bride, in addition to gold, oxen, cows, and horses.

A number of charters indicate that powers were being granted over persons but do not specify the latters' legal status. Sixteen documents, ranging in date from 871 x 877 to 1042 x 1066, declare that land was being given *mid mete and mid mannum*[12] or the Latin equivalent *cum uictu et cum hominibus*.[13] Similarly, in a lease of Archhishop Oswald's, dated 987, land was granted on condition 'that it should be returned without loss of all the things belonging to it, men and stock and provisions, just as it was there at that time',[14] a requirement very much like that imposed in the other ecclesiastical leases discussed earlier.[15] What is notable about these references to 'men' is that it was not deemed necessary to define their legal status.[16] From the perspective of the overlords the tribal status of persons living on their estates was not particularly relevant. For them what

---

[11] *Anglo-Saxon Charters*, §76 (ed. & transl. Robertson, p. 148) (text); *English Historical Documents c.550–1042*, §128 (transl. Whitelock, p. 593) (translation); *Anglo-Saxon Charters*, §77 (ed. & transl. Robertson, p. 150) (text); *English Historical Documents c.550–1042*, §130 (transl. Whitelock, pp. 596–7 [§129, p. 548, in the 1st edn]) (translation) (= Sawyer, *Anglo-Saxon Charters*, nos. 1459 and 1461 respectively).

[12] *Anglo-Saxon Charters* (ed. & transl. Robertson), §13, p. 24.11–12; §68, p. 140.3–4; §73, p. 146.5; §74, p. 146.19; §92, p. 178.16–17; §93, p. 178.26; §97, p. 184.7–8; §98, p. 184.23; §101, p. 188.10; §105, p. 200.17–18; §114, p. 212.12–13; and §117, p. 218.12 (= Sawyer, *Anglo-Saxon Charters*, nos. 357, 1661, 1219, 1422, 1224, 1225, 1468, 1391, 1471, 1474, 1476, and 1426 respectively). *Anglo-Saxon Charters*, §21 (ed. & transl. Robertson, p. 42.15–16) (= Sawyer, *Anglo-Saxon Charters*, no. 1289), grants land 'mid monnum 7 mid allum þæm nytnessum ge on fixnoðum ge on medwum ðe ðærto belympað' ('with its men and with all the profits from fisheries and meadows which belong to it').

[13] They are equivalent formulas in the Latin and English versions of Sawyer, *Anglo-Saxon Charters*, no. 1046 (= *Codex Diplomaticus Aevi Saxonici*, §§915 and 1346 [ed. Kemble, IV.252.31 and VI.206.4]), although it must be noted that Harmer in *Anglo-Saxon Writs*, p. 141, n. 2, considered them to be of dubious authenticity in their present form. *Codex Diplomaticus Aevi Saxonici*, §§938 (ed. Kemble, IV.272.6) and 941 (IV.277.4–5) (= Sawyer, *Anglo-Saxon Charters*, nos. 1223 and 1398), also have the Latin formula.

[14] 'ut tribuatur sine detrimento omnium rerum ad se pertinentium, hominum uel pecorum seu ciborum, sicuti tunc temporis inibi fuerit'. *Codex Diplomaticus Aevi Saxonici*, §660 (ed. Kemble, III.232.15–18) (= Sawyer, *Anglo-Saxon Charters*, no. 1353).

[15] *Cartularium Saxonicum*, §610 (ed. Birch II.269) (= Sawyer, *Anglo-Saxon Charters*, no. 380), of 899x909 records the transfer of the minster at Plympton in Devon *cum hominibus et pecoribus*, and on 16 April, 928 Æthelstan granted twelve hides at Odstock in Wiltshire *cum hominibus uictualibus*, etc., to the bishop of Winchester (*Cartularium Saxonicum*, §663 [ed. Birch, II.340.25]) (= Sawyer, *Anglo-Saxon Charters*, no. 400). *Cartularium Saxonicum*, §661 (ed. Birch, II.338.18–19) (11 September, 918) mentions *pratis, pascuis, silua, mancipiis quoque* ('with meadows, pastures, a wood, also slaves'), but this document was probably drawn up by a Flemish scribe.

[16] The legal status of many holding positions on estates is not known. This applies to those *qui osceptros uel falcones portant* ('who carry hawks and falcons'), the dog-handlers, and the grooms mentioned as being among the customary rights of princes from which Beorhtwulf released Æthelwulf at Pangbourne in Berkshire in 843 (*Cartularium Saxonicum*, §443 [ed. Birch, II.20.12–13]) (= Sawyer, *Anglo-Saxon Charters*, no. 1271); cf. *Cartularium Saxonicum*, §488 [ed. Birch, II.89.26–7) (= Sawyer, *Anglo-Saxon Charters*, no. 207). Elsewhere, in a charter of uncertain status (*Cartularium Saxonicum*, §450 [ed. Birch, II.32.18–19]) (= Sawyer, *Anglo-Saxon Charters*, no. 198), mention is made of *puerorum qui ducunt canes* ('boys who lead the dogs'); they may have been slaves but this cannot be proved.

was important was that the 'men' were tied to their lands through a nexus of rights and obligations which thereby provided some of the economic value of their estates.

A third group of charters illustrates that this situation already obtained in some measure by the end of the ninth century. In the case of the manor at Beddington leased to King Edward that has already been mentioned,[17] the slaves were not the only persons transferred with the estate since the document records that there were additional sheep and pigs which the herdsmen were to have. As these herdsmen are mentioned separately from the slaves, they were presumably freemen in terms of tribal law. But the word 'freeman' is no longer adequate to describe them. The lessor assumed that they were part of the permanent inhabitants of the estate. This had evidently received recognition on the manor through the development of some sort of customary arrangement whereby the herdsmen could own some of the livestock and be permitted to graze them on the estate.

Two charters connected with properties of the Worcester church mention a list of men in some way attached to an estate, who were to be transferred with the land mentioned in the charters. Their legal status is not recorded. The first document is dated 880, but if authentic must, in fact, date from 887.[18] It records that Æthelred, ealdorman of Mercia, granted, with King Alfred's permission, land at Brightwell Baldwin and Watlington in Oxfordshire to the bishopric of Worcester to be attached to the church at Pyrton in the same county. To this property were added six *homines* who previously were attached to the royal vill at Bensington, together with their offspring. After the date of the charter proper and preceding the bounds, the document adds: 'These were the names of the men which were granted in writing from Bensington to Pyrton in the diocese of Worcester with their family and that progeny which descends from them, for an everlasting possession. Ealhmund. Tidwulf. Tidheah. Lull. Lull. Eadwulf.'[19] The second document is a charter of 899 in which Wærferth, bishop of Worcester, recorded the lease by the ecclesiastical community at Worcester of five hides at Elmstone Hardwicke in Gloucestershire for a period of three lives. The charter declares that the land was acquired 'with the men attached to it whose names have been written a little below',[20] though the extant text unfortunately fails to provide the names.

At first sight one might think that these are lists of slaves, particularly in view of the early date. Yet the way in which they are described suggests that they were, in fact, serfs. They are called *homines*, which gives no indication of their legal status, and instead of being described as personal possessions of the king or the church, they are said to be attached (*pertinentes*) to a manor. This interpretation

---

[17] Above, p. 166 and n. 6.

[18] *Cartularium Saxonicum*, §547 (ed. Birch, II.166–7) (= Sawyer, *Anglo-Saxon Charters*, no. 217). On the date see *Asser's Life of King Alfred*, ed. Stevenson, p. 300.

[19] 'þis earon þara manna noman þe gewritene earon from Bynsincgtune to Readanoran in þ bisceoprice to uueorgerna cestre mid heara teame 7 mid þy tudre þe from him cume a on ece yrfewardnysse. Alhmund. Tidulf. Tidheh. Lull. Lull. Eaduulf.' *Cartularium Saxonicum*, §547 (ed. Birch, II.167.9–12) (= Sawyer, *Anglo-Saxon Charters*, no. 217). This document has been placed in a diplomatic context in Pelteret, 'Two Old English lists of serfs', 491–2.

[20] 'Cum hominibus ad illam pertinentibus quarum [*sic*] Nomina pau<lis>p<er> inferius scripta sunt'. *Cartularium Saxonicum*, §559 (ed. Birch, II.198.1–2) (= Sawyer, *Anglo-Saxon Charters*, no. 1415).

gains support from a lease of what must have been the same five hides of land at Elmstone, drawn up between 899 and 904 by Wærferth.[21] This records that he had made over to a kinswoman 'the three hides of land for three lives, and she shall have the right of cutting timber in the wood which the *ceorlas* enjoy; and likewise I let to her separately the copse of the *ceorlas*. And the remaining two hides of land and the *ceorlas* and the Elmstone Wood shall belong to Prestbury, as long as the lease of the land runs.'[22] No slaves are mentioned, and it seems reasonable to assume that the *ceorlas* in this document were the same as the men in the prior document.

A similar possessory attitude towards persons who might well have been legally free is evident in an early document (A.D. 909) in which the bishop of Winchester leased to one Alfred forty hides of land that his parents had held. Alfred had to agree that 'his men shall be ready both for harvesting and hunting'.[23] These people may, of course, have been demesne slaves, but it seems more likely from the wording that they were freemen who had to be prepared to give help to the church at Winchester when needed.

After these few documents from the turn of the century there is singularly little information on freemen for the next 150 years.[24] Two documents, however, lift the curtain of diplomatic formulas hiding the process of social change. The vernacular bounds of a charter issued in A.D. 955 x 957 disclose that the document is describing *geburland*, that is, land occupied by freemen, even though there is no mention of the inhabitants of the estate in the body of the charter.[25] Another document of A.D. 1050 recording the amalgamation of the dioceses of Devon and Cornwall included both freemen and slaves amongst the possessions of the diocese, showing that though the legal status of slave and free remained distinct in people's minds, their socio-economic position was merging.[26] With these last documents should also be included two that mention *weorcwyrðe* men, the first from *ca* 963 and the other of uncertain date.[27] It seems most likely that

---

[21] *Anglo-Saxon Charters*, §16 (ed. & transl. Robertson, pp. 28–30) (= Sawyer, *Anglo-Saxon Charters*, no. 1283).

[22] 'ðæt ðreora hida lond on ðreora monna daeg, 7 heo hæbbe ða wuduraeddenne in ðæm wuda ðe ða ceorlas brucaþ; 7 ec ic hire lete to ðæt ceorla graf to sundran. 7 elles ðæt twega hida lond 7 ða ceorlas 7 se Alhmunding snaed here into Preosdabyrig, ða hwile hit unagaen seo.' *Anglo-Saxon Charters*, §16 (ed. & transl. Robertson, p. 28.22–7) (text); *ibid.*, p. 29 (translation, emended) (= Sawyer, *Anglo-Saxon Charters*, no. 1283).

[23] 'his men beon gearuwe ge to ripe ge to huntoðe'. *Anglo-Saxon Charters*, §15 (ed. & transl. Robertson, p. 28.6) (text); *ibid.*, p. 29 (translation) (= Sawyer, *Anglo-Saxon Charters*, no. 1287).

[24] The vernacular bounds attached to many charters often record that the place-names given are those used by the local inhabitants, who are variously called *ruricoli, solicoli, indigeni, incoli,* etc. These terms, however, give no indication of legal status.

[25] *Cartularium Saxonicum*, §1002 (ed. Birch, III.201.14–27) (= Sawyer, *Anglo-Saxon Charters*, no. 663).

[26] *Codex Diplomaticus Aevi Saxonici*, §791 (ed. Kemble, IV.119.30) (= Sawyer, *Anglo-Saxon Charters*, no. 1021).

[27] *Anglo-Saxon Charters*, §39 (ed. & transl. Robertson, p. 72.28) (= Sawyer, *Anglo-Saxon Charters*, no. 1448) and appendix II, §3 (p. 248.19). On the term *weorcwyrðe* see appendix I below.

these also were freemen in terms of the tribal law, but were nevertheless legally obligated to perform labour services.

The post-Conquest royal charters and writs confirm that control over persons who would formerly have been termed 'free' was growing, though they do not afford any direct information on slaves.[28] For instance, a notification of January 1071 states that William the Conqueror had granted Archbishop Lanfranc the manor of Freckenham in Suffolk 'with all the lands, meadows, pastures, woods, *rustici* and sokemen, and all other things.' The Old English version describes these *rustici* as *geneatas*.[29] One recognises here the old diplomatic formula that lists the appurtenances of an estate. What has changed is that freemen are definitely included, whereas, with the single exception of the charter of 1050 issued by King Edward, all the earlier Anglo-Saxon charters had merely listed 'men' without defining their status.

In the post-Conquest period the conception that people formed part of the appurtenances of an estate is likewise to be seen in the notification of A.D. 1072 x 1077 to Abbot Æthelwig recording the granting of the Abbey of Evesham 'with the lands <and> the men';[30] the precept of *ca* 1080 that the Abbey of Ely was to have its customs 'over its own men in its own lands';[31] the record of a gift made sometime between 1066 and 1086 by Walter de Lacy to St Peter of Gloucester and St Peter of Hereford of ten villeins, one from each of ten vills, as well as tithes from those vills and four carucates of land;[32] a precept of William Rufus of A.D. 1087 x 1097 that 'the men of the Saint [Edmund]' did not have to attend shire or hundred courts except those who possessed sufficient land to do so in the time of King Edward' (a clear reference to freemen);[33] and a precept of A.D. 1093 x 1100 to seise St Benet of Holme and a monk of 106 acres and four men in Wynterton in Norfolk, and thirty acres and four *bordarii* in Burc.[34] Several more documents make unspecific references to 'men' who were granted.[35]

Finally, one should note a new injunction that appears in three late documents. In a precept of A.D. 1093 x 1097 William II granted to Eudo *Dapifer* in succession to his brother the manor formerly belonging to Dereman, with the command that those men who left after Dereman's death had to return with all their chattels.[36] A second precept of A.D. 1087 x 1099 declares: 'William, King

---

[28] Post-Conquest charters will be referred to by the number assigned them in Davis, *Regesta*, volume I.

[29] 'in omnibus terris, pratis, paschuis, sylvis, rusticis & sochemanis, & ceteris omnibus.' *Textus Roffensis*, facs. ed. Sawyer, fo 171r; *Textus Roffensis*, ed. Hearne, p. 141. The Old English version reads: '7 made 7 læse 7 weode 7 geneatas 7 socumen 7 ealle þing þe þas togebyriad': Davis, *Regesta*, §47 (I.13).

[30] 'cum terris, cum hominibus'. *Ibid.*, §106 (I.121).

[31] *Ibid.*, §129 (I.34).

[32] *Ibid.*, §225 (I.60).

[33] 'Et defendo etiam ut non cogatis homines Sancti ire ad schiras uel ad hundreda, nisi illos qui tantum terre habent, unde digni fuissent tempore regis Edwardi ire ad schiras uel ad hundreda.' *Ibid.*, §393 (I.135).

[34] 'de c. acris terre et vi acris prati et quatuor hominibus in Wyntertona et triginta acris in Burc et iii bordariis.' *Ibid.*, §468 (I.138).

[35] *Ibid.*, §§291 (I.76), 294 (I.77), 331 (I.86), 354 (I.91), 361 (I.93), 412 (I.103).

[36] *Ibid.*, §399 (I.101).

of England, to R. his chaplain and his sheriffs and officials, greetings. I order you that wherever the Abbot of Ramsey or his men are able to find fugitives who have fled from the land of the Abbey without permission and wrongly, make them return and see that no one in any way wrongly detain them.'[37] The same problem seems to have arisen with men from the Abbey of Eynsham, as a third precept of A.D. 1093 x 1100 shows: 'William, King of England, to all his sheriffs and officials of England, greetings. I order you that you justly and without delay act to hold all the men with their livestock of the Abbey of Evesham and its abbot, wherever the men of the same Abbey are able to find them. And I prohibit on pain of a fine of ten pounds that anyone should unjustly detain them, because I wish the Abbot to hold his men and his abbey with great honour.'[38] There is no indication in these three documents that the runaway men were slaves – in fact, they probably were not. They were men whose freedom had been defined according to an outmoded system of law, men whom a changed socio-economic system did not encourage to regard freedom of movement as one of their rights.

In closely analysing these documents we must take care not lose the wood for the trees. If we stand back and look at them as a whole, we can see a vast social transformation taking place. From the reign of Alfred up to 1066 there are over 800 charters purporting to be issued by kings (who unlike the bishops and laity presumably could convert folkland into bookland and who tended to alienate land in perpetuity). This compares with fewer than 350 charters for the whole of the preceding period.[39] Many of the earlier charters admittedly must have been lost because of warfare between tribal groups, the ravages of the Viking incursions[40] or accidents such as fire[41] or careless storage.[42] But the disparity in the

---

37 'Willelmus Rex Angliae R. capellano suo et uicecomitibus suis et ministris salutem. Praecipio uobis ut ubicunque abbas de Ramesia uel sui homines poterint inuenire fugitiuos qui de terra abbathiae sine licentia et iniuste aufugerint eos redire faciatis, et uidete ne aliquis eos ullo modo iniuste detineat.' *Chronicon Abbatiae Rameseiensis*, §193 (ed. Macray, p. 212).

38 'Willelmus, Rex Anglie, omnibus uicecomitibus suis & ministris Anglie, salutem. Precipio uobis ut iuste & sine dilatione habere faciatis abbatie de Egnesham & abbati eius homines suos omnes cum pecuniis eorum, ubicunque eos inuenire poterint homines eiusdem abbatie. Et defendo super x libras forisfacture ne aliquis eos iniuste detineat, quia uolo ut abbas homines suos & abbatiam suam cum magno honore teneat.' *Eynsham Cartulary*, ed. Salter, I.50–1; Davis, *Regesta*, §465 (I.113).

39 These are approximate figures based on Sawyer, *Anglo-Saxon Charters*. They include documents other than land-charters, such as writs and wills, and also include many forgeries; nevertheless, the numbers serve as an adequate basis for the generalisation made here.

40 Collections of documents may not merely have been burned but also looted. Cf. the case of the Golden Gospels, which were bought back from the Danes by Ealdorman Alfred: *Select English Historical Documents*, §9 (ed. & transl. Harmer, pp. 12–13) (text); *ibid.*, pp. 46–7 (translation).

41 *Codex Diplomaticus Aevi Saxonici*, §709 (ed. Kemble, III.327–30) (= Sawyer, *Anglo-Saxon Charters*, no. 909), is a copy replacing one destroyed when the Oxford citizenry set fire to St Frideswide's Minster in Oxford, where some Danes had taken refuge during what appears to have been the St Brice's Day massacre in 1002. On the charter see Stenton, 'St. Frideswide and her times', 105–6.

42 This is the reason behind the comparatively recent discovery of Æthelgifu's will. See Lord Rennell, 'The will of Æthelgifu: introduction and provenance', in *The Will of Æthelgifu*, ed. & transl. Whitelock, pp. 2–4. *Cartularium Saxonicum*, §757 (ed. Birch, II.482.19–20)

number of charters extant from before and after Alfred's reign is so great that one can only conclude that from the tenth century on there was a mighty growth in the use of the charter to convey landed property.

The growth in bookland gives the key to the very real change that took place in the structure of English society between the seventh and the eleventh centuries. Lordship is evident in the earliest Anglo-Saxon sources, but it was a lordship dependent on service and unprotected by the permanent superiority over land conferred by book-right. With the growth of estates, starting in the eighth century but particularly strong from the tenth century on, power passed to individuals and institutions.[43] This power was not merely political (as, for instance, the influence Wulfstan had over early eleventh-century legislation and Godwine possessed in the later years of Edward's reign) but also judicial.

For ordinary peasants their most important rights and obligations shifted from the tribal to the manorial sphere. As a result the concept of freedom changed, and with this change went the disappearance of the old slave-free dichotomy. And so these last documents order the return of men to the estate to which they had been tied without recording their legal status – for the old tribal distinction in status within this frame of reference was now an irrelevance.

SURVEYS AND CUSTUMALS

Charters merely record the transfer of estates and so they are not usually very informative about the inhabitants living on the land, as has been mentioned. Fortunately there are three tracts extant which afford some insight into the internal organisation of manorial estates. In this section we shall concentrate our attention on the longest and most informative of these documents, the *Rectitudines Singularum Personarum*, which evidently describes the customs observed on a number of estates. The broad social trends that it implies can be confirmed from two custumals of manors at Hurstbourne Priors in Hampshire and Tidenham in Gloucestershire, and the conclusion of this process of social change is evident in a twelfth-century charter recording the establishment of Revesby Abbey, which will be examined briefly in order to place the three custumals in perspective.

The exact date and provenance of the *Rectitudines* are not certain,[44] but Bethurum has adduced significant evidence to suggest that the document (at least in its present form) was compiled under the influence of Archbishop Wulfstan in the second decade of the eleventh century and has as its subject the extensive holdings of the Worcester church.[45]

(= Sawyer, *Anglo-Saxon Charters*, no. 469) of A.D. 940 provides an ancient example; it explains, 'Ideo scripsimus nouam cartulam quia antiquum non habebamus.' ('Therefore we have written a new charter because we did not have the old one.')

[43] This is particularly clear in the case of the monasteries. See John, *Orbis Britanniae*, pp. 154–209.

[44] Text in *Die Gesetze*, ed. Liebermann, I.444–53; translation in *English Historical Documents 1042–1189*, §172 (transl. Douglas & Greenaway, pp. 875–9).

[45] Bethurum, 'Episcopal magnificence in the eleventh century', in *Studies in Old English in Honor of Arthur G. Brodeur*, ed. Greenfield. P. D. A. Harvey in 'Rectitudines', has not

A close reading of the document reveals that the compiler organised the material into three main sections. The first four clauses are devoted to the rights and obligations of various socio-legal categories of freemen in descending social rank from *þegn* to *gebur*. The second section turns to specific occupational groups in which both those of free and slave legal status are to be found. The final section, running from clause 21 on, continues this discussion of occupational groups but makes no explicit comment about their legal status.

The first two socio-legal classes mentioned are too far removed from slaves to concern this study. The cottars, who are the third group to be discussed, are more relevant. They were required to work on the demesne every Monday or for three days in the week at harvest-time. Their land-holding was a minimum of five acres. Such a holding would have been inadequate to provide a reasonable livelihood, and they must have supplemented the produce they derived from their own lands by working as labourers on the lord's demesne (*inland*). To a later age, when the possession of land meant economic power, the cottar would have seemed less free than the *gebur*, who had a much bigger landholding. But this is not the view of the compiler: in his eyes to hold land was to be subject, with the corollary that if one performed labour services, one must hold land. Thus he wrote of the cottar's holding: 'it is too little if it ever be less [than five acres]; because his work must be frequent'.[46] This cast of thinking explains why the compiler dealt with the cottar before the *gebur*, thereby implying that the former enjoyed a superior status: though the cottar must have been in reality more heavily dependent on his lord to hire his labour in order to make ends meet, he was in a sense freer than the *gebur*, who had more compulsory services to perform in return for his larger acreage.[47]

According to the *Rectitudines* the *gebur* was to be given seven acres of sown land out of the thirty acres that comprised his holding. Seebohm provided a plausible explanation for this seemingly curious figure.[48] In a three-field system the farmer would plough ten acres for the autumn crop and a further ten for the spring crop. The remaining ten would lie fallow. Of this total, three acres would be *gafol-erðe*, that is, land whose produce was payable to the overlord as rent. In the first season of his tenure the tenant would be excused from this rent as he had

questioned the association with Wulfstan but has posited that the text as it survives has been through several changes, that it is at least as old as the tenth century, and that it originated in the south-west of England (possibly at St Peter's, Bath). His suggestions are tentative and the text will obviously have to undergo intensive linguistic scrutiny before they can be accepted. My comments, which are based on the extant text, should not be invalidated by future conclusions about the prior transmission of the text.

46 '7 to lytel hit biö, beo hit a læsse; forðan his weorc sceal beon oftræde.' *Rectitudines Singularum Personarum*, §3.3: *Die Gesetze*, ed. Liebermann, I.446 (text); *English Historical Documents 1042–1189*, §172 (transl. Douglas & Greenaway, p. 876) (translation).

47 Harvey in 'Rectitudines', 12–13, has also argued that this section is logical, although he came to this conclusion by a different route through interpreting it from the viewpoint of an estate manager: 'All the thegn's services are due to the king; the estate manager gets nothing from him. From the *geneat*, however, he gets occasional services and payments, from the *kote setla* some regular services as well, and from the *gebur* a great deal more. It is a straightforward progression.'

48 Seebohm, *The English Village Community*, p. 141. The document as a whole is discussed on pp. 129–47.

gained no return from the land to provide the seed to sow the three acres; from the second season on, however, he should have the wherewithal to do this. In addition to his rent, the *gebur* on some estates had to work on the lord's demesne for two days per week and had yet further services and renders to perform beside. The effect of holding land of another was thus inevitably to make one subject, which thereby blurred an old distinction between slave and freeman.

Another effect of manorialism, the interdependence of the inhabitants on an estate, tended in the same direction. The position of the *gebur* illustrates this well. The lord provided him with a quarter of a hide and a quarter of a plough-team. This implies that he would be expected to pool his resources with three of his neighbours to form a plough-team, a practice observed even in developed agricultural communities in many parts of the world today (except that the team has often been replaced by the tractor and combine-harvester). Strip farming must also have encouraged such co-operation. The *gebur's* possession of a cow and six sheep implies that these would be grazed on common land, which similarly required a measure of agreement amongst neighbours. Further evidence of co-operation is the explicit statement that two boors had to be responsible for a hunting dog (§4.2).

Though these persons were becoming increasingly subject to others, they were still freemen in terms of the world outside the manor. The compiler recognised this in the case of the cottar. He recorded that the cottar was obliged to pay Peter's Pence (§3.4) precisely because he was a freeman;[49] he also had to pay church dues at Martinmas, another obligation of freemen, as II Egbert, §2.3 indicates. One may reasonably assume that in addition to these obligations these men enjoyed the rights of freemen in matters covered by the royal laws, though the compiler does not state this.

After treating of these various groups of freemen the compiler then turns to specific occupational groups (§§5ff.). The first two occupations listed are bee-keeper and swineherd. These men could be either 'freemen' (in the sense described above) or slaves. The freeman is categorised as one who is liable to *gafol*, that is, rent. The swineherd is, in fact, called a *gafol-swine* (a 'rent-paying swineherd'). The free bee-keeper is simply called a *beo-ceorl*, but the hives he has charge of are called *gafol-heord*, implying that they were supplied by the lord in return for rent. His rent or *gafol* is described in §5.1.

Three significant differences between these freemen and their slave counterparts are evident. First, the freemen are defined in terms of their obligations towards the lord of the manor, the slaves in terms of the rights owed them by their lord. The document implies that the freeman's time was essentially his own, subject to the customary obligations expected of him on the estate; the slave's time, on the other hand, was essentially his master's (although, as has been seen, Alfred's legislation had limited this and estate custom may well have limited it further).

Second, the free bee-keeper and swineherd could keep the fruits of their labour, subject to the payment of *gafol*, which in the case of the swineherd

---

[49] See II Egbert, §4, VIII Æthelred, §10, and I Cnut, §9: *Die Gesetze*, ed. Liebermann, I.198, 265, and 292 respectively.

included fifteen pigs per annum. Out of these fruits they were presumably expected to feed themselves and their families. It was quite otherwise for the slaves. For instance, the *æhteswan* (the slave swineherd who worked on the lord's *æhteland* or demesne) with charge over the demesne herd (*inheord*, that is, the herd belonging to the *inland* or demesne) was allowed only a single young pig and certain (presumably inferior) portions of a pig after he had made bacon, plus the food rations appropriate to his status.[50] In other words, the freeman was given a lifetime's enjoyment of the lord's property subject to an annual rent whereas the slave was merely the guardian of the property of his lord, who retained full rights of ownership.

Third, it appears that the freeman could, potentially at least, own property that was not under the lord's control. 'When death befalls him [*sc.*, the bee-keeper] let his lord take charge of what he leaves unless there should be anything free' (§5.5).[51] What was there that could be free? Surely the property that the free bee-keeper brought with him when he entered into the lord's service on the estate. As this was not supplied him by his lord, it remained in his own possession and he retained the right of its free disposal.

Although there is a firm distinction between slaves and freemen in this portion of the tract, the *Rectitudines* makes it clear that slaves were not bereft of rights – rights that in some circumstances might have made the status of slave more attractive than that of freeman.[52] The document shows that by the eleventh century it was considered reasonable for a slave to be given food rations consisting of both corn and meat, as well as rights to cutting wood (§8). The right to food is confirmed by an unexpected source. To the question, 'Tell me what kinds of books and how many there are?' in that curious work, the prose *Solomon and Saturn*, comes the completely disjointed reply: 'In twelve months you must give to your slave seven hundred and twenty loaves, besides morning and afternoon meals.'[53] The food ration was presumably to compensate for the slaves' paucity of land and long working hours, both of which would have limited their opportunity to grow their own crops. The *Solomon and Saturn* text also gives an indirect indication that these slaves must have returned at the end of the day to their own homes, as one might expect, rather than to slave quarters, for otherwise one might presume their master would have supplied an evening meal as

---

[50] See appendix I below, s.v. *æhteswan*.

[51] 'ðonne his forðsið gebyrige, hede se hlaford ðæs he læfe, bute hwet friges sy.' *Rectitudines Singularum Personarum*, §5.5: *Die Gesetze*, ed. Liebermann, I.448 (text); *English Historical Documents 1042–1189*, §172 (transl. Douglas & Greenaway, p. 877) (translation).

[52] In the light of the suggestion that this document was influenced by Wulfstan (see n. 45 above), it is interesting that in his *Sermo ad Anglos* Wulfstan stressed the rights of slaves (*þræl-riht*). Cf. above, pp. 96–8.

[53] 'On xii mo<n>ðum þu sealt syllan þinon ðeowan men vii hund hlafa and xx hlafa buton morgeme<tt>en and nonmettum.' *The 'Prose Solomon and Saturn' and 'Adrian and Ritheus'*, §59 (edd. Cross & Hill, p. 34.20–2) (text); *ibid.*, p. 123 (translation, emended). Cross and Hill on p. 126 of their edition have suggested that the text should read '730' rather than '720', giving an average of two loaves a day. They relate this to the rations prescribed for monks in the Rule of St Benedict, an interesting observation, especially since the monks would have been known as *Godes þeowas*. Cross and Hill, whose edition has now superseded Kemble's study, *The Dialogue of Salomon and Saturnus*, have advanced our understanding of this text by placing it in the context of a literary genre: see *ibid.*, pp. 7–13.

well.[54] The two loaves they received daily presumably went towards the feeding of their families and would have been supplemented by whatever vegetables, fruit or meat their wives and children were able to produce from their tofts.[55]

The *Rectitudines* also declares: 'All slaves belonging to the estate ought to have food at Christmas and Easter, a strip of land for ploughing (*sulh-æcer*) and a harvest-handful (*hærfest-hand<f>ul*) besides their dues.'[56] The 'harvest-handful' is, I suggest, a quantity of seed sufficient to sow an acre. The fruits of an acre would most likely be considered insufficient to supply surplus grain for the following season's seeding, and consequently the slaves would have been given this annually. One cannot overemphasise the importance of this clause. Its significance lies in the fact that the slave was now considered to have a 'right' to work land *for himself*. It was but a small area compared to the thirty acres of the *gebur* or even the five acres of the cottar. The reference to a *sulhæcer* probably means that a slave had a share in the common fields, though it is not impossible that the term could refer to a croft that lay behind the toft. Whatever the term specifically denotes, it reveals that in that most important element of an agrarian society, the right to work the land, the slave's position differed now from a freeman's only in *degree*, no longer in kind. The freeman/slave distinction was thus becoming increasingly anachronistic in the manorial sphere.

The remaining section of the document deals with the rights and duties of people engaged in various occupations on an estate, but there is no explicit comment on their legal status. Yet it has been shown that the compiler was aware of legal distinctions between the free and unfree, so it is appropriate to consider the legal status of the persons mentioned.

First there is the *folgere*. Douglas and Greenaway have assumed that he was a privileged person on the estate.[57] I am not so certain. In II Cnut, §20a, where he is included among the freemen, he is contrasted with the *heorðfæst* men, that is, those who had their own home. Elsewhere the word glosses *assecla*.[58] In the *Rectitudines* the *folgere* was in a better position than the slave in that he was given two acres, but, like the slave, he was supplied with his food. The role he would best fit would be that of a hired servant in the *hired* or household. The land would have been to supplement his income. It would have reflected adversely on the lord if his domestic servant was badly clad, which would account for why his lord was responsible for his shoes and gloves.[59]

---

[54] This confirms the evidence of *Anglo-Saxon Wills*, §24 (ed. & transl. Whitelock, p. 68) (= Sawyer, *Anglo-Saxon Charters*, no. 1527) discussed on pp. 124–5 above.

[55] Writing of the post-Conquest period, D. Hinton in *Alfred's Kingdom*, pp. 119–20, has pointed to the importance of night soil and manure in making crofts potentially more fertile than the surrounding fields. Even if slaves did not possess crofts, their tofts may have been an important source of food for the same reason, especially if they approached the size of those at Holworth (see above, chapter IV, n. 84).

[56] 'Eallum æhtemannum gebyreð Midwintres feorm 7 Eastorfeorm, sulhæcer 7 hærfest-hand<f>ul toeacan heora nydrihte.' *Rectitudines Singularum Personarum*, §9.1: *Die Gesetze*, ed. Liebermann, I.450 (text); *English Historical Documents 1042–1189*, §172 (transl. Douglas & Greenaway, p. 877) (translation).

[57] *Ibid.*, p. 877, n. 4.

[58] Wright, *Anglo-Saxon and Old English Vocabularies*, ed. Wülcker, I, col. 189.30.

[59] Harvey, 'Rectitudines', 14–15, has argued that *folgere* means 'ploughman', though he has

The sower's legal position (§11) is also uncertain. He must have been dependent on the lord for food in the first year, yet a grant of seed at the end of that period implies that he was given land of his own for sowing. He may in the first year also have been in the position of a hired hand.

As it stands the clause on the ox-herd (§12) is elliptical and confusing. It appears to state that if the ox-herd possessed two or more oxen in his own right he had to have permission from the reeve of the estate to use the lord's grazing land. Presumably he then would also make them available for service on the lord's *inland*, for which he got clothing in recompense. The possession of cattle might indicate that he was a free hired hand, but by this time slaves could acquire property, and the possession of a *metecu* seems to indicate that he was a slave.

There is a clearer indication that the shepherd was a slave in that the flock was obviously not his since he was entitled only to a single lamb from each year's new-born. This lamb, however, together with a fleece and supplies of milk and whey, was over and above the rights to food and wood possessed by a slave. This applied to the goat-herd (§15) as well.

The remaining persons were specialised labourers or administrators. All seem to have performed tasks connected with the demesne. The cheesemaker, for instance, was required to make butter for the lord's table. In all cases they could have been slaves, although equally they might have been hired workmen.

In our analysis of this document we have followed the compiler through his description of both freemen and slaves. This is not merely because freemen could have been employers of slaves but also because, more importantly, his discussion of freemen gives valuable pointers as to how the two groups were able to merge. To begin with, there was the levelling effect that the co-operative farming described here must have had, particularly when enforced by estate custom. No longer was the community of the kindred the dominant factor; now it was the community of the estate. With the growth of such a community went a growth of interdependence. Formerly, many disputes were likely to have been within the kin and would have been adjudicated by the kin. Between kindreds disputes would have been in the jurisdiction of the tribal leader, that is, the king. Now the kin was less likely to be important. Disputes would still arise between members of the community, but the adjudicator was much more likely to be the head of the manor or his deputy rather than the king.

The lord of the manor was no less dependent on his workers than they were on him. The lord needed workers for the *inland*; the workers needed to supplement the produce from their sometimes meagre holdings by being hired to work on the demesne. The cement that bound the lord and peasant together was the *landlagu*, the customary relationships and practices that evolved on an individual estate. The *landlagu* is mentioned in clause 4.4. The aim of this customary law, as with all law, was to ensure stability. In these circumstances the purpose of the *land-lagu* must obviously have been to discourage freedom of movement on the part of the estate workers. Freedom of movement still existed to some degree at the time of the writing of the *Rectitudines*: that special customs applied to *geburas*

granted that this is a 'shot in the dark'. The reference to shoes and gloves makes this a very improbable interpretation.

in their first year of service implies they were able to move from an estate. But clearly the custom of the manor discouraged this. To most estate workers, in consequence, manorial custom would have been more important than the tribal law promulgated by the king. In the *Rectitudines* royal law, such as that governing Peter's Pence, was indeed enforced on the estate, but throughout the document the overriding emphasis is on the law of the manor: in day-to-day affairs that was what counted.

Under these circumstances the old slave-free polarity as defined by tribal law was simply no longer relevant. The results are visible in the very structure of the *Rectitudines* itself. Up to clause 4.6 the compiler sets down the rights of persons in accordance with their legal status. Thereafter he discusses estate personnel largely in terms of their social or economic roles. To be sure, he was still aware that there was a legal distinction between an ordinary bee-keeper or swineherd and a slave performing the same tasks, but he does not preserve this distinction for all the occupational groups. In other words the dichotomy between slave and free still had some validity in legal terms but, so far as their economic roles were concerned, the legal distinction was waning in importance. Nevertheless, it took a long time to disappear from view: Domesday Book proves that the dichotomy was to linger on for most of the eleventh century.

Here it must be stressed that these were general trends in a process of social change that nowhere led to absolutely uniform consequences. One can only talk in such generalisations when manorialism is looked at in 'soft focus'; when the focus is sharpened it is clear from even the exiguous extant documentation that rights and duties varied greatly from area to area. This local variation is emphasised throughout the *Rectitudines* and receives confirmation from the other English custumals, especially the one from Hurstbourne, and from the twelfth-century foundation charter of Revesby Abbey in the sections where it mentions customary holdings.

The custumal of the manor of Hurstbourne Priors in Hampshire describes the duties of *ceorlas* on the estate.[60] The date of this document has been presumed by Douglas and Greenaway to be *ca* 1050.[61] Robertson, too, seems to have accepted the eleventh century attribution.[62] Finberg has adduced strong evidence, however, to suggest that it is in fact a document of *ca* 900, as it purports to be.[63] If this be accepted as correct (and Finberg's views have thus far gone uncontested), it provides valuable supplementary evidence on the early growth of the manorial customary law that is occasionally also to be seen in the land-charters.

The document does not state how much land the *ceorl* possessed, but he had to plough three acres as part of his rent. This is the same as the *gebur* in the *Rectitudines*, which implies that the holding of the *ceorl* was likewise a quarter of a hide. Admittedly the rent of a Hurstbourne *ceorl* included a money payment

[60] *Anglo-Saxon Charters*, §110 (ed. & transl. Robertson, p. 206) (text); *ibid.*, p. 207 (translation) (= Sawyer, *Anglo-Saxon Charters*, no. 359).

[61] *English Historical Documents 1042–1189*, §173 (transl. Douglas & Greenaway, p. 879).

[62] Robertson, *Anglo-Saxon Charters*, §110 (ed. & transl. Robertson, p. 454).

[63] Finberg, 'The Churls of Hurstbourne', in *Lucerna*, pp. 131–43. Harvey has provided an explanation in 'Rectitudines', 17–18, for the late dating of this text by placing it in the context of English historiography of the past century.

based on a hide of land. But as has just been mentioned, the *gebur* must have had to co-operate with three others in order to raise a full team of eight oxen.[64] The hide, no doubt, was more convenient to the estate owner as a unit of assessment; exactly how the rent was raised could be left to the tenants, who presumably would use the same co-operative approach as they did in their ploughing. Just as with the *geburas* in the *Rectitudines*, each *ceorl* must have been given a flock of sheep, since he was expected to give an annual render at Easter, but unlike the *Rectitudines* the Hurstbourne custumal also lists specific duties that were required of him, such as an obligation to supply fencing poles. This must have been one of those customs that the *Rectitudines* alludes to as being peculiar to a particular estate.

The Hurstbourne custumal shows, then, that perhaps as early as A.D. 900 *ceorlas* were becoming obligated to engage in week work in addition to paying rent. However, even though their obligations were becoming more exacting, their position still differed materially from that of slaves in that they retained a large measure of control over their own labour. Thus, although their rent was specified, exactly how and when they obtained this was left up to them: they were to supply it 'in their own time', a phrase that appears no fewer than six times.

The custumal of an estate at Tidenham in Gloucestershire from *ca* 1060 in which the duties of *geneatas* and *geburas* are set out also discloses the growing subjection of freemen to customary manorial obligations.[65] The duties of the *geneatas* and *geburas* differed somewhat from those of their counterparts in the *Rectitudines*. The property was an estuarine one so it had regulations governing fishing rights, another reminder of the variation that existed between estates. Yet though it differs in its details from the other documents, it confirms the general trend towards the enserfment of those whom the tribal law would have declared to be freemen.

To put this trend in perspective we might conclude by looking briefly at the foundation charter of Revesby Abbey (A.D. 1133), where the new rights and obligations of tenants who had been displaced from their former holdings were recorded.[66] Among those who had not chosen freedom (which had now come to mean the right to leave an estate), these rights and obligations differed greatly from person to person. The socio-legal categories of *geneat* and *gebur* were no longer needed, and distinctions between slave and free had ceased to be relevant. Here we see the conclusion of the process of social change that the pre-Conquest custumals had already recorded as being in progress.

---

[64] On the plough-team see pp. 200–1 below.

[65] *Anglo-Saxon Charters*, §109 (ed. & transl. Robertson, pp. 204–6) (text); *ibid.*, pp. 205–7 (translation) (= Sawyer, *Anglo-Saxon Charters*, no. 1555).

[66] Text and analysis in *Facsimiles of Early Charters from Northamptonshire Collections*, ed. Stenton, pp. 1–7.

OTHER MISCELLANEOUS DOCUMENTS

The efficient administration of a large manor or a group of estates demanded a certain amount of documentation. Much of this would have been of an ephemeral nature and of only local importance. Fortunately a few estate documents survive to confirm the trends evident in the other texts examined in this chapter.

Farm accounts were one type of record that must have been common. A few fragments of a set of records of this type from Ely underline the fact that from the perspective of any manorial overlord, whether ecclesiastical or lay, a slave was basically a chattel.[67] Though the accounts are recorded in an early eleventh-century hand, the contents of the first entry suggest that they, in fact, date from not long after Bishop Æthelwold founded Thorney Abbey in 972.[68] Several of the entries deal with the stocking of the estates belonging to the newly founded abbey. The slaves are treated no differently from the rest of the stock. For instance, after listing the cost of two thousand herrings and bean seed, the document records that five *oras* (that is, between sixty and one hundred pence) were paid as the price of a man at Newton in Huntingdonshire.[69] A woman worth a similar amount was purchased for Stanground in the same county.[70] In addition, a swineherd worth half a pound was moved from an estate which Ely had earlier acquired at Milton in Cambridgeshire. (The text is defective at this point, so it is not clear where he moved to). Finally a *daia* or dairymaid,[71] who is specifically identified as a slave, was transferred to Linton in Cambridgeshire. Other accounts for the abbey of Ely in the same manuscript record that money was expended for the purchase of a woman at Stretham (also in Cambridgeshire). One should note that this account also mentions the payment of three mancuses for hired labour, showing that Ely had to depend on more than just slave labour to farm its demesne.

The list of estate-workers is another type of document of which only a few pre-Conquest examples survive. Evidence from two such lists incorporated into charters has already been discussed.[72] A list that is independent of a charter is to be found written in a hand of around the year 1000 in London, British Library, MS. Cotton Tiberius B.v, volume I, fo 76.[73] The persons named are described as *geburas*. The descendants of up to thirteen families and the estates on which they were currently resident are given.[74] Each family had originally been attached to

---

[67] *Anglo-Saxon Charters*, appendix II, §9 (ed. & transl. Robertson, pp. 252–6) (text); *ibid.*, pp. 253–7 (translation).

[68] On the date see Ker, *Catalogue*, §80 (p. 126) and *Anglo-Saxon Charters*, ed. & transl. Robertson, p. 503.

[69] Thorney Abbey held five hides there at the time of Domesday: see Domesday Book, volume I, fo 205r; *The Victoria History of the County of Huntingdon*, volume I, edd. Page & Proby, p. 345.

[70] The Abbey held eight hides there in 1086: *loc. cit.*

[71] On the *daia* see below, appendix I, s.v. *dæge*.

[72] Above, pp. 168–9.

[73] Pelteret, 'Two Old English lists of serfs', 472–3 (text); *ibid.*, 473–4 (translation).

[74] For a more detailed discussion see *ibid.*, 486–9. On p. 486 the estate is said to be at Mardlebury in Hertfordshire; in fact, this is where Ælfwold hailed from.

an estate at Hatfield in Hertfordshire (or, as the document puts it, they were *inbyrde to Hæðfelda*).

The uses to which such a list as this could be put become appparent in the light of a legal action reported in the *Liber Eliensis*, II.10. One Ælfwold claimed back some land at Stretham in Cambridgeshire, which he asserted he had sold under duress to Bishop Æthelwold. The abbot of Ely, Brihtnoth (970–996 x 999), counter-claimed that Ælfwold's wife and sons had been *innati* of Hatfield and that Ælfwold had sold the land in order that they should be free and without claim ('liberos et absque calumpnia eos habere'). Ælfwold's family must thus have been in the same socio-legal category as those in the Hatfield list, for *innatus* is the exact Latin equivalent of *inbyrde*. In both cases the words must refer to persons who, though they may have been defined as freemen in tribal law, were nevertheless legally bound to the estate on which they had been born. In short, they were serfs.[75]

The value of the Hatfield list lay in the protection it afforded to the Abbey's rights in any future cases hinging on personal legal status. The care with which it was drawn up is evident from the listing of two sisters whose ties with Hatfield were through their great-grandparents: their great-grandfather had been a *gebur* attached to Hatfield and their great-grandmother the daughter of a Hatfield *gebur*.[76] This association with the estate going back over five generations proves that servile tenures had been in existence for the very minimum of a century, that is, at least as early as Alfred's reign. We have seen that already in Alfred's day the concept of freedom was being transformed by the growth of manorialism.[77] Further evidence that rights over persons born on an estate were being claimed at this period is given by a Winchester charter of 902, which states:

The bishop gave permission to his kinsman Beornwulf to take into his service (?) the persons born on the estate at Ebbesbourne [in Wiltshire]. I have now taken them into my service(?) – Lufu and her three children and Luha and his six children. Now the community at Winchester had begged from me that these persons might remain on the estate, whether I had it or any of my friends. Moreover there were on it three penal slaves of peasant birth (*burbærde*) and three persons of slave birth (*ðeowbærde*); these the bishop and the community gave me as my rightful property, with their offspring.[78]

It is not an implausible suggestion that the families of Lufu and Luha at Ebbesbourne were *geburas*. *Gebur* certainly was a term used in the area, as is evident from the penal slaves who held that status at birth. And it is plain that this differed from a slave's status, since the three persons of slave origin are

---

[75] For a genealogical analysis of the document see *ibid.*, 475–86. The number of family groups may, in fact, be as few as eight, depending on how one interprets the names (*ibid.*, 484).

[76] *Ibid.*, 478, table I, no. 8.

[77] Above, pp. 55–6.

[78] 'Bisheop lyfde Beornulfe his mege þæt he most þa inberðan menn hamettan to Eblesburnan. Nu hebbe ic hi hamet – Lufe 7 hire ðreo bearn 7 Luhan 7 hie seax bearn. ðonne geærendodon me ða hiwan on Wintanceastre ðet þa men mostan on þan londe wunien, hæfde swa ic swa minra freonda swelce hit hæfde. Þonne weron þær ðreo witeðeowe men burbærde 7 ðreo ðeowberde; ða me salde bisceop 7 þa hiwan to ryhtre æhta 7 hire team.' *Select English Historical Documents*, §17 (ed. & transl. Harmer, p. 29.17–23) (text); *ibid.*, p. 60 (translation, emended) (= Sawyer, *Anglo-Saxon Charters*, no. 1285).

mentioned separately. The distinction in the grantor's mind between those born on the estate (the *inberðan*) and the slaves is quite clear. The former were attached to the land. The slaves, on the other hand, were given as the personal property of the grantee and so presumably could be kept or disposed of as Beornwulf wished. One may suspect that the bishop's concern with the former group stemmed from the possibility that the estate would be depleted of tenants rather than with the security of tenure of these families.

Hyams has suggested that the Hatfield document is evidence 'that lords used the procedure of suit of kin when they needed to prove their right to dependents of hereditary servile (but not necessarily slave) status.'[79] If this was the case, it would explain what motivated the entry of two documents in the *Textus Roffensis*. The first of these is another list, this time of *æhtemen* associated with the estate at Wouldham.[80] It is very like the Hatfield list, except that it names those who had transferred *into* rather than *out of* the estate. The reason why it was entered into this cartulary is apparent when one examines the document that immediately follows it.[81] In the latter Æthelsige is recorded as having lent his daughter and granddaughter 'out of Tottel's kin' and replaced them with other persons. Tottel is mentioned in the previous list together with his brother and an unnamed sister, who had a daughter with two children.[82] It seems most likely that Æthelsige either married the sister or himself was a brother of Tottel, whose daughter and granddaughter wished to leave the estate, probably in order for the daughter to remarry. Æthelsige made good this loss to the labour force of the estate by finding replacements, but the Cathedral wanted a written record of their continued rights in these persons and their progeny wherever they might move to in order to bring a suit of kin if it was necessary to regain control over them.[83]

Just such a suit of kin possibly lies behind a Bodmin record of A.D. 959 x 967, which supplies a list of men who, with the king's sanction, defended themselves against 'the accusation of evil men' that they were sons of *coloni* of the king.[84] (*Colonus* is an unusual word in early English documents but is a regular word for a serf in Continental sources.)[85] These men probably relocated, which would explain why their fathers' status was emphasised. Unfortunately the document discreetly avoids specifying who the 'evil men' were. Very likely they were powerful local magnates out to acquire these freemen's lands by proving that

---

[79] Hyams, 'The proof of villein status in the common law', 723, n. 8. See also Whitelock and Blake in *Liber Eliensis*, ed. Blake, pp. xii, xv, and 83, n. 6.

[80] Pelteret, 'Two Old English lists of serfs', 493 (text and translation) (= *Status Document*, §2.1).

[81] Pelteret, 'Two Old English lists of serfs', 493 (text and translation) (= *Status Document*, §2.2).

[82] For Tottel's genealogy see Pelteret, 'Two Old English lists of serfs', 501, table II, no. 1.

[83] See further *ibid.*, 494–503.

[84] *Manumission*, §3.50.

[85] The duties of a church *colonus*, for instance, were laid down in the *Lex Baiwariorum* of A.D. 744 x 748 (in *Leges Baiwariorum*, ed. Schwind, pp. 286–90, translated in part in Duby, *The Early Growth of the European Economy*, p. 41, and in a complete version in *Laws the Alamans and Bavarians*, transl. Rivers, p. 123). See further Latouche, *The Birth of the Western Economy*, 2nd. edn, pp. 182, 193, 195, and 199; Rivers, 'Seigneurial obligations and "Lex Baiuvariorum" I,13', and *idem*, 'The manorial system in the light of the "Lex Baiuvariorum" I,13'.

they were not entitled to hold them in their own right, but equally they might have been royal reeves trying to build up the labour force on the estates under their charge.

The estate documents examined in this chapter help one to understand how slavery came to disappear in England through a fusion of the slave and free peasantry, which was brought about by subjecting all those resident on an estate to the custom of the manor. Those who were free in tribal law found themselves becoming subject to obligations in the form of regular labour services, while those who were slaves gained rights that became protected by custom. The process was a slow one. Freemen had begun to incur obligations to overlords of estates by the end of the ninth century but the body of local manorial customary law had not grown sufficiently by the close of the Anglo-Saxon era to obliterate totally the distinctions that had existed in tribal law between slaves and freemen. That was a process that seems to have been completed in the century after the Norman Conquest.

A LACUNA IN THE DOCUMENTATION

The *Rectitudines* hints at a system of agriculture whereby peasants co-operated in the management of their fields and shared the teams of oxen they used in their ploughing.[86] The ridge-and-furrow that is the product of generations of plough-men is still visible if one gazes out of the train window when travelling up through the Midlands. Perhaps the most dominant characteristic of the English landscape, also to be seen from the train window, is the village. Yet the origins of the mediaeval English practice of farming the arable with common fields and the process of nucleation of settlement, events that seem from our perspective to be revolutionary, received very little notice in the written sources. Not surprisingly, therefore, they are subjects that have generated tremendous scholarly debate, especially in recent decades. As one of the leading researchers has written very recently,

'The last thirty years' work in mediaeval rural settlement in England has not produced any clear pattern. Indeed, matters, have become increasingly complex and confused. Nowhere is this more clearly demonstrated than in the late Saxon to early mediaeval period. All the recent work now seems to indicate that the English landscape was torn apart at this time and largely rebuilt over a period of perhaps 300 years. . . . [T]here remains one . . . basic problem which at the moment appears to be insoluble. This is the understanding of the mechanism by which all the changes to the landscape at this time were actually effected.'[87]

The reason for this confusion is that historians, archaeologists, and landscape geographers have passed from a happy state of ignorance when there were few facts – and consequently simple and satisfying generalisations were possible – to a position where they are swamped by an overwhelming mass of data which is,

---

[86] Above, p. 174.
[87] Taylor, 'Medieval rural settlement', 9.

however, not complete enough to enable new generalisations to emerge. This is especially evident when field systems are considered. Seebohm was able to suggest that the three-field system might have had its roots in Roman Britain.[88] Now we realise that the three-field system is largely limited geographically to the Midlands – and that the Midland region itself had a variety of field systems.[89]

In a book like this there seems little point in becoming mired in the controversies over the reorganisation of field systems and the origins of English villages at a time when the state of knowledge has moved from a stage of synthesis to intense analysis – when, for instance, one scholar has been moved to write twenty-five years after he had produced a cogent explanation for the settlement history of a particular village in Wiltshire that 'at present, there is no clear idea of its origin or development'![90] All one can safely say at this point is that the shift in agricultural practice whereby farmers took to ploughing their own strips of land within a common field *must* have had some impact on social relationships among the peasantry. Since there seems to be a general consensus that this practice had started by the tenth century,[91] it is hard to believe that it did not have some part to play in the disappearance of slavery. Until new syntheses are possible it seems foolish to make any more definite assertions.

[88] Seebohm, *English Village Community*, p. 417.
[89] *Studies of Field Systems in the British Isles*, edd. Baker & Butlin.
[90] Taylor, writing of Whiteparish in 'Medieval rural settlement', 10–11 at p. 11.
[91] C. Dyer has suggested that the development of the system of open fields started in the ninth century and the nuclear regrouping of villages a century or so later: 'Les problèmes de la croissance agricole', in *La Croissance agricole du haut moyen âge*, p. 124. For an introduction to these subjects, see *The Origins of Open-Field Agriculture*, ed. Rowley; Taylor, *Village and Farmstead*; *Studies in Late Anglo-Saxon Settlement*, ed. Faull; and *Medieval Villages*, ed. Hooke.

VII

'LIES, DAMNED LIES, AND STATISTICS':
DOMESDAY BOOK

INTRODUCTION

Domesday studies have played a long and honourable role in English historical scholarship.[1] Given the numerical prominence of those working on the land in the great survey, it is not surprising that some sections of the peasantry recorded there have attracted much attention from historians. Until very recently this attention did not extend to the Domesday Book slaves: apart from some scholars writing at the turn of the century such as Maitland, Vinogradoff, and Round,[2] a few of the contributors to the *Victoria County Histories*, and Professor Darby, who mapped the distribution of slaves in his *Domesday Geographies*, the slaves have been accorded rather cursory treatment by scholars.[3] The novocentenary celebrations of Domesday Book in 1986 acted as a spur to a renewed examination of the Domesday texts in which the slaves received some scholarly notice: John Moore presented a major paper on the topic in 1988[4] and a number of introductions to the county volumes designed to complement the facsimile issued in the novocentennial year contain several illuminating observations.

Yet there is abundant information on slaves in Domesday Book.[5] To treat this evidence exhaustively would require a monograph in itself. Instead, certain topics will be selected that offer insights into the lives of slaves and the institution of slavery, topics that only this source permits us to explore. We shall begin

---

[1] Bates, *A Bibliography of Domesday Book*, is an invaluable introduction to writings on the subject.

[2] See above, pp. 7–9 and 12, n. 54.

[3] See Clarke's valuable review of some of Darby's work in 'Domesday slavery'.

[4] Moore, 'Domesday slavery'.

[5] All references to the text of the Exchequer (Great) Domesday (Domesday Book, volume I) and Little Domesday (Domesday Book, volume II) are to the two volumes issued by the Record Commission under the editorship of A. Farley in 1783, which are now readily accessible with a translation in a series of 37 volumes (including indices) under the general editorship of John Morris. In the tables, references to specific holders and their estates use the numbering system employed in the translations in Morris's series but for the translations themselves I have preferred to cite the Victoria County History volumes. These editions and translations are used because they are more accessible than the *Great Domesday* facsimile and translations, edited by Williams & Erskine, which are likely to be available only in large research libraries. In the spelling of personal names, however, I have followed the practices of the translations in the *Great Domesday* volumes. The place-names in Domesday Book have been checked against Darby & Versey, *Domesday Gazetteer*.

with an examination of what the Domesday survey sought to learn about the slave population of England, how the Domesday commissioners obtained this information and what reliance we can place on the data collected. We shall then examine three out of the numerous categories of people listed in the survey: the *serui*, the *bouarii*, and the *ancillae*. This will be followed by a detailed treatment of four different Domesday counties, selected because of their varied mode of composition, the range of information they record about their inhabitants, and their geographic diversity.[6] Some general observations on this and other information in Domesday Book will follow in the third section. To put the insights we have gained in perspective, the chapter will conclude by considering the information on the agrarian workforce provided by several twelfth-century surveys.

Fortunately the terms of reference employed by the Domesday commissioners who visited Cambridgeshire are extant:

Then, what is the name of the manor, who held it in the time of King Edward, who holds it now, how many hides, how many ploughs on the demesne, how many belonging to the men, how many *uillani*, how many *cotarii*, how many slaves, how many *liberi homines*, how many sokemen, how much woodland, how much meadow, how much pasture, how many mills, how many fisheries, how much has been added or taken away, how much the whole was worth then and how much now, how much each *liber homo* or sokeman had or has. All this in three versions, namely, in the time of King Edward, and when King William gave it, and how it is now, and if more is able to be had than is had.[7]

None of the counties, in fact, follows these instructions in all their details, but nevertheless the terms of reference for the Cambridge commissioners in all likelihood represent substantially those received by all the Domesday Book commissioners. The amount of information the commissioners were required assemble appears to have been overwhelming.[8] Nor was their task made any easier by a certain imprecision in their terms of reference.

Exactly how the commissioners collected all their data is still a matter for debate. Some information was undoubtedly drawn from existing surveys, especially geld lists; hundredal juries must also have played an important part; but ultimately much of the information must have been dependent on the questions

---

6 In this I am following the example of Reginald Lennard, who in his *Rural England 1086–1135*, chapter II, used Oxfordshire as a sample county in his discussion of rural land tenure. He set out his justification (with which I concur) on p. 40. Convenient tables that could serve as a basis for further studies are contained in Baring, *Domesday Tables*.

7 'Deinde quomodo uocatur mansio, quis tenuit eam tempore R. E., quis modo tenet, quot hidae, quot carrucae in dominio, quot hominum [MS. hoi°m], quot uillani, quot cotarii, quot serui, quot liberi homines, quot sochemani, quantum silue, quantum prati, quantum pascuorum, quot molendarii, quot piscine, quantum est additum uel ablatum, quantum ualebat totum simul, et quantum modo, quantum ibi quisque, liber homo uel sochemanum habuit, uel habet. Hoc totum tripliciter scilicet tempore Regis Æduardi, et quondam Rex Willelmus dedit, et quomodo sit modo, et si potest plus haberi quam habeatur.' The text appears in London, British Library, MS. Cotton Tiberius A.vi, fo 38r, and was printed in full in Ellis, *A General Introduction to Domesday Book*, I.22–7.

8 Contemporaries of William evidently thought so too: see the entry in the *Anglo-Saxon Chronicle*, s.a. 1085 E, in *Two of the Saxon Chronicles Parallel*, ed. Plummer, p. 216, especially lines 26–30.

asked and the modes of collation employed by the commissioners.[9] The investigations of several generations of scholars have led to the conclusion that the commissioners' work was divided into seven circuits, which are analysed in table VI (the numbers in parentheses refer to the order in Domesday Book).[10]

TABLE VI: PUTATIVE DOMESDAY CIRCUITS

Circuit	Counties
I	Kent (1), Sussex (2), Surrey (3), Hampshire (4) Berkshire (5)
II	Wiltshire (6), Dorset (7), Somerset (8), Devonshire (9), Cornwall (10)
III	Middlesex (11), Hertford (12), Buckingham (13), Cambridge (18), Bedford (20)
IV	Oxford (14), Northampton (21), Leicester (22), Warwick (23)
V	Gloucester (15), Worcester (16), Hereford (17), Stafford (24), Shropshire (25), Cheshire (26)
VI	Huntingdon (19), Derby (27), Nottingham (28), Rutland (29), York (30), Lincoln (31)
VII	Essex (32), Norfolk (33), Suffolk (34)

Recently Alan Thacker and Peter Sawyer have argued that this widely-held interpretation is flawed: in their view, assessments were made instead county by county and the features found to be in common between certain counties lie in editorial decisions that were reached when the final version of Domesday was compiled in Winchester.[11] This should become a rich and fruitful subject of controversy between Domesday scholars for some time to come. Fortunately we do not have to be drawn into it. The mechanics of how the data were assembled need not detain us: what is relevant to us is that there are patterns discernible within the data, with groups of counties presenting different kinds of evidence. Whether these differences arose from the way in which various groups of commissioners accumulated and assessed the data which their extensive and somewhat vague terms of reference had enjoined them to assemble or whether they arose because editorial practice changed in Winchester does not affect our

---

[9] The debt of the Domesday commissioners to existing surveys has been emphasised by Harvey in 'Domesday Book and its predecessors'. Two of the introductions to county volumes in the *Great Domesday* facsimile series, discussing as they have done counties in different circuits, are particularly illuminating about the methods of compilation of Domesday Book: Lewis, 'An introduction to the Shropshire Domesday', in *The Shropshire Domesday*, edd. Williams & Erskine, pp. 6–12, and Roffe, 'An introduction to the Huntingdonshire Domesday', in *The Huntingdonshire Domesday*, edd. Williams & Erskine, pp. 2–6. Roffe, 'Domesday Book and northern society' is also essential reading.

[10] Table VI is drawn from Galbraith, *The Making of Domesday Book*, p. 8, who based it on earlier analyses by Eyton, Ballard, and Carl Stephenson. He suggested (p. 200, n. 2) that Staffordshire should perhaps be transferred from Circuit V to Circuit IV, an interpretation with which Dr David Roffe (*in litt.*) has agreed. Lewis, 'An introduction to the Shropshire Domesday', in *The Shropshire Domesday*, edd. Williams & Erskine, p. 6, n. 2, has also suggested that Staffordshire should be removed from Circuit V. Further evidence will be given below (see nn. 38 and 73) to suggest that it is wrongly placed in this circuit.

[11] Sawyer & Thacker, 'The Cheshire Domesday: introduction', in *A History of the County of Chester*, I, ed. Harris, pp. 293–4.

interpretation. Since Thacker and Sawyer have yet to prove in detail the general validity of their claim, we shall adopt a conservative position, employing as a working hypothesis the prevailing orthodoxy that the commissioners worked in circuits, while enjoying the luxury of declaring a disinterested agnosticism on the subject.

We do not only have to deduce from the record itself the methods employed by the commissioners to collect information: we also have to look to Domesday Book to answer the more fundamental question as to how the commissioners interpreted the terms they had received. This immediately presents us with the major dilemma of determining what the Domesday population-figures represent.[12] The problem is particularly acute in the case of the *serui*. Darby's *Domesday Geographies* offer two possibilities: the figures for *serui* either record the heads of slave households or else they represent all the members of slave families.[13]

In seeking an answer as to how to interpret these figures we must first dismiss from our minds any *a priori* assumptions about the legal and economic status of the slave that have been derived from a general view of English post-Conquest society. As will soon become apparent in this chapter, Domesday Book is in many ways *sui generis*, and one should start with the information furnished by the terms of reference and by Domesday Book itself.[14]

As can be seen, the terms of reference of the Cambridgeshire commissioners do not distinguish the *serui* from the other social groups they were required to enumerate. Had it been intended that one element of the population was to be treated differently from the rest, we might have expected this to have been noted. Then too, it is evident that whatever the overriding function of thc Domesday survey was,[15] a major goal must have been to provide an evaluation of the economic potential of the country – though we should think of this potential in terms of tribute and customary renders (including payments in the form of livestock) expressed in fiscal units rather than how a modern economist might conceive of it.[16] The evaluation of potential is most clearly revealed in the assessment of the plough-teams, where not only were the actual number of

---

[12] See Russell, *British Medieval Population*, pp. 36–41 and 51–4, and Brothwell, 'Palaeodemography and earlier British populations'.

[13] See, for example, *The Domesday Geography of Midland England*, edd. Darby & Terrett, 2nd edn, figs 149, 150, 152, and 153 (pp. 429, 431, 433, and 435); Darby, *Domesday England*, pp. 73–4.

[14] Cf. the comments of Finberg in *Tavistock Abbey*, p. 55: 'The language of Domesday Book is not the language of the Old English laws and charters, nor is it that of the later court rolls and manorial extents. It is a language peculiar to king William's great inquest; and no one key will unlock all its meanings.'

[15] The main purpose of Domesday Book is still a matter of scholarly controversy. Two older studies still contain much of value: see S. Harvey's excellent paper, 'Domesday Book and its predecessors', and V. H. Galbraith's *The Making of Domesday Book*. The millennium of Domesday Book encouraged a vast amount of scholarly activity, including the introductions to the county volumes of *Great Domesday*, edd. Williams & Erskine, which now are essential reading. In addition to Roffe's introduction mentioned in n. 9 above, his remarks in 'An introduction to the Derbyshire Domesday', in *The Derbyshire Domesday*, edd. Williams & Erskine, pp. 1–27, are also most informative.

[16] I owe this point to Dr David Roffe.

plough-teams noted but also how many there *could* be. Nor did the survey restrict itself only to the land and its animals; it included human-beings as well. Given an underlying economic motive for the survey, one can assume that the commissioners were interested only in those contributing economically to the estates they were assessing. In fact, one might go further and say that these economic contributions were defined in the commissioners' eyes as those that had an actual or potential fiscal outcome, though many scholars might contest this interpretation. The commissioners therefore would probably have excluded children under the age of twelve (or possibly fifteen),[17] who, though they were capable of working as domestic servants in the demesne hall, may have been too young to engage in full-time agricultural labour. The survey probably also excluded most women, though here the commissionere ran into a problem. Some women – presumably those who were unmarried and the widows – must have had agricultural (as opposed to domestic) duties that made an important contribution to the value of an estate.[18] Female slaves especially would have been capable of providing some economic return to their owners. In two circuits the commissioners got round this problem by recording *ancillae*, though in numbers that preclude the possibility that all female slaves were recorded.[19]

Thus the commissioners neither recorded all members of a socio-economic group (in other words, took a census) nor, I suspect, did they limit themselves solely to the heads of households. This approach would have applied to the *uillani* and *serui* alike because, as has been indicated, the commissioners were not instructed to vary their criteria of assessment according to the group being surveyed. If this interpretation is correct, it follows that the figures in Domesday Book record not merely the heads of households but also unmarried brothers and sons of working age who in some way contributed to the geldable value of a manor.[20] The Middlesex Domesday, which is unusually explicit about peasant

---

[17] This assumption is based on the age that youths were held legally responsible for crimes such as theft in Anglo-Saxon England (twelve years old according to II Æthelstan, §1 and VI Æthelstan, §1.1, but VI Æthelstan, §12 exempted those under fifteen from capital punishment: *Die Gesetze*, ed. Liebermann, I.150, 173, and 183). Either twelve or fifteen presumably represents what the Anglo-Saxons considered to be the age when adult status was attained.

[18] The Domesday commissioners occasionally gave recognition of this fact in listing such women as *feminae cotar.* (Salop.), *liberae feminae* (Norfolk), *mulier paupercula* (Kent), *uiduae feminae* (Salop.), and *uxores uillanorum defunctorum* (Gloucs.).

[19] See below, pp. 202–3.

[20] In this chapter the word 'manor' is always used in the Domesday sense, with one exception, which is clearly signalled in the text. This sense is not the one used elsewhere in this book, where the focus is on its seigneurial, tenurial, and economic dimensions. Recent scholarship has stressed the importance of the Domesday *manerium* in relation to the collection of geld, thus returning (with some modifications) to the views of Maitland first expressed nearly a century ago. Roffe has stressed that the Domesday 'manor', at least in the East Midlands, was not an economic unit nor was it 'necessarily a basic tenurial unit': 'it was primarily a nexus of delegated tribute' based on a hall where the dues were rendered (Roffe, 'An Introduction to the Nottinghamshire Domesday', in *The Nottinghamshire Domesday*, edd. Williams & Erskine, pp. 29–30 and cf. p. 3). He has suggested, however, that the concept was not a fixed one in Domesday Book but that it evolved in course of compilation: see 'Domesday Book and northern society', especially pp. 328–33. Palmer's analysis of the *manerium* is also very illuminating; he has concluded that it was 'a house at which geld is collected' (Palmer, 'The Domesday manor', in *Domesday Studies*, ed. Holt, p. 153).

land-holdings, supports this contention. There are numerous entries recording a group of *uillani*, *bordarii*, or *cotarii* resident on an extensive estate.[21] Many such entries can be interpreted to be the land-holding of a large family or a number of families related by marriage.

This suggests that however one calculates the total population of England in 1086, the proportion of slaves to the rest of the population will remain fixed. At first glance the only grounds for suggesting that the proportions could change would seem to be that slaves may have differed in family size or fertility from the rest of the population – but there is no evidence to support this. Unfortunately, the happy prospect of an untroubled amble through Domesday population statistics soon becomes shattered by uncomfortable facts Domesday Book itself and other related documentation thrust into our path. In reality Domesday's statistics are very unreliable for some of the purposes to which we might like to put them.

First, it must noted that the commissioners themselves seem to have exercised considerable discretion over what information they collected and how it was to be collated. As far as slaves are concerned this is most evident in the returns of Circuit VI. We shall search in vain for slaves in the Huntingdonshire Domesday. Unfortunately for our confidence in Domesday Book, the *Inquisitio Eliensis*, which appears to have been one of the documents stemming from the Domesday inquest, shows that the abbey of Ely possessed no less than sixteen slaves on four estates in that county.[22] Other counties in the circuit mention exiguous numbers of slaves: Nottinghamshire reported a mere twenty-four. One must conclude that in this circuit information on slaves was not sought, though their presence was noted on occasion, presumably when a tenant's documentation happened to record them.[23]

Nor was this the only element in the population that was probably under-recorded. If what Domesday Book calls *liberi homines* and sokemen did not owe soke outside the area where they were resident, they may well also have been omitted, since they did not affect the value of a tenant's manor, which was of primary interest to the commissioners.[24] Two other categories that probably are under-represented in the Domesday figures for some parts of England are the

21 For a full list see the figures given under the heading 'Tenures imprecisely recorded' in appendix II of Pinder's 'Domesday Survey', in *A History of the County of Middlesex*, edd. Cockburn *et al.*, I.132–5. See n. 144 below for the corrections that should be made to this appendix.

22 The estates were at Colne, Bluntisham, Somersham, and Spaldwick: *Inquisitio Comitatus Cantabrigiensis . . . subjicitur Inquisitio Eliensis*, ed. Hamilton, p. 169, and cf. Moore, 'Domesday slavery', p. 197, table II. For the *Inquisitio Eliensis* itself see Clarke, 'The Domesday satellites', in *Domesday Book: A Reassessment*, ed. Sawyer, especially p. 53.

23 The references to slaves in Nottinghamshire, found on fos 287–289v of Domesday Book, volume I, are evidently limited to three *breues* (that is, the full description in Domesday Book of the manorial holdings of three tenants-in-chief), namely, William Peverel, Walter d'Aincourt, and Geoffrey Alselin; the only mention in the county of *censarii* is also to be found there: see Roffe, 'An introduction to the Nottinghamshire Domesday', in *The Nottinghamshire Domesday*, edd. Williams & Erskine, p. 4, n. 7. Moore has conveniently tabulated the information on Nottinghamshire slaves in 'Domesday slavery', p. 197, table III.

24 On the recording of sokemen see Roffe, 'An introduction to the Huntingdonshire Domesday', in *The Huntingdonshire Domesday*, edd. Williams & Erskine, pp. 16–17.

bordarii and *cotarii*.[25] If people in these categories were full-time employees on the demesne or were employed by those called *uillani* in Domesday Book, they may well not have been included in Domesday's figures. Only if they directly added to the value of a manor (and we shall see that this appears very much to have been the case with the Essex *bordarii*) was there good reason to note their existence.

Yet another category that is rarely mentioned by name and which has to be sought for in Domesday Book is the *censarius* or rent-payer. Later documentation from Burton Abbey records that they formed an important element on its estates.[26] But the extant terms of reference for the Domesday commissioners did not include those who paid rent and so they frequently must simply have been omitted. Where such persons were commonly to be found, they may have been included in some of the circuit returns under other categories of person, which was perhaps the case in Essex, as will be discussed later.

The inadequacy of the Burton returns in Domesday Book suggests that the accuracy of the statistics recorded was heavily dependent on the quality of the manorial documentation, in spite of all the assistance that the commissioners sought from juries. This is likely to have been especially so with the slaves, who were probably answerable only to their owners and not to the peasants amongst whom they may have laboured.

Many slaves may have been doomed to anonymity by working, not for a tenant-in-chief or a sub-tenant, but for sokemen, who themselves were often omitted from the record. Indeed they may also on occasion have worked for the lesser categories of men such as *uillani*. In Exon Domesday slaves sometimes appear with *uillani* in association with ploughs. This *could* mean that the slaves were themselves the part-owners of these ploughs but it is equally possible that they were owned by the *uillani* concerned.[27]

One should not retreat into a reductionist position as a result of this lamentable catalogue of (from our point of view) statistical inadequacies. To decide that Domesday Book has nothing dependable to say about the English agrarian population of the latter part of the eleventh century would be a failure of nerve. The complexities, contradictions, and omissions simply warn us that the data require close evaluation at a regional, county and, if possible, local level. At the broadest levels of generalisation the Domesday statistics on slaves still have a value and table VII, using the figures calculated by H. C. Darby, is presented to that end.[28] One should have the gravest reservations about the percentages of slaves in specific counties; only at a regional level may these have any validity.

[25] *Ibid.*, p. 16, and Darby, *Domesday England*, pp. 69–71.
[26] Walmsley, 'The *censarii* of Burton Abbey and the Domesday population'; cf. Darby, *Domesday England*, pp. 85–6.
[27] For some examples see Moore, 'Domesday slavery', p. 214.
[28] Because of ambiguities in the record itself and variations between present-day county boundaries and those at the time of Domesday, every scholar is likely to arrive at a different total for the Domesday population. For the sake of convenience the figures for slaves in table VII have been drawn from Darby, *Domesday England*, appendix III, pp. 338–45, although somewhat different figures may be used elsewhere in this chapter for the some of the counties. The percentages of slaves as a proportion of the whole population in a county have been derived from Darby's book, as have been the figures for *ancillae* and *bouarii*, although Slack, 'The

In our present state of knowledge about Domesday Book and eleventh-century regional variations in agricultural practices, it would be folly to suggest multipliers that could provide the actual number of slaves in England in 1086. The most that can be asserted is that a single multiplier would have no intellectual validity.

TABLE VII: NUMBERS OF *SERUI* (INCLUDING *ANCILLAE*), *BOUARII*, AND *ANCILLAE* ALONE, AND THEIR PERCENTAGE OF THE TOTAL POPULATION PER COUNTY AS RECORDED IN DOMESDAY BOOK

	Serui and ancillae	%	*Bouarii*	%	*Ancillae*	%
Bedfordshire	480	13.4				
Berkshire	793	2.9				
Buckinghamshire	845	16.6				
Cambridgeshire	541	11.1				
Cheshire[a]	141	9.2	161	10.5	11	.7
Cornwall	1,149	21.4				
Derbyshire	20	0.3				
Devonshire	3,318	19.2			1	
Dorset	1,244	16.9			3	
Essex	1,809	12.9				
Gloucestershire[a]	2,140	26.1			223	2.7
Hampshire	1,765	18.0				
Herefordshire[a]	722	16.7	113	2.6	124	2.9
Hertfordshire	591	13.0				
Huntingdonshire	0	0.0				
Kent	1,160	9.9	4			
Lancashire (South)	20	7.7	12	4.6	3	1.1
Leicestershire	402	6.3			23	.4
Lincolnshire	0	0.0				
Middlesex	112	5.1				
Norfolk	973	3.7				
Northamptonshire	737	9.6			59	.8
Nottinghamshire	24	0.4			2	
Oxfordshire	1,002	14.9				
Roteland	0	0.0				

Shropshire ploughmen of Domesday Book', which has slightly lower figures, is used when discussing the *bouarii* of Shropshire. The figures for *ancillae* are almost certainly overstated: whenever Domesday Book employed the phrase *inter seruos et ancillas*, Darby divided the figure in half when calculating the number of *ancillae*, which seems the only practical way of dealing with the problem but which is not in accordance with the proportions of *ancillae* to *serui* in the counties where the phrase appears. As Moore has pointed out ('Domesday slavery', pp. 192, 194 and n. 7), Ellis's figures had been used in the past (see n. 7 above); they have long been recognised to be faulty. See, for example, Walker, 'On the measurements and valuations of the Domesday of Cambridgeshire', especially p. 125.

	Serui and *ancillae*	%	*Bouarii*	%	*Ancillae*	%
Shropshire[a]	918	19.5	389	8.3	88	1.9
Somerset	2,120	16.3				
Staffordshire	240	7.9			1	
Suffolk	892	4.7				
Surrey	503	12.3				
Sussex	416	4.3				
Warwickshire	781	12.4			34	
Wiltshire	1,588	16.0				
Worcestershire	718	15.6	79	1.7	128	2.8
Yorkshire	0	0.0				
England	28,164	10.5	757	2.7	706	2.5

[a] A further seventy-one slaves and four *bouarii* should be added if the parts of the Domesday counties that are now in Wales are added.

SOME SOCIO-LEGAL CLASSES IN DOMESDAY BOOK

Three groups of persons in Domesday Book are relevant to this study. These are the *serui*, the *bouarii*, and the *ancillae*. It has been suggested that a fourth group, the *coliberti*, may represent slaves who had been freed in groups,[29] but this hypothesis is not supported by the evidence. *Colibertus* is several times equated with the Old English *gebur* in Domesday Book,[30] and if one examines the position of the Continental *colliberti*, it is evident that the Domesday commissioners in some circuits adopted the term because it was used of a Continental agrarian group with rights and obligations similar to those of the Anglo-Saxon *geburas*.[31] The *coliberti* accordingly are excluded from consideration here.

[29] Vinogradoff, *English Society in the Eleventh Century*, p. 468.

[30] *burs i. coliberti*, Domesday Book, volume I, fo 38rb (Cosham [Hants.]); *uel bures* interlined above *coliberti*, Domesday Book, volume I, fo 38vb (Wallop [Hants.]); *coliberti* interlined above *buri*, Domesday Book, volume I, fo 174vb (Powick [Worcs.]). In Eckington (Worcs.) six *coliberti* paid 11s 2d *per annum*, and ploughed and sowed twelve acres with their own seed (Domesday Book, volume I, fo 174va). Translations in Round, 'The text of the Hampshire Domesday', in *A History of Hampshire and the Isle of Wight*, volume I, ed. Doubleday, pp. 451b and 453b, and *idem*, 'The text of the Worcestershire Domesday', in *The Victoria History of the County of Worcester*, volume I, edd. Willis-Bund & Doubleday, pp. 301 and 300 respectively.

[31] For the Domesday evidence, see Pelteret, 'The *coliberti* of Domesday Book' and cf. Van de Kieft, 'Les "Colliberti" '. Hallam has equated the *geburas* and the *coliberti* but has claimed that they were 'housed slaves who were decidedly unfree – the *nativi* or born serfs of later generations': 'England before the Norman Conquest', in *The Agrarian History of England and Wales*, volume II, ed. Hallam, p. 43. The latter part of his statement I would not contest and it would be foolish to deny the possibility that some *geburas* had originally been slaves. Their land-holdings seem to have been too large, however, for this to have generally been so.

THE *SERUUS*

Horace Round in his magisterial contributions to the *Victoria County Histories* always referred to the Domesday *seruus* as a 'serf' and the latter word was still used in the Cheshire volume published as recently as 1987.[32] This practice was also followed by Darby in his *Domesday Geographies*. Darby has been strongly criticised by Clarke, however, for not using the word 'slave' in these contexts,[33] and indeed this is how another Domesday authority, R. W. Finn, always translated it in his writings.[34] Darby was evidently persuaded by the criticism because he dropped the word 'serf' and referred only to 'slaves' in his book *Domesday England*, the volume that summarised his findings.

This is not a subject that demands a lengthy debate: *seruus* should simply be translated as 'slave'. 'Serf' is a generalised term expressing a relationship of a peasant who occupies land in return for certain services. The terms of reference of the Cambridgeshire commissioners in contrast show that *seruus* was one of a number of specific socio-legal categories. Only if several of these specific categories were to be lumped together might the generalised term 'serf' be applicable. If the distinction in meaning between 'slave' and 'serf' is to have any validity (and it is a contention of this book that it does), then 'serf' must be dropped hereafter from all discussions of the Domesday *seruus*.

THE *SERUUS*, THE *BOUARIUS*, AND THE PLOUGH

Both contemporary Anglo-Saxon and later mediaeval sources indicate that the plough and its attendant team were operated by two men. In many of the Domesday counties two *serui* are recorded for every demesne plough listed. Round was the first to notice this and he observed that the correlation also applied to the *bouarii*.[35] In this section of the chapter the evidence on the *seruus* as ploughman, on the *bouarius*, and on the plough itself will be examined.[36] Naturally, we shall focus on the Domesday Book evidence, but in the case of the plough it will be necessary to draw on other sources in order to make full use of the Domesday evidence to be reviewed later in this chapter.

Presumptive evidence for ploughing as the primary occupation of many slaves is widespread in Domesday Book and is to be found in counties as far apart as Essex and Worcester. In the case of Warwickshire, to take one county from among many as an example, there is a ratio of two slaves per demesne plough on fifty-five of the approximately 160 manors where slaves are recorded.[37]

---

[32] Sawyer, 'The Cheshire Domesday: translation of the text', in *A History of the County of Chester*, I, ed. Harris, pp. 342–70.

[33] Clarke, 'Domesday slavery', 42.

[34] See, for example, his book *The Norman Conquest and its Effects on the Economy*.

[35] Round, 'Introduction to the Worcestershire Domesday', in *The Victoria History of the County of Worcester*, volume I, edd. Willis-Bund & Doubleday, pp. 274–6; Round, 'Introduction to the Essex Domesday', in *The Victoria History of the County of Essex*, volume I, edd. Doubleday & Page, pp. 361–2; Round, 'Introduction to the Herefordshire Domesday', in *The Victoria History of the County of Hereford*, volume I, ed. Page, pp. 288–90.

[36] M. M. Postan in *The Famulus* provided an invaluable analysis of the *seruus* as ploughman and the *bouarius*, to which this section is heavily indebted.

[37] *Ibid.*, p. 6.

In Circuit V *bouarii* are found in four of the six counties and also in South Lancashire;[38] a single individual is reported from Warwickshire. The greatest number were in Shropshire. The figures for this county as tabulated by Slack[39] are presented in table VIII.

TABLE VIII: NUMBERS OF DEMESNE TEAMS, *BOUARII*, AND *SERUI* IN SHROPSHIRE IN 1086

	Manors	Demesne teams	Bouarii	Serui
Manors with excess *bouarii*	2	2.5	8	–
Manors with sufficient free ploughmen and no *serui*	66	142	284	–
Manors with insufficient free ploughmen and no *serui*	4	17.5	21	–
Manors with free and slave ploughmen	12	39	32	48
Manors with sufficient slave ploughmen	162	290.5	–	581
Excess *serui* on 93 of these manors	–	–	–	211
Manors with insufficient slave ploughmen	24	57	–	69
Manors with no recorded ploughmen	43	66.5	–	–
Serui on manors with no recorded demesne	–	–	–	8
TOTALS	313	615	345	917

Slack's figures show very clearly that both *serui* and *bouarii* were connected with ploughing but that the two classes of person were distinct from each other. In the case of the *bouarii* they were to be found in Shropshire by 1086 on eighty-four manors. Only seven of these were ecclesiastical holdings, whereas slaves were to be found on no less than sixteen ecclesiastical estates. As will be seen again later, there is other evidence to support the contention that the Church was highly conservative in its use of manpower in that slaves on ecclesiastical estates tended not to be freed.

Slack has no doubt that the Domesday *bouarii* were freemen. Their legal status has been a matter of scholarly controversy, however,[40] and there are two

---

[38] None is recorded in Staffordshire, which is perhaps an indication that it does not belong in Circuit V. Cf. nn. 10 and 73.

[39] Slack, 'The Shropshire ploughmen of Domesday Book.' The table appears on p. 35.

[40] *Ibid.*, 32. Round in his 'Introduction to the Worcestershire Domesday', in *The Victoria History of the County of Worcester*, volume I, edd. Willis-Bund & Doubleday, p. 276, argued on the

kinds of entry that might initially seem to indicate that the *bouarii* were slaves. The first is where *bouarii* are mentioned in association with *ancillae*. In such cases the same phraseology is employed as when *serui* and *ancillae* appear together. An example is the entry for the Shropshire estate of Edgmond: 'In demesne there are six ploughs and twelve ploughmen and one bondwoman';[41] compare the entry for Ford: 'In demesne there are ten ploughs, and twenty slaves and six bondwomen'.[42] There are two such entries in Shropshire, one in Worcestershire, and four in Herefordshire. In fact, this association proves nothing one way or the other, as a moment's reflexion will show. Since it was natural in the Edgmond entry to place the word *bouarii* in association with *VI car.*, the Exchequer scribe's only alternative to what he actually wrote would have been to place *ancillae* before *VI car.* – but this would not have been consistent with the stereotyped formulas that he strove for. The order that the scribe followed was thus probably dictated by nothing other than economy of labour.

The second argument, which was advanced by Round, is that one of the entries in the *Liber Niger* of Peterborough Abbey (A.D. 1125 x 1128) indicates that on the Abbey's property a *bouarius* could be either a slave (*seruus*) or free (*liber*).[43] The Domesday commissioners were sufficiently innovative and idiosyncratic in their terminology, however, for it to be foolish to base an interpretation primarily on other sources. All the Peterborough evidence suggests is that the term *bouarius* could be used of a slave but equally could be applied to a freeman.[44]

On the other hand, eleven *liberi bouarii* are recorded in Herefordshire and one in Shropshire. Round admitted: 'As the former are found within the compass of two columns, the *liber* may be only one of the Domesday scribe's pleonastic vagaries', but he did not commit himself further.[45] In fact, the scribe's practice is perfectly explicable in psychological terms. Faced with occasional *bouarii* in the

---

basis of Peterborough evidence that some *bouarii* were servile and others free. James Tait in his 'Introduction to the Shropshire Domesday', in *The Victoria History of Shropshire*, volume I, ed. Page, pp. 302–3, suggested that either *bouarii* were freemen, noted because they were doing tasks normally performed by slaves, or that 'while not exactly free, even with the restricted freedom of bordars and cottars, the "bovarii" of Domesday were men who were throwing off the slough of mere servitude' (*loc. cit.*). Round responded to Tait in 'Introduction to the Herefordshire Domesday', in *The Victoria History of the County of Hereford*, volume I, ed. Page, p. 289, but did not take a firm stand one way or the other.

[41] 'In dominio sunt VI carrucae 7 XII bouarii 7 una ancilla.' Domesday Book, volume I, fo 253vb (text); Drinkwater, 'Translation of the Shropshire Domesday', in *The Victoria History of Shropshire*, volume I, ed. Page, p. 317b (translation, emended).

[42] 'In dominio sunt X carrucae 7 XX serui 7 VI ancillæ.' Domesday Book, volume I, fo 253vb (text); Drinkwater, 'Translation of the Shropshire Domesday', in *The Victoria History of Shropshire*, volume I, ed. Page, pp. 316a–317b (translation, emended).

[43] *Liber Niger Monasterii S. Petri de Burgo*, in *Chronicon Petroburgense*, ed. Stapleton, p. 163.38–9; Round, 'Introduction to the Worcestershire Domesday', in *The Victoria History of the County of Worcester*, volume I, edd. Willis-Bund & Doubleday, p. 276. For the text see n. 49 below.

[44] For further discussion of the Peterborough entry, see Postan, *The Famulus*, p. 9, n. 2.

[45] Round, 'Introduction to the Herefordshire Domesday', in *The Victoria History of the County of Hereford*, volume I, ed. Page, p. 289. Round was criticised on this point by Postan, *The Famulus*, p. 10.

returns from Circuit V and suddenly realising that the term was ambiguous because *serui* frequently performed this function, he must have decided to prefix *bouarius* with *liber*. This he continued to do for a couple of columns, but either consciously or unconsciously then reverted to his earlier practice. Anyone who has engaged in a lengthy piece of writing will recognise this natural inclination towards inconsistency.

This interpretation might be dismissed as weak were it not for four entries from Hereford which decisively reveal the practice of whoever compiled this section. On folios 179v, 180rb, and 180vb the terms *serui* and *bouarii* appear together. At Marden there were four slaves and two *bouarii* with three ploughs on the demesne; at Kingsland there were five ploughs (though there could have been three more), ten *bouarii*, and two slaves; on the demesne of Cleve with the berewick of Wilton there were four ploughs, nine slaves, five bondwomen, and a single *bouarius*; at Ford, with three ploughs on the demesne, there were three slaves, two bondwomen, and three *bouarii*; and at Eldersfield, also with three ploughs on the demesne, there were five slaves and bondwomen together (*inter seruos et ancillas*) and six *bouarii*. The last entry shows that *serui* and *ancillae* were closely associated with each other, in contrast to the *bouarii*. The first entry, that for Marden, reveals that the *serui* and *bouarii* together could form plough-teams, and at both Wilton and Ford there were insufficient *bouarii* to man the demesne ploughs, so some of the *serui* listed must have performed this function.[46]

The significance of this has been pointed out by Postan.[47] What Domesday Book reveals is a process of social change whereby *serui* were becoming *bouarii*. Here it is necessary only to mention two pieces of evidence from the Peterborough *Liber Niger* in support of this. In the latter source it is noticeable that the land-holdings of the *bouarii* are located on the demesne. This suggests that these *bouarii* were descendants of slaves for whom the lord had carved out a plot of land from his demesne in return for rents and services. For example, at Glinton in Northamptonshire 'on the demesne there are three plough-teams of twenty-four oxen and six *bouarii*, and each of them holds nine acres'.[48]

Confirmation of this interpretation lies in the entry in the *Liber Niger* for Castor (Northants.), which declares: 'There are four plough-teams of thirty-two oxen and eight *bouarii*, each holding ten acres. . . . And each *bouarius* gives one penny (*denarius*) for his person, if he is free. And if he is a slave, he gives nothing.'[49] The reference to the *denarius* looks suspiciously like Peter's Pence,

---

46 Round, 'Translation of the Herefordshire Domesday', in *The Victoria History of the County of Hereford*, volume I, ed. Page, pp. 312b (Marden), 313a (Kingsland), 313b (Wilton), 315a–b (Ford; Round's translation has two ploughs on the demesne instead of three, an obvious error), 317b (Eldersfield).

47 *The Famulus*, especially pp. 7–11.

48 'In curia sunt iii carrucae, xxiiii bobus et vi bouarii, et unusquisque eorum tenet ix acras.' *Liber Niger Monasterii S. Petri de Burgo*, in *Chronicon Petroburgense*, ed. Stapleton, p. 163.13–14. Stapleton's reading of *xxxiiii* is an error. Cf. also Pitchley (Northants.), where there were 'eight oxherds, each of whom have half a virgate on the demesne' ('viii bubulci, quisque habet dimidiam uirgam de dominio'): *ibid.*, p. 162.7.

49 'Ibi sunt iiii carrucae de xxxii bobus et viii bouarii, quisque tenens x acras. . . . Et unusquisque bouarius dat i denarium pro capite suo, si liber est. Et si seruus est, nichil dat.' *Ibid.*, page 163.

the payment of which distinguished a freeman from a slave. We may wonder whether a contemporary royal court would have maintained such a distinction between a freeman and a slave, and indeed it is moot whether all the rights and obligations of an Anglo-Saxon slave would have been insisted upon at this time. What it proves is that ploughing was still remembered as an occupation characteristic of slave status, though the entry shows that by this time it was more relevant for an overlord to define a person by economic function than by legal status.

The *Liber Niger* also reveals that it was chiefly the wives of *bouarii* who sometimes had to perform certain labour services such as mowing and winnowing corn.[50] That these women were obligated to undertake labour services at all suggests that they were originally slaves bound to perform manorial duties. The only other woman required to perform these services was the wife of a cow-herd (*uaccarius*), who in the light of his occupation and small land-holding of four acres was probably also of slave origin.[51]

In early twelfth-century records *bouarii* are, in fact, ubiquitous. On the Evesham Abbey estates there were two to every plough.[52] Their presence was not simply limited to the west: the *Liber Niger* reports them in Lincolnshire, a county where Domesday Book records no slaves at all.[53] In Worcestershire the holdings of these *bouarii* tended to be half-virgates.[54] It is doubtful, however, whether this was always the case. Domesday Book records, for instance, that on the Bishop of Hereford's manor of Onibury (Salop.) there was only one slave to operate the demesne plough, but there was also one cottar (*cozet*) recorded, who may have been his partner.[55] On the Peterborough estates on the other side of the country *bouarii* tended, in fact, to be closer to the cottagers described in the *Rectitudines* or the *bordarii* of the Middlesex Domesday rather than to the Old English *gebur* or Middlesex *uillanus* with his virgate or half-virgate of land. The *Liber Niger* evidence on this is set out in table IX.

---

50 *Ibid.*, pp. 163.14–15 and 37–8 (Glinton and Castor [Northants.]), 164.29–30 (Fiskerton [Lincs.]), and 165.6–7 (Scotterthorpe [Lincs.]).

51 *Ibid.*, pp. 163.42–164.1 (Castor [Northants.]).

52 Slack, 'The Shropshire ploughmen of Domesday Book', 32.

53 *Liber Niger Monasterii S. Petri de Burgo*, in *Chronicon Petroburgense*, ed. Stapleton, pp. 164–5. Cf. Round, 'Introduction to the Worcestershire Domesday', in *The Victoria History of the County of Worcester*, volume I, edd. Willis-Bund & Doubleday, p. 275.

54 This seems to be the typical holding on the Evesham Abbey estates. Cf. Tait, 'Introduction to the Shropshire Domesday', in *The Victoria History of Shropshire*, volume I, ed. Page, p. 303.

55 Domesday Book, volume I, fo 252rb (text); Drinkwater, 'Translation of the Shropshire Domesday', in *The Victoria History of Shropshire*, volume I, ed. Page, p. 311b (translation).

TABLE IX: LAND-HOLDINGS OF *BOUARII* ON PETERBOROUGH ESTATES IN
A.D. 1125 x 1128

Acreage:	15	10	9	5	Unknown	Average Acreage
Bouarii (*bubulci*)	8	10[a]	6	9	16	9.7[a]
No. of estates recording *bouarii* (*bubulci*)	1	2	1	2	5	

[a] At Scotterthorpe (Lincs.) two *bouarii* 'held ten acres'. This possibly means that each
held five acres for a total of ten acres, rather than ten acres each, in which case the
average acreage for a ploughman would drop to 9.4.

The variations in the land-holdings of *bouarii* disclosed by table IX should not
surprise us, since if these men were freed slaves, the economic motives for their
release would have varied from estate to estate and from area to area. For
overlords intent on reducing their demesnes or wishing to increase the arable on
their estates it was obviously in their interests to give the men land. If, on the
other hand, they wanted the continued use of their former slaves' labour, it made
better economic sense simply to give them tofts.

As to the general duties of the eleventh-century slave ploughman and *bouarius* the sources are mute, but the twelfth-century Evesham Cartulary (London,
British Library, MS. Cotton Vespasian B.xxiv) tells us something about the
bouarius. On folio 49r the labour services required of those on a holding
described as *quatuor . . . uirge bouariorum*[56] were that each had to work for two
days in autumn. Furthermore, from the feast of St Michael to the feast of St
Martin (that is, from 29 September to 11 November) each was to carry fodder to
Evesham for the use of the abbot. At *Heuedlega* (folio 27r) they had to plough
for five days on the demesne; on the Saturday they could do their own work.
Furthermore, they had to guard thieves if there were any at the lord's court
(*curia*). If rent was paid on the land, it amounted to three shillings, and there
were other customary obligations they had to observe.

Since ploughmen will appear again in this chapter, it is perhaps appropriate to
conclude this section by describing with the help of various sources the social
and economic unit formed by a ploughman and his plough-team. According to
Ælfric the ploughman's assistant was a boy (*puer*) whose function to goad the
oxen with a whip and with his voice.[57] The illustrations in London, British
Library, MSS. Cotton Tiberius B.v and Cotton Julius A.vi perhaps confirm this,

[56] The meaning of this phrase is indicated in the entry for Hampton (by Evesham) on fo 79v of
the Evesham cartulary (London, British Library, MS. Harley 3763), where it states that each
of the 'uirge bouariorum' had to find 'two men for the lord's plough'. ('Per totum annum uirga
debet inuenire duos homines ad carucam domini et autumpno ii homines ad ebdomada et ad
Wedhoc. . . .') Cf. Round, 'Introduction to the Worcestershire Domesday', in *The Victoria
History of the County of Worcester*, volume I, edd. Willis-Bund & Doubleday, p. 274. (On the
relationship between this cartulary and London, British Library, MS. Cotton Vespasian
B.xxiv, see Davis, *Medieval Cartularies of Great Britain*, p. 44, no. 382).

[57] *Ælfric's Colloquy*, line 29 (ed. Garmonsway, p. 21).

as the figure in charge of the oxen is bare-footed, beardless, and smaller than the ploughman and the sower that follow the plough.[58] Evidence from the twelfth and thirteenth centuries suggests, however, that both ploughmen were adults.[59] The Anglo-Saxon illustrations show a team of four oxen and Ælfric might also have had a small team in mind, which might explain why he referred to a boy as performing the role of the twelfth-century *fugator*, who in general probably had a larger team to control.

The Domesday commissioners evidently considered the plough-team to consist of eight oxen.[60] This appears to have been a fiscal figure, however,[61] like the ploughland itself (also called a *carruca*, an ambiguous usage that reflects Continental practice),[62] and there are many exceptions mentioned within Domesday Book. For example, the Huntingdonshire folios of Domesday Book mention teams belonging to *uillani* consisting of five, three, and even two beasts, and the six-ox plough-team appears to have existed in the South-west at the time of Domesday.[63] The twelfth-century *Liber Niger* from Peterborough Abbey confirms that an uneven number of oxen could be employed and also supplies a few

---

[58] The two pictures are obviously iconographically related. They are reproduced in *An Eleventh-century Anglo-Saxon Illustrated Miscellany*, edd. McGurk *et al.*, frontispiece (MS. Cotton Tiberius B.v, in colour) and plate IX, no. 67 (MS. Cotton Julius A.vi). The relationship between the two manuscripts is discussed by McGurk, 'Labours of the months', in *ibid.*, pp. 41–3. The two illustration are §§192(2) and 167(1) in Ohlgren, *Insular and Anglo-Saxon Illuminated Manuscripts*, pp. 248 and 150 respectively.

[59] The matter was discussed by Postan in *The Famulus*, pp. 16–17. In the thirteenth century the man in charge of the plough was called the *tenens carruce, tenor*, or *conductor* and the person in charge of the team the *fugator*.

[60] Reginald Lennard argued in 'Domesday ploughteams: the south-western evidence' that the commissioners in the South-west worked on the basis of a six-ox plough-team. This was questioned by Finberg in 'The Domesday plough-team', but the six-ox team was certainly to be found in the twelfth century, as Lennard proved in 'The composition of demesne plough-teams in twelfth-century England'. The eight-ox plough was first recorded by Pliny the Elder in his *Naturalis Historia*, XVIII.xlvii.170 (ed. & transl. Rackham, V.297)

[61] See Van de Kieft, 'Les "Colliberti" ', 376 and nn. 39–42.

[62] On the origin of the unit as a fiscal assessment see Lennard, 'The origin of the fiscal carucate'. The interpretation of the term remains a matter of controversy. For S. P. J. Harvey it represents a new assessment devised to provide William the Conqueror with additional revenue ('Taxation and ploughland in Domesday Book', in *Domesday Book: A Reassessment*, ed. Sawyer, p. 103) and D. R. Roffe has concluded that it is 'an estimate of taxable potential', probably representing 'an attempt at reassessment undertaken in the course of the inquiry' ('An introduction to the Huntingdonshire Domesday', in *The Huntingdonshire Domesday*, edd. Williams & Erskine, p. 12). Nicholas Higham has taken a completely different tack in 'Settlement, land use and Domesday ploughlands', by relating it to how land was actually used. Following earlier work by John Moore, Higham has argued that 'the ploughland was used as a unit by which to measure the area of arable land in 1086' (p. 36). Although I applaud Higham for attempting to relate the abstractions of Domesday Book to the realities of landscape geography and land usage, on the basis of the Essex evidence discussed below I am more inclined to follow the fiscal interpretation.

[63] Domesday Book, volume I, fo. 206ra (Orton Longueville) and 206rb–va (Hemingford Grey) (text); Stenton, 'Text of the Huntingdonshire Domesday', in *The Victoria History of the County of Huntingdon*, volume I, edd. Page & Proby, pp. 348b–349b and 350a–b (translation). See Roffe, 'An introduction to the Huntingdonshire Domesday', in *The Huntingdonshire Domesday*, edd. Williams & Erskine, p. 14. For the South-west, see n. 60 above.

examples of teams of six oxen.[64] Anglo-Saxon illustrations show teams of two and four oxen, and even, in the case of the Bayeux Tapestry, a single donkey.[65] (The donkey is anomalous: although the Bayeux Tapestry shows a harrow being drawn by a horse with a horse-collar, suggesting that the technology already existed that would permit horses to draw a plough,[66] there is general agreement that equine traction was not customarily used for ploughing until after the eleventh century and that oxen were the norm as plough-beasts at the time of Domesday Book.[67])

The variation in the size of the teams is possibly due to the nature of the plough.[68] Like other agricultural implements, the plough in Britain has left little material evidence of its existence for archaeologists to find.[69] Late Saxon ploughshares from Westley Waterless (Cambridgeshire), St Neots (Huntingdonshire), and Thetford (Norfolk) are the only remnants of Anglo-Saxon ploughs excavated to date.[70] Instead one has to rely on the manuscript illustrations already alluded to. These illustrations all depict a wheeled symmetrical or scratch plough, which is best termed an 'ard' to distinguish it from the heavier asymmetrical plough. The latter possessed a mould-board and was capable of tackling heavier soils than the ard could. Lynn White has argued on philological

---

[64] *Liber Niger Monasterii S. Petri de Burgo*, in *Chronicon Petroburgense*, ed. Stapleton, pp. 158.10 (Tinwell [Rutland]), 159.39 (Cottingham [Northants.]), 160.41 (Alwalton [Hunts.]), 165.41 (Fletton [Hunts.]), 160.31 (Thurlby Ness [Lincs.]: 'i carruca de vii bobus'), 161.27 (Peterborough [Northants.]: 'iiii carrucae de xxix bobus'). It is possible that in this record the uneven numbers may have arisen through a failure to record *animalia otiosa*, which are reported on a number of estates. At Pytchley (Northants.), there were four ploughs with thirty oxen, so presumably three of the teams had eight oxen apiece and one six: *ibid.*, p. 162.7. Kathleen Biddick has pointed out that while the majority of Peterborough manors had the standard eight-ox teams in the twelfth century, '[m]anors located on lighter limestones and gravels held demesne plough teams composed of six oxen' (*The Other Economy*, p. 42).

[65] Apart from the illustrations in the two Cottonian manuscripts (see n. 58 above), there are two illustrations in Oxford, Bodleian Library, MS. Junius 11 (*S.C.* 5123) and three in London, British Library, MS. Harley 603, described in Ohlgren, *Insular and Anglo-Saxon Illuminated Manuscripts*, §§163(29 and 45) and 169(69, 73, and 96) (pp. 145, 147, 174–5, and 179 respectively). There is also a single illustration in the Bayeux tapestry. All except the one in London, British Library, MS. Cotton Julius A.vi, were conveniently reproduced and discussed by Steensberg, 'North West European plough-types'. See also *The Cædmon Manuscript of Anglo-Saxon Biblical Poetry*, ed. Gollancz, pp. 54 and 77, and *The Bayeux Tapestry*, ed. Stenton, 2nd edn, p. 12.

[66] See Clarke, 'Agriculture in late Anglo-Saxon England', in *Domesday Book: Studies*, edd. Williams & Erskine, p. 44 and Fig. 1.

[67] Langdon, *Horses, Oxen and Technological Innovation*, pp. 27–33.

[68] The amount of material on the European plough is now voluminous. In addition to other papers cited below see Bratanic's useful illustrated paper 'On the antiquity of the one-sided plough in Europe', and also Steensberg, 'Modern research of Agrarian History in Denmark'.

[69] The available archaeological evidence on agricultural implements has been reviewed by Wilson in 'Anglo-Saxon carpenters' tools', in *Studien zur europäischen Vor- und Frühgeschichte*, edd. Claus *et al*. The evidence could usefully be supplemented by an examination of Anglo-Saxon manuscript illumination. Some of the evidence on the plough was discussed by Payne, 'The British plough: some stages in its development', though this needs to be supplemented by the references cited in the following note.

[70] Westley Waterless: Fox, *Archaeology of the Cambridge Region*, p. 300; St Neots: Addyman, 'Late Saxon settlements in the St Neots area', p. 94 and fig. 19.30; Thetford: Rogerson & Dallas, *Excavations in Thetford 1948–59 and 1973–80*, p. 81 and fig. 121.

grounds that the heavy plough was a technological innovation introduced by the Viking invaders.[71] The heavy plough may, however, have been known in Britain as far back as Roman times.[72] This would not deny the possibility that its use was expanded by the Scandinavian settlers in England, and even more so by their Norman descendants. It could have provided the technological advance needed to enable the arable to be expanded to include heavier soils, a hypothesis that we shall briefly return to in our examination of the Essex Domesday.

THE *ANCILLA*

Perhaps because of the ambiguity in their terms of reference the commissioners of Circuit V evidently decided to record female slaves, since in all the counties of this circuit *ancillae* are to be found.[73] The commissioners of Circuit IV must have decided to do the same, but they were less diligent about this or, alternatively, they were dependent on less informative manorial records, because *ancillae* were recorded in lower numbers in the counties of this Circuit and they do not appear at all in Oxfordshire (see table VII). *Ancillae* were recorded in three other counties but in such small numbers (one in Devonshire, three in Dorset, and two in Nottinghamshire) that their inclusion must be interpreted as another of the numerous minor inconsistencies that abound in the survey.

This prompts the question as to which female slaves the commissioners decided to record. The figures in table VII show that the commissioners must have been selective, for in none of the counties does the number of *ancillae* in any way approach the number of *serui*. In the counties of Worcester and Hereford, where the largest number of *ancillae* are recorded, they are about one-fifth the number of the *serui*; in the other counties they form an even smaller fraction. Since there is no evidence to suggest that slaves in England were ever sexually segregated or that there were large gangs of male slaves, the difference in numbers cannot be explained on these grounds. Nor can it be argued that the figures for *serui* and *ancillae* denote the heads of slave households and their wives. The Worcestershire figures present no evident correlation between the number of male and female slaves on an estate. On the demesne of the king's manor at Kidderminster, for example, there were only two *serui*, yet there were four *ancillae*.[74] On the other hand, on the estate of Fladbury belonging to the bishop of Worcester only three *ancillae* were reported, though there were sixteen *serui*.[75]

The only reasonable conclusion is that the *ancillae* enumerated were women holding positions of responsibility on an estate. As has been mentioned,

---

[71] *Medieval Technology and Social Change*, pp. 39–57, especially pp. 51–3.

[72] This was the conclusion of W. H. Manning in 'The plough in Roman Britain', 65.

[73] Only one is recorded, however, in Staffordshire, another indication that this county may belong in Circuit IV (cf. nn. 10 and 38).

[74] Domesday Book, volume I, fo 172rb (text); Round, 'The text of the Worcestershire Domesday', in *The Victoria History of the County of Worcester*, volume I, edd. Willis-Bund & Doubleday, p. 286b (translation).

[75] Domesday Book, volume I, fo 172vb (text); Round, 'The text of the Worcestershire Domesday', in *The Victoria History of the County of Worcester*, volume I, edd. Willis-Bund & Doubleday, p. 289b (translation).

permanent staff such as slaves were important in the manorial economy, where they were needed to perform the daily services for which the occasional labour of the villein was unsuited.[76] One daily role that a woman could play was that of dairymaid and the Ely farm accounts attest this was indeed a function performed by an *ancilla*.[77] Domesday Book acknowledged the importance of this occupation by recording a *daia* or dairymaid on the king's estates of Bushley and Queenhill (Worcs.)[78] An *ancilla* was ideal as the cows would have required daily attention, just as daily work in caring for the oxen was needed from ploughmen. Domestic servants, particularly those engaged in some productive economic task like weaving, may also have been included among the *ancillae* who were enumerated.[79]

In Worcestershire the numbers on any one estate are small; apart from the king's manor of Feckenham, where five *ancillae* are recorded, and seven manors with four *ancillae* each,[80] on each of the remaining forty-nine manors only three or fewer *ancillae* are to be found.

SOME SAMPLE COUNTIES

The statistical information on slaves in Domesday Book is too extensive for every county to be surveyed in this study. Instead four sample counties, Essex, Middlesex, Cornwall, and Worcestershire, will be examined in order to highlight different facets of slavery in England in the latter half of the eleventh century. The selection of such geographically scattered counties is deliberate as it enables one to see some of the regional differences within the country. Essex has been

---

[76] See above, p. 116.

[77] See above, p. 180.

[78] Entered under Herefordshire: Domesday Book, volume I, fo 180vb (text); Round, 'The text of the Worcestershire Domesday', in *The Victoria History of the County of Worcester*, volume I, edd. Willis-Bund & Doubleday, p. 322a–b (translation); cf. Round, 'Introduction to the Worcestershire Domesday', in *ibid.*, p. 279.

[79] There is no direct evidence that slave-women engaged in weaving. But tapestries and cloth-making were probably already important cottage industries before the end of the eleventh century (the Bayeux Tapestry, for instance, is generally considered to be an English product: see *The Bayeux Tapestry*, ed. Stenton, pp. 11, 29–33). Æthelgifu's will mentions wall-hangings and clothing. Some of the latter were left by Æthelgifu to her household women, but unfortunately the status of these women is not mentioned: see *The Will of Æthelgifu*, ed. & transl. Whitelock, p. 7, line 7; p. 13, lines 45 and 49; and pp. 82–4.

[80] This includes Eadgifu's manor at Chaddesley Corbet (Domesday Book, volume I, fo 178ra [text]; Round, 'The text of the Worcestershire Domesday', in *The Victoria History of the County of Worcester*, volume I, edd. Willis-Bund & Doubleday, p. 320a [translation]), which records 'viii inter seruos 7 ancillas'. Round in *ibid.*, p. 277, showed that this phrase 'meant that the numbers of the class were given jointly, instead of separately'. Ellis, *A General Introduction to Domesday Book*, II.454, n. 4 and II.500, n. 1, wrongly assumed that when this phrase occurred no numbers were given, and he thus omitted them. The return for Feckenham was recorded under Herefordshire: see Domesday Book, volume I, fo 180va (text) and Round, 'Introduction to the Worcestershire Domesday', in *The Victoria History of the County of Worcester*, volume I, edd. Willis-Bund & Doubleday, p. 280, and *idem.*, 'The text of the Worcestershire Domesday', in *ibid.*, pp. 320b–321a (translation).

chosen because it is one of only three counties to record (albeit irregularly) the number of slaves on an estate in the time of both Edward the Confessor and William. Middlesex presents detailed information on the geldable land-holdings of the peasantry, permitting comparisons to be made between various Domesday categories of person. Cornwall was late in coming under Anglo-Saxon control and had a high percentage of slaves. Worcestershire, which is close to Wales and which had substantial ecclesiastical estates in 1086, permits one to test whether geographic location and size of landholdings were relevant factors in the distribution of slaves.

ESSEX

Domesday Essex was a large and well-wooded county. The land is characterised by extensive tracts of boulder clay extensively interrupted by river valleys, whose gravel floors have tended to attract settlement.[81] By 1086 the lineaments of its land-use had already long been in place: some of its field systems may be of Iron Age date; the Romans and Romano-British also left traces of their presence that can still be discerned.[82] Its landscape is more complex than a casual visitor might suspect. The greatest advances in our knowledge of the settlement history and geography of this county are likely to come from those with a detailed topographical knowledge of the area who are willing to apply their expertise to an informed interpretation of both the historical sources and the local archaeological evidence.[83]

Essex was one of the counties of England that had been settled longest by the Anglo-Saxons.[84] Any indigenous British groups would have been totally assimilated by the time of Domesday.[85] Yet slaves still accounted for nearly 13% of the recorded population. This percentage is low compared to the western shires, but Essex was a well-populated county, so that the number of slaves recorded there amounted to no fewer than 1,809 persons in 1086. A possible reason for this large number lies in the Viking raids in the time of Æthelred and their concomitant economic disruptions.

The Essex record lists some eighty-eight tenants-in-chief (excluding the king and an unspecified number of 'freemen of the King'). All but fifteen of these

---

[81] Woodward, 'Geology', in *The Victoria History of the County of Essex*, volume I, edd. Doubleday & Page, p. 1–23 and geological map opposite p. 1.

[82] Williamson, 'Settlement chronology and regional landscapes', in *Anglo-Saxon Settlements*, ed. Hooke.

[83] *Ibid.*, and Hart, 'Essex in the late tenth century', in *Battle of Maldon: Fiction and Fact*, ed. Cooper, have shown that there are those with the necessary skills who have begun this process of recovery. P. H. Dixon in 'The Anglo-Saxon settlement at Mucking' has provided a fascinating reconstruction based on first-hand ethnographic and topographic knowledge: it is to be hoped that work of this kind will be undertaken for the late Anglo-Saxon period.

[84] On archaeological evidence for early settlement see, for example, Barton, 'Settlements of the Iron Age and Pagan Saxon periods at Linford, Essex'; M. V. & W. F. Jones, 'The crop-mark sites at Mucking, Essex, England', in *Recent Archaeological Excavations in Europe*, ed. Bruce-Mitford, pp. 183–7.

[85] On Celtic survival in Essex see Reaney, *The Place-Names of Essex*, p. xxvii. Cf. also Chadwick, 'The Celtic background of early Anglo-Saxon England', in Jackson *et al.*, *Celt and Saxon*, pp. 323–52; she did not, however, discuss Essex.

owned slaves in 1086. Their social status varied from Odo, bishop of Bayeux and brother of the king, to the obscure Grim the Reeve. Their holdings in slaves also varied. Count Eustace owned 184, Turchil the Reeve a single person. The Essex figures are so detailed that they would permit one not merely to record the number of *serui* owned by the various tenants-in-chief, tabulated according to their geographic distribution in the twenty-four hundreds and half-hundreds in the county, but also in most instances to list the number of slaves held at two different periods: in the time of King Edward (*TRE*, the standard Domesday Book abbreviation for *tempore regis Edwardi*), and in 1086 (*TRW*, that is, *tempore regis Willelmi*). The reader would probably find, however, that the resulting mass of figures would obfuscate rather than clarify the position of slaves in the county.

Though slaves were widely distributed from a geographic point of view and most major land-holders owned some, their numbers were declining dramatically by 1086. In the two decades preceding the survey there had been an overall decline of 25% in the number of slaves across the county. On some holdings the drop had been dramatic: they had been reduced on the estates in Count Eustace's fee from 256 to 184, and on the estates of Suen of Essex, Robert Gernon, and Ralf Baignard there were only half the numbers recorded in 1066.

Two groups of estates do not fit into this pattern. On the king's manors the numbers decreased by 22.7%, somewhat less than the average. The reason may be that the king's lands would have been administered by reeves disinclined to release a man without the king's consent. Unlike the king, a resident tenant would have been more accessible to his reeve. He also would have been more sensitive to local economic trends than the king with his extensive holdings across the country, and so would be more likely to release slaves if he saw that it was to his economic advantage.

A far greater contrast to trends in the county is provided by the estates held by ecclesiastical foundations. Apart from the estates belonging to four communities (St Peter of Westminster, the Canons of Holy Cross of Waltham, St Martin of London, and the Abbey of St Ouen) the numbers of slaves on ecclesiastical holdings remained remarkably static and even in a few cases increased. In the time of King Edward St Walery had fourteen slaves on its estates and Holy Trinity of Caen seventeen; the same number were there in 1086. The canon's of St Paul's in London increased their slaves from twenty-eight to thirty-three.

At first sight this seems puzzling in the light of the Church's advocacy of manumission. One reason probably lies in the canonical rules which prohibited the alienation of church property.[86] As we have seen the Synod of Chelsea had specified that those slaves acquired during an incumbent's lifetime who were resident on a bishop's own property – as opposed to those living on the episcopal demesne – were to be released on his death.[87] Perhaps this is why the number of slaves on the lands of the Bishop of London increased from fifty-four to fifty-five during the twenty years before the Domesday survey, while the number on the bishop's fee (that is, the lands acquired during Bishop William's tenure of the

[86] See Sheehan, *The Will in Medieval England*, pp. 90–1, and references there cited.
[87] Cf. above, p. 83.

see [1051–75] rather than land traditionally attached to it)[88] declined by 40%, from forty-seven slaves to twenty-seven. For some of the ecclesiastical foundations located in the region such as Ely and St Edmund's the continued practice of demesne agriculture was a practical expedient in that food was needed to support the resident monks or canons. There was probably also more administrative continuity on ecclesiastical estates than on lay properties, where so many of the Anglo-Saxon holders were replaced by Normans: this continuity would have encouraged the perpetuation of conservative farming practices.

The terms of reference of the Cambridgeshire commissioners had prescribed that three sets of figures should be obtained.[89] In the Essex Domesday this injunction was followed on some estates. Unfortunately the second date is not specified in the records; it is usually expressed in the text by the vague word *tunc*. Table X lists the estates in which interim figures for slaves were supplied.[90]

TABLE X: NUMBER OF *SERUI* AND PLOUGHS RECORDED
AT THREE DIFFERENT TIMES IN ESSEX
(The number of *bordarii* is recorded in parentheses)

Holder	Estate	SLAVES			PLOUGHS		
		TRE	*Then*	TRW	TRE	*Then*	TRW
20, 25	Claret Hall, Hinckford	10 (?)	4 (12)	4 (12)	5	3	3
25	Little Yeldham, Hinckford	8 (?)	6 (8)	6 (8)	3	2	2
26	Belchamp Otten, Hinckford	4 (4)	4 (4)	2 (5)	2	2	2
52	Little Baddow, Chelmsford	6 (4)	6 (4)	3 (8)	3	3	3
63	St Osyth, Tendring	8 (?)	2 (?)	2 (2)	1	0	1
23, 6	Panfield, Hinckford	8 (8)	8 (8)	7 (15)	4	2	2
7	Great Yeldham, Hinckford	5 (5)	5 (5)	2 (8)	3½	3½	3½
13	Finchingfield, Hinckford	4 (?)	2 (?)	2 (4)	2	2	2
28	Boyton Hall, Hinckford	4 (7)	4 (8)	2 (8)	2	2	2
24, 53	Clavering, Clavering	8 (9)	8 (9)	12 (37)	4	4	5
54	Berden, Clavering	4 (?)	4 (?)	0 (5)	1	1	1
25, 16	Pledgdon Hall, Clavering	2 (2)	2 (2)	0 (16)	4	2	2
30, 18	Moze, Tendring	13 (17)	11 (?)	3 (13)	4	4	2
45	Saffron Walden, Uttlesford	16 (?)	16 (17)	20 (40)	8	8	10
32, 16	Stansted Mountfichet, Uttlesford	8 (4)	4 (4)	3 (18)	4	2	3
17	Takeley, Uttlesford	3 (?)	3 (?)	2 (8)	2	2	2
18	Wendens Ambo, Uttlesford	6 (?)	6 (?)	5 (5)	3	3	3
19	Bentfield Bury, Clavering	7 (2)	7 (2)	4 (11)	3	3	3
21	Farnham, Clavering	8 (8)	8 (8)	1 (8)	2	2	2
23	Great Maplestead, Hinckford	4 (2)	4 (2)	2 (6)	2	2	2
42	Shortgrove, Uttlesford	6 (0)	6 (0)	3 (0)	3	2	2

[88] On the distinction see Round, 'Introduction to the Essex Domesday', in *The Victoria History of the County of Essex*, volume I, edd. Doubleday & Page, p. 339.

[89] See above, p. 186 and n. 7.

[90] Excluded are estates where the figures for slaves are stated as 'always' having remained the same.

Holder	Estate	SLAVES			PLOUGHS		
		TRE	*Then*	TRW	TRE	*Then*	TRW
33, 19	Henham, Freshwell	8 (5)	8 (5)	0 (38)	4	4	4
34, 20	Stebbing, Hinckford	13 (14)	13 (14)	11 (31)	?	6	5
21	Great Henny, Hinckford	2 (?)	2 (?)	0 (11)	2	2	2
35, 4	Ugley, Clavering	6 (1)	6 (1)	2 (10)	3	3	3
36, 9	Binsley, Hinckford	2 (?)	2 (?)	1 (13)	1	1	1
12	North Weald Basset, Harlow	9 (3)	9 (3)	7 (8)	5	3	2
37, 12	Baythorne End, Hinckford	2 (?)	2 (?)	3 (7)	2	2	2
38, 6	Sturmer, Hinckford	1 (?)	1 (?)	2 (3)	2	2	2
39, 1	Rayne, Hinckford	4 (5)	4 (5)	3 (5)	2	2	2
2	Rayne, Hinckford	6 (?)	6 (?)	3 (3)	2	1	1
3	Sible Hedingham, Hinckford	4 (1)	2 (1)	2 (3)	2	2	2
40, 2	Great Saling, Hinckford	4 (3)	3 (3)	3 (5)	2	0	1
43, 4	Belchamp Otten, Hinckford	4 (9)	1 (9)	1 (12)	3	3	3
6	Weston Hall, Hinckford	9 (5)	9 (5)	4 (10)	5	5	5
44, 2	Goldingham Hall, Hinckford	6 (?)	6 (?)	2 (5)	3	2	2
46, 1	Mount Bures, Lexden	6 (9)	6 (9)	4 (9)	3	3	2
52, 3	Holland, Tendring	5 (10)	5 (10)	3 (11)	4	4	3
67, 1	Shalford, Hinckford	2 (?)	2 (?)	1 (3)	1½	1½	1
90, 22	Rockell's Farm, Uttlesford	5 (0)	7 (0)	7 (0)	2	2	1½
25	Farnham, Clavering	7 (4)	7 (4)	3 (15)	8	8	5
56	Toppesfield, Hinckford	4 (4)	4 (4)	0 (7)	1	1	1
58	Cornish Hall, Hinckford	3 (5)	3 (5)	2 (8)	1	2	2
63	Ovington, Hinckford	2 (3)	2 (3)	0 (8)	3	?	?
TOTAL		256	230	149	127 [124]	114 [108]	110 [105]

(The three sets of figures in square brackets exclude two groups of estates for which one of the three figures for ploughs is missing.)

In general there was a dramatic reduction in the number of slaves between 'then' and *TRW*. This cannot be said to be due to a decrease in demesne ploughs: decrease the ploughs did, but hardly at all between 'then' and *TRW* (124 > 108 > 105). The closer 'then' was to 1066 the less impressive, of course, the reduction. But it does at least prove that a major decline took place under the Normans.

This poses the question as to what became of these freed slaves. The only possible answer seems to be that they were included among the *bordarii*, as Round suggested.[91] Unlike the Middlesex Domesday, where the Anglo-Saxon *geburas* and *cotsetlas* were represented by two terms, in the Essex Domesday *bordarius* alone was used. Presumably this term covered both those holding half-virgates of land and those possessing only a toft.

---

[91] Round, 'Introduction to the Essex Domesday', in *The Victoria History of the County of Essex*, volume I, edd. Doubleday & Page, pp. 362–3.

The number of *bordarii* in Essex increased greatly in the twenty years preceding the survey.[92] Table XI, which compares the relative number of slaves and *bordarii* on certain estates, appears to confirm that freed slaves became *bordarii*.

TABLE XI: RELATIVE NUMBER OF *SERUI, BORDARII,* AND *UILLANI*
ON SELECTED ESSEX MANORS

Holder	Manor	Hundred	BORDARII		SERUI		UILLANI	
			Then	Now	Then	Now	Then	Now
18, 15	Beckney	Rochford	–	1	1	–	–	–
22, 9	Dunmow	Dunmow	–	3	3	–	–	–
24, 1	West Horndon	Barstable	7	10	4	1	(?	3)
64	Elmstead	Tendring	31	36	6	1	(14	13)
25, 1	Great Braxted	Witham	4	6	2	–	(5	6)
3	'Morrell' Roding	Dunmow	1	3	3	1	(9	3)
12	Broxted	Dunmow	3	5	3	1	(?	2)
26, 1	Great Hallingbury	Harlow	4	5	1	–	(18	8)
28, 5	Great Braxted	Witham	4	6	4	2	–	–
30, 37	Easton	Dunmow	–	1	1	–	–	–
32, 6	Matching	Harlow	1	4	3	–	(1	–)
12	Purleigh	*Wibertsherne*	–	1	1	–	–	–
36	Culvert's Farm	Chelmsford	–	2	1	–	1	–
34, 6	Terling	Witham	–	11	5	–	11	5
15	Layer Breton	Winstree	1	4	4	1	–	–

This could be verified only if those estates for which there are three sets of figures for both *serui* and *bordarii* were in exact correlation. Unfortunately the number of such estates is too small for valid statistical conclusions to be drawn (see table X) and only on one of them, Great Yeldham, was the decrease in *serui* on all three dates matched by a corresponding increase in *bordarii*. Nevertheless the evidence in table XI certainly points in this direction.

To ascertain the reasons for the sharp decrease in the number of slaves in Essex in the two decades after the Conquest is a complex task. As we have seen, during the last century of Anglo-Saxon rule a growing number of slaves were manumitted in East Anglia.[93] This trend is evinced by the release by testament of at least a substantial proportion, and often all, of the slaves on various lords' estates. Testamentary manumission of this kind, however, can have played little part in the reduction in numbers of slaves in Essex after the Conquest for, though there was a steady decline in the number of slaves on estates of lay tenants-in-chief right across the country, there are only four instances in Essex where the

---

[92] See the comments and examples cited by Maitland, *Domesday Book and Beyond*, p. 35 and n. 1 and p. 363, and Round, 'Introduction to the Essex Domesday', in *The Victoria History of the County of Essex*, volume I, edd. Doubleday & Page, pp. 359–61.

[93] See chapter IV above.

number of slaves dropped between 1066 and 1086 to zero – and in none of these four cases was more than seven slaves involved.[94]

Economic factors are far more likely to have led to the reduction. At this point certain other Domesday statistics that have puzzled historians should be considered. Basing his views on the reduction in swine on a number of Essex estates, Round suggested that this signified a concomitant reduction in woodland in the county between 1066 and 1086, with the formerly forested lands being devoted to assarts. At the same time one might note that the *ualets* of many manors and the number of *bordarii* increased during the same period.[95] These are probably not unrelated phenomena (though the interpretation of the data is more complicated than Round's explanation implied). What the figures suggest is that the Norman overlords were employing a different approach to land management.

Reginald Lennard called in question Round's claim that the loss of woodland was caused by an increase in assarts, pointing out that on most of the estates concerned there had also been a reduction in ploughs, which Round had failed to notice.[96] Curiously enough, Lennard himself failed to notice the increase in *ualets* evident on many of these same estates. Putting the information in tabular form will help point us to a solution.[97]

TABLE XII: NUMBER OF DEMESNE PLOUGHS; NUMBER OF *UILLANI* (v), *BORDARII* (b), AND *SERUI* (s) (PRIESTS EXCLUDED); AND VALUES ON MANORS WHERE THE NUMBER OF SWINE OR THE EXTENT OF WOODLAND DECLINED

(The figures are given in the order *TRE* > 'later' or 'when acquired' > *TRW*.
* indicates an increase in the total number of demesne and villein ploughs on the estate; x denotes a reduction in the value of the estate.)

Tenant	Estate	Demesne ploughs	Population	Values
1.13	Wethersfield	4 > 2 > 3	24 > 24 > 28v; 7 > 14 > 7s	£20 > £28
1.24	Writtle	12 > 9 > 9	97 > 73 > 73v; 36 > 60 > 60b; 24 > 18 > 18s	10 nights' provisions + £10; now £100 + 100/– in gifts
x14.4	Birchanger	2 > 2 > 1	1v; 5b; then 2s	60/– > 60/–> 50/–

[94] The estates of the Bishop of Hereford at Writtle; Edmund, son of Algot, at Horndon-on-the-Hill and Matching; Goscelm the Lorimer at Ilford; and William, son of Constantine, at Theydon: Domesday Book, volume II, fos 26r, 93v, 94, and 97r (text); Round, 'The text of the Essex Domesday', in *The Victoria History of the County of Essex*, volume I, edd. Doubleday & Page, pp. 460b, 558a, 559a, and 563a (translation).
[95] On woodland see Round, 'Introduction to the Essex Domesday', in *The Victoria History of the County of Essex*, volume I, edd. Doubleday & Page, pp. 377–8; on *ualets* see *ibid.*, pp. 363–5.
[96] Lennard, 'The destruction of woodland in the eastern counties under William the Conqueror' and *idem*, 'The destruction of woodland in the eastern counties, 1066–1086'.
[97] I have drawn the list of estates from Lennard, 'The destruction of woodland in the eastern counties under William the Conqueror', pp. 41 and 43.

Tenant	Estate	Demesne ploughs	Population	Values
20. 6	White Notley	3 > 2 > 2	10 > 10 > 6v; 3 > 16 > 16b; 9 > 4s	£10 always
20. 7	Coggeshall	3 always	11 > 9 > 9v; 22 > 31b; now 4s	£10 > £14 but it pays £20
x20. 9	Rivenhall	2 > 1	2 > 5v; 1 > 2b.; 5 > 4s	60/– > 30/–
22. 5	Gt Easton	2 always	3 > 8b; 3 > 2s	£8 > £9
22. 6	Ltl. Canfield	4 > 2	3 > 17b; 2s always	£8 > £9
22.13	Hunt's Hall	–	6b; 7 > 5s	£10 > £14/16/–
23. 2	Thaxted	8 > 7	55 > 52v; 24b & 16s always	£30 > £30 when acquired > £50
24.20	Eastwood	2 always	3v & 2s always; 21 > 30b	£4 > £6
24.45	Notley	2 > 1	4 > 2v; 4 > 5b; 2 > 0s	40/– > 60/–
*24.46	Ltl. Hallingbury	2 always	8 > 10v; now 17b; 4s always	100/– > £6
*24.53	Clavering	4 > 4 > 5	17v; 9 > 9 > 37b; 8 > 8 > 12s	£20 > £30
x28. 5	Gt Braxted	2 > 1	4 > 6b; 4 > 2s	100/– > £4 > 60/–
*30.45	Saffron Walden	8 > 8 > 10	66 > 66 > 46v; 17 > 17 > 40b; 16 > 16 > 20s	£36 > £36 > £50
33. 7	Wimbish	3 always	26v always; 19 > 55b; 6 > 0s	£12 > £20
*35. 3	Thunderley Hall	2 > 2 > 3	11v; 5b	£6 > £7
x40. 1	Notley	5 > 3	7 > 5v; 13 > 11b; 4 > 0s	£7 > £6
40. 2	Gt Saling	2 > 0 > 1	3 > 1 > 2v; 3 > 3 > 5b; 4 > 3 > 3s	60/–
x40. 3	Ltl. Maplestead	2 > 0 > 1	2 > 1 > 5v; 2s always	40/– > 30/–
42. 3	Ltl. Easton	6 > 4	5 > 3v; 2 > 25b; 7 > 1s	£7 > £8
44. 1	Stanstead Hall	2 always 4 > 3½	10 > 8 > 4v; 7b always; 7 > 6s 6 > 6 > 24b; 4 > 1s	£6 > £9
53. 1	Gt Easton	5 > 4 > 3	11 > 15v; 10 > 16b; 10 > 9s	£10 > £19
57. 3	Layer	4 > 2	1v; 17b; 8 > 3s	£7 always
65. 1	Elsenham	2 always	8v; 1 > 12b; 5s	£6 > £8
x90. 5	Layer	2 > 0 > 0	now 2b	40/– > 20/–
90.25	Farnham	8 > 8 > 5	6 > 6 > 3v; 4 > 4 > 15b; 7 > 7 > 3s	£6 always

When one takes into account the renders (*ualets*) of the twenty-eight estates where there was a reduction in woodland and pigs in table XII, it is striking that only six record a reduction and a further three no change in the *ualets*. The majority of these estates, in fact, increased in value to their holders. Yet only four of these twenty-eight estates record an increase in ploughs and in only three of those instances did the demesne ploughs increase. What changes noticeably on many of these estates is a growth in the number of *bordarii*. This increase in *bordarii* demands an explanation.

Reduction in woodland could be accomplished by importing labourers to clear it and then work the land. The increase in *bordarii* in the county as a whole is such as to suggest that owners of estates might occasionally have followed this course. But they had another option, namely, to give small parcels of land, either on parts of their estates hitherto not used as arable land or on their demesnes, to manumitted slaves to develop. This might explain at least some of the reduction in the slave numbers in the county. In doing so the owner could have used the traditional method of demanding food payments and labour services in return for the land granted. The increase in manorial values in the county suggests, however, that the owners found an alternative more attractive, namely, that of an annual cash payment. The fact that this was a relatively new practice would have meant that the rent-payers would not have developed much land yet for arable purposes and so the designation of *bordarius* may have seemed appropriate.

The increase in cash payments as opposed to payments in kind might in turn have inclined the owners to free yet more slaves in order to use them as hired labourers. As in other counties the ratio of two slaves per plough appears frequently, indicating that in Essex, as elsewhere, this was a common slave occupation.[98] But the correlation is much more common *TRE* than *TRW*, as table XIII indicates.

TABLE XIII: RATIO OF *SERVI* TO PLOUGHS *TRE* AND *TRW* IN ESSEX

	1:1	2:1	3:1	4:2	5:2	6:3	8:4	10:5	12:6	16:8	18:9	20:10	24:12
TRE	3	43	3	94	1	34	11	3	1	2	0	0	1
TRW	3	28	3	50	0	16	3	0	1	0	1	1	0

Even though the number of demesne ploughs did decline somewhat in the twenty years following the Conquest, they did not decrease to the extent that would explain the figures in table XIII. It can only be that these slaves were being freed and then used as hired labourers, presumably because this practice gave the overlord more flexibility in his estate management.[99]

All this begs a question. Presumably woodland had not been cleared before because it had not been profitable to do so. It could be argued that it was done at this time because of the increased rearing of sheep, which the Domesday figures also attest. But sheep-rearing tends not to be a labour-intensive activity (even though it may have required more personnel then because of the practice of milking ewes).[100] This does not provide, therefore, an explanation for the increased manpower on Essex estates in the twenty years after the Conquest.

Another possible explanation lies in the expanded use of the heavy plough under the Normans. As has been mentioned the Scandinavian settlers might have

---

[98] McDonald & Snooks in *Domesday Economy*, p. 110, have claimed on the basis of statistical legerdemain that 'the contribution of slaves to net production was about one-half that made by villeins', which suggests that they worked 'on average, no more than one-and-a-half days per week on the demesne'. Their conclusion that 'a large proportion were personal slaves' is not, however, a necessary one: slaves could also have contributed economically to the demesne in occupations other than ploughing such as being shepherds, woodsmen, etc., functions which would not necessarily have been recorded in Domesday's production figures.

[99] On hired labour see Postan, *The Famulus, passim*.

[100] The relatively few men needed in relation to the amount of land used in sheep-rearing has been emphasised by Domar, 'The causes of slavery or serfdom', 29. On the milking of ewes see Round, 'Introduction to the Essex Domesday', in *The Victoria History of the County of Essex*, volume I, edd. Doubleday & Page, pp. 368–9.

initially encouraged its wider use in England, but Viking settlement was probably relatively limited in Essex.[101] The Norman overlords, however, with their Scandinavian background are likely to have been fully conversant with the plough. By encouraging the use of the plough on the heavier, woodland soils they would have increased the arable land,[102] which could offer them increased revenues in the form of rent without incurring the expenses of feeding the labourers and plough-beasts (not to mention the management costs involved in supervising slaves and those who provided customary labour services on the demesne). This must surely have been attractive to the new Norman overlords, whose zest for wealth is evident from the frequent displacement of the original Anglo-Saxon tenants[103] and the long list of encroachments recorded in the Essex section of Little Domesday Book. The problem with this explanation lies in its simplicity – one need look for no *deus ex machina* to explain the disappearance of slavery: one has the *machina* itself in the form of the heavy plough to provide the answer. Major social changes, however, are usually far more complex, being the product of a nexus of changes in other spheres.

Yet another answer might lie in the increase in population that all demographers seem to agree was occurring in the eleventh century.[104] If labour was plentiful, to hire people cheaply and require them to develop the land in order to support themselves might be more effective than having to feed and manage them every day for work that might not always be needed.[105] This, of course does not explain why this change should have occurred in the twenty years after the Conquest.

The previous two answers might be part of the solution. But they point to a third solution, an unambiguous change that shattered the social fabric of Anglo-Saxon life: the coming of the Normans and their Continental allies. Here was a group of ruthless and ambitious men, eager to profit from their success at Hastings. Past traditions, old social ties, regional or tribal relationships are likely to have meant little to them – unless they could exploit them to some material advantage for themselves. A Norman taking over an estate staffed by Anglo-Saxons with a variety of statuses is thus less likely to have been inhibited in

---

101 Though Essex was part of the Danelaw, Reaney, *The Place-Names of Essex*, p. xxviii, pointed out that 'the strength of the Danes in this quarter lay farther north and no serious attempt was made to settle in Essex. Place-names show but slight traces of any Scandinavian settlement.'

102 Oliver Rackham, who has revolutionised knowledge about the history of English woodland, has accepted Lennard's objections to Round's case, and has suggested that more woodland was being used for coppicing (*Trees and Woodland in the British Landscape*, rev. edn, p. 55, and cf. Rackham, *The History of the Countryside*, p. 84). Rackham's explanation need not exclude other possibilities: a single explanation for the reduction in woodland seems inherently improbable.

103 Round, 'Introduction to the Essex Domesday', in *The Victoria History of the County of Essex*, volume I, edd. Doubleday & Page, p. 355, observed: '. . . in Essex the transfer of land was for all purposes complete. Every Englishman, small or great, who held his land "freely" seems to have forfeited its possession'.

104 This hypothesis is put forward rather tentatively because the interpretation of such mediaeval population data as exist is fraught with hazards. Richard Smith's paper, 'Human resources', in *The Countryside of Medieval England*, edd. Astill & Grant, pp. 188–212, has revealed some of the problems and provided an introduction to the secondary literature on the subject.

105 Cf. Hicks, *A Theory of Economic History*, p. 132, and above, p. 14.

making changes – be they in land-usage, adoption of technological developments, or redeployment of staff – than an Anglo-Saxon lord may have been,
particularly if, as has been suggested in earlier chapters, the distinctions between
slaves and the lower ranks of the free were weakening in any case. Nor in general
would they have been especially interested in food renders and a large demesne,
which required extensive management and was thus potentially less profitable.[106]
For absentee landlords especially, cash rents were an economically attractive
proposition. The evidence of this is there for all to see in the Essex Domesday:
almost without exception,[107] there was a reduction in slaves on the lands of the
major lay tenants-in-chief. Some of these reductions were dramatic: slaves on
Count Eustace's estates went down from 256 to 184, on Swein of Essex's lands
from 126 to 62, on the properties of Robert Gernon from 144 to 77, and on those
of Ralph Baignard from 109 to 54.

Seen from this perspective the overall position of the people who were freed
may have been no better than those who remained as slaves – in fact, in some
cases it might have been worse – but it is difficult to assess this, as the new status
would have involved a different set of rights and obligations.

If this appraisal of the evidence for Essex is correct, it suggests that the
Normans gave the *coup de grâce* to the institution of slavery in England. In spite
of manumission, slaves were still relatively plentiful in the Anglo-Saxon Essex
of 1066; by 1086 they were obviously on their way out as a legal class. The
Normans encouraged a different use of land resources and of manpower. The
latter change in general meant that those who had been slaves were transformed
into freemen in return for renders which we may suspect were more usually in
the form of cash rents rather than of services. These seem to be the only cogent
explanations for the many changes that took place in Essex in the two decades
following the Conquest.

WORCESTERSHIRE

The Worcester Domesday account contains several features that are of absorbing
interest for our study. First, the statistics that it contains confirm the close
association between slaves and ploughing that has already been noticed in other
sources. Second, information has been preserved that enables us to gain a much
clearer picture of the complexity of tenurial relationships which must have
existed throughout England, a complexity that has been masked in many of the
other county surveys. A concomitant of this is the recording of a wide diversity

---

[106] The qualification 'in general' is employed because S. P. J. Harvey has pointed out that several
Norman lords took an active interest in demesne farming and had a considerable number of
slaves, which suggests that the use of slaves rather than freemen was not necessarily economically inefficient, a point to which I shall return in the final chapter. Nevertheless, her
observation that '[t]here would seem to be little benefit to lords who did not wish to keep a
hall on the manor for residence in producing foodstuffs in times when transport was difficult
to organize' is eminently sensible, as is her conclusion, 'A set payment, be it by bailiff or a
group of husbandmen, was a more mobile return': 'Domesday England', in *The Agrarian
History of England and Wales*, volume II, ed. Hallam, p. 55, and on Norman lords who
exploited the demesne, *ibid.*, pp. 115–19.

[107] Among the major lay tenants-in-chief only Tihel the Breton had an increase in slaves on his
estates between 1066 and 1086 – and that was by a single person!

of social and occupational categories amongst those resident in the county.[108] Finally, a number of religious houses are prominent in the account, including the bishopric and monastery of Worcester, whose surviving records give it an important position in any study of Anglo-Saxon England.[109] Some important conclusions can be drawn from the statistics relatings to these ecclesiastical foundations. Taken together these factors make the Domesday record for Worcester much more informative than is the case for many of the other county returns.

Let us begin with an examination of what appears to have been the primary occupation of slaves in Worcester. Table XIV reveals a high correlation between the number of slaves and the number of ploughs; this also applies to the *bouarii* and the ploughs.[110]

TABLE XIV: PLOUGHS AND MEN ON WORCESTERSHIRE ESTATES

Ratio of ploughs to men:	1:2	2:4	3:6	4:8	5:10	6:12	7:14
No. of estates exhibiting this ratio (*serui*)	27	30	6	4	3	2	2
No. of estates exhibiting this ratio (*bouarii*)	7	5	–	–	–	–	–
No. of estates exhibiting this ratio (*serui* and *bouarii*)	–	–	–	1	–	–	–
No. of estates exhibiting this ratio (*serui* and *cotarii*)	–	1	–	–	–	–	–
No. of *serui*	54	121	36	34	30	24	28
No. of *bouarii*	14	20	–	6	–	–	–
No. of *cotarii*	–	3	–	–	–	–	–

Included in table XIV are six *bouarii* and two slaves with four ploughs on the demesne at Lindridge, and one slave with three *cotarii*, who were probably employed to act as ploughmen for the two demesne ploughs at Abberley.[111] There

---

[108] Cf. the observation of Round, 'Introduction to the Worcestershire Domesday', in *The Victoria History of the County of Worcester*, volume I, edd. Willis-Bund & Doubleday, p. 273: 'When we turn from the land to the men who dwelt on it, we are confronted by a hierarchy of classes bewildering enough in its variety. Indeed, it would be difficult in any county to find a greater variety.' See also A. Williams, 'An introduction to the Worcestershire Domesday', in *The Worcestershire Domesday*, edd. Williams & Erskine, pp. 3–5.

[109] For a history of the Priory in the Anglo-Saxon period see Calthrop, 'Priory of St. Mary of Worcester', in *The Victoria History of the County of Worcester*, volume II, edd. Willis-Bund & Page, pp. 94–7; Atkins, 'The Church of Worcester from the eighth to the twelfth century'; and cf. Bassett, 'Churches in Worcester before and after the conversion of the Anglo-Saxons'; for its landholdings see Dyer, *Lords and Peasants in a Changing Society*, pp. 7–38.

[110] Where the phrase *inter seruos et ancillas* occurs, the numbers have been divided between *serui* and *ancillae* in table XIV – but bear in mind the caveat in n. 28 above.

[111] Lindridge and Abberley: Domesday Book, volume I, fos 176ra and 176rb (text); Round,'The text of the Worcestershire Domesday', in *The Victoria History of the County of Worcester*, volume I, edd. Willis-Bund & Doubleday, pp. 309b and 310a (translation).

is, of course, the overwhelming probability that on many estates which do not exhibit the ratio of two slaves per demesne plough the slaves present acted as ploughmen. (This is most likely the case with the Worcester community's estates at Fladbury, for instance, where there were sixteen *serui* and nine demesne ploughs.)[112] Overall the figures show that 327 out of the 718 male slaves recorded in the county were definitely associated with ploughing. We shall return to this topic a little later when we come to examine the estates of the monastic cathedral church of St Mary, Worcester.

The Worcester Domesday is particularly helpful in enabling us to glimpse the incredible complexity of tenure over agricultural land in the late Anglo-Saxon period. Take the estate of Dormston, for instance.[113] This lay in the middle of Esch hundred but was in fact a detached portion of Pershore hundred. It was part of the endowment of the abbey of St Peter, Westminster.[114] It had been under the control of one Waland before 1066: in return for it he had reaped his lord's (that is, Westminster's) meadows and performed other services. In 1086 William fitzCorbucion was lord of its five hides and there were six *serui* and one *ancilla* on his property. But two of the five hides were held of William by one Albert, who had one plough and two slaves on his two hides. Furthermore, one *uillanus* held half a plough and presumably thus occupied part of Albert's two hides. Thus the entry for Dormston records not merely a tenant-controlled property with slaves but also land managed by a sub-tenant. What we do not know is whether the villein under-tenant of the sub-tenant also controlled slaves. This is at least a possibility that should be allowed for.

Agriculture was not the only economic force within the county. The Worcestershire Domesday mentions that the bishop's manor of Northwick had ninety houses in the city of Worcester. The borough itself had given every third penny to the bishop in the days of King Edward, though in 1086 the bishop had to share this with the king and Roger of Montgomery, the earl of Shrewsbury.[115] Droitwich was an incipient industrial centre. In addition to its brine pits, whose salt was widely distributed through the Midlands,[116] there is also mention of lead works in the town.[117] When the information on this county was compiled at Winchester, the editor fortunately preserved many of the social and economic

---

[112] Domesday Book, volume I, fo 172vb (text); Round, 'The text of the Worcestershire Domesday', in *The Victoria History of the County of Worcester*, volume I, edd. Willis-Bund & Doubleday, p. 289b (translation).

[113] Domesday Book, volume I, fo 174vb (text); Round, 'The text of the Worcestershire Domesday', in *The Victoria History of the County of Worcester*, volume I, edd. Willis-Bund & Doubleday, p. 302b (translation).

[114] Given the history of the Westminster lands in Worcester, which is discussed later in this section, Dormston may well have been linked earlier with Pershore. See further, pp. 220–1 below.

[115] Domesday Book, volume I, fo 173va (text); Round, 'The text of the Worcestershire Domesday', in *The Victoria History of the County of Worcester*, volume I, edd. Willis-Bund & Doubleday, p. 294a (translation).

[116] Hooke, *The Anglo-Saxon Landscape: The Kingdom of the Hwicce*, pp. 122–6. For additional information on salt-production in England, see Laurence Keen's two papers, 'Coastal salt production in Norman England' and 'Medieval salt-working in Dorset', and Hart, 'Essex in the tenth century', in *Battle of Maldon: Fiction and Fact*, ed. Cooper, pp. 185–6.

[117] Domesday Book, volume I, fo 173va (text); Round, 'The text of the Worcestershire Domes-

categories that must have appeared in his original returns. Most of these – the *radmanni* (*radmans*), burgesses, reeves, Frenchmen, priests, the *rustici porcarii*, even a hunter and a smith – are not relevant to our study.[118] There is mention of one person, however, who might give us pause to ponder.

In the record for Badsey, an estate belonging to the Church of Evesham, there is an arresting phrase: 'There are four slaves there and one widow.'[119] The collocation of a widow and slaves suggests that the lot of a poor woman could resemble that of a slave. For but a moment we are given a glimpse of this social category: she is the only widow mentioned in the county. Since elderly widows tend to be the most indigent in advanced capitalist societies, we may suspect that within many communities in late Anglo-Saxon and early Norman England there were widows who had literally to work like slaves in order to survive.

The compiler of the Worcestershire Domesday took particular pains to record the presence of sub-tenants. This is not the case is many other counties. This means that we should at least raise the possibility that in some counties the number of slaves is under-recorded. Presumably, if a tenant-in-chief kept accurate records, he would know with how many slaves an estate was stocked when it was granted to a tenant. We might assume, therefore, that the number of slaves recorded by a tenant-in-chief included those who were nominally controlled by his tenants. But two factors are likely to have reduced the accuracy of these figures. The first lay in the practice of granting an estate for a number of lives. Thus, Pershore's one-hide estate at Wadborough had been bought by a thegn of King Edward's for the life of three heirs. In 1086 the third heir was still occupying the property.[120] Under such circumstances an increase in the number of slaves on the estate was not likely to be known to the monastic house that had granted the manor. Another source of inaccuracy would have arisen if someone introduced additional slaves onto an estate after taking up the lease on the property.

When we turn to examine the slave-owners in Worcestershire, we see that they can be divided into two main groups: the four great abbeys of Worcester, Westminster, Evesham, and Pershore, and sundry lay tenants-in-chief. The number of *serui* and *ancillae* in each hundred of the county, tabulated according to the tenant-in-chief, is set out in table XV.

day, in *The Victoria History of the County of Worcester*, volume I, edd. Willis-Bund & Doubleday, p. 294a (translation).

[118] Domesday Book, volume I, fos 174va (burgesses at Pershore), 175va (*rustici porcarii*, that is, swineherds at Oldberrow), 174ra (hunter [*uenator*] at Lyppard), and 175va (smith at Mathon) (text); Round, 'The text of the Worcestershire Domesday', in *The Victoria History of the County of Worcester*, volume I, edd. Willis-Bund & Doubleday, pp. 300a, 306b, 296a, and 305b (translation).

[119] Domesday Book, volume I, fo 175vb (text); Round, 'The text of the Worcestershire Domesday', in *The Victoria History of the County of Worcester*, volume I, edd. Willis-Bund & Doubleday, p. 306b (translation).

[120] Domesday Book, volume I, fo 175rb (text); Round, 'The text of the Worcestershire Domesday' in *The Victoria History of the County of Worcester*, volume I, edd. Willis-Bund & Doubleday, p. 304b (translation).

TABLE XV: DISTRIBUTION OF *SERUI* (S) AND *ANCILLAE* (A) IN WORCESTERSHIRE IN 1086 (S/A = *Inter seruos et ancillas*)

Figures followed by * indicate that they were recorded under Hereford. Excluded are the 'several *bordarii* and slaves' owned by eight *radmen* at Powick (Domesday Book, volume I, fo 174vb)

Holder	Came S	A	Clent S	A	Oswaldslow S	A	Esch S	A	Cresselau S	A	Doddingtree S	A	Pershore S	A	Fishborough S	A	TOTAL S	A
King	11	1	–	–	– – / 8 S/A*		12* 5* / 6 S/A*		4	4	–	–	– – / 5 S/A*		–	–	27 10 / 19 S/A	
Church of Worcs.	4 1 / 7 S/A		–	–	217	41	16	6	12 3 / 6 S/A		17	–	–	–	–	–	266 51 / 13 S/A	
Bishop of Hereford	–	–	–	–	–	–	3	–	–	–	15	–	–	–	–	–	18	–
Church of Saint-Denis	–	–	–	–	–	–	–	–	–	–	–	–	–	–	–	–	–	–
Church of Coventry	–	–	–	–	–	–	–	–	–	–	–	–	–	–	–	–	–	–
Church of Cormeilles	–	–	–	–	–	–	–	–	–	–	–	–	–	–	–	–	–	–
Church of Gloucester	–	–	–	–	–	–	–	–	–	–	–	–	–	–	–	–	–	–
St Peter of Westminster	–	–	–	–	–	–	–	–	–	–	–	–	138	30	–	–	138	30
St Mary of Pershore	–	–	–	–	–	–	–	–	–	–	–	–	32	–	–	–	32	–
Church of Evesham	–	–	–	–	14	–	2	–	–	–	–	–	–	–	25	–	41	–
Bishop of Bayeux	–	–	–	–	–	–	4	–	–	–	12	–	–	–	–	–	16	–
Church of St Guthlac	–	–	–	–	–	–	–	–	–	–	–	–	–	–	–	–	–	–
Clerks of Wolverhampton	–	–	2	–	–	–	–	–	–	–	–	–	–	–	–	–	2	–
Earl Roger	–	–	11	5	–	–	–	–	–	–	–	–	–	–	–	–	11	5
Ralph de Tosny	–	–	–	–	–	–	–	–	–	–	34	–	–	–	–	–	34	–
Ralph de Mortimer	–	–	–	–	–	–	–	–	–	–	12	–	–	–	–	–	12	–
Robert of Stafford	–	–	–	–	–	–	6	–	–	–	–	–	–	–	–	–	6	–
Roger de Lacy	–	–	–	–	–	–	5	–	–	–	3	–	–	–	–	–	8	–
Osbern fitzRichard	–	–	3	–	–	–	3	–	–	–	26	4	–	–	–	–	32	4

Holder	Came S	Came A	Clent S	Clent A	Oswaldslow S	Oswaldslow A	Esch S	Esch A	Cresselau S	Cresselau A	Doddingtree S	Doddingtree A	Pershore S	Pershore A	Fishborough S	Fishborough A	TOTAL S	TOTAL A
Gilbert fitzTurold	–	–	–	–	–	–	–	–	–	–	6	–	–	–	–	–	6	–
Drogo fitzPonz	–	–															–	–
Harold, Son of Earl Ralph	–	–	–	–													–	–
William fitzAnsculf	4	1	10	–	–	–	–	–	–	–	–	–	–	–	–	–	14	1
William fitzCorbucion	–	–	4	1	–	–	–	–	–	–	–	–	–	–	–	–	4	1
William Goizenboded	–	–	–	–													–	–
Urse d'Abetot	2	2	12	–	–	–	–	–	4 – / 4 S/A		2	–	–	–	–	–	20 2 / 4 S/A	
Hugh l'Asne	–	1	–	–					–	–	–	–	–	–	–	–	–	1
Eadgifu	–	–	–	–	–	–	–	–	8 S/A		–	–	–	–	–	–	8 S/A	
TOTAL	21	6 / 7 S/A	42	6	231	41 / 8 S/A	51	11 / 6 S/A	20	7 / 18 S/A	127	4	170	30 / 5 S/A	25	–	687	105 / 44 S/A

Of these the four religious houses were the most important, as might be expected from their extensive land-holdings. The size of their land-holdings and the numbers of their estate workers are given in table XVI.

TABLE XVI: TOTAL LAND-HOLDINGS AND NUMBER OF WORKERS ON WORCESTERSHIRE ECCLESIASTICAL ESTATES

	Hidage	Serui	Ancillae	Inter seruos et ancillas	Bouarii	Bordarii	Uillani	Others	TOTAL
Worcester	393¼	266	51	13	–	475	648	42	1,495
Westminster	195¼	138	30	–	18	252	194	48[a]	680
Evesham	89½[b]	41	0	–	16	111	158	17	343
Pershore	106	32	0	–	–	113	121	6	272
TOTAL	784	477	81	13	34	951	1,121	113	2,790

[a] Excludes fifty-nine burgesses.
[b] Evesham had sixty-five hides in Fishborough hundred, 24½ hides in Oswaldslow and Esch hundreds (of which Urse d'Abetot allegedly held one hide illegally), and twenty-eight houses in Worcester, whose hidage is not reported.

As table XVI shows, the four religious houses had a total of 571 male and female slaves on their estates, comprising 20.5% of the recorded population (excluding land-holders) on these lands. In contrast, only 15.6% of the recorded

218

population of Worcestershire as a whole were slaves. These 571 slaves comprise nearly 80% of all the slaves (including *ancillae*) recorded in the county. Even if one excludes the slaves on the lands held by sub-tenants, the four ecclesiastical foundations owned a substantial number amounting to nearly 44% of all slaves in the county – nearly 30% of all slaves being on Worcester's demesnes alone, as can be seen from table XVII.

TABLE XVII: DEMESNE LAND-HOLDINGS AND NUMBER OF
SERUI AND *ANCILLAE* BELONGING TO
WORCESTERSHIRE ECCLESIASTICAL FOUNDATIONS

	Hidage	Serui	Ancillae	TOTAL
Worcester (bp & monks)	220¼[a]	177	36	213
Westminster	62½	30[b]	5[b]	35
Evesham	83½	42	0	42
Pershore	77	22	0	22
TOTAL	443¼	271	41	312

[a]   It is assumed that the manor of Tidenham contained Blackwell and Longdon, totaling six hides, so that seventeen rather than twenty-three hides were held in demesne by the bishop (Domesday Book, volume I, fos 173rb–174va).

[b]   Westminster is said to have had 200 hides but only 194¼ are enumerated. The initial entry mentioning the 200 hides also records eleven *serui* and one *ancilla*, which have been included in these figures.

That there was such a disparity between the number of slaves on these ecclesiastical manors and those resident on estates in the rest of the county is puzzling at first sight. Willis-Bund sought to explain this by arguing that Worcester, Evesham, and Pershore were useful to William as lines of defence both against rebellion and also against incursions from Wales.[121] He claimed that Worcester was in the vanguard of such a defence system: in the course of defending the border the servants of the cathedral would have made raids across the border which would have yielded both male and female slaves. Such raids, in his view, explain both the presence of *ancillae* and why Worcester had a greater number of slaves than Evesham or Pershore, whose lands were further from the border.

This explanation is unsatisfactory for several reasons. Had border raids been the source of resident slaves (as opposed to those traded abroad) one would have expected the highest concentrations of slaves to have been in the border hundreds, not only in Worcestershire, but in all the counties adjacent to Wales. This is by no means the case, as the *Domesday Geography* maps of the Midland counties show.[122] The inadequacy of Willis-Bund's explanation is particularly obvious when one realises that he has completely omitted the holdings of St

---

[121] Willis-Bund, 'Worcestershire Doomsday'.
[122] *The Domesday Geography of Midland England*, figs 152 and 153 (pp. 433 and 435).

Peter's, Westminster. Among the ecclesiastical land-holders this foundation had the second-largest number of slaves on its manors – and most of these slaves were on its lands in Pershore hundred, far from the Welsh border. A third objection lies in the figures for *ancillae* in this county, whose inclusion in the record seems to have been due to a decision of the commissioners of Circuit V to enumerate female slaves in a separate category, presumably because they played specific economic roles on manorial estates.[123] This makes Willis-Bund's hypothesis that the *ancillae* too were the product of border raids superfluous.

The reason for the discrepancy in numbers must surely instead lie in the history of the religious houses and their estates. The monastery with the longest and least chequered history among the four was Worcester. It had survived the passing of the Mercian supremacy with its lands intact, including the triple hundred of Oswaldslow. As it was the see of St Oswald, one of the leaders of the tenth-century monastic revival, the organisational upheavals of the Anglo-Saxon church – however much they may have discommoded the clergy – are unlikely to have affected its lands adversely.[124] The see prospered to the extent that Wulfstan at the beginning of the eleventh century may be considered to have possessed all the characteristics of an ecclesiastical magnate in the Continental tradition, as Bethurum pointed out.[125] The monastery suffered from the despoliation of lands by Harthacnut in 1014 and was in decline for some time thereafter until St Wulfstan took over as abbot and later bishop. There is no evidence that it suffered extensive losses of land during this period, however, and may even by dubious means have gained some.

Evesham's early history is shrouded in darkness.[126] Founded by St Ecgwine during the reign of King Coenred in the eighth century, it was held by secular clergy in the tenth century until the monastery was re-established by St Oswald in 970. On Edgar's death secular clerics resumed control and it was despoiled of many of its lands by Ælfhere, earl of Mercia. It also had a long-standing dispute over several estates with the Worcester community, which suggests that it was not even very effective in withstanding the aggression of other ecclesiastical foundations.[127]

Pershore was also refounded by St Oswald. Like Evesham, many of its estates

---

[123] Cf. above, pp. 202–3.

[124] Eric John's work on Worcester under Oswald, 'St Oswald and the Church of Worcester', in *Orbis Britannia*, pp. 234–48, needs to be revised in the light of Darlington's and Sawyer's work on the *Altitonantis* charter on which John's case depended. See Brooks, 'Anglo-Saxon charters: the work of the last twenty years', 229. One should, however, also note Ann Williams's conclusion: 'On balance, it seems quite feasible to accept the story told in Altitonantis, and accept Edgar as the creator of "Oswaldslow", and, by extension, of "Fishborough" and the triple-hundred of Pershore.' ('An introduction to the Worcestershire Domesday', in *The Worcestershire Domesday*, edd. Williams & Erskine, p. 16.)

[125] Bethurum, 'Episcopal magnificence in the eleventh century', in *Studies in Old English Literature in Honor of Arthur G. Brodeur*, ed. Greenfield, pp. 162–70.

[126] On the history of Evesham up till 1086 see Locke, 'Abbey of Evesham', in *The Victoria History of the County of Worcester*, volume II, edd. Willis-Bund & Page, pp. 112–16.

[127] Round, 'Introduction to the Worcestershire Domesday', in *The Victoria History of the County of Worcester*, volume I, edd. Willis-Bund & Doubleday, pp. 252–7.

suffered from Ælfhere's depredations, as its annals bear witness.[128] Also like Evesham, it reverted to secular control on the death of Edgar. Round has plausibly argued that the lands seized by Ælfhere from Pershore passed to Earl Odda.[129] When he died without leaving an heir, his lands passed to King Edward the Confessor, who instead of returning them to Pershore used them to establish the fourth of the great ecclesiastical foundations in the county, St Peter of Westminster. This explains why Westminster controlled so many estates in Pershore hundred.

This historical conspectus suggests that Worcester had the largest number of slaves because of the stability of its land-holdings. Many of the slaves on its lands must have been the descendants of indigenous inhabitants subjugated when the Anglo-Saxons first moved into the area. Many others must have been Anglo-Saxons enslaved because of debt or crime through the jurisdictional power which the bishop of Worcester had exercised independently of the king from an early period.[130]

When Ælfhere seized Pershore's lands, he probably took the wealthiest and best-stocked estates. These are precisely the ones that are likely to have had the most slaves. This would explain why Westminster owned so many more slaves than Pershore did. Here too lies the probable reason for Evesham's low numbers, as it also had had an internal upheaval within its community and had suffered extensive losses in land.

While this historical survey provides an explanation for the relative numbers of slaves on these ecclesiastical estates, tables XVI and XVII are really very crude statistical instruments that mask how carefully labour resources were utilised by these churches. A more probing examination of the Domesday material relating to the largest of the four foundations, the monastic cathedral of St Mary, is able to provide us with a much more nuanced insight into the part played by slaves within the economy of an ecclesiastical foundation.

The tenurial geography of Worcester's estates has recently been investigated by J. Hamshere. His approach has proved very useful, not least because it reveals how cautiously Domesday Book statistics must be handled, and will be drawn upon here. Because he did not restrict himself to the county of Worcestershire but included the church's estates in Gloucestershire and Warwickshire as well, his figures will differ somewhat from those given below.[131]

The lands of St Mary's, Worcester, were divided between the bishop and the monastery. Evidently, the latter's share must have been inadequate because at some point before 1086 the bishop made over three estates for the provisioning

---

[128] The annals, preserved in extracts made by Leland, mention a 'Delfero consuli' (Dugdale, *Monasticon Anglicanum*, ed. Caley *et al.*, II.415, s.a. 1259), whom Round, 'Introduction to the Worcestershire Domesday', in *The Victoria History of the County of Worcester*, volume I, edd. Willis-Bund & Doubleday, pp. 258–9, identified with Ælfhere (*ob.* 983).

[129] *Loc. cit.*

[130] Unfortunately John's work on Oswaldslow in *Land Tenure*, pp. 80–139, was also heavily dependent on the authenticity of the *Altitonantis* charter (see n. 124 above). Nevertheless, it appears that the bishop of Worcester had considerable powers in this part of the country.

[131] Hamshere, 'The structure and exploitation of the Domesday Book estate of the Church of Worcester'.

of the monks and in 1089 was to transfer another estate, Alveston, to the community.[132] (The three estates have been included in the church's rather than the bishop's lands in the tables below.) The total hidage for which St Mary's and the bishop was answerable was 393¼, of which 300 comprised the hundred of Oswaldslow. The hidage of these estates was remarkably faithfully recorded in the Exchequer Domesday. The bishop had manors totalling 225 hides (of which seven were under the control of the monks) and the monastic community had estates totalling a further 168¼ hides. The few ambiguous entries involve a very small number of hides and only ten hides are unaccounted for, all from the single manor of Cropthorne.[133] This encourages one to have some faith in the accuracy of the other figures recorded for St Mary's.

The relative proportion of slaves as a percentage of the population on the demesne of the bishop, the monastic community, and the sub-tenants varies significantly, as table XVIII shows.

TABLE XVIII: COMPOSITION OF THE POPULATION ON
ESTATES BELONGING TO ST MARY'S, WORCESTER

	Total Population	Villeins	Bordars	Slaves (both sexes)	Others
Bishop's demesne	484	241	158	72	13
% of population		49.8	32.6	14.9	2.7
Monastic demesne	502	216	131	141	14
% of population		43	26.1	28.1	2.8
Sub-tenants' lands	509	191	186	117	15
% of population		37.5	36.5	23	3

As a percentage of the population on the lands of an overlord, the slaves on the bishop's estates were the lowest – indeed, they were .7% below the proportion of slaves recorded in the county. Slaves formed approximately the same percentage of the population on both the monastic demesnes and on the lands controlled by sub-tenants, some 7.5–12.5% above the county average.

In the light of the evidence that slaves in Worcestershire were closely associ-

132 On Alveston, see *ibid.*, p. 50, and Pelteret, *Catalogue of English Post-Conquest Vernacular Documents*, §63 (pp. 86–7).
133 At Tredington, the phrase 'xvii hidae 7 ibi' has probably inadvertently been omitted between the words 'In *domanio* sunt' and 'v car.' (fo 173va; cf. Breedon, fo 173ra) and similarly at Grimley the words 'ii hidae 7 ibi' seem to have been left out, as can be deduced from the following entry for Knightswick, which is said to have formed one of Grimley's three hides (fo 173vb); Hallow with Broadwas had an extra half a hide, possibly the estate at Eastbury, which is described as 'villeins' land' (*terra uillanorum*; fos 173vb–174ra); the manor of Cropthorne included Netherton, which possibly accounted for the missing ten hides (fo 174ra); and finally I have assumed that the five hides that paid geld on the manor of Phepson comprised the berewick of Crowle described in the next entry (fo 174ra), especially since the values between these two estates would otherwise be so discrepant. If this interpretation be rejected, the holdings of the Priory of Worcester should be increased by five hides in tables XVI and XVII.

ated with the demesne ploughs, it is illuminating to examine the relationship between the size of the demesne, the numbers of ploughs and the population on the manors belonging to St Mary's in the county (see table XIX).

TABLE XIX: HIDAGE, POPULATION, AND PLOUGH-TEAMS ON THE ESTATES OF ST MARY'S, WORCESTER

	Hides	Slaves (male and female)	Demesne Ploughs	Villeins, bordars, and others	Ploughs
Bishop	92¾	72	38	412	203
Monastery	127¼	141	53	361	184
Sub-tenants	163¼[a]	117	93½	392	125¾

[a] Ten hides have been omitted from the manor at Cropthorne.

If it be granted that there was frequently a close relationship between slaves and ploughs, the bishop must have kept most of his slaves for ploughing.[134] The monastery, on the other hand, had a surplus of slaves over and above any that might be used for ploughing. These must have been employed, therefore, in other tasks on the monastic demesne. In contrast to the practice of the bishop and the monastery, the sub-tenants had too few slaves for ploughing to have been done by slaves alone. Much of the ploughing on the sub-tenants' demesnes must thus have been undertaken by the large number of villeins and bordars resident on their estates or by the sub-tenants themselves.

Hamshere has pointed out another important aspect of the use of resources on these estates. Relative to the size and value of his lands, Bishop Wulfstan had a considerably smaller number of ploughs on his demesne than the sub-tenants had. Both the bishop and, to a slightly lesser extent, the monastery must have relied to a much greater extent on the dependent peasantry to provide the ploughs and labour to work the demesne arable than the sub-tenants did.[135]

What are the implications of all these statistics for the relative numbers of slaves on the three estates? It appears that on the episcopal demesnes there was a tendency to reduce the number of slaves, reserving them for the specialist function of ploughing. Much of the ploughing was done, however, as an obligation performed by the dependent peasantry. If the bishops of Worcester were following the example of those in East Anglia, they must have freed many of

[134] Of the thirty-eight ploughs on the episcopal demesnes, twenty-five of them display a correlation of two slaves per plough. It thus seems likely that the sixteen slaves at Fladbury worked eight of the nine ploughs recorded on the bishop's demesne there. The remaining six slaves on the Worcester episcopal demesnes were women. John Hamshere has noted that 79% of the variance in the relationship between ploughteams and the total population in Worcestershire is statistically explained when r = .89, a strikingly high correlation. See further Hamshere, 'A computer-assisted study of Domesday Worcestershire', in *Field and Forest*, edd. Slater & Jarvis, pp. 107–8 and n. 6.

[135] Hamshere, 'The structure and exploitation of the Domesday Book estate of the Church of Worcester', pp. 46–7.

their slaves and given them land in return for continuing the duty of ploughing the demesne and engaging in other labour services.

The monastic community, however, did not show the same flexibility, possibly because to free slaves might have appeared to be alienating ecclesiastical property. Like the bishop, they too must have been heavily reliant on labour services for ploughing, but they seem to have retained more slaves for general agricultural purposes. Since the abbey would also have been heavily dependent on its estates for the food to support its monastic congregation, there was also no economic incentive to free slaves and give them land in return for monetary rents; the bishop may have not felt so constrained.[136]

The sub-tenants were given not merely the poorest land (as Hamshere has shown) but also properties that were the most poorly endowed with slaves.[137] In consequence, some of them probably had to plough their own lands in addition to using the services of the dependent peasantry resident on the estate.

The stability of Worcester's tenure of its lands suggests that on ecclesiastical estates it was not manorialism as such that led to a decline in the number of slaves. As long as slaves were regarded as the only section of the population that could be owned by a lord, there was a tendency for the number of slaves on ecclesiastical lands to remain stable because canon law proscribed the permanent alienation of church property. What the lords and institutions brought about through the development of the classic seigneurial manor (as opposed to the Domesday fiscal manor) was the growth of a system of customary law which subjected *all* those resident on their estates to their control. As already suggested this changed the nature of the concept of freedom so that only those permitted to leave an estate were considered 'free'. The rest of the residents – *ceorl* and *þeow* alike – 'belonged' to an estate. Only when the stage was reached that all residents were regarded in the same light was it possible for ecclesiastical lords (and especially monastic houses) to change the socio-economic relationship between themselves and part of this resident population, the slaves, by giving them dwellings and land in return for rents and services. It is evident from the Worcester figures that this last stage had not yet been reached on the Worcester ecclesiastical estates at the time of the Domesday survey.

We should note that Worcester's situation was not in conflict with the celebrated opposition of Bishop Wulfstan of Worcester to the slave trade, as has been

---

[136] This is very much in line with S. P. J. Harvey's views, based on a wider survey of the Domesday evidence. Noting that 'the economics of slavery and demesne agriculture seem closely allied', she has concluded that 'proportionally large demesnes, whether on great manors or small, clung tenaciously to slave labour'; the consequence that 'profits from demesne enterprise were small' may often have been the case, although she herself has pointed to Norman lords with large demesnes who were apparently agriculturally successful: see below, Conclusion, p. 254 and n. 61. Large demesnes are particularly characteristic of ecclesiastical land-holders, especially in the South-west; an obvious attraction to directly managing estates that were reasonably close to the home institution (and here one may think of the Worcester estates controlled by St Mary's) was 'the practical advantages of locally accessible foodstuffs'. See 'The extent and profitability of demesne agriculture', in *Social Relations and Ideas*, edd. Aston *et al.*, pp. 60, 69, 58, and 54.

[137] Hamshere, 'The structure and exploitation of the Domesday Book estate of the Church of Worcester', 48–9.

suggested.[138] Wulfstan's position, which was, in fact, entirely orthodox for his time, has been misrepresented. What he opposed was the sale of persons destined to be sent abroad; like his contemporaries he seems tacitly to have accepted the institution of slavery as such. Only the vigour of his opposition to the Bristol slave market excited comment. As has been already demonstrated, there was, in fact, a smaller than average proportion of slaves on his demesne but this can be ascribed to sound economic management by Wulfstan of his estates rather than to any moral opposition on his part to the principle of slavery.

MIDDLESEX

The Middlesex survey appears to be singularly valuable to the social and economic historian as it seems to reveal something about the holdings of each of the non-slave classes in the county, which should thereby enable one to get a picture of the relative economic status of the county's inhabitants.[139] Recently this orthodoxy has been challenged by A. R. Bridbury, who has argued that what we are presented with is a record of land for which geld must be paid.[140] Bridbury's case has a certain cogency in the light of the Huntingdonshire Domesday evidence. S. P. J. Harvey has noted that in Hurstingstone Hundred the villeins and sokemen there were responsible for paying the geld based on the recorded hidage[141] and David Roffe has observed that in that county 'in nearly 40 per cent of the instances in which the data can be determined, each virgate of land is represented by one villan.'[142] If this were the case, however, it would difficult to understand why the gardens of certain peasants find mention. Nevertheless, the possibility should not be rejected that in Middlesex the peasantry were required to pay the geld and that the original assessment for those called *uillani* in Domesday Book was based on a half-virgate holding. This conclusion need not affect the useful-

[138] Clarke, 'Domesday slavery', 40. Willis-Bund, 'Worcestershire Doomsday', 102, also commented: 'At first sight it is startling to find that the house of the sainted Dunstan, whose great glory it is always said was to do away with slavery in England, who devoted himself more than any of his age to that object, should have so far relapsed into the old paths as to have become a great slave owner.' There is no reference to such zeal on Dunstan's part in the B Life, which is the main source for his activities (see *Memorials of Saint Dunstan*, ed. Stubbs). Willis-Bund appears to have got his facts garbled; he was presumably thinking of St Wulfstan, who flourished a century later.

[139] See the excellent introduction by Pinder, 'Domesday Survey', in *A History of the County of Middlesex*, volume I, edd. Cockburn *et al.*, pp. 80–118.

[140] Bridbury, 'Domesday Book: a re-interpretation', especially pp. 295–6. Bridbury has cited the entry for Staines (fo 128rb–128va), where the number of hides (calculated at 120 acres per hide) almost equals the demesne hidage plus the acreage held by the peasantry. There are sufficient discrepancies in other entries, however, to give one cause to ponder the validity of Bridbury's interpretation. Note, for example, Fulham (answered for forty hides, but only twenty-six are listed), Harmondsworth (answered for thirty hides, though only seventeen-and-a-half are listed), and Enfield (answered for thirty hides, but only twenty-seven are listed): Domesday Book, volume I, 127va, 128vb, and 129vb (text); Pinder,'Domesday Survey', in *A History of the County of Middlesex*, volume I, edd. Cockburn *et al.*, pp. 123a (Staines), 121a, 123b–124a, and 126b (translation).

[141] Harvey, 'Taxation and the economy', in *Domesday Studies*, ed. Holt, p. 252.

[142] 'An introduction to the Huntingdonshire Domesday', in *The Huntingdonshire Domesday*, edd. Williams & Erskine, p. 11.

ness of the Middlesex figures for land-holding. There are a sufficient number of variants from this norm to suggest that even if the peasant holdings were originally divided according to a fiscal assessment, the holdings as enumerated in the survey had a close relationship to the areal reality in 1086.[143]

The peasantry of the Middlesex record are divided into *uillani*, *bordarii*, and *cotarii*. Their numbers, together with the land-holding that each was answerable for,[144] are presented in table XX.

TABLE XX: THE NUMBER OF *UILLANI* (U), *BORDARII* (B), AND
COTARII (C) IN MIDDLESEX AND THE AMOUNT OF LAND
EACH ANSWERED FOR EXPRESSED IN
HIDES (h), VIRGATES (v), AND ACRES (a)

2h	1h	3v	½h	60–40a	40–30a	1v	30–20a	20–15a	15a	15–10a	10a	10–5a	5a	5–3a	3–2a	1a or less	Gardens	No details	TOTAL
4	16	11	83	16	17	478	20	–	453	1	15	1	0	–	–	–	–	38	1,153
–	–	–	–	–	–	–	–	7	34	14	55	48	98	29	–	25	–	32ª	342
–	–	–	–	–	–	–	–	–	–	–	–	2	2	25	76	67	49	243	464

Excluding a number of *uillani* and *bordarii* at Fulham (fo 127va) and Isleworth (fo 130rb) whose land-holdings were not enumerated separately.

The distribution-pattern of the holdings is very informative. Table XX shows that three distinct economic classes at the time of Domesday Book can be discerned, although a trend towards two classes was already in progress. This is clearest when the statistical modes are examined. Among the *uillani* there are two modes; about 40% were answerable for a virgate and a nearly equal percentage a half a virgate. The mode for the *bordarii* is five acres. Most *bordarii*, however, were responsible for more property than this: fifty-five are recorded as having ten acres and an equal number more than ten and less than twenty acres. It is evident that the trend toward fifteen-acre (half-virgate) holdings which Round noted in the Essex Domesday and which was accomplished in the latter

---

143 My conclusion is thus at one with Lennard's and Pinder's as expressed by the latter in 'An introduction to the Middlesex Domesday', in *The Middlesex and London Domesday*, edd. Williams & Martin, p. 4, namely, that 'it is reasonable to accept Lennard's view that even if the Domesday Book figures were intended to be taken as a fiscal assessment rather than as indications of area, it is likely that the men's holdings were closely related to agrarian realities and their values'.

144 Pindar's appendix II ('Distribution of land among the peasantry') added to his 'Domesday survey', in *A History of the County of Middlesex*, volume I, ed. Cockburn *et al.*, pp. 132–5, is potentially very useful but the following errors need to be corrected: in entry 5, the one *uillanus* held two, not one hide; in entry 32, C (for *cotarius*) should be entered instead of '..' in the *Class* column; in entry 34 the reference to a single cottar under tenures imprecisely recorded should be deleted; in entry 78 for '2 on 1*h*' read '2 on 4*h*'; in entry 80 an additional eighteen *uillani* should be entered in the ½*v* (half a virgate) column.

county in the twelfth century was present in Middlesex as well, resulting in the coalescence of the *uillani* and *bordarii* into a single economic class.[145]

Most *cotarii* (243) were not recorded as holding land. There may be some inadequacy in the record here but Pinder is probably right in regarding the majority as landless men (though some may have occupied crofts).[146] Among the landed *cotarii* the mode figure is two to three acres. Most of those with land, however, answered for only a single acre or their gardens. Such a large number of landless and near-landless cottagers suggests that these must represent freed slaves. The figures imply that in Middlesex, unlike Essex, overlords found it more in their interests to create a class of *famuli* dependent on them for employment than to expand the arable by giving men a sufficient amount of land for them to pay geld on half-virgates. (This is, of course, a generalisation; probably some of the Middlesex *bordarii* were freed slaves also.)

It has been suggested above that in Essex the rise in the values of manors can only be explained in terms of the imposition of rents rather than of services, a practice that would have provided an attractive economic incentive to free slaves. In Middlesex rents are reported as being paid only by *cotarii*, which, if they represented freed slaves, lends support to this view. This shift from a traditional pattern of payment in services or kind would have been more easily imposed on freed slaves, who would have been less likely to have opposed such an innovation than a group not undergoing any status change.

Tables XXI and XXII show the numbers of *serui* in Middlesex and their distribution, both in geographical terms and as a proportion of the total population. The number of demesne ploughs on estates where slaves are recorded is given in parentheses.

TABLE XXI: *SERUI* IN THE MIDDLESEX DOMESDAY

Hundred:	Edmonton	Elthorne	Gore	Ossulstone	Spelthorne	Hounslow	TOTAL
1. King William	–	–	–	–	–	–	0
2. Archbishop of Canterbury	–	2(2)	2(4)	–	–	–	4
3. Bishop of London	–	–	–	2(2)	–	–	2
4. St Peter of Westminster	2(1) 2(1)	6(1) 1(1)	1(3)	1(1)	12(13)	–	25
5. La Trinité, Rouen	–	6(3)	–	–	–	–	6
6. Church of Barking	–	–	–	–	–	–	0

[145] Round, 'Introduction to the Essex Domesday', in *The Victoria History of the County of Essex*, volume I, edd. Doubleday & Page, p. 361. Pinder does not seem to have noticed this economic development.
[146] *A History of the County of Middlesex*, volume I, edd. Cockburn *et al.*, pp. 131, n. 3.

Hundred:	Edmonton	Elthorne	Gore	Ossulstone	Spelthorne	Hounslow	TOTAL
7. Earl Roger		1(2) 8(3)	–	–	–	–	9
8. Count of Mortain	–	–	–	–	2(1)	– 2(1)	4
9. Geoffrey de Mandeville	4(4) 6(4)	1(1) 6(2)	–	1(1)	–	–	18
10. Ernulf de Hesdin	–	4(3)			–	–	4
11. Walter fitzOther	–	–	–	–	8(3) 2(1)	–	10
12. Walter de Saint-Valery	–	–	–	–	–	–	0
13. Richard fitzGilbert	–	3(2)	–	–	–	–	3
14. Robert Gernon	–	–	–	–	–	–	0
15. Robert Fafiton	–	–	–	–	–	–	0
16. Robert fitzRoscelin	–	–	–	–	–	–	0
17. Robert Blund	–	–	–	–	–	–	0
18. Roger de Raismes	–	–	2(1)	–	6(1)	–	8
19. William fitzAnsculf	–	3(1)	–	–	–	–	3
20. Edward of Salisbury	–	–	–	3(2)	–	–	3
21. Aubrey de Vere	–	–	–	7(4)	–	–	7
22. Ranulf, brother of Ilger	–	–	–	1(1)	–	–	1
23. Deormann of London	–	–	–	–	–	–	0
24. Countess Judith	4(2)	–	–	–	–	–	4
25. Land given in alms	–	–	–	1(2)	–	–	1
TOTAL	18	41	5	16	30	2	112

TABLE XXII: *SERUI* AS A PROPORTION OF THE
TOTAL POPULATION IN MIDDLESEX[147]

Hundred:	Edmonton	Elthorne	Gore	Ossulstone	Spelthorne	Hounslow	TOTAL
Serui	18	41	5	16	30	2	112
Total pop.	265	454	193	753	350	151	2166
% of total pop.	6.8	9.0	2.6	2.1	8.6	1.3	5.2

There are extraordinarily few *serui* in Middlesex as table XXI shows. It is not easy to account for this. Sixty-three per cent of the slaves are recorded in the two westernmost hundreds, Elthorne and Spelthorne. Most of the manors in the Domesday survey of the county are also in these hundreds so there is clearly a correlation here.[148] Yet it seems puzzling that only sixteen slaves were reported from the large and populous south-eastern hundred of Ossulstone, which adjoins Essex, where the number of slaves was fairly high (see table XXII). The answer perhaps lies in the fact that Ossulstone was also adjacent to London, to which runaway slaves could escape. If this was the case it might explain why the compiler of the *Willelmi articuli Londoniis retractati* adopted from Continental sources the regulation that permitted slaves who had resided in a city for a year and a day to gain their freedom.[149]

The Abbey of St Peter of Westminster, with all its twenty-five slaves being resident on lands directly controlled by the abbot, and the rapacious Geoffrey de Mandeville, with sixteen out of eighteen slaves living on the manors under his direct control, between them owned 38% of the slaves enumerated in the county. As suggested above, prohibitions against the alienation of ecclesiastical property probably accounts for Westminster Abbey's twenty-five *serui*.

As in Essex and Worcester there is some evidence of a correlation between *serui* and demense ploughs: on eight out of the thirty-two estates with slaves a ratio of two *serui* to one demesne plough can be found.[150]

CORNWALL

Cornwall presents a very different picture from the preceding three counties. Finally brought under direct Anglo-Saxon control only in the reign of Æthelstan, it does not display either the administrative or the settlement structure of the rest of England. Unlike the Essex Domesday, with its clear division into geographic hundreds, the record for Cornwall as preserved both in Exon and the Exchequer versions of Domesday Book fails to mention any hundreds. Instead holdings are listed under tenants-in-chief, and, within these divisions, they are enumerated according to who the under-tenants were. Cornwall, like another Celtic territory,

---

[147] The figures for the total population are drawn from Pinder's table IV in his 'Domesday Survey', in *ibid.*, p. 94.

[148] For a map of the hundreds and the manors recorded in the Domeday survey see *ibid.*, p. 81.

[149] *Willelmi articuli Londoniis retractati*, §16 (*Die Gesetze*, ed. Liebermann, I.491).

[150] For a list of the manors see Pinder, 'Domesday Survey', in *A History of the County of Middlesex*, volume I, edd. Cockburn *et al.*, p. 94.

Wales, was a land of *trevs*, small non-nucleated settlements consisting on occasion of only a single house.[151] This gave the commissioners some trouble, which is reflected in Domesday Book; as Pounds pointed out: 'The occurrence in the West of large manors, where we know that large villages never existed, probably represents the complete failure of the royal commissioners to cope with the trevs, ever diminishing in size and accessibility as the western confines of the county were reached.'[152] That the commissioners experienced difficulty is not surprising since the Domesday survey depended heavily on the manor, a feature alien to the Cornish landscape.

These combined factors of history and of administrative and settlement structure will assist us in elucidating the Domesday figures for slaves in Cornwall.

TABLE XXIII: THE NUMBER OF *SERUI* AND THEIR OWNERS IN CORNWALL IN 1086 (Sub-tenants are inset)

	Holder	Estates	Slaves	Holder	Estates	Slaves
1.	King	18	194[a]	Hamelin	5	7
				Turstin	1	0
2.	Bishop of Exeter	7	36	Nigel	9	42
	Canons and sub-tenants	5	12	Jovin	13	20
3.	Church of Tavistock	6	14[b]	Nigel	1	8
4.	St Michael	1	–	Willelm	1	2
	Canons of St Stephen	1	–	Alvred	7	12
	Church of St Petroc	8	10	Erchenbald	3	8
	Berner	1	2	Osfrith	12	23
	Count of Mortain	9	51	Odo	6	13
	Richard	1	3	Algar	6	21
	Macco	1	1	Alward	2	3
	Canons of St Achebran	1	0	Alnoth	4	5
	Canons of St Probus	1	5	Eadnoth	1	0
	Canons of St Carantoc	1	0	Alnoth	1	0
	Canons of St Piran	1	2	Alric	2	1
	Canons of St Buryan	1	0	Alsige	1	1
	Clerks of St Neot	1	0	Almær	1	3
	St Constantine	1	0	Beorhtric	5	6
5.	Count of Mortain	22	182	Wulfsige	2	2
	Reginald (de Vautort)	33	132	Cola	1	0
	Richard (fitzTurold)	28	135	Leofnoth	2	12
	Turstin	18	59	Wulfweard	1	0
	Hamelin	17	46	Wulfsige	1	0
	Turstin	1	1	Wulfric	1	1
				Dodda	1	3
				Scirweald	1	1
				Gunnar	1	0

[151] Perhaps too much has been made of the isolated homestead, however; I. N. Soulsby has very cautiously concluded that '[a]t the very least there is mounting evidence from a number of directions . . . that the native population was not averse to group settlement': 'An introduction to the Cornwall Domesday', in *The Cornwall Domesday*, edd. Williams & Erskine, p. 6.

[152] Pounds, 'The Domesday geography of Cornwall', 71.

Holder	Estates	Slaves		Holder	Estates	Slaves
Godwine	1	3		Heldric	1	2
Wihumarc	2	2		Blohin	5	6
Hueche	1	1		Roger	4	7
Rabel	2	0				
Bernard	1	0	6.	Iudichael	1	4
Humphrey	1	0		of Totnes		
Seibert	1	0				
Frawin	1	5	7.	Goscelm	1	0
Andrew	2	4		Berner	10	8
Radulf	1	1		Brian	4	6

[a] This figure includes four slaves on an estate an under-tenant, Wulfweard, held of the Count of Mortain, who in turn held the land from the King. Two estates of Beorhtric, where no slaves were recorded, are entered under the King's lands.

[b] All Tavistock's estates were held by one Ermenald; four of the six manors recorded the presence of slaves.

TABLE XXIV: SUMMARY OF THE MAJOR CORNISH SLAVE-OWNERS
(Demesne holdings and numbers of slaves on those demesnes are given in parentheses)

Tenant-in-chief	Estates	Slaves
King	18(16)	194(190)
Ecclesiastics and Churches	47(24)	136 (57)
Count of Mortain (excl. St Petroc's sub-tenancy)	248(22)	794(182)
Count of Mortain (incl. St Petroc's sub-tenancy)	257(31)	845(221)
Other tenants-in-chief	2	4
TOTAL	315	1,128[a]

[a] Excluded are slaves recorded on detached estates located within the boundaries of Devonshire.

Slaves accounted for 21% of the recorded population of this sparsely inhabited county. This represents 1,128 persons (1,149 if those on estates located east of the Tamar are included), the eighth largest number of slaves in all the Domesday counties. The substantial numbers must have been the result of the relatively recent conquest of the West Country. Somerset and Devon similarly recorded large numbers: over a quarter of all England's slaves were to be found in these three counties.

The effect of this late conquest is also seen in the land-holdings. The king held eighteen estates, half of which had ten or more slaves. In all, the king owned one-sixth of the total slave population. In contrast, the Bishop of Exeter and his canons owned forty-eight slaves on twelve estates (most of them on the bishops' demesnes), and various churches a further eighty-eight slaves on thirty-five estates. The biggest holder in this latter group was St Petroc's, Bodmin, with sixty-seven slaves. There were, however, only ten slaves on the eight estates controlled directly by the monastery; most were on the nine estates held of St Petroc's by the Count of Mortain. Tavistock Abbey reported only fourteen slaves on its six estates, all of the latter being held by a sub-tenant.[153]

The biggest holder of both land and slaves was the Count of Mortain.[154] On the twenty-two estates he personally controlled (excluding the six he held of St Petroc's) there were 182 slaves; a further 612 were on the 226 estates of his sub-tenants.

The overall picture shows that the major slave-owners in the county were the king, who had an average of 10.1 slaves per estate, and the Count of Mortain, who had on the lands he personally controlled (including those held of St Petroc's) 8.2 slaves per estate. The ecclesiastical holders had far fewer: 5.1 per estate on the Bishop of Exeter's lands, 3.4 on those estates held of Tavistock Abbey and 1.25 on the manors directly controlled by St Petroc's. The sub-tenants of the Count of Mortain similarly averaged only 2.7 slaves per estate. This suggests that the king as conqueror kept the best-manned estates for himself or for his deputy in Cornwall, Robert, count of Mortain.[155] The rest had to be content with estates holding fewer indigenous inhabitants. Furthermore, the evidence of the Bodmin Gospels suggests that both ecclesiastical and lay lords had a long tradition of releasing slaves, which may also account for the smaller numbers on the estates of the lesser tenants.[156]

Only thirty-five estates record a ratio of two slaves per plough. This may be seen as strongly indicative of the relative lack of arable farming in the county. Cornwall was evidently agriculturally under-developed. Though religious tradition encouraged the release of slaves, there were not the economic incentives that existed in Essex for a rapid reduction in their numbers.

CONCLUSION

SOME GENERAL OBSERVATIONS

The Domesday statistics were crucially shaped by the purposes of the survey, the nature of the seigneurial returns, the methods employed by the commissioners in the various circuits to assemble and tabulate the data, and the editorial methods (which clearly changed as the work proceeded at Winchester). When one looks at this great compilation of figures, it is rather like looking at oneself in a cracked and fragmented distorting mirror at a fairground: some parts can be missing, some displaced, and some grotesquely misshapen – and yet one can still

---

153 On the slaves belonging to Tavistock see Finberg, *Tavistock Abbey*, especially pp. 57–61.

154 Half-brother of William the Conqueror and one of only eleven men who controlled half the land held by lay tenure in England under William (Douglas, *William the Conqueror*, p. 269), his position in Cornwall has been discussed by Soulsby, 'An introduction to the Cornwall Domesday', in *The Cornwall Domesday*, edd. Williams & Erskine, pp. 9–12.

155 They were the most populous estates: some 1008 persons (excluding thegns) or 18.5% of the total Domesday population for Cornwall were to be found on the lands of the king.

156 See chapter V above.

somehow be recognisable. Provided we are not misled into thinking that the seemingly definite outlines in Domesday Book are a precise replica of eleventh-century reality, we can still draw some conclusions from what we see.

The preceding studies have illustrated the great variation that existed in the social geography of England. The usage of land ranged from extensively or-ganised estates in Essex to small settlements in Cornwall. Control over land also varied. Worcester was heavily dominated by four great ecclesiastical foundations whereas most of the land in Essex was held by lay tenants-in-chief. The patterns of slave ownership likewise differed greatly from one part of the country to another. Local historical and geographic factors should be sought to explain this. The late conquest and economic under-development of Cornwall help account for the large numbers of slaves in that county. In Worcestershire the stable tenure by Worcester Priory of its large land-holdings and its continuing need to feed a resident monastic congregation, both of which may have fostered conservative land and labour practices, together with the traditional ecclesiastical prohibitions against the alienation of church property, explain the disproportionately large numbers of slaves on its estates. On the other hand, Middlesex, with its proximity to London, had very few slaves.

Geographic factors are likely to have been particularly important in determin-ing the level of the slave population in different parts of England. For instance, though the highest percentage of slaves was to be found in Gloucestershire, there were very few in the western areas of that county for the simple reason that it was heavily forested and the population was in general low in that region.[157] Geography could influence slave numbers in other ways. In the Sussex Weald, for instance, the population was probably devoted primarily to pig rearing be-cause of the woodland. The impracticability of exercising control over such men and also the difficulty of supplying them with food rations made it highly likely in consequence that swineherds would have been granted their freedom in return for regular dues in kind from their animals.[158]

One must be cautious, however, in the way in which one assembles and interprets this geographic evidence. The data tabulated above on the distribution of slaves warn us that it is easy to make false deductions from population maps such as some of those in the *Domesday Geographies*. Were one to draw a slave population map of Essex, say, one would find that a substantial proportion of slaves were in Hinckford hundred. Closer examination, however, would reveal that this happens also to be by far the largest hundred in Essex and one for which particularly detailed manorial statistics have been supplied. Other factors can also influence such maps. Spelthorne hundred with its thirty-five *serui* had nearly a third of the slaves recorded in Middlesex, but twenty of these prove to have been recorded on only two manors out of the eighteen in the hundred, showing that the distribution of slaves could vary widely even within a hundred.

The figures have emphasised that by 1086 slaves were very much a minority in England. But it was still a substantial one, ranging in many areas from 10 to 25% of the recorded population – though we should not place too much faith in

---

[157] See *The Domesday Geography of Midland England*, fig. 14 (p. 30) and pp. 23–31 (wood-land); figs 11 and 12 (pp. 24–5) (population).
[158] See Fleming, 'Pigs in Domesday Book', where the custom of pannage is discussed.

the precision of these percentages, given the lacunae and the variation in the recording of the population. The rapid disappearance of this minority during the late eleventh century must be ascribed to the Normans, who freed their slaves from motives largely inspired by a desire to exploit their newly-won lands in ways that would increase their wealth. By freeing men they could encourage the more intensive development of lands in return for rent, an undertaking that possibly would have been more feasible if there was concomitantly an expanded use of the heavy plough to tackle the more difficult clayland soils. The increased revenue may in turn have fostered the conversion into hired labourers of other slaves who had formed part of the permanent demesne staff, thereby both reducing the overlords' obligations to these persons and enhancing the flexibility with which they could utilise their labour-force. The arrival of the Normans thus provided the shock to the slave system necessary for its demise that Orlando Patterson has found to have characterised the disappearance of slavery else-where.[159]

The release of slaves is shown indirectly by the drop in their numbers in Essex over the twenty years preceding Domesday Book. The same pattern is likely to have been replicated all over the country. For instance, despite the high propor-tion of slaves in Cornwall as a whole, in fifty-nine out of the 315 estates for which detailed information has been supplied there were no slaves at all accord-ing to the Exchequer Domesday, and Finberg noted that there were something like one hundred such manors in Devonshire as well.[160] Evidence from earlier chapters in this book might suggest that formal manumission must in conse-quence have been a regular event all over the country in the latter part of the eleventh century. Indeed, even Domesday Book records that at Hailes in Glou-cestershire twelve slaves had been freed at some point before 1086.[161] Given the complex and gradual nature of the changes that took place in the concept of freedom during this period, however, one may doubt whether the change in status from slave to serf was always a formal event. A gradual change in status is particularly likely to have occurred in counties where slave numbers were so high that some found it possible to rise to the economic level of those who were legally free. There are several entries in the Exon Domesday that even suggest that in Devon a few persons who retained the appellation of *servus* possessed their own plough-oxen and were working land for themselves in 1086.[162] In the

---

[159] *Slavery and Social Death*, p. 285 ; cf above, p. 15.
[160] Finberg, *Tavistock Abbey*, p. 61.
[161] Domesday Book, volume I, fo 167va.
[162] At Gidcott two villeins and two slaves appear to have owned a plough-team, though the Exchequer version emended this to indicate that the oxen and the men belonged to the lord (Domesday Book, volume I, fo 113rb; Domesday Book, III.391, fo 420a); at Mowlish two *uillani* and two slaves owned a ferling of land between them, though the Exchequer version converted *serui* to *bordarii* (Domesday Book, volume I, fo 114ra; Domesday Book, III.316, fo 336v); a slave is recorded as the only inhabitant on a ferling that lay outside the demesne at Buckland, but the Exchequer version mentions another slave and a villein there as well (Domesday Book, volume I, fo 102vb, Domesday Book, III.120–1, fo 129v); the Exchequer version preserves the Exon Domesday record that at Buckfast the abbot has 'ten slaves who have two ploughs' (*x serui cum ii car.*: Domesday Book, volume I, fo 104ra; Domesday Book, III.169, fo 183r); and at Boasley the Exchequer version changed Exon Domesday's *Ibi*

course of time it would have been easy to drop the use of the word *seruus* to describe these men and to employ instead some other word such as *bordarius* (as the Exchequer version does in one of these instances in Devon).[163]

Domesday Book, therefore, emphasises that wide local differences existed in the ownership and distribution of slaves in the eleventh century and that the reasons for the disappearance of the institution of slavery are extremely diverse. Indeed, Domesday Book itself may have been a factor in the disappearance of slavery. Though William the Conqueror did not live to exploit its findings, there is every reason to believe that his son, William Rufus, and the latter's rapacious chancellor, Ranulf Flambard, did not ignore its information[164] in their eagerness to extract as much money as they could from the country[165] – and the Inquest evidently offered many apparent examples of the evasion of geld as well as its inexplicable reduction. To a lord presented with a demand for the payment of additional geld, the liberation of a slave in return for that person's becoming a geld-paying tenant may have proved to be as an attractive a proposition as the prospect of free status would have been to the slave.[166]

habet R[offus] vii seruos ('There Roffus has seven slaves') to *vii serui cum i carruca* ('[there are] seven slaves with one plough' (Domesday Book, volume I, fo 105vb; Domesday Book, III.265, fo 288v): Reichel, 'Translation of the Devonshire Domesday', in *The Victoria History of the County of Devon*, volume I, ed. Page, pp. 516a, 480b, 424a, and 433a. Finberg averred in his *Tavistock Abbey*, p. 60 and n. 3, that the last example is a mistake and suggested that the scribes of the Exchequer version considered the other Exon entries to be mistakes as well. While the Boasley entry may be a genuine error made in the compilation process at Winchester and the Exchequer scribes, who probably worked on the assumption that slaves could not possess plough-oxen or land, may well have considered the other Exon entries to be errors, that does not mean that Exon Domeday, which was probably closer to the 'original return' than the Exchequer version, made a mistake in this matter: there are too many examples for this to be explained away. See further Moore, 'Domesday slavery', p. 214. (For the identification of the Exchequer and Exon Domesday place-names with Gidcott and Mowlish see *Domesday Book: Devon*, Part 2, edd. & transl. C. & F. Thorn, §§34,13 and 28,5.) References to the Exon Domesday (Domesday Book, volume III) in this note are to the Record Commission edition, edited by Ellis (numbered as volume IV in some bindings).
163 At Mowlish: see the previous note.
164 See Hallam, *Domesday Book through Nine Centuries*, pp. 47–8. I consider the obituary of William found s.a. 1086 in the E version of the *Anglo-Saxon Chronicle* (*Two of the Saxon Chronicles Parallel*, ed. Plummer, p. 286.12–13) to be making a general characterisation of his reign in describing the hard bargains he drove in the sale of land; I do not think that it is referring to the opportunities Domesday Book may have provided him, as Hallam has suggested.
165 Barlow, *William Rufus*, pp. 217–22 and 243–7; Harvey, 'Domesday Book and Anglo-Norman governance', 188–93.
166 I owe this general point to Dr Roffe, who (*in litt.*) has commented that to judge from the satellite evidence, 'one of the chief concerns of the commissioners at the initial sessions of the survey was to find land which was illegally withholding geld. Demesne in the strictest sense was of course exempt, but many lords seem to have assumed that other types of demesne should have been included. The discovery of such evasions may have led to the liberation of tenants to pay the geld.'

THE TWELFTH-CENTURY EVIDENCE

As in the Loire valley in France,[167] the last vestiges of slavery did not disappear from England until the twelfth century. We have already seen evidence of this in the Exeter manumission-documents, and a number of monastic surveys confirm that this change was completed only in the fifty years of so after Domesday Book.

The cartulary of the nuns of Holy Trinity of Caen (Paris, Bibliothèque nationale, MS. latin 5650) is particularly informative about this change.[168] This monastery was dedicated just months before William's conquest of England and he offered his daughter, Cecilia, as an oblate at the ceremony. The nunnery benefited in consequence from William's success and received lands in several widely scattered parts of southern England, including Felsted in Essex, Pinbury in Gloucestershire, Tarrant Launceston in Dorset, Horstead in Norfolk, and *Dineslai* (probably Temple Dinsley in Hitchin, Hertfordshire).[169] Cecilia in due course became abbess and it may well be that it was under her guidance that the first surveys of the convent's English lands were undertaken. These surveys seem to have been made after 1106 but no later than 1130; a date shortly before 1113 seems likely.[170] They thus may have been compiled only a quarter of a century after Domesday Book. Most of Holy Trinity's records were lost at the time of the French Revolution; the survival of this cartulary is a happy chance. Only in 1982 was the record properly edited and as yet most scholars have not perceived its significance for Domesday studies.

Slaves were recorded on the four estates mentioned above. The account of Felsted, though somewhat imprecise, is the most informative. At the time of Domesday Book this Essex estate had twenty *uillani*, thirty-three *bordarii*, and eleven *serui*; in addition, four sokemen possessed fifty-five acres.[171] In the early twelfth-century survey ('Felsted A'), a substantial area had been given to one Ralph (*Radulfus*) to farm but there were still nineteen bordars on four virgates of land. Of these, we are told that fourteen worked three days a week (that is, on the demesne), four worked two days a week and the remaining one was a miller, who presumably ground the demesne grain whenever necessary. There were still eleven *serui* and mention is also made of three *ancillae*. Here the text becomes slightly incoherent but it appears to indicate that the slaves had to pay twopence per annum if they had a wife who was free and a further twopence if they had a free servant (*de seruiente libero denarios ii*). This cannot refer to the spouses and servants of the bordars as they are mentioned prior to the reference to the slaves. The slaves, provided they were able to work, had to do so during the whole week up to (but presumably not including) the Sabbath. The three female slaves were obliged to observe the same regimen. The slaves were permitted to have a cow

---

167 Van der Kieft, 'Les "Colliberti" ', especially pp. 394–5.

168 *Charters and Custumals of the Abbey of Holy Trinity Caen*, ed. Chibnall.

169 On the history of these acquisitions and the identification of *Dineslai*, see *ibid.*, pp. xxv–xxviii.

170 *Ibid.*, p. xxxi, especially n. 4.

171 Domesday Book, volume II, fo 21rb (text); Round, 'The text of the Essex Domesday', in *The Victoria History of the County of Essex*, volume I, edd. Doubleday & Page, p. 453 (translation).

free of tax; if they possessed more, they had to pay twopence for each one that was in milk.[172]

Here we will recognise evidence already seen in other sources: slaves were able to marry and they usually possessed at least a cow. More valuable to us is the way in which the Caen records clarify puzzling information found in these other sources. 'Felsted A' is not particularly concerned about the kindred of these eleven *serui* and three *ancillae*. If the males had spouses, the latter incurred, apparently through their marriage, the customary obligation of working twice a week on the demesne and, if they were free, they were subject to a personal tax to the nunnery. Whether or not they had children passed without notice. The marital relationships of the three female slaves likewise aroused no interest in the compiler. We must conclude, therefore, that these fourteen persons had specific offices to perform on the demesne. There may have been other slaves resident at Felsted, but these were also of no concern to the nuns. This will explain why the number of *serui* could remain stable at Felsted between 1086 and the date of the compilation of the cartulary record: the range of duties required of these men had not changed, so neither had their number. Quite conceivably three *ancillae* had been needed in 1086 but at some stage their presence was edited out of the Essex survey, like all other *ancillae* in this county.

What distinguishes the *serui* from the *bordarii* in this record is that they were allowed but a single day in the week – and that the Sabbath – to work for themselves. The overlord was thus entitled to almost all their labour. The concomitant of this was, of course, that their overlord had to support them. This finds no mention in the Holy Trinity record: it is a natural human failing to keep a precise record about what is owed oneself but to depend on one's memory and good will for what is owed others. (In this respect the sensitivity to reciprocal obligations in the *Rectitudines* is unusual.)

By this time, the status of slaves was no longer very significant. They had little freedom over their work habits, but that differed only in degree from many others living on an estate. It would not be surprising if they had 'free' spouses, even perhaps owned other slaves. What the kinship consequences of mixed marriages were do not get reported. But it is well to remember that the *Leges Henrici Primi* was contemporary with this text: 'Felsted A' shows us why the legal status of the children of such marriages is dealt with in that document.

A century later, the *seruus* had been forgotten at Felsted. A custumal, derived from a roll of 1224–1225 and called by its editor 'Felsted DE', does not mention *serui*. This does not mean that their labour functions ceased to be performed at Felsted. Ploughing was now undertaken by eight men who were called *acermanni*. There is no reason to disagree with Marjorie Chibnall when she interprets them as the successors of the *serui*.[173] These men now had land, which they received in return for looking after the demesne ploughs. Some of the old slave customs remained, however. They had the use of the demesne plough every other Sunday and received a meal at various times of the year, such as on

---

[172] See Postan, *The Famulus*, p. 9, n. 2.

[173] *Charters and Custumals of the Abbey of Holy Trinity Caen*, ed. Chibnall, p. 33, n. 2, referring to 'Felsted DE', §§71–8 (pp. 98–9).

Christmas Day and Easter Sunday. They also received in wintertime a full basket of seed-corn (*plenum seadleap frumenti*). On the other hand, the servile ties still remained: when the ploughs lay idle because of the freezing weather or for some other reason, they were required to go to the manorial courtyard (*ad curiam*) and follow the instructions of the reeve.

The earliest survey of Pinbury ('Pinbury A'), on the other side of the country in Gloucestershire, supplements what we have already deduced from the *Rectitudines* (which, as has been suggested, may come from the neighbouring county of Worcestershire). The text reads: 'uillanos vii operantes v diebus in ebdomada, bouarios vi, cocez iiii operantes tribus diebus, ancillas iii operantes tota ebdomada.'[174] Thus, the seven *uillani* worked five days in the week ('Pinbury BC' implies that this was in the autumn, when the harvest had to be brought in; eight virgates required only four days week-work in winter). The text is frustratingly defective when it moves on to the *bouarii*: one may suspect that *operantes iiii diebus* was dropped by the copyist through haplography. The cottars worked but three days on the demesne. Since they will have had very little land of their own (possibly only gardens), they will have needed to find additional employment elsewhere in the district in order to make ends meet. The three slaves at Pinbury seem to have been worse off than their counterparts at Felsted in that they worked all seven days in the week, perhaps because they were dairymaids.

At Tarrant Launceston in Dorset there had been three *ancillae*. Two of them, however, had died and had evidently not been replaced. Unfortunately the record is silent as to how their roles had been filled. Horstead in Norfolk had but a single *seruus* and one *ancilla*.[175] At *Dineslai* we again meet the familiar ploughman. We are told: 'There are five *bouarii*, and they hold thirty acres of land on the demesne, of whom three are free; the others, however, are slaves. Their wives work on Monday.'[176] Again, we must suppress our frustration at the opacity of the record. If all five ploughmen had an equal share of the thirty acres that had been carved out of the demesne for them (that is, six acres apiece), then it is difficult to see wherein the distinction in their status lay. Possibly the three free ploughmen had each received ten acres while their slave counterparts possessed no more than their houses. In either case, their personal legal status did not affect their spouses, all of whom had to work on Mondays.

No slaves are mentioned on the nuns' estates at Minchinhampton in Gloucestershire nor on the adjoining estate of Avening. We should not make too much of this, however, as the records are probably incomplete: at Avening there were eight ploughs, each with a team of eight oxen, but the only staff that find mention other than the millers are five bordars. The second survey of Avening made in *ca* 1170 ('Avening B') mentions two men who held ploughmen's holdings (*terram bubulcorum*) and a *daia*, presumably a dairymaid, who held six acres, which, as we have just seen, may also have been the holding of a ploughman at *Dineslai*. Incomplete though they may be, these records for Tarrant

---

174 *Ibid.*, pp. 34–5.
175 *Ibid.*, pp. 35 (Tarrant Launceston) and 36 (Horstead).
176 'Bouarii v, et tenent xxx acros terre de dominio quorum sunt iii liberi; alii uero serui. Femine eorum operantur die lune.' *Ibid.*, p. 37.

Launceston, Horstead, and *Dineslai* suggest that the slave status was in decline in most of the regions where the nuns held property.

At Evesham Abbey it was remembered that there were slaves in Edward the Confessor's day, though they had disappeared by the time the entry was made: 'Beckford consists of sixteen hides. Then five slaves and bondswomen. Then thirty-two villeins; now fourteen more. Then nine bordars; now six more. . . .'[177] But as the single chance reference to slave status in the *Liber Niger* shows,[178] the old legal status formerly recognised by the royal courts had become irrelevant to the monastic houses. The monks were primarily interested in the rents and services due to them from those living on their lands rather than in their legal status. This is particularly clear in the Evesham (Vespasian) Cartulary. On folio 34, for instance, there is a list of bordars with the rents they had to pay.[179] Several entries in the same cartulary list the customary dues of agricultural workers such the *bouarius*, *uaccarius* ('cow-herd') and *bercarius* ('shepherd').[180] It also contains detailed records of the various dues that were owed annually to the monks by other tenants.[181]

In most of the twelfth-century surveys *serui* do not appear at all. In some cases this is not surprising – Burton Abbey, for instance, is not recorded as owning any slaves at the time of Domesday Book.[182] Had the slave status survived into the latter half of the twelfth century, one might have expected them to be recorded in the Glastonbury Survey of 1184, given the large proportion of slaves in that area in 1086.[183] Yet they are not to be found. And so, though the antiquarian compiler of the *Leges Henrici Primi* knew about *serui*, the old slave-free dichotomy obviously had decreasing relevance to those who maintained manorial records in the twelfth century.

The laws enforced by the royal courts changed accordingly. It was important to be a freeman to be entitled to appeal to them – but no longer was this the sort of freeman known to the Anglo-Saxon laws. Paul Hyams's studies of the English law of villeinage has made this clear:[184] 'The free tenant had a bargaining position and could in theory leave the land if the new lord was completely unacceptable. Moreover, he had some security in the way he made his acknowledgement to the new lord. A villein would come and merely admit that he held

---

177 'Becchafort sunt xvi hid*ae*. . . . T*un*c serui *et* ancille v. T*un*c uillani xxxii; m*od*o xiiii pl*us*. T*un*c ix bord*ar*ii: m*od*o vi plus. . . .' (London, British Library, MS. Cotton Vespasian B.xxiv, fo 57v).

178 See above, p. 196 and n. 43.

179 There is also a list in the other Evesham cartulary, London, British Library, MS. Harley 3763, fo 79v.

180 London, British Library, MS. Cotton Vespasian B.xxiv, fos 27r, 49r.

181 *Ibid.*, fos 27r and 31v–32r.

182 See Lennard, *Rural England*, p. 94. Dr David Roffe (*in litt.*) has reminded me, however, that the Abbey's lands are poorly recorded in the Domesday returns as far as the population goes, as the omission of the *censarii* or rent-payers indicates; cf. n. 26 above.

183 *Liber Henrici de Soliaco*, ed. Jackson.

184 Hyams, 'Legal aspects of villeinage', substantially revised and expanded in *Kings, Lords and Peasants*.

in villeinage so much land. The free tenant, on the other hand, set out the terms on which he admitted holding the land for agreement at the outset.'[185]

This had serious implications for the villein at the level of the royal courts. While Hyams has felt that probably their lives were protected against their lords and that it was no defence in a case of homicide to assert that the dead man was one's own villein,[186] under common law 'the villein had no rights in land enforceable against his lord in the royal courts.'[187] This did not mean, however, that villeins were without rights in these courts. Though as litigants they might only sue their lords 'for sedition, homicide, and really serious physical maltreatment' and 'were for most purposes outside the common law', by 1300 they had become liable both to taxation and to engage in the defence of the realm.[188] Thus, '[t]he villein as subject had significantly higher pretensions than his predecessor of two centuries before had been permitted to have.'[189] Furthermore, most of their dealings would have been in a local context, and here they could look to the protection of manorial custom. Though the manorial lord undoubtedly had the power to influence custom, it would have been a foolish person who sought to manage an estate in flagrant breach of established tradition. As the compiler of the *Rectitudines* observed: '. . . one must delight among the people to learn laws if one does not oneself wish to lose honour on the estate.'[190] Villein descendants of former slaves could not, therefore, be said to have returned to the legal position of their slave forebears. They had gained rights at the manorial level which in general were probably respected by their overlords. Only if they had to take an unjust overlord to a royal court would they have found their customary rights unenforceable. Even in the public realm, however, they had gained in status through the dual obligations of taxation and military service. We may fairly claim, therefore, that a serf in the year 1300 in general had more rights than a slave of two centuries earlier.

---

[185] 'Legal aspects of villeinage', pp. 12–13. See further concerning the writ *Per que seruicia* in *Kings, Lords and Peasants*, pp. 6–8.

[186] Hyams, 'Legal aspects of villeinage', pp. 174–5. For a discussion of the three known cases where lords were impleaded for causing the deaths of their own villeins, see Hyams, *Kings, Lords and Peasants*, pp. 136–7.

[187] *Ibid.*, p. 49.

[188] For the quotations see *ibid.*, p. 150, and for public obligations see *ibid.*, pp. 151–60.

[189] *Ibid.*, p. 160.

[190] *Rectitudines Singularum Personarum*, §21.3: '. . . laga sceal on leode luflice leornian, lof se ðe on lande sylf nele leosan.' *Die Gesetze*, ed. Liebermann, I.452 (text); *English Historical Documents 1042–1189*, §172 (transl. Douglas & Greenaway, p. 878) (translation).

CONCLUSION

The time has now arrived when certain themes that have come to prominence in this examination of the Anglo-Saxon evidence on slavery must be drawn together. For comparative purposes the most important of these is a profile of those called 'slaves' in late Anglo-Saxon England. The various categories of evidence surveyed in the preceding chapters have provided many details that highlighted different aspects of this status. Thus, the literary evidence has delineated the social standing of slaves, the laws their rights and obligations, the wills some of the motivations for releasing them from that status, and the manumission-documents the mechanics whereby this change was accomplished. These elements will be assembled in the first section of this concluding chapter utilising the typology suggested by M. I. Finley.[1]

The disadvantage of Finley's method is that the approach must be largely synchronic if the resulting profile is to be useful for making comparisons with similar statuses in other societies. Yet it is abundantly clear that throughout the period examined in this study Anglo-Saxon slavery was undergoing a continuous – if at times barely perceptible – process of change that was to lead to its eventual demise. To compensate for what would otherwise be an unbalanced presentation the second section must, therefore, discuss the changes that took place in the institution of slavery over the centuries and suggest the reasons that lay behind its eventual disappearance from mediaeval English society.

Much of the evidence that has been used was a consequence of the activities of the Church. Inevitably the attitude towards slaves and slavery displayed by the Church, viewed both as an institution and as a body of individual christians, has frequently been mentioned and this book would not be complete without a discussion of this theme.

As is evident to any foreigner, Britain has never been immune from Continental influences. The forebears of the Anglo-Saxons who practised slavery and of the Normans under whom the institution came to an end both migrated from the Continent. It is thus fitting to conclude this study by comparing English slavery with that found elsewhere in early mediaeval Europe.

A PROFILE OF THE SLAVE IN LATE ANGLO-SAXON ENGLAND

1. CLAIMS TO PROPERTY

In the early Anglo-Saxon period slaves probably had no legal right to property at all. Alfred's legislation had permitted them, however, to sell goods acquired in

---

[1] See above, pp. 2–3 and n. 9. The order in which the various elements of this profile are examined follows that given in his paper 'Between slavery and freedom', 247–8.

their spare time or given as alms during the four Ember days. One may reasonably assume that the law regarded goods so acquired as the slaves' own property
rather than as belonging ultimately to their lords. Presumably because these
goods were – to use Anglo-Saxon legal parlance – 'free', they could devolve on a
slave's heirs, unlike the property given him by his lord, which reverted to the
latter on the slave's death.[2]

In an agrarian economy the value of goods obtained in this manner is not
likely to have been large. But there were opportunities for an energetic family to
acquire some goods through odd-jobbing on a villein's *utland*, bartering produce
grown on the toft or selling pottery or cloth produced in the home – provided its
members did not have to work as hard as Ælfric's ploughman. Domesday Book
suggests that by the second half of the eleventh century some slaves in Devon
owned ploughs,[3] no small investment in that society, and it is possible that some
of the ambiguous later manumission-documents should be seen as recording the
purchase of freedom by slaves themselves rather than recording a quittance
payment made by serfs.[4]

The Middlesex section of Domesday Book mentions the presence of cottagers
who possessed gardens.[5] At least some of these are very likely to have been
descendants of slaves who had been granted the properties on being liberated.
Unlike the estates of St-Germain-des-Prés, however, English manors did not
have servile *manses*.[6] Though one extant Anglo-Saxon will which granted liberated slaves their tofts implies that they did have the use of some land as slaves,[7]
in England this does not seem ever to have been big enough as a unit or general
enough as a practice for these properties to have been distinguished from other
types of land-holdings such as was the case with *geburland* and *thegnland*.

2. POWER OVER HUMAN LABOUR AND MOVEMENT

An Anglo-Saxon slave was unlikely to have had the resources to be able to buy
another slave, though Æthelgifu's will shows that a newly manumitted person
could be given a slave by the manumittor.[8] As far as the slave's own labour and
movements were concerned, he was totally under his owner's control. Lords
could probably move their slaves wherever they wished or sell them elsewhere in
the country, as happened to Imma[9] – the only limitation being that the slave
could not legally be sold out of the country to pagans. Lords were permitted to
work their slaves as long as they liked if one is to believe Ælfric's ploughman,

---

[2] *Rectitudines Singularum Personarum*, §5.5 (*Die Gesetze*, ed. Liebermann, I.448), discussed
above, p. 175.

[3] See above, p. 234 and n. 162.

[4] See above, pp. 158–9. It seems improbable that in a predominantly agrarian society slaves
used their capital to purchase other slaves as happened in Imperial Rome, where slaves very
often engaged in small-scale business undertakings which required assistants.

[5] See table XX, p. 226.

[6] On St-Germain-des-Prés see *Polyptique de l'Abbé Irminon*, ed. Guérard.

[7] See above, pp. 124–5.

[8] *The Will of Æthelgifu*, ed. & transl. Whitelock, lines 16 (Edwin the priest) and 54 (Mann the
goldsmith).

[9] *Bede's Ecclesiastical History*, IV.22(20) (edd. & transl. Colgrave & Mynors, pp. 400–5) (text
and translation).

though they were prohibited by law from making them work on Sundays, Ember days, and other fast days. On larger and more stable manors customs regulating the hours of work of slaves probably evolved in the same way as customs prescribing their food rations.

By Alfred's time some *ceorlas* had lost their freedom of movement;[10] in the late eleventh century this process had advanced so far that manumission-documents came to be used to record the granting of the right to move from an estate. Though *ceorlas* were perceived as being no different from slaves in this regard, their position in practical terms did differ from slaves. At least some of the *ceorlas* must voluntarily have waived their rights to freedom of movement by commending themselves to a lord, though unfortunately no Anglo-Saxon documentary proof of this survives; slaves, in contrast, did not have this right in the first place. *Ceorlas* on manorial estates also possessed far more time that was their own than the slave did, since they were obligated to work on the lord's estates only on specified days in the week or at set periods during the year. The rest of their time could be used to work the land that a lord had granted them or they could hire themselves out as labourers. They thus had greater opportunities to earn enough to free themselves and move elsewhere if they wished to.

3. POWER TO PUNISH AND IMMUNITY FROM PUNISHMENT

Vengeance was very much a means of social control throughout the Anglo-Saxon period, though the law codes sought to restrict it. There is no indication that this right sanctioned by social custom was ever extended to slaves, even for wrongs suffered at the hands of other slaves. Slaves were the property of others, so that any wrongs done them were committed, in effect, against their owners, who in consequence were the ones who possessed the right of vengeance.

The alternative to the law of talion was composition. There is some slight indication that slaves gained rights here. *Leges Henrici Primi*, §70.4 states that in Wessex it was customary law for a slave's relatives to be entitled to compensation if he was slain.[11] This was no doubt introduced, however, as an additional discouragement against damage to a lord's property.

IV Æthelstan, §6.5–7 made slaves the agents of punishment in the case of other slaves who had been found guilty of theft by requiring a group of slaves to put the convicted person to death.[12] This unpleasant provision, introduced as part of a collection of draconian laws against theft, had the effect of making the group of slaves both responsible to the owner for his financial loss caused by the slave's death and potentially the victims of acts of vengeance instigated by the slave's kin.

An enigmatic clause in the *Leges Henrici Primi* charges that lords claimed a man to be either a slave or a freeman according to which status would most protect him.[13] At first sight this might seem to imply that in certain matters slave

---

[10] See above, pp. 55–6; cf. pp. 168–9.
[11] *Leges Henrici Primi*, ed. & transl. Downer, pp. 218–19 (text and translation).
[12] *Die Gesetze*, ed. Liebermann, I.172 (text); *The Laws*, ed. & transl. Attenborough, p. 151 (translation).
[13] *Leges Henrici Primi*, §78.2b (ed. & transl. Downer, pp. 244–5) (text and translation).

status granted an immunity that was not available to freemen. More likely, however, it referred to misdemeanours that would have merited the death penalty for a slave (and thus the loss of the lord's property) but would have permitted a freeman to compound for the crime.

Traditional legal practice (derived no doubt from Continental sources) acknowledged that the only thing a slave could possess was his skin, since he was the property of someone else. Thus the characteristic punishment of a slave was a lashing because he did not have the wherewithal to compound for a crime. II Cnut, §46.2 softened this with respect to the breach of a fast by permitting him to pay a fine, though it must be noted that this was at the cost of weakening the slave economically.[14]

4. PRIVILEGES AND LIABILITIES IN THE JUDICIAL PROCESS

As has been discussed earlier, Anglo-Saxon England had three systems of law in operation, tribal, religious, and manorial. All three systems reveal some growth in the recognition of a legal personality of the slave.

Anglo-Saxon tribal law does not seem to have taken a conscious position on the legal personality of the slave. The clearest indication that he did not possess one in the early period is Ine, §47, which prohibited a slave from being vouched to warranty.[15] On the other hand, he did have legal obligations. He was subject to penalties if he stole (Æthelberht, §90, Wihtred, §27),[16] sacrificed to devils (Wihtred, §13),[17] ate during a fast (Wihtred, §15),[18] or worked on a Sunday (Ine, §3.1).[19] With the legislation of Alfred comes the first evidence of the positive recognition in tribal law of the slave's personality. Alfred, §43 permitted him to have two rights: to enjoy four holidays per annum and to keep what he earned or the alms given him on those days.[20] II Æthelstan, §24 added to his status by permitting him to be a principal in a sale.[21]

As early as Theodore's Penitential ecclesiastical regulations had permitted a slave to keep his earnings.[22] Later penitentials laid down that slaves should be treated differently from freemen in the penances imposed, but this clearly implies that slaves were subject to obligations just as freemen were (obligations which extended far beyond the regulations over the Sabbath observance and

---

[14] *Die Gesetze*, ed. Liebermann, I.344 (text); *The Laws of the Kings of England*, ed. & transl. Robertson, p. 199 (translation)

[15] *Die Gesetze*, ed. Liebermann, I.110 (text); *The Laws*, ed. & transl. Attenborough, p. 53 (translation).

[16] *Die Gesetze*, ed. Liebermann, I.8 and 14 (text); *The Laws*, ed. & transl. Attenborough, pp. 17 and 31 (translation).

[17] *Die Gesetze*, ed. Liebermann, I.13 (text); *The Laws*, ed. & transl. Attenborough, p. 27 (translation).

[18] *Die Gesetze*, ed. Liebermann, I.13 (text); *The Laws*, ed. & transl. Attenborough, p. 27 (translation).

[19] *Die Gesetze*, ed. Liebermann, I.90 (text); *The Laws*, ed. & transl. Attenborough, p. 37 (translation).

[20] *Die Gesetze*, ed. Liebermann, I.78 (text); *The Laws*, ed. & transl. Attenborough, pp. 85 and 87 (translation).

[21] *Die Gesetze*, ed. Liebermann, I.164 (text); *The Laws*, ed. & transl. Attenborough, p. 141 (translation).

[22] *Poenitentiale Theodori*, II.13.3 (*Councils*, edd. Haddan & Stubbs, III.202).

fasting embodied in the tribal laws). On the other hand, slaves were absolved from paying Peter's Pence.[23]

One has to depend almost entirely on the *Rectitudines* for information about manorial law. This document reveals that slaves had well-defined rights, chiefly in their entitlement to food rations.[24] Were more custumals extant, they may well have revealed that slaves had other rights in addition to those relating to their physical sustenance.

In all three areas it is impossible to assess how far these rights and obligations were enforced. Obligations were, no doubt, rigorously exacted under royal law, but one may doubt whether a slave could protect his rights by taking his lord to a royal court for depriving him of his holidays or earnings. In the ecclesiastical sphere the extent to which penitential discipline was imposed would have depended on the strength of the Church and on the degree of interest evinced by its leaders in imposing penitential sanctions. To judge from the extant texts enforcement appears to have been strong in the late tenth and in the eleventh century, though this may only be because so many texts associated with Wulfstan have survived. In the manorial realm enforcement is likely to have varied widely. At first blush it would seem that a dictatorial or unjust overlord would have had sufficient power to ride roughshod over the customary rights of all his under-lings, be they serfs or slaves. But there were many ways in which these people could strike back through non-cooperation, sabotage, and inefficient or tardy work. It would have been a foolish lord who ignored these sanctions, though the dislike of the lord's agent, the reeve, displayed in Anglo-Saxon literature suggests that injustices were certainly perpetrated, as might be expected.[25]

5. PRIVILEGES IN THE AREA OF THE FAMILY

Theodore's Penitential had permitted marriages between slaves and the free, which had the effect of eliminating the possibility that marriage might become an élitist ritual or a means of preserving a caste.[26] There is no reason, therefore, to believe that unions between slaves were any different in nature or frequency from those of freemen. Nor were slaves likely to be significantly less fertile, since there is no evidence to suggest that the Anglo-Saxons enslaved those of only one sex, worked them in chain gangs, or housed them *en masse* in special quarters, all of which might have restricted normal family relationships. (It must be admitted, however, that in an inegalitarian society like Anglo-Saxon England the upper classes may have been more fertile because they had ate better. Our information does not allow us, however, to measure this.) The manumission-documents often refer to wives and children. No special terminology was employed to indicate that these unions differed in kind from those of freemen. As slaves were subject to ecclesiastical regulations such as the obligation to fast, one would expect that the Church also encouraged them to observe the canonical

---

[23] *Rectitudines Singularum Personarum*, §3.4 (*Die Gesetze*, ed. Liebermann, I.446) observes that this was an obligation of a freeman.

[24] See above, pp. 175–6.

[25] See, for example, *Byrhtferth's Manual*, ed. Crawford, p. 242.6–7.

[26] *Poenitentiale Theodori*, II.13.5 (*Councils*, edd. Haddan & Stubbs, III.202).

rules on marriage, such as the obligation not to marry within the prohibited degrees of consanguinity.

Unions between those of unfree and free status inevitably must have resulted in questions about the status of the offspring. *Leges Henrici Primi*, §77.1 argues that 'the status established by birth is determined always by the father, not the mother'.[27] The only exception was when the lord decided: 'Yet the calf is the mother's, whosoever's bull has sported with her.'[28] Downer has suggested that the latter rule would have applied only in the case of an illegitimate birth where the father was unknown,[29] which seems a reasonable interpretation. But Theodore's Penitential had a principle exactly the opposite to the fundamental rule of the *Leges* by declaring that children took their status from their mother. This is perhaps supported by the Hatfield genealogies (*Status Document*, §1.1), where Ely laid claim to several *geburas* through the ties a female ancestor had had with its estate at Hatfield.[30] It is possible that here there was a clash between a native Germanic principle and an imported Roman ecclesiastical one which may well never have been resolved. If this is so, the pull on the offspring is in general likely to have been downwards wherever the lord was powerful (as in the case of Ely and the Hatfield *geburas*), with the offspring taking their status from whichever ancestor happened to be subject to an overlord, provided, of course, that the latter chose to lay claim to them. On the other hand, one could well see a lord's wanting an illegitimate child of his to have free status, though I know of no case in the literature where an Anglo-Saxon lord acknowledged paternity of a slave-woman's offspring.

The status of the children of slaves was not affected by the granting of free status to their parents. This is apparent from *Manumission*, §1.1, where it is specified that the son should receive the freedom granted his father. It explains why many of the manumission-documents also recorded the granting of freedom to the offspring of those being manumitted.

6. PRIVILEGES OF SOCIAL MOBILITY

Throughout the Anglo-Saxon period it was possible – theoretically at least – for a slave to become free. In the seventh century there may have been two ways of making this status change. The first was a Germanic practice in which the change took place over several generations. The *lætas* may well have represented this group.[31] But they are only recorded in the Kentish laws of the end of the sixth century, which suggests that by the time records became more common in the late seventh century this mode was yielding to the Roman practice of *manumissio in ecclesia*.

The nature of *manumissio in ecclesia* had important implications for the institution of slavery in England. In the first place it involved an immediate

---

[27] 'semper a patre, non a matre, generationis ordo texitur': *Leges Henrici Primi*, ed. & transl. Downer, p. 242 (text); *ibid.*, p. 243 (translation).

[28] 'Uitulus autem matris est, cuiuscumque taurus alluserit': *Loc. cit.*, §77.2a.

[29] *Ibid.*, p. 394.

[30] See Pelteret, 'Two Old English lists of serfs', 478, table I, no. 8, and 490–1, and above, p. 181.

[31] See below, appendix I, s.v. *læt*.

change in status from being a slave to becoming a member of a tribe. Though Wihtred, §8 specified that the former owner retained his *mund* over the freedman and hence presumably was still entitled to certain rights in him, those freed did not form a legally defined status group as was the case among the Lombards.[32] This perhaps accounts for the rarity of the word *freotmann* in Old English sources. The Law thus did not recognise a buffer group between slaves and freemen that would help preserve distinctions between the two.

This form of manumission also brought the act within the ambit of the Church, which gained thereby an interest in it. The Church encouraged the freeing of slaves as morally commendable, though institutional pressures usually discouraged the Church itself from manumitting such persons on its own lands, except on the death of a bishop, when those who had been penally enslaved were freed. The support of the Church for manumission probably became influential from the late tenth century on, when ecclesiastical reform enhanced the Church's influence over society. This was precisely the time when the establishment of compact manorial estates and expanding agrarian pressures presented economic incentives for the freeing of slaves and the right of bequest had been enlarged to include the freeing of slaves after a testator's death.

There are also records of persons being freed at crossroads, a symbolic form of manumission that appears to have been Germanic in origin and perhaps was imported from Lombard sources.[33] The presence of priests at the ceremony and the recording of the act in a gospel book suggest that this type of manumission had been influenced by its ecclesiastical counterpart and had the same legal effects. In the eastern part of the country the philological evidence shows that the Norse retained their own traditional form of manumission in the areas under their control. This, like the Kentish type, involved an inter-generational status change.[34]

From the tenth century on those being freed probably outnumbered those entering slavery, so that the Normans inherited what was essentially a dying institution.[35] But throughout the period – and in some places as late as the end of the eleventh century[36] – freemen were continually moving down into slavery while slaves were being freed. Enslavement by capture was probably the most common means in the early centuries of the Anglo-Saxon era, and it seems to have been prominent again in the time of Æthelred. A person might also be enslaved for a variety of criminal offences: Sunday labour (Ine, §3.2, Edward and Guthrum, §7.1),[37] theft under certain circumstances (Ine, §7.1, II Edward, §6, VI Æthelstan, §12.2),[38] incest (Edward and Guthrum, §4),[39] and as an alter-

---

[32] *Die Gesetze*, ed. Liebermann, I.13 (text); *The Laws*, ed. & transl. Attenborough, p. 27 (translation).

[33] See above, pp. 143–5.

[34] See below, appendix I, s.vv. *healf-freoh, lising*.

[35] See further below, pp. 252–4.

[36] See above, p. 163.

[37] *Die Gesetze*, ed. Liebermann, I.90 and 132 (text); *The Laws*, ed. & transl. Attenborough, pp. 37 and 107 (translation).

[38] *Die Gesetze*, ed. Liebermann, I.92, 144, and 183 (text); *The Laws*, ed. & transl. Attenborough, pp. 39, 121, and 169 (translation).

[39] *Die Gesetze*, ed. Liebermann, I.130 (text); *The Laws*, ed. & transl. Attenborough, p. 105 (translation).

native for a condemned man who had reached sanctuary (Grið, §16).[40] In the tenth century crime, debt, and voluntary enslavement because of poverty most likely became the major reasons why freemen became slaves. In theory any person in Anglo-Saxon society could have been enslaved but in practice ties of kinship would have protected the aristocracy, who were able to call on rich and powerful relatives to ransom them if captured or to shield them against legal penalties.[41]

7. PRIVILEGES AND DUTIES IN THE POLITICAL, MILITARY, AND SACRAL SPHERES

This book has repeatedly stressed that the slave was not a member of the tribe and that this exclusion defined his status. Throughout the Anglo-Saxon period slaves effectively neither possessed the privileges of nor were subject to the duties attendant on membership in the political and military spheres of society. At the tribal and national level the political aspects of the society lay in the hands of the aristocracy and the more able members of the free peasantry who were aspirants to this status. The slave was not so different from the ordinary *ceorl* in this area. At the local level, however, slaves were excluded from the tithing and the hundred court, which effectively marked them off from freemen, many of whom might in some economic and social respects have resembled them.

As has been argued above, the military sphere in the earlier part of the Anglo-Saxon era was likewise a preserve of the aristocracy.[42] By the tenth century there is some evidence that *ceorlas* fought in the *fyrd* but there is no hint in the sources that slaves were ever used as soldiers. It is entirely possible, of course, that in the disruptions that took place during the reign of Æthelred the Vikings were not averse to employing former Anglo-Saxon slaves as soldiers, as Wulfstan asserts,[43] but it seems improbable that the Anglo-Saxons ever used them as regular troops.

In the sacral sphere it was a long-standing rule of canon law that a slave could not become a priest unless he had first been manumitted.[44] Æthelgifu's will portrays, however, a woman of undoubted wealth and apparent piety who in the late tenth century had a priest of slave status on one of her estates.[45] How many such contraventions of canon law occurred in England is impossible to say. The monastic reformers of the tenth century may not have had the chance to regularise ecclesiastical practices on large estates, where it might have seemed quite natural to a person who possessed an *Eigenkirche* to have it served by one who, like the ecclesiastical building itself, was owned.

---

[40] *Die Gesetze*, ed. Liebermann, I.471 (text).

[41] Imma (above, n. 9) was redeemed from enslavement by King Hlothhere of Kent, nephew of Queen Æthelthryth, whose thegn he once had been. In the eleventh century Earl Godwine and his sons were able to protect themselves when outlawed by Edward the Confessor because of their powerful positions.

[42] See above, pp. 30–1 and n. 152.

[43] *The Homilies of Wulfstan*, §20 (EI), lines 100–6 (ed. Bethurum, p. 271), quoted above, p. 98 and n. 87.

[44] See *The Will of Æthelgifu*, ed. & transl. Whitelock, p. 32 and n. 6.

[45] See above, p. 15.

In contrast to this ecclesiastical stance, christianity has always possessed an egalitarian element in its concept of the universality of sin and the possibility of redemption for all from it. In England ecclesiastical regulations came to be imposed on slaves and freemen alike. The necessity of observing the Sabbath had early been given secular legal sanction, as was the practice of fasting. Evidence from the eleventh century shows that attempts were made to insist that slaves be subject to at least some of the regulations on fasting imposed by the penitentials, which makes it likely that they were expected to observe yet other ecclesiastical regulations as well (though penalties for their breach may have been less than those imposed on freemen).[46]

That slaves were from the early days of christianity in England subject to ecclesiastical obligations suggests that they were believed to be entitled to rights in the spiritual realm as well. Certainly Ælfric and Wulfstan argued forcefully in their writings that slaves were as equally open to Divine Grace as freemen. A belief in rights and obligations in the spiritual realm common to all persons thus implicitly ran counter to the divisions between slaves and freemen present in other spheres of existence. This aspect of christianity was counteracted in some measure by the acceptance of slavery in the Scriptures and by the use of the concept of slavery in religious imagery. The egalitarian element in christianity should not, therefore, be exaggerated. As a positive agent of social change its influence may not have been great in this period,[47] but equally it did not act as a barrier to such change.

8. ESTEEM

Finley does not include this category in his typology, and one can understand why, as one's assessment of it must needs be highly subjective. Yet it has to be considered if comparisons between slaves in various societies are to be made. It is clear, for instance, that the slave who worked in the Greek mines in Laurium and the slave on the Imperial staff in Rome were viewed quite differently by their respective societies.[48]

Anglo-Saxon society can be regarded as being divided in two ways. First, there were the privileged few who formed the landed élite and the ecclesiastical hierarchy on the one hand, and the rest of the society, both *ceorlas* and *þeowas*, on the other. Second, there were the freemen and the slaves. The task of assessing how the slave was regarded by the rest of the community is hampered by the absence of extant written evidence composed by the lower ranks of the free. Thus one cannot say what the standing of slaves was in the crucial social sphere

---

[46] See above, pp. 66–7; cf. pp. 90–1 (punishment).

[47] The christian support for manumission, however, was an agent of change. See further below, pp. 253 and 255.

[48] In the concept of esteem, I differ somewhat from Orlando Patterson, who instead has used the term 'dishonour', which he has considered to be integral to the concept of slavery: 'The slave could have no honor because of the origin of his status . . . but most of all because he was without power except through another' (*Slavery and Social Death*, p. 10). Apart from defining his concept in negative terms, Patterson has not allowed for differences in degree, in part because he was looking for the universal defining characteristics of slavery.

of the village community. Instead one has to see them through the eyes of the privileged.

Æthelgifu's will implicitly shows that slaves could be well regarded by their owner. Many of those freed in her will are mentioned by name, which suggests a personal bond between them and their mistress, and in the instances of the priest and Mann the goldsmith, they were not merely to be manumitted but were bequeathed men as well.

From the viewpoint of the overlord the slave undoubtedly had the lowest position in the hierarchy of statuses within the society. There are two hints in the sources of feelings of definite prejudice against slaves. The first is found in the *Riddles* and is based on tribal differences between Celts and Anglo-Saxons.[49] The second is the survival in English of the word *þræl*, which may have acquired an adverse moral connotation that the word *þeow* seems never to have possessed. Other than these instances, there is no direct indication in the literature that inferior moral or intellectual qualities were ascribed to slaves in virtue of their status. This is perhaps because the status was one that was relatively easy to acquire and to lose, and because the bulk of the free population were occupied in similar agricultural tasks. If one can judge from the nature of prejudice in other societies, however, it may also be because we have been presented only with selective evidence: the privileged were unlikely to become slaves and so did not feel threatened enough by the status to talk about it.

How necessary were slaves to the maintenance of the Anglo-Saxon economy? Provided there was interest on the part of an estate owner and adequate supervision, they could increase productivity and, because they must have lived close to a subsistence level, they may frequently have permitted their owners to acquire luxury items or leisure through their labours. In general, however, one may suspect that slaves were not essential to the economy and never had been. Certainly their numbers in Domesday Book suggest that they did not have the importance they had in the Classical world.[50] Yet that same source indicates that they were very useful on major estates, where they performed necessary daily tasks like ploughing and milking.[51] These were not roles that had to be filled by persons of slave status, however. Thus, by the close of the eleventh century the rights and obligations of those performing these tasks had changed sufficiently for the old status terminology to have virtually died out.

---

[49] See above, pp. 51–3.

[50] See Finley, 'Was Greek civilization based on slave labour?', in *Slavery in Classical Antiquity*, ed. Finley, pp. 53–72.

[51] I have discussed this question in slightly different terms in 'Slavery in Anglo-Saxon England', in *The Anglo-Saxons: Synthesis and Achievement*, edd. Woods & Pelteret, pp. 126–33.

WHEN AND WHY DID SLAVERY DISAPPEAR IN ENGLAND?

In the posthumously published paper by Marc Bloch discussed in the Introduction to this book, he attempted to determine the reasons for the disappearance of slavery in Western Europe[52] and found them to lie in the reduction in the availability of persons who could be enslaved, changing patterns of land usage, and the influence of the christian religion. The process of social transformation that led to the demise of slavery in most parts of Western Europe by the end of the tenth century was completed somewhat later in England. In the main Bloch's analysis can be seen to fit the Anglo-Saxon evidence. His was a synthetic paper, however, and a detailed study of the English evidence shows that the process was somewhat more intricate than he suggested.[53]

As has been seen, the slave's complex status stemmed from its dependence on political, economic, legal, and religious circumstances operating within the society as a whole. Major changes were occurring in all four spheres in England between the late ninth century and the end of the eleventh century. To understand fully the reasons for the decline of slavery one must disentangle these different elements, while recognising that changes in all four spheres were occurring simultaneously, with results that sometimes hindered and at other times promoted social change. For instance, both economic pressures and religious values can be seen to have acted in concert to encourage laymen to free slaves in the tenth and eleventh centuries. Yet the Scandinavian invasions of the late tenth century led to the kind of social disorder that promoted increases in the number of slaves.

As was stressed at the beginning of this book the introduction of Roman concepts of land-law into England brought about fundamental changes in Anglo-Saxon society. Slavery did not escape its effects. Through the permanent alienation of land from the tribal domain by means of the legal device of the land-charter the old multiple-estates could be broken up into more compact units divided between the lord's demesne and areas worked by resident peasants. On these estates customs arose that covered many areas of life not regulated by tribal law. These included the rent and services due to a landlord in return for use of the land, matters which were more relevant in day-to-day living than the penalties imposed by tribal law for such crimes as rape, theft, or physical injury. Subjection to the new obligations led to an alternative conception of freedom from that recognised by tribal law. Whereas the latter kind of law had considered the possessor of freedom, that is, a freeman, to be one who held the right to be granted the protection of the law, manorial custom came to recognise someone as free if he or she had the power to leave an estate. Embryo manors may have been coming into existence as early as the seventh century, when the land-charter was introduced into England, and changes in the concept of freedom may have

---

[52] See above, pp. 15–17.
[53] 'How and why ancient slavery came to an end', in *Slavery and Serfdom in the Middle Ages*, transl. Beer, pp. 1–31.

started at that time. But the earliest evidence of this change is in Alfred's translation of Orosius at the end of the ninth century.[54]

This long delay is not surprising, however, since the movement towards the acquisition of bookland – that is, land alienated from the tribe by use of the land-charter – was not a steady one. Inter-tribal warfare up till the ninth century, and then the Scandinavian incursions and settlements during that century, meant that landed estates were likely to have a chequered history. Only with the stability brought by Alfred's successors could there be the continuity of tenure necessary for the growth of manorial custom (and even that was disrupted by the renewed Scandinavian attacks in the late tenth century).

During this period of slow movement towards the subjection of the 'free' peasantry to manorial customs such as the obligation to perform week-work, slaves were acquiring rights and obligations characteristic of freemen. Among the rights they gained was the power to sell what they had been given or what they had made and to keep the fruits for themselves, a right first conceded them in law by Alfred. Manorial custom also decreed that they were entitled to a certain amount of food every day. As for obligations, the slave had long been subject to ecclesiastical regulations governing sabbath labour and fasting (both of which were enforced by tribal law). With the growing influence of penitential discipline under Wulfstan at the end of the tenth century, rules on fasting appear to have been more rigorously enforced, and it seems likely that slaves were also required to observe other penitential regulations.

There was thus a gradual merging of the peasantry of both free and slave origin in the tenth and eleventh centuries into a spectrum of unfree statuses. Yet slaves continued to be manumitted throughout the Anglo-Saxon period, which shows that the slave's status still remained distinct from other groups in the society.

There are grounds for believing that the number of slaves was substantially reduced in the century and a half preceding the Conquest, even though comparative figures cannot be given. To begin with one must note the decline in the wars of conquest after the first quarter of the tenth century. Once the Celtic South-west had been fully tamed, newly enslaved persons had to be brought from distant border regions or else they were local people enslaved for debt or crime. To be sure, the disruptions in the reign of Æthelred led to the enslavement of many, but it is likely that large numbers of those captured by Viking raiders were exported from England. At any rate, the movement towards the unification of Anglo-Saxon England made it more difficult for Anglo-Saxons themselves to enslave their fellow countrymen, even if they did come from another tribe.

In itself the drying up of the reservoirs of people suitable for enslavement (that is, those from outside the tribe) need not necessarily have led to a decrease in the number of slaves, as Bloch suggested.[55] We have observed already that late Anglo-Saxon slaves did not work in chain gangs nor did they live in sexually segregated quarters: instead, they shared a similar sort of existence to the

---

[54] See above, pp. 55–6.
[55] 'How and why ancient slavery came to an end', pp. 6 and 18–19.

cotsetas and *geburas*, and there is no reason to believe that their fertility and survival rate were strikingly different. But from the tenth century on there was a conjunction of economic and religious forces that encouraged the manumitting of slaves. From the point of view of the slave-owners the accumulation of large tracts of land under relatively stable tenure encouraged them to free their slaves by giving them land to work in return for dues and services, since they themselves were then released from the obligation of supervising them on a daily basis and supplying regular food rations.[56] At the same time the Church offered the owners spiritual benefits for their acts of manumission. The wills document this conjunction of interests by recording an increase in the proportion of persons freed on the estates of laymen over the last 150 years of the Anglo-Saxon era.[57]

This process of manumission would probably have led to the eventual disappearance of slavery in England, but it would have taken some time as social change is usually a slow process, unless there is a revolution. Just such a revolution occurred as a result of William's victory at Hastings, and within two generations slavery as a social institution was a thing of the past.[58]

The reasons for this lie in an acceleration of the processes that had already been taking place under the Anglo-Saxons. What happened in Essex may be used as an example.[59] The decrease in woodland and the increase in rents there point to a reorganisation in the exploitation of the resources of the land, made easier by the usurpation of many of the original landlords. Slaves who were not particularly productively employed were manumitted – in twenty years their numbers dropped in Essex by 25%.[60] It is unlikely that they were sent away from

---

[56] We can document in some detail the landed wealth of a number of tenth-century figures in addition to the otherwise unknown Æthelgifu discussed in chapter IV above. See Hart, 'Athelstan "Half King" and his Family', printed in revised form in *The Danelaw*, and Williams, '*Princeps Merciorum Gentis*'. Accumulation of manorial estates by particular individuals and families continued in the eleventh century. For the most notable example of this, the family of the Godwines, see Fleming, 'Domesday estates of the King and the Godwines' and Raraty, 'Earl Godwine of Wessex'.

[57] See table IV above, pp. 129–30. This is in line with Patterson's general observation on the relationship between monotheistic religions and manumission: 'Except in isolated cases none of these religions seem to have had any influence. Only when economic and political expediency coincided with piety did religion seem to count.' (*Slavery and Social Death*, p. 275.) However, I believe he goes too far when he claims that 'Christianity had no effect on the rate of manumission in medieval Europe' (*loc. cit.*). It at least provided a moral justification for an act that might, in fact, have been prompted by economic considerations.

[58] The displacement of the Anglo-Saxon landed élite by William and his followers is obvious from Domesday Book. As will be seen from the following paragraph, the issue of whether there was a tenurial revolution is not germane to the argument presented in this book since the change lay not in the nature of the estates held in 1086 but in the attitudes of the new overlords to those occupying these estates. For the debate on the issue see Sawyer, '1066–1086: a tenurial revolution?', in *Domesday Book: A Reassessment*, ed. Sawyer, pp. 71–85 and Fleming, 'Domesday Book and the tenurial revolution', in *Anglo-Norman Studies IX*, ed. Brown, pp. 87–102; Lewis has suggested a resolution to the controversy in 'The Domesday jurors', in *The Haskins Society Journal*, V, ed. Patterson, pp. 17–44.

[59] See above, pp. 204–13.

[60] Cf. Patterson's observation in *Slavery and Social Death*, p. 295, that 'for all but small lineage-based societies, manumission rates tended to be highest in those societies that were

the estate; instead they were probably given land to develop in return for rents and services. Those slaves essential to the continued productivity of the demesne could be manumitted but retained as hired labourers or *famuli* with the support of the increased revenues. This gave an overlord more flexibility in his use of the available labour, and perhaps also released him from certain obligations formerly due to his slaves. As newcowers the Normans were not inhibited by the traditional distinctions between slave and free, which were based on the outmoded notion of membership of the tribe. Instead they viewed people as being tied to their estates by a variety of obligations, all of whom could be considered to be unfree. Had the old divisions between slave and freeman remained clearly defined and the numbers of slaves been greater, the Normans may have been deterred from making so rapid a change.

As it was, there were several clear economic incentives to free slaves. Obviously a magnate like the Count of Mortain with lands in widely scattered areas had no particular incentive to retain the 'farm of one night', with its food supplies that had to be transported to a central location. Money rents were a much more attractive proposition – and this must also have been the case for many mesne lords as well. Once Domesday Book had been compiled, the evasion of geld became more difficult and demands by William Rufus for increased financial support provided another impulsion to free persons in return for annual payments of rent and the like.

We should not make the mistake of arguing that slavery by its very nature was inefficient. Sally Harvey has pointed to several Norman lords who seem to have taken an interest in agriculture and who retained large demesnes with a substantial slave work-force. Henry de Ferrers appears to have been influenced in his choice of location for Tutbury Castle by the strength of demesne agriculture there. Earl Roger of Montgomery was another lord who was interested in promoting his demesne lands; a lesser lord, Ernulf of Hesdin, was a third.[61] For those with the interest, the supervision of the demesne staff was evidently worthwhile – but for most Normans financial profit exempt from the disadvantages of managing slave labour was likely to be far more attractive.[62]

It would be a mistake, however, to visualise thousands of formal manumissions taking place throughout the country in the half-century or so after the Conquest, though the Exeter Book shows that such ceremonies were still a living institution in the twelfth century in the south-west of England.[63] There would have come a point when the numbers were so low that the legal terms *þeow* or *seruus* would simply have been dropped in favour of a generalised term like *rusticus* or a word denoting a person's occupation like *bouarius* or *daia*.[64] By the early 1100s the status was still remembered in a few places, but the substance had gone out of the institution.

subject to periodic structural shocks. Those shocks might be of an economic or political (military) nature, or of course both.'

[61] See Harvey, 'The extent and profitability of demesne agriculture', 55–7 and 'Domesday England', in *The Agrarian History of England and Wales*, II, ed. Hallam, pp. 115–19.

[62] See *ibid,*. p. 64, for these disadvantages.

[63] See above, pp. 160–1.

[64] See above, pp. 179 and 239.

THE CHURCH AND SLAVERY

Before we examine this topic a distinction must be drawn between the Church as an organisation which followed a set of *administrative* principles and the Church as a collection of individual christians who followed a set of *moral* principles. If this distinction is borne in mind, the contradictory attitudes of the Church towards slaves and slavery can be understood.[65]

Early in its history as an organisation the Church had adopted the principle that no ecclesiastical property should be alienated. As slaves were considered in law to be property, the Church was predisposed against freeing them on its own lands. It is probably for this reason that the Synod of Chelsea did not order the release of all slaves on ecclesiastical estates but only those acquired through jurisdictional processes during the tenure of a see: the latter could be regarded as the personal property of the bishop rather than the inalienable property of the diocese.[66] The Worcester Domesday illustrates the principle in action: the four great religious houses in the county possessed proportionally more slaves than the estates of the great lay tenants-in-chief.[67]

For ecclesiastical communities such as monasteries or collegiate churches an added incentive to retain slaves was the necessity for food to be provided for the monks or canons, especially when the estates were located close to the religious institution.

On the other hand, the ecclesiastical hierarchy had from the earliest days of the Church stressed the moral virtues inherent in freeing a person, a position no doubt influenced by the fact that the Church had traditionally drawn some of its support from the urban servile classes. The impact of this teaching will have varied; to have much influence it needed the right combination of extraneous social, economic, and political factors. As has been discussed in the previous section, this seems to have occurred in the England of the tenth and eleventh centuries. The growth in manumission was not solely responsible for the disappearance of slavery, but it did help reduce it to a level where other political and economic circumstances could bring about its total disappearance.

The Anglo-Saxon Church seems to have remained oblivious of the contradictions between its organisational and its moral principles. The Church was able to live with this contradiction because its members accepted the institution of slavery as part of the natural order of society. This was easy to do because the Bible portrayed slavery in that way. Not merely did slavery exist in the world of the Old and New Testaments,[68] but it was also employed in religious imagery.

[65] A. Szogs discusses the issue of the Church and slavery in Anglo-Saxon England in *Die Ausdrücke für 'Arbeit' und 'Beruf' im Altenglischen*, pp. 11–18. For a more general discussion of the Church and slavery in the early middle ages see Hoffmann, 'Kirche und Sklaverei im frühen Mittelalter'.

[66] In freeing 250 slaves at Selsey Bishop Wilfrid was doubtless acting like a tribal chieftain, using the powers granted him by King Æthelwealh. The freeing resulted in a change in status according to the local tribal law, but as pointed out above on p.137 and n. 34, his action is not likely to have meant that the former slaves left Selsey and were lost to the Church.

[67] See tables XV and XVI and pp. 219–21.

[68] The Epistle of Paul to Philemon and Jerome's commentary on it do not seem, however, to

The use of the metaphor 'slave of God' as a central image in christianity led to an unreflective attitude towards the secular institution from which the image was drawn. Having accepted the institution of slavery, the Church felt no qualms about keeping slaves on its own lands, while at the same time through its officers encouraging the manumission of slaves on secular estates. It was only after economic forces had transformed the concept of freedom from a status based on tribal law to the right to leave an estate, thereby rendering the slave status anachronistic, that the Church was able to countenance the disappearance of slavery on its own lands. This seems to have taken place in the fifty or sixty years after Domesday Book. The conservatism of the Church as an organisation meant that ecclesiastical records were the last to document the existence of slaves: Peterborough Abbey still reported them on its estates as late as the 1120s.[69]

SLAVERY IN ENGLAND AND CONTINENTAL EUROPE: SIMILARITIES AND CONTRASTS

The Germanic peoples, like the Romans before them, practised slavery,[70] though the reasons for their doing so have not been fully explained.[71] Slavery thus became a characteristic feature of early mediaeval European society from Iceland to Spain, and from Ireland to Byzantium.[72] The practice of Anglo-Saxon slavery, by and large, was similar to that of the rest of Europe, where parallels can be found for each of its major features. All that makes Anglo-Saxon slavery distinctive is the particular combination of elements.

War is attested throughout Europe as the major source of slaves. Verlinden has argued that slavery continued later in the Iberian peninsula than in France because of the fighting that took place between christians and muslims.[73] The late conquest of those of Celtic ethnic origin in the south-west of England at a time when the Church was comparatively weak might account in part for the fact that slavery lasted longer in England than it did in some parts of France, where the opportunities for the conquest of foreign peoples largely ended with Charlemagne. It should be noted, however, that war was not necessarily the primary means of recruitment of slaves in England during the difficulties of Æthelred's reign; debt and poverty were probably also major sources.

As for the legal status of slaves, Anglo-Saxon law like Roman law considered them originally to be things rather than persons. Roman law is probably also the

---

have been known to the Anglo-Saxons: familiarity with these writings would probably have reinforced their acceptance of the validity of the institution.

[69] See above, p. 196 and n. 43; cf. pp. 236–9.

[70] For a general introduction to Germanic slavery see Wergeland, *Slavery in Germanic Society during the Middle Ages*.

[71] B. J. Siegel in his paper on the Northwest-Coast Indians, 'Some methodological considerations for a comparative study of slavery', has some interesting suggestions as to why some societies adopt slavery and others do not.

[72] For references, see above, p. 24, n. 118.

[73] Verlinden, *L'Esclavage*, I.729–30.

Conclusion

source of the legal sanction of corporal punishment for crime, a practice adopted, for instance, by the Burgundians as well.[74]

Because Anglo-Saxon England was less urbanised than some parts of the Mediterranean, most slaves were involved in agricultural tasks rather than crafts (though Æthelgifu's will does mention a goldsmith). The Anglo-Saxon slave's common role of ploughman was an occupation filled by slaves elsewhere as well: the slave ploughman is also mentioned, for instance, in the Lombard laws.[75]

With respect to manumission, *manumissio in ecclesia* was widely diffused through Europe by the Church. England seems to have shared only with the Lombards, however, the use of the crossroads as a place of manumission. The eastern part of England was also familiar with Scandinavian forms of manumission because of the Norse invasion of that region.

It is in the disappearance of slavery that the greatest regional variation is to be found. By the middle of the ninth century the *Polyptych of the Abbey of St Rémi* makes no mention of slaves on its estates,[76] while in England there is still some slight evidence for their existence in the early twelfth century.[77] Bloch was not altogether correct, however, in his generalisation that slavery was later in disappearing from England than from France[78] in that the word *seruus* continued to appear in documents in the Loire area up till the twelfth century.[79] In the Iberian peninsula slavery had not died out by the time of the discovery of the New World, with the result that the practice was exported there and took on a new lease of life – perhaps the most baleful legacy bestowed by the middle ages on the modern world.

The effect of war as a contributory factor in the continuation of slavery has already been mentioned. The weakening of tribal bonds and the accumulation of property in large estates, which encouraged a different approach to the use of labour, must also be accounted major factors.[80] It took time for the tribal barriers to break down in England, and the development of manorial estates seems to have been retarded there. This is why slavery survived longer in England than in some parts of France, where the shift towards serfdom had started under the Merovingians.[81]

A key factor in change according to several contemporary historians of Western Europe was economic growth.[82] Verhulst has claimed that the distinction between freemen and slaves disappeared by the ninth century west of the Rhine,

---

[74] *Leges Burgundionum*, IV.4 (ed. Salis, p. 44).
[75] *Edictus Rothari*, §133 (ed. Bluhme), in *Monumenta Germaniae Historica, Legum Tomus IIII*, ed. Pertz, p. 31.
[76] *Polyptique de l'Abbaye de Saint-Rémi de Reims*, ed. Guérard.
[77] Presumably the Normans did not enslave the Welsh in the twelfth century because the Church was stronger then and could argue that the Welsh were fellow christians. Cf. Bloch's discussion of the *ciuitas christiana* mentioned above, p. 17.
[78] 'How and why ancient slavery came to an end', in *Slavery and Serfdom in the Middle Ages*, transl. Beer, p. 25.
[79] Van der Kieft, 'Les "colliberti" ', 392.
[80] As emphasised by Van der Kieft in *ibid.*, 393–4.
[81] Verlinden, *L'Esclavage*, I.731.
[82] For the material in the following two paragraphs see above, Introduction, pp. 20–3.

257

unlike the region to the east of that river.[83] Slave numbers were also smaller in the west, largely because of greater economic development.

This growth was brought about by a variety of factors, including technological change and increasing population. What seems to be central was the acquisition of power by local lords, which enabled them to force social change. Bois has suggested that in Lournand in the Mâconnais the transformation from an aristocratic society employing slaves to a feudal one which led to the suppression of slave and freeman alike took place abruptly in the tenth century.[84] In southern Europe Bonnassie has argued that slavery underwent its final crisis at the end of that century and the beginning of the next one – though one might be somewhat sceptical of his view that there was a brief halcyon period when servitude was in abeyance before a backlash from the rulers led to the imposition of new burdens on the free peasantry.[85] In Catalonia Freedman has claimed that the seizure of power by local lords early in the eleventh century enabled them to bring about the enserfment of the peasantry in the areas under their control.[86]

In England there was certainly a growth in local lordship in the tenth century, though central kingship (even if at times weak) probably kept excesses in check through the strength of Anglo-Saxon administrative processes. Economic growth received a powerful stimulus from the arrival of the Normans. Here the drive to extract more wealth from the land was as much centrally driven by William the Conqueror and his son, William Rufus, as by the power of local lords. As perhaps in Lournand – though for different reasons – the process of change seems also to have been a rapid one as far as the disappearance of slavery is concerned; unlike Continental Europe, this was made easier by the superimposition of a foreign landlord class on the native peasantry, whereby the merging of slave and free legal categories could easily be accomplished. Compared with some parts of western Europe, the disappearance of slavery in England appears to have been somewhat retarded, surely because its insular status fended off radical change – until one invasion too many led to a transformation in the central power structure of the country.

What seems with the hindsight of centuries to have been a dramatic social change took place without comment from the people of the age. The multiplicity of forces at work and the gradual nature of the social transformation must provide the reasons for this. The decline of slavery in England was the product of a combination of impersonal economic forces, purposeful human action, and chance. Continued exploitation of the land coupled with a reduction in the ready availability of persons enslaved through war impelled landholders to adopt approaches towards the use of manpower that gave them greater flexibility and increased the productivity of those under them. At the same time people came to see virtue in emancipating slaves, thus actively intervening in a continuing socio-economic development. What brought slavery to an end, however, was the conquest of England by an alien group who did not share the traditions of those

---

[83] 'Étude comparative', in *La croissance agricole du haut moyen âge*, p. 105.
[84] Bois, *The Transformation of the Year One Thousand*, transl. Birrell.
[85] *From Slavery to Feudalism in South-Western Europe*, transl. Birrell, p. 55.
[86] *The Origins of Peasant Servitude in Medieval Catalonia*, p. 64.

they subjugated – a conquest, it may be said, that was accomplished only through an arrow finding its mark on the field at Hastings. It was this shock to the body politic that ultimately spelled the doom of the institution of slavery in England.

The writing of history deals in the past but can shape the present and the future. What might this study say to us today? It suggests that purposeful social activity by individuals can foster change. Yet this statement has immediately to be qualified: the changes that result may not be the ones intended. It is unlikely that any who manumitted their slaves, whether out of piety or for profit, foresaw that they were destroying a social institution. On the other hand, two factors can be seen to have inhibited the process of change. The first arose when the interests of the Church in preserving itself as an institution caused it to act contrary to the principles on which it was established. This is a charge that is expressed by many today, though the object of their attention is now Government rather than the Church. The second inhibiter of change was the power of slavery as an image, an image originally employed to expand human perceptions in one sphere but which then served to restrict perceptions in another. Perhaps only the insights of great writers can help us throw off the shackles by which contemporary imagery holds us in thrall.

Though unnoticed by contemporaries, the passing of slavery in England and other parts of northern and western Europe marked a small step forward in the recognition of rights that should be shared by all humanity. The process continues today. We have still to attain the goal of a society affording equal economic, political, legal, and social rights for all.

APPENDIX I

The Old English Terminology of Servitude and Freedom

The following is a semantic analysis of the terminology of servitude and freedom employed in Old English. It was originally based on Bosworth's *Anglo-Saxon Dictionary* and its supplements by Toller and Campbell. Citations were drawn in the main from the examples given in these works but now, where necessary, these have been supplemented by examples drawn from *A Microfiche Concordance to Old English* by Venezky & Healey and the revised corpus of Old English texts maintained on an electronic data base at the Dictionary of Old English office.

The Dictionary naturally depends primarily on published editions, although the staff consults microfilms of the manuscripts in cases of doubt, as I have done. Pulsiano has recently pointed to the inadequacies of many editions of the Psalters[1] and the unreliability of the Wright-Wülcker edition of the glosses has long been known. I have had perforce to rely on the existing psalter editions, but in the case of the glossaries I have used the best published edition and have also employed the unpublished dissertation of Kindschi, in the latter instance with cross-references to Wright-Wülcker.

This study includes words used metaphorically, particularly in the context of religious writings and land transactions. Those that appear only in the latter contexts are prefixed by an asterisk. In order to avoid a plethora of spaced periods, the initial word of a quotation and translation is not capitalised if it is not the first word of a sentence in the original text; the period at the end of a quotation is to be regarded as an editorial one. Existing translations have been utilised wherever possible. References to and citations from the Vulgate version of the Bible are based on the version edited by Colunga & Turrado.

The following words have been omitted because their Old English meanings do not seem to be applicable to this study: *cnapa*, *cyfes*, *friþdom*, *gingre*, *gop*, *hors-wealh*, *hund-wealh*, *incniht*, *incnapa*, *inhired*, *inhiwan*, *inweorud*, *nidling*, *scielcen*, *scip-wealh*, and *wineard-wealh*.

ÆHT sb. (f)   1) 'A person owned by another, a slave.'

Æht was the general word for property. It was used especially of land, but also of moveables such a cattle. In the Old English version of the 'Penitential' it appears in the phrase 'Gif hwylc man his æht ofslehð' ('If any man kills his slave'), where the context shows that a slave was being referred to.[2] Another clear instance is to be found in the Old English version of Gregory's *Dialogues*: '7 hi genamon þær of þæs biscopes æhte twegen lytle cnihtas' ('and they took there from the bishop's property two little boys'), translating 'sed duos paruos puerulos de possessione abstulerant'.[3]

---

[1] Pulsiano, 'Old English glossed psalters'.
[2] *Die altenglische Version des Halitgar'schen Bussbuches*, II.3 (ed. Raith, p. 17.2).
[3] *Bischof Wærferths von Worcester Übersetzung*, I.10 (ed. Hecht, p. 80.6–8) (Old English); *Grégoire le Grand Dialogues*, I.10.12 (ed. de Vogüé, II.102.132–3) (Latin).

2) 'A serf.'

Status Document, §1.1, a late tenth-century Ely record, declares: 'Wærlaf . . . wæs riht æht to Hæðfelda.' ('Wærlaf was . . . the rightful property of Hatfield.') The context suggests that Wærlaf had the status of a *gebur*.[4]

ÆHT-BOREN adj. 'Born as a person who is owned by another, slave-born.'

The sole occurrence of this word is in the twelfth-century Old English copy of the *Benedictine Rule* preserved in London, British Library, MS. Cotton Faustina A.x, where it translates *ex conditione seruili*.[5] Cf. *æht, þeowboren*.

ÆHTE-MAN sb. (m) 'A person attached to the lord's demesne.'

The contexts in which this word appears suggest that the first element utilises *æht* in the sense of 'property, lands' rather than 'possession, power'. Its meaning is thus 'a man connected with the lord's landed property' rather than 'an owned man'.

A phrase in Ælfric's *Letter to Sigeweard* ('On the Old and New Testament') brings out the association with the land: *Laboratores sind . . . yrðlingas 7 æhtemen*. ('*Laboratores* are . . . ploughmen and persons on the demesne.')[6] A passage in his *Life of Saint Sebastian* implies they were the labourers on the demesne rather than the domestic staff of the manor or *innhyred*: 'Þa wearð gefullod fæder and sunu mid heora innhyrede and heora æhtamannum.' ('Then were baptized father and son, with their domestic staff and their estate workers.')[7]

The status of these men probably varied. In *Rectitudines singularum personarum*, §§8–9.1 the word is used in association with *esne* ('a male slave') and *ðeowan wifmen* ('female slaves').[8] But it seems very likely that the *æhtemen* mentioned in the *Textus Roffensis*, now Maidstone, Kent County Archives Office, MS. DR/Rc1 (*Status Document*, §2.1), were serfs.[9] The word is perhaps the vernacular equivalent of *famulus*. See further above, p. 182.

ÆHTE-SWAN sb. (m) 'A swineherd belonging to the demesne.'

Æhteswan occurs only in *Rectitudines singularum personarum*, §7. It need not necessarily have denoted legal status, but it is clear from *Rectitudines singularum personarum*, §6.4, which refers to the *ðeow swan* ('swineherd with the status of a slave') or *seruus porcarius* in the Latin version of the same sub-clause, that a slave was being referred to in this document.[10]

* A-FREON vb 'To free or release from a spiritual state.'

This form is found only four times in Old English in two Northumbrian texts. In the Rushworth Gospels at Luke 11:4 (part of the Lord's Prayer) the word appears in the phrase *afria usih from yfle*, glossing *libera nos a malo*,[11] and in the *Durham Ritual*

---

4 See Pelteret, 'Two Old English lists of serfs', 473 and 474–5.
5 *Die angelsächsischen Prosabearbeitungen der Benediktinerregel*, ed. Schröer, p. 138.20 (Old English); *ibid.*, p. 233 (Latin) (= Ker, *Catalogue*, §154B [pp. 194–5]).
6 *The Old English Version of the Heptateuch*, ed. Crawford, p. 71.1208–9 (text, emended).
7 *Ælfric's Lives of Saints*, §5 (ed. & transl. Skeat, I.136.307–8) (text); *ibid.*, I.137.307–8 (translation, emended).
8 *Die Gesetze*, ed. & transl. Liebermann, I.449–50 (text); *English Historical Documents 1042–1189*, §172 (transl. Douglas & Greenaway, p. 877) (translation).
9 Pelteret, 'Two Old English lists of serfs', 493 and 496–500.
10 *Die Gesetze*, ed. & transl. Liebermann, I.449.
11 *The Gospel according to Saint Luke*, ed. Skeat, p. 117.

liberemur is variously glossed *ve sie afriad*, *ve sie afriodo*, and *ve sie afriado* ('we are freed').[12]

A-LISAN vb   1) 'To release.'

A late eleventh-century document from Exeter, *Manumission*, §5.2, declares: 'Æilgyuu Gode alysde Hig . . . æt Mangode to XIII mancson.' ('Æthelgifu Good released Hig . . . from Mangod for thirteen mancuses.') It is not clear whether this is a record of the freeing of a slave (that is, a manumission) or whether it is a attestation of a release from an estate (in other words, a quittance).

2) 'To release from a contractual obligation to an estate.'

The word appears as a phrasal verb in a further two Exeter manumission-documents from the latter part of the eleventh century in the form *alysde ut* (*Manumission*, §§8.20 and 8.24). The second document states: 'Gedmer . . . hæfð alised Leofilde . . . ut of Toppeshamlande mid IIII 7 XX penuge at Ceolrice.' ('Eadmer . . . has released Leofhild. . . from the estate at Topsham from Ceolric for twenty-four pence.')

* A-LISEDNESS sb. (f) 'A (spiritual) redemption.'

This word and the variant form *alisedness* (q.v.) seem to have been the regular Old English equivalents of the Latin *redemptio*. In the mid-eleventh-century Stowe Psalter version of Psalm 48:9 *weorð alysednysse sawle his* ('the price of the redemption of his soul') glosses *pretium redemptionis anime suae*,[13] and in the Durham, Cathedral, MS. B.III.32 version of one of the Old English hymns *ure alysednyss* glosses *nostra redemptio*.[14] *Mine saule to alisednesse* ('for the redemption of my soul') is cited regularly in the charters as the motivation for a gift of property; the same reason is given by William, bishop of Exeter, for his release of Wulfric Pig as late as the year 1133.[15] In Psalm 27:8 in the Lambeth Psalter *alisedness* is extended slightly in meaning, being a gloss for *saluationum*.[16]

* A-LISENDLIC adj. 'That can release.'

Litteras solutorias is translated *ða alysendlecan rune* ('the releasing letters') in the ninth-century Mercian *Bede*.[17]

* A-LISENDNESS sb. (f) 'A (spiritual) redemption.'

Bosworth, *An Anglo-Saxon Dictionary*, ed. Toller, s.v. *a-lisendnes*, refers the reader to *a-lysednys*,[18] but the two forms are derived from different parts of speech and must originally have had slightly different meanings. *Alisendness* means 'a state arising out of the action of a redeemer (*alisend*)' whereas *alisedness* denotes 'a state arising out of having been redeemed'.

Alisendnes appears with only a religious sense. In the ninth-century Old English version of Gregory the Great's *Dialogues*, 'þæt lac . . . for alysendnesse his sawle' translates *pro absolutione eius animae . . . sacrificium*,[19] and in the Lindisfarne Gospels

---

12 *Rituale Ecclesiae Dunelmensis*, edd. Thompson & Lindelöf, pp. 53.2, 54.13, and 91.12.
13 *The Stowe Psalter*, ed. Kimmens, p. 91.7–8.
14 *Hymnar und Hymnen im englischen Mittelalter*, §71.1 (ed. Gneuss, p. 356, n. 1).
15 *Manumission*, §8.12 (= Pelteret, *Catalogue*, §103 [p. 104]).
16 *Der Lambeth-Psalter*, I.42, ed. Lindelöf.
17 *The Old English Version of Bede's Ecclesiastical History*, IV.23 (ed. & transl. Miller, I.2.328.6) (text; personal translation) (= *Bede's Ecclesiastical History*, IV.22[20] [edd. & transl. Colgrave & Mynors, p. 402]).
18 Bosworth, *An Anglo-Saxon Dictionary*, ed. Toller, p. 35, col. 1.
19 *Bischof Wærferths von Worcester Übersetzung*, IV.59 (ed. Hecht, I.347.13–14) (Old English); *Grégoire le Grand Dialogues*, IV.59.3 (ed. de Vogüé, III.198.24–5) (Latin).

at Matthew 20:28 *alesenis* (presumably with assimilation of the consonantal cluster *-ndn-*) glosses *redemptionem* as an alternative to *eftlising* (q.v.)[20] It is also to be found in a charter of King Æthelred to Christ Church, Canterbury, issued in 979, where redemption of the soul, *For mine saule alisendnesse*, is mentioned – as in so many other charters – as the motivation for the act.[21]

* A-LISING sb. (f) 'A (spiritual) redemption.'

Alysinge translates *redemptionem* in the metrical version of Psalm 110:6 in the Paris Psalter, which was copied in the first half of the eleventh century.[22] It is also used once in the Old English version of *Chrodegang's Rule*, which was copied in the eleventh century.[23]

A-LISNESS sb. (f) 1) 'A redemption (from captivity).'

In the Old English *Bede, þæt weorð his alesnesse* ('the price of his release') translates *pretium suae redemtionis*.[24]

2) 'A (spiritual) redemption.'

This sense is attested in several sources, such as the Old English *Bede: fore alysnesse his sawle* ('for the release of his soul'), translating *pro absolutione animae eius*,[25] and *Christ III*, line 1473.[26]

* AMBIHT-MÆCG sb. (m) 'A serving-man, slave.' (In a spiritual sense.)

According to Festus the Latin *ambactus* was of Celtic origin and meant 'slave'.[27] But the primary meaning of the word seems to have been 'one who serves'. In this sense it appears in Latin and also widely in the Germanic languages, including Old English, where it is both a masculine *nomen agentis* (often glossing *minister*) and a neuter abstract substantive meaning 'service'. With the exception of the compound here cited, neither *ambiht* nor its compounds (*ambihtman, ambihtscealc, ambihtsmið,* and *ambihtþegn*) seem to denote legal status but instead refer to a person who performed some kind of serving function.

Ambihtmæcg is used only twice, both times in the Paris Psalter: *þine scealcas ambyhtmæcgas*, glossing *seruis tuis* in Psalm 101:12,[28] and *þinne agenne ombihtmæcg* in Psalm 143:11, representing *seruum tuum* in the Vulgate version of Psalm 143:10.[29] The word expresses the relationship of servitude between Humanity and God, and parallels similar uses of *þeow* (q.v.). The simplex *mæcg* is found only in poetic texts; that the

---

20 *The Gospel according to Saint Matthew*, ed. Skeat, p. 165.
21 Dugdale, *Monasticon Anglicanum*, I.111, §38.2–3 (edd. Caley *et al.*) (= Sawyer, *Anglo-Saxon Charters*, no. 1636).
22 *The Paris Psalter*, ed. Krapp, p. 95 (= Vulgate Psalm 110:9).
23 *The Old English Version of the Enlarged Rule of Chrodegang*, §43 (ed. Napier, p. 51.33) (text). On the date of the extant manuscript see Ker, *Catalogue*, §46 (pp. 74–5).
24 *The Old English Version of Bede's Ecclesiastical History*, IV.23 (ed. & transl. Miller, I.2.330.5–6) (text; personal translation) (= *Bede's Ecclesiastical History*, IV.22[20] [edd. & transl. Colgrave & Mynors, p. 404]).
25 *The Old English Version of Bede's Ecclesiastical History*, IV.23 (ed. & transl. Miller, I.2.326.31) (text); *ibid.*, I.2.329.1 (translation) (= *Bede's Ecclesiastical History*, IV.22[20] [edd. & transl. Colgrave & Mynors, p. 420]).
26 *The Exeter Book*, edd. Krapp & Dobbie, p. 44.
27 'Ambactus apud Ennium lingua Gallica seruus appellatur.' ('A slave is called "ambactus" in Ennius from the Gallic tongue.') *Sexti Pompei Festi De Verborum Significatu*, ed. Lindsay, p. 4.20–1.
28 *The Paris Psalter*, ed. Krapp, p. 73 (= Vulgate Psalm 101:15).
29 *Ibid.*, p. 142.

compound is found only in the verse portion of the Paris Psalter suggests that it too was a poetic word.

BE-BICGAN vb 'To sell (a person as a slave).'

Ine's Law, §11 declares: 'Gif hwa his agenne geleod bebycgge, ðeowne oððe frigne, . . . ofer sæ, forgielde hine his were' ('If anyone sells one of his own countrymen, bond or free, over the sea, . . . he shall pay for him with his wergeld').[30] Lambard's version of the Preface to Alfred's Laws, §12, employs this verb as well;[31] other manuscripts use forms of *gebicgan* and *sellan* (qq.v.) This form also appears in several manuscripts of the same text, §15, translating Exodus 21:7 and 16.[32] The word was known in this sense in the Northumbrian dialect, since it appears as a gloss to *uenundari* in the Rushworth Gospels at Matthew 18:25.[33]

BE-FREON vb 'To free.'

This word appears only in the form *befreo* as the equivalent of the Latin *libera* in line 110 of a metrical version of Psalm 55 preserved in London, British Library, MS. Cotton Vespasian D.vi, a mid-tenth-century Kentish manuscript.[34]

(GE)-BICGAN vb   1) 'To buy someone into a state of slavery.'

In Genesis 47:19 Joseph's brothers declare to him, 'eme nos in seruitutem regiam, et praebe semina', which is rendered in Old English 'bige us to þæs cyncges þeowote 7 sile us sæd'.[35]

2) 'To buy someone who is in a state of slavery.'

The Old English 'Penitential' preserves this sense of the word: 'man gebicge man of þeowdome 7 hine syþþan gefreoge' ('if a person buys someone who is in a state of slavery and afterwards frees him').[36]

3) 'To buy (a release from an estate).'

(Ge)bicgan is used in manumission-documents from both Bath and Exeter (for example, *Manumission*, §§8.1, 8.2, 9.16, 9.22, 9.23). The full formula in which it appears is 'X hæfþ geboht Y (ut) mid/to A æt Z (to ecum freote)' ('X has bought a release for Y for A from Z [<to have> eternal freedom]'), where A is the purchase price of the release. See above, pp. 158–60.

4) 'To sell into a state of slavery.'

The Preface to Alfred's Laws, §12 employs a form of *gebicgan* to express the sale of a member of a free family into slavery in two of the primary manuscripts; the third uses a form of *sellan* [q.v.])[37]

---

[30] *Die Gesetze*, ed. Liebermann, I.94 (text); *The Laws*, ed. & transl. Attenborough, p. 41 (translation).

[31] Lexicographers should show caution in citing this example, however, in the light of the questions about the authenticity of the text: see above, p. 82, n. 10.

[32] *Die Gesetze*, ed. Liebermann, I.30.3. The two manuscripts are Cambridge, Corpus Christi College, MS. 173 (where this section is in West-Saxon and written in a hand of *ca* 925 according to *Die Gesetze*, ed. Liebermann, I.xxiv), and London, British Library, MS. Cotton Nero A.i, which is probably of Worcester origin and dates from the mid-eleventh century.

[33] *The Gospel according to Saint Matthew*, ed. Skeat, p. 151.

[34] *The Anglo-Saxon Minor Poems*, ed. Dobbie, p. 92 (= Vulgate Psalm 50:16). On the date and provenance of the manuscript see Ker, *Catalogue*, §207e (p. 269).

[35] *The Old English Version of the Heptateuch*, ed. Crawford, p. 203.

[36] *Die altenglische Version des Halitgar'schen Bussbuches*, IV.57b (ed. Raith, p. 67.12–13) (text). See also *Manumission*, §§8.8–10 (above, p. 158).

[37] *Die Gesetze*, ed. Liebermann, I.30 (text).

BIRELE sb. (f) 'A female slave (?cup-)bearer.'

Æthelberht, §§14 and 16 describe the legal status of the *birele*. Clause 14 states: 'Gif wið eorles birele man geligeþ, XII scill' gebete.' ('If a man lies with a nobleman's serving maid, he shall pay 12 shillings compensation.') Clause 16 adds: 'Gif wið ceorles birelan man geligeþ, VI scillingum gebete; aet þære oþere ðeowan L scætta; aet þare þriddan XXX scætta.' ('If a man lies with a serving maid of a *ceorl*, he shall pay 6 shillings compensation; <if he lies> with a slave of the second class, <he shall pay> 50 *sceattas* <compensation>; if with one of the third class, 30 *sceattas*.')[38]

Birele is etymologically related to the verb *beran* 'to bear'. Elsewhere in Old English texts the masculine equivalent denotes a cup-bearer or butler (*pincerna*),[39] which by the Norman period had risen to being a position of some standing in a lord's household.[40] It is not possible to say whether the word here retains the generalised sense of 'bearer' or whether it had already acquired the specialised sense of 'cup-bearer'. Æthelberht's Laws show that she was a slave of the first class (cf. *aet þære oþere ðeowan*). Presumably her relative standing was dictated by her economic function within her owner's household (which on the basis of the later use of the word seems to have been to serve at meals); from Æthelberht, §11 it appears that the second class of female slave had the role of grinding corn (*grindende þeowa*).[41]

CEAP-CNIHT sb. (m) 'A young man who is for sale as a slave.'

Variants of *ceapcniht* gloss *em(p)ticius* in the eighth-century Corpus Glossary (Cambridge, Corpus Christi College, MS. 144), the Erfurt Glossary (Erfurt, Codex Amplonianus f. 42) of the late eighth to early ninth centuries, and the mid-tenth-century Cleopatra Glossary (London, British Library, MS. Cotton Cleopatra A.iii).[42] Elsewhere the word appears only in the homily of Ælfric's where he recounts Bede's story of Pope Gregory's encounter in Rome with English youths on sale in a market there: 'ða gelamp hit . . . þæt Englisce cypmenn brohton heora ware to Romana-byrig. . . . Þa geseah he [*sc.* Gregorius] betwux ðam warum cypecnihtas gesette.' ('It happened then . . . that English chapmen brought their wares to Rome. . . . He then saw among their wares youths placed for sale.')[43]

CNIHT sb. (m) 1) 'A youth.'

'A youth' is the commonest meaning of this word. The words used for children of different ages are given in Ælfric's homily, *On the First Sunday after Pentecost*: 'þonne þæt cild wyxt, and gewyrð eft cnapa, and eft syððan cniht' ('then the child grew and became a *cnapa* and afterwards a *cniht*').[44]

---

[38] *Ibid.*, I.4 (text); *The Laws*, ed. & transl. Attenborough, p. 7 (translation, emended).

[39] For example, Wright, *Anglo-Saxon and Old English Vocabularies*, ed. Wülcker, I, col. 303.2.

[40] Stenton, *The First Century of English Feudalism*, pp. 71 and 105.

[41] *Die Gesetze*, ed. Liebermann, I.3 (text); *The Laws*, ed. & transl. Attenborough, p. 5 (translation).

[42] *The Corpus Glossary*, E151, ed. Lindsay, p. 63; *Old English Glosses in the Épinal-Erfurt Glossary*, ed. Pheifer, p. 19.349; Wright, *Anglo-Saxon and Old English Vocabularies*, ed. Wülcker, I, col. 392.5.

[43] *Ælfric's Catholic Homilies*, §9.53–7 (ed. Godden, p. 74) (= *The Sermones Catholici*, II.9 [ed. & transl. Thorpe, p. 120.14–18]) (text); *ibid.*, p. 121.13–17 (translation).

[44] Bäck, *The Synonyms for 'Child', 'Boy', 'Girl' in Old English*, pp. 110–32; *Homilies of Ælfric*, XII.120–1 (ed. Pope, II.484).

2) 'A follower of a more powerful man.'

This is the sense behind such lemmata as *cliens uel clientulus*[45] and *parasitorum*.[46] Cnihtas are beneficiaries of gifts in a number of charters.

3)a: 'A young man who serves.'

With this meaning *cniht* is the vernacular equivalent of *puer*, both in the Old English *Heptateuch* version of Genesis 24:65[47] and in the Old English translation of Psalm 68:17 in the Paris Psalter.[48]

3)b: 'A servant.' (Legal status unspecified.)

This sense appears in the Alfredian *Cura Pastoralis*: 'hit is niedðearf ðæt mon his hlaford ondræde, & se cneoht his magi<s>ter' ('it is necessary for a man to fear his lord, and the servant his master'), translating 'Et tamen necesse est ut rectores a subditis timeantur'.[49]

4) 'A slave.'

This rare usage appears in an anonymous homily, *Ammonitio amici*: 'Seruus, sciens uoluntatem domini sui et non faciens, plagis uapulabit multis. Þæt ys on englisc: se cniht, þe wat, hwæt his hlafordes willa syg, and he þæt forgægð, he byð wyrðe, þæt he beo teartlice geswungen.' ('That is in English: the slave who knows what his lord's wish is and goes against that, he is deserving of being severely beaten.')[50]

CYRE-LIF sb. (n)   1) 'One who has voluntarily enslaved himself to another.'

Eytmologically *cyre-* is related to *ceosan* 'to choose'; the basic meaning of the compound is 'choice of life'. Alfred in his will of 873 x 889 enjoins: '7 ic bidde on Godes naman 7 on his haligra þæt minra maga nan ne yrfewearda ne geswence nan nænig cyrelif þara þe ic foregeald.' ('And I pray in the name of God and of His saints that none of my kinsmen or legatees oppress any of the *cyrelif* for whom I have paid.') The passage goes on to make it clear that these persons were slaves. The prefix *cyre-* implies that this status was of their own choosing. That Alfred had to pay for them suggests that they may have been persons who had fallen into debt and who had then chosen to become slaves in order to discharge their debts, as well as to gain the advantages of the regular food rations that slavery would bring. Alfred's concern that 'no man put pressure on them . . . by pecuniary exactions' ('hy nan man ne brocie ne mid feos manunge') also suggests that debt lay behind their status.[51] See above pp. 110–11.

2) 'A state of voluntary enslavement.' (Used in a spiritual sense.)

The Old English version of the *Rule of Chrodegang* states: 'Gehicgon hig eac þæt hig gehealdon . . . heora clænnysse ungewemmedum lichaman, oððe witodlice beon geferlæhte þære gefæstnuncge anes gesynscypes, butan þam canonican þe on cyrelife sittað.'

---

[45] London, British Library, Additional MS. 32246, fo 18r, in 'The Latin-Old English glossaries', ed. Kindschi, p. 207.5 (= Wright, *Anglo-Saxon and Old English Vocabularies*, ed. Wülcker, I, col. 171.2).

[46] *Old English Glosses*, §1.4165 (ed. Napier, p. 110).

[47] *The Old English Version of the Heptateuch*, ed. Crawford, p. 149.

[48] *The Paris Psalter*, ed. Krapp, p. 25 (= Vulgate Psalm 68:18).

[49] *King Alfred's West-Saxon Version of Gregory's Pastoral Care*, §17 (ed. Sweet, I.109.13–14 = I.108.14–15) (Old English text); *ibid.*, I.108–9 (translation); *Grégoire le Grand Règle pastorale*, II.6.28–9 (edd. Judic *et al.*, I.204) (Latin).

[50] *Wulfstan*, §48 (ed. Napier, p. 248.9–13).

[51] *Select English Historical Documents*, §11 (ed. & transl. Harmer, p. 19.16–18 and 22) (text); *ibid.*, pp. 52–3 (translation, emended; Harmer translated *cyrelif* as 'dependants') (= Sawyer, *Anglo-Saxon Charters*, no. 1507).

('They determined also that they maintain . . . their purity with an undefiled body or truly be conjoined through the security of a single marriage, except for the canons who exist in a state of *cyrelif.*')[52] Napier pointed out that in the latter part of the sentence the translator did not follow the Latin text, which reads: 'exceptis his canonicis qui uictu et uestitu potiantur' ('except those canons who obtain food and clothing'). He was thus puzzled as to how the translator understood his original.[53]

When one recalls that the clergy were frequently called *Godes þeowas*, it becomes clear that the translator was influenced by certain aspects of the status of a *cyrelif*, namely,

1) that it as a state of life entered into by choice;
2) that it resulted in enslavement to another; and
3) that this involved the lord in supplying the dependant with basic necessities.

The translator's choice of the word *cyrelif* was thus entirely appropriate.

DÆGE sb. (f)   1) 'A (female) baker, a baxter.'

The existence of this word suggests that there must have existed an Old English verb **digan*, 'to knead'. Its relationship to the later English verb *dig* is problematic.[54] The Old English sense is most clearly revealed in the word *hlæfdige*, which by a variety of sound changes yields the Modern English *lady*. The simplex in this sense is to be found only once, as a gloss to *pristris* (= *pistrix*) in the glosses to Prosper's *Epigrammata* in London, British Library, MS. Cotton Tiberius A.vii.[55]

2) 'A dairymaid.'

This sense is not attested in the *Dictionary of Old English* microfiche of the letter *D*. Yet the word occurs in Domesday Book, where, in a good example of how important Mediaeval Latin texts can be for extending our knowledge of vernacular languages,[56] on one occasion it is fairly clear that a dairymaid is being referred to. Under Bushley (in Worcestershire, though recorded in the Herefordshire folios) Domesday Book records that the king held a manor of whose staff it is said, 'Ibi VIII inter seruos 7 ancillas 7 uaccarius 7 daia.' ('[There are] 8 there, among the slaves and bondwomen. And [there are] a cow-herd and a *daia*.')[57] The association of the *daia* (a latinised form of *dæge*) with the *uaccarius* or cowherd strongly suggests that they had a similar occupational function. We may further assume from the collocation of these two persons with *serui* that the *daia* and *uaccarius* were themselves legally slaves with a specialist role on the demesne. One can less certainly determine the legal status of the *daia* mentioned on the same folio who lived on the king's manor at Queenshill, but the association of this person with two *bouarii* implies involvement in animal husbandry rather than in bread-making: 'Ibi I porcarius 7 II bouarii 7 daia.' ('[There are] there 1 swineherd and 2

---

[52] *The Old English Version of the Enlarged Rule of Chrodegang*, §62 (ed. Napier, p. 77.6–9) (text).

[53] Napier, 'Contributions to Old English lexicography', 279–80.

[54] *To dig* appears to have entered Middle English *via* French. The noun seems to be more closely related to Modern English *dough*. See Simpson & Weiner, *The Oxford English Dictionary*, IV.646, col. 1, s.v. *dig*; IV.986, col. 2, s.v. *dough*; and VIII.582, col. 2, s.v. *lady*.

[55] Wright, *Anglo-Saxon and Old English Vocabularies*, ed. Wülcker, I, col. 277.3 (= Ker, *Catalogue*, §189 [p. 250]).

[56] See Pelteret, 'Expanding the word hoard'.

[57] Domesday Book, volume I, fo 180vb (text); 'Translation of the Herefordshire Domesday', transl. Round, in *The Victoria History of the County of Hereford*, volume I, ed. Page, p. 317b (translation, emended).

oxmen and a *daia*.')[58] Frank and Caroline Thorn in their translation of the Herefordshire folios of Domesday Book point out that *daia* can be masculine or feminine,[59] but both its association with the word *uaccarius* and the vernacular use of the word in Middle English suggest that a woman is being referred to. The *Middle English Dictionary*, in fact, gives as the primary meaning of the word, 'A woman in charge of milking and making butter and cheese, a dairymaid; also a woman who keeps cows and other farm stock.'[60] By the middle of the thirteenth century an Anglo-French suffix had been added to create the form *daierie*, the ancestor of Modern English *dairy*.[61] The word appears in an eleventh-century Bath manumission, *Manumission*, §8.14; in some farm accounts from the same century in the dative form *dægan*;[62] and in a twelfth century survey from Burton Abbey.[63] Unfortunately the contexts do not enable one to ascertain the precise meaning here but in all three instances the word can plausibly be interpreted as referring to a dairymaid (*pace* the editors of the *Dictionary of Old English*). The necessity of giving daily attention to cattle will have encouraged the employment of slaves for the purpose of milking and caring for cows.[64]

DRUNC-MENNEN sb. (f) 'A drunken female slave.'

This, the only reference to a drunken woman in Old English literature, appears in *Riddle*, §10.9.[65] Because of its unique sense Grein wanted to emend the text to read *dunc-mennen* 'a female steward', with the (hypothetical) first element being cognate with Old High German *tunc*.[66] This does not make much sense in the context, however, whereas the manuscript reading fits in with the derogatory epithets *wonfeax* and *dol*, which are used with reference to this same person. See further above, pp. 52–3.

* GE-EDFREOLSIAN vb 'To renew the declaration of freedom from any obligation to render the dues formerly associated with a property.'

This verb occurs in a single charter of A.D. 960: 'Þis is ealra þara landa freols þe Eadgar cyning geedfreolsade Wulfrice his þegene on ece yrfe.' ('This is the charter of freedom over all those lands whose rights of freedom King Edgar renewed as a perpetual possession for Wulfric his thegn.')[67]

* EFEN-ÞEOW, EFEN-ÞEOWA sb. (m) 'A fellow-slave.' (In a spiritual sense.)

Efenþeow was probably originally coined to translate the Latin *conseruus*. Its form follows a common pattern of substantival and adjectival compounds in *efen-/efn-* used to

---

[58] Domesday Book, volume I, fo 180vb (text); 'Translation of the Herefordshire Domesday', transl. Round, in *The Victoria History of the County of Hereford*, volume I, ed. Page, p. 317b (translation, emended).

[59] *Herefordshire*, transl. F. & C. Thorn, n. 1,44.

[60] See *Middle English Dictionary*, ed. Kurath, C–D, p. 823, col. 2, s.v. *daie*; cf. Simpson & Weiner, *The Oxford English Dictionary*, IV.588, col. 1, s.v. *dey*, and *The Will of Æthelgifu*, ed. & transl. Whitelock, p. 14, n. 1.

[61] *Middle English Dictionary*, ed. Kurath, C–D, p.823, col. 2, s.v. *daiere*; cf. Simpson & Weiner, *The Oxford English Dictionary*, IV.218, col. 3, s.v. *dairy*.

[62] *Anglo-Saxon Charters*, appendix §2.9 (ed. Robertson, p. 252).

[63] Bridgeman, 'The Burton Abbey twelfth century surveys', in *Collections for a History of Staffordshire*, ed. William Salt Archaeological Society, p. 235, col. 2.

[64] See above, p. 203.

[65] *The Old English Riddles*, ed. Williamson, p. 74 (= Riddle, §12.9, in *The Exeter Book*, edd. Krapp & Dobbie, p. 186).

[66] See *Die altenglischen Rätsel (Die Rätsel des Exeterbuchs)*, ed. Trautmann, p. 75.

[67] *Cartularium Saxonicum*, §1055 (ed. Birch, III.275.33–4) (= Sawyer, *Anglo-Saxon Charters*, no. 687).

express Latin substantives or adjectives beginning in *con-/co-* (for example, *efenedwist-lic – consubstantialis*; *efenbisceop – co-episcopus*).

The word appears as a gloss to *conseruus* in Matthew 18:29, 31, and 33 in the Rushworth Gospels;[68] in the West-Saxon Gospels found in Cambridge, Corpus Christi College, MS. 140, it is used in the identical verses and also in verse 28.[69] It represents the same word in the Old English versions of the *Cura Pastoralis*[70] and the *Benedictine Rule*.[71]

Variant forms of *efenþeow* also appear in the manuscripts of the Old English *Cura Pastoralis* translating *consenior* (quoting 1 Peter 5:1): 'Ic, eower emnðeowa 7 Cristes ðrowunge gewita' ('I, your fellow-slave and witness of Christ's suffering'), translating *consenior et testis Christi passionum*.[72] The context indicates that *consenior* refers to Peter, who as an elder may well have been considered *Godes þeow* by the translator.

It is no doubt from scriptural translations that the word came to be used in homiletic writings (cf. *efenþeowen*). Its meaning of 'fellow-slave' is clearly brought out in an anonymous homily on the Nativity of Mary the Virgin based on the Pseudo-Matthew Gospel: 'Hwi wylt þu la cweðan þæt ðu sy min þeowa, ac þu eart min efenþeowa, forðan þe wit syndon anes Godes þeow.' ('Lo, why do you wish to say that you are my slave, but you are my fellow-slave because both of us are the slave of the one God.')[73] As this word appears only in scriptural contexts it is not clear whether it was used more generally as a secular legal term.

EFEN-ÞEOWEN sb. (f) 'A fellow female slave.'

This word appears only in an anonymous homily drawn from the *Uitae Patrum*.[74] It probably arose by analogy with *efenþeow(a)* (q.v.).

EFNE-ESNE sb. (m) 'A fellow slave.'

Efne-esne is used once in the Lindisfarne Gospels at Matthew 18:33.[75] In verses 28, 29, and 31 of the same chapter the translator uses *efneþegn* (q.v.) to gloss *conseruus*, while the Rushworth and West-Saxon versions have *efenþeow*, as do the Rushworth Gospels in verses 29 and 31.[76] The *Durham Ritual* also glosses the latter word as *efne esne*.[77]

EFNE-ÞEGN sb. (m) 'A fellow slave.'

This form is to be found only in the parable of the wicked servant in the Lindisfarne Gospels version of Matthew 18:28, 29, and 31,[78] where other translations use

---

[68] *The Gospel according to Saint Matthew*, ed. Skeat, pp. 151.

[69] *Ibid.*, p. 150.

[70] *King Alfred's West-Saxon Version of Gregory's Pastoral Care*, §29 (ed. Sweet, I.201.20 = I.200.20) (Old English text); *Grégoire le Grand Règle pastorale*, III.5.12 (edd. Judic *et al.*, II.284) (Latin).

[71] *Die angelsächsischen Prosabearbeitungen der Benediktinerregel*, §64 (ed. Schröer, p. 123.4).

[72] *efnðeowa* in London, British Library, MSS. Cotton Otho B.ii and Cotton Tiberius B.xi; *emnðeowa* in Oxford, Bodleian Library, MS. Hatton 20 (*S.C.* 4113): see *King Alfred's West Saxon Version of Gregory's Pastoral Care*, §18 (ed. Sweet, I.136.17 and I.137.16 respectively) (Old English text); *ibid.*, I.137.16 (translation, emended); *Grégoire le Grand Règle pastorale*, II.7.134–5 (edd. Judic *et al.*, I.228) (Latin).

[73] *Angelsächsische Homilien und Heiligenleben*, §10.202–5 (ed. Assmann, p. 123, col. 1) (text).

[74] *Ibid.*, §18.256 (p. 203) (text).

[75] *The Gospel according to Saint Matthew*, ed. Skeat, p. 151.

[76] *Ibid.*, pp. 150–1.

[77] *Rituale Ecclesiae Dunelmensis*, edd. Thompson & Lindelöf, p. 70.22.

[78] *The Gospel according to Saint Matthew*, ed. Skeat, p. 151.

efenþeow(a) (q.v.). The translator uses this form doubtless because *þegn* in his dialect (tenth-century Northumbrian) had 'slave' as one of its senses. In verse 33 of the same chapter *efne-esne* (q.v.) is used.

* EFT-LISEND sb. (n) 'Redeemer.'

Redemptor is on one occasion glossed by this word in the *Durham Ritual* in the form *eftlesend*.[79]

* EFT-LISING sb. (f) 'A (spiritual) redemption.'

Eftlising glosses *redemtionem* in the Lindisfarne Gospels in Matthew 20:28 as an alternative to *alesenis* (see *alisendness* above) and *redem(p)turus* in Luke 24:21 in both the Lindisfarne and the Rushworth Gospels; it glosses *redemptione* in the *Durham Ritual*.[80]

ESNE sb. (m)   1) 'A hired labourer.'

This word goes back to the Indo-European roots **es-en-*, **os-en-*, **-er-*, 'harvest time, summer'.[81] It retains this sense in Gothic *asans*, 'harvest, crop, summer', and Old Icelandic *ǫnn* < **azno*, 'harvest'. By association of ideas the root came to be linked with the labour involved in the harvest. Thus one finds Old Saxon *asna*, 'wages; taxes, dues'. The verbal cognate of the root in this sense is Old English *earnian* and Old High German *arnen*, 'to earn'. From this there was yet another extension of meaning to 'one who serves, one who receives wages'. This has resulted in the cognates Gothic *asneis*, Old High German *asni* and Old English *esne*.

In Old English *esne* first appears in the Laws of Æthelberht, §§85–8. The *esne* here was clearly regarded as being to some degree under the sway of another: §88 mentions a *mannes esne* and declares that six shillings should be paid in compensation for laying bonds on such an *esne*. This presumably was to be paid to the lord since six shillings is the fine prescribed for the breach of a *ceorl's mundbyrd* ('protection') in §15. It should be compared to the compensation of twenty shillings for the same offence when committed against a freeman (§24).[82]

Yet the *esne* was in a better position than a slave. His marriage rights were respected to the extent that he was entitled to a two-fold compensation for his wife's adultery (§85). This does not seem to differ in real terms from the rights of a freeman, since the latter could obtain the wergeld of the adulterer (or possibly that of his own wife) and obtain another wife at the adulterer's expense (§31).

The *esne* seemingly could possess financial resources, unlike the slave: an *esne* who killed another was responsible for paying the full compensation according to §86. Yet the very existence of this clause suggests that there must have been some question about this, for otherwise §21 specifying the wergeld of a *ceorl* could have applied.

It seems unlikely that the *esne* was the same as a *læt*, since there is no hint of various classes of *esne*. In the light of its etymological origin we may conclude that at this period the word most probably denoted a landless *ceorl* who hired himself out as a labourer. In a land-oriented society landless freemen would have been in a very weak position, so it is natural that they would have come under the protection of landed men. Their poor economic status would have reduced their rights and this explains why the law had to

[79] *Rituale Ecclesiae Dunelmensis*, edd. Thompson & Lindelöf, p. 126.12.
[80] *The Gospel according to Saint Matthew*, ed. Skeat, p. 165; *The Gospel according to Saint Luke*, ed. Skeat, p. 233; *Rituale Ecclesiae Dunelmensis*, edd. Thompson & Lindelöf, p. 123.19 (*pro redemptione – fore eftlesing*).
[81] Pokorny, *Indogermanisches etymologisches Wörterbuch*, I.343, s.v. *es-en-*.
[82] *Die Gesetze*, ed. Liebermann, I.8 and 4 (text); *The Laws*, ed. & transl. Attenborough, pp. 7, 15, and 17 (translation).

insist that in the event of the death of an *esne* his full value had to be paid (§86), and that the same should apply for the loss of an eye or foot (§87), vital for a labouring man.

A similar interpretation could be applied to the *esne* referred to in the Laws of Hlothhere and Eadric, §§1–4.[83] In these clauses a lord had the duty of yielding up his *esne* if he was guilty of homicide and paying the dead man's wergeld. If the *esne* escaped, his lord had then to pay the value of a further man (that is, one hundred shillings), which was a *ceorl*'s wergeld and may well have been the value of an *esne* as well. If indeed the wergeld of an *esne* was the same as a *ceorl*'s, then the interpretation of the *esne* as a hired worker whose lord had taken responsibility for him because he himself did not have the security of land is a cogent one.

Esne is also used in the West-Saxon laws. Ine, §29 lays down the compensation due to an owner of an *esne* who leaves on being armed by another person.[84] Whoever added the title to the clause in the Cambridge, Corpus Christi College, MS. 383 version evidently thought of the *esne* as a slave (*ðeowa*) but there is no reason to believe that he was. Alfred, §43 specifically excludes *þeowum monnum 7 esnewyrhtan* from certain holidays enjoyed by freemen, implying that slaves and *esnas* were different, even if similar, social classes.[85] Attenborough is thus probably correct in translating *esnewyrhtum* as 'hired labourers'.[86] This sense is confirmed by another ninth-century West-Saxon source: Wærferth's Old English translation of Gregory's *Dialogues* renders the Latin *mercenarii* as *esnewyrhtan*.[87]

2) 'A worker.' (With no indication of legal status.)

In the Laws of Wihtred the word is ambiguous.[88] Both the legal position of the *esne* in this code and the social classes discussed seem to indicate that he was a slave. Yet §23 talks of a *þeuwne esne*, implying that he did not necessarily hold this status.

The ambiguity is most obvious in §§9 and 10. The lord was entitled to a fine from his *esne* if the latter performed servile work or made journeys on horseback on a Sunday, but as an alternative the *esne* could be lashed. The payment of a fine implies that he had the right to possess financial means, which was the mark of a freeman. Yet the punishment by lash was the mark of a slave, who could only pay with his hide. Furthermore, the contrasting position of the *esne* and *friman* over Sabbath labour (§§9–11) is immediately followed by the contrasting penalties for a *ceorl* and *þeuw* guilty of worshiping devils (§§12–13). This implies that the *esne* was the same as a *þeow*.

Esnas are again mentioned in §§22–4 in contrast to the *ceorlisc man* (§21). The former had to be defended either by their lord or by a reeve in the case of a king's or bishop's *esne*. If the defence failed the *esne* was to be scourged.

The best way of reconciling this apparently conflicting evidence is to posit that the word was applying to two social groups who had certain points in common in the legal sphere. On the one hand there were the landless hired labourers. These were free, insofar as they were members of the tribe and thus possessed certain rights, which were recognised at law. Yet they served under lords who took some legal responsibility for them. In this last respect they were like the slave, who did not, however, have legally

---

[83] *Die Gesetze*, ed. Liebermann, I.9 (text); *The Laws*, ed. & transl. Attenborough, p. 19 (translation).

[84] *Die Gesetze*, ed. Liebermann, I.102 (text); *The Laws*, ed. & transl. Attenborough, p. 45 (translation).

[85] *Die Gesetze*, ed. Liebermann, I.78.

[86] *The Laws*, ed. & transl. Attenborough, p. 85.

[87] *Bischof Wærferths von Worcester Übersetzung*, II.3 (ed. Hecht, I.107, col. 1.4) (Old English); *Grégoire le Grand Dialogues*, II.3.6 (ed. de Vogüé, II.144.57) (Latin).

[88] *Die Gesetze*, ed. Liebermann, I.12–14 (text); *The Laws*, ed. & transl. Attenborough, pp. 25–31.

recognised rights. No doubt it was the similarity in their positions that enabled the word *esne* to be applied to slaves as well as to the hired labourers it originally denoted. In the Laws of Wihtred it seems to represent a transitional phase in meaning, applying both to hired workers *and* slaves. The drafter of the code tried to remove this ambiguity at one point by adding the adjective *þeuwne* to *esne*.

Esne seems to have undergone the same semantic shift in Wessex two centuries later. The Prologue to Alfred's Laws, §17 renders the Latin *seruus* of Exodus 21:20 as *þeowne esne*.[89]

3) 'A slave.'

This sense had developed in Northumbrian by the latter half of the tenth century. The *Durham Ritual* uses *esne* to gloss both *seruus* and *famulus*.[90] In the Lindisfarne and Rushworth Gospel glosses to Mark 10:44, *seruus* is glossed *ðræl uel esne*;[91] the Rushworth Gospels, in fact, use *esne* throughout for *seruus*.[92] The Mercian *Bede* also usually translates *seruus* by this word.[93]

It also had gained this sense in the eleventh-century *Rectitudines singularum personarum*, §8 (possibly of Worcestershire provenance), which makes the *esne* the male counterpart of the *þeowan wifmen* in §9.[94]

4) 'A slave.' (Used in a spiritual sense.)

Esne is employed in a number of psalms in the Paris Psalter to express the idea of a 'slave of God'. Thus, of David it is said: 'And Him ða David geceas, deorne esne' ('And He chose David for Himself, a dear slave'), translating *elegit David, seruum suum*,[95] and 'Ic Dauide dyrum esne on aðsware ær benemde' ('I swore earlier to David, a dear slave, in an oath'), translating *Iuraui Dauid, seruo meo*.[96] In Psalm 115:6 in the Paris Psalter the translator renders 'O Domine, quia ego seruus tuus' as 'Eala, ic eom þin agen esne, Dryhten' ('Lo, I am Your own slave, Lord').[97]

5) 'A man.'

Like the word *ceorl*, *esne* also moved from a specific socio-legal sense to the generalised meaning of 'a man', probably by way of sense 2). This was by no means restricted to the North, as was asserted Gutmacher.[98] Byrhtferth of Ramsay used *esne* with this meaning on two occasions.[99] It is used of Orpheus in the Alfredian translation of Boethius's *Consolatio Philosophiae*,[100] and also appears in a number of Riddles.[101] This

---

[89] *Die Gesetze*, ed. Liebermann, I.32.

[90] For example, *Rituale Ecclesiae Dunelmensis*, edd. Thompson & Lindelöf, pp. 95.17 (*famulus*), 1.2 (*seruus*). *Famulus* is also glossed ðegn (for example, *ibid.*, p. 69.7, 13, etc.)

[91] *The Gospel according to Saint Mark*, ed. Skeat, p. 85.

[92] See Venezky & Healey, *A Microfiche Concordance*, s.v. *esne* in its various cases.

[93] *Ibid.*

[94] *Die Gesetze*, ed. Liebermann, I.449–50 (text); *English Historical Documents 1042–1189*, §172 (transl. Douglas & Greenaway, p. 877).

[95] *The Paris Psalter*, ed. Krapp, p. 44, Psalm 77:69 (= Vulgate Psalm 77:70).

[96] *The Paris Psalter*, ed. Krapp, p. 56, Psalm 88:3 (= Vulgate Psalm 88:4).

[97] *The Paris Psalter*, ed. Krapp, p. 100, Psalm 115:6 (= Vulgate Psalm 114/115:16).

[98] Gutmacher, 'Der Wortschatz des althochdeutschen Tatian', 68, s.v. *asni*.

[99] *Byrhtferth's Manual*, ed. Crawford, pp. 144.4 and 170.18; cf. Jordan, *Eigentümlichkeiten des anglischen Wortschatzes*, p. 91.

[100] *King Alfred's Old English Version of Boethius De Consolatione Philosophiae*, §35 (ed. Sedgefield, p. 103.5) (text); *King Alfred's Version of the Consolations of Boethius*, transl. Sedgefield, p. 117 (translation).

[101] For examples see *The Old English Riddles*, ed. Williamson, p. 420, s.v. *esne*. Riddle, §25 has

sense is particularly clear in *Riddle*, §25, where *esne* is a poetic variant for *wer*, *hæleð*, and *ceorl*.

It would seem, therefore, that *esne* in senses 4) and 5) existed side by side in both the North and the South. In the Mercian *Bede* King Penda is described as 'se fromesta esne of Mercna cyningcynne' ('the most valiant man of the Mercian royal race'), representing 'uiro strenuissimo de regio genere Merciorum',[102] while later in the same translation it is used of the slaves freed by Bishop Wilfrid: 'Betwih ða twa 7 hundteontig 7 fiftig þara manna, esna ond menena, gefulwade.' ('Of these he baptized 250, men and women slaves.')[103] In southern Old English *Riddle*, §42 uses *esne* in the sense 'slave' and *Riddle*, §20 also appears to do so: 'swa hine [*sc.* wægn] oxa, ne teah ne esna mægen,/ ne fæthengest' ('yet so that an ox did not draw it [*sc.* the wagon], nor did strong slaves nor did a draught horse').[104] In the West-Saxon *Heptateuch* version of Genesis 24:61, 42:11 and 13, and Exodus 2:1 and 11:2 *esne* represents the Latin *uir*, while in Genesis 24:66 it is the equivalent of *seruus*.[105]

  6) A personal name.

Probably derived from sense 5) (cf. Old English *Mann*), it is also to be seen in the patronymic *Esning*.[106]

ESNE-WYRHTA sb. (m) 'A hired labourer.'

For a discussion of the *esnewyrhtan*, see s.v. *esne* 1) above and notes 86 and 87.

FÆREWYRÞE adj. 'Having the legal right to go (?from an estate).'

This word is not listed in Bosworth, *An Anglo-Saxon Dictionary*, ed. Toller, nor its supplements. For the meaning of the second element see Bosworth, *An Anglo-Saxon Dictionary*, ed. Toller, s.v. *weorþ* VIII (1).[107] The word is discussed above, p. 159.

FÆR-FRIGE adj. 'Having the legal right to go where one wishes.'

The only attestations of this word are in two Wiltshire manumission-documents of the early to mid-tenth century, *Manumission*, §§2.1 and 2.2. For further discussion of *fær-frige* see above, pp. 157–8, and cf. s.v. *freoh* adj. 2).

been edited in *ibid*, pp. 83–4 (= *Riddle*, §27, in *The Exeter Book*, edd. Krapp & Dobbie, p. 194).

[102] *The Old English Version of Bede's Ecclesiastical History*, II.16 (ed. & transl. Miller, I.1.146.29 and I.1.148.1) (text); *ibid.*, I.1.147.26 and I.1.149.1 (translation, emended) (= *Bede's Ecclesiastical History*, II.20 [edd. & transl. Colgrave & Mynors, p. 202]).

[103] *The Old English Version of Bede's Ecclesiastical History*, IV.17 (ed. & transl. Miller, I.2.306.1–2) (text); *ibid.*, I.2.307.1–2 (translation, emended) (= *Bede's Ecclesiastical History*, IV.13 [edd. & transl. Colgrave & Mynors, p. 376]). Miller's translation, 'men and maids', is indefensible; *mennen* (q.v.) always means 'a female slave'. The Latin text, furthermore, uses *seruos et ancillas*.

[104] *Riddle*, §§42.4 and 20.13, in *The Old English Riddles*, ed. Williamson, pp. 96 and 81 (text; personal translation) (= *Riddle*, §§44.4 and 22.13–14, in *The Exeter Book*, edd. Krapp & Dobbie, pp. 204 and 192). In *Riddle*, §20 it may, however, mean 'man'. There is a similar ambiguity in *Daniel*, line 243 (*The Junius Manuscript*, ed. Krapp, p. 118).

[105] *The Old English Version of the Heptateuch*, ed. Crawford, pp. 149, 186–7, 214, 241, and 149 respectively.

[106] Searle, *Onomasticon Anglo-Saxonicum*, p. 236 (*Esne*); *Cartularium Saxonicum*, §416 (ed. Birch, I.583.4) (= Sawyer, *Anglo-Saxon Charters*, no. 190) (*Esning*); and see Bäck, *The Synonyms for 'Child', 'Boy', 'Girl' in Old English*, pp. 161–2.

[107] Page 1200, col. 1.

FOLC-FRIGE adj. 'Free in terms of the folk, that is, enjoying the status, rights, and obligations of a freeman as defined by the law of the tribe.'

For a discussion of this word, which is used only in Wihtred, §8 and II Cnut, §45.3, see above, pp. 135–6 and 138.[108]

FOR-STELAN vb 'To steal (a person).'

In §15 of the Preface to Alfred's Laws *Se ðe frione forstele* represents the phrase *Qui furatus fuerit hominem* of Exodus 21:16.[109]

FOSTOR-CILD sb. (n) 'A foster-child (possibly adopted as a slave in return for its sustenance).'

In the glosses to Prudentius's *Cathemerinon* found in Boulogne-sur-Mer, Bibliothèque municipale, MS. 189, the lemma drawn from the original text, *alumnum*, receives a very revealing Latin gloss, *seruum* ('slave') as well as the Old English gloss, *fostor-cild*.[110] This supports the interpretation that children could be adopted into slavery suggested in the following entry, s.v. *fostorling*.

FOSTOR-LING sb. (m) 'A child adopted as a household slave in return for its sustenance.'

In the glossary appearing on fo 4r of London, British Library, Additional MS. 32246 *fostorling* glosses *uernula*,[111] and on fo 18r of the same manuscript *inberdling uel wostorling* glosses *uerna, uel uernaculus* (where the *wynn* in *wostorling* is clearly an unthinking mistranscription by the scribe of an *f*, a mistake easily explicable on palaeographical grounds).[112] Amongst other senses Old English *foster* means 'feeding, giving food' and 'bringing up, fostering'.[113] The lemmata indicate that a *fosterling* was considered to be of slave status, and furthermore performed a domestic function. *Inberdling* goes even further, implying that the child was born in the house. Presumably, therefore, the *fostorling* was a child, born perhaps of domestic slaves, who received his food in return for serving in the lord's house.

FREO-BEARN sb. (n)   1) 'Free-born offspring.'

The sense of the *freo-* element here strays close to 'nobly born', especially evident in the gloss *freobearn uel æþelborene cild* to the word *liberi* in the glossary in London, British Library, Additional MS. 32246, fo 18v[114] and in its use to describe Christ in *Elene*, lines 671–3: 'ahangen wæs/ on Caluarie cyninges freobearn,/ godes gastsunu' ('the noble Son of the King, God's spiritual Son, was hanged upon Calvary').[115] The word appears mostly in poetic sources.

---

[108] *Die Gesetze*, ed. Liebermann, I.13 (*folc-fry*) and 344 (*folc-frig*).

[109] *Ibid.*, I.30.

[110] *The Old English Prudentius Glosses*, §229 (ed. Meritt, p. 24).

[111] 'The Latin-Old English glossaries', ed. Kindschi, p. 55.15 (= Wright, *Anglo-Saxon and Old English Vocabularies*, ed. Wülcker, I, col. 111.19).

[112] 'The Latin-Old English glossaries', ed. Kindschi, p. 206.6. Wright, *Anglo-Saxon and Old English Vocabularies*, ed. Wülcker, I, col. 170.26–7, gives the emended version and incorrectly records *imberdling* for *inberdling*.

[113] Toller, *Supplement*, p. 259, col. 1, s.v. *foster* (2) and (3).

[114] 'The Latin-Old English glossaries', ed. Kindschi, p. 212.13 (= Wright, *Anglo-Saxon and Old English Vocabularies*, ed. Wülcker, I, col. 173.23).

[115] *The Vercelli Book*, ed. Krapp, p. 84 (text); *Anglo-Saxon Poetry*, transl. Bradley, p. 182 (translation).

2) 'Nobly born.'

The word is used either of Abraham or God in line 446 of the poem *Exodus*.[116]

3) A personal name.

This name may well have derived from the second rather than the first sense of *freobearn* (cf. s.v. *freobeorn* below). It is to be found in a charter of Edward the Confessor to Waltham Abbey issued in 1062.[117]

FREO-BEORN sb. (m) A personal name.

This was the name held by one of two *fre socne men* ('free sokemen') who with others controlled an estate at Eversley in Hampshire in the latter part of King Edward the Confessor's reign.[118] Literally it means 'free man', though since *beorn* is a poetic word and so has aristocratic connotations, the first element might have meant 'noble' in the minds of the parents who bestowed the name.

FREO-BORH sb. (m) 'Someone who gives a pledge, a surety.'

The Latin post-Conquest legal code called *Leges Edwardi Confessoris* preserves this word in §20 in a context that enables one to have some sense of the institution but not the precise meaning of its first element: 'sub fideiussionis stabilitate, quam Angli uocant friborgas, preter Eboracenses, qui uocant eam tyen manna tale, hoc est numerum X hominum' ('under a surety, which the English call "friborgas", except for the inhabitants of York, who call it "tyen manna tale", that is, "the number of ten men" ').[119] *Freo-* here might have had either or both of the two senses 'belonging to one who is legally free' or 'voluntary'.

FREO-BROÞOR sb. (m) 'Free-born brother.'

The only occurrence of this word is in the poem *Exodus*, line 338: 'Him on leodsceare/ frumbearnes riht freobroðor oðþah,/ ead and æðelo' ('His own brother had taken over from him the firstborn's right in the nation, his wealth and his nobility').[120]

FREO-DOHTOR sb. (f) 'Free-born, that is, legitimate daughter.'

Freo- here connotes legitimate birth, drawing as it does on the association between freedom and the law of the tribe that was the basis of that freedom. It is attested only in the anonymous homily, *De Temporibus Anticristi*: 'his fæder hine strynð be his agenre freodehter, and he bið his moder twam sibbum getæht, þæt he bið ægðer ge sunu ge broðer' ('his father begot him by his own legitimate daughter, and he is assigned to two of his mother's relationships, so that he is both son and brother').[121]

FREO-DOM sb. (m) 1) 'The state of possessing the rights and obligations, together with the social status, of a freeman as defined in the written law and decreed by custom.'

The word glosses *emancipatio* in the glossary in London, British Library, Additional

116 *The Junius Manuscript*, ed. Krapp, p. 103.
117 *Codex Diplomaticus Aevi Saxonici*, §813 (ed. Kemble, IV.157.13) (= Sawyer, *Anglo-Saxon Charters*, no. 1036).
118 *Anglo-Saxon Writs*, §85.13 (ed. & transl. Harmer, p. 351) (= Sawyer, *Anglo-Saxon Charters*, no. 1129).
119 *Die Gesetze*, ed. Liebermann, I.645 (text).
120 *The Junius Manuscript*, ed. Krapp, p. 100 (text); *Anglo-Saxon Poetry*, transl. Bradley, p. 59 (translation).
121 *Wulfstan*, §42 (ed. Napier, p. 193.5–7) (text); see Toller, *Supplement*, p. 425, col. 1, s.v. *ge-tæcan* IVa, for part of the translation.

MS. 32246, fo 21r,[122] and *libertas* in the Old English *Bede* (*libertatem receperunt – freodom onfengon*).[123] For a full discussion of the idea of 'freedom' see above, pp. 156–62.

2) 'Freedom (from a spiritual state).'

This sense can be most explicitly illustrated from a passage in the *Blickling Homilies*: 'Nis hit þæt an þæt him anum þæm apostolum wære geofu seald, ac eac ðonne eallum manna cynne forgifnes wæs seald ealra synna, & eac se freodom þæs unaræfnedlican þeowdomes, þæt is ðæs deofollican onwaldes eallum welwyrcendum.' ('Not alone to the apostles was this gift bestowed, but also, indeed, to all mankind was given forgiveness of all sins, and also to all doers of good, freedom from intolerable slavery, that is, from the devil's power.')[124]

3) 'Freedom of choice (with respect to a spiritual condition).'

Freodom has this meaning in a discussion of free will appearing in the Old English translation of the *Elucidarium* of Honorius of Autun: 'Hwæt is agen cyre? Hwæt is frigdom to geceosan god oððe yfel? Þone frigdom hæfde mann on neorxenewange, ac nu is se fridom geðeowtod, for se mann ne cann nan god, bute God þurh his geofe him tæce.' ('What is free will? What is freedom to choose good or evil? That freedom Man had in Paradise, but now that freedom is enslaved, for Man does not know good unless God through His grace teaches him.')[125]

4) 'Freedom from dues payable to an overlord.'

The word occurs in several charters in this sense. A will of A.D. 845 x 853 grants 'min ærfe lond . . . ðe ic et Aeðeluulfe cyninge begæt 7 gebohte mid fullum friodome on æce ærfe' ('my heritable land which I obtained and bought from King Æthelwulf with full freedom as a perpetual inheritance').[126] Another will of A.D. 873 similarly states: 'Leafa gebohte æt Æðere . . . ðis gewrit 7 ðis land mið ðy friadome ðe hit hær gefriad wæs to Cristes cirican on ec erfe.' ('Leofu bought from Æthhere . . . this document and this land with the freedom with which it here was freed for Christ's church as a perpetual inheritance.')[127] This freedom did not mean that the dues were waived for the inhabitants of an estate; rather, they were now payable to the new overlord who had acquired the superiority over the property by means of the charter. This is implied, for instance, in the text known as the *History of the Kentish Royal Saints*, which states: '7 heo ða æt him gebohte his dæl ðæs eardes to freodome into ðam mynstre' ('and she then bought from him his share of the district and freed it and granted it to the monastery').[128]

5) 'Freedom to exercise rights without being subject to the control of another.'

This sense is seen in a spurious writ granting property to Ramsey Abbey, where the

---

122 'The Latin-Old English glossaries', ed. Kindschi, p. 245.5 (= Wright, *Anglo-Saxon and Old English Vocabularies*, ed. Wülcker, I, col. 188.25).

123 *The Old English Version of Bede's Ecclesiastical History*, III.18 and IV.27 (ed. & transl. Miller, I.2.240.11 and I.2.358.16) (text and translation) (= *Bede's Ecclesiastical History*, III.24 and IV.26 [edd. & transl. Colgrave & Mynors, pp. 294 and 428]).

124 *The Blickling Homilies*, §12 (ed. & transl. Morris, p. 137.10–14) (text); *ibid.*, p. 136 (translation, emended).

125 *Early English Homilies*, §45 (ed. Warner, p. 141.14–17) (text).

126 *Anglo-Saxon Charters*, §6 (ed. & transl. Robertson, p. 10.2–3) (text); *ibid.*, p. 11 (translation) (= Sawyer, *Anglo-Saxon Charters*, no. 1510).

127 *Cartularium Saxonicum*, §536 (ed. Birch, II.154.16–18) (= Sawyer, *Anglo-Saxon Charters*, no. 344).

128 'Die altenglischen Beigaben des Lambeth-Psalters', II b).25–6 (ed. Förster, 335). The manuscript was copied in the latter half of the eleventh century: Ker, *Catalogue*, §281 (p. 343).

context indicates that it refers to rights.[129] (This sense is probably implicit also in the citations given under sense 1) above.) The writ was allegedly issued by Edward the Confessor but was probably compiled in the early Norman period.[130] The document reads: '7 in ælcer scire þær Scs Benedictus hafð land inne his saca 7 his socne, tol 7 team 7 infangenþeof, wiðinne burhe 7 wiðuten, 7 on ælce styde be lande 7 be strande, be wude 7 be felde, swa hwylc man swa þa socne ahe Scs Benedictus habbe his freodom on eallen þingen swa wel 7 swa freolice swa ic hit me seolf betst ahe ahwær in Engelande.' ('And in every shire where St. Benedict has land, his sake and his soke, toll and team and infangentheof, within borough and without, and in every place, by land and by strand, in woodland and in open country, whosoever may own the soke, St. Benedict is to have his freedom in all things as well and as freely as I myself have it to the fullest extent anywhere in England.')

This sense seems also to apply in the fairly common phrase *full freodom* ('full freedom'). The phrase often occurs in conjunction with a list of rights, implying that it means 'the right to enjoy the customary privileges belonging to an estate'.

6) 'A charter granting rights over property.'

The transition from sense 5) to sense 6) is illustrated in a charter of King Edgar which uses the word in the former sense but relates it to the Latin *priuilegium*.[131] *Priuilegium* is frequently used of a charter rather than in the abstract sense of 'right'. The document states: '7 beo þis priuilegium, þ is sindorlice wyrðmynt oððe agen freodom into þære stowe, mid eallum þisum ðingum, Godes geoffrod. . . .' ('And this privilege, that is this special honour or peculiar freedom belonging to the foundation, along with all these things, shall be offered to God.'). The use of *freodom* in this sense occurs in several documents, for example, in an endorsement of *ca* 822 to a Worcester land-charter: 'Þa hio him to spræcon se biscop 7 his weotan ymb þæt lond þæt he his him geuþe, þæt hio maehten þone freodom begeotan.' ('Then they, the bishop and his *witan*, spoke to him about the land, that he should grant it to them, that they might obtain the freedom.')[132] The semantic development thus parallels *freols* (q.v.).

FREO-DRYHTEN sb. (m) 'Noble lord.'

This compound appears only in poetic sources. The concept of aristocratic birth is uppermost in the first element, *freo-*. Beowulf uses it of Hrothgar: 'Onfoh þissum fulle, freodrihten min,/ sinces brytta' ('Accept this cup, my noble lord, the giver of treasure')[133] and in *Christ and Satan* it is used in apposition to *þeoden ure* (referring to God) and *ealdor*, 'prince'.[134]

(GE)-FREOGAN vb   1) 'To free from a condition of legal bondage.'

The Old English *Orosius* mentions *mon þa þeowas freode* ('the slaves were freed'), which shows the legal class that the word applied to,[135] and the same text indicates the

---

129 *Anglo-Saxon Writs*, §61.19–24 (ed. & transl. Harmer, p. 259) (text); *ibid.*, p. 261 (translation) (= Sawyer, *Anglo-Saxon Charters*, no. 1109).

130 On the authenticity of the document, see *Anglo-Saxon Writs*, ed. & transl. Harmer, p. 474 and cf. p. 477, note to line 24.

131 *Anglo-Saxon Charters*, §48 (ed. & transl. Robertson, pp. 100.31–2 and 102.1) (text); *ibid.*, pp. 101 and 103 (translation) (= Sawyer, *Anglo-Saxon Charters*, no. 779).

132 *Cartularium Saxonicum*, §308 (ed. Birch, I.429.3–5) (text) (= Sawyer, *Anglo-Saxon Charters*, no. 1432).

133 *Beowulf*, lines 1169–70, in *Beowulf and Judith*, ed. Dobbie, p.37 (text); *Anglo-Saxon Poetry*, transl. Bradley, p. 442 (translation).

134 *Christ and Satan*, lines 545–6 and 565–6, in *The Junius Manuscript*, ed. Krapp, p. 153.

135 *The Old English Orosius*, IV.3 (ed. Bately, p. 87.19–20) (text).

legal status from which they were released: '7 ealle þa men þe hie on ðeowdome hæfdon hie gefreodon. . . . Ond sume, þa þe heora <hlafordas> freogean noldon, . . . þa consulas . . . freodon.' ('And all those men whom they held in servitude they freed. . . . And some of them whom their <lords> were unwilling to free, . . . the consul . . . freed.')[136] *Manumission*, §8.3 reveals the new status acquired: 'Ælfric Scot 7 Ægelric Scot synd gefreod . . . to ecan freote.' ('Ælfric Scot and Æthelric Scot are freed . . . to <have> everlasting freedom.') See further above, pp. 158–9.

2) 'To free land from dues (whether taxes or services).'

The form without the prefix occurs in the record of two land grants to Peterborough inserted in the *Peterborough Chronicle*, s.aa. 777 and 963.[137] The first records the proceedings of a land grant: 'He [*sc*. Ealdorman Brordan] geornde at se kyning [*sc*. Offa] þ he scolde for his luuen freon his ane mynstre Wocingas het forþi ðet he hit wolde giuen into Medeshamstede 7 Sēe Peter 7 þone abbote þe þa was . . . 7 seo kyning freode þa þ mynstre Wocingas wið cining 7 wið biscop 7 wið eorl 7 wið ealle men swa þ nan man ne hafde þær nan onsting buton S. Peter 7 þone aƀ.' ('He begged the king that he should free for the love of him his own church called Woking because he wished to give it to Peterborough and St Peter and him who was then abbot. . . . And the king then freed that church at Woking from the king and bishop and earl and every man so that no one had jurisdiction except St Peter and the abbot.') The second summarises a charter of King Wulfhere and his brother concerning Peterborough which told 'hu hi hit freodon wið king, 7 wið ƀ, 7 wið ealle weoruld þeudom' ('how they freed it from the king and the bishop and all secular service').

The prefixed form also appears in the *Parker Chronicle*, s.a. 885: '7 þy ilcan geare forþferde se goda papa Marinus, se gefreode Ongelcynnes scole be Ælfredes bene West Seaxna cyninges.' ('That same year died the good pope, Marinus, who had freed from taxation the English quarter at the request of Alfred, king <of the West Saxons>.')[138] The charters, too, use the word (for citations see s.vv. *freodom, þeodom*).

Implied with this grant of freedom from dues is the acquisition by the recipient of the superiority over the property with its concomitant return; it does not indicate that the customary dues of those living on the land were waived.

* GE-FREOGEND sb. (m) 'Liberator, Deliverer, Redeemer.'

In the ninth-century Vespasian Psalter the form *gefrigend* glosses *liberator*, used in a metaphorical sense, at Psalms 17:2(3), 17:46(48), and 39:21; *gefrigen* appears in the same text at Psalm 143:2.[139] A variant form, *gefreogynd*, is also to be found at Psalm 17:48 in the mid-eleventh-century Cambridge Psalter (Cambridge, University Library, MS. Ff.1.23 [1156]).[140]

FREOH sb. (n) 'A *liber homo*.'

A seemingly unique usage of the substantive occurs in a writ of A.D. 1041 x 1064 from the north-west of England: 'Gospatrik greot ealle mine wassenas 7 hyylkun man freo 7 ðrenge.' ('Gospatric sends friendly greetings to all my *wassenas* and to every

---

[136] *Ibid*., IV.9 (p. 102.2–7) (text).

[137] *Two of the Saxon Chronicles Parallel*, ed. Plummer, I.53.3–10 and 116.5–6 (text); *English Historical Documents c.500–1042*, §1 (transl. Whitelock, p. 198–9) (translation).

[138] *Two of the Saxon Chronicles Parallel*, ed. Plummer, I.80.4–6.

[139] *The Vespasian Psalter*, ed. Kuhn, pp. 12, 15, 38, and 141 respectively.

[140] *Der Cambridger Psalter*, ed. Wildhagen, p. 37.10.

man, free man and dreng.')[141] Harmer has plausibly argued that this refers to the class of men referred to as *liberi homines* in Domesday Book.[142]

FREOH adj.   1) 'Possessing the rights and obligations, together with the social status, of a freeman as defined in the written law and decreed by social custom.'

This sense is frequently attested, especially in the laws. An example that brings out its legal connotations is *Rectitudines singularum personarum*, §3.4: 'Sylle his heorðpænig on halgan ðunresdæg, ealswa ælcan frigean men gebyreð.' ('Let him give his hearth-penny on Ascension Day even as each freeman ought to do.')[143]

2) 'Not subject to the obligations imposed by the customs of an estate.'

Manumission, §4.1, which dates from 955 x 959, illustrates this usage: 'Eadwi cing het gefreon Abunet Ælfnoð . . . an Exanceastre, . . . fryo 7 færewyrþe.' ('King Eadwig ordered Ælfnoth . . . at Exeter to free Abunet <to be> free and permitted to travel.') For the changing meanings of this word see above, pp. 156–62.

3) 'Released from dues owing to an external authority.' (Used of land.)

That this word had special reference to taxes and obligations involving service is attested by its use in several charters. Mention of taxation, for instance, appears in a charter of A.D. 990 concerning land in Worcestershire: '7 hit seo þonne þæm agen æghwæs to brucenne to freon twegra manna dæg butan þæm circsceatte' ('and it shall be their own to enjoy freely in every respect for two lives except for church dues').[144] Other services are referred to in a charter of A.D. 967 leasing land in Gloucestershire: 'Si hyt ælces þinges freoh buton ferdfore 7 walgeweorce 7 brycgeweorce' ('Let it be free from everything except military service and construction of walls and bridges')[145] and a second lease of land in the same county dating from 990: 'hio hit hæbben to frion ælces þinges butan wealgeworce 7 brygcgeweorce 7 ferdsocne' ('they shall hold it free from every obligation except the construction of walls and bridges and military service').[146]

A number of compound adjectives are derived from *freoh* used in this sense: *scotfreo*, *gafol-freo*, *toll-freo*, and *geld-freo*. The first two appear together in the phrase *scotfreo 7 gafolfreo* in several writs.[147] Harmer considered that the two taken together referred to all rents and taxes.[148] *Toll-freo*, 'free from toll', is extant in a single spurious writ of post-Conquest fabrication[149] and *geld-freo*, 'exempt from the payment of geld', occurs only in Gospatric's eleventh-century writ from the north-west of England.[150]

141 *Anglo-Saxon Writs*, §121 (ed. & transl. Harmer, p. 423.1) (text); *ibid.*, p. 424 (translation) (= Sawyer, *Anglo-Saxon Charters*, no. 1243).
142 *Anglo-Saxon Writs*, ed. & transl. Harmer, p. 532.
143 *Die Gesetze*, ed. Liebermann, I.446 (text); *English Historical Documents 1042–1189*, §172 (transl. Douglas & Greenaway, p. 876) (translation).
144 *Anglo-Saxon Charters*, §64 (ed. & transl. Robertson, p. 132.11–13) (text); *ibid.*, p. 133 (translation) (= Sawyer, *Anglo-Saxon Charters*, no. 1363).
145 *Cartularium Saxonicum*, §1203 (ed. Birch, III.481.25–6) (text) (= Sawyer, *Anglo-Saxon Charters*, no. 1313).
146 *Anglo-Saxon Charters*, §65 (ed. & transl. Robertson, p. 134.12–13) (text); *ibid.*, p. 135 (translation) (= Sawyer, *Anglo-Saxon Charters*, no. 1362).
147 *Anglo-Saxon Writs*, §§76.7, 86.4, 87.3, 93.10, 104.4, and cf. §15.4 (ed. & transl. Harmer, pp. 343, 353, 353, 358, 369, and cf. p. 158) (= Sawyer, *Anglo-Saxon Charters*, nos 1120, 1130, 1131, 1137, 1148, and cf. no. 1075).
148 *Anglo-Saxon Writs*, ed. & transl. Harmer, p. 496, note to line 7.
149 *Ibid.*, §61.26 (p. 259) (= Sawyer, *Anglo-Saxon Charters*, no. 1109). On the use of the term *toll-freo* see *Anglo-Saxon Writs*, ed. & transl. Harmer, p. 252.
150 *Ibid.*, §121.14 (p. 424) (= Sawyer, *Anglo-Saxon Charters*, no. 1243). On toll see *Anglo-Saxon Writs*, ed. & transl. Harmer, p. 478, and on geld, *ibid.*, pp. 513–14.

FREO-LÆTA sb. (m) 'A freedman.'

Various forms of *libertus*, 'a freedman' are glossed by this word.[151] See further s.v. *læt* below.

FREOLIC adj.   1) 'Possessing the (positive) characteristics of a free person.'

'Free', which one might assume was the root sense of the adjective, is not attested in any of the extant sources. Instead, in poetic contexts it acquired a sense derived from what must have been deemed to have been the characteristics of a free person. The precise sense is impossible to determine: Doane has given its meaning as 'noble, beautiful, good', based on its attestations in *Genesis A*,[152] whereas Klaeber glossed it as 'noble, excellent' in his edition of *Beowulf*.[153]

2) 'Voluntary.'

Since one of the attributes of a free person was freedom of action, the development of the sense 'voluntary' was a natural one. It can been seen in the gloss *mid frium cyre uel freolicum* to the lemma *libero arbitrio iudicio* in one of the Aldhelm glossaries[154] and the gloss *freolice* to the word *liberae*, which appears in the phrase *mortis deinde gloria liberae* ('then the glory of her dying by her own will') in the version of Prudentius's *Peristephanon*, XIV.9, in Boulogne-sur-Mer, Bibliothèque municipale, MS. 189.[155]

FREOLICE adv.   1) 'Freely, in a state of freedom.'

The primary sense of the root of this word is preserved in a passage in the Old English *Boethius*: 'Ac sio sawl færð swiðe friolice to hefonum, siððan hio ontiged bið, 7 for þæm carcerne þæs lichoman onlesed bið.' ('For the soul passeth freely to heaven once she is set free and released from the prison of this body.')[156]

2) 'Freely, voluntarily.'

In *Christ III*, line 1290, appears the phrase *hi ær freolice fremedon unryht* ('they had freely done wrong before').[157] Another example is 'god wraca drihten god wraca freolice dyde', representing the Latin 'Deus ultionem dominus; deus ultionem libere egit' of Psalm 93:1 in the Arundel Psalter (London, British Library, MS. Arundel 60) of the second half of the eleventh century.[158]

3) 'Freely, not subject to restrictions or to the regulations of another.' (Used of land.)

In this sense *freolice* appears in the positive and superlative form in a writ of 1 August 1065 x 5 January 1066 issued by Edward the Confessor: '7 ic cyðe eou þ ic habbe

151 For example, *Libertabus – friglætan* and *Libertus – frioleta*, in *The Corpus Glossary*, L177 and L233 (ed. Lindsay, pp. 106–7), and cf. *Libertinus – freolætan sunu*, on fo. 4r of London, British Library, Additional MS. 32246, in 'The Latin-Old English glossaries', ed. Kindschi, p. 56.2 (= Wright, *Anglo-Saxon and Old English Vocabularies*, ed. Wülcker, I, col. 111.22). *Uernaculus – frioleta*, in *The Corpus Glossary*, U120 (ed. Lindsay, p. 183), must be an error.
152 *Genesis A*, ed. Doane, p. 352, s.v. *fréo-líc*.
153 *Beowulf and the Fight at Finnsburg*, ed. Klaeber, p. 334, s.v. *frēo-līc*.
154 *The Old English Glosses of MS. Brussels, Royal Library, 1650*, §1325 (ed. Goossens, p. 233).
155 *The Old English Prudentius Glosses*, §921 (ed. Meritt, p. 97); *Prudentius*, ed. & transl. Thomson, II.338 (text) and II.339 (translation).
156 *King Alfred's Old English Version of Boethius De Consolatione Philosophiae*, XVIII.4 (ed. Sedgefield, p. 45.26–8) (text); *King Alfred's Version of the Consolation of Boethius*, transl. Sedgefield, p. 47 (translation).
157 *The Exeter Book*, edd. Krapp & Dobbie, p. 39 (text); *Anglo-Saxon Poetry*, transl. Bradley, p. 239 (translation).
158 *Der altenglische Arundel-Psalter*, ed. Oess, p. 157.

geunnen Baldwine abbe onne menetere wið inne Seint Eadmundes byrig al swa freolice on ealle þing to habben al swa me mine on hande stonden ower on enig minre burge alre freolukeost.' ('And I inform you that I have granted to Abbot Baldwin a [*or* one] moneyer within St. Edmund's Bury, to have with the same freedom from restriction as I have my own anywhere in any of my boroughs where I have them more freely than anywhere else.')[159] Unlike most of the other words considered here, this term can refer to the property of an office rather than to an immoveable. For instance, in what claims to be a writ of King Edward there is reference to goods cast up on the seashore: 'ic habbe gegeofen Criste 7 Sc̄e Marie 7 Sc̄e Benedicte . . . þa sæupwarp on callan þingen æt Bramcæstre 7 æt Ringstyde swa wel 7 swa freolice swa ic hit me seolf betst habbe bi ða særime ahwær in Engelande.' ('I have given . . . to Christ and St. Mary and St. Benedict . . . what is cast up by the sea in all things at Brancaster and at Ringstead, as well and as freely as I myself have it to the fullest extent by the seacoast anywhere in England.')[160] The use of the superlative appears in an earlier charter, Æthelred's famous renewal of the privilege granted to St Frideswide, Oxford, on 7 December 1004 after the congregation's documents had been burned during the St Brice's Day massacre of the Danes: 'alle that fredome that any fre mynstre frelubest' ('all the liberty that any free monastery has most freely').[161]

FREOLS sb. (m)   1) 'Freedom, that is, the legal condition of personal freedom from slavery.'

This sense is attested in the Laws of Wihtred, §8, which outlines the grant of *manumissio in ecclesia*, the freedom so granted being described as *freols* (see s.v. *freolsgefa* for the citation).[162]

The only other attestation is in a mid-eleventh-century manumission-document from Durham, *Manumission*, §6.1: <*Geatfleda*> *geaf freols* . . . ('<Eadflæd> gave freedom . . .').

2) 'Freedom from dues payable to an overlord and/or freedom to exercise rights without being subject to the control of another.'

3) 'A charter granting the freedom described in 2).'

As with *freodom* (q.v.), with which the word seems to have been synonynous and which shared a parallel semantic development, it is not easy to distinguish *freols* in the negative sense of a release from an obligation from the positive sense of a right to a privilege.[163]

The two senses are used together in a writ issued in 1017 x 1020 by Cnut: '7 ic cyðe eow þ se arceb spæc to me ymbe Cristes cyrcean freols, þ heo hæfð nu læsse munde þonne hio hwilan ær hæfde. Þa lyfde ic him þ he moste niwne freols settan on minan

159 *Anglo-Saxon Writs*, §25.2–5 (ed. Harmer, p. 165) (text); *ibid.*, p. 166 (translation) (= Sawyer, *Anglo-Saxon Charters*, no. 1085).

160 *Anglo-Saxon Writs*, §61.4–9 (ed. & transl. Harmer, p. 259) (text); *ibid.*, p. 261 (translation) (= Sawyer, *Anglo-Saxon Charters*, no. 1109). This may, however, be a post-Conquest usage, as Harmer (*Anglo-Saxon Writs*, p. 252) considered the document to be an Anglo-Norman compilation.

161 *Codex Diplomaticus Aevi Saxonici*, §709 (ed. Kemble, III. 329.23–4) (text); *English Historical Documents c.500–1042*, §127 (transl. Whitelock, p. 592) (translation) (= Sawyer, *Anglo-Saxon Charters*, no. 909).

162 *Die Gesetze*, ed. Liebermann, I.13 (text); *The Laws*, ed. & transl. Attenborough, p. 27 (translation).

163 For a discussion of the senses in which the word is used see *Anglo-Saxon Writs*, ed. & transl. Harmer, pp. 447–8, and for examples of *freols* in its second sense see also *Anglo-Saxon Charters*, ed. & transl. Robertson, p. 548, Index rerum, s.v. *Freols*.

naman. Þa cwæð hc to me þ he freolsas genoge hæfde gyf hi aht forstodan. Þa nam ic me sylf þa freolsas 7 gelede hi uppan Cristes agen weofod . . . to ðan ylcan foreweardan þe hit Æþelbyrht cing gefreode 7 ealle mine foregencgan þ næfre nan man ne sy swa dyrsti . . . þ ænig þara þinga gelytlie þe on ðam freolse stænt.' ('And I inform you that the archbishop spoke to me about the freedom of Christ Church – that it now has less *mund* than it once had. Then I gave him permission to draw up a new charter of freedom in my name. Then he told me that he had charters of freedom in plenty if only they were good for anything. Then I myself took the charters of freedom and laid them on Christ's own altar . . . in the same terms as King Æthelberht freed it and all my predecessors: that no man . . . shall ever be so presumptuous as to diminish any of the things that stand in that charter of freedom.')[164]

4) 'A feast day.'

Whereas the Latin *dies festiualis* drew on the concept of feasting, the Old English word employed that of freedom, presumably freedom from labour. *Freols* in this sense was very productive of compounds in Old English.[165]

FREOLS adj.   1) 'Free, that is, personally free from slavery.'

In *Manumission*, §3.33, a Bodmin document of *ca* 1075, Putrael 'dide hine sylfne 7 his ofspreng æfre freols 7 saccles' ('made himself and his offspring forever free and without accusation') by means of a settlement that prevented his being made a *nyd-þeowetling*. The position of *nydþeowas* is also contrasted with *þa ðe syndon freolse* ('those who are free') in *Episcopus*, §13.[166]

2) 'Released from the obligation to render dues and/or be subject to the jurisdiction of others.' (Used of land.)

An example occurs in a charter of A.D. 1046 x 1053 granting land at Hill near Fladbury in Worcestershire, which states: '7 sy þiss land ælces þinges freols' ('and this land shall be free of everything').[167]

3) 'Having the right of superiority over land.'

Sense 2) is implicit in this, but in a Beverley writ issued by Edward the Confessor it connotes the wider sense of possession as well: '7 ic wille þ þ mynster 7 seo are þe þider innto hirð, þ hit beo swa freols swa ænig oþer mynster is æt eallan þingan.' ('And my will is that the minster and the property belonging thereto shall be as free as any other minster is in all things.')[168] This citation illustrates that the word could be applied not merely to the land itself but also to the whole estate with all its appurtenances.

* FREOLS-BOC sb. (f) 'A land charter granting superiority over land, with freedom from the jurisdiction of others.'

That *freolsboc* refers to a grant of land and not merely to an exemption from dues is indicated by a charter of A.D. 974: 'Þis his seo freolsboc to Cheolcan and ealra ðare landa ðe into ðæ mynechina life æt Wiltune forgifene synt.' ('This is the charter for

---

[164] *Anglo-Saxon Writs*, §26.3–12 (ed. & transl. Harmer, pp. 181–2) (text); *ibid.*, p. 182 (translation) (= Sawyer, *Anglo-Saxon Charters*, no. 985).

[165] *Freols-æfen, freols-bryce, freols-dæg, freols-gear, freols-niht, freols-stow, freols-tid, freol-sung, gal-freolsas, heah-freols, heahfreols-dæg,* and *heahfreols-tid.*

[166] *Die Gesetze,* ed. Liebermann, I.479.

[167] *Anglo-Saxon Charters*, §112 (ed. & transl. Robertson, p. 210.9–10) (text; personal translation) (= Sawyer, *Anglo-Saxon Charters*, no. 1406). The dating is Sawyer's; Robertson (*Anglo-Saxon Charters*, p. 460) ascribes it more narrowly to 1051 x 1052.

[168] *Anglo-Saxon Writs*, §7.4–6 (ed. & transl. Harmer, p. 137) (text); *loc. cit.* (translation) (= Sawyer, *Anglo-Saxon Charters*, no. 1067).

Chalke and all those lands which have been given to the monastic community at Wilton.')[169] This was not *inland* but land that passed out of the control of the king, as is proved by a will of A.D. 1002 x 1004: 'Þis is seo freolsboc to þam mynstre æt Byrtune þe Æþelred cyning <æf>re ecelice gefreode.' ('This is the charter of freedom to the monastery at Burton which King Ethelred freed eternally.')[170]

* FREOLS-DOM sb. (m) 'Immunity.' (Used of taxation or rent.)

This word occurs in the Laws of Wihtred, §1, which declares: *Cirice an freolsdome gafola* ('The Church shall enjoy immunity from taxation'),[171] and in a charter of King Edmund dating from 943: 'þa hagan þe to þam seofan hydum æt Ticceststede gebyriað to þon ilcan freolsdome þe he þæt land hæfð' ('the messuage which belong to the seven hides at Tisted, [Hampshire], with the same immunity that he possesses over that land').[172]

* FREOLSEND sb. (m) 'Redeemer.'

Freolsend appears only in the Psalter of Eadwine of Canterbury in the forms *friolsiend* at Psalm 69:6 and four times as *friolsend* at Psalm 17:3 and 48 and Psalms 77:35 and 143:2, in all instances as a gloss to *liberator. Alysend* is given as an alternative gloss in Psalms 17:3 and 69:6.[173]

FREOLS-GEFA sb. (m) 'A manumittor.'

The only time this word appears in the sources is in the Laws of Wihtred, §8: 'Gif man his mæn an wiofode freols gefe, se sie folcfry; freolsgefa age his erfe ænde wergeld 7 munde þara hina, sie ofer mearce ðær he wille.' ('If anyone grants one of his men freedom on the altar, his freedom shall be publicly recognised; <but> the emancipator shall have his heritage and his wergeld, and the guardianship of his household, wherever he [the freed man] may be, <even if it be> beyond the border.')[174]

As any word for 'manumittor' is rare in Old English one cannot assume from this single early attestation that the word died out within the Anglo-Saxon period. As suggested below (s.v. *healf-freoh*) the continued existence of this word might account for the failure of Old Norse *frjálsgjafi* to be adopted into Old English.

* (GE)-FREOLSIAN vb   1) 'To set free, liberate.' (From a spiritual state.)

This verb is used several times by the author of the Blickling Homilies, as in the following extract, where the underlying notion of imprisonment with its bonds, punishment, and darkness as a consequence of a judgment (*dom*, line 15) supply the imagery: 'þe Drihten of d<eaþe> aras mancynne to bysene æfter his <þro>wunga, & æfter þæm bendum his deaþes, & æfter þæm clammum helle þeostra; & þæt wite & þæt ece wræc asette on þone aldor deofla, & mancyn freolsode; swa se witga Dauid be þisse tide witgade, & þus cwæþ: "Ure Drihten us gefreolsode." ' ('the Lord arose from the dead after his passion, after the bonds of his death, and after the bonds of hell's darkness; and

169 *Cartularium Saxonicum*, §1304 (ed. Birch, III.625.23–4) (= Sawyer, *Anglo-Saxon Charters*, no. 799).
170 *Anglo-Saxon Wills*, §17 (ed. & transl. Whitelock, p. 50.25–6) (text); *ibid.*, p. 51 (translation) (= Sawyer, *Anglo-Saxon Charters*, no. 1536).
171 *Die Gesetze*, ed. Liebermann, I.12 (text); *The Laws*, ed. & transl. Attenborough, p. 25 (translation).
172 *Cartularium Saxonicum*, §786 (ed. Birch, II.529.36–530.1–2) (= Sawyer, *Anglo-Saxon Charters*, no. 488).
173 *Eadwine's Canterbury Psalter*, ed. Harsley, II.119, and II.22, 27, 138, and 236.
174 *Die Gesetze*, ed. Liebermann, I.13 (text); *The Laws*, ed. & transl. Attenborough, p. 27 (translation).

he laid upon the prince of devils eternal torment and vengeance, and delivered mankind, as the prophet David prophesied of this period, thus saying, "Our Lord delivered us." ')[175]

2) 'To consecrate.' (Used of property.)

A single gloss *gefreolsod* to the lemma *consecratur* among the glosses to Aldhelm's works copied at Abingdon in a mid-eleventh century manuscript, now Oxford, Bodleian Library, Digby MS. 146 (*S.C.* 1747),[176] and the form *ge-edfreolsian* (q.v.) both point to a sense of this word not otherwise recorded. The sense of 'to consecrate', referring to property dedicated to the Church, suggests that this meaning developed by association of ideas from an earlier sense 'to free from all obligations to render the secular dues formerly associated with a property'.

* **FREOLSLICE** adv.   1) 'Freely, without restraint.'

Freolslice occurs in this sense in a homily of Ælfric[177] and several times in the Old English *Bede*.[178]

2) 'Freely, not subject to the payment of dues to an overlord.' (Used of land.)

The adverb is used in this sense only in a writ of A.D. 1053 x 1058 of Edward the Confessor: '7 ic ciþe eow þ Urk min huskarl habbe his strand eall forn egen hys age land ouer eall wel 7 freo<l>slic<e>.' ('And I inform you that Urk my housecarl is to have his shore, all that is over against his own land, everywhere completely and freely.')[179]

FREO-MÆG sb. (m) 'A kinsman.'

Genesis A preserves the only examples of this word, using it on one occasion to describe Cain's brother, Abel, and on another occasion to describe Jared, son of Mahalaleel: 'Se eorl wæs æðele, æfæst hæleð,/ and se frumgar his freomagum leof.' ('That warrior was noble, a law-abiding man and that leader <was> dear to his kinsmen.').[180] Rare though it be, the word takes us to the heart of early Germanic society where kinship and freedom were inextricably related. A free person was, in essence, one who possessed kindred. Kinship is a central concept in the early laws, being the basis for the regulation of feud. Slaves were excluded from the protection of these early laws, unlike free men, and so were *ipso facto* regarded as kinless persons.

FREO-MAN sb. (m) 'A man possessing a free status in law.'

Although in most instances the form *freo man* can be interpreted as representing an adjective followed by a substantive,[181] there are a couple of ambiguous instances where

---

[175] *The Blickling Homilies*, §7 (ed. & transl. Morris, p. 83.18–23) (text); *ibid.*, p. 82 (translation).
[176] *Old English Glosses*, §1.1493 (ed. Napier, p. 40); on the date and provenance see Ker, *Catalogue*, §390 (iii) (pp. 382–3).
[177] *Feria VI in Prima Ebdomada Quadragesimæ*, in *Homilies of Ælfric*, §2.178 (ed. Pope, I.238).
[178] *The Old English Version of Bede's Ecclesiastical History*, III.19 and V.12 (ed. & transl. Miller, I.2.212.2 and I.2.434.28) (text); *ibid.*, I.2.213.1 and I.2.435.26 (translation) (= *Bede's Ecclesiastical History*, III.19 and V.12 [edd. & transl. Colgrave & Mynors, pp. 270 and 496]).
[179] *Anglo-Saxon Writs*, §1.2–4 (ed. & transl. Harmer, p. 120) (text); *ibid.*, p. 121 (translation) (= Sawyer, *Anglo-Saxon Charters*, no. 1063).
[180] *Genesis*, lines 983 and 1183 (cf. Genesis 5:16–18) and also line 1039, in *The Junius Manuscript*, ed. Krapp, pp. 32, 38, and 34.
[181] For instance, 'Gif friman wið fries mannes wif geligeþ, his wergelde abicge' ('If <one> freeman lies with the wife of <another> freeman, he shall pay <the husband> his <or her> wergeld'), in Æthelberht, §31 (*Die Gesetze*, ed. Liebermann, I.5 [text]; *The Laws*, ed. & transl. Attenborough, p. 9 [translation]); the inflected form *fries mannes* suggests that *friman* should be read as two words.

it seems to be a true compound, as in the *Textus Roffensis* version of Alfred, §43: 'Eallum freomonnum ðas dagas syn forgifene' ('The following days shall be granted <as holidays> to all free men'); the Cambridge, Corpus Christi College, MS. 173 version has *frioum mannum*.[182] The existence of this compound in Old English must remain open to question unless a clear example in an oblique case can be found.

FREO-NAMA sb. (m)   1) 'Noble name.'

The link between the concept of freedom and aristocratic birth is clearly illustrated in the pious asseveration used in a record: 'Ures Drihtnes Hælendes Cristes freonama a on ecnyssa sy gewurþod' ('May the noble name of our Lord the Saviour Christ be honoured for ever to all eternity').[183]

2) A *cognomen.*

Names are a valuable indicator of status in many societies. Owners of Black slaves in the Americas did not call them by their African names (thereby denying them their past and, symbolically, their personhood), and if slaves acquired surnames, they were frequently those of their erstwhile owners, who thus symbolically perpetuated their ownership. The existence of the word *freonama* suggests that, although Anglo-Saxon slaves may have retained their native names (as the Celtic names in the Bodmin manumission-documents seem to indicate), it was only those of free birth who could acquire a secondary proper name (as opposed to a byname), a matter of some significance in a society where the same name might be held by several people within a single community. The word could be used both of native names (as in Oeric Æsc)[184] and of a Latin name (as in 'Ædde . . ., þæs freonama wæs Steffanus).[185]

FREOND sb. (m). 'A kinsman, friend.'

A word with cognates in other Germanic languages, such as *vriend* in Dutch and *freund* in German, it derives from a Primitive Germanic form **fri-jond*, whose root element was the word 'free'. This illustrates how deeply imbedded in the Germanic world was the concept that the only socially recognised relationships (such as kinship and friendship, themselves closely intertwined concepts)[186] were ones that existed between free persons. Something of its root sense may survive in Ælfric's *Life of Saint Eugenia* in the declaration, 'Ne hate ic eow na þeowan, ac ge synd mine freond.' (I call you not slaves, but you are my friends.')[187]

* FREONESS sb. (f) 'Immunity, freedom of land from dues.'

This is used in a misdated act of the Council of Clovesho of 803 that appears as a marginal note in the London, British Library, MS. Cotton Domitian viii version of the

---

[182] *Die Gesetze*, ed. Liebermann, I.78 (text); *The Laws*, ed. Attenborough, p. 85 (translation). Hough, 'Freo man', 642, has pointed out that the *Textus Roffensis* reading is far from certain and has suggested that the apparent compound form to be found in *Genesis A*, line 2176, presents a textual crux in a metrically defective line. She has thus concluded that *freoman* did not exist as a compound in Old English.

[183] *Anglo-Saxon Charters*, §104 (ed. & transl. Robertson, p. 194.3–4) (text); *ibid.*, p. 195 (translation).

[184] *The Old English Version of Bede's Ecclesiastical History*, II.5 (ed. & transl. Miller, I.1.110.18) (text); *ibid.*, I.1.111.19 (translation) (= *Bede's Ecclesiastical History*, II.5 [edd. & transl. Colgrave & Mynors, p. 150.18–19]).

[185] *The Old English Version of Bede's Ecclesiastical History*, IV.2 (ed. & transl. Miller, I.2.258.28–9) (text); *ibid.*, I.2.259.29–30 (translation) (= *Bede's Ecclesiastical History*, IV.2 [edd. & transl. Colgrave & Mynors, p. 334.12–13]).

[186] For *freond* in the sense of 'kinsman' see *Leges Henrici Primi*, ed. Downer, pp. 437–9.

[187] *Ælfric's Lives of Saints*, §2.87 (ed. & transl. Skeat, I.30) (text); *ibid.*, I.31 (translation, emended).

Anglo-Saxon Chronicle under the year 796: 'Ic Aðelard ... mid anmodan ræde ealles sinoðes 7 mid ealra ðare gegaderunga ealra ðara mynstra ðam be ealdan dagan frignesse was geauen fram geleaffullan mannum ...' ('I Æthelheard ... with the unanimous counsel of all the synod and with ... all the congregation of all the monasteries to which in old days immunity was given by faithful men ...').[188] *Frigness* here represents the Latin *libertas*, as the Latin version of the text makes clear;[189] it refers to the granting of superiority over land to the monasteries, together with a release from any obligation to pay dues from it to any external authority. The word also appears several times in an alleged charter of A.D. 682, which Finberg believed dated in reality from well after the Norman conquest.[190] There is no extant evidence that *frigness* was used of personal freedom but such a sense seems entirely possible.

FREO-SCEATT sb. (m) 'A person who is the freely-disposable property of another.'

The single occurrence of this word is to be found in a twelfth-century Old English version of the *Benedictine Rule* in London, British Library, MS. Cotton Faustina A.x: 'na þa ane, þe freo synt, ac gyt ma þa, þe æhtborene synt and oþera manna freosceattas and for þam anum foroft gefreode' ('not those only that are free, but still more those that are born chattels and the freely-disposable property of other men, and for that particular purpose alone are very often freed').[191]

* FREO-SCIPE sb. (m) 'Immunity.' (With reference to taxation or service.)

The single attestation of this word is in a catalogue of rights granted in a bilingual writ of A.D. 1072 x 1078 issued by William the Conqueror: 'alle frioscipes bi strande 7 bi lande' ('all immunities on sea and land').[192]

FREOT sb. (m) 'The personal condition of being legally free.'

The suffix *-t* denotes an abstract condition. The antonym is *þeowet*, as seen in II Cnut, §68.1*b*: 'we sceolon ... todælan ... freot 7 þeowet' ('we should ... distinguish between ... the condition of being legally free and of being a slave').[193] Cf. *þeowet*.

Freot first appears in Ine, §3.2, a sub-clause which enacts that if a freeman (*frigea*) works on a Sunday except at his lord's command 'he shall lose his freedom' (*ðolie his freotes*).[194] The same formula is used in Edward & Guthrum, §7.1. The word is also to be found in II Edward, §6.[195] It occurs in several eleventh-century Bath manumissions, *Manumission*, §§8.2–4 and 8.12–14. In *Manumission*, §8.3 it is associated with *gefreod* (q.v.): 'Ælfric Scot 7 Ægelric Scot synd gefreod ... to ecan freote.' ('Ælfric Scot and Æthelric Scot are freed ... to <have> eternal freedom.') The other documents use it with the verb *geboht (ut)* (q.v.).

FREOT sb. (f) 'A grant of personal freedom.'

This sense is to be found only in a Bodmin manumission-document of the second half

---

[188] *The Anglo-Saxon Chronicle*, ed. Thorpe, I.102, n. 1 (746 F).
[189] 'Annales Domitiani Latini: an edition', ed. Magoun, 254.
[190] Finberg, *The Early Charters of Wessex*, pp. 252–4, at p. 254 (= Sawyer, *Anglo-Saxon Charters*, no. 74).
[191] *Die angelsächsischen Prosabearbeitungen des Benediktinerregel*, ed. Schröer, p. 138.21 (= Ker, *Catalogue*, §154B [pp. 194–5]). For the use of *freo* in this context see Simpson & Weiner, *The Oxford English Dictionary*, VI.160, col. 1, s.v. *free*, §28a.
[192] *Early Charters of the Cathedral Church of St. Paul, London*, §9.6 (ed. Gibbs, p. 13) (= Pelteret, *Catalogue*, §27 [pp. 64–5]).
[193] *Die Gesetze*, ed. Liebermann, I.354.
[194] *Ibid.*, I.90.
[195] *Ibid.*, I.132 and 144.

of the eleventh century (*Manumission*, §3.29): '7 gif hwa þas freot abrece, hebbe him wið Criste gemene.' ('And if anyone should destroy this grant of freedom, may he be responsible to Christ.') This is the Old English equivalent of the formula 'quicumque fregerit hanc libertatem, anathema sit' used in the Bodmin *Manumission*, §§3.18 and 3.21, and with some variations, in *Manumission*, §§3.1 and 3.30, also from Bodmin. It is most likely, therefore, that the Old English substantive has borrowed its gender here from the Latin equivalent, *libertas*.

FREOT-GIFA sb. (m) 'Giver of freedom, manumittor.'

This glosses *manumissor* in London, British Library, Additional MS. 32246, fo 21r, and in the Cleopatra Glossary, copied in the eleventh and mid-tenth centuries respectively.[196]

FREOT-GIFE sb. (f) 'Gift of freedom, manumission.'

Freotgift, an obviously erroneous form, glosses *manumissio* in London, British Library, Additional MS. 32246, fo 21r.[197]

FREOT-MANN sb. (m) 1) 'A man who has been freed from slavery, a freedman.'

In a will of A.D. 984 x 1016 one Wulfwaru declares: 'And ic wylle þ þa þe to minre are fon þ hi fi<n>don twentig freotmanna.' ('And I desire that those who succeed to my property provide twenty freedmen.')[198] Another will of perhaps *ca* 1000 concerning *Tardebigge* in Worcestershire states: 'Þis is Wulfgates gecwide æt Dunnintune; þ is þonne þ he geann . . . VI 7 twentig freotmonna for his sawle.' ('This is the will of Wulfgeat of Donington; namely, that he grants . . . twenty-six freedmen for his soul.')[199] The most natural interpretation of this latter passage is that it is a manumission clause, as Whitelock pointed out.[200] The word also appears in a synodal document, which may record a canon of the synod held in 977:[201] it urges abbots and abbesses to provide a freedman on the death of a bishop. In all three instances there is no suggestion that the manumittors' successors would retain any residual powers over the men who were to be freed.

2) 'A man who has been freed subject to the retention of certain powers over him by his former owner.'

A bequest of Wynflæd, possibly of the mid-tenth century, concerning an estate at ?Charlton Horethorne in Somerset states: 'æt Ceorlatune hio hyre an ealswa þere manna 7 þæs yrfes b<ut>an þam freotmannon.' ('At Charlton, also, she grants her the men and the stock except the freedmen.')[202] This implies that the testatrix possessed powers over the freedmen that could be bequeathed.

---

[196] 'The Latin-Old English glossaries', ed. Kindschi, p. 245.3 (= Wright, *Anglo-Saxon and Old English Vocabularies*, ed. Wülcker, I, col. 188.23), and *ibid.*, I, col. 450.23.

[197] 'The Latin-Old English glossaries', ed. Kindschi, p. 245.4 (= Wright, *Anglo-Saxon and Old English Vocabularies*, ed. Wülcker, I, col. 188.24).

[198] *Anglo-Saxon Wills*, §21 (ed. & transl. Whitelock, p. 64.22–4) (text); *ibid.*, p. 65 (translation) (= Sawyer, *Anglo-Saxon Charters*, no. 1538).

[199] *Anglo-Saxon Wills*, §19 (ed. & transl. Whitelock, p. 54.7–9) (text); *ibid.*, p. 55 (translation) (= Sawyer, *Anglo-Saxon Charters*, no. 1534).

[200] *Anglo-Saxon Wills*, ed. & transl. Whitelock, p. 165, note to line 9.

[201] For the text see Brotanek, *Texte und Untersuchungen*, pp. 27–8 and cf. p. 133.

[202] *Anglo-Saxon Wills*, §3 (ed. & transl. Whitelock, p. 10.11–13) (text); *ibid.*, p. 11 (translation) (= Sawyer, *Anglo-Saxon Charters*, no. 1539).

3) 'A man who is in the higher category of freedman as defined by Norse law, a *leysingr*.'

In an anonymous homily, *Be mistlican gelimpan*, preserved in Oxford, Bodleian Library, Hatton MS. 113 (*S.C.* 5210) of the third quarter of the eleventh century, *hwilum be freotmen* is followed by the phrase *hwilum be healffreon*, which implies that there was a distinction between a *freotman* and a *healffreon*.[203] It will be argued below (s.v. *healffreoh*) that the word suggested to the person who added the phrase that a *freotmann* was equivalent to the Norse *leysingr*. This sense is not applicable to the word as used in the other two manuscripts containing this homily, where it must have sense 2). (Had the freedman possessed exactly the same status, rights, and obligations as a freeman, the contrast between the *esenwite* and the *freotmann* employed in this homily would have been inapplicable.)

FREO-WIF sb. (n) 'A freeborn woman.'

This word survives only in §73 of Æthelberht's Code: 'Gif friwif locbore leswæs hwæt gedeþ, XXX scll' gebete.' ('If a freeborn woman, with long hair, misconducts herself, she shall pay 30 shillings as compensation.')[204] The reference to long hair is a fascinating one: long hair was an attribute of kingship in Merovingian society and the reference to it here could be taken as further evidence of the Frankish influence that has been noted in other elements of early Kentish society.[205]

FREO-WINE sb. (m)   1) 'Noble friend.'

Beowulf uses this word of Hrothgar in his formal speech of introduction, calling him *freowine folca* ('noble friend of the people').[206]

2) ?A personal name.

This is only to be found in an unprinted twelfth-century list of witnesses to land bought from Freowine's widow (*at Frewines laf*), probably in Exeter.[207] The first element may well have been *Frea-*, 'lord', however.[208]

HÆFT-INCEL sb. (m) 'A young male slave.'

There is only a single instance of this word in the sources, in the Cleopatra Glossary, where it glosses the lemma *empticius*.[209] Meritt has identified it as a gloss to Genesis 17:12: 'infans octo dierum circumcidetur in uobis . . . tam uernaculus quam emtitius circumcidetur.' The definitions 'slave, an enslaved captive', he pointed out, 'do not catch the diminutive force of the suffix *incel* which should give to *hæft*, "slave", the meaning "little slave", and in fact probably does give that meaning here since the *empticius* referred to is only eight days old.'[210] Meritt's new definition was accepted by Campbell

---

203 *Wulfstan*, §35 (ed. Napier, p. 171.4) (= Ker, *Catalogue*, §331.29 [p. 394]).
204 *Die Gesetze*, ed. Liebermann, I.7 (text); *The Laws*, ed. & transl. Attenborough, p. 15 (translation).
205 See Wood, 'Frankish hegemony in England', in *The Age of Sutton Hoo*, ed. Carver. Edward James has pointed out that the Burgundians also had heavy fines for cutting the hair of a freewoman; for this and other symbolic uses of hair-cutting in the early middle ages, see *idem*, 'Bede and the tonsure question', especially p. 92 and n. 3.
206 *Beowulf*, line 430, in *Beowulf and Judith*, ed. Dobbie, p. 15 (text); *Anglo-Saxon Poetry*, transl. Bradley, p. 423 (translation).
207 Pelteret, *Catalogue*, §115 (pp. 108–9).
208 It is indexed under the latter form in *ibid.*, p. 126.
209 Wright, *Anglo-Saxon and Old English Vocabularies*, ed. Wülcker, I, col. 394.3. The same glossary also gives *ceapcniht* (q.v.) as the gloss to this Latin word.
210 Meritt, *Some of the Hardest Glosses in Old English*, p. 101.

in his *Enlarged Addenda and Corrigenda* to Bosworth, *An Anglo-Saxon Dictionary*, ed. Toller.[211] For the diminutive suffix see s.vv. *þeowincel, wilnincel.*

The word suggests that the simplex *hæft* once had the generalised sense of 'a slave', which presumably developed from the sense 'one who has been captured'. This sense is not, however, attested in any of the extant examples of *(ge)hæft* (sb. and adj.) or *gehæftan* (vb) and its compounds.[212]

HAM-BYRDE(?) sb. (f) 'A female slave born in the lord's house(hold).'

On fo 76r of the late tenth- or early eleventh-century Cambridge, Corpus Christi College, MS. 326 *uernacula* is glossed *hm bir*. Page has suggested that this stands for a hitherto unrecorded word, *hambyrde*.[213]

HEALF-FREO adj. 'Possessing the legal status of a *frjálsgjafi*, the lower category of freedman as defined by Norse law.'

This word appears only twice in Old English, once as an adjective and in the other instance as a substantive (q.v.) The adjectival form is to be found in a bequest of probably eleventh-century date made to St Edmund's Abbey: '<Þ>urkil and Aþelgit vnnen Wigorham into seynt Eadmunde . . . and þo men halffre þeowe 7 lisingar.' Whitelock translated this as: '<We>, Thurkil and Æthelgyth, grant to St Edmund's . . . Wereham . . . and also the men, <both those who are> half-free and slaves and freedmen',[214] where the word seems to have been understood by her as a substantive. But the weight of the evidence goes against this. For *healf-freoh* here to be a substantive one would have to understand the punctuation to be 'þo men: halffre, þeowe 7 lisingar'. The main objection to this interpretation is the order, which is illogical: one would have expected *þeowe* to have preceded *halffre*. A subsidiary objection is that the other example of the word (where it is clearly a substantive) shows it to have been included in the weak declension.

This same lack of logical order is likewise the primary objection to interpreting *halffre* as an adjective qualifying *men*. This leaves the possibility of interpreting it instead as an adjective qualifying *þeowe*. The punctuation would then be 'þo men: halffre þeowe 7 lisingar'. Syntactically this would be perfectly acceptable, since many other *healf*- compounds are adjectives. In this instance it is strong (with monophthongisation of the final syllable), which is appropriate to the context.

This then leaves the problem of determining the exact sense of *halffre þeowe*, 'half-free slave'. The Old Norse legal codes supply an explanation for this seemingly contradictory term. Von Maurer showed in his investigation of the Old Norse legal evidence on freedmen that in the earliest laws this class fell into two categories, the *leysíngar* (q.v. *lising*) and the *frjálsgjafir*.[215] The latter class were men who had been granted only a limited degree of personal freedom. They did not have the right of marriage, could not freely dispose of their property, and had neither reciprocal rights of succession between parents and children, nor between brothers and sisters. Furthermore, they were subject to a nexus of obligations towards the manumittor and his family known as *þyrmslir*, which was binding on those freed up to the ninth generation.

For an Anglo-Saxon the Norse term would have posed a problem of verbal designa-

211 Campbell, *Enlarged Addenda and Corrigenda*, p. 39, col. 1, s.v. *hæftincel*.
212 Toller, *Supplement*, p. 336, col. 2, s.v. *gehæftan* VI, gives the meaning as 'to put into the power of another, bring into bondage, enslave' but 'to take into captivity' would adequately fit either of the citations Toller provided.
213 Page, 'More Aldhelm glosses from CCCC 326', 488.
214 *Anglo-Saxon Wills*, §36 (ed. & transl. Whitelock, p. 92.9–11 (text); *ibid.*, p. 93 (translation) (= Sawyer, *Anglo-Saxon Charters*, no. 1529).
215 Maurer, 'Die Freigelassenen nach altnorwegischem Rechte'.

tion. Since the time of Wihtred at least, the Old English cognate for the Old Norse word, *freolsgefa* (q.v.), had meant 'giver of freedom, manumittor' rather than 'one given freedom, a freedman'. Consequently some other term would have had to be found. Given the severe limitations on the freedoms granted under Norse law to the *frjálsgjafi*, the designation 'half-free slave' may have seemed not inappropriate.

Circumstantial evidence lends support to this interpretation. The will in which the term appears comes from East Anglia, an area in which Danish influence was very strong, and indeed the name of one of the manumittors was of Scandinavian origin. Furthermore the *halffre þeowe* are mentioned in association with *lisingar*, the second and more privileged group of Norse freedmen. In Norse law both groups had ties to the manumittors and their descendants. If the testators had wanted to transfer their rights in their freedmen out of the family, it would have been natural, therefore, to specify which categories of freedmen they had control over. In this particular will it appears that Thurkil and Æthelgyth were making over to St Edmund's Abbey the rights and obligations possessed by them in both categories of freedmen.

HEALF-FREO sb. (m) 'A freedman of the lower category as defined by Norse law, a *frjálsgjafi*.'

In the Oxford, Bodleian Library, Hatton MS. 113 (*S.C.* 5210) version of the anonymous homily, *Be mistlican gelimpan*, appears the following: 'hwilum be mannes efenwihte, hwilum be freotmen, hwilum be healffreon' ('sometimes in the case of a man's equal, sometimes in that of the freedman, sometimes the half-free').[216] The Cambridge, Corpus Christi College, MS. 201 and London, British Library, Cotton MS. Tiberius A.iii versions omit the words *hwilum be healffreon*.

The Hatton manuscript is one of three 'companion volumes' containing many works of Wulfstan II of York.[217] It was transcribed in the third quarter of the eleventh century at Worcester, possibly for Wulfstan's later successor, St Wulfstan of Worcester. This sermon was considered by Jost not to be a genuine Wulfstanian work, but the language is Wulfstanian in parts and he felt it had drawn on VIIa Æthelred, a Wulfstanian law code. This link with Wulfstan is important because of his ties with York, which had a Norse king till 954. Jost posited the following stemma for the version of *Be mistlican gelimpan* in MS. Hatton 113 (E):[218]

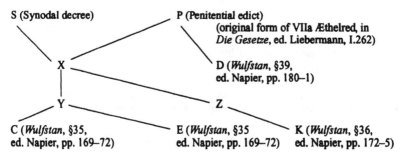

It would have been quite possible for Y to have been a York manuscript in which there could have been inserted (perhaps as an interlinear or marginal entry) the additional words contained in MS. Hatton 113.

---

[216] *Wulfstan*, §35 (ed. Napier, p. 171.3–4) (= Ker, *Catalogue*, §331.29 [p. 394])
[217] Ker, *Catalogue*, p. 399.
[218] Jost, *Wulfstandstudien*, pp. 213–16, at p. 215.

This link with York is, of course, pure conjecture – but it is not an improbable one. If the word *healffreon* was originally a York word (presumably in the Anglian form *half-freon*), its use becomes perfectly intelligible when one considers its context. The rhetoric of this section is based on the contrast between opposite pairs of words. It is unlikely, therefore, that *healffreon* can be read as a synonym for *freotmon*; the context demands instead a contrast, even though the addition of *hwilum be healffreon* breaks up the already existing contrast between *anne efenwihte* and *freotmen*.

Such a contrast can only be explained in the same way as the words *halffreo* and *lisingar* used in S 1529 (see s.v. *healf-freo* adj.) Here *freotman* (q.v.) must be equivalent to *lising*. The usage, therefore, reflects a Scandinavian legal practice that had been transferred to England. It is interesting to note that this is the only use of *healf-* plus an adjective having a substantival function. This, together with its assimilation into the weak substantive declension, suggests that it might have been a late compound formed after the Viking invasions.

HLAF-ÆTA sb. (m) 'Dependant of a freeman (probably with freedman status).'

This occurs only in the Laws of Æthelberht, §25: 'Gif man ceorlæs hlafætan ofslæhð, VI scillingum gebete.' ('If a man slay the dependant of a *ceorl*, he shall pay <the *ceorl*> 6 shillings compensation.')[219]

The word must be compared with other *hlaf-* compounds: *hlaford*, 'loaf-keeper, lord'; *hlæfdige*, 'loaf-kneader (?), lady'; and *hlafbrytta*, 'loaf-distributor, steward' (q.v.). These words must date from early in the Anglo-Saxon settlement of England, when social and economic conditions dictated that the main social unit be an extended household whose dominant activity was the production of food.

In order to determine the status of the *hlafæta* within this household one must examine the clause containing the word in the wider context of the code as a whole. First, one should note that the verb that signifies the paying of compensation for the killing of a *hlafæta* is *gebete*, which is used elsewhere in the code to denote the payment due to an overlord, presumably for the infringement of his *mund*. This contrasts with the word for the payment due to a man's kinsmen when he had been killed, namely, *forgeldan*. Thus Æthelberht, §13 declares that twelve shillings must be paid (*gebete*) to an *eorl* on whose premises a man had been killed, whereas in §26 payment for the slaughter of a *læt* is expressed by *forgeldan*. The essential difference between the two verbs is that the latter implies payment of wergeld, the former does not.

If the *læt* (q.v.) was a freedman, the collocation of §25 with its mention of the *hlæfæta* and §26 with its focus on the *læt* is significant. A *læt* is likely to have been under his former owner's *mund* because of his legal ties to him as a freedman. If the *læt* were killed, compensation would then be due both to the lord for infringement of his *mund* and to the *læt*'s kinsmen. And indeed Æthelberht, §15 sets a *ceorl*'s *mundbyrd* ('protection') at six shillings as in §25. It seems reasonable then to deduce that the *hlafæta* and *læt* were one and the same person. *Hlafæta* denoted his status *vis à vis* his lord, *læt* his tribal status.

HLAF-BRYTTA sb. (m) 'Steward.'

This occurs only once, in a manumission-document of A.D. 1030 x 1050 (*Manumission*, §5.9), where it is the by-name of a man whose daughter was freed. Etymologically it means 'one who distributes bread', and should be compared with other ancient formations like *hlaford*, *hlæfdige*, and *hlafæta*. The term is primarily an occupational

---

[219] *Die Gesetze*, ed. Liebermann, I.4 (text); *The Laws*, ed. & transl. Attenborough, p. 7 (translation, emended).

one, but if it does go back to the days of the earliest Anglo-Saxon settlement, it may have been reserved for those of slave status.

IN-BYRDE adj. 'Belonging to the lord's estate in virtue of birth there, servile.'

The prefix *in-* seems to have undergone successive transformations in meaning from 'associated with a place' to 'associated with a household' to 'associated with a manorial estate'. The suffix *-byrde* has strong status connotations (cf. the simplex *byrde* 'well-born, noble', and *burbyrde*, *efenbyrde*, and *þeowbyrde* [q.v.]). The compound *inbyrde* appears to have acquired a specialised legal sense. It is employed in a number of charters in both attributive and predicative positions. Denewulf in his lease of land in Wiltshire made in the year 902 states: 'he moste þa inberðan menn hamettan to Eblesburnan' ('he may take into his service [?] the persons born on the estate at Ebbesbourne'),[220] and *Status Document*, §1.1 declares: 'Wifus 7 Dunne 7 Seoloce syndan inbyrde to Hæðfelda' ('Wifus and Dunne and Seoloce belonged to the lord's estate at Hatfield by birth'). *Inbyrde* is equivalent to the Latin *innatus*, a word which occurs in the *Liber Eliensis* in connexion with a dispute at Hatfield.[221] Such persons were most probably serfs, that is, members of an estate who had customary rights based on the law of the manor but who did not have freedom of movement. See further above, pp. 180–2.

IN-BYRDLING sb. (m)   1) 'A native.'

The word etymologically means 'one born in a place'. Its Old Low German cognate, *in-burdig*, glosses *indigena* and the original sense of the Old English word also meant 'native'.[222] This sense is preserved in several glossaries; for example, *indigena id est iciuis* [sic] is glossed *inbyrdlinc, burleod*; *indigena i(d est) ciuis* is also equated with *inbyrdling* in another glossary.[223]

2) 'A young slave born in a master's household.'

The prefix here is used in the sense 'associated with a household'. It is used to translate *uernaculus* in the Old English *Heptateuch* version of Genesis 14:14, 15:3, 17:12, and 17:27;[224] *uerna uel uernaculus* are also the lemmata for the same word in several glossaries.[225] See s.v. *fostorling*.

IN-SÆTE adj. 'Belonging to one who is a member of a household.'

This informative gloss appears in London, British Library, Additional MS. 32246, fo 20v: '*casa, uel casula*, insæte hus, *uel* lytel hus'.[226] *Insæte* appears to be taken by the

220 *Select English Historical Documents*, §17 (ed. & transl. Harmer, p. 29.17–18 (text); *ibid.*, p. 60 (translation, emended) (= Sawyer, *Anglo-Saxon Charters*, no. 1285).
221 *Liber Eliensis*, ed. Blake, p. 83.
222 Gallée, *Vorstudien zu einem altniederdeutschen Wörterbuche*, p. 162, s.v. *in-burdig*. The Old High German equivalent is *inboran*, which also glosses *indigena*; the Old Icelandic cognate of *inboran* is *inn-borinn*, which means 'native'. No cognate of these two latter forms survives, however, in the extant Old English sources: see Starck & Wells, *Althochdeutsches Glossenwörterbuch*, p. 302, col. 1, s.v. *inboran*, and Cleasby & Vigfusson, *An Icelandic-English Dictionary*, 2nd edn, rev. Craigie, p. 314, col. 2, s.v. *inn-borinn*.
223 *Old English Glosses*, §§1.3957 and 2.275 (ed. Napier, pp. 105 and 144).
224 *The Old English Version of the Heptateuch*, ed. Crawford, pp. 121, 126, and 127.
225 London, British Library, Additional MS. 32246, fos 4r and 18r, in 'The Latin-Old English glossaries', ed. Kindschi, pp. 55.14 and 206.6, and also in Wright, *Anglo-Saxon and Old English Vocabularies*, ed. Wülcker, I, cols 111.18 (*uernaculus, inbirdling* [MS. *inbyrdlitig*]) and 170.26 (for the citation see *fostorling* above); *Aelfrics Grammatik und Glossar*, ed. Zupitza, p. 301.3; and *Old English Glosses*, §7.185 (ed. Napier, p. 160).
226 'The Latin-Old English glossaries, ed. Kindschi, p. 237.19 (= Wright, *Anglo-Saxon and Old English Vocabularies*, ed. Wülcker, I, col. 185.9).

glossator to be synonymous with *lytel* in this context. The lemmata also appear to be synonymous with one another. This implies that the members of the lord's household were not housed in the main house but in separate dwellings. As most Anglo-Saxon houses were probably timber-framed wattle-and-daub structures,[227] it is not surprising that those unrelated to the lord's immediate family lived in separate quarters; even in France, where something of the tradition of Roman stone architecture survived, the main house would have additional wooden buildings attached, which must have housed, *inter alia*, support staff.[228] It cannot be asserted that the word is used only of slaves, but there is other evidence that slaves lived in their own dwellings: see above, pp. 124–5.

IN-SWAN sb. (m) 'A swineherd in charge of the herd on the lord's demesne.'

For a discussion of this person mentioned in *Rectitudines Singularum Personarum*, §4.2, who must be the same as the *æhteswan* (q.v.) of §7 in the same text,[229] see above, pp. 174–5.

IN-ÞINEN sb. (f) 'A female domestic slave.'

Although other compounds of *þignen* (q.v.) probably do not denote legal status, the prefix *in-*, 'associated with a household', suggests that the second element, *þignen*, here has the sense 'female slave'. The word appears only in the Prudentius glosses in the eleventh-century manuscript, Boulogne-sur-Mer, Bibliothèque municipale, MS. 189, where the lemmata are *incola, urbicola*.[230]

IN-WEORC sb. (n) 'A task to be performed at the manorial *caput*.'

In the directions to reeves contained in the extension to the *Rectitudines singularum personarum* known as *Gerefa* they are told what agrarian duties they should supervise in winter or in frosty weather. In addition to specific tasks such as ploughing and cutting timber, there were many general ones to be performed at the headquarters of the manor, *manige inweorc wyrcean*.[231] Although the first element is probably cognate with the Modern English *inn*, which in turn is derived from the preposition *in*, the tasks were not necessarily to be performed inside, as Toller suggested in his gloss, 'indoor work'.[232] Though the text does not spell out who should do these tasks and under what conditions, one can legitimately deduce that these were labour services that the reeve could demand of serfs living on the manor.

LÆT sb. (m) 'A freedman.'

This word occurs as a simplex only in the Laws of Æthelberht, §26: 'Gif læt ofslæhð, þone selestan LXXX scll' forgelde; gif þane oþerne ofslæhð, LX scillingum forgelde; ðane þriddan XL scilling forgelden.' ('If he slays a *læt* of the best class, he shall pay 80 shillings; if he slays one of the second class, he shall pay 60 shillings; <for slaying one of> the third class, he shall pay 40 shillings.')[233] All scholars are agreed that *læt* is cognate with the *laetus* that appears in Continental Latin sources.

The *laeti* were Germanic peoples of various origins who after voluntarily submitting

---

[227] See Addyman, 'The Anglo-Saxon house'.
[228] For a detailed description of a *curtis* in Annapes see *Capitularia Regum Francorum*, ed. Boretius, I.254, and Duby, *The Early Growth of the European Economy*, pp. 83–4.
[229] *Die Gesetze*, ed. Liebermann, I.447 and 449.
[230] *The Old English Prudentius Glosses*, §952 (ed. Meritt, p. 103).
[231] *Gerefa*, §11, in *Die Gesetze*, ed. Liebermann, I.454.
[232] Toller, *Supplement*, p. 595, col. 1, s.v. *in-weorc*.
[233] *Die Gesetze*, ed. Liebermann, I.4 (text); *The Laws*, ed. & transl. Attenborough, p. 7 (translation).

to Rome became cultivators of the land in various parts of Gaul.[234] In other provinces they were called *inquilini*. They first appear in historical sources from the end of the third century A.D. In addition to being farmers, they were utilised by the Romans as soldiers. Their legal position was hereditary, and their status was intermediate between the slave and the freeman. The Romans doubtless took over the institution from Germanic sources, but transformed it for their own purposes. The word itself seems to be derived from the West-Germanic verb *lātan*, 'to let, permit', and probably meant 'freedman'.[235]

It seems inherently improbable, however, that the *laeti* of Roman Gaul were the same as the *lœtas* of Kent. To begin with, there is no evidence that this term was used by the Romans outside Gaul, and even if there were German federates settled in Britain, one would have to posit their continued existence as a social group for a hundred and fifty years after the Saxon uprisings in the 440s.[236] Admittedly the term did live on in France: *leti* were still recorded on the estates of St-Germain-des-Prés in the time of Abbot Irminon[237] – but then there was a clear social and economic continuity in Francia from Roman times. Some continuity there was in Kent, but it would be rash to assert that it was anything like that obtaining on the other side of the Channel.[238]

On the other hand, there does not seem to be anything against regarding the *lœtas* as an indigenous Germanic institution introduced into England by the Anglo-Saxon invaders. The strongest argument in favour of this lies in the tripartite class structure of the group. In this they are just like the *leysingar* of Norse law.[239] These three classes signified the three generations required for the descendants of a freedman to acquire full freedom.

That this group receive only a single mention in Anglo-Saxon sources can readily be explained, both in the light of recent evidence on Anglo-Saxon ethnology and later institutional developments. Myres provided a defence of Bede's description of the tribal composition of England. Previously a number of scholars had emphasised on the basis of archaeological evidence, notably that of jewellery, glassware and pottery, the links with Francia. Myres pointed out, however, that underlying this material are other fifth-century artefacts that provides definite links with Jutland. The superior standing of the Anglians and the influence of the Franks led to the Jutish role in Kent being forgotten, while in the south the Jutes came under the political domination of the West Saxons.[240]

It seems simplest to postulate, therefore, that the *lœtas* represent a Germanic system of manumission introduced into Britain by the Jutes, but that it is a system that was not observed by invaders from other tribal groupings.[241] If this is the case, the institution would probably have shared the decline of the people who practised it. The introduction

---

234 The following paragraph is drawn from W. Schönfeld's article on *laeti* in *Paulys Realencyclopädie der classischen Altertumswissenschaft*, edd. Wissowa & Kroll, XII.1, cols 446–8.

235 The Germanic forms are Old High German *lāz*, Old Frisian *lēt*, Middle Dutch *laet*. The Latinised form of the word was *litus* (cf. Jordanes *Liticiani*), *Letus*, *Latus*, and *Lassus*. The reason for the alteration in vowel length is obscure. See Schönfeld, 'Laeti', column 447.

236 For an analysis of the legal status of the *laeti* and a review of earlier writings on the subject see Balon, 'Les lètes chez les Francs'.

237 *Polyptique de l'Abbé Irminon*, ed. Guérard, I.273–6.

238 For some evidence of continuity see Wilson, 'The cult of St. Martin in the British Isles'.

239 See Seebohm, *Tribal Custom in Anglo-Saxon Law*, pp. 484–6.

240 Myres, 'The Angles, the Saxons, and the Jutes', especially pp. 167–72.

241 This seems a better explanation than to postulate that the institution was a borrowing from the Franks. Although *leti* were to be found on Frankish territory until the ninth century, there is no evidence that the class involved a three-generational status change. Furthermore, Balon, 'Les lètes chez les Francs', 443–4, has brought forward evidence to suggest that the function of the Frankish *leti* was to act as military defenders of seigneurial domains. Although these

of the Roman *manumissio in ecclesia* under the influence of the Church, with its immediate transformation in status from slave to freeman, would explain its demise. Only with the appearance of a people amongst whom the institution was a living one could the practice spring to life again. This is indeed what happened when the Vikings invaded England. Their terminology differed, however, and in consequence this class came to be called *lisingas* (q.v.)

If the *lætas* can be associated with the *hlafæta* (q.v.) of Æthelberht, §25,[242] it would appear that they possessed a wergeld but that their former lords were also entitled to compensation if they suffered injury.

The word survived into the eleventh century as a compound: in London, British Library, Additional MS. 32246, fo 4r, and the Cleopatra Glossary *freolæta/friglæta* glosses *libertus*.[243] This seems to be a common Germanic word, being found in the form *fra-lets* in Gothic, *frilaza* in the *Lex Baiuuariorum*, *frîlaz* and *frîlâz* in Old High German, and *vrilaet* in Middle Dutch.[244] It was possibly of wider provenance in England and more general in meaning than the simplex, which would account for its continued survival.

* (GE)-LISAN vb   1) 'To release from contractual obligations to an estate.'

Lisan occurs in this sense only in an Exeter manumission-document of the late eleventh century, *Manumission*, §9.21, probably as a variant of *alisan* (see s.v. *alisan* 2).

2) 'To free, to redeem (from a spiritual state).'

As has been pointed out in chapter II above, Anglo-Saxon writers employed three metaphors to express the theological concept of redemption:

1)   the legal concept of a state of slavery (to the devil, sin, etc.) drawn from the Bible and the structure of contemporary society;

2)   the legal concept of imprisonment, drawn ultimately from Biblical accounts of imprisonment;

3)   the social concept of captivity resulting from war, drawn in part no doubt from Biblical sources but reinforced by the warrior ethos of early Anglo-Saxon society.

A change from any of these three states was most frequently expressed by some form of the verb *lisan* or its compounds, while the agent of this release was described by the *nomen agentiua lisend* and its compounds.

The simplex *(ge)lisan* has as its basic sense 'to free', as can be seen in the Rushworth gloss *gelese us of yfle* representing the Latin, *libera nos a malo* ('free us from evil'), in Matthew 6:13,[245] but must have been extended to mean 'to loosen'. The phrase *eall his lichama <wæs> gelysed* ('all of His body <was> crushed') in the Blickling Homilies extends the latter sense yet further.[246]

The compounds *onlisan*, *tolisan*, and *unlisan*, as well as the simplex *lisian* all mean

---

estates may have survived from Roman times in Britain, it seems highly improbable that they were so widespread as to lead to the rise of a special social class like the *leti*.

[242] *Die Gesetze*, ed. Liebermann, I.4 (text); *The Laws*, ed. & transl. Attenborough, p. 7 (translation).

[243] 'The Latin-Old English glossaries', ed. Kindschi, p. 56.1 (= Wright, *Anglo-Saxon and Old English Vocabularies*, ed. Wülcker, I, col. 111.21), and *ibid.*, I, col. 432.31–2.

[244] Carr, *Nominal Compounds in Germanic*, p. 117, (ii) (a) 7.

[245] *The Gospel according to Saint Matthew*, ed. Skeat, p. 55.

[246] *The Blickling Homilies*, §19 (ed. & transl. Morris, p. 241.29–30) (text); *ibid.*, p. 240 (translation).

'to release (from a physical or mental state)', but none has reference to slavery in either its legal or spiritual senses.

* (GE)LISEDNESS sb. (f) '(Spiritual) redemption.'

Bishop Æthelmær in his bequest of A.D. 1047 x 1070 to Bury St Edmunds declared: 'ic wille þat þis stonde euere vnawent mine soule to lisidnesse' ('it is my wish that this shall ever remain unchanged for the redemption of my soul').[247] This was not simply a nonce usage: Canticle §9 in Eadwine's Psalter proclaims, 'gebletsod beo drihten god getreowa forðan he 7 dyde gelysednesse folces his' ('blessed be the Lord God of the faithful because he even brought about the redemption of his people'), representing the words of Luke 1:68, 'Benedictus dominus deus israhel quia uisitauit et fecit redemptionem plebis suae.'[248]

* LISEND sb. (m) 'Redeemer.'

Lesend glosses *redemptor* on three occasions in the *Durham Ritual*.[249]

LISING sb. (m) 'A freedman.'

Lising is from the same root as Old English *leosan*, 'to loose, release', from which the feminine substantive *lising*, 'a loosing, releasing, redemption' (q.v.), the masculine *lisend*, 'redeemer' (q.v.), and the compounds *crism-lising*, 'a leaving off of the baptismal vest', and *eftilisend*, 'redeemer' (q.v.), are derived. But it seems unquestionable that *lising* in the sense 'freedman' is a borrowing from Old Norse.[250] It occurs only twice in Old English texts, both of which have Scandinavian links.

In Norse law the *leysingr* or *leysingi* was the higher of two categories of freedman. To become a *leysingr* two separate acts of manumission were required.[251] The first was a grant of freedom (*gefa frelsi*), whereby the unfree person was led into a church, a gospel book placed on his head, and the words of freedom spoken. The second act was the celebration of the freedom-ale (*gera frelsisöl sitt*). Here the freedman was required to prepare a legally appointed quantity of beer for a banquet.[252] In the presence of witnesses the freedman then led in the manumittor and gave him the place of honour. In addition, a limited number of other guests, including the manumittor's wife, could be invited. On the first evening of the banquet, the freedman weighed out six ounces of gold for his manumittor as *leysingsaurar*. This payment was either accepted or remitted by the manumittor, which then concluded the matter: thereafter the freedman could not be claimed back. This second act was essential for the attainment of full manumission except in certain circumstances, such as when someone born unfree was released before his third birthday.

Leysingar differed from the *frjálsgjafir* in that they had the right of marriage, powers of disposal over their own property, and the right of inheritance (though this last was limited to the first rank of kinship).[253] Furthermore, they were not subject to the duties of *þyrmslir* (see s.v. *healf-freoh*). They were, however, responsible for certain subsidiary food dues, and were placed after the free in matters concerning social rank.[254]

In Old English the word first appears in *ca* 886 in Alfred and Guthrum, §2, where

---

[247] *Anglo-Saxon Wills*, §35 (ed. & transl. Whitelock, p. 92.6–7) (text); *ibid.*, p. 93 (translation) (= Sawyer, *Anglo-Saxon Charters*, no. 1499).

[248] *Eadwine's Canterbury Psalter*, Canticle, §9 (ed. Harsley, II.260.15–16).

[249] *Rituale Ecclesiae Dunelmensis*, edd. Thompson & Lindelöf, pp. 20.18, 30.17, and 33.8.

[250] See Maurer, 'Die Freigelassenen nach altnorwegischem Rechte', *passim*.

[251] *Ibid.*, pp. 26–30.

[252] On the quantity see *ibid.*, pp. 27–8.

[253] *Ibid.*, pp. 47–8.

[254] *Ibid.*, pp. 33–5.

lisingas were given the same social status as a *ceorle ðe on gafollande sit*.[255] Because these *ceorlas* were not in possession of their own land but were on rented land, they must have been to some degree subject to the lord of that land. This would have placed them in a position analogous to the Norse *leysingar* and it is natural that the two should have been associated with each other. It is noteworthy that the treaty specifies that the *lisingas* were to be found among the Danes, not the Anglo-Saxons (*heora* [that is, the Danes'] *liesingum*), implying that this was a Scandinavian legal category not found among the Anglo-Saxons. The second instance occurs in the East Anglian will discussed above, s.v. *healf-freoh*, where it is suggested that both Scandinavian categories of freedman are referred to.[256] There is also at least one instance where the Old English *freotmann* (q.v.) appears to have been used to designate a *leysingr*.

The rarity of the word in Old English texts is attributable to the limited number of texts extant from the Danelaw. Place-names such as Lazenby and Lazencroft (Yorkshire), Lazonby (Cumberland), and *Laysingthorpe* (Lincolnshire), show that freedmen (and by implication slaves as well) were to be found throughout the Danelaw.[257]

* LISING sb. (f) 'A (spiritual) redemption.'

Lesing glosses *redemtionem* (with reference to Jerusalem) in the Lindisfarne and Rushworth Gospels at Luke 2:38 as an alternative to *lesnis* (q.v.).[258] *Lesnise uel lesing* glosses the same word in the Lindisfarne Gospels at Luke 1:68[259] and glosses the same Latin word twice in the *Durham Ritual*.[260]

* LIS-NESS sb. (f) 'A (spiritual) redemption.'

At Mark 10:45 *Lesnise uel to lesinc* glosses *redemtionem* in the Lindisfarne Gospels and *lesnisse* in the Rushworth Gospels.[261] It also glosses *redemtionem* in both these gospel versions of Luke 1:68 and 2:38 (see s.v. *lising* above).[262]

MÆGDEN-MANN sb. (m) 1) 'Unmarried woman, virgin.'

Writing of Christ's mother Ælfric states: 'He geceas Him mæden-mann to meder.' ('He chose him a maiden for mother.')[263] This sense is confirmed by Ælfric's *Glossary*, where *mædenmann* glosses *uirgo*.[264] This was, no doubt, the regular sense of the word.

2) 'Unmarried woman belonging to another, a female slave.'

The Laws of Æthelberht, §10 refers to a *cyninges mægdenman*, which from the context clearly refers to a slave.[265] For a similar sense development see s.v. *mann*.

MANN, MANNA sb. (m) 1) 'A person of either sex.'

An example of this usage is to be seen in the Old English *Bede*: 'Þa æt nihstan geðafode se biscop, þæt he to þæm untruman men geeode. Þa he ineode to ðære

---

255 *Die Gesetze*, ed. Liebermann, I.126 (text); *The Laws*, ed. & transl. Attenborough, p. 99 (translation).
256 *Anglo-Saxon Wills*, §36 (ed. & transl. Whitelock, p. 92.11) (= Sawyer, *Anglo-Saxon Charters*, no. 1529).
257 Smith, *English Place-Name Elements*, II.24, s.v. *leysingi*.
258 *The Gospel according to Saint Luke*, ed. Skeat, p. 35.
259 *Ibid.*, p. 27.
260 *Rituale Ecclesiae Dunelmensis*, edd. Thompson & Lindelöf, pp. 21.7 and 38.22.
261 *The Gospel according to Saint Mark*, ed. Skeat, p. 85.
262 *The Gospel according to Saint Luke*, ed. Skeat, pp. 27 and 35.
263 *The Sermones Catholici*, I.21 (ed. & transl. Thorpe, p. 308.28–9) (text); *ibid.*, p. 309.28 (translation).
264 *Aelfrics Grammatik und Glossar*, ed. Zupitza, p. 301.5–6.
265 *Die Gesetze*, ed. Liebermann, I.3 (text); *The Laws*, ed. & transl. Attenborough, p. 5.

fæmnan, . . . þa genom he me mid hiene.' ('Then at last the bishop consented to visit the sick person. On going in to the maiden, . . . he took me with him.'), where the Old English uses *þæm untruman men* for the Latin *languentem*.[266]

2) 'A male person.'

This, the most common Modern English sense of the word, is frequently attested in Old English; for example, *uir uite* is glossed *lifes man* in the glosses to Aldhelm's *De Laudibus Uirginitatis* in Oxford, Bodleian Library, Digby MS. 146 (*S.C.* 1747).[267]

3) 'A person belong to another, a slave.'

a: Of persons of either sex: This occurs in a Durham manumission-document of A.D. 1030 x 1040, *Manumission*, §7.1: 'Her cyð þ Ælfred lareow hæfeð gefreolsad VII men . . .' ('Here is made known that Alfred the teacher has freed seven persons . . .' [a list of both men and women follows]).

b: Of men: This usage is attested from all periods. The earliest example appears in Hlothhere & Eadric, §5, the only weak declensional attestation in this sense: *Gif frigman mannan forstele* . . . ('If a freeman steals a man . . .').[268] Wihtred, §8 states: 'Gif man his mæn an wiofode freols gefe, se sie folcfry.' ('If anyone grants one of his men freedom on the altar, his freedom shall be publicly recognised.')[269] It again appears in the laws in the tenth-century *Forfang*, §2: 'æt men fiftene peningas 7 æt horse healswa' ('for a man fifteen pennies and for a horse likewise').[270] The eleventh-century *Rectitudines singularum personarum*, §8 records: 'Be manna metsunge. Anan esne gebyreð to metsunge . . .' ('About men's provisioning. Every slave ought to have as provisions . . .').[271] Here *esne*, which clearly must refer to a slave (see s.v. *esne*), is synonymous with *mann*. In the Alfredian translation of Pope Gregory's *Pastoral Care mann* is the Old English equivalent of *seruus*: 'Ge hlafordas, doð ge eowrum monnum ðæt ilce' ('Ye masters, do the same to your men'), translating Ephesians 6:9, 'Et uos domini eadem facite illis'.[272] Here, as with *þeow* (q.v.), there is the familiar social contrast between slave and *hlaford*.

c: Of women: The word is employed in a record of disputes over land in Surrey and Middlesex dating from 950 x 968: 'Se fruma wæs þ mon forstæl ænne wimman . . . Ælfsige. . . . Þa befeng Ælfsige þone mann æt Wulfstane. . . . Æfter þam bæd Ælfsige ægiftes his mannes.' ('The beginning <of this case> was that a woman was stolen . . . from Ælfsige. . . . Then Ælfsige attached the woman in the possession of Wulfstan. . . . After that Ælfsige asked for the return of the woman.')[273] It is also used in a Bath manumission-document dating from 1065 x 1066, *Manumission*, §8.8: '7 ofer his dæg 7 hys wifes dæg beo se man [*sc.* Sæþryþ (f)] freoh.' ('And after his lifetime and his wife's lifetime may that person be free.')

---

[266] *The Old English Version of Bede's Ecclesiastical History*, V.3 (ed. & transl. Miller, I.2.392.20–3) (text); *ibid.*, I.2.393.18–20 (translation) (= *Bede's Ecclesiastical History*, V.3 [edd. & transl. Colgrave & Mynors, p. 460]).

[267] *Old English Glosses*, §1.3699 (ed. Napier, p. 98).

[268] *Die Gesetze*, ed. Liebermann, I.9 (text); *The Laws*, ed. & transl. Attenborough, p. 19 (translation).

[269] *Die Gesetze*, ed. Liebermann, I.13 (text); *The Laws*, ed. & transl. Attenborough, p. 27 (translation).

[270] *Die Gesetze*, ed. Liebermann, I.390 (text; personal translation).

[271] *Ibid.*, I.449 (text); *English Historical Documents 1042–1189*, §172 (transl. Douglas & Greenaway, p. 877) (translation).

[272] *King Alfred's West Saxon Version of Gregory's Pastoral Care*, §29 (ed. Sweet, I.201.24 = I.200.24) (Old English text) and *ibid.*, I.201 (translation); *Grégoire le Grand Règle pastorale*, III.5.15–16 (edd. Judic *et al.*, II.284 (Latin).

[273] *Anglo-Saxon Charters*, §44 (ed. & transl. Robertson, p. 90.1–6) (text); *ibid.*, p. 91 (translation) (= Sawyer, *Anglo-Saxon Charters*, no. 1447).

4) 'Man belonging to another, a slave.' (Used in a spiritual context.)

This sense is clearest in an anonymous homily, *Sermo ad populum dominicis diebus*, copied in the first quarter of the eleventh century in London, Lambeth Palace, MS. 489, which is probably of Exeter provenance: 'Nis na ma hlafordinga on worulde þonne twegen, God Ælmihtig and deofol. Forþan se þe Godes beboda hylt, he is Godes man . . .; and se deofles worc begæð, he is deofles man.' ('There are no more than two lords in the world, God Almighty and the devil. Therefore, he who holds to God's commands is God's man . . . ; and he who does the devil's work is the devil's man.')[274]

MANN-LAF sb. (f) 'The remainder of the men belonging to someone.'

The only attestation of this word is in line 54 of Æthelgifu's will: *of þære manlafe . . . ii men.* ('from the residue of men . . . two men.')[275] The context makes it clear that the men referred to were slaves. Cf. *mann(a)* 3)*b*.

MANN-SILEN sb. (f) 'The selling of men (into slavery abroad).'

Wulfstan uses this word in his *Sermo ad Anglos*,[276] and it also appears in two homilies written in the Wulfstanian style.[277] In the *Sermo* and the first of these anonymous homilies, *To eallum folce*, it forms part of a catalogue of wrongs of a sort not uncommon in homilies, which perhaps derive their form from confessional prayers:[278] 'ðurh man-sylene 7 þurh hæðene unsida' ('through the selling of men and through heathen vices') and 'þurh mansilcna and þurh fela misdæda' ('through the selling of men and through many misdeeds'). In the second anonymous homily it is used in a relative clause appendant to a catalogue similar to the previous two: 'leogeras and liceteras and leodha-tan hetele ealles to manege, þe ðurh mansylene bariað þas þeode' ('liars and hypocrites and hostile tyrants all too many, who through the sale of men denude this people'). That the people were 'denuded' implies that they were being sold abroad. This was proscribed in many laws and was a crime which Wulfstan explicitly attacked in his *Sermo ad Anglos*. This explains the word's association with *misdæda* and with *hæþene*, as the Church's primary objection to the practice lay in the sale of Christians into heathendom. Although *silen* normally means 'gift', the word has here probably been influenced by *sellen* (q.v.) in the sense 'to sell'.[279]

MENNEN sb. (f)   1) 'A female slave.'

Mennen is derived from *mann* with the same feminine suffix *-en* < *-in* to be seen in *þeowen*, *þinen*, and *wiln* (qq.v.). It appears to have undergone the same sense development as *mann*: from 'woman (in general)' it became 'a woman owned by another', that is, 'a slave'. Unlike *mann*, however, 'slave' is the only sense preserved in the simplex.

The generalised sense survives in a number of compounds. *Meremenin* glosses

---

[274] *Wulfstan*, §57 (ed. Napier, p. 298.7–11). On the date and provenance see Ker, *Catalogue*, §283 (pp. 344–5).

[275] *The Will of Æthelgifu*, ed. & transl. Whitelock, p. 13 (text); *ibid.*, p. 12 (translation) (= Sawyer, *Anglo-Saxon Charters*, no. 1497).

[276] *The Homilies of Wulfstan*, §20(C) (ed. Bethurum, p. 264.133) (text); *English Historical Documents c.500–1042*, §240 (transl. Whitelock, p. 932).

[277] *Wulfstan*, §§27 and 60 (ed. Napier, pp. 130.1 and 310.3–5). Bethurum considered the latter homily, *Be hæðendome*, to have at least been assembled by Wulfstan (*The Homilies of Wulfstan*, p. 39); Jost (*Wulfstanstudien*, p. 268) declared it to be '[s]prachlich in der Haupt-sache echt, literarisch unecht.'

[278] For an example of such a prayer see 'Die altenglischen Beigaben des Lambeth-Psalters', I 2) (ed. Förster, 329–31) (= Ker, *Catalogue*, §280.2 [p. 342]).

[279] Bosworth, *An Anglo-Saxon Dictionary*, ed. Toller, p. 861, col. 2, s.v. *sellan* IV; Simpson & Weiner, *The Oxford English Dictionary*, XIV.935, col. 2, s.v. *sell*, B.3.

sirina, 'sea woman, mermaid', in the eighth-century Corpus Glossary and *meremennena* (genitive plural) has the lemma *sirena* in the Cleopatra Glosses.[280] Here the second part of the compound cannot be an indicator of the legal status of the *sirena*; it must refer to her sex as it indubitably also does in the compound *þeowmennen* (q.v.)

Alfred's laws illustrate how the simplex *mennen* gained its servile sense. Under the heading *Be ceorles mennenes nedhæmde* in the Cambridge, Corpus Christi College, MS. 383 version (written in a hand of A.D. 1125 x 1130) Alfred, §25 sets out the penalty 'gif mon ceorles mennen to nydhæmede geðreata' ('if anyone rapes the slave of a *ceorl*').[281] Here the possessive genitive *ceorles* makes the qualifying *þeow*- unnecessary. From this it was easy for the word to acquire the sense 'a woman in a legal state of slavery'.

    2) 'A female slave.' (Used in a spiritual context.)

In the Lambeth Psalter at Psalm 85:16 *filium ancillae tuae* is glossed *sunu þinre þinenne uel mennenne*,[282] and in twice in Wærferth's translation of Gregory's *Dialogues Godes mennen* is evidently used as the equivalent of *ancilla Dei*.[283]

NID-ÞEOW, NID-ÞEOWA sb. (m)   1) 'One compelled to enter the state of slavery as a result of a judicial process.'

This word appears in the Wulfstanian tract, *Episcopus*, §§10, 11, 13, and 14.[284] The connexion of the *nydþeow* with a judicial process is shown in §14, where men are deemed to be God's *nydþeowan* because He judges us 'swa we her demað þam þe we on eorðan dom ofer agan' ('just as we here judge those over whom we have jurisdiction on earth'). Such men are considered to be in some way different from the lord's *men* (presumably here meaning 'slaves') as the writer stresses in §10 that they must receive good treatment like the rest of his men. §11 decrees that *nydþeowan* must work for their lord 'ofer ealle þa scire, þe he on scrife.' This paraphrases the technical term *scriftscir*, 'the district in which a confessor exercises his functions'. As the tract is entitled *Episcopus*, this *scir* must refer to a diocese, which gives a strong indication that bishops had jurisdictional powers to enslave men. It also shows that such men lost what must have been the most precious asset of those who were not slaves in late Anglo-Saxon England, namely, security of tenure.

    2) 'One compulsorily enslaved to God.'

In addition to its metaphorical use in *Episcopus* the word is also used in the poem *Christ I*, line 361, where it is in apposition to *hæft* 'a captive'.[285] This suggests that the word could be used in a more generalised way than 1) with some such sense as 'one compulsorily enslaved'.

NID-ÞEOWETLING sb. (m) 'One compelled to enter the state of slavery as a result of a judicial process.'

Nydðeowetlinge (dative case) occurs in a Bodmin document from the second half of the eleventh century, *Manumission*, §3.33, where it refers to someone under threat of

---

[280] *The Corpus Glossary*, S349 (ed. Lindsay, p. 164) and Wright, *Anglo-Saxon and Old English Vocabularies*, ed. Wülcker, I, col. 506.5.

[281] *Die Gesetze*, ed. Liebermann, I.62 and 64 (text); *The Laws*, ed. & transl. Attenborough, p. 75 (translation, emended).

[282] *Der Lambeth-Psalter*, ed. Lindelöf, I.137.

[283] *Bischof Wærferths von Worcester Übersetzung*, I.4 and IV.14 (ed. Hecht, I. 29.20 and 280.12), translating *quamdam sanctimonialem feminam* in the latter instance (Old English); *Grégoire le Grand Dialogues*, I.4.5 and IV.14.4 (ed. de Vogüé, II.42.54 and III.58.37) (Latin).

[284] *Die Gesetze*, ed. Liebermann, I.478-9.

[285] *The Exeter Book*, edd. Krapp & Dobbie, p. 13.

being forced to become a slave. It is not clear from the context whether the second half of the compound is derived from *þeowetling* (q.v.) in the neutral sense 3) or in sense 2), which has a derogatory connotation.

* NID-ÞEOWIAN vb 'To force a property to render dues to one.'

The single occurrence of this word is in *Northumbrian Priest's Law*, §21, a text which dates from shortly before the Norman Conquest: *Gif man cirican nydþeowige* . . .[286] Presumably the manner in which a church was 'enslaved' was by diverting its revenues into private hands and probably also by determining who would be the incumbent of the living. This would give the church the characteristics of an *Eigenkirche*.[287] Cf. also s.v. *þeowian* 4).

* ON-LISEND sb. (m) 'Redeemer.'

A confessional prayer written in an eleventh-century hand in London, British Library, MS. Royal 2.B.v, fo 6v, contains the only instance of this word.[288]

* ON-LISENDLIC adj. 'That can be released.'

In Wærferth's translation of Gregory's *Dialogues* the Latin clause 'ut et illum amaritudo mortis a culpa solubilem faceret' is translated 'þæt þone sweltendan seo biternes 7 strecnes þæs deaðes gedyde onlysendlicne fram þære scylde' ('that the bitterness and severity of death caused the one who had died to be released from blame').[289] Cf. *alisendlic*, which has an active sense.

* ON-LISNESS sb. (f) 'A (spiritual) redemption.'

Onlesnisse glosses *redemtio* in the Lindisfarne and Rushworth Gospels at Luke 21:28.[290] It is also used twice in the Blickling Homilies.[291]

RIHT-ÞEOWA sb. (m) 'Lawfully-owned slave.'

This appears only once, in Wærferth's translation of Gregory's *Dialogues*: 'sæge þæt ic þin rihtþeowa sy' ('declare that I am your lawfully-owned slave'), representing the Latin 'me seruum iuris tui esse profitere'.[292] The prefix *riht-* is used in many compounds in the sense 'in accordance with the law'.

SCEALC sb. (m)   1) 'A slave.' (Used in a spiritual context.)

This is a common Germanic word, appearing in Gothic *skalks*, Old Saxon and Old Frisian *skalk*, Old High German *scalc*, '*seruus*', and Old Icelandic *skalkr*, 'rogue', with the word perhaps originally meaning 'a person who carries an obligation'.[293] The sense 'slave' remains in Old English but the word is used only in religious contexts. In the Paris Psalter at Psalm 115:6 it is equated with *esne* and *þeowa*: 'Eala, ic eom þin agen esne, Dryhten,/ and þin swylce eom scealc ombehte/ and þinre þeowan sunu on ðe acenned' ('Lo, I am your own slave, Lord, and likewise your slave in function and

286 *Die Gesetze*, ed. Liebermann, I.381.
287 On the *Eigenkirche* see Boehmer, 'Das Eigenkirchentum in England', in *Texte und Forschungen zur englischen Kulturgeschichte*, ed. Boehmer *et al.*
288 Logeman, 'Anglo-Saxonica minora', 500.5 (= Ker, *Catalogue*, §249c [p. 319]).
289 *Bischof Wærferths von Worcester Übersetzung*, IV.57 (ed. Hecht, I.345.1–2) (Old English); *Grégoire le Grand Dialogues*, IV.57.12 (ed. de Vogüé, III.190.88–9) (Latin).
290 *The Gospel according to Saint Luke*, ed. Skeat, p. 203.
291 *The Blickling Homilies*, §6 (ed. & transl. Morris, pp. 67.3 and 81.23).
292 *Bischof Wærferths von Worcester Übersetzung*, III.1 (ed. Hecht, I.180.6) (Old English); *Grégoire le Grand Dialogues*, III.1.2 (ed. de Vogüé, II.258.15–16) (Latin).
293 Hempl, 'G. *skalks*'; Hamp, 'Germanic **skalkaz*'.

begotten for you as a son of your slave'), translating 'O Domine, quia ego seruus tuus; Ego seruus tuus, et filius ancillae tuae'.[294] The word does not seem, however, to have had quite the neutral sense that *þeow* had; rather it appears to have been used of a slave who had some direct personal relationship with his lord. This is particularly clear in the Paris Psalter, the text where the word most frequently occurs. For instance, the Latin *tuus sum ego* in Psalm 118:94 is extended in translation to *ic eom þin hold scealc*. ('I a Your loyal slave.')[295]

It can also be used of slaves of the devil as *Christ and Satan*, line 133 shows: 'Hwilum ic gehere hellescealcas, gnornende cynn.' ('At times I hear Hell's slaves, a sorrowing tribe.')[296]

    2) 'A man.'

The word seems to have been generalised in meaning to 'man' in poetic contexts. It appears in this sense in *Beowulf*, lines 918 and 939,[297] in *Judith*, line 230,[298] in the *Metres of Boethius*, 8.21 and 15.14,[299] and in *Whale*, line 31.[300] Its sense development was probably 'one belonging to another, a slave' and then 'one belonging to a lord's company, a retainer'. From this considerably elevated sense it became suitable as a poetic synonym for 'man'. Its usage in *The Battle of Maldon*, line 181 may represent the intermediate sense: *ða hine heowon hæðene scealcas*. ('Then heathen retainers hacked him.')[301] But there may be deliberate ambiguity here: the original sense, 'slave', gives the line an added edge.

The feminine form, *scilcen*, seems only to have been used of a young woman;[302] there are no examples where it could refer to a female slave, though its attested meaning when compared to the masculine cognate suggests that it could have had this meaning at one time in Old English.

SELLAN vb 'To sell (a person as a slave).'

This sense appears in the twelfth-century *Textus Roffensis* version of the Preface to Alfred's Laws, §12, representing the Latin *uendendi* of Exodus 21:7.[303] Other manuscripts use the word *bebycg(g)an* (q.v.)

* SUNDOR-FREODOM sb. (m) 'A special right.' (Used of land.)

This word appears twice in a translation of a Latin grant of privileges made by Pope Sergius I to the Abbot Aldhelm and the abbeys of Malmesbury and Frome in Wiltshire in *ca* 701.[304] The translation was entered in London, British Library, MS. Cotton Otho C.i, Vol. I, fo 68, in the mid-eleventh century.[305] The word is used in the phrase *mid*

---

[294] *The Paris Psalter*, ed. Krapp, p. 100 (= Vulgate Psalm 114/115:16).

[295] *The Paris Psalter*, ed. Krapp, p. 111 (= Vulgate Psalm 118:94).

[296] *The Junius Manuscript*, ed. Krapp, p. 140.

[297] *Beowulf and Judith*, ed. Krapp, pp. 29 and 30.

[298] *Ibid.*, p. 105.

[299] *The Paris Psalter*, ed. Krapp, pp. 162 and 174.

[300] *The Exeter Book*, edd. Krapp & Dobbie, p. 172.

[301] *The Anglo-Saxon Minor Poems*, ed. Dobbie, p. 12 (text); *The Battle of Maldon AD 991*, ed. Scragg, p. 25 (translation, emended).

[302] For instance, *iuuencula* is glossed *scilcen*, *uirguncula*, and *fœmne*: see *The Old English Glosses of MS. Brussels, Royal Library, 1650*, §2075 (ed. Goossens, p. 282).

[303] *Die Gesetze*, ed. Liebermann, I.31.

[304] *Cartularium Saxonicum*, §106 (ed. Birch, I.154.20 and I.155.16–17); cf. *ibid.*, §105 (I.153.10).

[305] Ker, *Catalogue*, §181.2 (p. 235).

apostolicum sunderfreodomum, which in the second instance renders the Latin *apostolicis priuilegiis*.

* SUNDOR-FREOLS sb. (m) 'A special charter granting rights over property.'

This is used several times in a translation of a Latin charter, which, though the date is wrong, appears to have been entered in the manuscript in the eleventh century.[306] In its first use *on ðisum sunderfreolse ic gestrangige* paraphrases 'in huius libelli corroboratione priuilegioque confirmo'. In the other instances it represents *confirmationem* once and *priuilegium* twice. Cf. s.v. *freols* 3).

ÞEGN sb. (m) 1) 'One who serves another.'

Þegn glosses the Latin *minister* in several sources.[307]

2) 'A freeman who serves a noble or king.'

This specialisation in meaning covering a group of freemen who performed official duties for kings or nobles became the normal sense of the word in late Old English.[308]

3) 'A slave.'

Aldred, who wrote in the North Northumbrian dialect, frequently used the word *þegn* to gloss the Latin *seruus* in the Lindisfarne Gospels. The gloss was probably made between A.D. 950 and 970.[309] Aldred did not use *þegn* for this purpose in the *Durham Ritual*, which was glossed in *ca* 970.[310] Ross *et al.* suggested in the facsimile edition of the Lindisfarne Gospels that its absence from the *Durham Ritual* glosses is to be accounted for by the difference in the time between which the two works were completed.[311] This is no doubt true as far as it goes, but it does not explain *why* Aldred did not use it in the later text.

Þegn also glosses *discipulus* and *minister* in the Lindisfarne Gospels.[312] On the other hand, Aldred used *esne*, *ðea* (= *ðeow*), and *þræl* to gloss *seruus*.[313] That it is not used to gloss *seruus* in the *Durham Ritual* may simply be due to chance, as *seruus* rarely appears there.[314] (When it does, it is glossed *esne*, *ðea*, or *ðræl*). But the explanation is more likely to be that *þegn* was being employed less often in Aldred's dialect in the sense 'slave' in the face of the growing use of *þegn* as a replacement for *gesith*, which Loyn has shown was in declining use in the tenth century.[315]

306 *Codex Diplomaticus Aevi Saxonici*, §715 (ed. Kemble III.349.26, 350.12, 16, and 32) (= Sawyer, *Anglo-Saxon Charters*, no. 914); cf. Ker, *Catalogue*, §185 (p. 239).

307 For example, *Aelfrics Grammatik und Glossar*, ed. Zupitza, p. 315.11; *The Old English Version of Bede's Ecclesiastical History*, IV.25 (ed. & transl. Miller, I.2.346.28) (text); *ibid.*, I.2.347.29 (translation) (= *Bede's Ecclesiastical History*, IV.24 [edd. & transl. Colgrave & Mynors, p. 418]); *The Gospel according to Saint Matthew*, ed. Skeat, pp. 162–3 and 186–7 (Matthew 20:26 and 23:11: West-Saxon and Rushworth Gospels).

308 See Loyn, 'Gesiths and thegns in Anglo-Saxon England'.

309 For the date see *Evangeliorum Quattuor Codex Lindisfarnensis*, edd. Kendrick *et al.*, II.2.31–2.

310 For the date see *The Durham Ritual*, edd. Brown *et al.*, p. 17.

311 *Evangeliorum Quattuor Codex Lindisfarnensis*, edd. Kendrick *et al.*, II.2.31.

312 *Ibid.*, II.2.147–8.

313 *Ibid.*, II.2.80, s.v. *esne*; II.2.147, s.v. *ðea*; and II.2.149–50, s.v. *ðræl(l)*.

314 *The Durham Ritual*, edd. Brown *et al.*, p. 69, s.v. *esne*; p. 86, s.v. *ðea*; p. 87, s.v. *ðræl*.

315 Loyn, 'Gesiths and thegns in Anglo-Saxon England', 538–40.

ÞEOW, ÞEOWA (Northumbrian **ÞEA**) sb. (m) 1) 'A man in a legal state of slavery, a slave.'

This is the standard Old English word for a slave. Apart from its metaphorical use in religious contexts, the word seems always simply to denote legal status with no other connotations, unlike some of the other words for 'slave' (e.g. *cniht*, which has connotations of youth, and *esne*, which primarily refers to service). It is the usual gloss for the Latin word *seruus* (sometimes replaced by *þræl* or *þegn* in the Northumbrian dialect, and there and elsewhere by *esne*, qq.v.). It also glosses *mancipium* and occasionally *famulus*.[316]

In Genesis 17:12 in the Old English *Heptateuch*[317] and in London, British Library, Additional MS. 32246, fo 18r, *geboht þeowa* glosses *emptitius/empticus*.[318] Since *emptitii* in Genesis 17:27 is translated *gebohte ðeowan*, with an inflected ending to the adjective, Bosworth and Toller were probably correct in excluding the phrase from their dictionary, evidently interpreting it as an adjective plus substantive rather than a compound substantive.[319]

Þeow is used in association with *þeowen* in Genesis 32:5[320] and the Prologue to Alfred's Laws, §20,[321] and with *wyln* in Ælfric's *Grammar*.[322]

2) 'A slave.' (Used in a spiritual sense.)

This is the standard Old English equivalent of *seruus Dei*. It is found particularly frequently in Wulfstan's writings. See above, pp. 68–70 and 90 and cf. below, s.v. *þræl* 2).

ÞEOW, ÞEOWE (Northumbrian **ÐIO**) sb. (f) 'A woman in a legal state of slavery, a female slave.'

As with its masculine equivalent (q.v.), this word seems only to denote legal status, except when it is used in religious contexts. It glosses *ancilla* and *famula*.[323] In Matthew 26:69 in the Rushworth Gospels it is considered synonymous with *mennen*: *ancilla – an menen uel þeowæ* (*ðiua* is the equivalent gloss in the Lindisfarne Gospels).[324] It is not nearly as common as the masculine form is. It is used in the tenth-century *Blickling Homilies*,[325] but does not appear in eleventh-century sources. It was probably in declining use because of the confusion that could arise with its homophonous masculine equivalent.

ÞEOW adj. 'Legally servile, slave-.'

This is the standard adjective used to indicate the legal status of a slave. There is no

---

316 For example, Wright, *Anglo-Saxon and Old English Vocabularies*, ed. Wülcker, I, col. 497.37, and *Aelfrics Grammatik und Glossar*, ed. Zupitza, p. 102.1 (*mancipium*); *Rituale Ecclesiae Dunelmensis*, edd. Thompson & Lindelöf, p. 97.2 (*famulus*).
317 *The Old English Version of the Heptateuch*, ed. Crawford, p. 126.
318 'The Latin-Old English glossaries', ed. Kindschi, p. 206.5 (= Wright, *Anglo-Saxon and Old English Vocabularies*, ed. Wülcker, I, col. 170.25).
319 Bosworth, *An Anglo-Saxon Dictionary*, ed. Toller, p. 375, col. 1, s.v. *ge-boht*; cf. *The Old English Version of the Heptateuch*, ed. Crawford, p. 127.
320 *Loc. cit.*
321 *Die Gesetze*, ed. Liebermann, I.32.
322 *Aelfrics Grammatik und Glossar*, ed. Zupitza, pp. 100–1.
323 For example, *þinre þeowan sunu* glosses *filium ancillae tuae*, in *The Paris Psalter*, 85:15 and 115:6 (ed. Krapp, pp. 54 and 100) (= Vulgate Psalms 85:16 and 114/115:16), and *ðiua* glosses *famula*, in *Rituale Ecclesiae Dunelmensis*, edd. Thompson & Lindelöf, p. 103.14.
324 *The Gospel according to Saint Matthew*, ed. Skeat, p. 227.
325 *The Blickling Homilies*, §13 (ed. & transl. Morris, p. 157.3).

evidence to suggest that it held anything other than this legal denotation. It is frequently used with *mann* in the sense 'a slave'.[326] Its antonym is *freoh*.[327]

ÞEOWAN vb 'To serve (as a slave).'

Like its cognate *þeowian*, this verb's most common meaning is 'to serve', with no necessary implication that the subject is performing in the capacity of a slave. The word is rather rare, presumably because it could be confused both with the common homophonous verb, *þeowan*, which has such senses as 'to press, drive on, threaten, subjugate', and with the plural form of *þeowa* and *þeowe*, 'a (male/female) slave'.

a. Intransitive use: The two verbs, *þeowan* and *þeowian*, are to be found in successive sentences in one of Ælfric's *Catholic Homilies*: 'Ælc ðeowt bið geendod on ðisum andweardan life buton ðæra anra þe synnum ðeowiað. Hi habbað ecne ðeowt and ða oðre beoð frige, ðeah ðe hi on life lange ær ðeowdon.' ('Every servitude will be ended in this present life, save of those only who minister to sins, they will have everlasting servitude, and the others will be free, although they in life long before had served.')[328]

b. Followed by the object in the dative case: Another of Ælfric's homilies illustrates this usage: 'Ic bebead ðeowum mannum, þæt hi getreowlice, and swa swa God heora hlafordum þeowdon.' ('I commanded slaves faithfully and as God to serve their masters.')[329]

ÞEOW-BOREN adj. 'Born as a slave.'

The word appears only in the Old English *Benedictine Rule*, where it is contrasted with *æþelboren*, 'nobly-born'.[330]

ÞEOW-BYRD adj. 'Born as a slave.'

There is only a single appearance of this word in the sources, namely, in a lease of land made in 902 by Denewulf, bishop of Winchester, where the compound *burbærde*, 'born as a *gebur*', also appears.[331] Cf. also *eorlgebyrd*, 'nobly-born', and *inbyrde* (q.v.)

ÞEOW-CNAPA sb. (m) 'A slave boy.'

The word appears only once, in a homily of Ælfric's on the Deposition of St Martin of Tours, where it refers to the slave of a heathen thegn whom Martin healed. The boy's slave status is proved by his being called *se ðeowa* a few lines later.[332]

ÞEOW-DOM sb. (m)   1) 'The state of being a slave, slavery, servitude.'

The basic meaning of the word has few unambiguous attestations. The clearest example occurs in the description of the descendants of Ham in London, British Library, MS. Cotton Domitian iii: 'þ cynn was geseald . . . þam oðrum cynnum twam on heaftnead 7 on þeowdom' ('that kindred was given into captivity and slavery under the other

[326] As in Ælfric's *Grammar*, where *þeowa man* is used synonymously with *wealh* in glossing *mancipium*: *Aelfrics Grammatik und Glossar*, ed. Zupitza, p. 101.19–21.
[327] For example, *Genesis A*, lines 2747 and 2754, in *The Junius Manuscript*, ed. Krapp, pp. 81 and 82.
[328] *Ælfric's Catholic Homilies*, §19.224–7 (ed. Godden, p. 187) (= *The Sermones Catholici*, I.21 [ed. & transl. Thorpe, p. 326.30–3]) (text); *ibid.*, p. 327.29–32 (translation).
[329] *The Sermones Catholici*, I.26 (ed. Thorpe, p. 378.31–3) (text); *ibid.*, p. 379.29–30 (translation, emended).
[330] *Die angelsächsischen Prosabearbeitungen der Benediktinerregel*, §2 (ed. Schröer, p. 12.13).
[331] *Select English Historical Documents*, §17 (ed. Harmer, p. 29.22) (= Sawyer, *Anglo-Saxon Charters*, no. 1285).
[332] *Ælfric's Catholic Homilies*, §34.199 (ed. Godden, p. 293 and cf. line 201) (= *The Sermones Catholici*, II.39 [ed. & transl. Thorpe, p. 510.27 and cf. line 29]) (text); *ibid.*, p. 511.29 and cf. line 31 (translation).

two kindreds').[333] The word glosses *mancipatio* once[334] and *famulatus* twice.[335] Ælfric gives *þes þeowdom* as the gloss for *haec seruitus* in his *Grammar* but this probably represents its frequently attested sense of 'service'.[336] The latter meaning often occurs in ecclesiastical contexts, but it is not always possible to distinguish which sense is required in some instances. Ælfric was cognisant of the two meanings and makes use of the ambiguity in one of his homilies, *On the Nativity of One Apostle*: 'Ege is twyfeald, and ðeowdom is twyfeald. . . . Swa is eac oðer ðeowt neadunge buton lufe, oðer is sylfwilles mid lufe, se gedafenað Godes ðeowum.' ('Awe is twofold, and service is twofold. . . . So also one service is compulsory without love, the other is voluntary with love, which befits God's slaves.')[337]

2) 'Spiritual service.'

From sense 1) *þeowdom* was extended in meaning to 'work characteristic of a state of slavery'; it is most convenient to translate it 'service' but whether it ever lost its connotation of legal servitude is moot. The word is frequently used of service to God or to the devil, and in some contexts at least it would appear from associated words that the legal connotation remained. Thus in the fourth Blickling Homily one reads: 'gif se Godes þeow nelle þære cyrican on riht þeowian, þæt he þonne mid læwedum mannum onfo þæs heardestan þeowdomes' ('if the slave of God will not rightly serve the church, then let him receive along with the laity the hardest service').[338] So, also, the following two extracts referring to the redemptive acts of Christ imply through their verbs that a similar connotation is present: 'he wolde . . . us gefreolsian from deofles þeowdome' ('he would . . . release us from the devil's servitude') and *us alesde of deofles þeowdome* ('he released us from the devil's servitude').[339] It also occurs in the phrase *Godes þeowdom*.[340]

3) 'Service due from a property to an overlord.'

This appears, usually in the plural, in a number of charters, for example, one of King Edward the Confessor's to Horton Abbey in A.D. 1061: 'þ hyt sy . . . gefreod ealra cynelicra 7 ealdordomlicra þeowdoma' ('that it shall . . . be freed from all royal and official services').[341] The citation shows that the word no longer retained the root sense of 'slavery'. (For a similar semantic development cf. *þeowet*.) That the underlying idea of servitude was not entirely lost, however, is suggested by the use of the verb *freod* here

---

[333] Napier, 'Altenglische Kleiningkeiten', 2.49–51 (text) (= Ker, *Catalogue*, §186.8 [p. 243]).

[334] London, British Library, Additional MS. 32246, fo 21r, in 'The Latin-Old English glossaries', ed. Kindschi, p. 245.2 (= Wright, *Anglo-Saxon and Old English Vocabularies*, ed. Wülcker, I, col. 188.22).

[335] *Famulatus* in the Harley Glossary and *famulatibus – þeowdomum* in the Cleopatra Glossary: *ibid.*, I, cols 235.45 and 400.23.

[336] *Aelfrics Grammatik und Glossar*, ed. Zupitza, p. 60.6–7.

[337] *Ælfric's Catholic Homilies*, §35.45–8 (ed. Godden, p. 300) (= *The Sermones Catholici*, II.40 [ed. & transl. Thorpe, p. 524.3–6]) (text); *ibid.*, p. 525.3–6 (translation, emended).

[338] *The Blickling Homilies*, §4 (ed. & transl. Morris, p. 49.3–5) (text); *ibid.*, p. 48 (translation, emended).

[339] *Ibid.*, §6 (pp. 65.31–2 and 73.7–8) (text); *ibid.*, pp. 64 and 72 (translation; the second extract slightly emended).

[340] For example, *Homilies of Ælfric*, §18.94 (ed. Pope, II.594).

[341] *Anglo-Saxon Charters*, §120 (ed. & transl. Robertson, p. 222.8–10) (text); *ibid.*, p.223 (translation, emended) (= Sawyer, *Anglo-Saxon Charters*, no. 1032). Cf. also *Anglo-Saxon Charters*, §11 (ed. & transl. Robertson, p. 18.6) (= Sawyer, *Anglo-Saxon Charters*, no. 333); *Anglo-Saxon Wills*, §17 (ed. & transl. Whitelock, p. 48.4) (= Sawyer, *Anglo-Saxon Charters*, no. 1536); and in the singular, *Anglo-Saxon Charters*, §25 (ed. & transl. Robertson, p. 50.2) (= Sawyer, *Anglo-Saxon Charters*, no. 427).

and the contrasting use of *freodom* in a charter of Æthelstan of *ca* 934: '7 ic wulla ðæt þas land durhwunien on æcelecum freodomæ from æghwelcum eorðlecum ðeowdomæ butan firdæ 7 festæn gewæorcæ 7 brycggewæorce.' ('And I desire that these estates shall enjoy perpetual freedom from every secular service, except military service and the construction of fortifications and bridges.')[342]

* ÞEOWDOM-HAD sb. (m) 'The condition of being in slavery.' (In a spiritual sense.)

The word is found only in the Old English *Bede*, where 'monige . . . hi seolfe 7 hira bearn ma gyrnað in mynster ond on Godes þeowdomhad to sellenne, þonne hie syn begongende weoroldlicne comphad' ('many . . . are more desirous to give up themselves and their children to monastic life and God's service, than they are to pursue worldly warfare') somewhat freely translates 'plures . . . se suosque liberos, depositis armis satagunt magis, accepta tonsura, monasterialibus adscribere uotis quam bellicis exercere studiis'.[343]

ÞEOWEN, ÞEOWENE sb. (f)   1) 'A female slave.'

Þeowen is formed from a combination of the masculine substantive *þeow* and the feminine suffix *-en* seen also in *mennen*, *þinen* and *wyln* (qq.v.). That it is the exact feminine equivalent of *þeow* (q.v.) is proved by such examples as the translation *þeowas 7 ðeowena* for *seruos et ancillas* in the Old English *Heptateuch* at Genesis 32:5,[344] and the pair *his ðeowe oððe his ðeowenne* in the Prologue to Alfred's Laws, §20.[345]

   2) 'A female slave.' (In a spiritual sense.)

This is used in the phrases *Drihtnes þeowen* and *Godes ðeowen* in prose[346] and, in a poetic context, *nergendes þeowen* ('Saviour's slave') in *Judith*, lines 73–4,[347] all no doubt derived from the Latin *ancilla Dei*.

   3) 'A state of being a (female) slave.'

The single attestation in this sense occurs in the Preface to Alfred's Laws, §12: 'ðeah hwa gebycgge his dohtor on þeowenne' ('Though anyone sell his daughter to be a slave'). This is a literal translation of Exodus 21:7: 'Si quis uendiderit filiam suam in famulam', which may have been regarded as unidiomatic in Old English as *on þeowenne* is replaced by *to þeowte* in the *Textus Roffensis* version of Alfred's Laws.[348]

ÞEOWET sb. (m)   1) 'A legal state of slavery.'

In II Cnut, §68.1b *þeowet* is contrasted with *freot*.[349] In the Old English *Heptateuch* it represents the Latin *seruitute* of Leviticus 25:39.[350]

---

[342] *Anglo-Saxon Charters*, §25 (ed. & transl. Robertson, p. 50.1–3) (text); *ibid.*, p. 51 (translation) (= Sawyer, *Anglo-Saxon Charters*, no. 427).

[343] *The Old English Version of Bede's Ecclesiastical History*, V.22 (ed. & transl. Miller, I.2.480.9–11) (text); *ibid.*, I.2.481.9–12 (translation) (= *Bede's Ecclesiastical History*, V.23 [edd. & transl. Colgrave & Mynors, p. 560]).

[344] *The Old English Version of the Heptateuch*, ed. Crawford, p. 164.

[345] *Die Gesetze*, ed. Liebermann, I.32.

[346] For example, *The Blickling Homilies*, §1 (ed. & transl. Morris, p. 9.20) and *Select English Historical Documents*, §4 (ed. & transl. Harmer, p. 7.24: *Godes ðiwen*) (text); *ibid.*, p. 43 (translation) (= Sawyer, *Anglo-Saxon Charters*, no. 1197).

[347] *Beowulf and Judith*, ed. Dobbie, p. 101.

[348] *Die Gesetze*, ed. Liebermann, I.30–1.

[349] *Die Gesetze*, ed. Liebermann, I.354 (text); *The Laws of the Kings of England*, ed. & transl. Robertson, p. 209 (translation).

[350] *The Old English Version of the Heptateuch*, ed. Crawford, p. 300.

2) 'A spiritual state of slavery.'

This word was much favoured by Ælfric to describe servitude to the devil or to sin. The only possible instance where it could refer to divine service appears in his homily, *On the Nativity of One Apostle* (cited s.v. *þeowdom*); the sentence is elliptical and it would be unwise to assert that *þeowet* was used more widely in such a context.[351] An example of the pejorative use of *þeowet* is to be seen in Ælfric's contrast between legal and spiritual bondage: 'Ælc ðeowt bið geendod on ðisum andweardan life, buton ðæra anra þe synnum ðeowiað, hi habbað ecne ðeowt, and ða oðre beoð frige, ðeah ðe hi on life lange ær ðeowdon.' ('Every servitude will be ended in this present life, save of those only who minister to sins, they will have everlasting servitude, and the others will be free, although they in life long before had served.')[352] Another example appears in the Old English translation of Gregory's *Cura Pastoralis*, where the word is used in opposition to *freodom*, 'a (spiritual) state of freedom', representing *seruitus* and *libertas*, which are in the Latin source.[353]

3) 'Service due from a property to a superior authority.'

The single occurrence of this word shows by its context that it had moved from the abstract concept 'slavery' to the more concrete 'the payment through labour service, cash or kind due from a property to an overlord'. It appears in a charter of A.D. 963: 'ic Oswald . . . sumne dæl landes, þ synd III hida æt Þorndune Æþelstane minum þegne his dæg freoh ælces weoruldcundes þeowetes geuþe buton þreom þingum: an is circsceat 7 þ he mid eallum cræfte twuga on geare æne to mæþe 7 oþre siðe to ripe.' ('I, Oswald, . . . have granted a certain piece of land, namely 3 hides at Thorne, to my thegn Æthelstan for his lifetime, free from every secular service except for three things, one is church dues and that he <work> with all his might twice a year, once at hay-making and the other time at harvest.')[354] Its widespread use in other contexts in the sense 'slavery' suggests that it must originally have been applied metaphorically in this sense to land also.

* ÞEOWET-DOM sb. (m) 'A service.'

This word appears only once, in the plural forms *ðeowutdomas* (London, British Library, MSS Cotton Tiberius B.xi and Otho B.ii) and *ðiowotdomas* (Oxford, Bodleian Library, Hatton MS. 20 [*S.C.* 4113]), in Alfred's Preface to his translation of the *Cura Pastoralis*, where the words refer to services that are performed for God.[355] The word itself is probably synonymous with *þeowdom* (q.v.), the only difference being that it is derived from *þeowet* rather than *þeow*.

ÞEOWET-LIC adj. 'Servile, characteristic of a slave.'

An anonymous homily, *Sermo ad populum dominicis diebus*, uses the technical expression derived from canon law *þeowetlicum weorcum* (cf. s.v. *þeowweorc*).[356] Ælfric

---

351 *Ælfric's Catholic Homilies*, §35.47 (ed. Godden, p. 300) (= *The Sermones Catholici*, II.40 [ed. & transl. Thorpe, p. 524.5]).

352 *Ælfric's Catholic Homilies*, §19.224–7 (ed. Godden, p. 187) (= *The Sermones Catholici*, II.21 [ed. & transl. Thorpe, p. 326.30–3]) (text); *ibid.*, p. 327.29–32 (translation).

353 *King Alfred's West Saxon Version of Gregory's Pastoral Care*, §37 (ed. Sweet, I.265.5) (Old English text); *ibid.*, I.265 (translation); *Grégoire le Grand Règle pastorale*, III.13 (ed. Judic et al., II.336.24–5) (Latin).

354 *Anglo-Saxon Charters*, §36 (ed. & transl. Robertson, p. 66.6–11) (text); *ibid.*, p. 367 (translation) (= Sawyer, *Anglo-Saxon Charters*, no. 1305).

355 *King Alfred's West-Saxon Version of Gregory's Pastoral Care*, ed. Sweet, pp. 2.10 and 3.10 (text and translation).

356 *Wulfstan*, §55 (ed. Napier, p. 292.7).

also uses the phrase in his discussion of the day of rest in his first sermon on Midlent Sunday, but he takes the technical expression and renews it as a metaphor drawn from the terminology of servitude: 'Ac se Sunnandæg is nu gehalgod þurh soðfæstnysse his æristes of deaðe. Oðer restendæg is us eac toweard, þæt is, þæt ece lif, on ðam bið an dæg buton ælcere nihte, on þam we us gerestað ecelice, gif we nu ðeowtlicera weorca, þæt sind synna, geswicað.' ('[B]ut Sunday is now hallowed by the truth of his resurrection from death. Another day of rest for us is also to come, that is, the everlasting life, in which will be one day without any night, in which we shall rest eternally, if we now cease from servile works, that is, from sins.')[357] *Þeowetlic* glosses *seruilis* in several texts.[358]

ÞEOWETLING sb. (m) 1) 'A little or young slave.'

The diminutive force of the suffix can be seen in one of Ælfric's *Catholic Homilies* entitled *The Octaves and Circumcision of Our Lord*: 'Ælc hysecild . . . ægðer ge æþelboren ge þeowetling' ('every male child . . . both the noble-born and the slave').[359]

2) 'Slave.' (With some derogatory connotation.)

a: The phrase *earm þeowetling* appears twice, where an attitude of pity on the part of the speaker is implied. In Ælfric's *Sermon on the Fifth Sunday in Lent earm* is used in the sense 'pitiful, wretched': 'þeah ðe he bruce brades rices, he is earm ðeowtling, na anes hlafordes' ('though he enjoy a broad realm, he is a miserable slave, not of one master').[360] In VIII Æthelred, §6 *earm* is used in the sense 'destitute': 'þridde Godes þearfum 7 earman þeowetlingan' ('the third portion to God's poor and poverty-stricken slaves').[361] The implicit notion of weakness arising out of the legal condition of slavery perhaps governed Wulfstan's choice of this word in his *Institutes of Polity*: 'þearfena helpan and þeowetlingan beorgan' ('to help the needy and protect slaves'); it is possible, however, that he used it in sense 3).[362] The word may originally have been coined under the influence of the Latin *seruulus*; it glosses the latter several times in the hymns in London, British Library, MSS Cotton Julius A.vi and Vespasian D.xii.[363]

b: Two passages show by their context that the person concerned was being disparaged. In the *Life of Saint Agatha* in Ælfric's *Lives of the Saints* it is said of Quintinianus: 'Se wæs grædig gitsere . . . deofles þeowetlincg.' ('He was a greedy miser . . . the devil's slave.')[364] The word is also twice used of a priest's slave in Wærferth's translation of Gregory's *Dialogues* (*mancipium* is used in the original), where the slave is addressed by the priest: 'Cum, deoful, hider 7 unsco me!' ('Come here, devil, and take off my shoes!')[365]

---

[357] *Ælfric's Catholic Homilies*, §12.307–11 (ed. Godden, pp. 118–19) (= *The Sermones Catholici*, II.12 [ed. & transl. Thorpe, p. 13.208.3–7]) (text); *ibid.*, p. 209.4–7 (translation).

[358] *Aelfrics Grammatik und Glossar*, ed. Zupitza, p. 55.1 (*þeowtlic*); *Liber Scintillarum*, §11 (ed. Rhodes, p. 63.13); *Hymnar und Hymnen im englischen Mittelalter*, §44.2 (ed. Gneuss, p. 320).

[359] *The Sermones Catholici*, I.6 (ed. & transl. Thorpe, p. 90.29–92.1) (text); *ibid.*, p.91.28–93.2.

[360] *Ælfric's Catholic Homilies*, §13.78–9 (ed. Godden, p. 129) (= *The Sermones Catholici*, II.13 [ed. & transl. Thorpe, p. 228.10–11]) (text); *ibid.*, p. 229.9–10 (translation, slightly emended).

[361] *Die Gesetze*, ed. Liebermann, 1.264 (text); *The Laws of the Kings of England*, ed. & transl. Robertson, p. 121 (translation).

[362] *Die 'Institutes of Polity, Civil and Ecclesiastical'*, §2.87 (ed. Jost, p. 79.6–7).

[363] *Hymnar und Hymnen im englischen Mittelalter*, §§25.3, 104(2).3, 117.8, 121.4, and 124.4 (ed. Gneuss, pp. 292, 387, 393, 398, and 402).

[364] *Ælfric's Lives of Saints*, §8.5–6 (ed. & transl. Skeat, I.196) (text); *ibid.*, I.197.5–6 (translation).

[365] *Bischof Wærferths von Worcester Übersetzung*, III.20 (ed. Hecht, I.221.21–2 and 222.1) (Old English); *Grégoire le Grand Dialogues*, III.20.1 and 2 (ed. de Vogüé, II.350.5 and 13) (Latin).

3) 'The legal status of slave.'

The diminutive denotation and derogatory connotations of the *-ling* suffix seem to have been lost in the anonymous homily, *Be mistlican gelimpan*: 'alces mannes þeowet-lingas ealle þa ðry dagas . . . weorces beon gefreode' ('everyone's slaves are to be freed from work on all those three days') in the Cambridge, Corpus Christi College, MS. 201 and Oxford, Bodleian Library, MS. Hatton 113 (*S.C.* 5210) versions.[366] In the other version of the sermon in London, British Library, MS. Cotton Tiberius A.iii, it is replaced by *þeowlincgas* (q.v.).[367] Cf. *nydþeowetling*. In an untitled variant of the ninth of the Vercelli Homilies to be found in Oxford, Bodleian Library, MS. Hatton 115 (*S.C.* 5135), the word similarly seems to be devoid of any derogatory connotation and its use seems rather to have been based on stylistic grounds: '7 se deaþ is iunglic, for þon þe cild sweltaþ 7 unmagan, 7 he is freolic 7 þeowlic, for þon cyningas sweltaþ 7 þeowet-lingas' ('And Death is youthful, because the child dies and the needy person, and it is free and servile, because kings die and slaves).[368] The rhetorical balancing evident in *cild/unmagan* and *freolic/þeowlic* has undoubtedly dictated the choice of the noun, *þeowetlingas*, so as to rhyme with the *-inges* of *cyningas*.

* **ÞEOWETSCIPE** sb. (m) 'The condition of being in servitude, service.' (In a spiritual sense.)

Derived from *þeowet*, the word is used once in a description of the monk Zosimus in Ælfric's *Death of St Mary of Egypt*: 'And he ealle þæs regoles bebodu and fulfremed-nysse þæs munuclican þeowtscypes untallice geheold.' ('And he blamelessly observed all the directions of the rule, and the perfection of the monastic service.')[369] The associ-ation of the word with slavery is appropriate as monks were considered to be God's slaves.

* **ÞEOW-FÆST** adj. 'Acting in the manner of a slave', hence, 'obedient.'

The second of the Vercelli Homilies illustrates this usage: '7 sien we snotre 7 soðfæste . . . 7 larsume 7 þeowfæste' ('and let us be wise an true . . . and willing to learn and obedient').[370]

* **ÞEOWFÆSTNESS** sb. (f) 'Behaviour appropriate to a slave', hence, 'obedience.'

The Winteney version of the *Benedictine Rule* translates the Latin, 'Pueri parui uel adolescentes in oratorio uel ad mensas cum disciplina ordines suos consequantur' as 'Ða child 7 þeo geogad mid styre þeowfætnesse hire endebyrdnesse filian' ('the child and the youth should follow their order with obedience').[371]

* **ÞEOW-HAD** sb. (m) 'The condition of being a slave.' (In a spiritual sense.)

The word appears only in the Old English *Bede*, where it is used both of a nun and of a monk. In the first instance *accepto uelamine sanctimonialis habitus* is paraphrased 'heo þær haligrefte onfeng 7 Godes þeowhade' ('she received the veil and accepted the condition of a slave of God'), and in the second *acceptaque tonsura* is rendered in Old English as '7 he þer Godes þiohade 7 scare onfeng' ('And he there accepted the state of

366 *Wulfstan*, §35 (ed. Napier, p. 171.19–20).
367 *Ibid.*, §36 (p. 173.23–4).
368 *The Vercelli Homilies*, §9.46–8 (ed. Scragg, p. 163).
369 *Ælfric's Lives of Saints*, §23B (ed. & transl. Skeat, II.4.25–6) (text); *ibid.*, II.5.25–6 (trans-lation).
370 *The Vercelli Homilies*, II.110 (ed. Scragg, p. 64).
371 *Die Winteney-Version der Regula S. Benedicti*, §63 (ed. Schröer, p. 129.29–30) (Old Eng-lish); *The Rule of Saint Benedict in Latin and Old English*, ed. & transl. McCann, p. 144 (Latin).

slavery to God and the tonsure').[372] The translator clearly was influenced by the phrase *Godes þeow(en)* in his choice of *þeowhad* to paraphrase the Latin.

(GE)-ÞEOWIAN vb 1) 'To serve (as a slave).'

a: An unambiguous example of *geþeowian* in this sense is in Exodus 21:2 in the Old English *Heptateuch*: 'Gyf ðu Ebreiscne ðeow bigst, þeowige he syx gear, 7 beo him freoh on ðam seofoðan' ('If you buy a Hebrew slave, let him serve you for six years, and let him be free on the seventh'), translating 'Si emeris seruum Hebræum, sex annis seruiet tibi: in septimo egredietur liber gratis.'[373] In *Grið*, §17, the three verbs, 'gylde he, þeowige he 7 þolige he' ('he should pay, he should serve as a slave, and he should suffer punishment') equate to the three substantives in the preceding clause, *wergyld, ece þeowet, hengenwitnuncg* ('wergeld, perpetual enslavement, imprisonment').[374]

b (followed by the dative case): In Genesis 47:25 in the Old English *Heptateuch* Joseph's brothers declare: 'we þeowiaþ bliðelice þam cyninge', which translates *læti seruiemus regi*.'[375]

2) 'to be enslaved, to serve (as a slave, in a metaphorical sense).'

Ælfric was clearly making a play on the concept of slavery in his statement, 'Witodlice se synfulla ðeowaþ ðam wyrstum ðeowte þeah ðe he bruce brades rices; he is earm ðeowtling. Soð soð ic eow secge, ælc ðæra ðe synne wyrcð, he bið þonne ðære synne ðeow.' ('But a sinful man is a slave in the worst servitude: though he enjoy a broad realm, he is a miserable slave. Truly, truly, I say to you, each of those who sin, he is then a slave of sin.')[376]

3) 'To enslave, to reduce to a legal state of slavery.'

The word appears in an Exeter manumission-document of the second half of the eleventh century, *Manumission*, §5.1, and in the manumission clause of a will of A.D. 966 x 975;[377] in both instances it is contrasted with its antonym *freogan*: 'Halwun Hoce . . . freode Hægelflæde hire wimman. . . . Him wurþe wrað þe hi hæfre geþywie' ('Alwynn Hook . . . freed her woman, Æthelflæd. . . . May He be angry with whoever enslaves her') and 'man freoge on ælcum tunæ ælne witæþæownæ mann þæ undær hiræ geþeowuð wæs' ('every penally enslaved man who was subject to her shall be freed'). It is twice attested in this sense in Ine, §48[378] and also appears in the various versions of Wulfstan's *Sermo ad Anglos*.[379] This wide (if infrequent) attestation probably indicates that it was the standard verb to denote the act of enslavement.

4) 'To subject property to one's overlordship.'

V Æthelred, §10.1–2 (cf. VI Æthelred, §15) enacts: '1) 7 sy ælc cyrice on Godes

---

[372] *The Old English Version of Bede's Ecclesiastical History*, IV.21 and V.13 (ed. & transl. Miller, I.2.318.7–8 and I.2.424.11) (text); *ibid.*, I.2.319.8–9 and I.2.425.12–13 (translation, emended in both instances) (= *Bede's Ecclesiastical History*, IV.19 and V.12 [edd. & transl. Colgrave & Mynors, pp. 392 and 488]).

[373] *The Old English Version of the Heptateuch*, ed. Crawford, p. 263.

[374] *Die Gesetze*, ed. Liebermann, I.471.

[375] *The Old English Version of the Heptateuch*, ed. Crawford, p. 204.

[376] *Ælfric's Catholic Homilies*, §13.76–8 (ed. Godden, p. 129) (partially recorded in *The Sermones Catholici*, II.13 [ed. & transl. Thorpe, p. 228.9–11]) (text); *ibid.*, p. 229.8–10 (translation, emended and supplemented).

[377] *Anglo-Saxon Wills*, §8 (ed. & transl. Whitelock, p. 20.8–9) (text); *ibid.*, p. 21 (translation) (= Sawyer, *Anglo-Saxon Charters*, no. 1484).

[378] *Die Gesetze*, ed. Liebermann, I.110.

[379] *The Homilies of Wulfstan*, §§20(BH).41–2, 20(C).47, and 20(EI).46 (ed. Bethurum, pp. 257, 262, and 269).

griðe 7 on ðæs cynges 7 on ealles Cristenes folces. 2) 7 ænig man heonan forð cyrican ne ðeowige.' ('§1. And all churches shall be under the special protection of God and of the king and of all Christian people. §2. And no-one henceforth shall enslave the Church.')[380] The effect of 'enslaving' a church was that the lord would get any dues accruing from the property, turning the church in effect into an *Eigenkirche*. Cf. s.v. *nidþeowian*.

ÞEOW-INCEL sb. (n) 'A little/young slave.'

The word occurs in one of the hymns in the Vespasian Psalter (London, British Library, MS. Cotton Vespasian A.i), written in the Mercian dialect probably in the middle of the ninth century, where the plural form *ðiowincelu* glosses *familici*, 'households'.[381] The glossator must have (incorrectly) assumed the latter word to be a diminutive form of *famulus*, 'a slave'. The mid-eleventh-century Cambridge Psalter (Cambridge, University Library, MS. Ff.1.23 [1156]) preserves this *faut pas*.[382] The suffix -*incel* is also to be seen in *wilnincel* (q.v.).

ÞEOW-LIC adj. 'Appropriate to the condition of a slave, servile.'

This glosses *seruilis* in the Worcester, Cathedral, MS. F.174 version of Ælfric's *Grammar*, written in the thirteenth century. The other manuscripts have forms derived from *þeowetlic* (for example, *þeowtlic*, *þeowotlic*).[383] That *þeowlic* is a valid form and not a scribal error is proved by its use in an anonymous homily for the Second Sunday after Epiphany, where *ðeowlic* (Vercelli, Biblioteca Capitolare, MS. CXVII actually reads *deoplic*) is contrasted with *freolic*.[384] An even less ambiguous attestation appears in the phrase *þone ðeowlice ege*, 'the servile fear', in an Old English translation of Alcuin's *De Uirtutibus et Uitiis*.[385]

* ÞEOW-LICE adv.   1) 'In the manner of a slave, servilely.'

The single example of *þeowlice* in this sense is to be found in one of the Blickling Homilies: 'He þonne gecyrde to us, þa he hider becom of his Fæder rice, 7 hine ungyrede þæs godcundan mægenþrymmes, 7 gegyrede hine þeowlice mid þære menniscan tydernesse.' ('He turned to us when he came hither from his father's realm and divested himself of the divine majesty and invested himself humbly with human frailty.')[386]

2) 'With an obligation to render the customary dues from a property to an overlord.'

This usage occurs is in what purports to be a writ of A.D. 1045 x 1049 of King Edward: 'ic [*sc.* Edward] cyðe eow þ ic habbe gegiuen Criste 7 Sce Peter into Westmunstre þ land æt Ældenham, mid saca 7 mid socna, mid tolle 7 mid teame 7 infangeneþeofe, swa full 7 swa forð swa Sihtric eorl of þan munstre þiowlice hit hyold.' Harmer translated this as: 'And I inform you that I have given to Westminster, to Christ and to St. Peter, the land at Aldenham with sake and with soke, with toll and with team

---

[380] *Die Gesetze*, ed. Liebermann, I.240 (and cf. *ibid.*, I.250) (text); *The Laws of the Kings of England*, ed. & transl. Robertson, p. 83 (translation, emended).

[381] *Hymn*, §4.7, in *The Vespasian Psalter*, ed. Kuhn, p. 148. On the dating of the hand see Ker, *Catalogue*, §203 (p. 267).

[382] *Canticle*, §3.5, in *Der Cambridger Psalter*, ed. Wildhagen, p. 375.7 (*þeowinclu*).

[383] *Aelfrics Grammatik und Glossar*, ed. Zupitza, p. 55.1; Ker, *Catalogue*, §398 (pp. 466–7). The manuscript is one of several written in a 'tremulous' hand by a Worcester scribe.

[384] *The Vercelli Homilies*, §9 (ed. Scragg, p. 162.53 = p. 163.47).

[385] *Early English Homilies*, §35 (ed. Warner, p. 105.7).

[386] *The Blickling Homilies*, ed. Morris, p. 103.1–4 (text); *ibid.*, p. 102 (translation).

and infangenetheof, as fully and as completely as Earl Sihtric held it humbly (?) of the monastery.'[387]

In the light of the analysis in chapter I above of the terminology of servitude as applied to land, it seems that Harmer was wise in indicating uncertainty over glossing *þiowlice* as 'humbly'.[388] The use of such words as *freodom*, *freolice*, and *þeowdom* (qq.v.) suggest that a different explanation is required. The most reasonable one is that Sihtric had been granted some sort of use of the estate at Aldenham (possibly the usufruct in the *inland* or demesne) but that the estate as a whole still had to return dues to the monastery rather than to Sihtric. He would thus not hold the land 'freely' (*freolice*, q.v.). Alternatively, it might mean that Sihtric could not alienate the estate. If either of these suggested meanings (and *freolice* as an antonym) is reasonable, then Harmer was probably incorrect in asserting that the word 'is not part of the normal legal phraseology of the Anglo-Saxon period'.[389]

ÞEOWLING sb. (m) 'A person in a legal condition of slavery, a slave.'

The word is used once in an anonymous homily (possibly composed by Wulfstan)[390] beginning *Be mistlican gelimpan*: 'þeowlincgas þa þry dagas ælces weorces beon frige.' ('slaves are to be free from work on those three days.')[391] Here the *-ling* suffix seems to have lost its diminutive and pejorative connotations, as in *þeowetling* 3) and *nidþeowetling* (qq.v.). Wulfstan uses *þeowetling* (q.v. 3) in the same context; the variant version of the anonymous sermon also uses the latter word.

ÞEOW-MAN sb. (m) 'Slave.'

This word is used over a wide chronological and geographic range in Old English. Its earliest use is in the Laws of Ine, §3: 'Gif þeowmon wyrce on Sunnandæg be his hlafordes hæse, sie he frioh' ('If a slave works on Sunday by his lord's command, he shall become free').[392] It also appears in Alfred's Laws, §25.1,[393] and is found as late as the twelfth century in one of the homilies in Oxford, Bodleian Library, MS. Bodley 343 (*S.C.* 2406): 'Soðlice nylt þu nan þing yfeles habben on þin æhte; þu nelt habben yfel wif, ne yfel child, ne yfele þeowmen.' ('Truly thou wilt not have anything bad in thy possession. Thou wilt not have a bad wife or a bad child or bad slaves.')[394] This latter example, together with its use in a Kentish marriage agreement of A.D. 1016 x 1020 in which an intending husband pledges to his bride-to-be various gifts including *tyn ðeowmen* ('10 slaves'),[395] indicates by the plural form that this was regarded by Anglo-Saxons as a true compound and not simply an adjective plus a substantive. Ælfric in his *Grammar* regarded it is the vernacular equivalent of *mancipium*[396] and in the *Northumbrian Priest's Law*, §56, it is contrasted with *friman*, 'a freeman'.[397]

387 *Anglo-Saxon Writs*, §78.2–5 (ed. & transl. Harmer, p. 345) (text); *ibid.*, p. 346 (translation) (= Sawyer, *Anglo-Saxon Charters*, no. 1122).

388 *Anglo-Saxon Writs*, ed. & transl. Harmer, p. 346.

389 *Ibid.*, p. 314.

390 Whitelock in *Sermo Lupi ad Anglos*, p. 21, considered it to be in Wulfstan's style. Cf. Jost, *Wulfstanstudien*, pp. 213–16.

391 *Wulfstan*, §36 (ed. Napier, p. 173.23–4).

392 *Die Gesetze*, ed. Liebermann, I.90 (text); *The Laws*, ed. & transl. Attenborough, p. 37 (translation).

393 *Die Gesetze*, ed. Liebermann, I.64 (text); *The Laws*, ed. & transl. Attenborough, p. 75 (translation).

394 *Twelfth-Century Homilies in MS. Bodley 343*, §13 (ed. Belfour, p. 134.19–20).

395 *Anglo-Saxon Charters*, §77 (ed. & transl. Robertson, p. 150.6) (text); *ibid.*, p. 151 (translation) (= Sawyer, *Anglo-Saxon Charters*, no. 1461).

396 *Aelfrics Grammatik und Glossar*, ed. Zupitza, pp. 88.19–89.1.

397 *Die Gesetze*, ed. Liebermann, I.383.

ÞEOW-MENNEN sb. (f) 'A female slave.'

In the compound *þeowmennen*,[398] the first element would be pleonastic if *-mennen* did not have the generalised sense of 'a female person'. The word is to be found in the Prologue to Alfred's Laws, §21[399] and, with reference to Hagar, in the poem *Genesis A*, line 2248.[400]

ÞEOW-NID sb. (f) 'Enslavement by compulsion, subjugation.'

This word occurs only in the context of religious poetry. It has the same semantic structure as *þreanyd*, 'force or compulsion that punishes or causes the misery or affliction that comes from punishment', and the two words appear in the same formulaic contexts:

> we nu hæðenra/ þeowned (Daniel, lines 306–7)
>
> we þær hæþenra/ þreanyd (Azarias, lines 27–8)

and

> for þreaum and for ðeonydum (Daniel, line 293)
>
> for þearfum ond for þreanydum (Azarias, line 14).[401]

In the second example *þeownid* appears to have a more generalised sense of 'oppression'. It is particularly associated with the verb *þolian*, 'to suffer': the formula *þeownid þolian* appears in *Daniel*, *Genesis A*, and *Elene*.[402]

* (GE)-ÞEOWTIAN vb 'To enslave.' (Used in a metaphorical sense.)

This word is used in the Old English translation of the *Elucidarium* of Honorius of Autun in a discussion of free will where the homilist utilises the terminology of servitude to express his meaning through paradox.[403] For the citation see s.v. *freodom* 3).

* ÞEOW-WEORC sb. (n) 'Work appropriate to be done by a slave, servile work.'

Þeowweorc appears only three times in the corpus of Old English. Its literal meaning is exemplified by II Edward, §6, which decrees: 'Gif hwa . . . freot forwyrce . . . ðonne sy he ðæs ðeowweorces wyrðe, ðe ðærto gebyrige.' ('If any man . . . forfeits his freedom, . . . he shall do such servile labour as may be required.')[404]

In the second extract it has the same meaning ('servile work') as in the previous one, but in this instance it holds a technical sense within the context of canon law: 'Gif esne ofer dryhtnes hæse þeowweorc wyrce an sunnan æfen efter hire setlgange . . .' ('If a servant, contrary to his lord's command, does servile work between sunset on Saturday

---

398 Bosworth, *An Anglo-Saxon Dictionary*, ed. Toller, p. 1056, col. 1, s.v. *þeow-mennen*, seems to reveal uncertainty as to whether to regard this as an adjective plus a substantive or as a compound substantive. The opposition *ðeow oððe ðeowmennen* in the Cambridge, Corpus Christi College, MS. 173 version of the Prologue to Alfred's Laws, §21 (*Die Gesetze*, ed. Liebermann, I.34) suggests that it should be taken as a compound substantive and one would expect such a form on the analogy of *þeowman*. But *þeow* could be a strong form of the adjective; unfortunately, it nowhere appears after a definite article where an adjectival usage would have dictated an inflected form.

399 *Die Gesetze*, ed. Liebermann, I.34.

400 *The Junius Manuscript*, ed. Krapp, p. 67.

401 *Daniel: The Junius Manuscript*, ed. Krapp, p. 119; *Azarias: The Exeter Book*, edd. Krapp & Dobbie, p. 89.

402 *Daniel*, line 307, and *Genesis*, line 2030, in *The Junius Manuscript*, ed. Krapp, pp. 119 and 61; *Elene*, line 769, in *The Vercelli Book*, ed. Krapp, p. 87.

403 *Early English Homilies*, §45 (ed. Warner, p. 141.16).

404 *Die Gesetze*, ed. Liebermann, I.144 (text); *The Laws*, ed. & transl. Attenborough, p. 121 (translation).

evening . . .') (Wihtred, §9).[405] The legislation is derived from the biblical prohibition against work on the Sabbath.[406] It holds the latter sense also in one of Ælfric's letters to Bishop Wulfsige.[407]

ÞIGNEN sb. (f)   1) 'A female slave.'

Ancilla is glossed by *þignen* in the Lindisfarne Gospels (Luke 22:56 and John 18:17) and *þegnen* in the Rushworth Gospels at John 18:17;[408] in the Corpus Glossary the lemma is *pedisequa*.[409] In the Old English *Bede þignen* is associated with *þeow*: 'Þa wæs heo gelæded from hire þeowum 7 þignenum to þæm mynstre' ('Then she was led by her male and female slaves to the monastery'), which rather imprecisely renders the Latin, 'Perducta namque a puellis suis ad monasterium'.[410]

2) 'A female slave.' (In a spiritual sense.)

The word is considered by the eleventh-century glossator to the Lambeth Psalter to be synonymous with *mennen* (q.v.)[411] It is used of those bound both to God and to the devil. Thus Ælfric quotes in his sermon, *The Annunciation of St Mary*, Mary's declaration in Luke 1:38: *Ic eom Godes ðinen* ('I am God's handmaid'),[412] and in his *Sermon on the Passion of St Matthew* Matthew blesses the Abbess Effigenia and her nuns with the words: 'ðu eart ealra Scyppend, and gelice Alysend; geheald þas Ðine þinena wið ælcere gewemmednysse.' ('Thou art of all Creator and likewise Redeemer, hold thine hand-maids against all pollution.')[413] On the other hand, in the Old English *Martyrology* under 19 October (St Pelagia) one reads: 'heo . . . cwæð to him: "Ic eom deofles ðinen." ' ('She . . . said to him: "I am the devil's slave." ')[414]

ÞIR sb. (f) 'A female slave.'

This is used only in the Lindisfarne and Rushworth Gospels at John 18:17, where *ancilla* is glossed *ðir uel sio ðignen* (*ðegnen* in Rushworth).[415] The word is a borrowing from Old Norse *þýr* 'bondwoman' with unrounding of the vowel. The final *-r* is an Old Norse feminine suffix. The glossators to both Northumbrian texts also use *þræl*, which is employed as the masculine equivalent to *þýr* in a number of Old Norse texts.[416]

ÞRÆL sb. (m) 1) 'A slave.'

There is no doubt that this word is a borrowing from Old Norse. It does not appear in

---

[405] *Die Gesetze*, ed. Liebermann, I.13 (text); *The Laws*, ed. & transl. Attenborough, p. 27 (translation).

[406] See McReavy, 'The Sunday repose from labour'.

[407] *Die Hirtenbriefe Ælfrics*, I.150 (ed. Fehr, p. 32).

[408] *The Gospel according to Saint Luke*, ed. Skeat, p. 215; *The Gospel according to Saint John*, ed. Skeat, p. 159.

[409] *The Corpus Glossary*, P190 (ed. Lindsay, p. 133).

[410] *The Old English Version of Bede's Ecclesiastical History*, IV.13 (ed. & transl. Miller, I.2.292.24) (text); *ibid.*, I.2.293 (translation) (= *Bede's Ecclesiastical History*, IV.10 [edd. & transl. Colgrave & Mynors, p. 364]).

[411] *Der Lambeth-Psalter*, ed. Lindelöf, I.137.

[412] *The Sermones Catholici*, I.13 (ed. & transl. Thorpe, p. 200.10) (text); *ibid.*, p. 201.9–10 (translation).

[413] *The Homilies of Ælfric*, §32.176–8 (ed. Godden, p. 278) (= *The Sermones Catholici*, II.37 [ed. & transl. Thorpe, p. 478.9–11]) (text); *ibid.*, p. 479.9–11 (translation).

[414] *Das altenglische Martyrologium*, §210 (ed. Kotzor, II.234.7).

[415] *The Gospel according to Saint John*, ed. Skeat, p. 159.

[416] See Cleasby & Vigfusson, *An Icelandic-English Dictionary*, 2nd edn, rev. Craigie, p. 756, s.v. *þýr*.

Old English before the time of the Scandinavian invasions, and its use in Old English is limited to three contexts, all related to the Norse world:

i) writings derived from the northern parts of England;
ii) legal documents, possibly drawn up outside the Norse sphere of influence but nevertheless directly concerning that people;
iii) writings of Wulfstan.

In the first category fall the Northumbrian glosses in the Lindisfarne and Rushworth Gospels and the *Durham Ritual*, all of which date from the latter half of the tenth century. With but a single exception *þræl* glosses *seruus* in these texts.[417]

The word is used twice in the laws of Æthelred. II Æthelred, §5.1 refers to a *Deniscne ðræl*, so is obviously influenced by Norse terminology.[418] The second attestation is in VIIa Æthelred, §3, a code drawn up under Wulfstan's influence.[419] *Grið*, another piece of legislation showing Wulfstanian influence, employs in §21.2 one of his favourite jingles: 'þræl wearð to ðegene 7 ceorl wearð to eorle' ('a thrall becomes a thegn and a churl becomes an earl').[420]

Finally, *þræl* is the standard word for a slave in Wulfstan's own writings.

The only example of the word in a possible southern context is in the gloss to *Colloquy*, line 201, where the Latin text contrasts *coci* with *dominus*.[421] The glossator, obviously thinking of the standard contrast between slave and lord, glossed *coci* with the word *þrælas*. The gloss dates from the eleventh century, when West Saxon was the standard literary dialect. Thus the text could have a northern provenance, even though written in West Saxon.[422]

2) 'A slave.' (In a spiritual sense.)

In Wulfstan's ideolect *þræl* and *þeow* seem to have had slightly different connotations in religious contexts, a point that hitherto seems to have escaped attention. *Þeow* is used in a phrase much loved by Wulfstan, *Godes þeowas*. *Þræl* appears to have acquired a pejorative connotation, which does not seem to have been the case with *þeow*. A passage in Wulfstan's homily, *De Septiformi Spiritu*, illustrates this: '7 Antecristes þrælas þe his weg rymað, þeah hy swa ne wenan' ('and Antichrist's slaves who clear the way for him, though they do not think so').[423] Here one might have expected *þeow* to have been used on the analogy of *Godes þeowas*.

ÞRÆL-RIHT sb. (n) 'The legal rights possessed by a slave,'

For a discussion of this word, which appears only in the the various versions of Wulfstan's *Sermo ad Anglos*, see above, pp. 97–8.[424]

---

[417] For example, *The Gospel according to Saint Mark*, ed. Skeat, p. 85 (Mark 10:44); *The Gospel according to Saint Luke*, ed. Skeat, p. 135 (Luke 12:46); *The Gospel according to Saint John*, ed. Skeat, pp. 83 and 141 (John 8:34 and 15:15); *The Durham Ritual*, edd. Brown *et al.*, p. 21.11.
[418] *Die Gesetze*, ed. Liebermann, I.222 (text); *The Laws of the Kings of England*, ed. & transl. Robertson, p. 59 (translation).
[419] *Die Gesetze*, ed. Liebermann, I.262 (text); *The Laws of the Kings of England*, transl. Robertson, p. 115 (translation).
[420] *Die Gesetze*, ed. Liebermann, I.472.
[421] *Ælfric's Colloquy*, ed. Garmonsway, p. 37.
[422] The evidence of the spelling is too ambiguous or inadequate for localisation of the dialect. See *ibid.*, pp. 15–17.
[423] *The Homilies of Wulfstan*, §9.128 (ed. Bethurum, p. 190).
[424] *The Homilies of Wulfstan*, §20(BH).43, (C).48, (EI).47 (ed. Bethurum, pp. 256, 262, 269).

ÞYFTEN sb. (f) 'A female domestic slave.'

This word seems ultimately to be derived from the same root as Old English *þoft*(?) sb. (f), 'a rower's bench', from which the form *geþofta* sb. (m), 'a bench fellow, companion', was derived.[425] The feminine substantive must have referred to domestic slaves who perhaps sat separately at meals from the family they served. The word illustrates the use of the feminine suffix *-en* seen also in *þeowen, þignen, wiln*, etc. (qq.v.)

It appears four times in Old English manuscripts in the form of two glosses to Aldhelm's *De Laude Uirginitatis* appearing in Bruxelles, Bibliothèque royale, MS. 1650 (1520), where the glosses date from the first half of the eleventh century,[426] and in Oxford, Bodleian Library, Digby MS. 146 (*S.C.* 1747), whose glosses probably date from the middle of that same century.[427] Ker suggests that most of the glosses in the latter manuscript were copied from the former one with some corrections and alterations.[428] In the Brussels glosses the word first appears as *þeftan* (with Kentish *-e-* and late Old English vowel confusion in the unstressed suffix) glossing *uernacula, seruula, ancilla*, and in then in the form *þyften*, glossing *uerna, famula, seruus* [sic].[429] MS. Digby 146 eliminates the Kenticism but retains the *-an* suffix and the error of *seruus* for *serua*: 'uernacula id est ancilla uel serua, þyftan' and *uerna id est seruus, þyften*.[430] The domestic connotation of the word is indicated by the lemma *uerna(cula)*.

* **TO-LISING** sb. (f) 'A (spiritual) redemption.'

In the Lindisfarne Gospels at Mark 10:45 'þte he salde sawel his lesnise uel tolesinc fore monigum' ('that he gave his soul as a release or redemption for many') glosses 'et daret animam suam redemtionem pro multis'.[431] See s.v. *lisness* above.

* **UN-ALISENDLIC** adj. 'Not able to be redeemed.'

This word occurs only in a phrase in Ælfric's *Sermon on the Seventeenth Sunday after Pentecost*: *þonne bið his scyld unalysendlic* ('then shall his sin be unredeemable').[432] Cf. s.v. *alisendlic*.

UNDER-ÞEOW sb. (m) 'A slave subjugated in war.'

Underþeow appears only in the Alfredian *Orosius*, where it is used five times.[433] On no occasion can it be said to translate a specific Latin word or phrase. In every case, however, the general context shows that it refers to the position of persons who were conquered in war. As it is used only in this single translation it may be a nonce-word, a possibility supported by the *hapax legomena underfolgeþ*, 'a subordinate office',[434] and *underlatteow*, 'a subordinate ruler', employed only in this work.[435]

---

[425] Simpson & Weiner, *The Oxford English Dictionary*, XVIII.30, col. 1, s.v. *thuften*.

[426] Ker, *Catalogue*, §8 (pp. 6–7).

[427] *Ibid.*, §320 (iii) (pp. 382–3).

[428] *Loc. cit.*; cf. *ibid.*, §8 (pp. 6–7).

[429] *The Old English Glosses of MS. Brussels, Royal Library, 1650*, §§2307 and 2633 (ed. Goossens, pp. 297 and 319).

[430] *Old English Glosses*, §1.2349 and 2716 (ed. Napier, pp. 63 and 73).

[431] *The Gospel according to Saint Mark*, ed. Skeat, p. 85.

[432] *The Sermones Catholici*, I.33 (ed. & transl. Thorpe, p. 500.18) (text); *ibid.*, p. 501.17 (translation).

[433] *The Old English Orosius*, II.8, IV.13, V.11, V.12, and V.15 (ed. Bately, pp. 52.11, 112.17–18, 125.18, 128.10, and 132.10).

[434] *Ibid.*, VI.31 (p. 150.18, where the form *sunderfolgeþa* of the main manuscripts is represented by *underfolgoþa* in London, British Library, MS. Cotton Tiberius B.i [MS. C in Bately's edition]).

[435] *Ibid.*, II.2 (p. 40.13; again the word appears only in Bately's MS. C).

One can but speculate on the development of its semantic form. Possibly the word was linked with *underþeodan*, 'to subjugate' (found in the form *underþieded*) (q.v.):[436] the translator, knowing that those 'subjugated' in war were enslaved, may thus have coined the form *underþeow* on the analogy of a form like *undercyning*, 'a dependant or tributary king, one who rules under another' (found as a gloss in the Lindisfarne Gospels, but the Latin equivalent, *subregulus*, is found in English sources from the early eighth century).[437]

UNDER-ÞEOW adj. followed by dative. 'Enslaved to.'

As with the substantival form of this word, *underþeow* appears only in the Old English *Orosius*, where the translator did not employ it to represent a specific Latin word but used it to describe what was perceived to be a subjugated city or people.[438]

WEALE sb. (f) 'A female Celtic slave.'

This purely literary usage is found in two of the Old English *Riddles*.[439] See above, pp. 51–3.

WEALH sb. (m)   1) 'A foreigner.'

The appearance of *walh-* as an element in words a diverse as Old English *wealh-hnutu*, 'foreign nut, walnut', and Old Icelandic *Valhöll*, 'Valhalla', suggests that 'foreign' is a primary rather than a derivative meaning, as Faull has implied.[440] *Wealh* glosses *barbarus* (in the form *walch*) in the Cleopatra Glosses,[441] and in London, British Library, Additional MS. 32246, fo 4v, *Ius quiritum* is glossed *weala sunderriht*.[442] The word may have been given the specialised sense 'Roman' in the latter instance, as Bosworth & Toller suggested,[443] but it would seem more likely that it was simply the nearest equivalent Ælfric could find (in the sense 'foreign law') for a distinction that an Anglo-Saxon would not be familiar with; Ælfric glossed the preceding lemma *Ius publicum* as *ealdormanna riht*. This sense also appears in one of the Exeter Book riddles: 'ic . . . mearcpaþas wala [manuscript: *walas*] træd, moras pæðde.' ('I trod the roads of foreigners, I traversed the moors.')[444]

Wealh is also a fairly common element in place-names such as Walcot, Wallington, Walton, and Walworth. The pioneering work of Zachrisson on these names[445] has been superseded by the thorough investigation made by Kenneth Cameron,[446] although

---

[436] *Ibid.*, I.10 (p. 28.24).

[437] Matthew 27:2: *undercynige* (dative), in *The Gospel according to Saint Matthew*, ed. Skeat, p. 227; Latham, *Revised Medieval Latin Word-List*, p. 460, s.v. *subregulus*.

[438] *The Old English Orosius*, IV.11 and 12 (ed. Bately, pp. 110.23 and 111.23).

[439] *The Old English Riddles*, §§10.8 and 50.6 (ed. Williamson, pp. 74 and 99) (= *Riddle*, §§12.8 and 52.6, in *The Exeter Book* [edd. Krapp & Dobbie, pp. 186 and 207]).

[440] Faull, 'The semantic development of Old English *wealh*', 20. Hers is the fullest study of this word.

[441] Wright, *Anglo-Saxon and Old English Vocabularies*, ed. Wülcker, I, col. 361.29.

[442] 'The Latin-Old English glossaries', ed. Kindschi, p. 63.4 (= Wright, *Anglo-Saxon and Old English Vocabularies*, ed. Wülcker, I, col. 115.25).

[443] Bosworth, *An Anglo-Saxon Dictionary*, ed. Toller, p. 1173, col. 2, s.v. *wealh*, Ib.

[444] *The Old English Riddles*, §70.12 (ed. Williamson, p. 108; Williamson has removed *walas* from his text completely) (= *Riddle*, §72.12, in *The Exeter Book* [edd. Krapp & Dobbie, p. 232; the editors retain the manuscript reading]).

[445] Zachrisson, 'List of place-names containing O.E. wealh, weall, weala-', in *idem, Romans, Kelts and Saxons in Ancient Britain*, pp. 67–75.

[446] Cameron 'The meaning and significance of Old English *walh* in English place-names', with appendices by Todd & Insley. See also Tolkien, 'English and Welsh', in *Angles and Britons*, pp. 26–8.

additional examples, especially of field names, will continue to be found.[447] Although some of these may contain elements such as *weall* 'wall' (Zachrisson believed that the majority did), many must contain *w(e)alh* as an element. Ekwall's argument that as a rule this element must have had the sense 'Briton'[448] seems more convincing than Smith's claim that most of the names had the sense 'serf, slave'.[449] There are two objections to Smith's viewpoint. The first is Faull's substantial argument that the Old English synonym *þeow*, 'slave', does not appear as an element in English place-names.[450] This argument has greater cogency when one considers the rarity with which the word *wealh* in the sense 'slave' is attested in the literary sources, where one would expect it to be far more common if Smith were right because of the widespread occurrence of place-names with the *wealh-* element. Cameron in his study felt that the word meant 'Briton, Welshman', that is, a person who could be regarded as ethnically Celtic.[451]

Smith did raise a reasonable argument against the view that *wealh* referred to people of Celtic origin in that many of the extant examples are late.[452] The presence of names with this element in Surrey and south-west of London seems puzzling in the light of Anglo-Saxon settlement geography if the word always had this sense.[453]

The possibility that *wealh-* had the sense 'foreigner' in these place-names does not seem to have been considered by these scholars. Yet pockets of settlers of diverse origins, such as Flemings, Norsemen, or Normans might account for a number of *wealatun* forms, and dwellings of outsiders, such as traders, would explain the place-name *wealacot*. Place-names with this element could thus have been created at any time in the Anglo-Saxon period. This suggestion will be disappointing to those who would like to argue for the widespread survival into the Anglo-Saxon period of Celtic-speaking persons in England.[454]

2) 'A Briton, a person of Celtic-speaking origin.'

This sense is most clearly attested in the early laws and the *Anglo-Saxon Chronicle*.[455]

3) 'A slave.'

a: This sense sees to have been limited to the south of England. In biblical translations it appears only in those composed in the West-Saxon dialect. Thus in the West-Saxon versions of Matthew 24:50 *weales* (*weles, wieles*) translates *serui* (but *[efen]þeow* is used in verses 45–9).[456] In the Vespasian Psalter, undoubtedly in the Mercian dialect even though transcribed in Canterbury,[457] *seruus* is always glossed *þiow*; in the Rush-

447 Watts & Prince, 'OE *walh* in English place-names: an addendum', and Wakeford, 'Two *walh* names in the fields of Kingston'.
448 Ekwall, 'Tribal names in English place-names', 160.
449 See Smith, *English Place-Name Elements*, II.242–3.
450 Faull, 'The semantic development of Old English *wealh*', 33.
451 Cameron, 'The meaning and significance of Old English *walh* in English place-names', 29.
452 Smith, *English Place-Name Elements*, II.242–3.
453 For examples see Cameron, 'The meaning and significance of Old English *walh* in English place-names', 28 and n. 56.
454 For instance, Finberg, 'Roman and Saxon Withington', in *idem, Lucerna*, p. 34.
455 For example, Ine, §23.3 (*Die Gesetze*, ed. Liebermann, I.100) and Plummer, *Two of the Saxon Chronicles Parallel*, pp. 14.3–4 and 15.3–4 (s.a. 473 AE).
456 *The Gospel according to Saint Matthew*, ed. Skeat, p. 200.
457 *Pace* Kuhn, this provenance must now be accepted in the light of the manuscript evidence adduced by Wright in *The Vespasian Psalter*, pp. 41–3.

worth Gospels the corresponding word is *esne*;[458] and the Lindisfarne Gospels have either *esne, ðea,* or *þræl*.[459]

In Ælfric's works *wealh* occurs fairly frequently in his *Grammar*, where, however, it glosses only *mancipium* (and sometimes it is replaced by *þeowman* or *þeowa man*:[460] for instance, *hic manceps* is glossed by him *þes ðeowa mann*).[461] He seems in general to have used *ðeowa* in his sermons, though *wealh* does appear in one of them.[462] It is used in the Old English *Heptateuch* in Genesis 20:14 (where *seruos et ancillas* is translated *wealas 7 wylna*) and 21:25,[463] both of which are of Ælfrician authorship according to Clemoes,[464] as well as in the allegedly non-Ælfrician portion of the *Heptateuch* at Exodus 14:5.[465]

Ælfric's use of *wealh* thus seems to have been limited to his earlier writings, and is even then its appearance is a rare occurrence. His use of it in his *Grammar* only to gloss *mancipium*, the less common Latin word for a slave, suggests that it was not in regular use in his vocabulary and that he eliminated it over a period of time, perhaps because of the possibility of confusing it with sense 2).

In London, British Library, Additional 32246, fo 7v, *crudum uinum* is glossed *weala win* in contrast to *honorarium uinum*, which is glossed *hlaforda win*.[466] This must be derived from *wealh* in the sense of 'slave', and its use in this context must be based on the common status contrast *þeow/hlaford*. The manuscript is most likely from Abingdon.[467]

In the fragmentary *History of the Kentish Royal Saints* appears the phrase, 'ðrittegum gearum ne gestilde næfre stefen cearciendes wænes ne ceoriendes wales' ('for thirty years the sound of the creaking waggon and the chiding slave never stilled').[468] Although the text presumably emanated from the south-east of England, it should be noted that the extant manuscript leaves (London, Lambeth Palace, MS. 427, fos 210–11) are written in a hand of an Exeter type.[469]

The only other attestation is in II Æthelred, §6.2: '7 þæt naðor ne hy ne we ne underfon oðres wealh ne oðres ðeof ne oðres gefan.' ('And . . . neither they nor we shall

---

[458] See, for example, *The Gospel according to Saint Matthew*, ed. Skeat, pp. 200, at Matthew 24:50.

[459] See *Evangeliorum Quattuor Codex Lindisfarnensis*, edd. Kendrick *et al.*, II.2.80, s.v. *esne*; II.2.147, s.v. *ðea*; and II.2.149–50, s.v. *þræl*.

[460] In his declension of *meum mancipium* (*Aelfrics Grammatik und Glossar*, ed. Zupitza, pp. 101–2) Ælfric alternates between *min weal* and *min þeowa man*.

[461] *Ibid.*, p. 67.2.

[462] *On the Greater Litany*, in *Ælfric's Catholic Homilies*, §19.52 (ed. Godden, p. 181) (= *The Sermones Catholici*, II.21 [ed. & transl. Thorpe, p. 316.23]) (text); *ibid.*, p. 317.22 (translation). For an example of *seruus* glossed as *ðeowa* see *Aelfrics Grammatik und Glossar*, ed. Zupitza, p. 12.18.

[463] *The Old English Version of the Heptateuch*, ed. Crawford, pp. 137 and 140.

[464] Clemoes, 'The chronology of Ælfric's works', in *The Anglo-Saxons*, ed. Clemoes, p. 218.

[465] *The Old English Version of the Heptateuch*, ed. Crawford, p. 249. The usage of *wealh* might have possible implications for determining which portions of the *Heptateuch* are by Ælfric, a question that must still be considered to be an open one: see Pope in *The Homilies of Ælfric*, I.143, n. 4.

[466] 'The Latin-Old English glossaries', ed. Kindschi, pp. 94.15 and 95.2 (= Wright, *Anglo-Saxon and Old English Vocabularies*, ed. Wülcker, I, col. 128.25 and 27).

[467] Ker, *Catalogue*, §2 (p. 3).

[468] 'Die altenglische Beigaben des Lambeth-Psalters', II b).21–2 (ed. Förster, 335).

[469] On the provenance of the manuscript see Ker, *Catalogue*, §281 (p. 343).

harbour a slave belonging to the other party, or a thief pursued by them, or anyone who is involved in vendetta with them.')[470]

This sense probably came about through the late conquest of the Celtic-speakers in the West Country and their subsequent enslavement. The transformation in sense from 'Celt' to 'slave' displays the same semantic development as the Modern English 'slave'.[471]

b: Margaret Faull has very acutely observed that in a single instance in the West-Saxon Gospels the Latin *seruus* is translated by *wealh*, where in all other instances *þeow* is used: in Matthew 24:50 'Ueniet dominus serui illius in die, qua non sperat' is translated 'þanne cymð þas weales hlaford on þam daige þe he ne wenð',[472] which possibly suggests that the word had acquired a pejorative sense like the word *þræl*.[473]

4) 'A British or Celtic slave.'

Ine, §23.3 reads: 'Wealh gafolgelda CXX scill., his sunu C, ðeowne LX, somhwelcne fiftegum; Weales hyd twelfum.' (<The wergeld of> a British taxpayer <is> 120 shillings; of his son 100 shillings. <The amount to be paid for killing> a slave <is normally> 60 <shillings>, but in some cases 50 <shillings>. A Briton may compound for a scourging by the payment of 12 shillings.')[474] In this very early text, the sense of 'slave' is implied only by the context and arises out of the elliptical nature of the early laws.[475] This sense is better exemplified in the feminine substantive form *weale* (q.v.): see above, p. 51, n. 6, for further discussion.

WEAL-SADA sb. (m) 'A slave shackle.'

For the Latin *absconderunt superbi laqueum mihi* Psalm 139:5 in the Paris Psalter has:

> forhyddan oferhygde me   inwitgyrene,
> wraðan wealsadan   wundnum rapum

('proud ones hid treacherous snares from me, cruel slave shackles with plaited ropes').[476] *Mið sada* glosses *laqueo* (ablative case), 'a cord, halter, snare', in the Lindisfarne Gospel version of Matthew 27:5; the simplex is also used in the Lindisfarne and Rushworth Gospels at Luke 21:35 (*sado, sade*) and in Psalm 123:7 in the Paris Psalter.[477] *Weal-* must be derived from *wealh* in the sense 'slave'. Bound slaves are mentioned in the *Uita Wulfstani*.[478]

---

[470] *Die Gesetze*, ed. Liebermann, 1.224 (text); *The Laws of the Kings of England*, ed. & transl. Robertson, p. 59 (translation, emended).

[471] See Verlinden, 'L'Origine de *sclavus*'.

[472] *The Gospel according to Saint Matthew*, ed. Skeat, p. 200.

[473] Faull, 'The semantic development of Old English *wealh*', 27.

[474] *Die Gesetze*, ed. Liebermann, 1.100 (text); *The Laws*, ed. & transl. Attenborough, p. 43 (translation, emended).

[475] The sense is given in full in Ine, §74 in the two words ðeow Wealh: *Die Gesetze*, ed. Liebermann, 1.120. *Contra* Liebermann and Faull ('The semantic development of Old English *wealh*', 22) these should not be interpreted as a single compound substantive.

[476] *The Paris Psalter*, ed. Krapp, p. 136 (= Vulgate Psalm 139:6).

[477] *The Gospel according to Saint Matthew*, ed. Skeat, p. 229; *The Gospel according to Saint Luke*, ed. Skeat, p. 205; *The Paris Psalter*, ed. Krapp, p. 121 (Vulgate Psalm 123:7).

[478] *The Vita Wulfstani*, II.20 (ed. Darlington, p. 43). On this passage see above, p. 77. For further discussion of this word and the archaeological evidence for slave shackles see above, pp. 58–9.

WENCEL sb. (n) 'A slave.'

The basic meaning of this word is 'child'. Probably by an association of ideas similar to that seen in the sense development of *cniht* (q.v.) *wencel* appears twice in the sense 'slave' in Wærferth's translation of Gregory's *Dialogues*, where for instance, 'cum situla lignea . . . mancipium ad fontem perrexit' is translated as 'þa arn an wencel mid treowenum æscene . . . to þære wyllan' ('then a slave ran with a wooden bucket . . . to the well').[479]

WEORC-ÞEOW sb. (m) 'A workman with the status of a slave, a slave.'

This word is only found in the poems *Genesis A* and *Daniel*. In *Genesis A*, line 2721 the form *weorcþeos* (the manuscript reads *weorc feos* with the *s* altered from *h* = *?þeowas*) seems to paraphrase the *seruos et ancillas* of Genesis 20:14. The feminine equivalent (in the dative) appears in *Genesis A*, line 2262 with reference to Hagar, who is described as an *ancilla* in Genesis 16:5–6.[480] In *Daniel*, lines 72–4,

Nabochodonossor	him on nyd dyde
Israela bearn	ofer ealle lufen,
wæpna lafe	to weorcþeowum

('Nebuchadnezzar forced the children of Israel who survived the sword to become his slaves'),[481] seems to paraphrase 'si quis euaserat gladium, ductus in Babylonem seruiuit regi' (II Chronicles 36:20). In none of these extracts is there any apparent semantic reason why the simplex *þeow(e)* should not have been employed. The compound was probably chosen for metrical reasons in the above passages, but it would be hazardous to assert that it was a purely poetic word as the parallel Old Icelandic form *verk-þræll* suggests that the words had a common Germanic origin. The form was probably developed by analogy with *weorcmann* (cf. Old Icelandic *verk-maðr*), possibly with the purpose of indicating legal status as well as occupation.[482]

WEORC-ÞEOWE sb. (f) 'A female worker with the status of a slave, a slave.'

See the preceding entry.

WEORC-WYRÐE adj. 'Legally bound to engage in labour services.'

A notification of a grant of estates to Peterborough by Bishop Æthelwold in *ca* 963, records 'xvi weorcwurðe men 7 viii iunge men' ('16 *weorcwurðe* men and 8 young men') at Farcet in Huntingdonshire. The same document reports that at Yaxley in Huntingdonshire there were 'þryttene wepmen weorcewyrþe 7 v wimmen 7 æhta geonge men' ('13 *weorcwyrþe* men and 5 women and 8 young men'), as well as oxen, sheep, pigs, flitches of bacon, corn, sown land, barrels, tubs, etc.[483]

The only other use of the word is in a fragmentary eleventh-century list in a manuscript that formerly belonged to Bury St Edmunds: '<x>l weorcwyrðra manna, xviii oxana <7> xxxvi faldhriþera, hundteontig swina 7 vi <7 hu>ndnigontig sceapa, sifon hund flicca, <. . .>nhund ceasa, vii systras huniges, oþar <he>alfhund foþra cornes, ccc æcera asawen.' ('40 *weorcwyrðe* men, 18 oxen <and> 36 stalled oxen, 100 swine and 96

---

[479] *Bischof Wærferths von Worcester Übersetzung*, I.1 (ed. Hecht, I.11.20, and see also *ibid.*, I.11.23) (Old English); *Grégoire le Grand Dialogues*, I.1.2 (ed. de Vogüé, II.18.15–16) (Latin).

[480] *The Junius Manuscript*, ed. Krapp, pp. 81 and 68.

[481] *Ibid.*, p. 113.

[482] Cleasby & Vigfusson, *An Icelandic-English Dictionary*, 2nd edn, rev. Craigie, p. 698, s.vv. *verk-þræll* and *verk-maðr*.

[483] *Anglo-Saxon Charters*, §39 (ed. & transl. Robertson, pp. 72.28 and 74.17–18) (text); *ibid.*, pp. 73 and 75 (translation, emended) (= Sawyer, *Anglo-Saxon Charters*, no. 1448).

sheep, 700 flitches of bacon, . . . hundred cheeses, 7 sesters of honey, 150 fothers of corn, 300 acres sown.')[484]

As a prefix indicating 'labour services' *weorc-* is attested in the compound *weorcland* used in a document of A.D. 1020 x 1030 entered on fos 156v–157r of the York Gospels, where it is specifically contrasted with *inlande*.[485] *Inland* was demesne land and so the former must mean 'land subject to labour service'. The latter part of the compound, *-wyrðe*, has the sense 'subject to, liable to' seen in the simplex.[486] The compound, therefore, must be seen as referring to serfs rather than to slaves.

To interpret the inventories it is helpful to turn to the *Rectitudines singularum personarum*.[487] This text discloses that a lord was entitled *inter alia* to the following from his estates:

    i)   labour services from his tenants;
    ii)   an annual render from the livestock on the estate (two hens at Martinmas and a young sheep at Easter);
    iii) an annual render of grain (twenty-three sesters of barley);
    iv) a certain acreage to be sown with the peasants' own seed (three acres);
    v)   on the death of a *gebur* his property (because the lord had initially to supply him with livestock and sown land): the compiler notes that on some estates a *gebur* may pay tribute in the form of honey, food, or ale.

If the East Anglian inventories are interpreted as lists of what the lord was entitled to, one can see a clear parallel with the *Rectitudines*. Thus in East Anglia the lists include:

    i)   the 'ownership' of the labour services of the tenants of the land;
    ii)   the ownership of the livestock and its increase (in which presumably the tenants enjoyed the usufruct);
    iii) a render of corn;
    iv) a certain acreage to be sown;
    v)   certain items of farm equipment, which probably fall into the same category as 5) in the *Rectitudines*.

The only difference between these dues and the ones listed in the *Rectitudines* is that in the latter a small annual render of live-stock was required, which does not seem to have been the case in the East Anglian documents. It appears that the *weorcwyrðe* men were required to sow an average of just over six acres of the lord's land at Yaxley and seven and a half at (?) Bury St Edmunds, as opposed to three acres in the *Rectitudines*. But as the author of the *Rectitudines* insisted, customs varied, and given the likelihood that these documents emanated from opposite sides of the country, variation is not surprising.[488]

[484] *Anglo-Saxon Charters*, appendix 2, §3 (ed. & transl. Robertson, p. 248.19–23) (text); *ibid.*, p. 249 (translation, emended). On the date see Ker, *Catalogue*, §77 (p. 125).

[485] *Anglo-Saxon Charters*, §84 (ed. & transl. Robertson, p. 166.7–8) (text); *ibid.*, p. 167 (translation). Keynes has discussed this passage in 'The additions in Old English', in *The York Gospels*, ed. Barker, pp. 88–9.

[486] On *weorc* see Campbell's *Enlarged Addenda and Corrigenda*, p. 65, col. 2, s.v. *weorcland*, and *Anglo-Saxon Charters*, ed. & transl. Robertson, p. 415, note to lines 7f.; on *weorð* see Bosworth, *An Anglo-Saxon Dictionary*, ed. Toller, p. 1200, col. 2, s.v. *weorþ* VIII (2).

[487] *Die Gesetze*, ed. Liebermann, I.444–53 (text); *English Historical Documents 1042–1189*, §172 (transl. Douglas & Greenaway, pp. 875–9) (translation).

[488] One cannot compare the grain renders in the various documents as they are given in different measures whose capacities are not known. On the basis of its French and German cognates, a *sester* as a dry measure must have been about twelve bushels. For a discussion of the *sester* see Grierson, 'Weights and Measures', in *Domesday Book: Studies*, edd. Williams & Erskine,

It may be wondered why 'young men' are listed at Farcet and Yaxley, with women also being listed on the latter estate. The probable reason is that these indicate the additional labour potential of the estate. The 'young men' were presumably too young both to engage in the physical labour required and to take the responsibility for farming their own land. (This distinction, in itself, is probably indicative of free status – a slave would most likely have been considered 'work-worthy' at any age.) The women, on the other hand, probably were liable for certain services but as this document does not pretend to be a detailed custumal, their duties were not listed.

WIF-MANN sb. (m) 'A woman belonging to another woman, that is, a female slave.'

This sense appears in the Old English 'Penitential': 'Gif hwylc wif . . . hire wifman swingeð 7 heo þurh þa swingele wurð dead . . . fæste seo hlæfdige VII gear.' ('If any woman beats her woman . . . and she dies as a result of the beating . . . let that mistress fast for seven years.')[489] It is also attested in this sense in an Exeter manumission-document of the latter half of the eleventh century (*Manumission*, §5.1): 'Halwun Hoce . . . freode Hægelflæde, hire wimman.' ('Alwynn Hood . . . freed Æthelflæd, her woman.') From the context, *an minra wimmanna* ('one of my women') in Ælfric's *Life of St Eugenia* appears to refer to her personal female servants, one of whom is referred to as *seo wyln* (q.v.) in line 211.[490]

The usage parallels the semantic development of *mann* (q.v.).

WILISC adj.   1) 'Foreign.'

In the regulations of the Thegn's Guild in Cambridge, a tenth-century document, the contribution of members toward the wergeld of a *wylisc* man is put at one *ore*, half that of a man who was a *ceorl*.[491] It is highly unlikely that there was a Celtic-speaking population with second-class status surviving in this area, even if some survived in the fen district in Guthlac's day.[492] Thus the meaning 'Celtic' should be ruled out. This leaves two possibilities. The first is that it means 'servile', which is the sense that Whitelock accepted with some hesitation.[493] But *wealh* (q.v.) in the sense 'slave' appears to have been largely a south-western word and it seems rash to assert that this sense existed in the east, where Celtic slaves are likely to have been uncommon.

Wealh, the word from which *wylisc* is derived, can, however, mean 'foreigner'. Usually *wylisc* refers to Celtic-speakers, in other words, the people of a specific foreign nationalities characterised by their speech. But in the *Peterborough Chronicle* entry for the year 1048, where *wealh* refers to the Normans, it seems to have the more general sense of 'foreign'.[494] This last sense would have been appropriate in these guild regulations. Foreigners such as Flemings are likely to have been familiar as traders in an eastern town like Cambridge.[495] These men, being lordless, would have been in a weaker position than indigenous members of the community and so might well have had a lower

---

pp. 82–3. A *fother* was a cartload: see Bosworth, *An Anglo-Saxon Dictionary*, ed. Toller, p. 328, col. 1, s.v. *FÓÐER*.

[489] *Die altenglische Version des Halitgar'schen Bussbuches*, II.4 (ed. Raith, p. 17.5–8).

[490] *Ælfric's Lives of Saints*, §2 (ed. & transl. Skeat, I.36.189) (text); *ibid.*, I.37 (translation).

[491] *Diplomatarium Anglicum Ævi Saxonici*, ed. Thorpe, pp. 611.33–612.1 (text); *English Historical Documents c.500–1042*, §136 (transl. Whitelock, p. 604) (translation).

[492] *Felix's Life of Saint Guthlac*, §34 (ed. & transl. Colgrave, pp. 108–11).

[493] *English Historical Documents c.500–1042*, §136 (transl. Whitelock, p. 604; she translated the passage: 'if he is servile [or Welsh?], one ore').

[494] *Two of the Saxon Chronicles Parallel*, ed. Plummer, p. 173.16 (1048E); cf. *ibid.*, II.237 (text); *English Historical Documents 1042–1189*, §1 (transl. Douglas & Greenaway, p. 119 and n. 2) (translation).

[495] See Grierson, 'The relations between England and Flanders', especially pp. 94–5.

wergeld. It was to protect these foreigners that the king or *eorl* and the bishop were created their 'kinsmen and protectors' (*for mæg 7 for mundboran*) in Edward & Guthrum, §12.[496] One should thus reject the sense 'servile' in this context, as Finberg did,[497] and should translate *wilisc* here as 'foreign'.

2) 'British, Celtic.'

This sense is found in the entry for A.D. 465 in the *Anglo-Saxon Chronicle*[498] and several times in the Laws of Ine.[499] *Wilisc eala*, 'Celtic ale', seems to have been a favoured medicine to judge from the frequency of its occurrences in the Leechdoms.[500]

3) 'Of slave status.'

In a note on Adam in London, British Library, MS. Cotton Tiberius A.iii the descendants of the three sons of Noah are divided into three social classes equivalent to the major divisions in Anglo-Saxon society, the slaves, the *ceorlas*, and the nobility: 'He on ðreo towearp ða cneordnysse þ wæs wælisc 7 on cyrlisc cynn 7 on gesyðcund cynd.' ('He separated those races into three, namely slave and the *ceorl* class and the *gesith* class.') *Wælisc* clearly refers to the descendants of Ham, of whom it is said elsewhere in the same work: 'þ cynn wæs geseald . . . þam oðrum cynnum twam on heaftnead 7 on þeowdom' ('that kindred was given into captivity and slavery under the other two kindreds').[501]

4) 'British (language).'

'7 her sind on þis iglande fif geþeode Englisc 7 Brittisc 7 Wilsc [Bryt Wylsc D] 7 Scyttisc 7 Pyhtisc 7 Boc Leden.' ('and here in the island there are five languages, English, British, Scottish, Pictish and Latin.') The preface to three versions of the *Anglo-Saxon Chronicle* contains this use of *wealh*. Perhaps the textual confusion arose because *Wilsc* had not yet acquired a Celtic ethnic sense in everyone's idiolect and a scribe felt that a gloss *Brittisc* was needed to give greater specificity; *Scyttisc* also had a somewhat different meaning from its modern cognate, being usually employed in the sources before the tenth century to denote the inhabitants of Ireland (though presumably the Irish resident in the west of Scotland were being referred to here).[502]

5) 'Welsh.'

Only from the middle of the eleventh century do various versions of the *Anglo-Saxon Chronicle* record *wilisc* several times in this, the sense that has survived into Modern English.[503]

---

[496] *Die Gesetze*, ed. Liebermann, I.134 (text); *The Laws*, ed. & transl. Attenborough, p. 109 (translation).

[497] *The Agrarian History of England*, I.2, ed. Finberg, p. 396 and n. 1.

[498] *Two of the Saxon Chronicles Parallel*, ed. Plummer, I.12.28 (465 A) (text); *English Historical Documents c.500–1042*, §1 (transl. Whitelock, p. 154) (translation).

[499] Ine, §§32, 46.1, 54.2, and 70.1, in *Die Gesetze*, ed. Liebermann, I.102, 110, 114, and 118.

[500] For example, *Leechdoms, Wortcunning, and Starcraft of Early England*, I.47 and II.65 (ed. Cockayne, II.118.4 and II.294.3).

[501] Napier, 'Altenglische Kleinigkeiten', 3.62–3; cf. *ibid.*, 2.49–51 (= Ker, *Catalogue*, §186.8 [p. 243]).

[502] *Two of the Saxon Chronicles Parallel*, ed. Plummer, I.3.3 (text); *English Historical Documents c.500–1042*, §1 (transl. Whitelock, p. 148 and n. 9) (translation).

[503] The *Anglo-Saxon Chronicle*, s.a. 1050 D, seems to be the first certain example: *Two of the Saxon Chronicles Parallel*, ed. Plummer, I.170 (text); *English Historical Documents 1042–1189*, §1 (transl. Douglas & Greenaway, p. 114) (translation, where the *Wylisca Axa* is given its modern name of Usk).

WILN sb. (f) 'A female slave.'

An example of this word is to be found in Oxford, Bodleian Library, Bodley MS. 340 (*S.C.* 2404), fo 125v, line 7, in the form *wyln* as a gloss to *an mennen* (*mænnen* is glossed *wylin* in line 10). This is the work of a Rochester scribe of the middle of the eleventh century.[504] This form is the feminine cognate of *wealh*, being derived from an earlier **walhīn*,[505] which contains the feminine suffix *-en* < **-in* that appears in *mennen*, *þeowen*, and *þignen*. West Germanic *a* > Old English *æ*, and in the West Saxon dialect *æ* > *ea* by breaking; in turn *ea* > *ie* in West Saxon by *i-mutation* (cf. the masculine form *wielh*), and then *ie* > *y*. Subsequently *y* was occasionally unrounded to *i*.[506]

The association of the word with *wealh* is to be seen in the alliterative tag *wealas and wylna*, which is used in the Old English *Heptateuch* as the equivalent of *seruos et ancillas* (Genesis 20:14, cf. Exodus 20:17 and Leviticus 25:44).[507] This tag quite possibly reflects an earlier sense, when the words would have meant 'male and female Celts'. Unlike *wealh*, however, the word is never used as any sort of national appellative for the Celts in extant sources. In the glossaries, the Old English *Heptateuch* (Genesis 16:6, 20:14, 21:10, 21:13, Exodus 20:17, 21:20, 21:32, and Leviticus 25:44), and Ælfric's *Grammar* the word always represents *ancilla*.[508]

In every case where the word appears it seems to refer to legal status, unlike *þeow*, which sometimes denotes a state of spiritual dependancy, as in *Godes þeow*. This is most clearly evident in a passage in Ælfric's homily *On the Epiphany of the Lord*: 'Hit gelimpþ forwel oft þæt on anre tide acenð seo cwen and seo wyln, and ðeah geðicð se æðeling be his gebyrdum to healicum cynesetle, and ðære wylne sunu wunað eal his lif on ðeowte.' ('It happens very often that the queen and the slave bring forth at one time, and yet the prince, through his birth, grows up for the lofty throne, and the son of the slave continues all his life in servitude.')[509] The phrase *wunað . . . on ðeowte* shows that the son had a servile status inherited from his mother.

There are several indications that the word was not just used to denote a female slave in general but that it referred more specifically to one who had a personal relationship with her owner. Ælfric's *Sermon on Auguries* in his *Lives of Saints* provides one example: 'Ac seo sawl is ðæs flæsces hlæfdige and hire gedafnað þæt heo simle gewylde ða wylne þæt is þæt flæsc to hyre hæsum. Þwyrlice færð æt ðam huse þær seo wyln bið þære hlæfdian wissigend and seo hlæfdige bið þære wylne underðeodd.' ('But the soul is the flesh's mistress, and it befits her that she should ever rule the bondmaid, that is the flesh, according to her commands. It fares ill with the house where the bondmaid is the ruler of the mistress and the mistress is in subjection to the bondmaid.')[510] In another passage Ælfric uses *seo wyln* of a slave who is elsewhere referred to as *an minra*

---

[504] Ker, *Catalogue*, §309 (p. 361).

[505] Holthausen, *Altenglisches etymologisches Wörterbuch*, p. 393, s.v. *wielen*.

[506] Campbell, *Old English Grammar*, §§132(3), 143, 200(1), 300, and 317 (pp. 52, 55, 79, 127–8, and 132).

[507] *The Old English Version of the Heptateuch*, ed. Crawford, pp. 137; cf. *ibid.*, pp. 262 (*ne his weales, ne his wylne*) and 300 (*ge wealas ne wylna*).

[508] *Ibid.*, pp. 123, 137, 138 (2x), 262, 265, 266, and 300; London, British Library, Additional MS. 32246, fos 3r and 18r, in 'The Latin-Old English glossaries', ed. Kindschi, pp. 50.12 and 206.3 (= Wright, *Anglo-Saxon and Old English Vocabularies*, ed. Wülcker, I, cols 108.28 and 170.23); *Aelfrics Grammatik und Glossar*, ed. Zupitza, pp. 100.20–101.12 and 301.4.

[509] *The Sermones Catholici*, I.7 (ed. & transl. Thorpe, p. 110.26–9) (text); *ibid.*, p. 111.25–8 (translation).

[510] *Ælfric's Lives of Saints*, §17 (ed. & transl. Skeat, I.364.8–12) (text); *ibid.*, I.365.8–11 (translation, emended).

wimmanna (q.v.).[511] The relationship between a slave and her master in a law of Cnut supports this interpretation. II Cnut, §54 lays down penalties for a married man who has sexual relations with his own slave.[512] The latter is referred to as a *wyln*. The most likely category of persons that the word would describe is domestic slaves: in the Prudentius glosses in Boulogne-sur-Mer, Bibliothèque municipale, MS. 189, the lemma *uernae*, which is glossed *ignobiles – wylna*, supports this hypothesis.[513] The passage in Ælfric's *Lives of the Saints* cited above is particularly suggestive of this.

One should note that most of the citations of this word are from the works of Ælfric of Eynsham. It also occurs at Psalm 115:16 in the eleventh-century Arundel Psalter in the form *wilne* and probably also in the same verse in the Vitellius Psalter, both manuscripts being of Winchester provenance.[514] The word appears once in a homily of Wulfstan[515] and, as has just been noted, in one of Cnut's laws, which was probably subject to Wulfstanian influence.[516] Its rarity in the Archbishop's writings might suggest that it was a borrowing from Ælfric and not a normal part of Wulfstan's idiolect. Kent had been in the West-Saxon sphere of influence since the time of Alfred, which perhaps accounts for its occurrence in the south-east. The sense 'female slave' was probably thus a southern one (cf. *Wealh* 3) above).

WILN-INCEL sb. (f) 'A little or young slave.'

This appears in the Prudentius glosses in Boulogne-sur-Mer, Bibliothèque munici-pale, MS. 189, as the Old English equivalent of *mancipium*.[517] Meritt pointed out that the glossator in using the Old English diminutive was influenced by the context of the word: it refers to St Agnes, who is described as a *puellula* in the text.[518] *Wilnincel* itself is derived from *wiln* (q.v.) with the addition of the diminutive suffix *-incel* seen in *þeowincel* (q.v.)

WITE-FÆST adj. 'Enslaved as a punishment.'

This has the common suffix *-fæst* 'firm in punishment'. The word appears to be synonymous with *witeþeow* (q.v.), but it is rare, being attested only in the will of Archbishop Ælfric of A.D. 1003 x 1004 and that of Ætheling Æthelstan of A.D. 1014 x 1015. Both documents make it clear that the term was used of those found guilty through a judicial decision: 'man freoge . . . ælene witefæstne man þe on his timan forgylt wære' ('every penally enslaved man who was condemned in his time be set free')[519] and 'man gefreoge ælcne witefæstne mann þe ic on spræce ahte' ('every

[511] *Ibid.*, §2 (I.36.211) (text); *ibid.*, I.37 (translation). Cf. p. 299 and n. 273 above.
[512] *Die Gesetze*, ed. Liebermann, I.348 (text); *The Laws of the Kings of England*, ed. & transl. Robertson, p. 203 (translation).
[513] *The Old English Prudentius Glosses*, §367 (ed. Meritt, p. 39).
[514] *Die altenglische Arundel-Psalter*, ed. Oess, p. 190; *The Vitellius Psalter*, ed. Rosier, p. 290, where the word was recorded as damaged in the manuscript. On the date and provenance of the two manuscripts see Ker, *Catalogue*, §§134 and 224 (pp. 166–7 and 298–301).
[515] *The Homilies of Wulfstan*, §8b.60 (ed. Bethurum, p. 173).
[516] See Whitelock, 'Wulfstan's authorship of Cnut's laws'.
[517] *Wilincel* in Bosworth, *An Anglo-Saxon Dictionary*, ed. Toller, p. 1225, col. 1, is a ghost form: for the correct reading see Meritt, 'Old English glosses to Gregory, Ambrose and Pruden-tius', 67, and for the context see *The Old English Prudentius Glosses*, §925 (ed. Meritt, p. 98).
[518] Meritt, 'Old English glosses to Gregory, Ambrose and Prudentius', p. 67.
[519] *Anglo-Saxon Wills*, §18 (ed. & transl. Whitelock, p. 54.4–5) (= Sawyer, *Anglo-Saxon Char-ters*, no. 1488).

penally enslaved man whom I acquired in the course of jurisdiction be freed').[520] It is not clear, however, whether this term was used of those who had fallen into debt or was restricted to those who were guilty of a crime.

WITE-ÞEOW sb. (m) 1) 'One who has become a slave as a punishment, a penal slave.'

There are three attestations: in the Laws of Ine, §48,[521] in Æthelstan's *Ordinance relating to Charities*, §1,[522] and in the will of Ælfwold, bishop of Crediton (988–1008 x 1012). The last instance illustrates the contrast in this status with the condition of being free (*freot*, q.v.): 'ælcon men freot þe witeþeow wære, oððe he mid his feo gebohte' ('freedom to every man that is a penal slave, or whom he bought with his money').[523]

2) 'One who has become a slave as a punishment.' (Used in a spiritual sense.)

In *Christ I*, lines 150–1, the souls in hell declare: *Bring us hælolif,/ werigum witeþeowum*. ('Bring us, weary penal slaves, salvation.')[524]

WITE-ÞEOW adj. 'In slavery as a punishment, penally enslaved.'

This legal-status term appears in Ine, §§24 and 54.2,[525] in a land lease,[526] and in several wills dating from the tenth century.[527] In every instance the word qualifies *man* or *men* (in Ine, §24, *Engliscmon*). Unfortunately, when this word is used, nowhere do the sources state the reason for enslavement. Work on a Sunday (Ine, §3.2, Edward & Guthrum, §7.1),[528] theft under certain circumstances (Ine, §7.1, II Edward, §6, VI Æthelstan, §12.2),[529] incest (Edward & Guthrum, §4),[530] and as an alternative for a condemned man who had reached sanctuary (*Grið*, §16)[531] were grounds for punishment by enslavement. It is legitimate to assume that men who fell into these categories would have been called *witeþeowas*. What is not clear is whether those enslaved for debt could be so described (when, for example, a man enslaved himself to another who had paid his fine for him, as laid down in Ine, §62).[532] Ine, §54.2 makes it clear that both

---

[520] *Anglo-Saxon Wills*, §20 (ed. & transl. Whitelock, p. 56.14–15) (text); *ibid.*, p. 57 (translation) (= Sawyer, *Anglo-Saxon Charters*, no. 1503).

[521] *Die Gesetze*, ed. Liebermann, I.110 (text); *The Laws*, ed. & transl. Attenborough, p. 53 (translation).

[522] *Die Gesetze*, ed. Liebermann, I.148 (text); *The Laws*, ed. & transl. Attenborough, p. 127 (translation).

[523] *The Crawford Collection of Early Charters and Documents*, §10.28–9 (edd. Napier & Stevenson, p. 23) (text); *ibid.*, p. 126 (translation) (= Sawyer, *Anglo-Saxon Charters*, no. 1492).

[524] *The Exeter Book*, edd. Krapp & Dobbie, p. 7.

[525] *Die Gesetze*, ed. Liebermann, I.100 (text); *The Laws*, ed. & transl. Attenborough, p. 44 (translation).

[526] *Select English Historical Documents*, §17 (ed. & transl. Harmer, p. 29.22) (= Sawyer, *Anglo-Saxon Charters*, no. 1285).

[527] *Anglo-Saxon Wills*, §§3, 4, 8, and 9 (ed. & transl. Whitelock, pp. 12.10, 16.2, 20.8, and 24.7) (= Sawyer, *Anglo-Saxon Charters*, nos 1539, 1491, 1484, and 1485).

[528] *Die Gesetze*, ed. Liebermann, I.90 and 132 (text); *The Laws*, ed. & transl. Attenborough, pp. 37 and 107 (translation).

[529] *Die Gesetze*, ed. Liebermann, I.92, 144, and 183 (text); *The Laws*, ed. & transl. Attenborough, pp. 39, 121, and 169 (translation).

[530] *Die Gesetze*, ed. Liebermann, I.130 (text); *The Laws*, ed. & transl. Attenborough, p. 105 (translation).

[531] *Die Gesetze*, ed. Liebermann, I.471.

[532] *Die Gesetze*, ed. Liebermann, I.116 (text); *The Laws*, ed. & transl. Attenborough, p. 57 (translation).

ethnic Celts (*Wyliscne*) and Anglo-Saxons (*Engliscne*) could be penally enslaved and be lashed, though the latter penalty required an accusation based on different levels of oaths, with the Celts – not surprisingly – being subject to punishment on the basis of a lesser oath.

Under Ine's laws both Anglo-Saxons and Celts could be penally enslaved (Ine, §54.2).[533] The presence of such men on both episcopal and private estates (the latter as early as the time of Ine, see §24)[534] implies that persons other than the king could enslave people as part of the profits of jurisdiction.

[533] *Die Gesetze*, ed. Liebermann, I.114 (text); *The Laws*, ed. & transl. Attenborough, p. 55 (translation).
[534] For examples see n. 527 above and cf. also nn. 520–21. See further *Anglo-Saxon Wills*, ed. & transl. Whitelock., pp. 111–12.

APPENDIX II

Analysis of Sections 3 and 5 of Æthelgifu's Will
(lines 3–44 and 50–9 in Whitelock's edition)

An initial major difficulty in these two sections lies in the sentence and phrase divisions. The copyist affords us no help here. There is no discernible pattern in the pointing and a number of instances of faulty word division and dittography do not lead one to place much faith in the scribe's understanding of the document or his accuracy.[1] All one can do is weigh up the possible interpretations against syntactic patterns to be found elsewhere in the text and consider the contextual position of the passages in question. In seeking links between sentence and sentence or phrase and phrase one must discard any notion of an argument presented according to the dictates of objective logic: such thinking is more the product of a society with a long tradition of conveying its thoughts through the medium of the written word. Though there is some logic in the broad framework of the will, as we have seen, within this overall structure facts are given in an order governed by an association of ideas.

The first problem of interpretation lies in lines 9–11. The relevant section of the manuscript reads: '7 þ land æt lan/gaforda ælfnoðe his dæg. 7 v. men 7 mangod 7 mantat freo . . . 7 wine mylnere 7 þæs swanes sunu 7 wif 7 þone gingran sceaphyrde/ hæbbe æ'l'fnoð 7 cc. sceapa .c. hund ewna 7 c. geldsceapa. . . .'[2] The problems, caused by our uncertainty about the original sentence division, are: whether Ælfnoth is initially granted anyone; who precisely is freed; and whether Ælfnoth, when mentioned the second time, is given anyone other than the younger shepherd.

Originally the scribe wrote *freoge* but the *-ge* has been erased. This suggests corruption, a view supported by the absence of *freo* anywhere else in a like context, where the formula that is usually employed is '7 freoge man X 7 Y'. The context is such as to encourage scribal error since it contains the repeated syllables *men . . . man . . . man . . . .* It seems reasonable, then, to postulate that the original had *freoge man* but that the scribe omitted the word *man* and a subsequent corrector then attempted to make sense of the now-subjectless verb *freoge* by converting it into the adjective *freo*.

Comparison with the syntactic patterns elsewhere in the will suggests furthermore that this phrase has been misplaced. Nowhere else does the pattern *X 7 Y freoge man* appear; it is always *freoge man X* or *freoge man X 7 Y*.[3] Where should

---

[1] Cf. p. 112, n. 17 above.

[2] Whitelock translated this as follows: 'And the land at Langford (is to be given) to Ælfnoth for his lifetime, and five men; and Mangod and Mantat are to be freed. And Ælfnoth is to have Wine the miller and the swineherd's son and wife and the younger shepherd, and 200 sheep, 100 ewes, and 100 sheep which yield no milk. . . .' (*The Will of Æthelgifu*, ed. & transl. Whitelock, p. 6.)

[3] Lines 6, 8, 9, 13, 15, 16, 18, 21, 23, 25 (2x), 32, 35, 50, 52 (2x), 53, 55, 58.

331

it be placed then? Both on syntactic and contextual grounds it seems inherently unlikely that it precedes *v. men*. The pattern 'þ land . . . ælfnoðe . . . 7 v. men', with the separation of the elements of a compound subject or object, is regular in Old English. The reading 'freoge man v. men 7 mangod . . .' with the unspecific preceding the specific seems improbable in this context. The most reasonable explanation, therefore, is that *freoge man* originally preceded *mangod*, but that the repetition of *men/man* led the scribe initially to omit the phrase, and when he realized his error, he simply inserted *freoge* to try to restore the sense.

This is not, however, the end of the problem, for now one must determine who is freed and who is to be bequeathed to Ælfnoth. Unfortunately, the comparable use elsewhere in this document of Object + *hæbbe* + Subject + Extension of Object is just as ambiguous as this extract; one cannot say whether the object that preceded the verb is compound or not.[4] The only answer is to try to discern an association of ideas. I would suggest that only the unnamed persons, a younger generation, were the ones who were to be given to Ælfnoth, namely, the swineherd's son and his wife, and the younger shepherd. This prompted Æthelgifu to bequeath the sheep she then describes and the herd of swine. This same association of ideas can be seen in line 18: *7 ælfwyðe*, which is set off by a point from the preceding list of those freed, is co-ordinate with the deferred object *7 hire cild*. The three named men, Mangod, Mantat, and Wine the miller, are to be freed.

Admittedly there are other possible interpretations of the manuscript as it stands. One could justify *freo* in that it does appear elsewhere in the document (although it has a different syntactic function there);[5] one could argue that *freoge* (with or without *man*) is syntactically reasonable (although it appears nowhere else in this document) and that Wine the miller as well as the swineherd's son and his wife are not to be freed but are bequeathed to Ælfnoth. These are all possible; all that can be said is that the balance of probability favours the interpretation that has been put forward here.

The section from line 9 to line 19 is devoted primarily to the Langford estate. The bequest of the land at Clifton, as Whitelock noted,[6] is parenthetical. (As the two parishes adjoin, it is possible that the two estates were contiguous, which would explain why it is mentioned at this point.) After the Clifton reference Æthelgifu returns to Langford in order to record to which estates sheep are to be transferred. The remainder are to go to her priests. She then concentrates on a single priest, Edwin. He is to be freed, and is to be given a church in an unspecified locality and a man. To this church is given 'the half hide which Wineman possessed'. The location of this land is not stated, but the mention of the transfer of Byrhstan's sister to Stondon for Edwin a few lines later suggests that it may be there – since otherwise, if the estate is at Langford, it is difficult to see why Byrhstan's sister is being moved to Stondon. It seems most likely that she is, in fact, being drawn *from* Langford. If this is the case, then one can detect a pattern in the writer's thought and get an inkling as to where the church was

4 Lines 18, 33–4.
5 Line 18.
6 *The Will of Æthelgifu*, ed. & transl. Whitelock, p. 6, n. 16.

located. The overriding concern in these lines is with Langford: other estates may be mentioned through an association of ideas, but the writer returns to Langford. It is likely, therefore, that the church itself was at Langford and that all the people mentioned, including Ufic and the fuller and also the miller's wife and child(ren), are drawn from Langford. The land at Stondon was thus an outlying estate given to the priest to supply financial support for him and his church.

It also seems probable that the miller whose wife is given to Edwin is the man called Wine the miller who, I have suggested, is granted his freedom in line 10. If this is so, one can understand the grounds for freeing him: it would enable him to move to an estate nearer to the one where his wife and children were to be employed.

The next problem concerns the identity of the four *wæpmen* mentioned in line 21. Whitelock considered it more probable that this refers to four unnamed men, rather than Oswig, Cinesige, Brihtwine, and Godere.[7] She did not make it clear why this should be so, and her next note reveals that it got her into difficulties.[8]

Once again association of ideas was at play here. The four men being given to Ælfwold are named, but in doing so the testatrix also directs how their families are to be treated.[9] Part of Whitelock's difficulties stemmed from her misinterpretation of the word *heord*. She assumed that it means 'herd', and indeed elsewhere in the will it means just that, but here the more logical meaning is surely that given by Toller: 'a family under the care of its head'.[10] Thus Oswig and Cinesige with their wives and Godere and his family are given to Ælfwold, together with Brihtwine, but Cinesige's children are to be freed. It is, of course, appropriate that four men be granted to Ælfwold as this was the regular number needed to work two plough-teams.

Another problem of interpretation concerns the phrase '7 freoge man leofric æt weowdune'.[11] Whitelock translated this as 'And Leofric of Weedon is to be freed'. This seems the least likely interpretation. It is more likely that *æt weowdune* has been misplaced and should follow *man*, exemplifying the same syntactic patterns as one gets above in line 32: '7 freoge man æt offanlege cyneleofe 7 mærtin . . .'. But even if the reading be retained, syntactically *æt weowdune* can be taken to apply to all that follows. Thus 'at Weedon' not merely Leofric, but also Ælfric, Brihtelm, and his sister are to be freed.[12]

Finally there is the phrase *his ginra sunu* in line 41. It is impossible to say whether this is nominative (in which case Leofwine is given the herd of swine that Brihtelm *and* his son controlled), or accusative (in which case Leofwine gets

---

7 *Ibid.*, p. 8, n. 8.
8 *Loc. cit.*, n. 9.
9 Dr Bruce Mitchell considers this the most reasonable interpretation, although he stresses that the passage is ambiguous. I am grateful to him for the time he gave me in discussing this document.
10 Toller, *Supplement*, p. 535, col. 1, s.v. *heord*, III.
11 Line 35.
12 Whitelock moved some way towards validating this interpretation in the alternative translation she supplied in note 7 on p. 10 of her edition: 'Leofric is to be freed at Weedon.'

the herd *and* the younger son of Brihtelm). It seems best to go along with Whitelock in assuming that it is an accusative, on the pattern of Eatstan, the swineherd at Standon, who was freed, but whose son did not receive his freedom and instead was put in charge of the herd.[13]

[13] Line 26.

BIBLIOGRAPHY OF WORKS CITED

Abels, Richard P. *Lordship and Military Obligation in Anglo-Saxon England* (Berkeley & Los Angeles, CA & London 1988)

Addyman, P. V. 'Late Saxon settlements in the St. Neots area: the village or township at St. Neots', *Proceedings of the Cambridge Antiquarian Society* 64 (1973) 45–99

Addyman, P. V. 'The Anglo-Saxon house: a new review', *Anglo-Saxon England* 1 (1972) 273–307

Anderson, Alan O. (transl.) *Scottish Annals from English Chroniclers A.D. 500 to 1286* (London 1908)

Anderson, E. R. 'Social idealism in Ælfric's *Colloquy*', *Anglo-Saxon England* 3 (1974) 153–62

Andersson, T. M. 'The thief in *Beowulf*', *Speculum* 59 (1984) 493–508

Andrews, D. D., & Milne, G. (edd.) *Wharram: A Study of Settlement on the Yorkshire Wolds*, volume I: *Domestic Settlement, 1: Areas 10 and 6* (London 1979)

Angles and Britons. O'Donnell Lectures (Cardiff 1963)

Anstey, R. [Review of D. B. Davis, *The Problem of Slavery in the Age of Revolution 1770–1823* (1976)], *English Historical Review* 91 (1976) 141–8

Árni Pálsson. 'Um lok þrældóms á Íslandi', *Skírnir* 106 (1932) 191–203

Arnold, Morris S., *et al.* (edd.) *On the Laws and Customs of England: Essays in Honor of Samuel E. Thorne* (Chapel Hill 1981)

Arnold, Thomas (ed.) *Symeonis Monachi Opera Omnia. Historia Regum* (2 vols, London 1882/85)

Assmann, Bruno (ed.) *Angelsächsische Homilien und Heiligenleben* (Kassel 1889; rptd with supplementary intro. by Peter Clemoes, Darmstadt 1964)

Astill, G. 'Rural settlement: the toft and the croft', in *The Countryside of Medieval England*, ed. G. Astill & A. Grant (Oxford & New York 1988), pp. 36–61

Astill, Grenville, & Grant, Annie (edd.) *The Countryside of Medieval England* (Oxford & New York 1988)

Aston, T[revor] H., *et al.* (edd.) *Social Relations and Ideas: Essays in Honour of R. H. Hilton* (Cambridge 1983)

Aston, T. H. 'The origins of the manor in England', *Transactions of the Royal Historical Society*, 5th S., 8 (1958) 59–83; rptd '*with a postscript*', in *Social Relations and Ideas*, edd. T. H. Aston *et al.* (Cambridge 1983), pp. 1–43

Atkins, I. 'The Church of Worcester from the eighth to the twelfth century', *Antiquaries Journal* 17 (1937) 371–91; 20 (1940) 1–38 *and* 203–29 + plates 39–40

Attenborough, F[rederick] L. (ed. & transl.) *The Laws of the Earliest English Kings* (Cambridge 1922)

Bäck, Hilding. *The Synonyms for 'Child', 'Boy', 'Girl' in Old English. An Etymological-Semasiological Investigation* (Lund 1934)

Bak, J. M. 'Serfs and serfdom: words and things', *Review* 4.1 (Summer 1980) 3–18

Baker, Alan R. H., & Butlin, Robin A. (edd.) *Studies of Field Systems in the British Isles* (Cambridge 1973)

Balon, J. 'Les lètes chez les Francs', *Tijdschrift voor Rechtsgeschiedenis* (= *Revue d'Histoire du Droit*) 33 (1965) 1–17

335

Balzaretti, R., *et al.* 'Debate: Trade, industry and the wealth of King Alfred', *Past and Present* no. 135 (May 1992) 142–88

Baring, Francis Henry. *Domesday Tables for the Counties of Surrey, Berkshire, Middlesex, Hertford, Buckingham and Bedford and for the New Forest. With an Appendix on the Battle of Hastings* (London 1909)

Barker, Nicholas (facs. ed.) *The York Gospels* (London 1986)

Barlow, Frank. *William Rufus* (Berkeley & Los Angeles, CA 1983)

Bartchy, S. Scott. ΜΑΛΛΟΝ ΧΡΗΣΑΙ. *First Century Slavery and the Interpretation of 1 Corinthians 7:21* (Missoula, MT 1973)

Bartlett, Robert. *Trial by Fire and Water. The Medieval Judicial Ordeal* (Oxford 1986)

Barton, K. J., with contributions by Genrich, A., *et al.* 'Settlements of the Iron Age and Pagan Saxon periods at Linford, Essex', *Transactions of the Essex Archaeological Society*, 3rd S., 1 (1961/5) 57–104

Bascombe, K. N. 'Two charters of King Suebred of Essex', in *An Essex Tribute*, ed. K. Neale (London 1987), pp. 85–96

Bassett, S. 'Churches in Worcester before and after the conversion of the Anglo-Saxons', *Antiquaries Journal* 69 (1989) 225–56

Bassett, Steven (ed.) *The Origins of Anglo-Saxon Kingdoms* (London & New York 1989)

Bately, J. M. 'King Alfred and the Latin MSS of Orosius' History', *Classica et Mediaevalia* 22 (1961) 69–105

Bately, Janet (ed.) *The Old English Orosius* (London 1980)

Bates, David. *A Bibliography of Domesday Book* (Woodbridge & Dover, NH 1986)

Belfour, A[lgernon] O. (ed.) *Twelfth-Century Homilies in MS. Bodley 343. Part I. Text and Translation* (London 1909)

Benson, Larry D. (ed.) *The Riverside Chaucer* (3rd edn, Boston 1987)

Beresford, Guy, *et al.* *Goltho: The Development of an Early Medieval Manor c 850–1150*, ed. J. Geddes (London 1987)

Beresford, Maurice, and Hurst, John G. (edd.) *Deserted Medieval Villages. Studies* (London 1971)

Beresford, Maurice, & Hurst, John. *English Heritage Book of Wharram Percy Deserted Medieval Village* (London 1990)

Bessinger, Jess B., Jr, & Creed, Robert P. (edd.) *Medieval and Linguistic Studies in Honor of Francis Peabody Magoun, Jr.* (London 1965)

Bethmann, L., & Waitz, G. (edd.) *Pauli Historia Langobardorum*, in *Scriptores Rerum Langobardicarum et Italicarum Saec. VI–IX*, ed. Societas Aperiendis Fontibus Germanicarum Medii Aevi (Hannover 1878), pp. 12–192

Bethurum, D. 'Archbishop Wulfstan's commonplace book', *Publications of the Modern Language Association* 57 (1942) 916–29

Bethurum, D. 'Episcopal magnificence in the eleventh century', in *Studies in Old English Literature in Honor of Arthur G. Brodeur*, ed. S. B. Greenfield (Eugene, OR 1963), pp. 162–70

Bethurum, D. 'Six anonymous Old English codes', *JEGP: Journal of English and Germanic Philology* 49 (1950) 449–63

Bethurum, Dorothy (ed.) *The Homilies of Wulfstan* (Oxford 1957)

Beyerle, Franz & Buchner, Rudolf (edd.) *Lex Ribuaria* (Hannover 1954)

Bieler, Ludwig (ed.) *The Irish Penitentials* (Dublin 1975)

Biddick, K. 'People and things: power in early English development', *Comparative Studies in Society and History* 32 (1990) 3–23

Biddick, Kathleen. *The Other Economy. Pastoral Husbandry on a Medieval Estate* (Berkeley & Los Angeles, CA & London 1989)

Biddle, Martin (ed.) *Object and Economy in Medieval Winchester* (2 vols, Oxford 1990)

Birch, Walter de Gray (ed.) *Cartularium Saxonicum* (3 vols & Index, London 1885/93)

Blair, John. *Early Medieval Surrey: Landholding, Church and Settlement before 1300* (Stroud 1991)

Blair, J. 'Introduction: from minster to parish church', in *Minsters and Parish Churches*, ed. J. Blair (Oxford 1988), pp. 1–19

Blair, John (ed.) *Minsters and Parish Churches. The Local Church in Transition 950–1200* (Oxford 1988)

Blair, John, & Sharpe, Richard (edd.) *Pastoral Care Before the Parish* (Leicester, London & New York 1992)

Blake, E[rnest] O. (ed.) *Liber Eliensis* (London 1962)

Bloch, Marc. *Feudal Society*, transl. L. A. Manyon (2 vols, Chicago, IL 1964)

Bloch, M. 'How and why ancient slavery came to an end', in *idem, Slavery and Serfdom in the Middle Ages*, trans. W. R. Beer (Berkeley & Los Angeles, CA & London 1975), pp. 1–31

Bloch, Marc. *Mélanges historiques* (2 vols, Paris 1963)

Bloch, Marc. *Slavery and Serfdom in the Middle Ages: Selected Essays by Marc Bloch*, transl. William R. Beer (Berkeley & Los Angeles, CA & London 1975)

Bluhme, F. (ed.) *Edictus Rothari*, in *Monumenta Germaniae Historica, Legum Tomus IIII*, ed. G. H. Pertz (Hannover 1868), pp. 1–95

Bluhme, Friedrich (ed.) *Leges Liutprandi Regis*, in *Monumenta Germaniae Historica, Legum Tomus IIII*, ed. G. H. Pertz (Hannover 1868), pp. 96–182

Blunt, C. 'The coinage of Offa', in *Anglo-Saxon Coins*, ed. R. H. M. Dolley (London 1961), pp. 39–62 + plates IV–VII

Boddington, A. 'Models of burial, settlement and worship: the final phase reviewed', in *Anglo-Saxon Cemeteries*, ed. E. Southworth (Stroud 1990), pp. 177–99

Boddington, A. 'Raunds, Northamptonshire: analysis of a country churchyard', *World Archaeology* 18 (1986) 411–25

Boehmer, H. 'Das Eigenkirchentum in England', in *Texte und Forschungen zur englischen Kulturgeschichte*, edd. H. Boehmer *et al.* (Halle 1921), pp. 301–53

Boehmer, Heinrich *et al.* (edd.) *Texte und Forschungen zur englischen Kulturgeschichte: Festgabe für Felix Liebermann zum 20. Juli 1921* (Halle 1921)

Bøgholm, N[ils], *et al.* (edd.) *A Grammatical Miscellany offered to Otto Jespersen on his Seventieth Birthday* (Copenhagen & London 1930)

Bois, Guy. *La Mutation de l'an mil. Lournand, village mâconnais, de l'antiquité au féodalisme* (Paris 1989)

Bois, Guy. *The Transformation of the Year One Thousand. The Village of Lournand from Antiquity to Feudalism*, transl. Jean Birrell (Manchester & New York 1992)

Bolin, S. 'Mohammed, Charlemagne and Ruric', *Scandinavian Economic History Review* 1 (1953) 5–39

Bonnassie, Pierre. *From Slavery to Feudalism in South-Western Europe*, transl. Jean Birrell (Cambridge & Paris 1991)

Bonnassie, P. 'The survival and extinction of the slave system in the early medieval West (fourth to eleventh centuries)', in *idem, From Slavery to Feudalism in South-Western Europe*, transl. J. Birrell (Cambridge & Paris 1991), pp. 1–59

Boretius, Alfred. *Capitularia Regum Francorum* (Hannover 1883)

Boretius, A. (ed.) *Liber Legis Langobardorum Papiensis*, in *Monumenta Germaniae Historica, Legum Tomus IIII*, ed. G. H. Pertz (Hannover 1868), pp. 289–606

Bosanquet, Geoffrey (transl.) *Eadmer's History of Recent Events in England* (London 1964)

Bosworth, Joseph. *An Anglo-Saxon Dictionary: Based on the Manuscript Collections of the Late Joseph Bosworth, D.D., F.R.S.*, ed. T. Northcote Toller (Oxford 1898)

Bradley, S. A. J. (transl.) *Anglo-Saxon Poetry. An Anthology of Old English Poems in Prose Translation with Introduction and Headnotes* (London, Melbourne, & Toronto, ON 1982)

Brady, Robert. *A Complete History of England. From the First Entrance of the Romans under the Conduct of Julius Cæsar, unto the End of the Reign of King Henry III. . .* (London 1685)

Bratanic, B. 'On the antiquity of the one-sided plough in Europe, especially among the Slavic peoples', *Laos: Études comparées de folklore ou d'ethnologie régionale* 2 (1952) 51–61

Bresslau, Harry (ed.) *Die Urkunden Konrads II. Mit Nachträgen zu den Urkunden Heinrichs II* (Hannover & Leipzig 1909)

Bretholz, Bertold (ed.) *Die Chronik der Böhmen des Cosmas von Prag (Cosmae Pragensis Chronica Boemorum)* (Berlin 1923)

Bridbury, A. R. 'Domesday Book: a re-interpretation', *English Historical Review* 105 (1990) 285–309

Bridgeman, C. G. O. 'The Burton Abbey twelfth century surveys', in *Collections for a History of Staffordshire. 1916*, ed. William Salt Archaeological Society (London 1918), pp. 209–300

Brisbane, M. 'Hamwic (Saxon Southampton): an 8th century port and production centre', in *The Rebirth of Towns in the West AD 700–1050*, edd. R. Hodges & B. Hobley (London 1988), pp. 101–8

Bromberg, E. I. 'Wales and the mediaeval slave trade', *Speculum* 17 (1942) 263–9

Brooks, N., *et al.* 'A new charter of King Edgar', *Anglo-Saxon England* 13 (1984) 137–55

Brooks, N. 'Anglo-Saxon charters: the work of the last twenty years', *Anglo-Saxon England* 3 (1974) 211–31

Brooks, Nicholas. *The Early History of the Church of Canterbury. Christ Church from 597 to 1066* ([Leicester] & Atlantic Highlands, NJ 1984)

Brotanek, Rudolf (ed.) *Texte und Untersuchungen zur altenglischen Literatur und Kirchengeschichte* (Halle 1913)

Brothwell, D. 'Palaeodemography and the earlier British populations', *World Archaeology* 4 (1972/3) 75–87

Brown, P. 'Society and the supernatural: a medieval change', *Daedalus* 104, no. 2 (Spring 1975) 133–51

Brown, R. Allen (ed.) *Anglo-Norman Studies IX: Proceedings of the Battle Conference 1986* (Woodbridge 1987)

Brown, R. Allen (ed.) *Anglo-Norman Studies XI: Proceedings of the Battle Conference 1988* (Woodbridge 1989)

Brown, T[homas] J[ulian], *et al.* (facs. edd.) *The Durham Ritual: A Southern English Collectar of the Tenth Century with Northumbrian Additions (Durham Cathedral Library A. IV. 19)* (Copenhagen 1969)

Bruce-Mitford, Rupert [L. S.] (ed.) *Recent Archaeological Excavations in Europe* (London, 1975)

Bruce-Mitford, Rupert [L. S.] *The Sutton Hoo Ship Burial* (3 vols in 4 parts, London 1975/83)

Brühl, Carlrichard, & Violante, Cinzio (edd.) *Die "Honorantie Civitatis Papie". Transkription, Edition, Kommentar* (Köln & Wien 1983)

Brunner, Heinrich. *Deutsche Rechtsgeschichte* (2nd edn, Leipzig 1906)

Buckland, W[illiam] W. *The Roman Law of Slavery. The Condition of the Slave in Private Law from Augustus to Justinian* (Cambridge 1908)

Bullough, D. A. 'Anglo-Saxon institutions and early English society', *Annali della fondazione italiana per la storia amministrativa* 2 (1968) 647–59

Cabaniss, Allen. *Agobard of Lyons: Churchman and Critic* ([Syracuse, NY] 1953)

Calthrop, M. M. C. 'Priory of St. Mary of Worcester', in *The Victoria History of the County of Worcester*, volume II, edd. J. W. Willis-Bund & W. Page (London 1906), pp. 94–112

Cameron, A. 'A list of Old English texts', in *A Plan for the Dictionary of Old English*, edd. R. Frank & A. Cameron (Toronto, ON & Buffalo, NY 1973), pp. 25–306

Cameron, A. 'The boundaries of Old English literature', in *The Anglo-Saxons. Synthesis and Interpretation*, edd. J. D. Woods & D. A. E. Pelteret (Waterloo, ON 1985), pp. 27–36

Cameron, K. 'The meaning and significance of Old English *walh* in English place-names'; Appendix 1: Malcolm Todd, 'The archaeological significance of place-names in *walh*'; Appendix 2: John Insley, 'The Continental evidence: OHG *wal(a)h*, OSax *walh*', *Journal of the English Place-Name Society* 12 (1979/80) 1–53

Campbell, Alistair. *Enlarged Addenda and Corrigenda* to T. N. Toller, *Supplement to An Anglo-Saxon Dictionary* (Oxford 1972)

Campbell, Alistair (ed.) *Frithegodi Monachi Breuiloquium Vitæ Beati Wilfredi et Wulfstani Cantoris Narratio Metrica de Sancto Swithuno* (Zurich n.d. [1950])

Campbell, A[listair]. *Old English Grammar* (Oxford 1959)

Campbell, J. 'Some agents and agencies of the late Anglo-Saxon state', in *Domesday Studies: Papers read at the Novocentenary Conference of the Royal Historical Society and the Institute of British Geographers Winchester, 1986.* ed. J. C. Holt (Woodbridge & Wolfeboro, NH 1987), pp. 201–18

Carr, Charles T. *Nominal Compounds in Germanic* (London 1939)

Carver, M[artin] O. H. (ed.) *The Age of Sutton Hoo. The Seventh Century in North-Western Europe* (Woodbridge 1992)

Carver, M. O. H. 'The Anglo-Saxon cemetery at Sutton Hoo: an interim report', in *The Age of Sutton Hoo*, ed. M. Carver (Woodbridge 1992), pp. 343–71

Chadwick, H[ector] Munro. *Studies on Anglo-Saxon Institutions* (Cambridge 1905)

Chadwick, H[ector] Munro. *The Heroic Age* (Cambridge 1912)

Chadwick, Nora K., *et al. Studies in the Early British Church* (Cambridge 1958)

Chadwick, N. K. 'The British or Celtic part in the population of England', in *Angles and Britons: The O'Donnell Lectures* (Cardiff 1963), pp. 111–47

Chadwick, N. K. 'The Celtic background of early Anglo-Saxon England', in K. Jackson *et al.*, *Celt and Saxon: Studies in the Early British Border* (Cambridge 1964), pp. 323–52

Chambers, R[aymond] W., *et al.* (facs. edd.) *The Exeter Book of Old English Poetry* (London 1933)

Chaney, William A. *The Cult of Kingship in Anglo-Saxon England. The Transition from Paganism to Christianity* (Manchester 1970)

Charles, B[ertie] G. *Old Norse Relations with Wales* (Cardiff 1934)

Charles-Edwards, T. 'Early medieval kingships in the British Isles', in *The Origins of Anglo-Saxon Kingdoms*, ed. S. Bassett (London & New York 1989), pp. 28–39

Charles-Edwards, T. 'The pastoral role of the church in the early Irish laws', in *Pastoral Care Before the Parish*, edd. J. Blair & R. Sharpe (Leicester, London & New York 1992), pp. 63–80

Chibnall, Marjorie (ed.) *Charters and Custumals of the Abbey of Holy Trinity Caen* (London 1982)

Clack, Peter, & Ivy, Jill (edd.) *The Borders* (Durham 1983)

Claessen, Henri J. M., & Van de Velde, Pieter (edd.) *Early State Dynamics* (Leiden, New York, Copenhagen, & Cologne 1987)

Claessen, Henri J. M., & Skalník, Peter (edd.) *The Early State* (The Hague, Paris, & New York 1978)

Claessen, Henri J. M., & Skalník, Peter (edd.) *The Study of the State* (The Hague, Paris, & New York 1981)

Clarke, H. 'Agriculture in late Anglo-Saxon England', in *Domesday Book: Studies*, edd. A. Williams & R. W. H. Erskine (London 1987)

Clarke, H. B. 'Domesday slavery (adjusted for slaves)', *Midland History* 1, no. 4 (Autumn 1972) 37–46

Clarke, H. B. 'The Domesday satellites', in *Domesday Book: A Reassessment*, ed. P. Sawyer (London 1985), pp. 50–70

Claus, Martin, *et al.* (edd.) *Studien zur europaischen Vor- und Frühgeschichte* (Neumünster 1968)

Cleasby, Richard & Vigfusson, Gudbrand. *An Icelandic-English Dictionary* (2nd edn, with a Supplement by William A. Craigie, Oxford 1957)

Clemoes, Peter, & Hughes, Kathleen (edd.) *England before the Conquest: Studies in Primary Sources presented to Dorothy Whitelock* (Cambridge 1971)

Clemoes, Peter (ed.) *The Anglo-Saxons. Studies in Some Aspects of their History and Culture presented to Bruce Dickins* (London 1959)

Clemoes, P. 'The chronology of Ælfric's works', in *The Anglo-Saxons*, ed. P. Clemoes (London 1959), pp. 212–47

Cockayne, Oswald (ed.) *Leechdoms, Wortcunning, and Starcraft of Early England. Being a Collection of Documents, for the Most Part never before Printed, Illustrating the History of Science in this Country before the Norman Conquest* (3 vols, London 1864/6)

Cockburn, J[ames] S., *et al.* (edd.) *A History of the County of Middlesex*, volume I (London 1969)

Cohn, H. H. 'Slavery', in *Encyclopaedia Judaica*, ed. C. Roth, volume XIV (Jerusalem & [New York] 1971), cols 1655–60

Colgrave, Bertram & Mynors, R. A. B. (edd. & transl.) *Bede's Ecclesiastical History of the English People* (Oxford 1969)

Colgrave, Bertram (ed. & transl.) *Felix's Life of Saint Guthlac* (Cambridge 1956)

Colunga, Alberto, & Turrado, Laurenzo (edd.) *Biblia Sacra iuxta Vulgatam Clementinam. Nova Editio Logicis Partitionibus Aliisque Subsidiis Ornata* (5th edn, Madrid 1977)

Cooper, Janet (ed.) *The Battle of Maldon: Fiction and Fact* (London & Rio Grande, OH 1993)

Craster, H. H. E. 'Some Anglo-Saxon records of the see of Durham', *Archaeologia Æliana*, 4th S., 1 (1925) 189–98

Crawford, S[amuel] J. (ed.) *Byrhtferth's Manual (A.D. 1011): Now edited for the First Time from MS. Ashmole 328 in the Bodleian Library*, volume I: Text, Translation, Sources and Appendices (London 1929)

Crawford, S[amuel] J. (ed.) *The Old English Version of the Heptateuch, Ælfric's Treatise on the Old and New Testament and his Preface to Genesis*, etc. (London 1922; rptd, with the Text of Two Additional Manuscripts transcribed by Neil R. Ker, London 1969)

Cross, J. E., & Brown, A. 'Literary impetus for Wulfstan's *Sermo Lupi*', *Leeds Studies in English*, N.S., 20 (1989) 271–91

Cross, James E., & Hill, Thomas D. (edd.) *The 'Prose Solomon and Saturn' and 'Adrian and Ritheus': Edited from the British Museum Manuscripts with Commentary* (Toronto, ON, Buffalo, NY, & London 1982)

Cummings, William Hayman. *Dr. Arne and 'Rule Britannia'* (London 1912)

Damico, Helen. *Beowulf's Wealhtheow and the Valkyrie Tradition* (Madison 1984)

Darby, H[enry] C. *Domesday England* (Cambridge 1977)

Darby, H[enry] C., & Versey, G[eorge] R. *Domesday Gazetteer* (Cambridge 1975)

Darby, H[enry] C., & Terrett, I[an] B. (edd.) *The Domesday Geography of Midland England* (2nd edn, Cambridge 1971)

Darlington, R. R. 'Ecclesiastical reform in the late Old English period', *English Historical Review* 51 (1936) 385–428

Darlington, Reginald R. (ed.) *The Vita Wulfstani of William of Malmesbury: To which are added the Extant Abridgements of this Work and The Miracles and Translations of St. Wulfstan* (London 1928)

Davidson, H. E. 'Human sacrifice in the late Pagan period in North Western Europe', in *The Age of Sutton Hoo*, ed. M. O. H. Carver (Woodbridge 1992), pp. 331–40

Davidson, J. B. 'Some Anglo-Saxon boundaries, now deposited at the Albert Museum, Exeter', *Transactions of the Devonshire Association* 8 (1876) 396–419

Davies, W., & Vierck, H. 'The contexts of Tribal Hidage. Social aggregates and settlement patterns', *Frühmittelalterliche Studien* 8 (1974) 223–93

Davies, W. 'The Latin charter-tradition in western Britain, Brittany and Ireland in the early mediaeval period', in *Ireland in Early Mediaeval Europe*, edd. D. Whitelock *et al.* (Cambridge 1982), pp. 258–80

Davis, David Brion. *The Problem of Slavery in Western Culture* (Ithaca, NY & London 1966)

Davis, G[odfrey] R. C. *Medieval Cartularies of Great Britain. A Short Catalogue* (London 1958)

Davis, H[enry] W. C. (ed.), with the assistance of R. J. Whitwell. *Regesta Regum Anglo-Normannorum 1066–1154*. Volume I: *Regesta Willelmi Conquestoris et Willelmi Rufi 1066–1100* (Oxford 1913)

Davis, N. 'Note to the Second Edition', in *Beowulf*, ed. J. Zupitza (2nd edn, London 1959), pp. v–xvii

Davis, R. H. C. 'Alfred the Great: propaganda and truth', *History* 56 (1971) 169–82

Deanesly, Margaret. *The Pre-Conquest Church in England* (2nd edn, London 1963)

Diamond, Stanley (ed.) *Culture in History: Essays in Honor of Paul Radin* (New York 1960)

Dickins, B. 'The beheaded manumission in the Exeter Book', in *The Early Cultures of North-West Europe. (H. M. Chadwick Memorial Studies)*, edd. C. Fox & B. Dickins (Cambridge 1950), pp. 363–7 + 1 plate

Dickinson, Tania M. *Cuddesdon and Dorchester-on-Thames, Oxfordshire. Two Early Saxon 'Princely' Sites in Wessex* (Oxford 1974)

Dimock, James F. *Giraldi Cambrensis Topographia Hibernica, et Expugnatio Hibernica* (London 1867)

Dixon, P. H. 'The Anglo-Saxon settlement at Mucking: an interpretation', in *Anglo-Saxon Studies in Archaeology and History*, volume VI , ed. W. Filmer-Sankey (Oxford 1993), pp. 125–47

Doane, A. N. (ed.) *Genesis A. A New Edition* (Madison, WI & London 1978)

Dobbie, Elliott Van Kirk (ed.) *Beowulf and Judith* (New York & London 1953)

Dobbie, Elliott Van Kirk (ed.) *The Anglo-Saxon Minor Poems* (New York & London 1942)

Doble, Gilbert H. *The Saints of Cornwall*. Part Four. *Saints of the Newquay, Padstow and Bodmin District* (Truro 1965)

Dockès, Pierre. *Medieval Slavery and Liberation*, transl. Arthur Goldhammer (Chicago, IL & London 1982)

Dodgson, J. McN. 'Place-names from *hām*, distinguished from *hamm* names, in relation to the settlement of Kent, Surrey and Sussex', *Anglo-Saxon England* 2 (1973) 1–50

Dolley, R[eginald] H. M[ichael] (ed.) *Anglo-Saxon Coins. Studies Presented to F. M. Stenton on the Occasion of his 80th Birthday 17 May 1960* (London 1961)

Domar, E. D. 'The causes of slavery or serfdom: a hypothesis', *Journal of Economic History* 30 (1970) 18–32

Doubleday, H[erbert] Arthur (ed.) *A History of Hampshire and the Isle of Wight*, volume I (Westminster 1900)

Doubleday, H[erbert] Arthur, & Page, William (edd.) *The Victoria History of the County of Essex*, volume I (Westminster 1903)

Douglas, David C., & Greenaway, George W. (transl.) *English Historical Documents 1042–1189* (2nd edn, London & New York 1981)

Douglas, David C. *William the Conqueror: The Norman Impact upon England* (Berkeley & Los Angeles, CA 1964)

Downer, L. J. (ed. & transl.) *Leges Henrici Primi* (Oxford 1972)

Dozy, R[einhart P. A.]. *Recherches sur l'histoire et la littérature de l'Espagne pendant le Moyen Age* (3rd edn, 2 vols, Paris & Leyde 1881)

Drew, Katherine Fischer (transl.) *The Lombard Laws* (Philadelphia, PA 1973)

Drinkwater, C. H. 'Translation of the Shropshire Domesday', in *The Victoria History of Shropshire*, volume I, ed. W. Page (London 1908), pp. 309–49

Drinkwater, John, & Elton, Hugh (edd.) *Fifth-century Gaul: A Crisis of Identity?* (Cambridge 1992)

Duby, Georges. *L'Economie rurale et la vie des campagnes dans l'Occident médiéval (France, Angleterre, Empire, IXᵉ–XVᵉ siècles)*. Essai de synthèse et perspectives de recherches (2 vols, Paris 1962)

Duby, G. 'Preface', in G. Bois, *The Transformation of the Year One Thousand*, transl. J. Birrell (Manchester & New York 1992), pp. ix–x

Duby, Georges. *Rural Economy and Country Life in the Medieval West*, transl. Cynthia Postan (London 1968)

Duby, Georges. *The Early Growth of the European Economy. Warriors and Peasants from the Seventh to the Twelfth Century*, transl. Howard B. Clarke (London & Ithaca, NY 1974)

Duby, Georges. *The Three Orders: Feudal Society Imagined*, transl. Arthur Goldhammer, with a Foreword by Thomas N. Bisson (Chicago, IL & London 1980)

Dugdale, William. *Monasticon Anglicanum. A History of the Abbies and Other Monasteries, Hospitals, Frieries, and Cathedrals and Collegiate Churches, with their Dependencies, in England and Wales. . . . ,* volume II, edd. John Caley *et al.* (London 1846)

Dumville, D. N. 'The ætheling: a study in Anglo-Saxon constitutional history', *Anglo-Saxon England* 8 (1979) 1–33

Dunbabin, J. [Review of Guy Bois, *La Mutation de l'an mil. Lournand, village mâconnais de l'antiquité au féodalisme* (1989)], *English Historical Review* 108 (1993) 697–8

Dyer, C. 'Les problèmes de la croissance agricole du haut moyen âge en Angleterre', in *La Croissance agricole du haut moyen âge* (Auch 1990), pp. 117–30

Dyer, Christopher. *Lords and Peasants in a Changing Society. The Estates of the Bishopric of Worcester, 680–1540* (Cambridge 1980)

Earle, John (ed.) *A Hand-Book to the Land-Charters and Other Saxonic Documents* (Oxford 1888)

Earle, Timothy (ed.) *Chiefdoms: Power, Economy, and Ideology* (Cambridge 1991)

Eckhardt, Karl August (ed. & transl.) *Leges Anglo-Saxonum 601–925* (Göttingen 1958)

Einar Ólafur Sveinsson (ed.) *Laxdœlasaga; Halldórs Þættir Snorrasonar; Stúfs Þáttr* (Reykjavik 1934)

Ekeh, P. P. 'Social Anthropology and two contrasting uses of Tribalism in Africa', *Comparative Studies in Society and History* 32 (1990) 660–700

Ekwall, E. 'Tribal names in English place-names', *Namn och Bygd* 41 (1953) 129–77

Ellis, Henry [J.] *A General Introduction to Domesday Book: Accompanied by Indexes of the Tenants in Chief, and Under Tenants at the Time of the Survey*, etc. (2 vols, London 1833)

[Ellis, Henry J. (ed.)] *Liber Censualis, vocati Domesday-Book. Additamenta ex codic. antiquiss. Exon' Domesday. Inquisitio Eliensis. Liber Winton'. Boldon Book* (London 1816)

Emerton, Ephraim (transl.) *The Letters of Saint Boniface* (New York 1940)

Erskine, R. W. H. (general ed.) *Great Domesday: Facsimile . . . including All Folios subsequently added to the Manuscript* (London 1987)

Evans, Angela Care. *The Sutton Hoo Ship Burial* (London 1986)

Evans, D[aniel] Simon (ed.) *Historia Gruffud Vab Kenan. Gyda Rhagymadrodd a Nodiadau* (Caerdydd [= Cardiff] 1977)

Evans, J[ohn] Gwenogvryn (ed.), with the co-operation of John Rhys. *The Text of the Book of Llan Dâv reproduced from the Gwysaney Manuscript* (Oxford 1893)

Fabbrini, Fabrizio. *La Manumissio in Ecclesia* (Milano 1964)

[Farley, Abraham. (ed.)] *Domesday Book seu Liber Censualis Willelmi Primi Regis Angliæ, inter Archivos Regni in Domo Capitulari Westmonasterii asservatus* (2 vols, [London] 1783)

Faull, Margaret L. (ed.) *Studies in Late Anglo-Saxon Settlement* (Oxford 1984)

Faull, M. L. 'The semantic development of Old English *wealh*', *Leeds Studies in English*, N.S., 8 (1975) 20–44

Fehr, Bernhard (ed.) *Die Hirtenbriefe Ælfrics: in altenglischer und lateinischer Fassung* (Hamburg, 1914; rptd with a Supplement to the Introduction by Peter Clemoes, Darmstadt 1966)

Ferro, K. 'The king in the doorway: the "Anglo-Saxon Chronicle", A.D. 755', in *Kings and Kingship*, ed. J. Rosenthal (Binghamton, NY 1986), pp. 17–30.

Filmer-Sankey, William (ed.) *Anglo-Saxon Studies in Archaeology and History*, volume VI (Oxford 1993)

Finberg, H[erbert] P. R. *Lucerna. Studies of Some Problems in the Early History of England* (London & New York 1964)

Finberg, H[erbert] P. R. *Tavistock Abbey. A Study in the Social and Economic History of Devon* (2nd edn, New York 1969)

Finberg, H[erbert] P. R. (ed.) *The Agrarian History of England and Wales*. I. ii. *A.D. 43–1042* (Cambridge 1972)

Finberg, H. P. R. 'The Domesday plough-team', *English Historical Review* 66 (1951), 67–71

Finberg, H[erbert] P. R. *The Early Charters of Wessex* (Leicester 1964)

Finberg, H. P. R. 'The House of Ordgar and the foundation of Tavistock Abbey', *English Historical Review* 58 (1943) 190–201

Finley, M. I. 'Between slavery and freedom', *Comparative Studies in Society and History* 6 (1963/4) 233–49

Finley, M[oses] I. (ed.) *Slavery in Classical Antiquity. Views and Controversies* (Cambridge 1960; rptd with supplement to bibliography, Cambridge & New York 1968)

Finley, M. I. 'The servile statuses of ancient Greece', *Revue Internationale des Droits de l'Antiquité*, 3e série, 7 (1960) 165–89

Finley, M. I. 'Was Greek civilization based on slave labour?', in *Slavery in Classical Antiquity*, ed. M. I. Finley (Cambridge & New York 1968), pp. 53–72

Finn, R[ex] Welldon. *The Norman Conquest and its Effects on the Economy: 1066–86* (London 1970 & New York 1971)

Finsterwalder, Paul Willem (ed.) *Die Canones Theodori Cantuariensis und ihre Überlieferungsformen* (Weimar 1929)

Fleming, L. 'Pigs in Domesday Book', *Sussex Notes and Queries* 11, no. 2 (May 1946) 32 *and* 34.

Fleming, R. 'Domesday Book and the tenurial revolution', in *Anglo-Norman Studies IX: Proceedings of the Battle Conference 1986,* ed. R. Allen Brown (Woodbridge 1987), pp. 87–102

Fleming, R. 'Domesday estates of the King and the Godwines: a study in late Saxon politics', *Speculum* 58 (1983) 987–1007

Foard, G. [Review of *Anglo-Saxon Settlements*, ed. D. Hooke (1988)], *Medieval Archaeology* 35 (1991) 251–3

Foote, P. 'Þrælahald á Íslandi', *Saga* 15 (1977) 41–54

Förster, Max. *Der Flussname Themse und seine Sippe. Studien zur Anglisierung keltischer Eigennamen und zur Lautchronologie des Altbritischen* (München 1941)

Förster, M. 'Die altenglischen Beigaben des Lambeth-Psalters', *Archiv für das Studium der neueren Sprachen und Literaturen* 132 (1914) 328–35

Förster, M. 'Die Freilassungsurkunden des Bodmin-Evangeliars', in *A Grammatical Miscellany offered to Otto Jespersen on his Seventieth Birthday*, ed. N. Bøgholm *et al.* (Copenhagen & London 1930), pp. 77–99

Foulke, William Dudley (transl.) *History of the Langobards by Paul the Deacon* (New York, 1907; rptd as Paul the Deacon, *History of the Lombards*, ed. Edward Peters, Philadelphia, PA 1974)

Fournier, Marcel. *Essai sur les formes et les effets de l'affranchissement dans le droit gallo-franc* (Paris 1885)

Fournier, P. 'Le *Liber ex lege Moysi* et les tendances bibliques du droit canonique irlandais', *Revue celtique* 30 (1909) 221–34

Fowler, R. 'A late Old English handbook for the use of a confessor', *Anglia* 83 (1965) 1–34

Fox, Cyril [F.] *The Archaeology of the Cambridge Region. A Topographical Study of the Bronze, Early Iron, Roman and Anglo-Saxon Ages, with an Introductory Note on the Neolithic Age* (Cambridge 1923)

Fox, Cyril [F.], & Dickins, Bruce (edd.) *The Early Cultures of North-West Europe. (H. M. Chadwick Memorial Studies)* (Cambridge 1950)

Frank, Roberta, & Cameron, Angus (edd.) *A Plan for the Dictionary of Old English* (Toronto, ON & Buffalo, NY 1973)

Frantzen, Allen J. *King Alfred* (Boston, MA 1986)

Frantzen, Allen J. *La Littérature de la pénitence dans l'Angleterre anglo-saxonne*, transl. Michel Lejeune (Fribourg, Switzerland 1991)

Frantzen, Allen J. *The Literature of Penance in Anglo-Saxon England* (New Brunswick, NJ 1983)

Frantzen A. J. 'The penitentials attributed to Bede', *Speculum* 58 (1983) 573–97

Frantzen, A. J. 'The tradition of penitentials in Anglo-Saxon England', *Anglo-Saxon England* 11 (1982) 23–56

Freedman, Paul. *The Origins of Peasant Servitude in Medieval Catalonia* (Cambridge 1991)

Fried, M. H. 'On the evolution of social stratification and the State', in *Culture in History. Essays in Honor of Paul Radin*, ed. S. Diamond (New York 1960), pp. 713–31

Galbraith, V[ivian] H. *The Making of Domesday Book* (Oxford 1961)

Gallée, J[ohan] H[endrik]. *Vorstudien zu einem altniederdeutschen Wörterbuche* (Leiden 1903)

Garmonsway, G[eorge] N. (ed.) *Ælfric's Colloquy* (2nd edn, London 1947)

Garmonsway, G. N. 'The development of the Colloquy', in *The Anglo-Saxons*, ed. P. Clemoes (London 1959), pp. 248–61

Gelling, Margaret. *Place-Names in the Landscape* (London & Melbourne 1984)

Gelling, Margaret. *Signposts to the Past. Place-Names and the History of England* (2nd edn, Chichester 1988)

Gibbs, Marion (ed.) *Early Charters of the Cathedral Church of St. Paul, London* (London 1939)

Giles, John A. (transl.) *William of Malmesbury's Chronicle of the Kings of England: From the Earliest Period to the Reign of King Stephen* (London 1847)

Gleissner, Reinhard. *Die 'zweideutigen' altenglischen Rätsel des 'Exeter Book' in ihrem zeitgenössischen Kontext* (Frankfurt am Main, Bern, New York, & Nancy 1984)

Gneuss, H. 'A preliminary list of manuscripts written or owned in England up to 1100', *Anglo-Saxon England* 9 (1981) 1–60

Gneuss, Helmut. *Hymnar und Hymnen im englischen Mittelalter. Studien zur Überlieferung, Glossierung und Übersetzung lateinischer Hymnen in England; Mit einer Textausgabe der lateinisch-altenglischen Expositio Hymnorum* (Tübingen 1968)

Godden, Malcolm (ed.) *Ælfric's Catholic Homilies: The Second Series Text* (Oxford 1979)

Godfrey, C. J. 'The Archbishopric of Lichfield', *Studies in Church History* 1 (1964) 145–53

Gollancz, Israel (facs. ed.) *The Cædmon Manuscript of Anglo-Saxon Biblical Poetry, Junius XI in the Bodleian Library* ([London] 1927)

Goodall, I. H. 'Locks and keys', in *Object and Economy in Medieval Winchester*, ed. M. Biddle (Oxford 1990), II.1001–36

Goodspeed, Edgar J. *Problems of New Testament Translation* (Chicago, IL [1945])

Goossens, Louis (ed.) *The Old English Glosses of MS. Brussels, Royal Library, 1650 (Aldhelm's* De Laudibus Virginitatis*) Edited with an Introduction, Notes and Indexes* (Brussels 1974)

Gordon, E[ric] V. (ed.) *The Battle of Maldon* (London 1937)

Gordon, E. V. 'Wealhþeow and related names', *Medium Ævum* 4 (1935) 169–75

Graves, Edgar B. *A Bibliography of English History to 1485. Based on the Sources and Literature of English History from the Earliest Times to about 1485 by Charles Gross* (Oxford 1975)

Green, Charles. *Sutton Hoo. The Excavation of a Royal Ship-Burial* (2nd rev. edn, London 1988)

Green, D[ennis] H. *The Carolingian Lord. Semantic Studies on Four Old High German Words, Balder, Frô, Truhtin, Herro* (Cambridge 1965)

Greenfield. Stanley B. (ed.) *Studies in Old English Literature in Honor of Arthur G. Brodeur* (Eugene, OR 1963)

Gregson, N. 'The multiple estate model: an adequate framework for the analysis of early territorial organisation?', in *The Borders*, edd. P. Clack & J. Ivy (Durham 1983), pp. 49–80

Gregson, N. 'The multiple estate model: some critical questions', *Journal of Historical Geography* 11 (1985) 339–51

Grierson, P. 'La Fonction sociale de la monnaie en Angleterre aux VIIᵉ–VIIIᵉ siècles', in *Moneta e scambi nell'alto Medioevo* (Spoleto 1961), pp. 341–62; 'La discussione sul tema: Isole Brittanniche – Relazione Grierson', *ibid.*, pp. 363–85

Grierson, P. 'The relations between England and Flanders before the Norman Conquest', *Transactions of the Royal Historical Society*, 4th S., 23 (1941) 71–112

Grierson, P. 'Weights and measures', in *Domesday Book: Studies*, edd. A. Williams & R. W. H. Erskine (London 1987), pp. 80–5.

Grimm, J[akob] L. K. *Deutsche Rechtsalterthümer*, edd. Andreas Heusler & Rudolf Hübner (4th edn, 2 vols, Leipzig 1899)

Grosjean, P. [review of Eric John, *Land Tenure in Early England* (1960)], *Analecta Bollandiana* 79 (1961) 210–13

Guérard, B[enjamin E. C.] (ed.) *Polyptique de l'Abbaye de Saint-Rémi de Reims, ou dénombrement des manses, des serfs et des revenus de cette abbaye, vers le milieu du neuvième siècle de notre ère* (Paris 1853)

Guérard, B[enjamin E. C.] (ed.) *Polyptique de l'Abbé Irminon. Ou dénombrement des manses, des serfs et des revenus de l'abbaye de Saint-Germain-des-Prés sous le règne de Charlemagne publié d'après le manuscrit de la Bibliothèque du Roi, avec des prolégomènes pour servir à l'histoire de la condition des personnes et des terres depuis les invasions des barbares jusqu'à l'institution des communes* (2 vols, Paris 1844)

Gutmacher, E. 'Der Wortschatz des althochdeutschen Tatian in seinem Verhältnis zum Altsächsischen, Angelsächsischen und Altfriesischen', *Beiträge zur Geschichte der deutschen Sprache und Literatur* 39 (1914) 1–83

Haas, Jonathan (ed.) *The Anthropology of War* (Cambridge 1990)

Haddan, Arthur West, & Stubbs, William (edd.) *Councils and Ecclesiastical Documents relating to Great Britain and Ireland* (3 vols in 4 parts, Oxford 1869/78)

Härke, H. ' "Warrior graves"? The background of the Anglo-Saxon weapon burial rite', *Past and Present*, no. 126 (February 1990) 22–43

Hall, Richard. *The Viking Dig: The Excavations at York* (London, Sydney, & Toronto, ON 1984)

Hallam, Elizabeth M. *Domesday Book through Nine Centuries* (London 1986)

Hallam, H. E. 'England before the Norman Conquest', in *The Agrarian History of England and Wales*, volume II, ed. H. E. Hallam (Cambridge 1988), 1–44

Hallam, H. E. (ed.) *The Agrarian History of England and Wales. Volume II. 1042–1350* (Cambridge 1988)

Hamerow, H. F. 'Settlement mobility and the "Middle Saxon Shift": rural settlements and settlement patterns in Anglo-Saxon England', *Anglo-Saxon England* 20 (1991) 1–17

Hamilton, N[icholas] E. S. A. *Inquisitio Comitatus Cantabrigiensis Nunc Primum e Manuscripto Unico in Bibliotheca Cottoniana Asservato Typis Mandata. Subjicitur Inquisitio Eliensis* (London 1876)

Hamp, E. P. 'Germanic **skalkaz*', *Nowele: North-Western European Language Evolution* 16 (September 1990) 99

Hamshere, J. D. 'A computer-assisted study of Domesday Worcestershire', in *Field and Forest: An Historical Geography of Warwickshire and Worcestershire*, edd. T. R. Slater & P. J. Jarvis (Norwich 1982), pp. 105–24

Hamshere, J. D. 'The structure and exploitation of the Domesday Book estate of the Church of Worcester', *Landscape History* 7 (1985) 41–52

Harmer, F[lorence] E. (ed. & transl.) *Anglo-Saxon Writs* (Manchester 1952)

Harmer, F[lorence] E. (ed. & transl.) *Select English Historical Documents of the Ninth and Tenth Centuries* (Cambridge 1914)

Harris, B[rian] E. (ed.), assisted by Thacker, A. T. *The Victoria History of the County of Chester*, volume I (London 1987)

Harsley, Fred (ed.) *Eadwine's Canterbury Psalter* (London 1889)

Hart, C. R. 'Athelstan "Half King" and his family', *Anglo-Saxon England* 2 (1973), 115–44; rptd in revised form in C. Hart, *The Danelaw* (London & Rio Grande, OH 1992), chapter XXI

Hart, C. R. 'Essex in the late tenth century', in *The Battle of Maldon: Fiction and Fact*, ed. J. Cooper (London & Rio Grande, OH 1983), pp. 171–204

Hart, Cyril [R.] *The Danelaw* (London & Rio Grande, OH 1992)

Hart, C[yril] R. *The Early Charters of Eastern England* (Leicester 1966)

Hart, C. R. 'The Tribal Hidage', *Transactions of the Royal Historical Society*, 5th S., 21 (1971) 135–57

Harvey, P. D. A. 'Rectitudines singularum personarum and Gerefa', *English Historical Review* 108 (1993) 1–22

Harvey, S. P. J. 'Domesday Book and Anglo-Norman governance', *Transactions of the Royal Historical Society*, 5th S., 25 (1975) 174–93

Harvey, S. [P. J.] 'Domesday Book and its predecessors', *English Historical Review* 86 (1971) 753–73

Harvey, S. [P. J.] 'Domesday England', in *The Agrarian History of England and Wales*, volume II, ed. H. E. Hallam (Cambridge 1988), pp. 45–136

Harvey, S. P. J. 'Taxation and the economy', in *Domesday Studies*, ed. J. C. Holt (Woodbridge & Wolfboro, NH 1987), pp. 249–64

Harvey, S. P. J. 'Taxation and the ploughland in Domesday Book', in *Domesday Book. A Reassessment*, ed. P. Sawyer (London 1985), pp. 86–103

Harvey, S. P. J. 'The extent and profitability of demesne agriculture in England in the later eleventh century', in *Social Relations and Ideas*, edd. T. H. Aston *et al.* (Cambridge 1983), pp. 45–72

Haslam, Jeremy (ed.) *Anglo-Saxon Towns in Southern England* (Chichester 1984)

Haslam, J. 'Market and fortress in England in the reign of Offa', *World Archaeology* 19 (1987) 76–93

Hazeltine, H. D. '[General Preface.] Comments on the Writings Known as Anglo-Saxon Wills', in *Anglo-Saxon Wills*, ed. & transl. D. Whitelock (Cambridge 1930), pp. vii–xl

Hearne, Thomas (ed.) *Textus Roffensis: Accedunt Possessionum Antiquorum Angliæ Episcoporum Formulæ, De Canonica Obedientia Archiepiscopis Cantuariensibus Præstanda, et Leonardi Hutteni, de Antiquitatibus Oxoniensibus* (Oxford 1720)

Hecht, Hans (ed.) *Bischof Wærferths von Worcester Übersetzung der Dialoge Gregors des Grossen über das Leben und die Wundertaten italienischer Väter und über die Unsterblichkeit der Seelen. Aus dem Nachlasse von Julius Zupitza nach einer Kopie von Henry Johnson* (2 vols, Leipzig & Hamburg 1900/7)

Heers, Jacques. *Esclaves et domestiques au moyen âge dans le monde méditerranéen* (Paris 1981)

Hempl, G. 'G. *skalks*, NHG. *schalk*, etc., G. *kalkjo*, ON. *skækja*, OHG. *karl*, NHG. *kerl*, *kegel*, etc.', *Journal of Germanic Philology* 1 (1897) 342–7

Hennessy, William M. (ed. & transl.) *The Annals of Loch Cé. A Chronicle of Irish Affairs from A.D. 1014 to A.D. 1590*, volume I (London 1871)

Henning, J. 'Gefangenenfesseln im slawischen Siedlungsraum und der europäische Sklavenhandel im 6. bis 12. Jahrhundert. Archäologisches zum Bedeutungswandel von "sklābos-sakaliba-sclavus" ', *Germania* 70.2 (1990) 403–26

Hermann, John P. *Allegories of War. Language and Violence in Old English Poetry* (Ann Arbor 1989)

Heywood, Samuel. *A Dissertation upon the Distinctions in Society, and Ranks of the People, under the Anglo-Saxon Governments* (London 1818)

Hickes, George. *De Antiquae Litteraturae Septentrionalis Utilitate, sive De Linguarum Veterum Septentrionalium Usu Dissertatio Epistolaris, ad Bartholomæum Showere, Equitem Auratum, Non ita pridem Jurisconsultum apud Anglos, & Causarum Patronum Celeberrimum* (Oxford 1703)

Hicks, John [Richard]. *A Theory of Economic History* (Oxford 1969)

Higham, Nicholas. *Rome, Britain and the Anglo-Saxons* (London 1992)

Higham, N. 'Settlement, land use and Domesday ploughlands', *Landscape History* 12 (1990) 33–44

Hill, David. *An Atlas of Anglo-Saxon England* (Toronto, ON & Buffalo, NY 1981)

Hill, D. 'The Burghal Hidage – the establishment of a text', *Medieval Archaeology* 13 (1969) 84–92

Hill, R. M. T. 'Holy kings – the bane of seventh-century society', *Studies in Church History* 12 (1975) 39–43

Hill, T. D. ' "Wealhtheow" as a foreign slave: some Continental analogues', *Philological Quarterly* 69 (1990) 106–12

Hill, T. D. '*Rígsþula*: some medieval christian analogues', *Speculum* 61 (1986) 79–89

Hilton, C. B. 'The Old English *Seasons for Fasting*: its place in the vernacular complaint tradition', *Neophilologus* 70 (1986) 155–9

Hinton, David A. *Alfred's Kingdom. Wessex and the South 800–1500* (London 1977)

Hodges, Richard. *Dark Age Economics. The Origins of Towns and Trade A.D. 600–1000* (London 1982)

Hodges, Richard, & Whitehouse, David. *Mohammed, Charlemagne & the Origins of Europe: Archaeology and the Pirenne Thesis* (Ithaca, NY 1983)

Hodges, Richard. *The Anglo-Saxon Achievement. Archaeology and the Beginnings of English Society* (London 1989)

Hodges, Richard, & Hobley, Brian (edd.) *The Rebirth of Towns in the West AD 700–1050* (London 1988)

Hoffmann, H. 'Kirche und Sklaverei im frühen Mittelalter', *Deutsches Archiv für Erforschung des Mittelalters* 42 (1986) 1–24

Hoffmann, Otto. *Reimformeln im Westgermanischen* (Darmstadt 1885)

Holdsworth, William S. *A History of English Law*, rev. A[rthur] L. Goodhart & H[arold] G. Hanbury, with an Introductory Essay and Additions by S[tanley] B. Chrimes, volume I (7th edn, London 1956)

Holm, P. 'The slave trade of Dublin, ninth to twelfth centuries', *Peritia: Journal of the Medieval Academy of Ireland* 5 (1986) 317–45

Holt, J[ames] C. (ed.) *Domesday Studies. Papers read at the Novocentenary Conference of the Royal Historical Society and the Institute of British Geographers Winchester, 1986* (Woodbridge & Wolfboro, NH 1987)

Holt, Richard. *The Mills of Medieval England* (Oxford & New York 1988)

Holthausen, F[erdinand]. *Altenglisches etymologisches Wörterbuch* (Heidelberg 1934)

Hoogewerf, G. J. 'Friezen, Franken en Saksen te Rome', *Mededeelingen van het Nederlandsche historische Institute te Rome* 5 (1947) 1–69 + plates I–IV

Hooke, Della (ed.) *Anglo-Saxon Settlements* (Oxford & New York 1988)

Hooke, Della (ed.) *Medieval Villages* (Oxford 1985)

Hooke, Della. *The Anglo-Saxon Landscape. The Kingdom of the Hwicce* (Manchester & Dover, NH 1985)

Hough, C. A. 'Freo man: a note on word division', *Neophilolgus* 75 (1991) 641–3

Howlett, Richard (ed.) *Chronicles of the Reigns of Stephen, Henry II., and Richard I.*, volume IV, *The Chronicle of Robert of Torigni, Abbot of the Monastery of St Michael-in-Peril-of-the-Sea* (London 1889)

Hughes, Kathleen. *The Church in Early Irish Society* (London 1966)

Hyams, Paul R. *Kings, Lords and Peasants in Medieval England. The Common Law of Villeinage in the Twelfth and Thirteenth Centuries* (Oxford 1980)

Hyams, Paul R. 'Legal aspects of villeinage between Glanvill and Bracton' (Oxford D. Phil. dissertation, [Oxford] 1968)

Hyams, P. R. 'The proof of villein status in the common law', *English Historical Review* 89 (1974) 721–49

Hyams, P. R. 'Trial by ordeal: the key to proof in the early common law', in *On the*

Laws and Customs of England: Essays in Honor of Samuel E. Thorne, edd. M. S. Arnold *et al.* (Chapel Hill, NC 1981), pp. 90–126

Ianning, Conrad *et al.* (edd.) *Acta Sanctorum. Iulii . . . Tomus I* (New edn, ed. Jean Carnandet, Paris & Roma 1867)

Ianning, Conrad *et al.* (edd.) 'Historia Translationis et Miraculorum, Auctore, ut videtur, Lantfredo a, Monacho Wintoniensi in Anglia', in *Acta Sanctorum. Iulii . . . Tomus I* (New edn, ed. Jean Carnandet, Paris & Roma 1867), pp. 292–3

Ianning, Conrad *et al.* (edd.) 'Miracula S. Swithuni ex antiquissimis membranis Reginae Sueciae in Cod. num. 769', in *Acta Sanctorum. Iulii . . . Tomus I* (New edn, ed. Jean Carnandet, Paris & Roma 1867), pp. 294–9

Jackson, John Edward (ed.) *Liber Henrici de Soliaco Abbatis Glaston. et vocatur A. An Inquisition of the Manors of Glastonbury Abbey, of the Year M.C.LXXXIX. From the Original Manuscript in the Possession of the Marquis of Bath* (London 1882)

Jackson, Kenneth, *et al.* *Celt and Saxon: Studies in the Early British Border* (Cambridge 1964)

Jacob, Walter (ed.) *Cassiodori-Epiphanii Historia Ecclesiastica Tripartita* (Vindobona 1952)

James, E. 'Bede and the tonsure question', *Peritia: Journal of the Medieval Academy of Ireland* 3 (1984) 85–98

Janssen. W. 'Some major aspects of Frankish and medieval settlement in the Rhineland', in *Medieval Settlement*, ed. P. Sawyer (London 1976), pp. 41–60

Jastrow, Ignaz. *Zur strafrechtlichen Stellung der Sklaven bei Deutschen und Angelsachsen* (Breslau 1878)

Jenner, H. 'The manumissions in the Bodmin Gospels', *Journal of the Royal Institution of Cornwall* 21 (1924) 235–60

John, E. 'A note on Bede's use of "facultas" ', *Revue Bénédictine* 72 (1962) 350–5

John, Eric. *Land Tenure in Early England. A Discussion of Some Problems* (2nd impression [corrected], Leicester 1964)

John, Eric. *Orbis Britanniae and Other Studies* (Leicester 1966)

Johnson, Charles & Cronne, H[enry] A. (edd.) *Regesta Regum Anglo-Normannorum 1066–1154*. Volume II: *Regesta Henrici Primi 1100–1135* (Oxford 1956)

Jón Stefánsson. 'The Vikings in Spain. From Arabic (Moorish) and Spanish sources', *Saga-Book* 6 (1909/10) 31–46

Jones, A. 'The rise and fall of the manorial system: a critical comment', *Journal of Economic History* 32 (1972) 938–44

Jones, Arthur (ed. & transl.) *The History of Gruffydd ap Cynan* (Manchester 1910)

Jones, G. R . J. 'Multiple estates and early settlement', in *Medieval Settlement*, ed. P. Sawyer (London 1976), pp. 15–40

Jones, G. R. J. 'Multiple estates perceived', *Journal of Historical Geography* 11 (1985) 352–63

Jones, M. U., & Jones, W. T. 'The crop-mark sites at Mucking, Essex, England', in *Recent Archaeological Excavations in Europe*, ed. R. [L. S.] Bruce-Mitford (London 1975), pp. 133–87

Jonsson, Kenneth (ed.) *Studies in Late Anglo-Saxon Coinage. In Memory of Bror Emil Hildebrand* (Stockholm 1990)

Jordan, Richard. *Eigentümlichkeiten des anglischen Wortschatzes. Eine wortgeographische Untersuchung mit etymologischen Anmerkungen* (Heidelberg 1906)

Jost, Karl (ed.) *Die 'Institutes of Polity, Civil and Ecclesiastical'. Ein Werk Erzbischof Wulfstans von York* (Bern 1959)

Jost, K. 'Einige Wulfstantexte und ihre Quellen', *Anglia* 56 (1932) 265–315

Jost, Karl. *Wulfstanstudien* (Bern 1950)

Judic, Bruno, *et al.* (edd.) *Grégoire le Grand Règle pastorale* (2 vols, Paris 1992)

Kapelle, William E. *The Norman Conquest of the North. The Region and its Transformation, 1000–1135* (Chapel Hill, NC 1979)

Karras, R. M. 'Concubinage and slavery in the Viking Age', *Scandinavian Studies* 62 (1990) 141–62

Karras, Ruth Mazo. *Slavery and Society in Medieval Scandinavia* (New Haven, CT & London 1988)

Keen, L. 'Coastal salt production in Norman England', in *Anglo-Norman Studies XI: Proceedings of the Battle Conference 1988*, ed. R. Allen Brown (Woodbridge 1989), pp. 133–79

Keen, L. 'Medieval salt-working in Dorset', *Proceedings of the Dorset Natural History and Archaeological Society* 109 (1987) 25–8

Kemble, John M. (ed.) *Codex Diplomaticus Aevi Saxonici* (6 vols, London 1839/48)

Kemble, John M. (ed. & transl.) *The Dialogue of Salomon and Saturnus, with an Historical Introduction* (London 1848)

Kemble, John Mitchell. *The Saxons in England. A History of the English Commonwealth till the Period of the Norman Conquest* (New edn, rev. Walter de Gray Birch, 2 vols, London 1876)

Kendrick, T[homas] D. *et al.* (facs. edd.) *Evangeliorum Quattuor Codex Lindisfarnensis: Musei Britannici Codex Cottonianus Nero D.IV Permissione Musei Britannici Totius Codicis Similitudo Expressa* (2 vols, Olten & Lausanne 1956/60)

Ker, N[eil] R. *Catalogue of Manuscripts Containing Anglo-Saxon* (Oxford 1957)

Ker, N. [R.] 'The handwriting of Archbishop Wulfstan', in *England before the Conquest*, edd. P. Clemoes & K. Hughes (Cambridge 1971), pp. 315–31

Ker, N. R. 'Three Old English texts in a Salisbury pontifical, Cotton Tiberius C 1', in *The Anglo-Saxons*, ed. P. Clemoes (London 1959), pp. 262–79

Keynes, S. 'A charter of King Edward the Elder for Islington', *Historical Research* 66 (1993) 303–16

Keynes, Simon, & Lapidge, Michael (transl.) *Alfred the Great. Asser's 'Life of King Alfred' and Other Contemporary Sources* (Harmondsworth 1983)

Keynes, S. 'A lost cartulary of St Albans Abbey', *Anglo-Saxon England* 22 (1993) 253–79

Keynes, Simon. *Anglo-Saxon Charters: Archives and Single Sheets* (forthcoming, Oxford)

Keynes, S. 'King Athelstan's Books', in *Learning and Literature in Anglo-Saxon England. Studies presented to Peter Clemoes on the Occasion of his Sixty-Fifth Birthday*, edd. M. Lapidge & H. Gneuss (Cambridge 1985), pp. 143–201 + plates I–XVI

Keynes, S. 'The additions in Old English', in *The York Gospels*, ed. N. Barker (London 1986), pp. 81–99

Keynes, Simon. *The Diplomas of Æthelred 'The Unready' 978–1016. A Study in their Use as Historical Evidence* (Cambridge 1980)

Keynes, S. 'The lost cartulary of Abbotsbury', *Anglo-Saxon England* 18 (1989) 207–43

Kieft, C. van de. 'Les "Colliberti" et l'évolution du servage dans la France centrale et occidentale (Xᵉ–XIIᵉ Siècle)', *Tijdschrift voor Rechtsgeschiedenis* (= *Revue d'Histoire du Droit*) 32 (1964) 363–95

Kimmens, Andrew C. (ed.) *The Stowe Psalter* (Toronto, ON, Buffalo, NY, & London 1979)

Kindschi, Lowell (ed.) 'The Latin-Old English glossaries in Plantin-Moretus MS 32 and British Museum MS Additional 32,246' (Stanford University Ph.D. dissertation, [Stanford, CA] 1955)

Kirby, D[avid] P. (ed.) *Saint Wilfrid at Hexham* (Newcastle upon Tyne 1974)

Kirby, D[avid] P. *The Earliest English Kings* (London 1991)

Klaeber, F[rederick] (ed.) *Beowulf and the Fight at Finnsburg* (3rd edn, Boston, MA 1950)

Kobishchanow, Yurii M. 'The phenomenon of *gafol* and its transformation', in *Early State Dynamics*, ed. H. J. M. Claessen & P. van de Felde (Leiden, New York, Copenhagen, & Cologne 1987), pp. 108–28

Kopytoff, I., & Miers, S. 'African "slavery" as an institution of marginality', in *Slavery in Africa. Historical and Anthropological Perspectives*, edd. S. Miers & I. Kopytoff (Madison, WI & London 1977), pp. 3–81

Kotzor, Günter (ed.) *Das altenglische Martyrologium* (2 vols, München 1981)

Krapp, George Philip, & Dobbie, Elliott Van Kirk (edd.) *The Exeter Book* (New York & London 1936)

Krapp, George Philip (ed.) *The Junius Manuscript* (New York & London 1931)

Krapp, George Philip (ed.) *The Paris Psalter and The Metres of Boethius* (New York & London 1932)

Krapp, George Philip (ed.) *The Vercelli Book* (New York & London 1932)

Krueger, Paul (ed.) *Codex Iustinianus* (9th edn, Berlin 1915)

Kuhn, Sherman M. (ed.) *The Vespasian Psalter* (Ann Arbor, MI 1965)

Kurath, Hans, *et al.* (edd.) *Middle English Dictionary* (7 vols to date, Ann Arbor, MI 1952–)

La Croissance agricole du haut moyen âge. Chronologie, modalités, géographie (Auch 1990)

Lambard(e), William. Αρχαιονομια, sive De Priscis Anglorum Legibus Libri . . . (London 1568)

Langdon, John. *Horses, Oxen and Technological Innovation. The Use of Draught Animals in English Farming from 1066 to 1500* (Cambridge 1986)

Lapidge, Michael, & Gneuss, Helmut (edd.) *Learning and Literature in Anglo-Saxon England. Studies presented to Peter Clemoes on the Occasion of his Sixty-Fifth Birthday* (Cambridge 1985)

Lapidge, Michael, & Winterbottom, Michael (edd. & transl.) *Wulfstan of Winchester. The Life of St Æthelwold* (Oxford 1991)

Latham, R. E. *Revised Medieval Latin Word-List from British and Irish Sources* (London 1965)

Latouche, Robert. *The Birth of the Western Economy. Economic Aspects of the Dark Ages*, transl. E. M. Wilkinson (2nd edn, London 1967)

Lee, R[obert] W. *The Elements of Roman Law. With a Translation of the Institutes of Justinian* (4th edn, London 1956)

Lendinara, P. 'The Abbo Glossary in London British Library, Cotton Domitian i', *Anglo-Saxon England* 19 (1990) 133–149

Lendinara, P. 'The Third Book of the *Bella Parisiacae Urbis* by Abbo of Saint-Germain-des-Prés and its Old English gloss', *Anglo-Saxon England* 15 (1986) 73–89

Lennard, R. 'Domesday plough-teams: the south-western evidence', *English Historical Review* 60 (1945) 217–33

Lennard, Reginald. *Rural England 1086–1135: A Study of Social and Agrarian Traditions* (Oxford 1959)

Lennard, R. 'The composition of demesne plough-teams in twelfth-century England', *English Historical Review* 75 (1960) 193–207

Lennard, R. 'The destruction of woodland in the eastern counties, 1066–1086', *Economic History Review*, N.S., 1 (1948/9) 144

Lennard, R. 'The destruction of woodland in the eastern counties under William the Conqueror', *Economic History Review* 15 (1945) 36–43

Lennard, R. 'The economic position of the bordars and cottars of Domesday Book', *Economic Journal* 61 (1951) 342–71

Lennard, R. 'The origin of the fiscal carucate', *Economic History Review* 14 (1944) 51–63

Levison, Wilhelm. *England and the Continent in the Eighth Century* (Oxford 1946)

Lewis, C. P. 'An introduction to the Shropshire Domesday', in *The Shropshire Domesday*, edd. A. Williams & R. W. H. Erskine (London 1990), pp. 1–27

Lewis, C. P. 'The Domesday jurors', in *The Haskins Society Journal: Studies in Medieval History*, ed. R. B. Patterson, volume V (Woodbridge 1993), pp. 17–44

Lexikon des Mittelalters (7 vols to date, München & Zürich 1977–)

Liebermann, F[elix] (ed.) *Die Gesetze der Angelsachsen* (3 vols, Halle a. S. 1903/16)

Lindelöf, U[no] (ed.) *Der Lambeth-Psalter: Eine altenglische Interlinearversion des Psalters in der Hs. 427 der erzbischöflichen Lambeth Palace Library, zum ersten Male vollständig herausgegeben* (2 vols, Helsingfors 1909/14)

Lindsay, Wallace M. (ed.) *Sexti Pompei Festi De Verborum Significatu quae supersunt cum Pauli Epitome. Thewrewkianis copiis usus edidit* (Leipzig 1913)

Lindsay, W[allace] M. (ed.), with an Anglo-Saxon Index by Helen McM. Buckhurst. *The Corpus Glossary* (Cambridge 1921)

Locherbie-Cameron, M. A. L. 'The men named in the poem', in *The Battle of Maldon AD 991*, ed. D. Scragg (Oxford 1991), pp. 238–49

Locke, A. A. 'The Abbey of Evesham', in *The Victoria History of the County of Worcester*, volume II, edd. J. W. Willis-Bund & W. Page (London 1906), pp. 112–27

Logeman, E. 'Anglo-Saxonica minora', *Anglia* 12 (1889) 497–518

Lohaus, Annethe. *Die Merowinger und England* (München 1974)

Lombard, Maurice. *The Golden Age of Islam*, transl. Joan Spencer (Amsterdam, Oxford, & New York 1975)

Loomis, G. 'Further sources of Ælfric's Saints' Lives', *Harvard Studies and Notes in Philology and Literature* 13 (1931) 1–8

Lopez, Robert S., & Raymond, Irving W. *Medieval Trade in the Mediterranean World: Illustrative Documents translated with Introductions and Notes* (New York 1955)

Lowe, K. A. (ed.) 'A new edition of the will of Wulfgyth', *Notes and Queries* 234 (1989) 295–8

Loyn, Henry R. (facs. ed.) *A Wulfstan Manuscript, containing Institutes, Laws and Homilies. British Museum Cotton Nero A. 1* (Copenhagen 1971)

Loyn, H. R. 'Gesiths and thegns in Anglo-Saxon England from the seventh to the tenth century', *English Historical Review* 70 (1955) 529–49

Loyn, Henry [R.] *The Free Anglo-Saxon* (Cardiff [1975])

Mac Airt, Seán, & Mac Niocaill, Gearóid (edd. & transl.) *Annals of Ulster (To A.D. 1131)*, Part I: Text and Translation (Dublin 1983)

McCann, Justin (ed. & transl.) *The Rule of Saint Benedict in Latin and English* (London 1952)

McDonald, John, & Snooks, G. D. *Domesday Economy: A New Approach to Anglo-Norman History* (Oxford 1986)

McGurk, P., et al. (edd.) *An Eleventh-Century Anglo-Saxon Illustrated Miscellany. British Library Cotton Tiberius B. V Part I together with Leaves from British Library Cotton Nero D. II* (Copenhagen 1983)

Mackie, W[illiam] S. (ed.) *The Exeter Book, Part II: Poems IX–XXXII* (London 1934)

MacLean. G. E. 'Ælfric's version of Alcuini Interrogationes Sigeuulfi in Genesin. (Fortsetzung.) The A.S. and Latin texts', *Anglia* 7 (1884) 1–59

MacMullen, R. 'Late Roman slavery', *Historia* 36 (1987) 359–82

Macray, W[illiam] Dunn (ed.) *Chronicon Abbatiæ Rameseiensis, a Sæc. x. usque ad An. circiter 1200: in Quattuor Partibus* (London 1886)

McReavy, L. L. 'The Sunday repose from labour: an historico-theological examination of the notion of servile work. (From the era of the Apostles to the advent of Charlemagne.)', *Ephemerides Theologicae Lovanienses* 12 (1935) 291–323

Maddicott, J. R. 'Trade, industry and the wealth of King Alfred', *Past and Present* no. 123 (May 1989) 3–51

Magoun, F. P., Jr. '*Annales Domitiani Latini*: an edition', *Mediaeval Studies* 9 (1947) 235–95

Maitland, Frederic William. *Domesday Book and Beyond. Three Essays in the Early History of England* (Cambridge 1897)

Manning, W. H. 'The plough in Roman Britain', *Journal of Roman Studies* 54 (1964) 54–65 + plate VIII

Mansi, Giovanni Dominico (ed.) *Sacrorum Conciliorum Nova et Amplissima Collectio. . . .*, volume XIX (Venetiis 1774)

Margulies, C. S. 'The marriages and the wealth of the Wife of Bath', *Mediaeval Studies* 24 (1962) 210–16

Marx, Karl. *Pre-Capitalist Economic Formations*, transl. Jack Cohen, ed. and with an Introduction by E. J. Hobsbawm (New York 1965)

Mason, Emma. *St Wulfstan of Worcester c.1008–1095* (Oxford 1990)

Maurer, K. von. 'Die Freigelassenen nach altnorwegischem Rechte', *Sitzungsberichte der philosophisch-philologischen und historischen Classe der königlich bayerischen Akademie der Wissenschaften.* Jahrgang 1878, Erster Band (München 1878), pp. 21–87

Mayr-Harting, Henry. *The Coming of Christianity to Anglo-Saxon England* (3rd edn, University Park, PA 1991)

Melvinger, Arne. *Les Premières Incursions des Vikings en Occident d'après les sources arabes*, [transl. Jacques Gengoux] (Uppsala 1955)

Meritt, H. D. 'Old English glosses to Gregory, Ambrose and Prudentius', *JEGP: Journal of English and Germanic Philology* 56 (1957) 65–8

Meritt, Herbert Dean. *Some of the Hardest Glosses in Old English* (Stanford, CA 1968)

Meritt, Herbert Dean (ed.) *The Old English Prudentius Glosses at Boulogne-sur-Mer* (Stanford, CA 1959)

Metcalf, D. M., & Northover, J. P. 'Debasement of the coinage in southern England in the Age of King Alfred', *Numismatic Chronicle* 145 (1985) 150–76 + plates XXIV–XXVII

Miers, Suzanne, & Kopytoff, Igor (edd.) *Slavery in Africa. Historical and Anthropological Perspectives* (Madison, WI & London 1977)

Migne, J[acques]-P[aul] (ed.) *Hermanni Monachi De Miraculis S. Mariae Laudunensis, De Gestis Venerabilis Bartholomaei Episcopi et S. Nothberti Libri Tres*, in *Venerabilis Guiberti Abbatis S. Mariae de Novigento Opera Omnia* (Paris 1880), cols 962–1018

Migne, J[acques]-P[aul] (ed.) *S. Agobardi Lugdunensis Episcopi, Eginhardi Abbatis Opera Omnia . . .* (Paris 1864)

Migne, J[acques]-P[aul] (ed.) *Venerabilis Guiberti Abbatis S. Mariae de Novigento Opera Omnia* (Paris 1880)

Milani, Piero A. *La schiavitù nel pensiero politico. Dai Greci al basso medio evo* (Milano 1972)

Miller, Thomas (ed. & transl.) *The Old English Version of Bede's Ecclesiastical History of the English People* (4 vols, London 1890/8)

Mollat, Michel. *The Poor in the Middle Ages. An Essay in Social History*, transl. Arthur Goldhammer (New Haven, CT & London 1986)

Mommsen, Theodor & Krueger, Paul (edd.) *Theodosiani Libri XVI cum Constitutionibus Sirmondianis* (3rd edn, Berlin 1962)

Mone, F[ranz] J. (ed.) *Quellen und Forschungen zur Geschichte der teutschen Literatur und Sprache* (Aachen & Leipzig 1830)

Moneta e scambi nell'alto Medioevo (Spoleto 1961)

Moore, J. S. 'Domesday slavery', in *Anglo-Norman Studies XI. Proceedings of the Battle Conference 1988*, ed. R. A. Brown (Woodbridge 1989), pp. 191–220

Mor, C. G. 'La "manumissio in ecclesia" ', *Rivista di storia del diritto italiano* 1 (1928) 80–150

Morris, John (general ed.) *Domesday Book* (37 vols, Chichester 1975/92)

Morris, R[ichard] (ed. & transl.) *The Blickling Homilies: With a Translation and Index of Words together with 'The Blickling Homilies'* (2 vols, London, 1874/80; rptd in 1 vol., London 1967)

Murray, Alexander. *Reason and Society in the Middle Ages* (Oxford 1978)

Musset, L. 'Le Satiriste Garnier de Rouen et son milieu (début de XIᵉ siècle)', *Revue de Moyen Age Latin* 10 (1954) 237–58

Myres, J. N. L. 'The Angles, the Saxons, and the Jutes', *Proceedings of the British Academy* 56 (1970) 145–74

Mytum, Harold. *The Origins of Early Christian Ireland* (London & New York 1992)

Napier, A. 'Altenglische Kleinigkeiten', *Anglia* 11 (1889) 1–10

Napier, A. S. 'Contributions to Old English lexicography', *Transactions of the Philological Society, 1903–1906* (1906) 265–358

Napier, A[rthur] S. *Old English Glosses: Chiefly Unpublished* (Oxford 1900)

Napier, A[rthur] S. & Stevenson, W[illiam] H. (edd.) *The Crawford Collection of Early Charters and Documents Now in the Bodleian Library* (Oxford 1895)

Napier, Arthur S. (ed.) *The Old English Version of the Enlarged Rule of Chrodegang together with the Latin Original. An Old English Version of the Capitula of Theodulf together with the Latin Original. An Interlinear Old English Rendering of the Epitome of Benedict of Aniane* (London 1916)

Napier, Arthur [S.] (ed.) *Wulfstan. Sammlung der Ihm zugeschriebenen Homilien nebst Untersuchungen über ihre Echtheit. Erste Abteilung: Text und Varianten* (rptd with Appendix by Klaus Ostheeren, Dublin & Zurich 1967)

Neale, Kenneth (ed.) *An Essex Tribute: Essays presented to Frederick G. Emmison as a Tribute to his Life and Work for Essex History and Archives* (London 1987)

Nelson, Lynn H. *The Normans in South Wales, 1070–1171* (Austin, TX & London 1966)

Nieboer, H[erman] J. *Slavery as an Industrial System. Ethnological Researches* (2nd, rev. edn, The Hague 1910)

Noble, Frank. *Offa's Dyke Reviewed*, ed. Margaret Gelling (Oxford 1983)

Nock, Arthur Darby. *Early Gentile Christianity and its Hellenistic Background* (New York, Evanston, IL & London 1964)

North, D. C., & Thomas, R. P. 'The rise and fall of the manorial system: a theoretical model', *Journal of Economic History* 31 (1971) 777–803

Oakley, Thomas Pollock. *English Penitential Discipline and Anglo-Saxon Law in their Joint Influence* (New York 1923)

O'Donovan, John (ed.) *Annals of Ireland. Three Fragments copied from Ancient Sources by Dubhaltach Mac Firbisigh* (Dublin 1860)

Oess, Guido (ed.) *Der altenglische Arundel-Psalter. Eine Interlinearversion in der Handschrift Arundel 60 des Britischen Museums* (Heidelberg 1910)

Ohlgren, Thomas H. *Insular and Anglo-Saxon Illuminated Manuscripts: An Iconographic Catalogue c. A.D. 625 to 1100* (New York & London 1986)

Oliver, Roland. *The African Experience* (London 1991)

Olson, Lynette. *Early Monasteries in Cornwall* (Woodbridge & Wolfeboro, NH 1989)

Orrick, Allan H. (ed.) *Nordica et Anglica. Studies in Honor of Stefán Einarsson* (The Hague & Paris 1968)

Ott, J. H[einrich]. *Ueber die Quellen der Heiligenleben in Ælfrics Lives of Saints*, volume I (Halle a S. 1892)

Owen, D. 'Chapelries and rural settlement: an examination of some of the Kesteven evidence', in *Medieval Settlement. Continuity and Change*, ed. P. H. Sawyer (London, 1976), pp. 66–71

Page, R. I. 'More Aldhelm glosses from CCCC 326', *English Studies* 56 (1975) 481–90

Page, William (ed.) *The Victoria History of Shropshire*, volume I (London 1908)

Page, William (ed.) *The Victoria History of the County of Devon*, volume I (London 1906)

Page, William (ed.) *The Victoria History of the County of Hereford*, volume I (London 1908)

Page, William, & Proby, Granville (edd.), assisted by Norris, H. E. *The Victoria History of the County of Huntingdon*, volume I (London 1926)

Palmer, J. J. N. 'The Domesday manor', in *Domesday Studies*, ed. J. C. Holt (Woodbridge & Wolfboro, NH 1987), pp. 139–53

Patterson, Orlando. *Slavery and Social Death: A Comparative Study* (Cambridge, MA & London 1982)

Patterson, O. 'The structural origins of slavery: a critique of the Nieboer-Domar hypothesis from a comparative perspective', in *Comparative Perspectives on Slavery in New World Plantation Societies*, edd. V. [D.] Rubin & A. Tuden (New York 1977), pp. 12–34

Patterson, Robert B. (ed.) *The Haskins Society Journal: Studies in Medieval History*, volume V (Woodbridge 1993)

Payne, F[rances] Anne. *King Alfred and Boethius: An Analysis of the Old English Version of the Consolation of Philosophy* (Madison & Milwaukee, WI & London 1968)

Payne, F. G. 'The British plough: some stages in its development', *Agricultural History Review* 5 (1957) 74–84

Pearson, R. 'Some aspects of social mobility in early historic Indo-European societies', *Journal of Indo-European Studies* 1 (1973) 155–61

Pelteret, David A. E. *Catalogue of English Post-Conquest Vernacular Documents* (Woodbridge & Wolfboro, NH 1990)

Pelteret, D. A. E. 'Expanding the word hoard: opportunities for fresh discoveries in early English vocabulary', *Indiana Social Studies Quarterly* 31 (1978) 56–65

Pelteret, D. A. E. 'Slave raiding and slave trading in early England', *Anglo-Saxon England* 9 (1980) 99–114

Pelteret, D. A. E. 'Slavery in Anglo-Saxon England', in *The Anglo-Saxons: Synthesis and Achievement*, edd. J. D. Woods & D. A. E. Pelteret (Waterloo, ON 1985), pp. 117–33

Pelteret, D. [A. E.] 'Slavery in the Danelaw', in *Social Approaches to Viking Studies*, ed. R. Samson (Glasgow 1991), pp. 179–88

Pelteret, D. A. E. 'The *coliberti* of Domesday Book', *Studies in Medieval Culture* 12 (1978) 43–54

Pelteret, D. A. E. 'Two Old English lists of serfs', *Mediaeval Studies* 48 (1986) 470–513

Pertz, Georg Heinrich (ed.) *Monumenta Germaniae Historica, Legum Tomus IIII* (Hannover 1868)

Peters, H. 'Two suffixes reconsidered: Old English -ild and -incel', *English Studies* 72 (1991) 106–22

Peyer, H. C. 'Das Reisekönigtum des Mittelalters', *Vierteljahrschrift für Sozial- und Wirtschaftsgeschichte* 51 (1964) 1–21

Pharr, Clyde (transl.) *The Theodosian Code and Novels and the Sirmondian Constitutions* (Princeton, NJ 1952)

Pheifer, J. D. (ed.) *Old English Glosses in the Épinal-Erfurt Glossary* (Oxford 1974)

Phillips, William D., Jr. *Slavery from Roman Times to the Early Transatlantic Trade* (Minneapolis, MN 1985)

Picken, W. M. M. 'Bishop Wulfsige Comoere: an unrecognised tenth-century gloss in the Bodmin Gospels', *Cornish Studies* 34 (1986) 34–8

Pinder, T. G. 'An Introduction to the Middlesex Domesday', in *The Middlesex and London Domesday*, edd. A. Williams & G. H. Martin (London 1991)

Pinder, T. G. 'Domesday survey', in *A History of the County of Middlesex*, edd. J. S. Cockburn *et al.*, volume I (London 1969), pp. 80–138

Plummer, Charles (ed.) *Two of the Saxon Chronicles Parallel: With Supplementary Extracts from the Others* (2 vols, Oxford 1892/9; re-issued with Bibliographical Note by Dorothy Whitelock, 1952)

Plummer, Charles (ed.) *Venerabilis Baedae Opera Historica* (2 vols, Oxford 1896)

Pohl, Walter. *Die Awaren. Ein Steppenvolk in Mitteleuropa 567–822 n.Chr.* (München 1988)

Pokorny, Julius. *Indogermanisches etymologisches Wörterbuch* (2 vols, Bern & München 1959/69)

Pope, John C. (ed.) *Homilies of Ælfric: A Supplementary Collection* (2 vols, London 1967/8)

Postan, M[ichael] M. *The Famulus. The Estate Labourer in the XIIth and XIIIth Centuries* (London & New York [1954])

Pounds, N. J. G. 'Mining', in *Dictionary of the Middle Ages*, ed. J. R. Strayer, volume VIII (New York 1987), pp. 397–404

Pounds, N. J. G. 'The Domesday geography of Cornwall', *The One Hundred and Ninth Annual Report of the Royal Cornwall Polytechnic Society*, N.S., 10 (1942) 68–81

Pulleyblank, E. G. 'The origins and nature of chattel slavery in China', *Journal of the Economic and Social History of the Orient* 1 (1958) 185–220

Pulsiano, P. 'Old English glossed psalters: editions versus manuscripts', *Manuscripta* 35 (1991) 75–95

Rackham, H[arris] (ed. & transl.) Pliny [the Elder]. *Natural History*, volume V (London & Cambridge, MA 1940)

Rackham, Oliver. *The History of the Countryside* (London & Melbourne 1986)

Rackham, Oliver. *Trees and Woodland in the British Landscape* (rev. edn, London 1990)

Radford, C. A. R. 'The later pre-Conquest boroughs and their defences', *Medieval Archaeology* 14 (1970) 83–103

Raftis, J. A. 'The trends towards serfdom in mediaeval England', *Report of the Canadian Catholic Historical Association* 22 (1955) 15–25

Rahtz, Philip, *et al.* (edd.) *Anglo-Saxon Cemeteries 1979. The Fourth Anglo-Saxon Symposium at Oxford* (Oxford 1980)

Rahtz, P. A. 'Holworth, medieval village excavation 1958', *Proceedings of the Dorset Natural History and Archaeological Society* 81 (1959) 127–47, 12 figures + plates I–XII

Rahtz, P., & Bullough, D. 'The parts of an Anglo-Saxon mill', *Anglo-Saxon England* 6 (1977) 15–37

Raith. Josef (ed.) *Die altenglische Version des Halitgar'schen Bussbuches (sog. Poenitentiale Pseudo-Egberti)* (Hamburg 1933)

Raraty, D. G. J. 'Earl Godwine of Wessex: the origins of his power and his political loyalties', *History* 74 (1989) 3–19

Raymond, I[rving] W. (transl.) *Seven Books of History against the Pagans. The Apology of Paulus Orosius* (New York 1936)

Reaney, P[ercy] H. *The Place-Names of Essex* (Cambridge 1935)

Reichel, O. J. 'The Devonshire "Domesday". IV. The "Domesday" churches of Devon', *Transactions of the Devonshire Association* 30 (1898) 258–315

Reichel, O. J. 'Translation of the Devonshire Domesday', in *The Victoria History of the County of Devon*, volume I, ed. W. Page (London 1906), pp. 403–549

Rella, F. A. 'Continental manuscripts acquired for English centers in the tenth and eleventh centuries: a preliminary checklist', *Anglia* 98 (1980) 107–16

Rendall, T. 'Bondage and freeing from bondage in Old English religious poetry', *JEGP: Journal of English and Germanic Philology* 73 (1974) 497–512

Rennell [of Rodd], Lord. 'The will of Æthelgifu: introduction and provenance', in *The Will of Æthelgifu*, ed. & transl. D. Whitelock (Oxford 1968), pp. 1–4

Rhee, Florus van der. *Die germanischen Wörter in den langobardischen Gesetzen* (Rotterdam 1970)

Rhodes, E[rnest] W. (ed.) *Defensor's Liber Scintillarum: With an Interlinear Anglo-Saxon Version made Early in the Eleventh Century* (London 1889)

Richards, Julian D. *English Heritage Book of Viking Age England* (London 1991)

Richardson, H[enry] G., & Sayles, G[eorge] O. *Law and Legislation from Æthelberht to Magna Carta* (Edinburgh 1966)

Richardson, H[enry] G., & Sayles, G[eorge] O. *The Governance of Mediaeval England from the Conquest to Magna Carta* (Edinburgh 1963)

Riggs, Charles H., Jr. *Criminal Asylum in Anglo-Saxon Law* (Gainesville, FL 1963)

Rivers, Theodore John (transl.) *Laws of the Alamans and Bavarians* ([Philadelphia, PA] 1977)

Rivers, T. J. 'Seigneurial obligations and "Lex Baiuvariorum" I,13', *Traditio* 31 (1975) 336–43

Rivers, T. J. 'The manorial system in the light of "Lex Baiuvariorum" I,13', *Frühmittelalterliche Studien* 25 (1991) 89–95

Robertson, A[gnes] J. (ed. & transl.) *Anglo-Saxon Charters* (2nd edn, Cambridge 1956)

Robertson, A[gnes] J. (ed. & transl.) *The Laws of the Kings of England from Edmund to Henry I* (Cambridge 1925)

Robertson, J[ames] Logie (ed.) *The Complete Poetical Works of James Thomson* (London 1908)

Robinson, F. C. 'Lexicography and literary criticism: a caveat', in *Philological Essays*, ed. J. L. Rosier (The Hague & Paris 1970), pp. 99–110

Robinson, Fred C. *The Tomb of Beowulf and Other Essays on Old English* (Oxford & Cambridge, MA 1993)

Robinson, P. 'Mapping the Anglo-Saxon landscape: a land systems approach to the study of the bounds of the estate of Plaish', *Landscape History* 10 (1988) 15–24

Roffe, D. R. 'An introduction to the Derbyshire Domesday', in *The Derbyshire Domesday*, edd. A. Williams & R. W. H. Erskine (London 1989), pp. 1–27

Roffe, D. R. 'An introduction to the Huntingdonshire Domesday', in *The Huntingdonshire Domesday*, edd. A. Williams & R. W. H. Erskine (London 1989), pp. 1–23

Roffe, D. R. 'An introduction to the Nottinghamshire Domesday', in *The Nottinghamshire Domesday*, edd. A. Williams & R. W. H. Erskine (London 1990), pp. 1–31

Roffe, D. R. 'Domesday Book and Northern society: a reassessment', *English Historical Review* 105 (1990) 310–36

Rogerson, Andrew, & Dallas, Carolyn. *Excavations in Thetford 1949–58 and 1973–80* (Dereham 1984)

Rosenthal, Constance L. *The 'Vitae Patrum' in Old and Middle English Literature.* (Philadelphia, PA 1936)

Rosenthal, J. T. 'A historiographical survey: Anglo-Saxon kings and kingship since World War II', *Journal of British Studies* 24 (1985) 72–93

Rosenthal, Joel (ed.) *Kings and Kingship* (Binghamton, NY 1986)

Rose-Troup, F. 'Exeter manumissions and quittances of the eleventh and twelfth centuries', *Transactions of the Devonshire Association* 69 (1937) 417–45 + plates 57–9

Rose-Troup, Frances. *The Consecration of the Norman Minster at Exeter 1133* (Yeovil n.d. [1932])

Rosier, James L. (ed.) *Philological Essays. Studies in Old and Middle English Language and Literature in Honour of Herbert Dean Meritt* (The Hague & Paris 1970)

Rosier, James L. (ed.) *The Vitellius Psalter. Edited from British Museum MS Cotton Vitellius E. xviii* (Ithaca, NY 1962)

Roth, Cecil (editor-in-chief). *Encyclopaedia Judaica* (16 vols, Jerusalem [& New York] 1971/2)

Round, J. H. 'Introduction to the Essex Domesday', in *The Victoria History of the County of Essex*, volume I, edd. H. A. Doubleday & W. Page (Westminster 1903), pp. 333–425

Round, J. H. 'Introduction to the Herefordshire Domesday', in *The Victoria History of the County of Hereford*, volume I, ed. W. Page (London 1908), pp. 263–307

Round, J. H. 'Introduction to the Worcestershire Domesday', in *The Victoria History of the County of Worcester*, volume I, edd. J. W. Willis-Bund & H. A. Doubleday (London 1901), pp. 235–80

Round, J. H. 'Text of the Essex Domesday', in *The Victoria History of the County of Essex*, volume I, edd. H. A. Doubleday & W. Page (Westminster 1903), pp. 427–528

Round, J. H. 'The text of the Hampshire Domesday', in *A History of Hampshire and the Isle of Wight*, volume I, ed. H. A. Doubleday (Westminster 1900), pp. 449–526

Round, J. H. 'The text of the Worcestershire Domesday', in *The Victoria History of the County of Worcester*, volume I, edd. J. W. Willis-Bund & H. A. Doubleday (London 1901), pp. 282–323

Round, J. H. 'Translation of the Herefordshire Domesday', in *The Victoria History of the County of Hereford*, volume I, ed. W. Page (London 1908), pp. 309–45

Rowe, J. H. 'Anglo-Saxon manumissions', *Devon and Cornwall Notes and Queries* 12 (1922/3) 251–4

Rowley, Trevor (ed.) *The Origins of Open-Field Agriculture* (London 1981)

Rubin, Vera [D.], & Tuden, Arthur (edd.) *Comparative Perspectives on Slavery in New World Plantation Societies* (New York 1977)

Rule, Martin (ed.) *Eadmeri Historia Novorum in Anglia, et Opuscula Duo de Vita Sancti Anselmi et Quibusdam Miraculis Eius* (London 1884)

Runciman, W. G. 'Accelerating social mobility: the case of Anglo-Saxon England', *Past and Present* no. 104 (August 1984) 3–30

Russell, Josiah Cox. *British Medieval Population* (Albuquerque, NM 1948)

Russom, G. R. 'A Germanic concept of nobility in *The Gifts of Men* and *Beowulf*', *Speculum* 53 (1978) 1–15

Salis, Ludwig Rudolf von (ed.) *Leges Burgundionum* (Hannover 1892)

Salter, H[erbert] E. (ed.) *Eynsham Cartulary* (2 vols, Oxford 1907/8)

Salway, Peter. *Roman Britain* (Oxford 1981)

Samson, R. 'Slavery, the Roman legacy', in *Fifth-Century Gaul: A Crisis of Identity?*, edd. J. Drinkwater & H. Elton (Cambridge 1992), pp. 218–27

Samson, Ross (ed.) *Social Approaches to Viking Studies* (Glasgow 1991)

Sauvage, E. P. (ed.) 'Sancti Swithuni Wintoniensis episcopi translatio et miracula auctore Lantfredo, monacho Wintoniensi ex Codice olim Gemeticensi, jam Rotomagensi nunc primum edidit', *Analecta Bollandiana* 4 (1885) 367–410

Sawyer, P[eter] H. *Anglo-Saxon Charters. An Annotated List and Bibliography* (London 1968)

Sawyer, Peter [H.] (ed.) *Domesday Book. A Reassessment* (London 1985)

Sawyer, P[eter] H., & Wood, I[an] N. (edd.) *Early Medieval Kingship* (Leeds 1977)

Sawyer, P. H. 'Introduction: early medieval English settlement', in *Medieval Settlement. Continuity and Change*, ed. P. H. Sawyer (London 1976), pp. 1–7

Sawyer, P. H. 'Kings and merchants', in *Early Medieval Kingship*, edd. P. H. Sawyer & I. N. Wood (Leeds 1977), pp. 139–58

Sawyer, P[eter] H. *Kings and Vikings: Scandinavia and Europe AD 700–1100* (London & New York 1982)

Sawyer, P[eter] H. (ed.) *Medieval Settlement. Continuity and Change* (London 1976)

Sawyer, P. '1066–1086: a tenurial revolution?', in *Domesday Book. A Reassessment*, ed. P. [H.] Sawyer (London 1985), pp. 71–85

Sawyer, Peter [H.] (facs. ed.) *Textus Roffensis. Rochester Cathedral Library Manuscript A.3.5.* (2 vols, Copenhagen 1957/62)

Sawyer, P[eter] H. *The Age of the Vikings* (2nd edn, London 1971)

Sawyer, P. H., & Thacker, A. T. 'The Cheshire Domesday: introduction', in *A History of the County of Chester*, volume I, ed. B. E. Harris (London 1987), pp. 293–341

Sawyer, P. H. (transl.) 'The Cheshire Domesday: translation of the text', in *A History of the County of Chester*, volume I, ed. B. E. Harris (London 1987), pp. 342–70

Sawyer, P. H. 'The density of the Danish settlement in England', *University of Birmingham Historical Journal* 6 (1957/8) 1–17

Sawyer, P. H. 'The wealth of England in the eleventh century', *Transactions of the Royal Historical Society*, 5th S., 15 (1965) 145–64

Schiaparelli, Luigi (ed.) *Codice diplomatico longobardo*, volume I (Rome 1929)

Schönfeld, W. 'Laeti', in *Paulys Realencyclopädie der classischen Altertumswissenschaft*, edd. G. Wissowa & W. Kroll, volume XII.1 (Stuttgart 1924), cols 446–8

Schott, C. 'Freiheit, Freie. I. Rechsgeschichtlich', in *Lexikon des Mittelalters*, volume IV (München & Zürich 1987/9), columns 896–9

Schröer, Arnold (ed.) *Die angelsächsischen Prosabearbeitungen der Benedictinerregel* (Kassel 1885/8; rptd with an appendix by Helmut Gneuss, Darmstadt 1964)

Schröer, Arnold (ed.) *Die Winteney-Version der Regula S. Benedicti* (Halle 1888)

Schwind, Ernst von (ed.) *Leges Baiwariorum* (Hannover 1926)

Scott, A. B[rian], & Martin, F[rancis] X. (edd.) *Expugnatio Hibernica: The Conquest of Ireland by Giraldus Cambrensis* (Dublin 1978)

Scott, Alexander (ed.) *Alfred. Thomas Augustus Arne* (London 1981)

Scott, A. 'Arne's "Alfred" ', *Music and Letters* 55 (1974) 385–97

Scott, B. G. 'Iron "slave-collars" from Lagore crannog, Co. Meath', *Proceedings of the Royal Irish Academy* 78C (1978) 213–30

Scragg, Donald (ed.) *The Battle of Maldon AD 991* (Oxford 1991)

Scragg, D. G. (ed.) *The Vercelli Homilies and Related Texts* (Oxford 1992)

Searle, William George. *Onomasticon Anglo-Saxonicum. A List of Anglo-Saxon Proper Names from the Time of Beda to That of King John* (Cambridge 1897)

Sedgefield, Walter John (ed.) *King Alfred's Old English Version of Boethius De Consolatione Philosophiae* (Oxford 1899)

Sedgefield, Walter John (transl.) *King Alfred's Version of the Consolations of Boethius* (Oxford 1900)

Seebohm, Frederic. *The English Village Community: Examined in its Relation to the*

Manorial and Tribal Systems and to the Common or Open Field System of Husbandry. An Essay in Economic History (4th edn, London 1890)

Seebohm, Frederic. *Tribal Custom in Anglo-Saxon Law: Being an Essay Supplemental to (1) 'The English Village Community' (2) 'The Tribal System in Wales'* (London, New York, & Bombay 1902)

Service, Elman R. *Primitive Social Organization. An Evolutionary Perspective* (2nd edn, New York 1971)

Sheehan, Michael M. *The Will in Medieval England. From the Conversion of the Anglo-Saxons to the End of the Thirteenth Century* (Toronto, ON 1963)

Siegel, B. J. 'Some methodological considerations for a comparative study of slavery', *American Anthropologist*, N.S., 47 (1945) 357–92

Simpson, J[ohn] A., & Weiner, E[dmund] S. C. (edd.) *The Oxford English Dictionary* (2nd edn, 20 vols, Oxford 1989)

Sims-Williams, Patrick. *Religion and Literature in Western England 600–800* (Cambridge 1990)

Sisam, Kenneth. *Studies in the History of Old English Literature* (Oxford 1953)

Skeat, Walter W. (ed. & transl.) *Ælfric's Lives of Saints. Being a Set of Sermons on Saints' Days formerly observed by the English Church* (4 vols, London 1881/1900; rptd in 2 vols, London 1966)

Skeat, Walter W. (ed.) *The Gospel according to Saint John* (Cambridge 1878)

Skeat, Walter W. (ed.) *The Gospel according to Saint Luke* (Cambridge 1874)

Skeat, Walter W. (ed.) *The Gospel according to Saint Mark* (Cambridge 1871)

Skeat, Walter W. (ed.) *The Gospel according to Saint Matthew* (New edn, Cambridge 1887)

Slack, W. J. 'The Shropshire ploughmen of Domesday Book', *Transactions of the Shropshire Archaeological Society* 50 (1939/40) 31–5

Slater, T[erry] R., & Jarvis, P[eter] J. (edd.) *Field and Forest: An Historical Geography of Warwickshire and Worcestershire* (Norwich 1982)

Smith, A[lbert] H. *English Place-Name Elements* (2 vols, Cambridge 1956)

Smith, A. H. 'Place-names and the Anglo-Saxon settlement', *Proceedings of the British Academy* 42 (1956) 67–88

Smith, A. H. 'The *Hwicce*', in *Medieval and Linguistic Studies in Honor of Francis Peabody Magoun, Jr.*, edd. J. B. Bessinger Jr. & R. P. Creed (London 1965), pp. 56–65

Smith, R. 'Human resources', in *The Countryside of Medieval England*, edd. G. Astill & A. Grant (Oxford & New York 1988), pp. 188–212

Smyth, Alfred P. *Scandinavian Kings in the British Isles 850–880* (Oxford 1977)

Smyth, Alfred P. *Scandinavian York and Dublin. The History and Archaeology of Two Related Viking Kingdoms* (2 vols, Dublin 1975/9)

Societas Aperiendis Fontibus Rerum Germanicarum Medii Aevi (ed.) *Scriptores Rerum Langobardicarum et Italicarum Saec. VI–IX* (Hannover 1878)

Soulsby, I. N. 'An introduction to the Cornwall Domesday', in *The Cornwall Domesday*, edd. A. Williams & R. W. H. Erskine (London 1988)

Southall, A. W. 'The illusion of tribe', *Journal of Asian and African Studies* 5 (1970) 28–50

Southworth, Edmund (ed.) *Anglo-Saxon Cemeteries: A Reappraisal. Proceedings of a Conference held at Liverpool Museum 1986* (Stroud 1990)

Spindler, Robert (ed.) *Das altenglische Bussbuch (sog. Confessionale Pseudo-Egberti): Kritische Textausgabe nebst Nachweis der mittellateinischen Quellen, sprachlicher Untersuchung und Glossar* (Leipzig 1934)

Stafford, P. A. 'The "farm of one night" and the organization of King Edward's estates in Domesday', *Economic History Review*, 2nd S., 33 (1980) 491–502

Stanley, Eric Gerald (ed.) *Continuations and Beginnings. Studies in Old English Literature* (London 1966)

Stapleton, Thomas (ed.) *Chronicon Petroburgense* (London 1849)

Stapleton, Thomas (ed.) *Liber Niger Monasterii S. Petri de Burgo*, in *Chronicon Petroburgense*, ed. *idem* (London 1849), pp. 157–83

Starck, Taylor, & Wells, J. C. (edd.) *Althochdeutsches Glossenwörterbuch (mit Stellennachweis zu sämtlichen gedruckten althochdeutschen und verwandten Glossen*, 10 parts (Heidelberg 1971/84)

Steensberg, A. 'Modern research of Agrarian History in Denmark', *Laos: Études comparées de folklore ou d'ethnologie régionale* 1 (1951) 187–201

Steensberg, A. 'North West European plough-types of prehistoric times and the middle ages', *Acta Archaeologica* [Copenhagen] 7 (1936) 244–80

Stenton, Doris Mary (ed.) *Preparatory to Anglo-Saxon England. Being the Collected Papers of Frank Merry Stenton* (Oxford 1970)

Stenton, F[rank] M. *Anglo-Saxon England* (3rd edn, Oxford 1971)

Stenton, F. M. 'Early manumissions at Staunton, Nottinghamshire', *English Historical Review* 26 (1911) 93–7

Stenton, F[rank] M. (facs. ed.) *Facsimiles of Early Charters from Northamptonshire Collections* (Lincoln & London 1930)

Stenton, F. M. 'St. Frideswide and her times', *Oxoniensia* 1 (1936) 103–12

Stenton, F. M. 'Text of the Huntingdonshire Domesday', in *The Victoria History of the County of Huntingdon*, volume I, edd. W. Page & G. Proby (London 1926), pp. 337–55

Stenton, Frank [M.] (ed.) *The Bayeux Tapestry. A Comprehensive Survey* (2nd edn, London 1965)

Stenton, Frank [M.] *The First Century of English Feudalism 1066–1166. Being the Ford Lectures delivered in the University of Oxford in Hilary Term 1929* (2nd edn, Oxford 1961)

Stenton, F. M. 'The supremacy of the Mercian kings', *English Historical Review* 33 (1918) 433–52

Stenton, F. M. 'The thriving of the Anglo-Saxon ceorl', in *Preparatory to Anglo-Saxon England*, ed. D. M. Stenton (Oxford 1970), pp. 383–93

Stephenson, C. 'The problem of the common man in early medieval Europe', *American Historical Review* 51 (1945/6) 419–38

Stevenson, William Henry (ed.) *Asser's Life of King Alfred. Together with the Annals of Saint Neots erroneously ascribed to Asser* (Oxford 1904; New Impression with article on recent work on Asser's Life of Alfred by Dorothy Whitelock, Oxford 1959)

Stewart, I. 'Coinage and recoinage after Edgar's reform', in *Studies in Late Anglo-Saxon Coinage. In Memory of Bror Emil Hildebrand*, ed. K. Jonsson (Stockholm 1990), pp. 455–85

Stone, Lawrence. *Sculpture in Britain. The Middle Ages* (2nd edn, Harmondsworth 1972)

Strayer, Joseph R. (ed.) *Dictionary of the Middle Ages* (13 vols, New York 1982/9)

Stubbs, William (ed.) *Memorials of Saint Dunstan, Archbishop of Canterbury* (London 1874)

Stubbs, William (ed.) *Select Charters and Other Illustrations of English Constitutional Hstory from the Earliest Times to the Reign of Edward the First*, rev. H[enry] W. C. Davis (9th edn, Oxford 1921)

Stubbs, William (ed.) *Willelmi Malmesbiriensis Monachi De Gestis Regum Anglorum Libri Quinque; Historiae Novellae Libri Tres* (2 vols, London 1887/9)

Swanton, Michael (transl.) *Three Lives of the Last Englishmen* (New York & London 1984)

Sweet, Henry (ed. & transl.) *King Alfred's West-Saxon Version of Gregory's Pastoral Care* (London 1871)

Szogs, Arthur. *Die Ausdrücke für 'Arbeit' und 'Beruf' im Altenglischen* (Heidelberg 1931)

Tainter, Joseph A. *The Collapse of Complex Societies* (Cambridge 1988)

Tait, J. 'Introduction to the Shropshire Domesday, in *The Victoria History of Shropshire*, volume I, ed. W. Page (London 1908), pp. 279–307

Tangl, Michael (ed.) *Die Briefe des heiligen Bonifatius und Lullus* (Berlin 1916)

Taylor, C. 'Medieval rural settlement: changing perceptions', *Landscape History* 14 (1992) 5–17

Taylor, Christopher. *Village and Farmstead. A History of Rural Settlement in England* (London 1983)

Thompson, A[lexander] Hamilton, & Lindelöf, U[no] (edd.) *Rituale Ecclesiae Dunelmensis: The Durham Collectar. A New and Revised Edition of the Latin Text with the Interlinear Anglo-Saxon Version* (Durham & London 1927)

Thomson, H[enry] J[ohn] (ed. & transl.) *Prudentius* (2 vols, Cambridge, MA & London 1949/53)

Thorn, Frank & Caroline (edd. & transl. from a Draft Translation prepared by Caroline Thorne & Agnes O'Driscoll). *Domesday Book*, general ed. J. Morris, volume IX, *Devon*, Parts 1 & 2 (2 vols, Chichester 1985)

Thorn, Frank & Caroline (edd. & transl. from a Draft Translation prepared by Veronica Sankaran). *Domesday Book*, general ed. J. Morris, volume XVII, *Herefordshire* (Chichester 1983)

Thorpe, Benjamin (ed.) *Diplomatarium Anglicum Ævi Saxonici. A Collection of English Charters from the Reign of King Æthelberht of Kent, A.D. DC.V to That of William the Conqueror* (London 1865)

Thorpe, Benjamin (ed. & transl.) *The Anglo-Saxon Chronicle, According to the Saxon Original Authorities* (2 vols, London 1861)

Thorpe, Benjamin (ed. & transl.) *The Homilies of the Anglo-Saxon Church. The First Part, containing the Sermones Catholici, or Homilies of Ælfric. In the Original Anglo-Saxon, with an English Version* (2 vols, London 1844/6)

Tolkien, J. R. R. 'English and Welsh', in *Angles and Britons. O'Donnell Lectures* (Cardiff 1963), pp. 1–41

Toller, T[homas] Northcote. *Supplement to An Anglo-Saxon Dictionary. Based on the Manuscript Collections of the Late Joseph Bosworth* (Oxford 1921)

Trautmann, Moritz (ed.) *Die altenglischen Rätsel (Die Rätsel des Exeterbuchs)* (Heidelberg & New York 1915)

Troya, Carlo (ed.) *Codice diplomatico longobardo dal DLXVIII al DCCLXXIV, con note storiche, osservazioni e dissertazioni di Carlo Troya, ordinate principalmente a chiarir la condizione de' Romani vinti da' Longobardi e la qualità della conquista*, volume IV (Napoli 1854)

Turk, Milton Haight (ed.) *The Legal Code of Ælfred the Great* (Boston, MA 1893)

Ullmann, W. 'Public welfare and social legislation in the early medieval councils', *Studies in Church History* 7 (1971) 1–39

Venezky, Richard L., & Healey, Antonette diPaolo. *A Microfiche Concordance to Old English* (Toronto, ON 1980)

Verhulst, A. 'Étude comparative du régime domanial classique à l'est et à l'ouest du Rhin à l'époque carolingienne', in *La Croissance agricole du haut moyen âge* (Auch 1990)

Verhulst, A. 'The decline of slavery and the economic expansion of the early middle ages', *Past and Present* no. 133 (November 1991) 195–203

Verlinden, Charles. *L'Esclavage dans l'Europe médiévale. I: Péninsule ibérique-France* (Brugge 1955)

Verlinden, Charles. *L'Esclavage dans l'Europe médiévale. II: Italie, Colonies italiennes du Levant, Levant latin, Empire byzantin* (Ghent 1977)

Verlinden, C. 'L'Origine de *sclavus* = esclave', *Bulletin Du Cange. Archivum Latinitatis Medii Aevi* 17 (1942) 97–128

Verlinden, Charles. *Wo, wann und warum gab es einen Grosshandel mit Sklaven während des Mittelalters?* (Köln 1970)

Vince, Alan. *Saxon London. An Archaeological Investigation* (London 1990)

Vince, A. 'The economic basis of Anglo-Saxon London', in *The Rebirth of Towns in the West AD 700–1050*, edd. R. Hodges & B. Hobley (London 1988), pp. 83–92

Vinogradoff, Paul. *English Society in the Eleventh Century. Essays in English Mediaeval History* (Oxford 1908)

Vinogradoff, Paul. *Roman Law in Medieval Europe* (2nd edn, with Preface by F[rancis] de Zulueta, Oxford 1929)

Vinogradoff, Paul. *The Collected Papers of Paul Vinogradoff*. With a Memoir by H[erbert] A. L. Fisher (2 vols, Oxford 1928)

Vinogradoff, Paul. *The Growth of the Manor* (2nd edn, London & New York 1911)

Vogt, Joseph. *Ancient Slavery and the Ideal of Man*, transl. Joseph Wiedemann (Oxford 1974)

Vogüé, Adalbert de (ed.) *Grégoire le Grand Dialogues* (3 vols, Paris 1978/80)

Wade, K. 'Ipswich', in *The Rebirth of Towns in the West AD 700–1050*, edd. R. Hodges & B. Hobley (London 1988), pp. 93–100

Wakeford, J. 'Two *walh* names in the fields of Kingston', *Surrey Archaeological Collections* 75 (1984) 251–6

Walker, B. 'On the measurements and valuations of the Domesday of Cambridgeshire', *Cambridge Antiquarian Communications* 5 (1880/4) 93–127

Wallace-Hadrill, J[ohn] M. *Bede's 'Ecclesiastical History of the English People'. A Historical Commentary* (Oxford 1988)

Wallace-Hadrill, J[ohn] M. *Early Germanic Kingship in England and on the Continent* (Oxford 1971)

Wallace-Hadrill, J[ohn] M. *The Barbarian West 400–1000* (3rd rev. edn, London 1967)

Walmsley, J. F. R. 'The *censarii* of Burton Abbey and the Domesday population', *North Staffordshire Journal of Field Studies* 8 (1968) 73–80

Wanley, Humphrey. *Librorum Veterum Septentrionalium, qui in Angliæ Bibliothecis extant, nec non Multorum Veterum Codicum Septentrionalium alibi Extantium Catalogus Historico-Criticus, cum Totius Thesauri Linguarum Septentrionalium Sex Indicibus* (Oxford 1705)

Warner, Rubie D-N. (ed.) *Early English Homilies from the Twelfth Century MS. Vesp. D. XIV* (London 1917)

Warren, F. E. 'Slavery and serfdom in England, with special reference to East Anglia', *Proceedings of the Suffolk Institute of Archaeology and Natural History* 15 (1914) 183–99

Warren, F[rederick] E. (ed.) *The Leofric Missal: As used in the Cathedral of Exeter during the Episcopate of its First Bishop, A.D. 1050–1072.* . . . (Oxford 1883)

Wasserschleben, F[riedrich] W. H. *Die Bussordnungen der abendländischen Kirche nebst einer rechtsgeschichtlichen Einleitung* (Halle 1851)

Waterhouse, R. 'The theme and structure of 755 *Anglo-Saxon Chronicle*', *Neuphilologische Mitteilungen* 70 (1969) 630–40

Watts, V. E., & Prince, E. F. M. 'OE *walh* in English place-names: an addendum', *Journal of the English Place-Name Society* 14 (1981/2) 32–6

Weiss, E. 'Manumissio', in *Paulys Realencyclopädie der classischen Altertumswissenschaft*, edd. G. Wissowa & W. Kroll, volume XIV.2 (Stuttgart 1930), cols 1366–77

Wergeland, Agnes Mathilde. *Slavery in Germanic Society during the Middle Ages* (Chicago, IL [1916])

White, Lynn, Jr. *Medieval Technology and Social Change* (Oxford 1962)

Whitelock, Dorothy (ed. & transl.) *Anglo-Saxon Wills* (Cambridge 1930)

Whitelock, D. 'Archbishop Wulfstan, homilist and statesman', *Transactions of the Royal Historical Society*, 4th S., 24 (1942) 25–45

Whitelock, D[orothy], *et al.* (edd.) *Councils & Synods: With Other Documents relating to the English Church. I. A.D. 871–1204* (2 vols, Oxford 1981)

Whitelock, Dorothy (transl.) *English Historical Documents c. 500–1042* (2nd edn, London & New York 1979)

Whitelock, Dorothy, *et al.* (edd.) *Ireland in Early Mediaeval Europe: Studies in Memory of Kathleen Hughes* (Cambridge 1982)

Whitelock, D. [Review of E. John, *Land Tenure in Early England* (1960)], *American Historical Review* 66 (1960/1) 1009–10

Whitelock, Dorothy (ed.) *Sermo Lupi ad Anglos* (3rd edn, London 1963)

Whitelock, D. 'The prose of Alfred's reign', in *Continuations and Beginnings*, ed. E. G. Stanley (London 1966), pp. 67–103

Whitelock, Dorothy (ed. & transl.) *The Will of Æthelgifu: A Tenth Century Anglo-Saxon Manuscript* (Oxford 1968)

Whitelock, D. 'Two notes on Ælfric and Wulfstan', *Modern Language Review* 38 (1943) 122–6

Whitelock, D. 'Wulfstan and the Laws of Cnut', *English Historical Review* 63 (1948) 433–52

Whitelock, D. 'Wulfstan and the so-called Laws of Edward and Guthrum', *English Historical Review* 56 (1941) 1–21

Whitelock, D. 'Wulfstan *Cantor* and Anglo-Saxon law', in *Nordica et Anglica*, ed. A. H. Orrick (The Hague & Paris 1968), pp. 83–92

Whitelock, D. 'Wulfstan's authorship of Cnut's laws', *English Historical Review* 70 (1955) 72–85

Whitman, F[rank] H. (ed.) *Old English Riddles* ([Ottawa, ON] 1982)

Wickham, Chris. *Early Medieval Italy. Central Power and Local Society 400–1000* (London & Basingstoke 1981)

Wilde-Stockmeyer, Marlis. *Sklaverei auf Island. Untersuchungen zur rechtlich-sozialen Situation und literarischen Darstellung der Sklaven im skandinavischen Mittelalter* (Heidelberg 1978)

Wildhagen, Karl (ed.) *Der Cambridger Psalter. Zum ersten Male herausgegeben mit besonderer Berücksichtigung des lateinischen Textes* (Hamburg 1910)

Williams, A. 'An introduction to the Worcestershire Domesday', in *The Worcestershire Domesday*, edd. A. Williams & R. W. H. Erskine (London 1988)

Williams, Ann, & Erskine, R. W. H. (edd.) *Domesday Book: Studies* (London 1987)

Williams, A. '*Princeps Merciorum gentis*: the family, career and connections of Ælfhere, ealdorman of Mercia, 956–83', *Anglo-Saxon England* 10 (1981) 143–72

Williams, Ann, & Erskine, R. W. H. (edd.) *The Cornwall Domesday* (London 1988)

Williams, Ann, & Erskine, R. W. H. (edd.) *The Derbyshire Domesday* (London 1990)

Williams, Ann, & Erskine, R. W. H. (edd.) *The Huntingdonshire Domesday* (London 1989)

Williams, Ann, & Martin, G. H. (edd.) *The Middlesex and London Domesday* (London 1991)

Williams, Ann, & Erskine, R. W. H. (edd.) *The Nottinghamshire Domesday* (London 1990)

Williams, Ann, & Erskine, R. W. H. (edd.) *The Shropshire Domesday* (London 1990)

Williams, Ann, & Erskine, R. W. H. (edd.) *The Worcestershire Domesday* (London 1988)

Williams, Carl O. *Thraldom in Ancient Iceland* (Chicago, IL 1937)

William Salt Archaeological Society (ed.) *Collections for a History of Staffordshire. 1916* (London 1918)

Williamson, Craig (transl.) *A Feast of Creatures. Anglo-Saxon Riddle Songs* (Philadelphia, PA 1982)

Williamson, Craig (ed.) *The Old English Riddles of the 'Exeter Book'* (Chapel Hill, NC 1977)

Williamson, T. 'Settlement chronology and regional landscapes: the evidence from the claylands of East Anglia and Essex', in *Anglo-Saxon Settlements*, ed. D. Hooke (Oxford & New York 1988), pp. 153–75

Willis, G[eoffrey] G. *Essays in Early Roman Liturgy* (London 1964)

Willis-Bund, J[ohn] W., & Doubleday, H[erbert] Arthur (edd.) *The Victoria History of the County of Worcester*, volume I (Westminster 1901)

Willis-Bund, J[ohn] W., & Page, William (edd.) *The Victoria History of the County of Worcester*, volume II (London 1906)

Willis-Bund, J. W. 'Worcestershire Doomsday', *Associated Architectural Societies' Reports and Papers* 22, no. 2 (1894) 88–108

Wilson, D. M. 'Anglo-Saxon carpenters' tools', in *Studien zur europaischen Vor- und Frühgeschichte*, edd. M. Claus *et al.* (Neumünster 1968), pp. 143–50

Wilson, David M., with appendices by R. L. S. Bruce-Mitford & R. I. Page. *Anglo-Saxon Ornamental Metalwork 700–1100 in the British Museum* (London 1964)

Wilson, P. A. 'The cult of St. Martin in the British Isles: with particular reference to Canterbury and Candida Casa', *Innes Review* 19 (1968) 129–43

Winterbottom, Michael (ed.) Gildas. *The Ruin of Britain and Other Works* (London & Chichester 1978)

Winterfeld, Paul von. *Poetae Latini Aevi Carolini*, volume IV.1 (Berlin 1899)

Wissowa, Georg, & Kroll, Wilhelm (edd.) *Paulys Realencyclopädie der classischen Altertumswissenschaft*, volumes XII.1 & XIV.2 (Stuttgart 1924 & 1930)

Witney, K. P. *The Jutish Forest. A Study of the Weald of Kent from 450 to 1380 A.D.* (London 1976)

Wolfram, Herwig. *History of the Goths*, transl. Thomas J. Dunlap (Berkeley & Los Angeles, CA & London 1988)

Wood, I. N. 'Frankish hegemony in England', in *The Age of Sutton Hoo*, ed. M. O. H. Carver (Woodbridge 1992), pp. 235–41.

Wood, Ian, & Lund, Niels (edd.) *People and Places in Northern Europe 500–1600. Essays in Honour of Peter Hayes Sawyer* (Woodbridge 1991)

Woods, J. Douglas, & Pelteret, David A. E. (edd.) *The Anglo-Saxons: Synthesis and Achievement* (Waterloo, ON 1985)

Woodward, H. B. 'Geology', in *The Victoria History of the County of Essex*, volume I, edd. H. A. Doubleday & W. Page (Westminster 1903), pp. 1–23 + Geological Map

Wormald, P. 'A handlist of Anglo-Saxon lawsuits', *Anglo-Saxon England* 17 (1988) 247–81

Wormald, P. 'Bede, the *Bretwaldas* and the origins of the *Gens Anglorum*', in *Ideal and Reality in Frankish and Anglo-Saxon Society*, ed. P. Wormald with D. Bullough & R. Collins (Oxford 1983), pp. 99–129

Wormald, Patrick (ed.), with Bullough, Donald, & Collins, Roger. *Ideal and Reality in Frankish and Anglo-Saxon Society. Studies Presented to J. M. Wallace-Hadrill* (Oxford 1983)

Wormald, P. 'In search of King Offa's "Law Code" ', in *People and Places in Northern Europe 500–1600*, edd. I. Wood & N. Lund (Woodbridge 1991), pp. 25–45

Wright, David H. (facs. ed.), with a Contribution on the Gloss by Alistair Campbell. *The Vespasian Psalter. British Museum Cotton Vespasian A. 1* (Copenhagen 1967)

Wright, J. 'On slavery, as it existed in England during the Saxon era, and the substitution of villenage after the Norman Conquest, until its gradual extinction', *Transactions of the Historic Society of Lancashire and Cheshire* 10 (1857/8) 207–30

Wright, Thomas (ed.) *Anglo-Saxon and Old English Vocabularies* (2nd edn, ed. Richard Paul Wülcker, 2 vols, London 1884)

Yorke, Barbara. *Kings and Kingdoms in Early Anglo-Saxon England* (London 1990)

Zachrisson, R[obert] E. *Romans, Kelts and Saxons in Ancient Britain. An Investigation into the Two Dark Centuries, 400–600, of English History* (Uppsala 1927)

Zangemeister, Karl (ed.) *Pauli Orosii Historiarum adversum Paganos Libri VII, accedit eiusdem Liber Apologeticus* (Vindobona 1882)

Zeumer, Karl (ed.) *Formulae Merowingici et Karolini Aevi* (Hannover 1886)

Zeumer, K. (ed.) *Formulae Salicae Merkelianae*, in *Formulae Merowingici et Karolini Aevi*, ed. K. Zeumer (Hannover 1886), pp. 239–64

Zupitza, Julius (ed.) *Aelfrics Grammatik und Glossar* (Berlin 1880; rptd with intro. Helmut Gneuss, Berlin, Zürich, & Dublin 1966)

Zupitza, Julius (ed.) *Beowulf. Reproduced in Facsimile from the Unique Manuscript British Museum MS. Cotton Vitellius A. xv* (2nd edn, Introductory Note by Norman Davis, London 1959)

GENERAL INDEX

References to primary texts and to modern scholars are included only if they are mentioned in the main body of the text. Names and places appearing in the tables are omitted. Old English and Latin words and phrases are indexed if they are subject to extended treatment in the book itself; Old English words that are discussed only in Appendix I are omitted. Primary sources and modern scholars mentioned in Appendix I are not indexed.

INDEX OF MANUSCRIPTS